TRAVELLER'S
Literary Companion

FRANCE

JOHN EDMONDSON

PASSPORT BOOKS
NTC/Contemporary Publishing Company

Series Foreword © 1995 Margaret Drabble

Published by Passport Books
an imprint of NTC/Contemporary Publishing Company
4255 West Touhy Avenue
Lincolnwood (Chicago), Illinois 60646-1975 U.S.A.

First published by In Print Publishing Ltd.
9 Beaufort Terrace
Brighton BN2 2SU, UK

ISBN 0-8442-8965-5
Library of Congress Catalog Card Number: on file

Typeset by MC Typeset
Printed by Bell & Bain, Glasgow
Front cover photo by Photo Network, © Paul Thompson
Back cover photo by Photo Network, © Ehlers

Also available in the Traveller's Literary Companion series:
South and Central America
Africa
Japan
Indian Subcontinent
South-east Asia
Eastern & Central Europe
Caribbean

To my late parents, Mac and Ken Edmondson

Series Foreword

This series of *Traveller's Literary Companions* is the series I have been looking for all my travelling life. Discovering new writers and new countries is one of the greatest pleasures we know, and these books will greatly increase the enjoyment of all who consult them. Each volume is packed with scholarly and entertaining historical, geographical, political and above all literary information. A country lives through its literature, and we have here an illustrated survey not only of a country's own writers, but also of the views of foreigners, explorers, tourists and exiles. The only problem I foresee is that each volume will bring about a compulsive desire to book a ticket on the next flight out.

The writers take us back in the past to each country's cultural origins, and bring us right up to the present with extracts from novels, poems and travel writings published in the 1980s and 1990s. The biographical information about the writers is invaluable, and will give any traveller an easy and immediate access to the past and present state of each nation. Conversation with hosts, colleagues or strangers on trains will be greatly assisted. An enormous amount of work has gone into the compiling and annotating of each volume, and the balance of fact and comment seems to me to be expertly judged.

Margaret Drabble

CONTENTS

LIST OF MAPS

USING THE COMPANION

Within each chapter, the literary sites and landmarks are organized by *département*, and are listed alphabetically by town. Maps indicate the locations of the places highlighted. In the Paris chapter, the literary landmarks are organized into the three major divisions of the Left Bank, the two islands, and the Right Bank and within those into *quartiers*, and are listed alphabetically street by street. Also in the Paris chapter is a comprehensive list of writers' graves in the main cemeteries and churches.

The extracts are arranged by place, alphabetically, and each has a number to make it easy to locate from elsewhere in the chapter. A quick list of published sources can be found in the Booklist, where the extract numbers are highlighted in bold type. Fuller references are included in 'Acknowledgments and Citations' at the end of the book.

The Booklists include recommended novels, short stories, plays and poetry and occasionally books of particular interest for general background reading. Recommended biographies, however, are detailed in the 'Lives and Works' sections.

The symbol ◊ after an author's name indicates that there is an entry in 'Lives and Works'. Where this entry is in another chapter, this is indicated after the symbol, which is then printed in parentheses: eg 'Pagnol (◊ Provence)'.

Bold type is used throughout to highlight references to particular places, such as cities and towns, museums, writers' houses, and so on.

Title dates given in the text normally indicate the date of first publication (occasionally dates of premières for plays). In the Booklists, the date in square brackets is the date of first publication of the original work in its original language.

At the end of the book, there are indexes of authors, places outside Paris, and streets in Paris.

Finally, some words of caution for literary travellers may be useful. Details are provided of literary museums and writers' houses which may be visited. The opening times of many of these are limited and subject to change, and in addition houses may be temporarily closed from time to time for renovation work. Times are not stated here, and it is very advisable to check in advance with a tourist office before setting out on a visit.

Many addresses with literary connections are given in the Companion. In cases where a house may be visited, this is always explicitly stated – in all other cases visiting is not an option.

About the author

John Edmondson studied French, English and American Literature at the University of Warwick, UK, and has worked in book and journal publishing for some twenty years. His abiding interest in French literature and culture has taken him to France many times. He lives and works in London.

INTRODUCTION

This book is about the relationships between writers and places, and the light they shed on each other. It is both a geographically oriented guide to literature by French and expatriate writers, and a literary tour of the country, highlighting literary landmarks and viewing the many and varied regions of France through the works and experiences of novelists and poets.

With this dual aim in mind, each chapter is divided into several sections. First, there is a town-by-town guide to each *département* (street-by-street for Paris), highlighting writers' houses and museums, significant settings in fiction, and other places of literary interest. Then a Booklist gives publishing details of all the novels, poetry and plays recommended, as well as other suggested reading. This is followed by a selection of short extracts from books highlighted in the chapter – the extracts are chosen both for what they convey about a place or an aspect of local culture, and also to give a brief taste of the style and approach of the work from which they are taken. Finally the 'Lives and Works' section of each chapter offers detailed biographical and literary information about the authors extracted, together with reviews of the works highlighted and other recommended books (for expatriate writers, only those aspects of their lives and works which relate to France are included).

The emphasis is on 'creative writing' – principally novels and poetry – rather than on travel literature. With the odd rare exception, travel writing is included only when it is by an author principally known for his or her prose fiction or poetry (thus there are extracts, for example, from travel books by Stendhal and Henry James). Similarly, I have occasionally selected extracts from memoirs or journals, especially where these constitute major literary works, as they do, for instance, in the cases of Gide and Chateaubriand.

Throughout, titles of works of French literature are first given in French, followed by the title and date of publication of an English translation. As this is a guide for readers of English, it concentrates on literature in translation. Partly for this reason, there are comparatively few extracts from French poetry, although there are many references to and descriptions of the work of French poets in the course of the book. Apart from the obvious and often insuperable problems of rendering French verse successfully into English verse, which make the available choice fairly narrow, many of the volumes of French poetry on the shelves of British and American bookshops wisely provide the original French verse with a literal English prose translation. Nevertheless, readers will find here effective verse translations of pieces by, among others, Baudelaire, Rimbaud, Verlaine, and Valéry. There is too a sample of Lawrence Ferlinghetti's outstanding renderings of poems from Jacques Prévert's *Paroles*. On the other hand, I regret the absence of, for example, Apollinaire's 'Le Pont Mirabeau' – although there have been several impressive attempts to render it in verse, it is virtually untranslatable, even into literal prose.

With regard to French prose fiction, there are many excellent translations in English of contemporary authors – Pat Goodheart's rendering of Marie Cardinal's *Les Mots pour le dire*, 1975 (*The Words To Say It*, 1984) and Ralph Manheim's of Jean Rouaud's *Les Champs d'honneur*, 1990 (*Fields of Glory*, 1992) are just two of numerous fine examples – and translations of pre-20th-century authors continue to appear (within the last two years, for instance, new translations of previously hard-to-find novels by George Sand and Gérard de Nerval have been published). In selecting from the huge range available, I have tried to strike a balance between the famous names and the less well known, and between the 'classics' and recent French fiction. I have followed the same process in selecting samples of work by British and American writers, so that, I hope, the guide does not constitute too predictable a litany of names while at the same time paying due attention to the many great authors readers will expect and want to see included.

Geographically, the tour starts in the north and meanders around the east to the south, working its way up again through the western areas of the country, taking in the central region as it goes, and leaving the Île-de-France and Paris until the last. Inevitably the section on Paris constitutes a major portion of the book, not only because of its central place in the development of French literature, but also because it has sheltered and influenced so many expatriate writers in its long literary history – each moved by the city and distilling something of its essence in his or her own way. As I researched the book, it was the unique quality of each writer's experience of the city and the particular way in which it influenced his or her work that interested me most and I have tried to reflect this in the guide – the relationship between writer and place is ultimately personal and intimate. As Arthur Koestler puts it in his *Scum of the Earth*, 1941, 'This town has always been thought of by her lovers as a person alive – not metaphorically, but as a psychological reality.' At the same time, I have paid due respect to the significance of Paris as a centre for the many groups and communities of writers that have flourished there over the centuries. There are deliberate omissions, though, which relate to the editorial scope of this book. For example, I have made little reference to the great wealth of African francophone literature (although Sembène Ousmane is among the authors highlighted), despite the fact that Paris has long been a major centre for African writers, with publishing houses such as Présence Africaine and L'Harmattan playing key roles in the promotion and dissemination of their work. The literature, however, very predominantly relates to Africa and the African experience and is more appropriately covered elsewhere in this series of literary guides (see Oona Strathern's *Traveller's Literary Companion to Africa*, 1994).

The choice of writers and works for inclusion was, of course, vast and daunting and this is inevitably a personal selection – of both books and places – which could easily have been twice as long and still left me regretting that I had to leave out so much. I hope at least that you will enjoy what is here and will look kindly on the gaps and omissions. Whether treading the streets of Paris, touring the countryside of Burgundy, taking in the Riviera sun, or sitting at home in your armchair, I hope you will find something to entertain you and many temptations to make new literary acquaintances and revisit old friends.

John Edmondson
London, 1997

Acknowledgments

The road from conception to completion was a long and winding one, and along the way I received numerous helpful and encouraging suggestions, many of which set me off in rewarding directions I would otherwise have missed. I am especially grateful to Martine Bretéché for her advice, her knowledge of Paris, and the hard-to-find little pamphlets and books that dropped through my mailbox from time to time. I am very grateful also to Ray Keenoy, publisher of the excellent Babel guides to modern fiction in translation, for kindly supplying me with an advance copy of his database of English translations of French literature – now published in the *Babel Guide to French Fiction* – so saving me considerable time and trouble and furnishing me with a valuable research resource. I also acknowledge with gratitude the suggestions of Catherine de Crignis, Alastair Dingwall, Martin Garrett, Stefan Howald, Peter Lake, Gillian Page, and Christa Schwarz. Thanks too to Luc Maillebuau of the Centre National des Lettres for an early conversation which helped me order my thoughts in the planning stages. I contacted a number of French tourist offices, large and small, in the course of researching the book, and found them invariably efficient and informative. Some went to considerable trouble to furnish me with newspaper articles and other documentation from their archives which went well beyond the answer to my initial enquiry and provided me with interesting and useful additional information. In this respect, I would like to thank in particular Marie-Héllène Devillard of the Comité Départemental du Tourisme, Saône & Loire, Claudine Levy of the Office Départemental du Tourisme du Bas-Rhin, and Judith Richard of the Comité Régional de Tourisme, Nord–Pas-de-Calais. Acknowledgments for the use of extracts and pictures are presented at the end of the book, but I would like to mention here the help of Margaret Sherry of Princeton University Library in selecting pictures from the Papers of Sylvia Beach and Hamish Crooks at Magnum for digging out the right images from my vague descriptions. Thanks too to Russell Townsend for his work on the maps. Finally, I am grateful to Alastair Dingwall for editing the text and for his patience in waiting for the arrival of a book which took me a little longer to write than I had anticipated.

The information contained in the guide is based primarily on the works themselves, authors' correspondence, autobiographies, published interviews, authoritative biographies, and first-hand observation. Details such as house numbers and dates have been cross-checked as thoroughly as possible – where I have been in doubt I have omitted the reference (there are numerous inconsistencies in published sources, arising from typographical errors, changes in street numbering systems, etc). Any remaining inaccuracies are entirely my own responsibility.

Other guides and general reference

In the course of researching and writing this book I picked up many general travel guides and a few with a specifically literary orientation. Some provided me with leads and pointed up connections between writers and places I might otherwise have missed. I acknowledge their thoroughness with gratitude and also highly recommend them for further reading.

In French, Jean-Paul Clébert has written two fascinating and luxuriously illustrated guides to French literature – *Les Hauts Lieux de la littérature à Paris* (Bordas, 1992) and *Les Hauts Lieux de la littérature en France* (Bordas, 1990). In the same series is Colette Becker's engrossing *Les Hauts Lieux du Romantisme en France* (Bordas, 1991). Georges Poisson's *Guide des maisons d'hommes célèbres* (Pierre Horay, 1988) is an authoritative and detailed selection which includes some writers' houses in its coverage. Along the same lines, the recently published *Guide des maisons d'artistes et d'écrivains en région Parisienne* by Dominique Camus (La Manufacture, 1995) gives substantial detail, with full-colour illustrations, of a number of writers' houses within 120 km of Paris. Marcel le Clere's *Guide des cimetières de Paris* is not particularly literary in its leanings but does include some interesting histories of the major Paris cemeteries, as well as helpful diagrams of their layouts. In English, Ian Littlewood's *Paris: A Literary Companion* is an absorbing literary tour of the city, highlighting passages from both French and expatriate literature. Brian N. Morton's *American Writers in Paris* (Quill, 1986) is a street by street listing of homes and hang-outs with many entertaining anecdotes. Of the general travel guides, Ian Robertson's *Blue Guide to France* and *Blue Guide to Paris* stand out both for the amount of literary information they contain and for their accuracy – a high standard which is not always met by their competitors.

For readers in search of general reference guides to French, British and American writers the Oxford Companions remain pre-eminent. The *New Oxford Companion to Literature in French*, edited by Peter France (OUP, 1995) is a recent and worthy successor to the *Oxford Companion to French Literature*, which manages to be far-reaching, entertaining, and scholarly all at once, and covers francophone writing throughout the world. For British and American literature, see the well established *Oxford Companion to English Literature*, edited by Margaret Drabble (OUP, revised 1995) and *Oxford Companion to American Literature* by James D. Hart and Phillip W. Leninger (OUP, sixth edition 1995).

The *Babel Guide to French Fiction in Translation* by Ray Keenoy, Laurence Laluyaux and Gareth Stanton (Boulevard Books, 1996) is an accessible and entertaining guide to 20th-century novels from France and other francophone countries in English translation, comprising informative and critical reviews of selected titles and an extensive listing of translations available.

Finally, for in-depth studies of British and American expatriate writers and publishers in literary Paris in the 20th century, see especially Shari Benstock's *Women of the Left Bank: Paris 1900–1940* (University of Texas Press, 1986), Noel Riley Fitch's *Sylvia Beach and the Lost Generation* (Penguin, 1985), Hugh Ford's *Published in Paris: American and British Writers, Printers and Publishers in Paris, 1920–1939* (Pushcart, 1975), and Christopher Sawyer-Lauçanno, *The Continual Pilgrimage: American Writers in Paris, 1944–1960* (Bloomsbury, 1992).

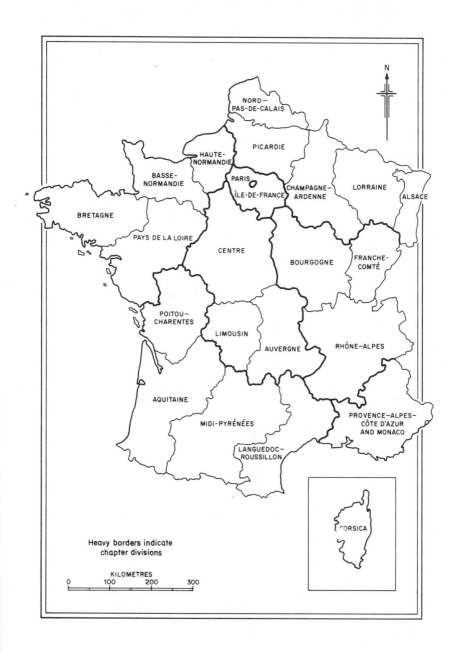

N

NORD–
PAS-DE-CALAIS

PICARDIE

HAUTE–
NORMANDIE

BASSE–
NORMANDIE

PARIS
ÎLE-DE-FRANCE

CHAMPAGNE–
ARDENNE

LORRAINE

ALSACE

BRETAGNE

PAYS DE LA LOIRE

CENTRE

BOURGOGNE

FRANCHE–
COMTÉ

POITOU–
CHARENTES

LIMOUSIN

AUVERGNE

RHÔNE–ALPES

AQUITAINE

MIDI-PYRÉNÉES

PROVENCE–ALPES–
CÔTE D'AZUR
AND MONACO

LANGUEDOC–
ROUSSILLON

CORSICA

Heavy borders indicate
chapter divisions

KILOMETRES
0   100   200   300

xiii

Nord–Pas-de-Calais; Picardie; Champagne–Ardenne; Alsace–Lorraine

> 'Yes, he could see it was a mine now, for the scattered lanterns showed up the yards, and a door which suddenly opened gave him a glimpse of the furnaces in a blaze of light. He could understand it all now, even the exhaust of the pump, the long heavy, monotonous panting, like the snorting breath of a monster.'
>
> Émile Zola, *Germinal*

NORD

Cambrai. Fénelon (1651–1715), author of *Télémaque*, c1695 (*The Adventures of Telemachus*, 1979), was appointed archbishop here in 1695. His tomb is in the **Cathedral** (rebuilt since his time – the cathedral Fénelon knew was destroyed in the Revolution). **Le Musée Municipal** includes a bust and portrait of this churchman, mystic, and prolific writer.

Douai. The Romantic and until recently greatly undervalued poet Marceline Desbordes-Valmore (1786–1859) was born in **rue de Valenciennes** (it was then rue Notre-Dame). If the plaque is still on No 34, ignore it – **32** is the correct number. The statue of her behind the church of Notre-Dame is the third to have been erected – its predecessors were destroyed in the First and Second World Wars.

Lille. The poet Albert Samain (1858–1900) was born in Lille – hence the bust of him in the **Jardin Vauban**.

A plaque at **26 rue Jean-Moulin**, with an appropriate quotation from her autobiographical *Archives du Nord*, reveals that Marguerite Yourcenar (see below under Saint-Jans-Cappel) lived in the house during the first two years of her life. It was then owned by her grandmother.

Roubaix. Novelist Maxence Van der Meersch (1907–51) was born at **76 rue Cuvier**. He spent much of his life in this industrial region, where most of his stories are set, characteristically evoking the hardships of the textile workers and the mists and canals of Flanders. He won the Prix Goncourt in 1936 for his novel *L'Empreinte du Dieu*. Several of his books were translated in the 1950s – including *Maria, fille de Flandre*, 1948 (*The Bellringer's Wife*, 1951).

1

Saint-Jans-Cappel. There is a small but rewarding museum here dedicated to the novelist Marguerite Yourcenar (1903–87) – **rue Marguerite Yourcenar**, Saint-Jans-Cappel, 59270 Bailleul. Opening times are limited and seasonal, so it is very advisable to check in advance with a tourist office if you are making a special detour. Yourcenar was brought up by her father (her mother died when she was a baby) at the nearby family property of **Mont-Noir** – the family name was Crayenour (of which Yourcenar was an anagram devised by her father). The château in which she spent much of her early childhood was destroyed in the First World War and another building now occupies the site, although it is still surrounded by the large park which Yourcenar knew and remembered with great affection throughout her life. She left Mont-Noir when she was eight, and travelled widely with her father. In 1939 she moved permanently to the USA, but her childhood here in French Flanders remained a cherished and influential memory. Near the end of her life, in 1980, Yourcenar became the first woman ever to be elected to the Académie Française. In France for the associated ceremonies, she revisited, on 15 December 1980, the places of her childhood, where she was welcomed as a star. 'All the photographs taken that day show her astonishingly young and smiling,' writes Josayne Savigneau (*Marguerite Yourcenar: L'Invention d'une vie*, 1991). At Mont-Noir, Yourcenar found the same view from the existing house that she had known as a young child from her bedroom window in the old château. 'Le temps était aboli,' she wrote in a letter of thanks.

For Yourcenar's own exploration of her roots in the Nord, see in particular the second volume of her autobiographical *Le Labyrinthe du monde – Archives du Nord*, 1977 (translated as *How Many Years – A Memoir*, 1995).

Sars-Poteries. In May 1940, just outside this village in the farming country near the Belgian border, a French cavalry captain, riding with a lieutenant and two troopers, was shot dead by a German sniper. The three other soldiers ran for cover. One of the troopers was Claude Simon ◊, who was later rounded up and sent to a prisoner-of-war camp. Some 20 years afterwards, his innovative and complex novel *La Route des Flandres*, 1960 (*The Flanders Road*, 1985) was published, with the shooting of the captain as its central incident (Extract 10). Readers of the 1985 John Calder/Riverrun edition of *The Flanders Road* will find in John Fletcher's brief but illuminating introduction a precise location of the ambush in which Simon was involved.

Valenciennes. The chronicler and poet Jean Froissart (1337–?) was born here – in the square named after him you can see his statue.

Early in 1884 Émile Zola ◊ was in the initial stages of planning his great novel of industrial struggle, *Germinal*, 1885 (*Germinal*, 1954), and it was in the mining region around Valenciennes that he did his 'field research'. On 19 February a major conflict broke out at the nearby mining community of **Anzin**, involving some 12 000 miners. The memorable and evocative portrayal of the fictional mining community of Montsou in *Germinal* has its basis in Zola's observations of the miners and the mines at Anzin during this period (see Extract 9). Biographer Philip Walker tells the story: 'Four days later, he rushed up to the scene of action. During his summer vacation in Brittany in 1883, he had, as luck would have it, established a friendly relationship with Alfred Giard, a Lille professor who also happened to be a left-wing Deputy from the constituency of Valenciennes. Posing as Giard's secretary, he had been able to attend strike meetings in Anzin, visit miners' dwellings and cafés, question miners and their wives, form an idea of their mores, interview Émile Basly, one of their leaders, and inspect from close up the miners' behaviour

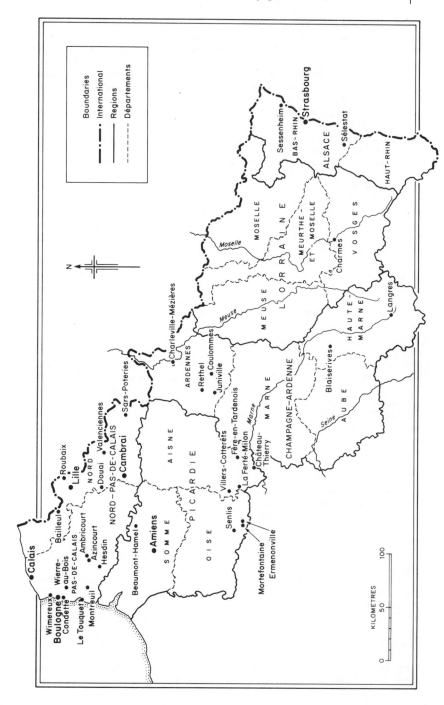

during the strike. He had also managed, during the little more than a week he stayed in the region, to familiarize himself with actual mines. Accompanied by an engineer, he had, despite his fear of the dark and of being buried alive, descended into the bottom of one of them, the Fosse Renard.' (Philip Walker, *Zola.*)

PAS-DE-CALAIS

Ambricourt. This village is the setting for *Journal d'un curé de campagne*, 1936 (*The Diary of a Country Priest*, 1956) by Georges Bernanos (1888–1948). The novel tells the story of the heroic struggle of a young country priest against the corrupting evil and apathy which he finds all around him in the local community.

Azincourt. The site of the famous battle, better known as Agincourt, in which Henry V won his famous but bloody victory on 25 October 1415 (St Crispin's Day), on which Shakespeare's play is based.

Boulogne. 'This house is on a great hill-side, backed up by woods of young trees. It faces the Haute Ville with the ramparts and the unfinished cathedral – which capital object is exactly opposite the windows. On the slope in front, going steep down to the right, all Boulogne is piled and jumbled about in a very picturesque manner. The view is charming – closed in at least by the tops of swelling hills; and the door is within ten minutes of the post-office, and within quarter of an hour of the sea. The garden is made in terraces up the hill-side, like an Italian garden; the top walks being in the before-mentioned woods. The best part of it begins at the level of the house, and goes up at the back, a couple of hundred feet perhaps. There are at present thousands of roses all about the house, and no end of other flowers.' (Dickens, letter of 26 June 1953.) Boulogne became a

favourite resort of Charles Dickens ◊ during the 1850s, and he spent three summers here in 1853, 1854 and 1856. He stayed at two villas owned by the same landlord – the 'Villa des Moulineaux' (1853 and 1856), **rue Beaurepaire**, described above, and the 'Villa du Camp de Droite' nearby. The Villa des Moulineaux, the pride and joy of the landlord, was demolished after the Second World War – the **Lycée Mariette** now stands on the site. The Villa du Camp de Droite, which stood in what are now the college grounds, was demolished in 1917. Dickens writes of his attraction to Boulogne, and also of his great liking for his French landlord, in his 1854 essay 'Our French Watering-Place' (Extract 3). The landlord in question, fictionalized in 'Our French Watering-Place' as 'M. Loyal Devasseur', was one Ferdinand Beaucourt-Mutuel, by all accounts a loyal and committed citizen and an extremely generous and gracious man. Dickens and Beaucourt-Mutuel became good friends. Later, in the 1860s, when the financially stressed Frenchman had to sell his Boulogne properties and move to nearby **Condette**, Dickens continued to visit him – see below under Condette for the continuation of the story. For a detailed and meticulous investigation of the relationship between Dickens and Beaucourt-Mutuel and of Dickens's stays in Boulogne and Condette, see Janine Watrin's *De Boulogne à Condette: une histoire d'amitié*, 1992.

The Boulevard Sainte-Beuve recalls the fact that the novelist and critic Charles-Augustin Sainte-Beuve (1804–69) was born in Boulogne (in **rue Pot d'Étain**).

The town is atmospherically evoked in Elizabeth Bowen's ◊ *The House in Paris*, 1935 (Extract 2).

Two British poets died in Boulogne – Charles Churchill (1732–64) and Thomas Campbell (1777–1844).

Calais. At the beginning of Sterne's ◊ *A Sentimental Journey*, 1768 (Extract

Dickens crossing the Channel – cartoon by Gill

4), the narrator/protagonist Yorick stays in Calais at the Hôtel Dessin (Sterne spells it 'Dessein'). This large inn, where you could also hire travelling carriages and exchange currency, was already well known among English travellers to the continent. Sterne himself stayed at it in 1765 and features its owner in the opening chapters of his novel. As a result, Pierre Quillacq, known as Dessin, became famous and his hotel an essential port of call – thanks to Sterne, he grew to be one of the richest men in Calais.

In *Tristram Shandy*, Volume VII, Sterne has Tristram pass through Calais at the beginning of his travels in France and satirizes the fact-obsessed and opinionated travel books of the period: "'Now before I quit Calais,' a travel writer would say, "it would not be amiss to give some account of it." Now I think it very much amiss – that a man cannot go quietly through a town, and let it alone, when it does not meddle with him, but that he must be turning about and drawing his pen at every kennel he crosses over . . . For my own part, as heaven is my judge, and to which I shall ever make my last appeal – I know no more of Calais (except the little my barber told me of it, as he was whetting his razor) than I do this moment of Grand Cairo; for it was dusky in the evening when I landed, and dark as pitch in the morning when I set out, and yet by merely knowing what is what, and by drawing this from that in one part of the town, and by spelling and putting this and that together in another – I would lay any travelling odds, that I this moment write a chapter upon Calais as long as my arm; and with so distinct and satisfactory a detail of every item, which is worth a stranger's curiosity in the town – that you would take me for the town-clerk of Calais itself . . .'. And he proceeds to do exactly that, simply lifting facts from other sources.

Condette. In 1860, Ferdinand Beaucourt-Mutuel moved from Boulogne (see above) to the quiet, secluded village of Condette. Recent researchers, including Peter Ackroyd, Claire Tomalin, and Janine Watrin, have established that Dickens, in all probability, paid a number of short, and it seems secretive, visits to his French friend's new home between 1862 and 1865. The supposition is that during this time the young actress Ellen Ternan and her mother were staying at Beaucourt-Mutuel's chalet and that therein lay the motive for Dickens's visits. The nature of the relationship between the middle-aged internationally famous novelist and Ellen Ternan, then in her early twenties, is a matter of speculation, but he was certainly to an extent, to use Ackroyd's word, 'obsessed' with her. That Condette became a place of considerable importance for Dickens at this stage of his life is in little doubt.

Unlike the two villas in which Dickens stayed in Boulogne, Beaucourt-Mutuel's Condette home, known as the **Chalet Dickens**, has survived. However, it has been extensively rebuilt since his time – it was all but destroyed by the Germans in the Second World War. It is private property and cannot be visited, but you can see it on the **allée**

Charles Dickens. In the **cemetery** you will find the grave of Ferdinand Beaucourt-Mutuel, with the inscription in English, 'The landlord of whom Charles Dickens wrote, "I never did see such a kind and gentle heart"'.

Hesdin. Birthplace of L'Abbé Prévost (1697–1763), author of *Manon Lescaut*, 1731 (*Manon Lescaut*, 1949) and the first translator of Samuel Richardson's *Clarissa*, which appeared in French as *Lettres anglaises*, 1751. Prévost spent the first 16 years of his life in Hesdin, where he was educated by the Jesuits.

Montreuil. Formerly known as Montreuil-sur-Mer, this town is a key setting in the early part of Hugo's *Les Misérables*, 1862 (*Les Misérables*, 1976) – Extract 8.

Le Touquet. P.G. Wodehouse ◊ bought a house here in the 1930s. He stayed in Le Touquet when war broke out, was arrested by the Germans in 1940, and spent the next year in internment camps. In *French Leave*, 1956, Wodehouse creates a typical fashionable resort on the Picardie/Pas-de-Calais coast (Extract 6).

Wierre-au-Bois. Sainte-Beuve came to this village many times in his youth – the manor house in which he stayed still stands in the square, where there is also a statue of him.

Wimereux. John McCrae (died 1918) is buried here. He wrote 'In Flanders Fields', which appeared in *Punch* in December 1915 and which made the poppy the symbol of remembrance – 'If ye break faith with us who die/We shall not sleep, though poppies grow/In Flanders fields.'

PICARDIE: SOMMME

First World War. Of the many remarkable works of literature that this notoriously wasteful, brutal and incompetent conflict produced, the following selection is especially recommended. For novels, see Henri Barbusse's ◊, *Le Feu*, 1916 (*Under Fire*, 1926 – Extract 16) ; Ford Madox Ford's ◊ *Parade's End*, 1924–28 (Extract 12); Erich Maria Remarque's *Im Westen nichts Neues*, 1929 (*All Quiet on the Western Front*, 1929 – Extract 17); Siegfried Sassoon's ◊ semi-autobiographical *Memoirs of an Infantry Officer*, 1930 (Extract 15); and *Three Soldiers*, 1921, by John Dos Passos (1896–1970) about the war experiences of three privates and the effects on their very different personalities. Although, unlike all of the above, he did not have direct experience of the war, William Boyd's (1952–) *The New Confessions*, 1987, contains startlingly vivid descriptions of trench warfare, as does Sebastian Faulks's *Birdsong*, 1993. For autobiography, see Robert Graves's ◊ *Goodbye to All That* (Extract 13). See also Edmund Blunden's (1896-1974) *Undertones of War*, 1928. In the theatre, R.C. Sherriff's *Journey's End*, 1929, remains a powerful portrayal of relationships among soldiers in the trenches. For poetry, turn to Wilfred Owen's ◊ *Collected Poems*, 1963 (Extract 14); Charles Sorley's (1895–1915) *Marlborough and Other Poems*, 1916; Isaac Rosenberg's (1890–1918) *Collected Works*, 1937; and Siegfried Sassoon's *The Old Huntsman*, 1917. (Owen, Sorley and Rosenberg were killed in action.)

Amiens. Birthplace of Choderlos de Laclos (1741–1803), author of the great epistolary novel, *Les Liaisons dangereuses*, 1782 (*Les Liaisons Dangereuses*, 1961).

Novelist Jules Verne (1828–1905) lived for much of his life in Amiens, and served for many years on the city council. Among his various addresses were **44 boulevard Jules-Verne**, where he lived from 1872 to 1882 and from 1902 until his death, and **2 rue Charles-Dubois**, which was his home from 1882 until 1902. The latter is now the **Centre de Documentation Jules-Verne**, and part of the house is open to the public. There is a reconstruction of Verne's study, various of his personal belongings, a huge collection of books and papers on his work, and a permanent exhibition relating to his life and his writing. Verne is buried in the **Cimetière de la Madeleine**.

John Ruskin (◊ Auvergne) began writing *The Bible of Amiens* while staying in the city in October 1880. Describing Amiens as the 'Venice of Picardy', Ruskin explores the city's historical, cultural and geographical significance, culminating in a detailed discourse on the sculpture of its **Cathedral**, the 'Bible' of the title.

Beaumont-Hamel. H.H. Munro, alias Saki, was killed here in 1916 (1870–1916). He was shot in the head while taking refuge in a crater.

PICARDIE: OISE

Aumont-en-Halatte. Henri Barbusse ◊, author of *Le Feu*, 1916 (*Under Fire*, 1926) bought a house here (about 2 km from Senlis) in 1910 which he called *Villa Sylvie* in honour of Nerval ◊. His widow (the daughter of writer and critic Catulle Mendès) requested in her will that the house be dedicated to the memory of her husband. Her wish was honoured and, under the guardianship of the Société des Amis d'Henri Barbusse, the **Maison d'Henri Barbusse**, 60300 Aumont, may be visited. There is a bust of the writer in the garden and inside a small museum evokes his life and career through photos, personal possessions, and of course his work. You can see among other things his royalty statement for *Le Feu* – in 1917 it sold 10 000 copies per month.

Chaalis. A Cistercian **abbey** was founded here (near Senlis) in the 12th century and its ruins became an attraction for painters and Romantic poets. It was treasured as a place for reflection by Rousseau and Nerval and now there is a museum which includes in its exhibits manuscripts and memorabilia of Rousseau. In Nerval's novel *Sylvie*, 1853 (*Sylvie*, 1993), the narrator, back in his native region searching for identity and continuity through the landmarks of his past, remembers the abbey of Chaalis.

Ermenonville. The Château here was acquired in 1763 by the Marquis de Girardin (1735–1808), an ardent admirer of the works of Jean-Jacques Rousseau (1712–78) and the author of a respected book on landscape gardening. He rebuilt the Château and created a magnificent English-style park around it, a picturesque expression of the harmonious potentials between people and nature – potentials symbolized in monuments he erected in some of the most attractive parts of the park, such as 'Le Temple de la Philosophie', 'L'Autel de la Rêverie', and 'Le Tombeau de l'Inconnu'. In May 1778, Rousseau visited the Marquis and was captivated by the park. He stayed, teaching music to Girardin's children and living in a small house near the Château. It was to be his last home – he died here suddenly on 2 July 1778. He was buried on an island wooded with poplar trees – **L'Île des Peupliers**. The building where Rousseau lived no longer exists, but his tomb, which Girardin had erected on the island and which rapidly became a place of pilgrimage (Robespierre was an early visitor), can still be seen. Rousseau's remains, however, were moved to the Panthéon in 1794. The Château itself may not be visited.

Ermenonville was a treasured refuge for Gérard de Nerval, who visited it frequently and describes it affectionately in, among other works, *Sylvie*.

Mortefontaine. Gérard de Nerval was brought up here by his uncle, and the countryside and villages of the **Valois** left a profound impression on him. The house in which he spent his childhood is now demolished, but the neighbouring **Château de Mortefontaine**, which

he knew well, may still be seen (though not visited). He writes in *Sylvie*, 'My mind's eye saw again a castle of the time of Henry IV, with its slate-roofed, pointed towers and its reddish façade quoined in yellow stone, and near by a great open greensward surrounded by elm and linden trees, their foliage pierced through by the fiery rays of a setting sun.' When Nerval was a child, the Château was the home of the awesome Baronne de Feuchères, real name Sophie Dawes, an English prostitute who had become the mistress of the Prince de Condé and by that route had risen to her present state of nobility. She was shrouded in mystery and scandal – when the old Prince was found hanged, the Baronne was tried (but acquitted) for involvement in his murder. This aura of mystery, coupled with her controversial lifestyle, and heightened by the fact that he saw her only at a distance riding in the grounds of her estate, bought her a permanent place in Nerval's vivid and treasured memory of his childhood. He mentions her in *Sylvie*, demonstrating that the childhood admiration remained with him – 'Except for Madame de F . . ., they had never seen a woman so imposing in appearance and yet so gracious to everyone she encountered.' Key scenes in the novel are set in and around Mortefontaine – for example, there is a fête at the Château, Sylvie lives in the village of **Loisy** (Extract 7), and there is an outing to a lake island in the park of Mortefontaine reputedly painted by Watteau in his *L'Embarquement pour l'Île de Cythère*, 1717.

PICARDIE: AISNE

Château-Thierry. Birthplace of the poet Jean de La Fontaine (1621-95), whose *Fables*, 1668-94, continue to delight and impress adults and children alike. The house in which he was born still stands. It has been considerably altered over the years, but at least retains its fine 16th century façade (the original house dates from 1559). It is now a museum dedicated to La Fontaine (**Le Musée Jean de La Fontaine**, 12 rue La Fontaine, 02400 Château-Thierry). The museum includes an impressive illustrated collection of his works and various documents and manuscripts. Although he spent long periods of his life in Paris, La Fontaine always felt a profound attachment to his home region. The house remained his property until 1676, and in his adult life here he took over from his father the role of Maître des Eaux et Forêts.

La Ferté-Milon. Birthplace of Jean Racine (1639–99). Racine's mother died in 1841, and he became an orphan at the age of four when his father died two years later. He spent the rest of his early childhood, until he was ten, with his grandmother, Marie Desmoulins. Her house still exists and has been restored. It is now **Le Musée Jean-Racine**, 2 rue des Bouchers, 02460 La Ferté-Milon. The material relating to Racine is rather sparse – little more than a collection of letters and documents – but there are sculptures and paintings of interest and some local history. Opening times are seasonal and limited, so it is important to check in advance if you are making a special visit.

Villeneuve-sur-Fère. Paul Claudel (1868–1955) was born in this village near **Fère-en-Tardenois**, and spent his childhood here, until he left for Paris in 1882. The house in which he grew up is not open to the public, but there is a small **museum** dedicated to Claudel in the village church.

Villers-Cotterêts. Alexandre Dumas (◊ Provence) was born at what is now **No 54 rue Alexandre-Dumas**, and he and his parents are buried in the cemetery here. There is a **Musée Alexandre-Dumas** at 24 rue Demoustier, 02600 Villers-Cotterêt, with an impressive collection of documents, portraits and manuscripts (including that of *Le Com-*

te de Monte-Cristo). There are also exhibits relating to the life of his father, and Alexandre Dumas *fils*.

CHAMPAGNE–ARDENNE: ARDENNES

Charleville-Mézières. When Arthur Rimbaud ◊ was born in **Charleville** in 1854, it had not yet been united by suburban sprawl with neighbouring Mézières. Charleville, founded in 1606, was much newer than its neighbour and was a quiet, conservative town populated predominantly by unexciting middle-class business people. Rimbaud spent the first 16 years of his life here, and came to despise what was for him the town's stifling provincial culture – witheringly portrayed in his poem 'À la Musique', 1870 (Extract 5). The wild child was born at **14 rue Thiers**. When he was six, his parents separated and he spent the next two years with his mother in the less salubrious neighbourhood of **rue de Bourbon**. After that, they moved to **13 cours d'Orléans**, in one of the best *quartiers* of Charleville. Around this time, Rimbaud, until then educated by his mother, was sent to school at the pension Rossat, at **11 rue de l'Arquebuse**. From the age of 11, he attended the Collège de France, which is now the municipal library on **place de l'Agriculture**. Here he became a star pupil, and was befriended by a young teacher, George Izambard, who was influential in his early poetic development. Apparently a model student, Rimbaud abandoned his college studies when he was 15; by then he was unruly and rebellious and refused to return when the college reopened after the disruptions of the Franco–Prussian war in 1870. While he was attending the Collège de France, he moved to his final home in Charleville – on quai de la Madeleine, now **quai Arthur-Rimbaud**. It was here that he wrote 'Le Bateau ivre' before leaving for Paris and Verlaine in 1871. Rimbaud returned for visits throughout his life to Charleville and to nearby **Roche**, then a small rural community where his mother had a farm. Towards the end of his stormy relationship with Verlaine, in April 1873, he stayed at the farm and began to write *Une Saison en enfer*, 1873 (*A Season in Hell and Other Poems*, 1994) – he came back later in the year, when the affair with Verlaine had ended with the shooting incident in Brussels, and finished it. Rimbaud's last visit to the Ardennes was in 1891, following the amputation of his leg in Marseille, due to a tumour which had forced him to return from Africa – he stayed at Roche for a month in deteriorating health and increasing pain, and then left again for Marseille, where he died a few weeks later.

Ironically, there is a statue to Rimbaud in **place de la Gare** in Charleville – the square which serves as a setting for his bitterly sardonic 'À la Musique'. **Le Musée Rimbaud** at Le Vieux Moulin (quai Arthur-Rimbaud, 08100 Charleville-Mézières) presents an impresssive collection of documents, manuscripts and photographs, and some personal memorabilia, including a piece of his luggage. You will also see there the picture by Fantin-Latour entitled *Le Coin de table*, painted in January 1872 and featuring Verlaine and Rimbaud at the time of their early days together in Paris, in the company of several other, now obscure, poets of the day. Rimbaud is buried in the **cemetery** at Charleville.

The Conseil Général des Ardennes has mapped out itineraries for those wishing to visit places in the area connected with Rimbaud and Verlaine. For details of the **Route Rimbaud-Verlaine** contact Vitrine Touristique et Culturelle du Conseil Général, 24 place Ducale, F-08000 Charleville-Mézières. (See also below under Rethel.)

Forest of the Ardennes. Julien Gracq ◊ sets his atmospheric novel *Un Balcon en forêt*, 1958 (*A Balcony in the Forest*, 1960) high up in the forest, near the Belgian border (Extract 1). Here, remote from the familiar world and seemingly suspended in time, Lieutenant Grange awaits the enemy at the beginning of the Second World War.

Rethel. While Verlaine (◊ Paris) was teaching in Rethel at the Institution Notre Dame in 1877–79 he befriended Lucien Létinois, a pupil at the school. They spent the next few years together, until Létinois died in 1883. In 1880, Verlaine and Létinois tried their hand at farming, setting up home in March 1880 in nearby **Juniville** – they failed, fell into debt and lost the farm. There is a small museum in Juniville dedicated to Verlaine (**Café Verlaine**). The poet was back in the Ardennes in 1883–85, once again trying rural life on a small farm in **Coulommes** (coincidentally the birthplace of Létinois), this time with his widowed mother keeping house. He drank heavily during this period and ended up with a one-month prison sentence in **Vouziers** for attacking her. In 1885, he left the Ardennes for good, returning with his mother to Paris, where she died in 1886 and he declined steadily into his own death 10 years later.

CHAMPAGNE–ARDENNE: HAUTE-MARNE

Cirey-sur-Blaise. In 1734, Voltaire (1694–1778) fled Paris to escape arrest and persecution at the hands of the Ancien Régime – his *Lettres philosophiques* had turned him from a nuisance into a distinctly perceived threat to the political establishment. He came here to the **Château de Cirey**, the property of his long-term companion and mistress Émilie, the physicist and mathematician Madame Du Châtelet (1706–49). It was then in a state of disrepair and Voltaire himself supervised the rebuilding and redecoration, although not, according to Nancy Mitford in her *Voltaire in Love*, 1957, without some significant alterations to his plans by

Madame du Châtelet. He spent much time with her here between 1734 and 1744 – and during these years at Cirey, he worked intensively, often with Madame du Châtelet, on a wide range of scientific, mathematical, historical and philosophical issues. Among his publications in the period were his verse satire in praise of luxury, *Le Mondain*, 1736, and his important contribution to the popularization of science, *Éléments de la philosophie de Newton*, 1736 (*Elements of Sir Isaac Newton's Philosophy*, 1967). He also wrote several of his dramatic tragedies at Cirey (including *Mérope* and *Mahomet*), which, given his situation, he could not see performed at the time. Deprived of the Paris stage, his solution was to create a small amateur theatre in the Château – it is still there. The Château de Cirey (Cirey-sur-Blaise, 52110 Blaiserives) may be visited.

Langres. Birthplace of Denis Diderot (1713–84). There is a statue of the author in the square where he was born (now **place Diderot** – he was born at No 6). The **Musée du Breuil de St-Germain** in **place de Verdun** has exhibits relating to him.

LORRAINE: VOSGES

Charmes. Birthplace of the novelist, journalist and right-wing politician Maurice Barrès (1862–1923), who is buried in the **cemetery** here. The house in which he was born, on **rue des Capucins**, no longer exists – instead he is remembered by a statue in the square which is named after him. Out of the town centre, on the **route d'Épinal**, is the house where Barrès's grandparents lived, where he spent holidays in his childhood, and which he himself bought in 1910. Barrès was preoccupied with what he saw as the importance of maintaining links with one's native, national and regional, tradition and culture. His trilogy *Le Roman de l'énergie nationale*, comprising *Les Déracinés*,

Julien Gracq

1897, *L'Appel au soldat*, 1900, and *Leurs figures*, 1902, explores the effects of cultural separation and alienation – in *Les Déracinés*, seven young men, natives of Lorraine, are first separated philosophically from their native culture by their education and then physically, when they leave for Paris to pursue their various careers: the novel follows their fortunes. In the early years of the century, Barrès campaigned in his journalism and his fiction – *Au service de l'Allemagne*, 1905; *Colette Baudoche*, 1908 – for the restitution of the ceded provinces of Alsace–Lorraine. The nearby ridge **La Colline de Sion-Vaudémont**, is *La Colline inspirée* of his 1913 novel, which pursues themes of the importance of regional consciousness and loyalty in the context of a religious community – the hill, in its mystical and physical presence, becomes a symbol of regional solidarity and pride.

ALSACE: BAS-RHIN

Sélestat. This town is home to one of the oldest public libraries in France.

The Humanist Library at 1 rue de la Bibliothèque comprises the ancient collections of the libraries of the Humanist School of Sélestat, to which donations began in 1452, and the library of Beatus Rhenanus (1485–1547), a friend of Erasmus, which he bequeathed to his native town in 1547. Some of the most impressive manuscripts (7th–15th centuries) and samples of early Alsatian printed books (15th and 16th centuries) are on display. There are also display cases dedicated to Beatus Rhenanus and to the Sélestat Humanists.

Sessenheim. In October 1970, Goethe (see under Strasbourg below) accompanied his fellow student Friedrich Léopold Weyland on a visit to this village close to the Rhine (formerly 'Sesenheim'). Weyland introduced him to the local pastor, Jean-Jacques Brion, and his family. Goethe promptly fell in love with one of the pastor's daughters, Frédérique. He became obsessed with her, dedicating verses to her, and wanting nothing more than to be in her company. He returned to Sessenheim for Christmas in 1770, and again in 1771 at Easter and then in May for a stay of some five weeks. The love affair, in its idyllic rural setting (Extract 11), flourished for a time, but Goethe's passion soon began to fade. On his return to Strasbourg in June, he concentrated his attentions on his studies, forcing his now mixed feelings about Frédérique into the background. Partly because of the difference in their social status, partly because of Frédérique's country upbringing, which had left her unsuited to urban society, and partly because Goethe was young and ambitious and did not want to commit himself to a bourgeois married life, it was clear to him that he would never marry her. Although he continued to visit her during the summer, for him the affair was already over. When he had completed his studies at Strasbourg, Goethe wrote a letter to Frédérique ending the relationship. He paid a farewell visit to Sessenheim in August

1771 and returned to Frankfurt the same month. It was then, he tells us in his appendix to *Poetry and Truth*, when he received Frédérique's reply to his letter, that he felt guilty for the pain he had caused her with the rise and fall of his heartfelt but transient passion. Frédérique remained, it seems, understanding and sympathetic – when Goethe revisited her in 1779, worried that his letters to her had fallen into the hands of an enemy, she reassured him of her loyalty to him and he left easier in his mind about her. The last evidence of correspondence between them is a letter from Frédérique to Goethe of March 1780. Goethe never revisited Alsace.

The pastor's home at Sessenheim no longer exists – a restored barn is all that remains of the presbytery. However, there is a small **museum** in the village dedicated to Goethe and his time in Alsace. You will find there a bust of him (in old age) by David D'Angers, documentation, portraits, manuscripts, souvenirs and explanations relating to the history of his stay here and his relationship with France and its culture generally. **Le Mémorial Goethe** is in rue Frédérique Brion, 67770 Sessenheim.

Strasbourg. Goethe ◊ lived in Strasbourg from April 1770 to August 1771, while completing his law studies at the university. He lodged in the **rue du Vieux-Marché-aux-Poissons** at what is now No 36, and took his meals, along with a group of other students, at a *pension* at **No 22 rue de l'Ail**. In his autobiography *Dichtung und Wahrheit*, 1811–32 (*Poetry and Truth*, 1994/*Truth and Fantasy*, 1949), Goethe recounts in entertaining detail the various important formative experiences of this period of his life. Among the most significant was his meeting and friendship with the philosopher and critic Johann Gottfried Herder (1744–1803), who happened to be staying in Strasbourg at the same time. Herder introduced Goethe to the works of

Shakespeare and encouraged and influenced him in his early writings. The **Cathedral** too was a revelatory experience: 'The more I studied its façade, the surer I became that my first impression was right and that here sublimity and loveliness had merged to form a whole. If we are not to be over-powered by the sheer mass of a huge building and not to be bewildered by its complexity of detail, immensity must combine with grace and beauty, in a way that is unnatural and even, apparently, impossible. The very fact that we cannot formulate our impressions of the minster except in terms of this apparently irreconcilable conflict and its solution is in itself an indication of the building's greatness.' (From the translation entitled *Truth and Fantasy*.) It was also during this period that Goethe met and fell in love with Frédérique Brion at nearby **Sessenheim** (see above) – a different kind of formative experience that would find its way more than once into his work.

Georg Büchner (1813–37) came to Strasbourg to study medicine when he was 18 and stayed for two years. He returned in 1835 to take refuge after his involvement in a failed revolution in Hesse. It was during this latter stay that he wrote his great play *Dantons Tod* (*Danton's Death*), published in 1835 but not performed until 1902.

Among the many admirers of the **Cathedral**, apart from Goethe, have been Alexandre Dumas, who called it the 'eighth wonder of the world', and sculptor and poet Jean Arp (1887–1966). Arp, a co-founder of the Dadaist movement and later a Surrealist, was born here ('i was born in nature. i was born in strasbourg. i was born in a cloud. i was born in a pump. i was born in a robe.'). In his poem 'La cathédrale est un coeur', 1963 ('The Cathedral is a Heart'), he portrays the Cathedral surrealistically as feeling, mutating, growing – 'The cathedral is a heart./The tower is a bud./Have you counted the steps/that lead up to the platform?/ They become more and more numerous every evening.' (from *Collected French Writings* – see Booklist.) The devout Catholic poet and dramatist Paul Claudel (1868–1955) celebrates it less eccentrically in his long poem 'Strasbourg' – although he too perceives it as a living being: 'La Cathédrale, toute rose entre les feuilles d'avril, comme un être que le sang anime, à demi humain.' ('The Cathedral, quite pink amid the April leaves, like a being given life by blood, half-human.') The poem is included in *The Penguin Book of French Verse*.

Strasbourg was also the birthplace of poet Sebastian Brant (1457–1521), and of Gottfried von Strassburg (?–c1210), author of *Tristan und Isolde*.

BOOKLIST

For most of the extracted works, the original publisher in English can be found in 'Acknowledgments and Citations' at the end of the volume, as can the exact location of the extracts and the editions from which they are taken. The date in square brackets is that of the original publication of the work in its original language. For additional titles by the authors highlighted in this chapter and for recommended biographies, see 'Lives and Works'.

Arp, Jean, *Collected French Writings*, Marcel Jean, ed, Joachim Neugroschel, trans, Calder and Boyars, London, 1974/as *Arp on Arp*, Viking Press, New York, 1972.

Barbusse, Henri, *Under Fire* [1915], Fitzwater Wray, trans, Everyman's Library, Dent, London, 1929. **Extract 16.**

Bernanos, Georges, *The Diary of a Country Priest* [1936], P. Morris, trans, Collins, London, 1956.

Blunden, Edmund, *Undertones of War* [1928], Penguin, London, 1992/ Harcourt Brace, Orlando, FL, 1985.

Bowen, Elizabeth, *The House in Paris* [1935], Penguin, London and New York, 1976. **Extract 2.**

Boyd, William, *The New Confessions* [1987], Penguin, London, 1988/ Viking Penguin, New York, 1989.

Claudel, Paul, 'Strasbourg', in *The Penguin Book of French Verse*, Brian Woledge, Geoffrey Brereton and Anthony Hartley, eds, Penguin, London and New York, 1975. (French verse with prose translations.)

Dickens, Charles, *Dickens in France*, In Print Publishing, Brighton, 1996. (Selected non-fiction and correspondence, includes 'Our French Watering-Place'). **Extract 3.**

Dos Passos, John, *Three Soldiers* [1921], Penguin, London, 1990/ Carroll and Graf, New York, 1988.

Faulks, Sebastian, *Birdsong* [1993], Vintage, London, 1994.

Ford, Ford Madox, *Parade's End* [1924–28], Penguin, London, 1990/Knopf, New York, 1992. **Extract 12.**

Goethe, Johann Wolfgang von, *Truth and Fantasy* [1811–32], selected passages from *Dichtung und Wahrheit*, Eithne Wilkins and Ernst Kaiser, trans, Weidenfeld and Nicolson, London, 1949. **Extract 11.** Also translated in full in two volumes in *From My Life: Poetry and Truth*, Princeton University Press, Princeton, NJ, 1994.

Gracq, Julien, *A Balcony in the Forest* [1958], Richard Howard, trans, Harvill, London, 1992/Columbia University Press, New York, 1987. **Extract 1.**

Graves, Robert, *Goodbye to All That* [1929], Penguin, London, 1960/ Doubleday, New York, 1957. **Extract 13.**

Hugo, Victor, *Les Misérables* [1862], Norman Denny, trans, Penguin, London, 1982/C.E. Wilbur, trans, Random House, New York, 1980. **Extract 8.**

Laclos, Choderlos de, *Les Liaisons Dangereuses* [1782], P.W.K. Stone, trans, Penguin, London and New York, 1961.

La Fontaine, Jean de, *Selected Fables*, J. Michie, trans, Penguin, London, 1982.

Meersch, Maxence Van der, *The Bell-ringer's Wife* [1948], Kimber, 1951.

Mitford, Nancy, *Voltaire in Love* [1957], Hamish Hamilton, London, 1976.

Nerval, Gerard de, *Aurélia* [1855] and *Sylvie* [1853], Kendall Lappin, trans, Asylum Arts, Santa Maria, CA, 1993. **Extract 7.**

Owen, Wilfred, *The Collected Poems of Wilfred Owen*, C. Day Lewis, ed, Chatto and Windus, London, 1963/New Directions, New York, 1964. **Extract 14.**

Prévost, L'Abbé, *Manon Lescaut* [1731], Leonard Tancock, trans, Penguin, London, 1949/Viking Penguin, New York, 1988.

Remarque, Erich Maria, *All Quiet on the Western Front* [1929], Triad Granada, London, 1977/ Buccaneer Books, Cutchogue, NY, 1981. **Extract 17.**

Rimbaud, Arthur, *Collected Poems*, Oliver Bernard, ed and trans, Penguin, London, 1962. (French originals with prose translations.)

Rimbaud, Arthur, *Complete Works*, HarperCollins, New York, 1976.

Rimbaud, Arthur, *Poems*, Everyman's Library Pocket Poets, London, 1994. (English verse translations only.) **Extract 5.**

Rimbaud, Arthur, *A Season in Hell and Other Poems*, Norman Cameron, trans, Anvil Press Poetry, London, 1994. (Bilingual.)

Rosenberg, Isaac, *Collected Works*, Chatto and Windus, London, 1989.

Sassoon, Siegfried, *Memoirs of an Infantry Officer* [1930], Faber and Faber, London, 1965. **Extract 15.**

Sassoon, Siegfried, *The War Poems of Siegfried Sassoon*, Faber and Faber, London, 1983.

Sherriff, R.C., *Journey's End* [1929], Penguin, London, 1983/Viking Penguin, New York, 1984.

Simon, Claude, *The Flanders Road* [1960], Richard Howard, trans, John Calder, London, 1985/ Riverrun Press, New York, 1985. **Extract 10.**

Sorley, Charles, *Collected Poems*, C. Woolf, London, 1985.

Sterne, Laurence, *The Life and Opinions of Tristram Shandy* [1759–67], Penguin, London and New York, 1967.

Sterne, Laurence, *A Sentimental Journey* [1768], Penguin, London and New York, 1986. **Extract 4.**

Wodehouse, P.G., *French Leave* [1956], Penguin, London, 1992/ Simon and Schuster, New York, 1959. **Extract 6.**

Yourcenar, Marguerite, *How Many Years – A Memoir* [1977], Maria Louise Ascher, trans, Aidan Ellis, Henley-on-Thames, 1995/Farrar, Straus and Giroux, New York, 1995. (This is a translation of *Archives du Nord*.)

Zola, Émile, *Germinal* [1885], Leonard Tancock, trans, Penguin, London and New York, 1954. **Extract 9.**

Extracts

(1) ARDENNES

Julien Gracq, *A Balcony in the Forest*

At the beginning of the Second World War, Lieutenant Grange is taken to the blockhouse and chalet which he is to man with three other soldiers, deep in the Forest of Ardennes. Instantly affected by the silence and remoteness of the place, Grange begins to enter what will be for him a kind of parallel and idyllic reality, as he waits tensely for the war to find him or pass by him.

The truck climbed quite slowly up the bumpy path. As soon as the zigzags stopped and they had lumbered onto the plateau, the truck turned into a straight road that seemed to run on through the underbrush as far as the eye could reach. The forest was stunted – the trees were mostly birches, dwarf beech, ash, and pin oaks, all gnarled like pear trees – but seemed extraordinarily dense, without a rent or clearing anywhere; on each side of the ribbon of river it was as if this earth had been shaggy with trees for all eternity, had exhausted axe and saber alike by the resurgence of its greedy fleece. Occasionally, a service path ran through the trees, as narrow as an animal trail. The solitude was complete, and yet the possibility of a meeting did not seem altogether unlikely; sometimes, in the distance, there seemed to be a man standing by the roadside in a long pilgrim's cape: at close range, this turned out to be a small fir, its shoulders black and square against the curtain of bright leaves. The road they were on must have followed the plateau's watershed, for there was never the sound of a stream, though two or three times Grange noticed a stone trough, half-buried in a recess of trees, from which a thread of clear water ran: it added to the silence of the fairy-tale forest.

Where am I being taken, he wondered. He calculated that they must have gone a good twelve kilometers since leaving the Meuse: Belgium couldn't be far away. But his mind floated in a comfortable obscurity: he asked for nothing better than to go on driving through the calm morning, between these moist thickets that smelled of squirrels' nests and fresh mushrooms. As they were about to take a turn, the truck slowed down, then, all its springs protesting, plunged left beneath the branches across a grass-grown breach. Among the trees, Grange made out a house with a peculiar looking silhouette as if a kind of Savoyard chalet were caught in the branches, fallen like a meteorite among these forgotten thickets.

'This is where you live,' Captain Vigaud said.

(2) BOULOGNE

Elizabeth Bowen, *The House in Paris*

Boulogne is the setting for the unveiling of a pivotal romantic scene in Bowen's richly textured novel. This passage demonstrates her use of location to illuminate and explain the action she describes.

At three they left, to walk up the battlements. The wide uphill Grande Rue of Boulogne is certainly not gay. Trams crawl unwillingly up it to the boulevards. It is without interest, uncertainly modern, abstract; its steepness, so tiring to the body, is calm to the eye. Shut shops, this afternoon, made its blankness absolute; massed trees at the top were summer-dark with heat. Max and Karen walked up silently, in what shade there was. They found themselves in the tranquil leafy dullness of the boulevards, out of which the old citadel rose.

The utter silence of the glaring, shuttered streets inside the citadel oppressed them. Everyone in here must be asleep, if not dead of a plague. Karen's feet began to ache from the cobbles; an afternoon unreality fell on her. The cathedral had the same stricken look: its façade was caked with autumn greyness, as though mists left a sediment. People in love, in whom every sense is open, cannot beat off the influence of a place. Max and Karen looked about them vaguely, not knowing why, they were not sightseeing – lost to each other in fatigue and vacancy. Then they turned back to the archway they had come in by and climbed the steps beside it, up inside the old wall to the ramparts.

Trees growing up here, and deep silent grass, make the walk round the ramparts dark green. Between branches there were rifts of blue; the bright sea-lit day shimmered and broke in. They passed the first angle, where a tower-top bulges, then sat down on the parapet. No one else was in view; the afternoon was too hot. The stone up here gave out heat, even in shadow. On the outside, below the parapet, the wall dropped sheer to the boulevards: there were seats the other side of the path, but they preferred this unsafe parapet. Having looked up and down the perspective of green walk they turned to look at each other, still with afternoon vacancy in their eyes.

'You're tired,' he said.

'It's the time of day. And the stones. Will you give me a cigarette?'

The leaves behind their heads and the leaves under them kept sifting in the uncertain air that drew out the flags. An incoming tide of apartness began to creep between Max and Karen, till, moving like someone under the influence of a pursuing dream, he drew the cigarette from between her fingers and threw it over on to the boulevard. Moving up the parapet, he kissed her, and with his fingers began to explore her hand. Their movements, cautious because of the drop below, were underlined by long pauses. They were hypnotized by each other, the height, the leaves . . .

(3) BOULOGNE

Charles Dickens, *Our French Watering Place*

In this short essay, originally published in his magazine Household Words in the 1850s, Dickens explains his fondness for Boulogne. He even temporarily deserted his favourite Broadstairs for 'two or three seasons' to spend holiday time here.

There is a charming walk, arched and shaded by trees, on the old walls that form the four sides of this High Town, whence you get glimpses of the streets below, and changing views of the other town and of the river, and of the hills and of the sea. It is made more agreeable and peculiar by some of the solemn houses that are rooted in the deep streets below, bursting into a fresher existence a-top, and having doors and windows, and even gardens, on these ramparts. A child going in at the courtyard gate of one of these houses, climbing up the many stairs, and coming out at the fourth-floor window, might conceive himself another Jack, alighting on enchanted ground from another bean-stalk. It is a place wonderfully populous in children; English children, with governesses reading novels as they walk down the shady lanes of trees, or nursemaids interchanging gossip on the seats; French children with their smiling bonnes in snow-white caps, and themselves – if little boys – in straw headgear like beehives, work-baskets and church hassocks. Three years ago, there were three weazen old men, one bearing a frayed red ribbon in his threadbare button-hole, always to be found walking together among these children, before dinner-time. If they walked for an appetite, they doubtless lived en pension – were contracted for – otherwise their poverty would have made it a rash action. They were stooping, blear-eyed, dull old men, slip-shod and shabby, in long-skirted short-waisted coats and meagre trousers, and yet with a ghost of gentility hovering in their company. They spoke little to each other, and looked as if they might have been politically discontented if they had had vitality enough. Once, we overheard red-ribbon feebly complain to the other two that somebody, or something, was 'a robber'; and then they all three set their mouths so that they would have ground their teeth if they had had any. The ensuing winter gathered red-ribbon unto the great company of faded ribbons, and next year the remaining two were there – getting themselves entangled with hoops and dolls – familiar mysteries to the children – probably in the eyes of most of them, harmless creatures who had never been like children, and whom children could never be like. Another winter came, and another old man went, and so, this present year, the last of the triumvirate left off walking – it was no good, now – and sat by himself on a little solitary bench, with the hoops and the dolls as lively as ever all about him.

(4) CALAIS

Laurence Sterne, *A Sentimental Journey*

Shortly after arriving at Calais, Sterne's narrator Yorick finds himself temporarily left alone in a small rickety chaise (the 'desobligeant') which he is considering hiring for his travels. He decides to use the opportunity to write the Preface to his story, and accordingly muses on the subject of travelling until he is interrupted. (A 'vis a vis' is a carriage in which people sit face to face.)

. . . Even so it fares with the poor Traveller, sailing and posting through the politer kingdoms of the globe in pursuit of knowledge and improvements.

Knowledge and improvements are to be got by sailing and posting for that purpose; but whether useful knowledge and real improvements, is all a lottery – and even where the adventurer is successful, the acquired stock must be used with caution and sobriety to turn to any profit – but as the chances run prodigiously the other way both as to the acquisition and application, I am of opinion, That a man would act wisely, if he could prevail upon himself to live contented without foreign knowledge or foreign improvements, especially if he lives in a country that has no absolute want of either – and indeed, much grief of heart has it oft and many a time cost me, when I have observed how many a foul step the inquisitive Traveller has measured to see sights and look into discoveries; all which, as Sancho Pança said to Don Quixote, they might have seen dry-shod at home. It is an age so full of light, that there is scarce a country or corner of Europe whose beams are not crossed and interchanged with others – Knowledge in most of its branches, and in most affairs, is like music in an Italian street, whereof those may partake, who pay nothing – But there is no nation under heaven – and God is my record, (before whose tribunal I must one day come and give an account of this work) – that I do not speak it vauntingly – But there is no nation under heaven abounding with more variety of learning – where the sciences may be more fitly wooed, or more surely won than here – where art is encouraged, and will soon rise high – where Nature (take her altogether) has so little to answer for – and, to close all, where there is more wit and variety of character to feed the mind with – Where then, my dear countrymen, are you going –

– We are only looking at this chaise, said they – Your most obedient servant, said I, skipping out of it, and pulling off my hat – We were wondering, said one of them, who, I found, was an *inquisitive traveller* – what could occasion its motion. – 'Twas the agitation, said I coolly, of writing a preface – I never heard, said the other, who was a *simple traveller*, of a preface wrote in a *Desobligeant*. – It would have been better, said I, in a *Vis a Vis*.

– *As an Englishman does not travel to see Englishmen*, I retired to my room.

(5) CHARLEVILLE

Arthur Rimbaud, from *À La Musique*

These stanzas from Rimbaud's early satirical poem articulate his alienation from and contempt for the provincial society and environment of Charleville, where he was brought up. Subtitled 'Place de la Gare, à Charleville' the poem depicts a summer evening scene on the town square, the citizens revealing their characters to the accompaniment of the music of a military band. This translation is from the selection published by Everyman's Library (see Booklist) – the translator has chosen to retitle it 'By the Bandstand'.

On the green benches, clumps of retired grocers
Poke at the sand with their knob-top canes,
Gravely talk of treaties, of war, move closer,
Take snuff from little boxes, then begin: 'Which means . . .'

Flattening his global bottom on a bench,
A bourgeois with shiny-buttoned gut – Flemish, not French –
Sucks his smelly pipe, whose flaky tobacco
Overflows – 'It's real imported stuff you know . . .'

On the green grass, slum kids yell and throw stones;
Chewing on roses, fresh-faced young soldiers
Feel sexy at the sound of slide trombones,
And wink at babies on pretty nurses' shoulders.

– And I go running after girls beneath the trees,
In my messy clothes, just like a student:
They know exactly what I'm after, and their eyes
On me can't hide the things I know they want.

I don't say anything: I just keep staring
At the white skin on their necks, their tousled hair,
At what's beneath the silly dresses they're wearing
That show their backs and leave their shoulders bare.

Pretty soon I see a shoe, then a stocking . . .
I put it all together: shoulders, back, hips;
They think I'm strange; they whisper, laughing, mocking . . .
And my brutal wishes bite their little lips . . .

(6) A Coastal Resort

P.G. Wodehouse, *French Leave*

Wodehouse introduces 'Roville-sur-mer', a fashionable resort on the Picardie/Pas-de-Calais coast and one of the main settings for his comic romantic novel.

Roville-sur-mer stands on the shore of the English channel, and in Paris and other French centres you see a good many posters on the kiosks urging you to take your summer vacation there. They all speak very highly of the place.

Like so many of the popular seashore resorts of France, Roville started out in life as a modest fishing village, inhabited by sons of the sea in blue jerseys who, when not fishing, played interminable games of boule on the water-front. Then progress hit it. The boule arena is now the mile-long Promenade des Anglais, there are two casinos, and large white hotels stand gleaming wherever you look – notably the Carlton, the Prince de Galles, the Bristol, the Miramar and – most luxurious of all – the Splendide. Roville points with pride at the Hotel Splendide, and with reason. It has all the latest improvements, including an American bar presided over by Philippe, formerly of Chez Jimmy, Paris, a first-class orchestra and cuisine, a garden for the convenience of guests wishing to commit suicide after visiting one or other of the Casinos, and ruinously expensive suites, mostly on the first floor, with balconies overlooking the water.

Terry was on the balcony of her first-floor suite this morning, standing at the rail and looking down at the beach. The golden sands dotted with striped umbrellas – you get a suggestion of them on the posters – made an attractive picture, but it was with a discontented frown that she eyed the scene, and the frown was still on her face as she turned and went back into the suite to talk to Kate.

'Kate,' she said, 'I'm bored.'

(7) Loisy

Gérard de Nerval, *Sylvie*

The narrator in Nerval's autobiographical novella returns to his native Valois region to see Sylvie, the girl he loved in his youth, and arrives towards the end of a local fête in the village of Loisy. Characteristically, Nerval vividly and lovingly evokes the culture and countryside of the area where he was raised.

I arrived at the Loisy dance at that melancholy, still-quiet hour when lights are turning pale and trembling at the approach of day. The tops of the linden trees were taking on a bluish cast, lighter than their underparts. The rustic flute was no longer getting so much competition from the trilling of the nightingale. Everyone looked pale, and I had difficulty finding any familiar faces among the depleted groups of dancers. At last I espied a tall girl named Lise, a friend of Sylvie's. She gave me a kiss. 'We haven't seen you around here in a long time, Parisian!' she said.

'Yes, it has been a long time.'

'And you've just arrived?'

'Yes, by mail coach.'

'And none too soon!'

'I wanted to see Sylvie. Is she still here?'

'She never leaves till morning, she's so keen on dancing.'

A moment later, I was at her side. She looked tired, but those dark eyes still shone with that old Athenian smile of hers. There was a young man standing near her. She signaled to him that she was not dancing the next quadrille. He withdrew, with a bow.

Dawn was breaking. We left the dance, holding hands. Sylvie's hair was undone, the flowers in it all askew; the nosegay at her bosom was shedding petals on the crumpled lace, some of her own fine handiwork. I offered to see her home. It was full daylight by now, but the weather was threatening. On our left the Thève went murmuring along, leaving at every bend an eddy of quiet water where yellow and white water-lilies were in bloom, an embroidery of delicate water-stars shining like daisies. The fields were bestrewn with bundles and stacks of hay, whose odour went to my head without making me drunk, as the fresh scent of woods and copses of flowering hawthorn used to do.

It didn't occur to us to go walking in the woods again. 'Sylvie,' I said to her, 'you don't love me any more!'

(8) MONTREUIL

Victor Hugo, *Les Misérables*

The Thénardiers, the unscrupulous guardians of Fantine's daughter Cosette, try to extract more money from Fantine by lying to her about her daughter's health. Penniless, Fantine turns to ever more desperate measures, quite literally destroying herself in her attempts to help her daughter.

'Cosette has caught the disease that is sweeping through the region, what they call a military fever. The medicine is very expensive. It is ruining us and we can no longer pay. If you do not send us forty francs within a week the child will die.'

This caused Fantine to burst into hysterical laughter, and she said to Marguerite:

'How wonderful! A mere forty francs! Two napoléons. Where do they expect me to get them? Are they mad?'

She re-read the letter standing by a window on the landing, and then, still laughing, ran downstairs and out into the street. To someone who asked what she found so funny she replied:

'A silly joke in a letter I've just had from some country people. They want forty francs from me, the poor, ignorant peasants!'

Crossing the market-square she saw a crowd gathered round a strangely shaped vehicle from which a man clad in red was addressing them. He was an itinerant dentist selling sets of false teeth, opiates, powders, and elixirs. Drawing closer, Fantine joined in the laughter at his oratory, in which slang for the common people was interlarded with highflown language for the well-to-do; and seeing her laugh, the dentist cried:

'You've got a fine set of teeth, my lass. If you'd care to sell me your two incisors I'll pay you a gold napoléon for each.'

'What are my incisors?'

'Your two top front teeth.'

'How horrible!' exclaimed Fantine.

'Two napoléons,' grumbled a toothless old woman standing near. 'She's in luck!'

Fantine fled, covering her ears to shut out the man's hoarse voice as he shouted after her:

'Think it over, my girl. Two napoléons are worth having. If you change your mind you'll find me this evening at the Tillac d'argent.'

Fantine ran home in a fury of indignation and told Marguerite what had happened.

'Would you believe it! The abominable man – how can they allow such creatures to travel round the country? He wanted to pull my two front teeth out. I should be hideous! Hair grows again, but not teeth. Oh, the monster! I'd sooner throw myself out of a top-storey window. He said he'd be at the Tillac d'argent this evening.'

'How much did he say he'd pay?' asked Marguerite.

'Two napoléons.'

'That's forty francs.'

'Yes,' said Fantine. 'That's forty francs.'

(9) NORD: MINING

Émile Zola, *Germinal*

Étienne Lantier, after his first experience of working in the pit of Le Voreux, wonders whether to move on or stay. Surveying the scene from his room at the local inn, he begins to be fascinated and challenged by its evil and ugly influence which subdues the workers and invades the land.

While he was turning all this over in his mind, his eyes wandered out over the wide plain and gradually took in what they saw. And it surprised him, for he had not imagined that the horizon was like this, when old Bonnemort had pointed it out in the darkness with a wave of the hand. True, he recognized Le Voreux in front of him, lying in a hollow with its timber and brick buildings, the tarred screening shed, the slated headgear, the winding-house and the tall, pale red chimney. There it all was, squat and evil-looking. But the yards round the buildings were much more extensive than he had imagined, like a lake of ink with heaps of coals for waves, bristling with high trestles supporting the rails of the elevated tracks, cluttered up at one end with the stock of timber, looking like a forest that had been mown down and gathered in. The view to the right was blocked by the slag-heap, rising colossal like a giant's earthwork; it was already grass-covered on its older parts, but at the other end it was being consumed by an inner fire, which had been burning for a year with dense smoke, and as it burned had left long trails of bloody rust on the surface of dull grey shale and sandstone. Further away stretched fields, endless fields of corn and beet, all bare at this time of the year, marshes with coarse vegetation and here and there a stunted willow, distant meadows cut up by slender rows of poplar. In the far distance, towns showed like small white patches – Marchiennes to the north, Montsou to the south – whilst eastwards the forest of the Vandame, with its leafless trees, made a purplish line on the horizon. And on this dull winter afternoon, beneath the colourless sky, it seemed as if all the blackness of Le Voreux and all the flying coal-dust had settled on the plain, powdering the trees, sanding the roads, sowing seed in the ground.

(10) SARS-POTERIES

Claude Simon, *The Flanders Road*

In May 1940, it was near this village of rural north-eastern France, close to the Belgian border, that Simon, then a cavalry trooper retreating from the German advance, saw the captain with whom he was riding shot dead by a sniper. His memory of the incident became the basis for his extraordinary multi-layered novel. Here, Georges, the narrator is, as Simon was, riding behind the captain as they approach the unseen sniper – in his narration he tries and fails, as ever, to pin down what actually happened through the search for precision in his memory and in the language with which he expresses it.

. . . and still pretending to see nothing pensive and futile on that horse as he advanced to meet his death whose finger was already pointed at him laid on him his stiff bony body cambered on his saddle at first a blur no larger than a fly for the concealed sniper a thin vertical figure above the gun sight, growing larger as he approached the motionless and attentive eye of his patient murderer index finger on the trigger seeing so to speak the reverse of what I could see or I the back and he the front, that is, between us – I following him and the other man watching him advance – we possessed the totality of the enigma (the murderer knowing what was going to happen to him and I knowing what had happened to him, that is, after and before, that is, like the two parts of an orange cut in half and that fit together perfectly) in the centre of which he rode ignoring or wanting to ignore what had happened as well as what would happen, in that kind of nothingness (as it is said that in the eye of a hurricane there exists a perfectly calm zone) of knowledge, that zero point: he would have needed a mirror with several panels, then he could have seen himself, growing larger until the sniper gradually made out the stripes, the buttons of his coat even the features of his face, the gun sight now choosing the best spot on his chest, the barrel shifting imperceptibly, following him, the glint of sunlight on the black steel through the sweet-smelling hawthorn hedge. But did I really see him or think I saw him or merely imagine him afterwards or even only dream it all, perhaps I was asleep had I never stopped sleeping eyes wide open in broad daylight lulled by the monotonous hammering of the shoes of the five horses trampling their shadows not walking at quite the same gait so that it was like a crepitation alternating catching up with itself superimposing mingling moments as if there were now only one horse, then breaking apart again disintegrating starting over apparently running after itself and so on over and over, the war somehow stagnant, somehow peaceful around us, the sporadic cannon-fire landing in the deserted orchards with a muffled monumental and hollow sound like a door flapping in the wind in an empty house, the whole landscape empty uninhabited under the motionless sky, the world stopped frozen crumbling collapsing gradually disintegrating in fragments like an abandoned building, unusable, left to the incoherent, casual, impersonal and destructive work of time.

(11) SESSENHEIM

Johann Wolfgang von Goethe, *Poetry and Truth*

*Goethe visited Sessenheim with his Alsatian friend Weyland in 1770
while he was a student at Strasbourg. At the home of a country
pastor, he met and fell in love with Frédérique Brion, one of the two
daughters of the family. This passage, taken from the selective
translation entitled 'Truth and Fantasy', finds Goethe playing a
practical joke on the daughters, dressed in the clothes of the suitor to
Frédérique's sister.*

Then I walked up and down in the garden. So far it had all gone very well, but
I drew a deep breath when I thought that Weyland and the girls would soon be
coming along. Then I was suddenly taken off my guard by the mother's coming
up to me; she was just going to ask me something when she looked me in the
face and, recognising me, broke off in the midst of what she was saying. 'I was
looking for George,' she said after a pause. 'And it is you I find, young man.
How many shapes have you, really?' 'Seriously, only one,' I said, 'but for a
joke's sake as many as you like.' 'Then I shall not spoil the joke,' she said
smiling. 'Go down the garden and out into the meadow until it strikes midday,
then come back and I shall have paved the way for your joke.' I did this. Only
when I came out from between the hedges round the village gardens and was
about to go into the meadows, some country people came along the footpath,
which was rather awkward. I thought it best to turn aside into a little wood on
a hill nearby, to hide there until it was time. But how strangely moved I was
when I went into the wood: for there was a little clearing with benches, from
which one had a delightful view out across the countryside. There below me
was the village, with its church steeple, then Drusenheim, and beyond it the
wooded islands in the Rhine; away on the other side were the Vosges
mountains, and Strasbourg Minster, too. Each of these sky-bright pictures was
set in a leafy frame. Nothing could be more charming and delightful. I sat
down on one of the benches and noticed a narrow little board on the mightiest
tree, with the inscription: 'Friederike's Repose.' It did not occur to me that I
might have come only to disturb this repose; for the delightful thing about
falling in love is that just as one does not know how it begins, so too one does
not think of how it will end, and, feeling all gladness and gaiety, one has no
forebodings of any grief one may be about to cause.

(12) SOMME: FIRST WORLD WAR

Ford Madox Ford, *Parade's End*

In the second volume of Ford's tetralogy, No More Parades,
Christopher Tietjens finds himself in the trenches on the Somme.
Here he muses on the deceptive effects of alcohol.

He took a sip from the glass of rum and water on the canvas chair beside him. It was tepid and therefore beastly. He had ordered the batman to bring it him hot, strong and sweet, because he had been certain of an incipient cold. He had refrained from drinking it because he had remembered that he was to think cold-bloodedly of Sylvia, and he had made a practice of never touching alcohol when about to engage in protracted reflection. That had always been his theory: it had been immensely and empirically strengthened by his warlike experience. On the Somme, in the summer, when stand-to had been at four in the morning, you would come out of your dug-out and survey, with a complete outfit of pessimistic thoughts, a dim, grey, repulsive landscape over a dull and much too thin parapet. There would be repellent posts, altogether too fragile entanglements of barbed wire, broken wheels, detritus, coils of mist over the positions of revolting Germans. Grey stillness; grey horrors, in front, and behind amongst the civilian populations! And clear, hard outlines to every thought . . . Then your batman brought you a cup of tea with a little – quite a little – rum in it. In three or four minutes the whole world changed beneath your eyes. The wire aprons became jolly efficient protections that your skill had devised and for which you might thank God; the broken wheels were convenient landmarks for raiding at night in No Man's Land. You had to confess that, when you had re-erected that parapet, after it had last been jammed in, your company had made a pretty good job of it. And, even as far as the Germans were concerned, you were there to kill the swine; but you didn't feel that the thought of them would make you sick beforehand . . . You were, in fact, a changed man. With a mind of a different specific gravity. You could not even tell that the roseate touches of dawn on the mists were not really the effects of rum . . .

(13) SOMME: FIRST WORLD WAR

Robert Graves, *Goodbye to All That*

Graves joined the fighting on the Somme in July 1916, just before his
21st birthday. He had come out to France in early 1915 and had
already been in the trenches further north near Béthune and
Laventie.

The next two days we spent in bivouacs outside Mametz Wood. We were in fighting kit and felt cold at night, so I went into the wood to find German overcoats to use as blankets. It was full of dead Prussian Guards Reserve, big men, and dead Royal Welch and South Wales Borderers of the New Army battalions, little men. Not a single tree in the wood remained unbroken. I collected my overcoats, and came away as quickly as I could, climbing through the wreckage of green branches. Going and coming, by the only possible route, I passed by the bloated and stinking corpse of a German with his back propped against a tree. He had a green face, spectacles, close-shaven hair; black blood was dripping from the nose and beard. I came across two other unforgettable corpses: a man of the South Wales Borderers and one of the Lehr Regiment had succeeded in bayoneting each other simultaneously. A survivor of the fighting told me later that he had seen a young soldier of the Fourteenth Royal Welch bayoneting a German in parade-ground style, automatically exclaiming: 'In, out, on guard!'

I was still superstitious about looting or collecting souvenirs. 'These greatcoats are only a loan,' I told myself. Our brigade, the Nineteenth, was the reserve brigade of the Thirty-third Division; the other brigades, the Ninety-ninth and Hundredth, had attacked Martinpuich two days previously, but had been halted with heavy losses as soon as they started. We were left to sit in shell-holes and watch our massed artillery blazing away, almost wheel to wheel. On the 18th, we advanced to a position just north of Bazentin-le-Petit, and relieved the Tyneside Irish. I had been posted to 'D' Company. Our Irish guide was hysterical and had forgotten the way; we put him under arrest and found it ourselves. On the way up through the ruins of Bazentin-le-Petit, we were shelled with gas-shells. The standing order with regard to gas-shells was not to bother about respirators, but push on. Hitherto, they had all been lachrymatory ones; these were the first of the deadly kind, so we lost half a dozen men.

(14) Somme: First World War

Wilfred Owen, *Anthem for Doomed Youth*

Owen's sonnet, written in 1917, with its control and restraint heightened by the verse form, is a moving and powerful expression of the waste and devastation of the war.

> What passing-bells for these who die as cattle?
>   Only the monstrous anger of the guns.
>   Only the stuttering rifles' rapid rattle
> Can patter out their hasty orisons.
>
> No mockeries now for them; no prayers nor bells,
>   Nor any voice of mourning save the choirs, –
> The shrill, demented choirs of wailing shells;
>   And bugles calling for them from sad shires.
>
> What candles may be held to speed them all?
>   Not in the hands of boys, but in their eyes
> Shall shine the holy glimmers of good-byes.

The pallor of girls' brows shall be their pall;
Their flowers the tenderness of patient minds,
And each slow dusk a drawing-down of blinds.

(15) Somme: First World War

Siegfried Sassoon, *Memoirs of an Infantry Officer*

*George Sherston, the hero in Sassoon's strongly autobiographical
novel, reflects on the catastrophic changes wrought by trench
warfare on the local countryside and rural life. It is spring 1916.*

We went into the line again on Tuesday. For the first three days Barton's
Company was in reserve at 71. North, which was an assortment of dug-outs
and earth-covered shelters about a thousand yards behind the front line. I
never heard anyone ask the origin of its name, which for most of us had meant
shivering boredom at regular intervals since January. Some map-making
expert had christened it coldly, and it had unexpectedly failed to get itself
called the Elephant and Castle or Hampton Court. Anyhow it was a safe and
busy suburb of the front line, for the dug-outs were hidden by sloping ground
and nicely tucked away under a steep bank. Shells dropped short or went well
over; and as the days of aeroplane aggressiveness had not yet arrived, we could
move about by daylight with moderate freedom. A little way down the road
the Quartermaster-sergeant ruled the ration-dump, and every evening Dottrell
arrived with the ration-limbers. There, too, was the dressing station where
Dick Tiltwood had died a couple of months ago; it seemed longer than that, I
thought, as I passed it with my platoon and received a cheery greeting from our
Medical Officer, who could always make one feel that Harley Street was still
within reach.

The road which passed 71. North, had once led to Fricourt; now it skulked
along to the British Front Line, wandered evilly across No Man's Land, and
then gave itself up to the Germans. In spite of this, the road had for me a queer
daylight magic, especially in summer. Though grass patched and derelict,
something of its humanity remained. I imagined everyday rural life going along
it in pre-war weather, until this business-like open air inferno made it an
impossibility for a French farmer to jog into Fricourt in his hooded cart.

(16) SOUCHEZ: FIRST WORLD WAR

Henri Barbusse, *Under Fire*

In this scene from Barbusse's novel, the narrator accompanies his friend Poterloo who wants to revisit his home village of Souchez (Pas-de-Calais), 'to see again the village where he lived happily in the days when he was only a man.' The war, Barbusse reminds us, robbed people of their roots and memories as well as their lives. Souchez is near Noeux-les-Mines – to its north-west is the spur of Notre-Dame de Lorette, a height gained by the French in May 1915, where there is now a cemetery and monument.

We take the road again, which at this point begins to slope down to the depth where Souchez lies. Under our feet in the whiteness of the fog it appears like a valley of frightful misery. The piles of rubbish, of remains and of filthiness accumulate on the shattered spine of the road's paving and on its miry borders in final confusion. The trees bestrew the ground or have disappeared, torn away, their stumps mangled. The banks of the road are overturned and overthrown by shell-fire. All the way along, on both sides of this highway where only the crosses remain standing, are trenches twenty times blown in and re-hollowed, cavities – some with passages into them – hurdles on quagmires.

The more we go forward, the more is everything turned terribly inside out, full of putrefaction, cataclysmic. We walk on a surface of shell fragments, and the foot trips on them at every step. We go among them as if they were snares, and stumble in the medley of broken weapons or bits of kitchen utensils, of water-bottles, fire-buckets, sewing-machines, among the bundles of electric wiring, the French and German accoutrements all mutilated and encrusted in dried mud, and among the sinister piles of clothing, stuck together with a reddish-brown cement. And one must look out, too, for the unexploded shells, which everywhere protrude their noses or reveal their flanks or their bases, painted red, blue, and tawny brown.

'That's the old Boche trench, that they cleared out of in the end.' It is choked up in some places, in others riddled with shell-holes. The sandbags have been torn asunder and gutted; they are crumbled, emptied, scattered to the wind. The wooden props and beams are splintered, and point all ways. The dug-outs are filled to the brim with earth and with – no one knows what. It is all like a dried bed of a river, smashed, extended, slimy, that both water and men have abandoned. In one place the trench has been simply wiped out by the guns. The wide fosse is blocked, and remains no more than a field of new-turned earth, made of holes symmetrically bored side by side, in length and in breadth.

I point out to Poterloo this extraordinary field, that would seem to have been traversed by a giant plough. But he is absorbed to his very vitals in the metamorphosis of the country's face.

He indicates a space in the plain with his finger, and with a stupefied air, as though he came out of a dream – 'The Red Tavern!' It is a flat field, carpeted with broken bricks.

(17) WESTERN FRONT, 1918

Erich Maria Remarque,
All Quiet on the Western Front

In the last months of the war, the German soldiers face defeat and grapple with their suffering and deprivation.

Behind us lay rainy weeks – grey sky, grey fluid earth, grey dying. If we go out, the rain at once soaks through our overcoat and clothing; – and we remain wet all the time we are in the line. We never get dry. Those who will wear high boots tie sand bags round the tops so that the mud does not pour in so fast. The rifles are caked, the uniforms caked, everything is fluid and dissolved, the earth, one dripping, soaked, oily mass in which lie yellow pools with red spiral streams of blood and into which the dead, wounded, and survivors slowly sink down.

The storm lashes us, out of the confusion of grey and yellow the hail of splinters whips forth the childlike cries of the wounded, and in the night shattered life groans painfully into silence.

Our hands are earth, our bodies clay and our eyes pools of rain. We do not know whether we still live.

Then the heat sinks heavily into our shell-holes like a jelly fish, moist and oppressive, and on one of these late summer days, while bringing food, Kat falls. We two are alone. I bind up his wound; his shin seems to be smashed. It has got the bone, and Kat groans desperately: 'At last – just at the last –'

Lives and works of extracted writers

BARBUSSE, Henri (1873–1935). Born in **Asnières**, a suburb of Paris, and educated at the Sorbonne, Barbusse found his sympathies firmly with the political left. He became a radical journalist in the years before the First World War. He also, in that period, published poetry, stories and two novels, including the naturalistic *L'Enfer*, 1908 (*Hell*, 1966), which attracted some attention. The experience of war, however, was to inspire his greatest work and ensure his enduring reputa-

tion. *Le Feu*, 1916 (*Under Fire*, 1926) is France's most famous novel about the First World War. Written partly in the trenches and partly in hospital, it won the Prix Goncourt in 1916. Based on Barbusse's own experiences, *Le Feu* is a novel about the desolation and squalor of the war, and about the comradeship which became the soldiers' one defence against the insanity and brutality of the conflict. Narratively, the book simply follows the experiences of a particular group of soldiers in the **Pas-de-Calais**, vividly evoking the reality of trench warfare, as well as life behind the lines and on brief periods of leave. Barbusse is especially effective at conveying the physical impact of the war on the landscape, the complete destruction of towns and villages and with it the destruction of people's memories and their sense of belonging (Extract 16). Unfortunately, the English translation by Fitzwater Wray is over-literal and may irritate some readers.

Among Barbusse's other publications is *Clarté*, 1919 (*Light*, 1919), another war novel. *Clarté* was also the title of the journal which he established in 1919 and of its associated revolutionary movement, initially internationalist and humanist but later moving closer to Soviet Communism, which attracted the support of left-wing writers from a number of countries.

Barbusse died suddenly in Moscow in 1935.

BOWEN, Elizabeth (1899–1973). Anglo–Irish novelist and short story writer Bowen's *The House in Paris*, 1935, is an intriguing and 'modernist' novel, with twists of time and narrative position. The story focuses on two children, temporarily crossing paths in a house in Paris, where Leopold is waiting to meet his mother whom he does not know and Henrietta is passing through, waiting to be taken on to catch a train. The book gradually reveals and explores the sexual and emotional relationships behind the children's situation and how their present has been determined by a past in which they have played no part. Paris, like the lives of the adults who impact on them, remains largely in the background, but at the same time is ever-present. Henrietta is never taken out to be shown the sights, as she had hoped. An old woman lies dying in the house, 'never not hearing the vibrations of Paris, a sea-like stirring, horns, echoes indoors, electric bells making stars in the grey swinging silence that never perfectly settles in volutions of streets and empty

courts of stone.' *The House in Paris* contains many rich and atmospheric descriptions of the locations where the action takes place – place itself plays an important part in the novel, illuminating and reflecting the sexual and emotional tensions which are developed. Among the most vivid descriptions are the passages relating to **Boulogne** where, in flashback, some of the key scenes are set (Extract 2).

Recommended biography: Victoria Glendinnning, *Elizabeth Bowen: Portrait of a Writer*, Weidenfeld and Nicolson, London, 1977.

DICKENS, Charles (1812–70). Dickens visited France many times and developed a considerable affection for the country and its culture. After his initial English suspicion and alienation, he felt increasingly at home there, becoming proficient in the language and taking great pleasure in the huge success of his books with French readers ('. . . I can't go into a shop and give my card without being acknowledged in the pleasantest manner possible.'). He developed a special liking for **Boulogne**, where he spent several summers in the 1850s (see introduction), and made frequent visits to **Paris**, wandering, in his leisure time, through the streets as he did in London, fascinated and excited by the city. As an internationally famous writer, he wined and dined in the top Parisian literary circles, meeting, among others, Hugo, Lamartine, Sand, and the historian Jules Michelet.

Dickens's travels in and experiences of France find their way into his writing, both fiction and non-fiction. The opening sections of his travelogue *Pictures from Italy*, 1867–68, record a tour through France of 1844 and include sketches of, among other places, **Paris**, **Lyon**, **Avignon**, **Aix** and **Marseille**. He writes entertainingly on France and the French in a number of essays originally published in the periodicals *All the Year Round* and *Household Words* and subsequently included in *The Uncommercial Traveller*, 1890, and *Reprinted Pieces*,

1868. An accessible selection, as well as the French sections of *Pictures from Italy* and some of his correspondence from France, is available in *Dickens in France*, 1996. Among the best of these essays are 'Our French Watering-Place' (Extract 3), on **Boulogne**; 'The Calais Night Mail', on a ferry crossing from Dover to **Calais**; 'A Flight', on a train journey to **Paris;** and 'Travelling Abroad', in which he discusses his fascination with the Paris Morgue.

With regard to his fiction, the novel with a French setting that everybody knows is *A Tale of Two Cities*, 1859 – a story of personal suffering, redemption and sacrifice acted out against the background of the French Revolution. The *Tale* vividly evokes Paris at the time of the Revolution, a city in the grips of violence and greed, against which individual integrity is pitted. Among the many dramatic passages are a stirring portrayal of the storming of the Bastille and wonderfully brooding descriptions of the atmosphere in the working-class *quartier* of **faubourg Saint-Antoine** as the storm clouds of the Revolution gather (see Paris, Extract 32). The book also presents Dickens's views of the contrast between the Revolution's ideals and its reality, and his characteristic distrust of mass movements as opposed to individual action (compare, for example, the treatment of trade unions in *Hard Times*).

Among the other French connections in Dickens's fiction, the opening chapter of *Little Dorrit*, 1857, set in **Marseille**, is outstanding (see also Book 1, Chapter 11 of this novel, on **Chalons**).

Readers wanting to know more about Dickens's relationship with France should also explore the published correspondence (in the Nonesuch edition or the more complete and admirably scholarly Pilgrim edition).

Recommended biography: Peter Ackroyd, *Dickens*, Minerva, London, 1991.

FORD, Ford Madox (1873–1939). Ford, the grandson of the Pre-Raphaelite painter Ford Madox Brown, was born Ford Hermann Hueffer (he changed his name by deed poll in 1919). He was a prolific writer, publishing in many different genres and styles. He wrote novels, poetry, literary and artistic criticism, and autobiography (about 80 books in all), published numerous articles in periodicals on literary topics, and founded and edited two short-lived but important literary reviews (the *English Review* in Britain and the *Transatlantic Review* in France).

Ford enlisted in the army in 1915 – his experiences in the First World War led to a mental breakdown and he was invalided out in 1917. The war experience became the basis for what would be, along with his novel *The Good Soldier*, 1915, his most significant literary achievement – *Parade's End* (Extract 12). This substantial and memorable work, with its combination of broad social-historical canvas and minutely detailed exploration of the psychology and emotions of its hero, originally appeared as a series of four novels published between 1924 and 1928 – *Some Do Not . . .*; *No More Parades*; *A Man Could Stand Up*; and *Last Post*. Also known as the 'Tietjens Saga' after its protagonist Christopher Tietjens, *Parade's End* is concerned with break-up and change, depicting the fall of the old order and traditional values of pre-war Britain, with the trauma of change reflected in the particular crises and agonies of Tietjens's own life and personality. Volumes 2 and 3 (*No More Parades* and *A Man Could Stand Up*) portray life and death in the trenches of the Somme. *A Man Could Stand Up* in particular includes many vivid passages, evoking the war as seen through the eyes and mind of Tietjens.

In 1922 Ford moved to **Paris**, where he became an important and influential figure in ex-pat literary circles. In 1924, he founded the *Transatlantic Review*, which he planned in discussion with his friend Ezra Pound. The *Review* published new Anglo–American writing, by established as well as young un-known authors – the more famous con-tributors included Joyce, Cummings, Stein, Pound, and Hemingway. Hemingway also 'assisted' editorially (imposing his own ideas whenever he could), as did the English poet Basil Bunting (1900–85). The *Review* lasted only a year – it ran into financial trouble and Ford was forced to close it. He continued to live in Paris through the 1920s, and retained a home there well into the 1930s. However, in 1930 his long relationship with Stella Bowen ended (she was the original of Mrs Braddocks in Hemingway's *The Sun Also Rises*) – the beginning of the end was likely Ford's unfortunate affair with Jean Rhys (◊ Paris). During a visit to New York in 1930 Ford met Janice Biala, with whom he was to spend the rest of his life. In the 1930s he kept a home in Paris but for the most part lived with Biala in **Provence**, a region whose culture, food and scenery he loved (see his book *Provence*, 1934, part travel guide, part personal re-miniscence). In 1936, his financial problems became too acute and Ford moved to the USA. He returned to France in 1939, convinced that a visit to his favourite country would improve his rapidly declining health. He was taken seriously ill in **Le Havre** and died in a hospital at **Deauville**, where he is buried.

Recommended biography: Arthur Mizener, *The Saddest Story: A Biography of Ford Madox Ford*, Carroll and Graf, New York, 1985. In 1996, as this book was going to press, an extensive new two-volume biography appeared: Max Saunders, *A Dual Life* (Vol 1 – *The World before the War*; Vol 2 – *The After-War World*), Oxford University Press, Oxford, 1996.

GOETHE, Johann Wolfgang von (1749–1832). Goethe's stay in **Stras-bourg** was short but formative in both personal and literary terms. He arrived in April 1770 to perfect his French and to complete his law studies at the university. He recollects this period in entertaining detail in his autobiography *Dichtung and Wahrheit* (*Poetry and Truth*, 1994/selections as *Truth and Fantasy*, 1949). It was published in four parts between 1811 and 1832, the last part appearing in the year of Goethe's death and written when he was over 80. His aim was to highlight those elements he considered most influential to him in his development as an artist. It is therefore intentionally not a fac-tual account of his life event by event but a collection of key episodes, artisti-cally shaped by the author's editing, selection and emphasis. The section concerning his residence in Strasbourg includes, in particular, a long account of his response to the **Cathedral** (see introduction); a detailed description of the passage of Marie-Antoinette through the city on her way back to Paris from Vienna; his embarrassing experience with a dancing master's daughters; his chance and crucial meet-ing, in terms of his development as an artist, with the German philosopher and critic Johann Gottfried Herder; a walking tour in Alsace; and his first visit to nearby **Sessenheim** (see intro-duction and Extract 11) where he met and fell in love with Frédérique Brion. Goethe's portrait of his early years presents us with a vivid and entertain-ing portrait of a young man recollected with an old man's tolerance and nostal-gia.

Recommended biography: Nicholas Boyle, *Goethe: The Poet and His Age, Vol 1: The Poetry of Desire, 1749–1790*, Clarendon, Oxford, 1991.

GRACQ, Julien (1910–). Julien Gracq, real name Louis Poirier, was born in **Saint-Florent-le-Vieil** (Maine-et-Loire) on 27 July 1910. He was educated in **Nantes** and **Paris** and subsequently pursued a career as a teacher of history in *lycées* in **Quimper**, **Nantes**, **Amiens**, and, from 1947 until 1970, in **Paris** (at the Lycée Claude Bernard). In his later years he returned to Saint-Florent-Le-Vieil.

Primarily a novelist, Gracq has also published literary criticism, most notably an essay on André Breton, two plays, and personal reminiscences. Despite his own literary renown, he has shunned 'literary society' and has been outspoken about what he considers the undesirability of prizes and the commercialization of literature. In 1951, his novel *Rivage des syrtes*, 1951 (*The Opposing Shore*, 1986) won the Prix Goncourt, but he refused to accept it.

Un Balcon en forêt, 1958 (*A Balcony in the Forest*, 1960) – Extract 1 – is characteristic of Gracq's writing and shows the influence of the Surrealist movement behind a more obvious Romantic lyricism. Set in the Forest of **Ardennes** during the first year of the Second World War, the novel focuses on Lieutenant Grange, assigned to a concrete 'blockhouse' in a remote high part of the forest near the Belgian border and waiting for the war to come to him. His senses heightened by the waiting, Grange finds himself cocooned in a dream-like world of natural calm and sensuous experience, where time seems suspended – a Forest of Arden in fact – with the war a distant, dimly realized threat until the final pages of the novel, when it bursts in with grim reality. The strength of the work lies in its minutely observed and atmospheric descriptions, while Grange's character, although the constant focus of the narrative, remains curiously remote and 'unfinished'. Gracq slows the pace almost to soporific, and yet the reader remains fascinated, drawn into the world which the author so mesmerically creates, and in suspense, constantly aware of impending danger.

Also available in translation is *Un Beau ténébreux*, 1945 (*A Dark Stranger*, 1951), set in an out-of-season seaside resort in **Brittany**.

GRAVES, Robert (1895–1985). Graves was a prolific writer in a range of genres – poetry, novels, short stories, biography, children's literature, and essays (especially on poetry and Greek mythology). Born in London and educated at the prestigious Charterhouse school, he joined the army in 1914 and saw considerable and courageous active service in the trenches in the First World War. His war experiences inspired the most powerful section of one of his finest works – *Goodbye to All That*, 1929 (Extract 13). The book is an autobiographical account of his childhood through to the break-up of his first marriage in 1929 and his departure for Majorca ('So I went abroad, resolved never to make England my home again; which explains the "Goodbye to All That" of this title.'). Graves writes in detail of life at the front, in a matter-of-fact prose which often contrasts sharply and effectively with the horrors it describes. He fought in the trenches near **Béthune** and **Laventie** and later on the **Somme**. He was wounded badly in 1916 by an exploding shell – Graves was actually reported dead due to an administrative error and for a short time his family and friends (including Siegfied Sassoon) thought they had lost him. He returned briefly to the front, but proved unfit for further active service (he later fully recovered from his wounds).

Apart from the war, Graves's connections with France were slight. He met Gertrude Stein in **Paris** in 1928 – largely on account of Laura Riding (1901–91), the American poet and critic with whom Graves was then living and working. Riding was interested in and influenced by Stein's work (although the two were later critical of each other). The following year, 1929, Stein invited them to spend time with her and Alice B. Toklas at their summer home in **Belley**, and it was then that Stein whetted their appetite for the island of Majorca, where Riding and Graves lived together for several years and where Graves made his permanent home after the Second World War (with his second wife, Beryl Hodge).

Riding and Graves also lived for a few months in **Brittany**. In the summer

of 1938, towards the end of their relationship, they took a run-down country
house in **Montauban-de-Bretagne**,
near **Rennes**. They lived there until
April 1939, sharing it with their friends
Alan and Beryl Hodge – Beryl, as noted
above, was to become Graves's second
wife.

Recommended biography: Miranda
Seymour, *Robert Graves: Life on the
Edge*, Doubleday, London and New
York, 1995.

NERVAL, Gérard de (1808–55). Nerval (real name Gérard Labrunie) was
born in **Paris** on 22 May 1808. His
mother died some two years after his
birth. His father – a military surgeon in
Napoleon's army until he returned to
France wounded in 1814 – was a distant
parent, both physically and emotionally. Nerval was brought up by his great-
uncle in the **Valois** district in **Picardie**,
at **Mortefontaine** – the region left a
deep impression on him, and he more
than once describes in his work the
woods, lakes, villages and landmarks
around Mortefontaine which so
affected him in his early life (see introduction). His childhood over, he returned to Paris where he lived with his
father and attended the Lycée Charlemagne – among the other students was
Théophile Gautier (1811–72), with
whom he established a lifelong
friendship. In his early adult life, Nerval shared an apartment with Gautier
and fellow Romantic bohemian Arsène
Houssaye (1815–96) – according to
Houssaye, Nerval was an easy person to
live with because he was almost always
out. He was in the habit of wandering
around the streets of Paris at night, his
creative energy flowing, and just went
to sleep wherever he happened to be
when he grew tired – throughout his
life, he had no permanent home and
his lifestyle often verged on the vagabond. Around 1833–34, Nerval met
the actress Jenny Colon, with whom he
fell obsessively in love, idealizing her
and in effect rendering her unattainable
(she married someone else in 1838) –

whether or not they ever had a sexual
relationship is unknown. His examination of his feelings for her, and for the
other most important woman in his
life, the pianist Marie Pleyel, is evident
in some of his best work. In 1834,
Nerval inherited a substantial fortune
from his grandfather, but it disappeared
rapidly into the black hole of a catastrophic publishing venture (*Le Monde
dramatique*, a magazine which seemed
designed primarily to promote the
career of Jenny Colon). Financial problems remained with him for the rest of
his life, and he became evermore foot-
loose, travelling widely but rough and
publishing frequently to make money
but without much success – his literary
value was not properly recognized until
long after his death. In 1841, Nerval
suffered his first mental crisis, foresha-
dowing the illness which was to recur
with increasing frequency and severity
– he apparently suffered from schi-
zophrenia and depression. He explores
his own insanity and dreams in his
remarkable and innovative novel *Aurélia*, 1855 (*Aurélia*, 1991) – later to be
much praised by the Surrealists. Nerval
died in January 1855 – he was found
hanged in a dingy cul-de-sac in Paris, in
all probability by his own hand.

Nerval was a committed Romantic.
Along with Dumas and Gautier, he was
one of 'Les Jeunes-France' (the second-
generation Romantic writers and artists
who were characterized by their extreme views and often eccentric behaviour), and a member of the Petit
Cénacle (the group of younger Romantic poets which spun off from Hugo's
Cénacle in the 1830s). He published
his translation of *Faust*, that great work
of German Romanticism, when he was
only nineteen (according to Gautier,
the translation was much admired by
Goethe himself). His work ranged
widely – theatre criticism, essays, travel
writing, plays, translations of German
writers, short stories, novels, and poetry. Characteristically, it is highly personal and often formally innovative,
playing especially with the interaction

of memory and dreams, reality and illusion.

Perhaps his best known work is *Sylvie*, 1853, fortunately available in a recent excellent translation (*Sylvie*, 1993). This short autobiographical novel tells of the narrator's love of three women and his search for identity, exploring his passions through recollections of emotions and influences. Of the three women, one is a nun, another an acclaimed actress (an idealized version no doubt of Jenny Colon) and the third Sylvie, a down-to-earth country girl, ingenuous and direct, whom the narrator has known since his childhood in the **Valois**. The nun and the actress are unattainable objects of desire – as Aurélie, the actress, puts it, '. . . you're looking for a drama, that's all, and the dénouement escapes you.' Returning to his roots in the Valois the narrator seeks to re-encounter Sylvie the narrator seeks to re-connect himself to his past and anchor himself in the region he loves and in the 'sweet reality' represented by Sylvie (Extract 7). Unfortunately, it is too late and his one-time sweetheart is now herself unattainable. He is, it seems, irrevocably separated from his past – 'I sadly discover within myself the ephemeral traces of a time when I affected a simplistic love of naturalness.' The story is rich in detail about the area in which Nerval grew up – like George Sand, he had a deep feeling not only for the countryside of his childhood but also for the traditions and songs of the local communities, and these too play their part in the novel.

OWEN, Wilfred (1893–1918). When the First World War broke out, Owen was in **Bordeaux** where he had been teaching English since 1913. It was in Bordeaux that he first saw the horrific wounds sustained by soldiers in the trenches – when he visited a hospital which was trying, with inadequate resources, to cope with casualties just brought back from the front. In 1915, Owen returned to Britain and enlisted in the army. He received his commission in June 1916, and left for the Somme at the end of the year. He first saw action in January 1917. In June, he was invalided home, suffering from concussion, the result of a serious fall, and trench fever. For convalescence, he was sent to the Craiglockhart War Hospital in Edinburgh, and it was here that he met Siegfried Sassoon ◊, who had just made a courageous public protest against the war. Their friendship played a key part in Owen's poetic development: at Craiglockhart, Sassoon commented and advised on his work, and edited several important poems which Owen produced during this period, including 'Anthem for Doomed Youth'. He also met Robert Graves at Craiglockhart, and Graves too encouraged him with constructive literary advice.

After several months service in Britain, Owen took a decision to return to the front, believing that only from the trenches could he make his protest effectively, and only there could he support his fellow soldiers. He left again for France at the end of August 1918 and was back in the thick of it in September. In October, he was awarded the Military Cross. On 4 November, one week before the Armistice, he was killed by machine-gun fire while trying to get his company across the **Sambre Canal**, just north of **Ors**.

In his short lifetime, Owen had seen only a handful of his poems published. He has since become the most widely read of all war poets. Much of his finest work was written in the last 12 months of his life – his talent accelerated and his skills rapidly honed in the urgent necessity to communicate the horror and trauma of the trenches. His greatest poems are technically brilliant expressions of controlled indignation mingled with intense compassion. The poem chosen here (Extract 14) is among the best known. 'Anthem for Doomed Youth', 1917, went through many drafts – with revisions by Sassoon – to achieve its immense power. Using the concise and constraining form of the sonnet, it is a timeless expression both of restrained anger at the brutal wastage of war and deep sadness at the widening, rippling circles of its tragedy from battlefield to home. As Owen famously explained, 'Above all I am not concerned with poetry. My subject is War and the pity of War. The Poetry is in the pity.'

Recommended biography: Jon Stallworthy, *Wilfred Owen: A Biography*, Oxford University Press, Oxford, 1977.

REMARQUE, Erich Maria (1898–1970). Remarque (real name Erich Paul Remark) fought in the German trenches in the First World War. He was wounded twice, but survived to produce his great war novel *Im Westen nichts Neues*, 1929 (*All Quiet on the Western Front*, 1929 – Extract 17). The book, together with the famous 1930 film by Lewis Milestone, made an enormous impact. *All Quiet on the Western Front* is a fictionalized account, intense and uncompromisingly realistic, of Remarque's experiences in the trenches. With its action seen subjectively through the eyes of the narrator, the novel deals powerfully with suffering, comradeship, and the enduring effects of war. It is not specific about place, beyond its location on the Western Front, and is concerned with the immediate experience of the war rather than its political and historical contexts. As such, it is perhaps even more powerful than the narratives of the other key prose writers of the period, achieving a special universality with its vivid evocations and deep humanity. Its disgust with the war conveyed an essential pacifism which found it a place on the National Socialists' blacklist – it was among the books they subjected to public burning in Berlin in 1933.

Among Remarque's other novels are *Der Weg zurück*, 1931 (*The Road Back*, 1931), a sequel to *All Quiet on the Western Front*, and *Arc de Triomphe*, 1946, a revenge story set in Paris during the Second World War.

In 1938, Remarque went to Switzerland, and declined to return to Germany. He lost his German citizenship as a consequence, and became a US citizen in 1947.

RIMBAUD, Arthur (1854–91). Rimbaud was born at **Charleville** on 20 October 1854. His father was an army officer, and his mother came from an established Ardennais farming family – their contrasting backgrounds and temperaments led to an early separation. From the age of six Rimbaud was brought up by his strict and rigidly moralistic mother. At the Collège de France in Charleville he was an outstanding pupil, regularly winning annual prizes. In his mid teens, however, he began to voice his hatred of the stifling routine and banality of the provincial bourgeois culture he found all around him. His early poem 'À la Musique', 1870, is a withering portrayal of the citizens of Charleville going

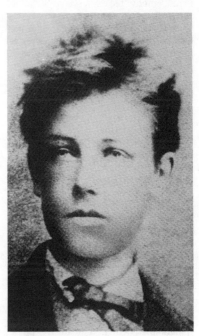

Arthur Rimbaud, 1872

through their predictable motions on the town square (Extract 5).

In the summer of 1870, after the outbreak of the Franco–Prussian war with its attendant excitement and disruptions, Rimbaud took to running away from home, first heading for Paris, where he was arrested and sent back, and then for Belgium, where he spent two weeks of happy wandering. The poems he wrote after this latter escapade, like 'Ma Bohème', reflect his enjoyment of the vagabond lifestyle he had tasted. He became more unruly than ever, expressing his rebellion in his increasing dishevelment, his unremitting insolence, and his rejection of any further attendance at college. He ran away again to Paris in spring 1871, and may have been briefly in the capital when the Commune was at its height.

Rimbaud expounded his famous *théorie du voyant* in his letters of 13 and 15 May 1871 to George Izambard and Paul Démeny. He expresses his belief in the visionary potential of poetry – declaring that 'Le Poëte se fait voyant par un long, immense et raisonné dérèglement de tous les sens. Toutes les formes d'amour, de souffrance, de folie; il cherche lui-même, il épuise en lui tous les poisons, pour n'en garder que les quintessences.' ('The poet becomes a seer through a long, boundless and rational disordering of all the senses. All kinds of love, suffering, madness; he searches his own self, uses up all the poisons within him, keeping only their quintessences.').

In the autumn of 1871, desperate to get to Paris, Rimbaud wrote to Verlaine (◊ Paris), enclosing samples of his poetry. Verlaine, impressed by the brilliance and originality of the work, and encouraged by the similar responses of his Parisian literary friends, replied enthusiastically 'Venez, chère grande âme, on vous appelle, on vous attend.' Before he left, Rimbaud, inspired by the success of his appeal, wrote his remarkable poem 'Le Bateau ivre' ('The Drunken Boat'), an allegorical explora-

tion, packed with startling, momentarily vivid images, of the visionary process – the 'drunken' rudderless and crewless boat deliriously at the mercy of the wild and stormy seas. When the poem was written, Rimbaud was still only 16.

In Paris, Rimbaud first stayed with Verlaine, but his coarseness and dirtiness were more than Verlaine's wife could stand for long. In fact, no-one except Verlaine seems to have been able to tolerate his depravity and arrogance and he soon alienated potential literary friends. With kindred spirit Verlaine, however, he was able to pursue that 'disordering of the senses' which was his purpose. In the summer of 1872, they left Paris together for two years of wandering, with stays in London and Brussels, Verlaine besotted, Rimbaud increasingly experiencing a cooling passion and returning now and then to France. In the final of a series of drunken arguments, in Brussels in July 1873, Verlaine shot and wounded Rimbaud, and so ended the tempestuous affair.

A few weeks earlier, in April 1873, Rimbaud had returned to **Roche** in the Ardennes, where his mother had a small farm. Here, he began *Une Saison en enfer*, 1873 (*A Season in Hell and Other Poems*, 1994), a collection of short pieces in prose and verse bound together by their intense self-analysis, confessional intent, and the ultimate rejection of the tormenting paths to creativity which he had chosen – collectively the 'hell' of the title. *Une Saison en enfer* was published in October 1873 – the printing was paid for by Rimbaud's mother. When he went to Paris to ascertain the impression his book had made, only a few months after the scandalous conclusion of his affair with Verlaine, Rimbaud was snubbed and the book virtually ignored. Back in the Ardennes, he burned his manuscripts and papers in a gesture, presumably, of rebellion against the literary circles which had rejected him, or perhaps as a symbolic repudiation of his own past. As for most things Rimbaud did and wrote, various interpretations are possible.

The remainder of Rimbaud's life had little to do with literature. He seems to have written nothing after the mid-1870s and makes no reference to poetry in the many letters he wrote home from abroad in the last 12 years of his life. After several years wandering in Europe, earning a living from casual jobs, Rimbaud decided to embark on a career. In 1880, employed by a coffee exporter in Aden, he travelled to Harar in Ethiopia (he was the first European to live there) where he eventually set up on his own as a trader and explorer, and where he also became involved in gun-running and, possibly, slave-trading. A tumour on the knee forced him to return in 1891 to **Marseille** where his right leg was amputated. After a brief stay at Roche, he tried to return to Harar but ended up back in hospital at Marseille, where he died on 10 November 1891, aged 37.

Despite his poetic links to his contemporaries, Rimbaud's extraordinary genius stands alone. His achievement is represented above all by the intensely personal, stunningly inventive and ultimately impenetrable prose poems of *Illuminations*, first published in 1886 by Verlaine without Rimbaud's knowledge and consent. The publication of *Illuminations*, plus Verlaine's essay on him in *Les Poètes maudits*, 1884, brought him into the foreground of poetic debate, where he has remained ever since. Rimbaud's innovations in content and technique, and his attempts to fuse language with the senses – see 'L'Alchimie du verbe' ('The Alchemy of the Word') section of *Une Saison en enfer* – have played their part in the development of modern poetry from the Surrealists through to the rock poets of the 1960s and 1970s (superficial similarities between Rimbaud's career and that of Jim Morrison have been made much of). One of the most influential and most discussed poets in French literature, Rimbaud completed his slim *oeuvre* before he was 21, pub-

lished very little of it, and then walked away from it for good, as if it were nothing more than an embarrassing episode of his adolescence.

Recommended biography: Enid Starkie, *Arthur Rimbaud*, Faber and Faber, London, 1973.

SASSOON, Siegfried (1886–1967). When he joined the army in 1914, Sassoon had had no previous employment – his wealthy background had allowed him to spend his days much as he pleased, often hunting or playing golf in the Kent and Surrey countryside and socializing at his London club. His literary output had been limited to privately published poetry. Sassoon experienced the worst of the war – he was involved in the fierce fighting at **Mametz Wood** and in the **Somme Offensive**. He distinguished himself as a soldier, earning the nickname Mad Jack for his bravery, and was awarded the Military Cross. He was shot in spring 1917 and invalided home. Back in Britain, Sassoon became an outspoken opponent of the war, issuing a courageous and defiant public statement to his commanding officer which included such comments as 'I have seen and endured the sufferings of the troops, and I can no longer be a party to prolong these sufferings for ends which I believe to be evil and unjust.' He also threw his MC into the Mersey. Thanks to an intervention by Graves, and presumably to save further embarrassment, the army did not court martial Sassoon, but instead decided he was 'shell-shocked' and despatched him to Craiglockhart War Hospital in Edinburgh, where he met Wilfred Owen and an important literary friendship began (see Owen, above).

As it did for his friends Graves and Owen, the experience of the war took Sassoon's writing ability to a new level – witness the fine war poems of *The Old Huntsman*, 1918, and *Counter-Attack*, 1918. His prose is no less effective: *Memoirs of an Infantry Officer*, 1930, is the second part of a semi-autobiographical trilogy narrating the life of its protagonist George Sherston. It follows on from *Memoirs of a Fox Hunting Man*, 1928, and begins in 1916, with the protagonist already in the trenches (the final part of the trilogy is *Sherston's Progress*, 1936). *Memoirs of an Infantry Officer* maps Sherston's wartime experiences, his final return home, and his formal protest against the continuation of the war. Sassoon's clear and easily accessible prose makes his descriptions and reflections direct and powerful (Extract 15) – conveying with eloquence and control the compassion of a rational man in an irrational world. Sassoon also wrote three volumes of 'straight' autobiography, remembering his life from his childhood through to 1920 – *The Old Century and Seven More Years*, 1938; *The Weald of Youth*, 1942; and *Siegfried's Journey*, 1945. His diaries of the war years were published in 1983.

SIMON, Claude (1913–). Simon was born in Tananarive in Madagascar on 10 October 1913. His father was killed in the First World War and his mother died when he was only 11. He was brought up in south-west France and subsequently studied in Paris. Simon was briefly active in the Spanish Civil War, fighting for the Republicans. When the Second World War broke out in 1939 he was called up, serving in a calvary regiment which was wiped out by German forces. After several months in a prisoner-of-war camp, Simon escaped and returned to France. His wartime experiences were to resurface in some of his most significant fiction – notably *La Route des Flandres* (see below), *La Palace*, 1962 (*The Palace*, 1987), and *Les Géorgiques*, 1981 (*The Georgics*, 1989). In his subsequent life, he continued to involve himself in political campaigns – in 1960, for example, he was one of the signatories of the *Manifeste des 121* (along with Breton, Sartre and Sarraute) against the war in Algeria. Simon is generally associated with the Nouveau Roman movement, especially for his innovative use of subjective and fragmentary narrative. He is, though, also an intuitive and emotive writer, and in some ways a unique talent in contemporary French fiction. One of his persistent themes is the impossibility of pinning down reality, the essential subjectivity of history, and this dominant concern is perhaps what drives his disruptions of conventional narrative forms – in this context a linear narrative becomes impractical. Simon's national reputation was formally recognized when he won the prestigious Prix Médicis for *Histoire*, 1967 (*Histoire*, 1969), dealing precisely with this theme in an associative narrative that combines the protagonist's reminiscences of his parents and other aspects of his personal life with his personal memories of the 'historical' event of the Spanish Civil War. Simon's international standing was appropriately acknowledged with the award of the Nobel Prize for Literature in 1985.

The novel highlighted here (Extract 10) is arguably his greatest. *La Route des Flandres*, 1960 (*The Flanders Road*, 1985) is about, among other things, war, the nature of personality, sexual relationships, and, again, the subjectivity of history, the impossibility of finding one simple 'true' interpretation of events. At the centre of the story is a real-life incident in which Simon himself was involved – the shooting by a sniper of a captain in a French calvary regiment as the captain, a lieutenant and two troopers (Simon was one) were riding away from the Belgian border in May 1940 in retreat from the Germans' advance (see introduction, under **Sars-Poteries**). The narrative of *La Route des Flandres* is dense and complex – sometimes in the first person, sometimes in the third, sometimes ambiguous as to who is 'speaking', it interweaves the perspectives of the three characters who survive the ambush and, arguably, also of the captain's mistress who becomes an important player in the drama. There are, too, many sudden and seamless time shifts, with the associative narrative constantly looping back to the central incident after departures into the time before or the time after. There are moving portrayals of the devastation of war, and effective illustrations of the complexities and ambiguities of sexual relationships. At the novel's heart, though, is the hopeless search for precision, for the truth about what actually happened – did the captain deliberately go into the ambush, in effect to commit suicide, or was his death a routine tragedy of war? The exploration of his past and of the events that follow the incident, the constant returning to the central action of the ambush, the search for the precise word or phrase, all end in ambiguity – as the novel draws to a close the words 'but how can you tell?' recur repeatedly. The form of the novel, with its rejection of linear narrative and its fragmentary structure, reflects its point – that our perception of reality, of the truth behind events, is necessarily limited, selective and ultimately untrustworthy.

STERNE, Laurence (1713–68). Sterne contracted tuberculosis early in his life, and his physical condition deteriorated steadily as he grew older. In 1761, when he had only recently become famous as the author of *Tristram Shandy*, the first two volumes of which had appeared in 1759, he decided to go to France in search of a healthier climate. He spent the first months of 1762 in **Paris**, where he met many of the leading intellectuals of the time – associating especially with Diderot and D'Alembert, and others involved in the *Encyclopédie*. He subsequently moved to the south with his wife and daughter, living in **Toulouse** and **Montpellier** until 1764, when he returned to England on his own – his family remained in the south of France until 1767. He crossed the channel again in October 1765, and spent several months touring in France and Italy.

A Sentimental Journey was no doubt inspired partly by this trip and partly by the publication of Tobias Smollett's (◊ Provence) *Travels Through France and Italy*, which appeared in May 1766, shortly before Sterne stopped in Paris on his way home. Smollett's book, with its caustic comments on France and the French, aroused considerable disapproval among Sterne's Parisian acquaintances, and out of his understanding of his French friends' objections, and his own reactions to it, came the idea for his comic novel *A Sentimental Journey Through France and Italy*, 1768, in which he satirizes Smollett as 'Smelfungus'.

Although the full title implies otherwise, Mr Yorick, the narrator and traveller in *A Sentimental Journey* (Extract 4), never gets to Italy – whether further volumes were intended or whether the title was used simply to mirror that of Smollett's travelogue, is open to speculation. The novel follows the journey through France of the gentle Yorick, a parson (like Sterne himself), who exhibits a consistently positive attitude towards French people and customs, and approaches his many encounters with compassion and sensitivity – a model of the 'Sentimental Traveller', as Sterne defines it (there is, however, irony to be found in the portrayal of Yorick's adventures which undermines the ideal). Although vaguely based on Sterne's own travels, *A Sentimental Journey* is anything but a travel book: places are insignificant, and the focus is on Yorick's musings and his responses to the people he meets on his journey. The style and structure are startlingly innovative. The narrative is consciously informal – it starts in mid-conversation ('They order, said I, these matters better in France'), ends in the middle of a sentence, and is written in a prose that recreates the rhythm of speech, or spoken thoughts – an experiment that stream-of-consciousness exponents would return to around 150 years later.

Sterne also makes fun of travel books and travellers in Volume VII of *Tris-*

tram Shandy, which describes Tristram's wanderings and adventures in France (see introduction, under Calais).

Recommended biography: Arthur H. Cash, *Laurence Sterne: The Early & Middle Years*, and *Laurence Sterne: The Later Years*, Methuen, London, 1975 and 1986.

WODEHOUSE, P.G. (1881–1975). Sir Pelham Grenville Wodehouse bought a house in **Le Touquet** in 1935, and he was there when the Germans arrived in 1940. Wodehouse was arrested, because he was English and under 60, and spent over a year in internment camps. He was released in 1941, but his wife and he were forced to stay in Germany, where his harmless but ill-advised radio broadcasts caused temporary hostility towards him in Britain and the USA. The Wodehouses were moved to **Paris** in 1943 and lived there for the rest of the war. Towards the end of his stay in Paris, Wodehouse noted, in his own special way, the respect for personal freedom that so many before him had valued: 'One thing I love about the French is that they are not hicks, – I mean that if they see anything unusual they accept it politely and don't guffaw. Not a single pedestrian who has passed me during my morning exercises has even turned his head. They see a man in a white sweater and golf bags bending and stretching and they say to themselves, "Ah, a man in a white sweater and golf bags bending and stretching. No doubt he has excellent motives, and in any case it has nothing to do with me."' (from letter of 27 November 1945 quoted by biographer Francis Donaldson). After the war, faced with the likelihood of legal proceedings in Britain because of his broadcasts (although he had many defenders, including George Orwell), and with the Le Touquet house severely damaged, Wodehouse decided to settle in America, where he had already lived for several years. He spent the rest of his life there, taking US citizenship in 1955.

His novel *French Leave*, 1956, is set in coastal **Brittany** and **Picardie** with the odd scene in **Paris**. Unfortunately, it is not one of Wodehouse's better books – it lacks the spark and original wit of the novels which centre around the Jeeves–Wooster relationship, and is essentially a run-of-the-mill farce with minimal characterization and all the sense of place of a Hilton International. However, for Wodehouse fans it is a book by the master in a French setting with a holiday mood. He sets the action in fictional 'exclusive' resorts where tourism has turned small fishing ports into major holiday destinations, with the inevitable casinos and smart hotels (Extract 6).

Recommended biography: Frances Donaldson, *P.G. Wodehouse*, Weidenfeld and Nicolson, London, 1982.

ZOLA, Émile (1840–1902). Although Zola also wrote short stories, plays, libretti, critical essays, and numerous newspaper articles, his reputation rests on his work as a novelist. He was born in **Paris** on 2 April 1840. He grew up in **Aix-en-Provence**, where he formed a close friendship with Paul Cézanne (1839–1906). His father died of pleurisy when he was only seven, and, in some financial difficulty, his mother took him back to Paris in 1858. After failing the *baccalauréat* Zola eventually found employment with the publisher Hachette. In the 1860s, he published his first collection of short stories and two novels, but at that time he attracted attention rather through his committed journalism, especially his defence of the challenging artistic innovations of Manet and his criticism of the regime of the Second Empire.

After 1868, following the publication of *Thérèse Raquin* in 1867, Zola concentrated on his great enterprise, the series of novels which he conceived and wrote over some 25 years, entitled collectively *Les Rougon-Macquart: Histoire naturelle et sociale d'une famille sous le Second Empire*, 1871–1893. As the title implies, the aim of the series (ultimately comprising 20 novels) was to portray a society through the story of one family, and to explore the impacts of both heredity and social environment on individuals. A huge undertaking following in the footsteps of Balzac's *La Comédie humaine*, *Les Rougon-Macquart* employs a vast array of characters, many of whom re-appear in various novels, and settings around the country. The series was conceived in the context of the 'Naturalist' movement (which effectively began in the 1860s although it did not really become a discernible 'movement' until the late 1870s). Driven essentially by socialist principles, and motivated by the considerable political and social changes in progress at the time, *le naturalisme* took as key subjects for treatment capitalist bosses, the corrupt bourgeoisie, the oppressed daily life of workers, the dehumanizing effects of industrial work, and so on. The theoretical framework had its roots in science – Zola was interested in the findings of Charles Darwin and Claude Bernard, in the impacts of natural evolution, the constant struggle with the environment to adapt and survive, and in the importance of heredity in determining a person's physical destiny. The basis of the Naturalist method lay in the goal of scientific experiment – a precise imitation of nature. Zola's *Le Roman expérimental*, 1880, sets out the principles of his Naturalist approach, drawing on the works of Claude Bernard and envisaging the novelist as scientist, using the scientific methods of experiment and observation. However, despite his stated intention that his novels would be less 'social than scientific', the huge impact of Zola's books lies paradoxically in their emotive power, in the engagement of the author's visionary imagination with his humanitarian and social conscience, and in the evocative richness of his prose with all its imagery and symbolism.

In 1877, *L'Assommoir* scored a major success and made him both famous and wealthy – it also made him a target for hostile criticism and moral outrage with its uncompromising portrayal of working class life in Paris. With the royalty earnings from the novel, he bought his country house at Médan (see under 'Île de France') which gave its name to 'Le Groupe de Médan', the loose association of Naturalist writers which met at Zola's house and from which the collection of stories *Les Soirées de Médan*, 1880, arose, including pieces by Zola himself and five of his then 'disciples' – Maupassant, Huysmans, Céard, Hennique, and Alexis.

In 1893, Zola ended his *Rougon-Macquart* series and produced several novels in a different, more optimistic vein – including his *Trois Villes* trilogy, comprising *Lourdes*, 1894 (*Lourdes*, 1993), *Rome*, 1896 (*Rome*, 1993), and *Paris*, 1898 (*Paris*, 1993), which charts the progress of a priest away from the institutionalized religion of Catholicism towards a true commitment to and belief in humanity. Zola's most famous piece of work in these later years was, however, his open letter published in the newspaper *L'Aurore* under the headline 'J'accuse', which made him a central figure on the side of the Dreyfusards in the Dreyfus Affair – the great controversy over a miscarriage of justice which divided France at the turn of the century. The letter, addressed to the President of the Republic, comprised an impassioned protest against the acquittal of Commandant Esterhazy, who was suspected of having committed the crime (spying) for which Captain Dreyfus had been imprisoned. The Affair finds its way into his fiction in the novel *Vérité*, 1903 (*Truth*, 1994). Whether or not his outspoken role in the Dreyfus Affair had anything to do with Zola's death remains a matter of speculation. On 28 September 1902, he was found dead in his Paris apartment – he had died from carbon monoxide poisoning, the result of a blocked chimney. His funeral, with no religious ceremony in accordance with his request, was attended by huge crowds, many among them attesting to the power of his work and his reputation – not least the now released Alfred Dreyfus and the delegations of miners chanting 'Germinal!'. Zola was buried in the cemetery at Montmartre – Anatole France gave the final oration. In 1908, there was a second funeral ceremony, when the coffin was transferred to the **Panthéon**, where Zola now shares a small vault with another great novelist and humanist, Victor Hugo.

The novel given special attention here is one of Zola's most accomplished. *Germinal*, 1885 (*Germinal*, 1954) uses the horrors of 19th century coal mining to paint a grim and sordid picture of the brutalizing and divisive effects of industrial capitalism. The novel is set in northern France, in the *département* of **Nord** (Extract 9), and is a graphic, often brutal examination of human misery and suffering and of the struggle of the oppressed against the system that oppresses them. The novel is, technically, 'historical' – when it was published in 1885 reforms had already alleviated the cruelties and abuses described. However, like Dickens and his condemnation of Squeers's school in *Nicholas Nickleby*, Zola is more concerned with the far-reaching implications of such events and with what they reveal about human nature, than with their immediate sociopolitical context. In a rough outline sent to his publisher, he set out the main subject of the novel – '. . . en un mot, la lutte du travail et du capital. C'est là qu'est l'importance du livre, je le veux prédisant l'avenir, posant la question la plus importante du XXe siècle.' ('. . . in a word, the struggle between labour and capital. That is where the importance of the book lies – I want it to look into the future, to put the key question for the twentieth century.')

If the thematic struggle in *Germinal* is between labour and capital, the essential struggle that informs Zola's work as a whole is between his particular vision of evil (social disintegration, human greed and malevolence, the ex-ploitation of industrialism) and the forces of hope and resistance (fertility, social progress, revolution, the human capacity to withstand suffering). At the end of the bleak and tragic story of *Germinal* he writes, 'On and on ever more insistently, his comrades were tapping, tapping, as though they too were rising through the ground. On this youthful morning, in the fiery rays of the sun, the whole country was alive with this sound. Men were springing up, a black avenging host was slowly germinating in the furrows, thrusting upwards for the harvests of future ages. And very soon their germination would crack the earth asunder.'

Zola's novels convey a strong sense of place and his stories are often located precisely. His evocations of 19th century **Paris** are especially memorable. Here, there is room only for a recommended selection – so see, in particular, *Thérèse Raquin*, 1867 (*Thérèse Raquin*, 1962), with its key setting of a dismal covered passage on the Left Bank near the **Pont-Neuf**; *L'Assommoir*, 1877 (*L'Assommoir*, 1970), a story of working-class life in the **Goutte d'Or** *quartier*; *Le Ventre de Paris*, 1873 (*The Belly of Paris*, 1996), set in **Les Halles**, then the central markets of Paris; *Nana*, 1880 (*Nana*, 1972), his story of the life of a courtesan in the wealthy middle-class environment of **Auteuil**; *La Bête humaine*, 1890 (*The Beast in Man*, 1977), his dark novel set among railway workers and with atmospheric descriptions of the **Gare Saint-Lazare**; and *L'Oeuvre*, 1886 (*The Masterpiece*, 1968), evoking the artistic milieux of Paris and with the **Île Saint-Louis** as a key location. For novels featuring other parts of France, aside from *Germinal*, see especially *La Terre*, 1887 (*The Earth*, 1980), set in a village in the **Beauce** region; and *La Conquête de Plassans*, 1874 (*The Conquest of Plassans*, 1994) – Plassans is Zola's fictionalization of **Aix-en-Provence**.

Recommended biography: Philip Walker, *Zola*, Routledge and Kegan Paul, London, 1985.

Burgundy (Bourgogne); Franche-Comté; Rhône–Alpes

> 'The sight of the awful and majestic in nature had indeed always the effect of solemnising my mind, and causing me to forget the passing cares of life. I determined to go without a guide, for I was well acquainted with the path, and the presence of another would destroy the solitary grandeur of the scene.'
>
> Mary Shelley, *Frankenstein*

BOURGOGNE: YONNE

Sacy. Restif (or Rétif) de la Bretonne (1734–1806) was born at Sacy (near Auxerre) into a well-off peasant family, one of 14 children. His parents' house still exists but cannot be visited (it is opposite the church), as does the family farm, outside the village, from which he took his name (he was born Nicolas Restif). This prolific author, best known for his portrayal of the darker side of Paris in the last years of the 18th century (see under Paris, Latin Quarter), spent the first 12 years of his life here. In his immense (16-volume) autobiography *Monsieur Nicolas*, 1794–97, he recalls his childhood in detail and with nostalgia – vividly evoking the reality of everyday life in Sacy in the mid-18th century. This rural community is also portrayed in arresting detail in Restif's *La Vie de mon père*, 1779, which is available in a recent English translation (*My Father's Life*, 1986).

Saint-Sauveur-en-Puisaye. In 1873 Colette ◊ was born in this village in La Puisaye, which she re-named 'Montigny-en-Fresnois' in the Claudine novels. The house where she was born, and where she lived until 1890, can still be seen in **rue Colette** (formerly **rue de l'Hospice**), and is identified by a plaque. See Extract 11 for her description of it. The village school which she attended – described in *Claudine à l'école*, 1900 (*Claudine at School*, 1963) – has, however, been demolished. Colette's happy childhood here, largely attributable to the enormously positive influence of her mother Sidonie, is memorably evoked in *La Maison de Claudine*, 1922, and *Sido*, 1929 (*My Mother's House and Sido*, 1969). In 1890, financial disaster struck the family and so the house in Saint-Sauveur, and its contents, had to be sold. Shortly afterwards, Colette married Henri Gauthier-Villars and moved to Paris, where she lived for the rest of her eventful life – her early years in the house in Saint-Sauveur, though, always remained vivid in her memory.

TERRITOIRE
DE BELFORT

Y O N N E

HAUTE-SAÔNE

•Luxeuil-
les-Bains

Saint-Sauveur
en-Puisaye
•Sacy

CÔTE D'OR

•Dijon

•Besançon

Urcy•

Saône

D O U B S

N I È V R E

FRANCHE-COMTÉ

B O U R G O G N E

MONTS DU MORVAN

J U R A

SAÔNE-ET-LOIRE

Lac Leman

Milly-Lamartine
Cluny• •Bussières
Saint-Point• •Prissé
•Mâcon

Ferney-Voltaire•

A I N

•Taninges

HAUTE-SAVOIE
•Annecy   Chamonix•

RHÔNE

Loire

Saint-Étienne-
le-Molard •

Belley•

*Lac du
Bourget*

MONT
BLANC ▲

Rhône

•Lyon

Morestel•

Aix-
les-Bains•
•Chambéry

L O I R E

Les Échelles•

I S È R E

S A V O I E

LA GRANDE CHARTREUSE

•Grenoble
•Claix
Villard-de-Lans•

R H Ô N E - A L P E S

A R D È C H E

D R Ô M E

•Ruoms   •Grignan

N

Boundaries

▬·▬·▬· International

▬▬▬ Regions

▬ ▬ ▬ Départements

KILOMETRES
0   50   100

Colette, 1949

Although her actual birthplace is still a private house, a **Musée Colette** has been established in the **Château de Saint-Sauveur**. Opened in 1995, the museum includes recordings and a film documentary. Several rooms recreate Colette's homes in Paris and Burgundy and evoke the connections between her life and her literature.

BOURGOGNE: NIÈVRE

Monts du Morvan. Sylvie Germain's ◊ powerful novel *Jours de colère*, 1989 (*Days of Anger*, 1993) is set in a remote village in a forest of the Morvan, overhanging the River Cure (see Extract 10).

BOURGOGNE: CÔTE-D'OR

Dijon. The playwright Crébillon *père* (1674–1762) was born at **32 rue Monge.** William Carlos Williams ◊ visited Dijon in 1924 and includes the city in his fictionalized travel narrative *A Voyage to Pagany,* 1928 (Extract 4).

Urcy. Here, about 25 km from Dijon, is the **Château de Montculot** which was once the property of the Abbé de Lamartine, uncle of Alphonse de Lamartine (see under Saône-et-Loire below). The young poet was a frequent visitor to the Château, attracted especially by the beauty and solitude of its setting. He inherited it in 1826, but was forced by financial pressure to sell it in 1831. Now a farm, it cannot be visited.

BOURGOGNE: SAÔNE-ET-LOIRE

Bussières. In his childhood, Lamartine came to school here from nearby Milly (see below). He was taught by the young Abbé Dumont, who later became his close friend. On Dumont's death, he wrote the epitaph which you can see on the tombstone displayed at the village church. Dumont's affair with the daughter of a local aristocrat (the comte de Pierreclau – now **Pierreclos** – whose château Lamartine visited frequently) inspired his epic *Jocelyn,* 1836. See under Mâcon for main entry on Lamartine.

Cluny. The remains of the once great Benedictine abbey, founded in 910, are the main attraction here. Abélard (◊ Paris) spent the last years of his life at the abbey (he died in 1142) under the protection of one of its most famous abbots, Peter the Venerable (1092–1156).

Mâcon. Birthplace of Alphonse de Lamartine (1790–1869), with whom the town and the surrounding region are strongly associated. Lamartine is best remembered in literary history for his role in the development of Romantic poetry with his early collection *Méditations poétiques,* 1820 (*Poetical Meditations,* 1993) – introspective verse of sensibility and melancholic lyricism, characteristically relating mood and emotion to aspects of the natural environment. He also wrote travel, history and educational books, and popular pot-boiler novels. In political history, he is famous for his central role in the provisional government during the 1848 Revolution. While he is not so fêted outside his own country, Lamartine is a household name of French culture – as evidenced by the huge tourist industry that has developed around him in this region.

He was born in a house in the grounds of a hotel owned by the Lamartine family in what is now **rue Bauderon-de-Senecé.** The main building can still be seen, but the actual house in which Lamartine was born was demolished in 1970. The **Hôtel d'Ozenay,** rue Lamartine, was bought by his father in 1805 and was the family home in the cold months – Lamartine wrote much of his *Méditations poétiques* while living here. There is a **Musée Lamartine** in the Hôtel Senecé, 41 rue Sigorgne, which includes documents relating to his life and work, as well as furniture, tapestries, and paintings. The Hôtel was formerly the headquarters of l'Académie des Arts et de Belles-Lettres de Mâcon, of which Lamartine was President. What is now the **Musée des Ursilines,** 5 rue des Ursulines, close to Lamartine's birthplace, was formerly a convent. During the Revolution it was used as a prison, and his father was incarcerated there for a time. On the **quai Lamartine** there is a statue of the poet, erected in 1878. It was not much admired by the touring Henry James, who refers to it in his *A Little Tour in France,* 1884: '. . . representing the poet in a frogged overcoat and top-boots, improvizing in a high wind, [the statue] struck me as even less casual in its attitude than monumental sculpture usually succeeds in being.' The mosaic at the corner of **rue Edouard-Herriot** and **rue Gambetta**, done in 1983, depicts the huge banquet given by the city in Lamartine's honour on 18 June 1847. For other key Lamartine landmarks in this region, see entries on Bussières; Milly-Lamartine; Prissé; and Saint-Point.

Milly-Lamartine. In his poem 'Milly ou La Terre natale' (*Harmonies poétiques et religieuses*, 1830), Lamartine sings the praises of the village and the country-side where he spent his childhood. Although his family lived in Mâcon in the winter months, this was the home that most influenced the poet and he remained devoted to it throughout his life – he was heartbroken when, under financial pressure, he was forced to sell it in 1860. The house and grounds have been scrupulously conserved and may be visited. There is also a bust of Lamartine near the **town hall**, and you can still see the family's bench in the **church**.

Prissé. The stately **Château de Monceau** (Prissé, 71960 Pierreclos), was Lamartine's last residence – he and his wife moved here in 1833 from Saint-Point, following the death of their daughter Julia. He was here at the peak of his political fame, and in his quieter old age. The Château cannot be visited and has been substantially changed inside. From the outside, however, it is as Lamartine would have known it – and you can still see in the grounds, amid the vines, the small wooden pavilion which served him as a retreat and where he wrote part of his influential *Histoire des Girondins*, 1847.

Saint-Point. Lamartine inherited the Château here from his father when he married in 1820. He had it substantially altered to his own tastes, and moved in with his English wife, Marianne Birch, in 1823. He kept the property all his

Alphonse de Lamartine (by Decaisne)

life, adding further alterations in the 1850s in the Gothic style reminiscent of Walter Scott. The Château now contains a museum dedicated to the poet (**Château de Lamartine**, Saint-Point, 71360 Tramayes). Among the rooms on exhibition are his bedroom (including the bed, with decorations by his wife, in which he died in Paris on 28 February 1869) and his study. There are many personal and moving exhibits here – including Marianne's portrait of their daughter Julia who died suddenly in 1832, causing the devastated parents soon after to quit permanent residence of the Château – in 1833 they made Monceau their principal home (see above, under Prissé). Lamartine is buried in a sealed chapel in the cemetery of the local **church** along with his wife, daughter, and other members of his family – the chapel was built at the request and with the money of Lamartine himself, in the *gothique troubadour* style which he favoured. In the church, you can see the bench on which he used to sit and two paintings of saints by his wife.

FRANCHE-COMTÉ: HAUTE-SAÔNE

Luxeuil-les-Bains. The stately **Hôtel du Card. Jouffroy**, rue Victor-Genoux, built in the 15th century, has several literary connections. Madame de Sévigné (1626–96) stayed here; it was home for a time to Lamartine (1790–1869); and the historian Augustin Thierry (1795–1856) lived here from 1831 to 1835.

FRANCHE-COMTÉ: DOUBS

Besançon. Charles Nodier (1780–1844), novelist and host of the important Romantic *salon* at the Bibliothèque de l'Arsenal in Paris, was born here, in the street named after him. Victor Hugo (◊ Paris) was born at **No 140** in the **Grande Rue** in 1802 (the house cannot be visited). In the same street were born the Lumière brothers, pioneers of cinematography (Auguste, 1862–1954, and Louis, 1864–1948).

The city features in Stendhal's ◊ *Le Rouge et le noir*, 1830 (*Scarlet and Black*, 1953) – see Extract 2 for Julien Sorel's first impressions.

RHÔNE–ALPES: LOIRE

Saint-Étienne-le-Molard. Honoré d'Urfé (1567–1625), author of the famous but now little read pastoral novel *L'Astrée*, 1607–27 (*Astrea*, 1657–58), was brought up at the country manor house known as **La Bastie**. He also spent part of his adult life at the house, where he conceived and worked on *L'Astrée*. This vast, unfinished prose romance, set in 5th century Gaul, is clearly located here in the **Lignon val-**

ley and celebrates the countryside of the Forez (the Lyonnais) which Urfé knew and loved, with precise topographical detail – although the novel transforms it into an idealized utopian environment, peopled by nymphs and shepherds and noblemen who have renounced all worldly ambitions.

Carefully restored by La Diane, Société Historique et Archéologique du Forez, La Bastie may be visited (**La Bastie d'Urfé**, Saint-Étienne-le-Molard, 42130 Boën-sur-Lignon). The house, in its overall appearance and structure, is broadly as Urfé would have known it, and several of the rooms are as they were when he lived in them. Among these are the 'grotto', decorated with shells and pebbles, the kitchen, with its original stone floor and oven, the chapel, and the *pavillon* in the garden. Also of particular interest are the authentic furniture from the period on display in various rooms, family portraits, including one of Honoré, original Renaissance ceilings, and tapestries depicting pastoral scenes from *L'Astrée*.

RHÔNE–ALPES: RHÔNE

Beaujolais district. Gabriel Chevallier's ◊ comic novel *Clochemerle*, 1936 (*Clochemerle*, 1951) is set in a small town in the Beaujolais hills and includes, as well as affection and satire, accurate and atmospheric descriptions of Beaujolais country (Extract 1). Chevallier is also a stout defender of the local wine: 'There is a tendency among all those who live far from the Department of the Rhône to believe that Morgon is but a pale imitation of Corton. This is a gross and unpardonable error, committed by people who drink with no power of discrimination, trusting to a mere label or to some headwaiter's questionable assertions . . . In reality, the Beaujolais wine has its own peculiar merits and a flavour which cannot be confused with that of any other wine.'

Lyon. Rabelais (◊ Centre) practised as a doctor at the **Hôtel-Dieu** in the 1530s – but the earliest parts of the present hospital (on the same site) date from the 17th century. It was here also that Rabelais had his *Pantagruel* and *Gargantua* printed: the **Musée de l'Imprimerie** at 13, rue de la Poulaillerie is testimony to the city's historically important role as a centre of printing and publishing.

Antoine de Saint-Exupéry (1900–44) was born in Lyon.

RHÔNE–ALPES: AIN

Belley. Alphonse de Lamartine (1790–1869) attended school here in 1803–1807. The school still stands and is now named after him. There is a statue (depicting him in his adolescence) near the entrance.

Belley is also, appropriately in light of the region's traditional reputation for good food, the birthplace of the writer on gastronomy Anthelme Brillat-Savarin (1755–1826), author of the highly regarded *Physiologie du goût*, 1825 (*The Physiology of Taste*, 1994). On their way to visit Picasso in Antibes, Gertrude Stein (◊ Paris) and Alice B. Toklas visited the town, as recorded in *The Autobiography of Alice B. Toklas*, 1933. Attracted by its gastronomic reputation ('Belley is its name and Belley its nature, as Gertrude Stein's elder brother remarked'), they liked the town and the countryside and stayed for longer than they had intended, enjoying the scenery and the food ('. . . Gertrude Stein says that wherever Lamartine stayed any length of time one eats well'), and Belley became a regular summer destination for them: 'All these summers we had continued to go to the hotel in Belley. We now had become so fond of this country, always the valley of the Rhône, and of the people of the country, and the trees of the country, that we began looking for a house. One day we saw the house of our dreams across a valley. Go and ask the farmer there whose house that is, Gertrude

Stein said to me. I said, nonsense it is an important house and it is occupied. Go and ask him, she said. Very reluctantly I did. He said, well yes, perhaps it is for rent, it belongs to a little girl, all her people are dead and I think there is a lieutenant of the regiment stationed in Belley living there now, but I understand they were to leave. You might go and see the agent of the property. We did. He was a kindly old farmer who always told us to allez doucement, go slowly. We had the promise of the house, which we never saw any nearer than across the valley, as soon as the lieutenant should leave. Finally three years ago the lieutenant went to Morocco and we took the house still only having seen it across the valley and we liked it always more.' The house was in nearby **Bilingnin**, and it became a second home for Stein and Toklas. During the Second World War, they lived here permanently. Stein recalls her wartime experiences in the village in *Wars I Have Seen*, 1945.

In 1929, Robert Graves (◊ Picardie) and Laura Riding spent a couple of weeks in Belley with Stein and Toklas, at Stein's suggestion. Stein talked of the happy time she and Toklas had had in Majorca in 1914 ('paradise, if you can stand it'). Graves and Riding, looking for a place to call home, were attracted by her description and shortly afterwards travelled to the island – they ended up living there for several years (Graves himself returned to live in Majorca permanently after the Second World War).

Ferney-Voltaire. In 1759, at the age of 65, Voltaire (1694–1778) bought an estate in the village of Ferney, in French territory but very close to the Swiss border, where he was finally to enjoy both prosperity and security from persecution (far from Paris and near the border but not subject to the control of the Swiss authorities). He spent the last 20 years of his life here, 'one foot in France and the other in Switzerland', managing and developing his estate profitably, making substantial improvements to the village and economy of Ferney, campaigning for many humanitarian causes, writing prolifically, generating a vast correspondence (sometimes 40 letters in a day), and receiving guests from all over the world – for he was by now internationally famous. James Boswell (◊ Corsica) spent a night at Ferney in December 1764 – 'I returned yesterday to this enchanted castle. The magician appeared a very little before dinner. But in the evening he came into the drawing-room in great spirits. I placed myself by him. I touched the keys in unison with his imagination. I wish you had heard the music. He was all brilliance.' (Letter dated 'Château de Ferney, 28 December 1764.')

Voltaire worked and campaigned hard to bring prosperity to his local community, and to alleviate the poverty generally of the Pays de Gex, the small province of which Ferney was then a part. He introduced the cultivation of tobacco, revived the production of silk, encouraged the draining and reclaiming of marshland. In the realm of trade and industry, he brought in tanners, and watch-makers from Geneva, and assisted in the establishment of industries such as lace-making and pottery. He also made civic improvements – he gave the town a theatre (**26 Grand-Rue**), a public fountain (at the intersection of **rue de Mayrin** and **rue de Genève**), and was responsible for much new housing development – you can still see at Ferney various houses from the period which are attibutable to the building plans conceived and implemented by Voltaire. His statue at the intersection of the **Grand-Rue** and **avenue Voltaire** dates from 1890.

The **Château** and its park may be visited and you can see there reconstructions of Voltaire's bedroom and living room, with items of his furniture, tapestries, portraits, etc – and the monument which was supposed to contain his heart (but this, so it is said, is in the base of the statue by Houdon in the Bibliothèque Nationale in Paris). In the entrance hall there are statues of Voltaire and, surprisingly, of Rousseau, his old adversary, who never came to Ferney. In the grounds, there is a disused chapel, built by the philosopher, with the inscription *Deo erexit Voltaire* – 'I prefer to build a church to the Master rather than to his servants,' declared Voltaire, the scourge of institutionalized religion.

In February 1778, in failing health, Voltaire left Ferney for a triumphal return to Paris to see the production of his last tragedy *Irène*. He promised to return soon, but he was not to see Ferney again – he died in Paris within a few weeks of his arrival there.

During his years at Ferney, Voltaire truly established his reputation as the enemy of intolerance and injustice, and an untiring defender of the Enlightenment – not only through his writing but also through his endless campaigning and his determined and hugely energetic practical application of his ideas. At the end of *Candide*, 1759 (*Candide*, 1947), the hero cuts short a philosophical discourse of Pangloss – ' "I also know," said Candide, "that we must go and work in the garden." "You are quite right," said Pangloss. "When man was placed in the Garden of Eden, he was put there 'to dress it and to keep it', to work, in fact; which proves that man was not born to an easy life." '

Le Château de Voltaire, 01210 Ferney-Voltaire, is about 10 km south of Gex.

RHÔNE–ALPES: HAUTE-SAVOIE

Annecy. It was here, at **No 10** in what is now the **rue Jean-Jacques-Rousseau**, that Rousseau first met Madame de Warens (see below under Chambéry, Savoie). In *Les Confessions* he recounts episodes from the time he spent in Annecy before moving with her to Chambéry. The house in which Madame de Warens lived was demolished in 1784 to be replaced by the building which still stands on its site – and which was originally the bishop's palace. There is a bust of Rousseau in the courtyard to commemorate what was for him one of the most important encounters of his life. At **No 13** in the same street was the choir school which he attended, and he sang in the choir at the **Cathédrale Saint-Pierre**.

Novelist Eugène Sue (1804–57) came here in exile from Paris after Napoleon III's *coup d'état* of 2 December 1851. He died in a lakeside village and was buried in Annecy.

Chamonix. Early literary visitors to this now famous Alpine resort at the foot of **Mont Blanc** included Wordsworth ◊, Southey, Byron, Ruskin (◊ Auvergne), and the Shelleys ◊. Of course they did not come to see the town, but the awesome mountain and the dramatic Alpine scenery all around it. Shelley came sightseeing here with Mary Godwin while they were staying in Geneva in the summer of 1816 (she became Mary Shelley at the end of the year). The trip was a productive one in literary terms – Shelley was inspired to write his famous poem 'Mont Blanc' (Extract 9), and Mary found a setting for a key scene in *Frankenstein*, 1818, in which Frankenstein confronts the monster on the **Mer de Glace**, a huge river of ice formed by three converging glaciers (best viewed from the summit of **Montenvers**) – Extract 8. The descriptions of Frankenstein's journey from Geneva to Chamonix and of the mountain scenery are based on her own trip – of which she also provides a factual record in her *Journal* (see Booklist).

Taninges. John Berger ◊ has lived for many years in a village in this region. Although he is careful to stress the broader applicability of the pictures of peasant village life he paints in *Pig Earth*, 1979 (Extract 7) and *Once in Europa*, 1989, the books nevertheless vividly evoke peasant society and landscape in the French Alps where he has made his home.

RHÔNE–ALPES: SAVOIE

Aix-les-Bains. In October 1816, the poet Alphonse de Lamartine (1790–1869) visited this fashionable spa, and met Julie Charles, the consumptive young wife of a famous, but much older, doctor. Whether they met here for the first time or had already encountered each other in Paris and arranged a liaison at Aix-les-Bains is unclear. What is certain is that it was here that their love affair flourished, the banks of the **Lac du Bourget** providing a romantic setting for their encounters. The affair continued in Paris and they arranged to meet at the Lac du Bourget again the following summer. But Lamartine waited in vain for Julie to arrive – she was too ill to make the trip and she died shortly afterwards. The emotional crisis that followed inspired him to write his famous poem of lost love and the transience of life, 'Le Lac' (*Méditations poétiques*, 1820), the last stanza of which reads 'Que le vent qui gémit, le roseau qui soupire,/Que les parfums légers de ton air embaumé,/Que tout ce qu'on entend, l'on voit ou l'on respire,/Tout dise: "Ils ont aimé!" ' ('Let the moaning wind, the sighing reed, let the light perfumes of your balmy air, let everything that is heard, seen or breathed, everything say "They loved!" '). One of the favourite places of the lovers was on the lakeside at the village of **Tresserve** where Lamartine is said to have composed the poem – the spot is now marked by a commemorative monument (erected in 1927). The Benedictine monastery of **Hautecombe** (accessible by boat from Aix-les-Bains) features both in 'Le Lac' and in Lamartine's short novel *Raphaël*, 1849, another of his works inspired by the affair.

Lamartine stayed several times in Aix-les-Bains, at the *pension* of the celebrated Dr Perrier – the building was demolished in 1931, but furniture from his room there is on display at **Le Musée du Docteur-Faure**, 18 boulevard Côtes.

The **Lac du Bourget** is also described by Balzac in *Le Peau de chagrin*, 1831 (*Wild Ass's Skin*, 1977).

Chambéry. In 1736, the 'country house' known as **Les Charmettes** was acquired by Madame de Warens (1700–62). A beautiful woman, separated from her husband, she was an agent of the King of Savoy and was also employed by the priesthood to provide assistance to new converts to Catholicism. In 1728 she had met Jean-Jacques Rousseau (1712–78) in **Annecy** – he was then only 16. They developed a close friendship; she became something like a mother to him (he called her *maman*) and he something like a son to her (she called him *petit*). It seems that they became lovers in 1733 or 1734. The precise details of their relationship and exact places and dates are not certain. However, between 1736 and 1742 Rousseau stayed with Madame de Warens at Les Charmettes several times. 'Here,' he writes in *Les Confessions*, 'begins the short period of happiness in my life.' It was certainly short – he returned to Chambéry from Montpellier in 1737 to find that Madame de Warens had taken another lover. However, it seems that their relationship, whatever form it took, did not end until 1742, when Rousseau left for Paris – and he remained grateful to her for her love and protection throughout his life. Perhaps it is that lasting gratitude which infuses his memory of his stays here in *Les Confessions* with idyllic happiness – 'I rose with the sun, and was happy; I walked, and was happy; I saw Maman, and was happy; I left her, and was happy; I journeyed through the woods and hills, I wandered in the little valleys, I read, I was an idler; I worked in the garden, I gathered fruit, I helped in the house, and happiness followed me everywhere; it was not attributable to anything tangible, it was entirely within myself, it couldn't leave me for a moment.' The house rapidly became a place of pilgrimage after Rousseau's death – Lamartine, Stendhal, and George Sand were among its nineteenth-century visitors.

Les Charmettes is open to the public (**Musée des Charmettes–Maison Jean-Jacques Rousseau**, chemin des Charmettes, Chambéry). The garden (restored) and the outside of the house are more or less as Rousseau would have known them, but inside the decor and furnishings are of a later period. Among the exhibits are a useful map indicating places in Savoie connected with Rousseau and various facsimile documents, including his will.

Rousseau pilgrims will find other places of interest in Chambéry. For example, he worked as a music teacher at several addresses in the town, including the **Hôtel Costa de Beauregard**, 14 rue de la Croix-d'Or. In 1735, Rousseau and Madame de Warens lived in a town house in the **place Saint-Léger**. When he arrived in 1732, Rousseau took an office job which he hated in the **Château des ducs de Savoie** (working for the land registry). And Madame de Warens is buried in the churchyard of **Saint-Pierre**.

The tourist office (24 boulevard de la Colonne) organizes tours of the town highlighting its connections with Rousseau, and will also be able to inform you about the *son-et-lumière* which takes place at Les Charmettes and the dramatization of the life of the young Rousseau which is performed in the streets of the old part of the town.

Les Échelles. In his *Vie de Henry Brulard*, Stendhal (see below, under Grenoble, Isère) writes with uncharacteristic effusiveness about the impression left on him by a visit to Les Échelles in 1791 when he was eight years old. Staying with his elegant and charming uncle, Romain Gagnon, whom the boy admired, and his attractive young wife, he was enraptured by the combination of lively society and the captivating mountain countryside that surrounded him. It was, he said, 'like staying in heaven: everything about it I found ravishing. The noise of the Guiers, the torrent that flowed 200 paces in front of my uncle's windows, became a sacred sound for me, which carried me instantly up into heaven . . .'.

RHÔNE–ALPES: ISÈRE

Brangues. The Catholic poet and dramatist Paul Claudel (1868–1955) acquired the **Château de Brangues** near the town of **Morestel** in 1927. He stayed here as often as he could when he was on leave from his various diplomatic positions (Claudel was ambassador to the USA in 1927–33 and to Belgium in 1933–35). After his retirement he spent every summer at Brangues – and he lived here permanently during the Second World War. The Château is now owned by the Fondation Paul-Claudel, and may be visited on request. You can see, among other rooms, Claudel's study (left exactly as it was when he used it), bedroom and library. He was buried at Brangues, in accordance with his wishes: his grave is in the grounds.

La Grande-Chartreuse. Literary tourists who have travelled to the famous monastery include Wordsworth ◊, who recalls his tour in *The Prelude* (Extract 6); Matthew Arnold ◊, whose visit in 1851 inspired his 'Stanzas from the Grande Chartreuse', 1855 (Extract 5); and Robert Browning, who found it noisy and touristy – 'The acceptance of the Hospitality of the Convent means that you dine there at your own expence (very moderate indeed, but still exacted:) and the consequence is anything but a *conventual* behaviour on the part of the multifarious guests, who make merry as at an eating house, in a mean-looking room . . .'.

Grenoble. Henri Beyle, better known

as Stendhal ◊, was born here in 1783, at the house which is now **No 14, rue Jean-Jacques-Rousseau**. Although it still stands (currently a museum dedicated to the Resistance) it has been much changed since Stendhal lived in it. In his autobiographical *Vie de Henry Brulard*, left unfinished in 1835 (*The Life of Henry Brulard*, 1995), Stendhal writes of his childhood in Grenoble, his antagonism towards his father and his aunt (his mother died when he was seven) and his hatred of what he considered the narrow selfish provincialism of the town. 'Grenoble is for me,' he wrote, 'like the memory of a dreadful bout of indigestion.' He left for Paris in 1799 and returned here only for a few brief visits.

There were, however, happier memories – many of which revolved around Henri's visits to the house of his maternal grandfather, Dr Gagnon. Gagnon was a favourite companion for Stendhal in his childhood and adolescence, and his fine house was for the boy a frequent refuge from his hated aunt, where he played and learned (he was given the freedom of the well stocked library). He writes of his grandfather's home in *The Life of Henry Brulard* – 'He owned an old house situated in the best position in the town, on the Place Grenette, at the corner of the Grande-Rue, facing due south, with in front of it the town's most beautiful square, the two rival cafés and the centre of fashionable society.' The house is now **La Maison Stendhal**, 20 Grande Rue, where the Société des Amis du Musée et de la Maison Stendhal organizes exhibitions and conferences on Stendhal's life and works. It has undergone major alterations since Stendhal knew it, although the terrace looking onto place Grenette, which he remembered with particular affection, still remains, with its trellised vine planted by Dr Gagnon in 1789. Grenoble also has a museum dedicated to Stendhal – **Le Musée Stendhal**, 1 rue Hector-Berlioz – which includes portraits of the writer and his relatives, manuscripts, correspondence, etc. The **municipal library** houses many of his manuscripts, including, of interest to readers of this book, the notebooks which form the basis of *Travels in the South of France* (see under Languedoc–Roussillon, Extract 6). In his last three years at Grenoble, Henri attended the École Centrale, now the **lycée Stendhal**.

Some 10 km to the south is **Claix**, where Stendhal's father had a country house, called **Les Furonières** – the young Henri Beyle spent summer holidays here where, away from the depressing Grenoble home, he learned to appreciate the pleasures of the countryside. The house still exists, but cannot be visited.

Villard-de-Lans. As a child, Georges Perec (◊ Paris), of Polish-Jewish parents, was hidden from Nazi eyes in a Catholic boarding school here called Collège Turenne. Perec's biographer David Bellos comments, 'Collège Turenne has since been converted into an apartment house named Immeuble Diamant, but the building still has the tower that earned the school its nickname, "Le Clocher" (The Belltower).' Perec recalls his time here in *W ou le Souvenir d'enfance*, 1975 (*W or the Memory of Childhood*, 1988).

RHÔNE–ALPES: DRÔME

Grignan. The impressive **Château de Grignan**, 26230 Grigan, extensively restored in 1913, and with a fine Renaissance façade, has associations with Madame de Sévigné (1626–96). Her daughter married the Comte de Grignan, and Sévigné stayed at the Château shortly after the wedding in the 1670s. She was also here from October 1690 to November 1691, and, for the last two years of her life, in 1694–96. She writes of the Château and the region in her celebrated correspondence, revealing a considerable affection for the beauty of the countryside (although she complains about the mistral) and for the Château itself. She died here – her tomb is in the church of **Saint-Sauveur** at Grignan. Various parts of the Château, as well as the gardens and terraces, are now open to the public. The rooms where Sévigné slept and wrote while living at Grignan survive and may be visited – they have of course been completely refurbished and refurnished (the Château has seen interesting times since Sévigné lived in it, not least the ravages of the Revolution).

RHÔNE–ALPES: ARDÈCHE

Ruoms. The family of Alphonse Daudet's mother lived at the nearby **Mas de la Vignasse**, and Daudet (◊ Provence) stayed here in 1855, when he was 15, after his parents, in dire financial straits, had been forced to move away from Lyon. He never returned to the house, but the **Musée Alphonse Daudet et d'Arts et Traditions Populaires** (Saint-Alban-Auriolles, 07120 Ruoms), contains various exhibits relating to him (portraits, manuscripts, photographs, memorabilia, etc).

BOOKLIST

For most of the extracted works, the original publisher in English can be found in 'Acknowledgments and Citations' at the end of the volume, as can the exact location of the extracts and the editions from which they are taken. The date in square brackets is that of the original publication of the work in its original language. For additional titles by the authors highlighted in this chapter and for recommended biographies, see 'Lives and Works'.

Arnold, Matthew, *The Complete Prose Works of Matthew Arnold*, R.H. Super, ed, University of Michigan Press, Ann Arbor, MI, 1960–77 (11 vols).

Arnold, Matthew, 'Stanzas from the Grande Chartreuse', in *The Poems of Matthew Arnold*, Kenneth Allott, ed, Longman, London, 1965. **Extract 5.**

Balzac, Honoré de, *Wild Ass's Skin* [1831], H.J. Hunt, trans, Penguin, London and New York, 1977.

Berger, John, *Once in Europa*, Granta Books, Cambridge, 1989/ Pantheon, New York, 1987.

Berger, John, *Pig Earth*, Writers and Readers Publishing Cooperative, London, 1979/Pantheon, New York, 1992. **Extract 7.**

Boswell, James, *The Journals of James Boswell 1762–1795*, selected and introduced by John Wain, Mandarin, London, 1992. (Includes correspondence and journal entries on meetings with Rousseau and Voltaire.)

Brillat-Savarin, Anthelme, *The Physiology of Taste* [1825], Viking Penguin, New York, 1994.

Chevallier, Gabriel, *Clochemerle* [1936], Jocelyn Godefroi, trans, Mandarin, London, 1993. **Extract 1.**

Colette, *Claudine at School* [1900], Antonia White, trans, Penguin, London, 1990/Ballantine, New York, 1982.

Colette, *My Mother's House and Sido* [1922, 1929], E. Mcleod and U.V. Troubridge, trans, Penguin, London, 1966. **Extract 11.**

Germain, Sylvie, *Days of Anger* [1989], Christine Donougher, trans, Dedalus, Sawtry, 1993/ Godine, Boston, MA, 1993. **Extract 10.**

Hebden, Mark, *Pel and the Predators* [1984], Futura, London, 1985/ Walker & Co, New York, 1985. **Extract 3.**

Lamartine, Alphonse de, *Poetical Meditations* [1820], G. Hittle, trans, E. Mellen Press, Canada, 1993.

Perec, Georges, *W or the Memory of Childhood* [1975], David Bellos, trans, Harvill, London, 1988/ Godine, New York, 1988.

Restif de la Bretonne, *My Father's Life* [1779], R. Veasey, trans, Alan Sutton, Gloucester, 1986.

Rousseau, Jean-Jacques, *The Confessions*, J.M. Cohen, trans, Penguin, London, 1970/Viking Penguin, New York, 1995.

Sévigné, Madame de, *Selected Letters*, Leonard Tancock, trans, Penguin, London and New York, 1982.

Shelley, Mary, *Frankenstein* [1818], Oxford University Press, Oxford and New York, 1980. **Extract 8.**

Shelley, Mary, *Mary Shelley's Journal*, Frederick L. Jones, ed, University of Oklahoma Press, Norman, OK, 1947.

Shelley, Percy Bysshe, 'Mont Blanc', in *Poetical Works*, Oxford University Press, Oxford and New York, 1970. **Extract 9.**

Stein, Gertrude, *The Autobiography of*

Alice B. Toklas [1933], Penguin, London and New York, 1966.

Stein, Gertrude, *Wars I Have Seen* [1945], Brilliance Books, London, 1994.

Stendhal, *The Life of Henry Brulard* [unfinished MS, 1835], John Sturrock, trans, Penguin, London and New York, 1995.

Stendhal, *Scarlet and Black* [1830], Margaret R.B. Shaw, trans, Penguin, London and New York, 1953. **Extract 2.**

Urfé, Honoré d', *Astrea: A romance* written in French and translated by a person of quality, London, 1657–58 (3 vols).

Williams, William Carlos, *A Voyage to Pagany* [1928], New Directions, New York, 1970. **Extract 4.**

Wordsworth, William, *The Prelude* [MS 1805], Ernest de Selincourt, ed, revised by Stephen Gill, Oxford University Press, Oxford and New York, 1970. (Book VI – 'Cambridge and the Alps'; Books IX and X – 'Residence in France'.) **Extract 6.**

Extracts

(1) BEAUJOLAIS

Gabriel Chevallier, *Clochemerle*

Chevallier's comic novel is set in the 1920s in the fictional town of Clochemerle, which he locates in Beaujolais country and to which he ascribes many physical and cultural characteristics of small towns in the region. Here the mayor and his right-hand man, the schoolmaster Tafardel, enjoy an autumn evening and discuss the location of the public urinal which the mayor, Piéchut, has decided to build for the town.

It was the loveliest moment of the day, an autumn evening of rare beauty. The air was filled with the shrill cries of birds returning to roost, while an all-pervading calm was shed upon the earth from the heavens above, where a tender blue was gently turning to the rose pink which heralds a splendid twilight. The sun was disappearing behind the mountains of Azergues, and its light now fell only upon a few peaks which still emerged from the surrounding ocean of gentle calm and rural peace, and upon scattered points in the crowded plain of the Saône, where its last rays formed pools of light. The harvest had been a good one, the wine promised to be of excellent quality. There was cause for rejoicing in that corner of Beaujolais. Clochemerle re-echoed with the noise of the shifting of casks. Puffs of cool air from the still-rooms, bearing a slightly acid smell, cut across the warm atmosphere of the square when the chestnuts were rustling in the north-easterly breeze. Everywhere stains from the wine-press were to be seen and already the brandy was in the process of being distilled.

Standing at the edge of the terrace, the two men were gazing at the peaceful decline of the day. This apotheosis of the dying summer season appeared to them in the light of a happy omen. Suddenly, with a touch of pomposity, Tafardel asked:

'By the way, Monsieur le Maire, where are we going to place our little edifice? Have you thought of that?'

A rich smile, in which every wrinkle on his face was involved, overspread the mayor's countenance. All the same, his jovial expression was somehow menacing. It was a smile that afforded an admirable illustration of the famous political maxim – 'To govern is to foresee.' In that smile of Barthélemy Piéchut's could be read the satisfaction he felt in his consciousness of power, in the fear he inspired, and in his ownership of lovely sun-warmed vineyards and of cellars which housed the best of the wine grown on the slopes that lay between the mountain passes of the West and the low ground of Brouilly. . . .

'Come and let us see the place, Tafardel!' he said simply, making his way towards the main street.

A great utterance. The utterance of a man who has made every decision in advance. An utterance comparable with Napoleon's when crossing the fields of Austerlitz: 'Here, I shall give battle.'

(2) Besançon

Stendhal, *Scarlet and Black*

The ambitious Julien Sorel travels for the first time to Besançon, where he is to enter a seminary. Knowing only rural and small-town life, he is overawed by the provincial capital.

At length, on the summit of a distant mountain, he caught a glimpse of black walls; it was the citadel of Besançon. How different it would be for me, he said sighing, if I were entering this fortified town to become a second lieutenant in one of the regiments in charge of its defence!

Besançon is not only one of the prettiest towns in France, it also abounds with high-hearted and intelligent people. But Julien was only a simple peasant and had no means of approach to distinguished men.

He had got a layman's suit from Fouqué, and was wearing it as he passed over the drawbridge. His mind full of the story of the siege of 1674, he wanted to look at the ramparts and the citadel before shutting himself up in the seminary. Two or three times he came near to being arrested by the sentry as he was making his way into places where military acumen, intent on getting a yearly sum of twelve or fifteen francs by selling hay, forbids the public to enter.

The height of the walls, the depth of the moats, the terrible aspect of the cannon had for several hours been absorbing his attention when he happened to pass by the big café situated on the public walk along the ramparts. He remained motionless with admiration; it was no use his reading the word 'Café' inscribed in large letters above two enormous doors – he could not believe his eyes. He made an effort to overcome his shyness, and, venturing to go inside, found himself in a large room some thirty or forty feet long, with a ceiling at least twenty feet high. Everything seemed magic to him that day.

Two games of billiards were in progress. The waiters were calling out the score; the players were running round the billiard-tables in the midst of a crowd of spectators; floods of tobacco smoke, surging out of everyone's mouth, enveloped them all in a bluish cloud. The high stature of the men, their round shoulders, their ponderous way of walking, their enormous whiskers, the long frock coats in which they were clad, all attracted Julien's attention. These noble scions of ancient Vesontio never spoke without shouting; they affected the pose of formidable warriors. Julien stood still, admiring them, and musing on the vastness and magnificence of a great capital like Besançon. He did not by any manner of means feel brave enough to ask those gentlemen, looking so aloof as they called out the score at billiards, to bring him a cup of coffee.

(3) BURGUNDY: SPRING IN THE CITY

Mark Hebden, *Pel and the Predators*

Hebden uses Burgundy as the atmospheric backdrop for his detective novels centred around Inspector Pel, whom he introduces here. The city is fictitious.

In Burgundy, spring had come early and the enamelled roofs for which the city was famous glowed in the golden light of the warm sunshine. Though it was an up-to-date thriving city packed with pedestrians and traffic, there were always odd corners which belonged to the Middle Ages, so that the solemn buildings, old courtyards and dim alleys seemed in the dusk as if they ought to be peopled in the bizarre splendour of the Valois court, with women in wimples and trailing dresses and men with swords and striped hose. It was often referred to as 'the city of a hundred belfries' but so was Rouen and doubtless a dozen other places too, and Evariste Clovis Désiré Pel of the Brigade Criminelle of the Police Judiciare wasn't one to dwell much on fantasies. A Burgundian to his finger tips, he was as proud of his city as he was of the rolling land that surrounded it, land that produced fat cattle, rich grain and the finest wine in France. When the wine of Bordeaux was mentioned, Pel usually looked blank and asked 'What's that?' though he had recently begun to notice that, for a late evening meal, Burgundy sat somewhat heavily on the stomach while the lighter wine of Bordeaux gave no trouble. As a good Burgundian, it seemed blasphemy to admit it but one had to face the facts of advancing age.

At the moment, however, his heart was light and that was a change because with Evariste Clovis Désiré Pel it often wasn't. A policeman's life, he felt was too real and too earnest for such frivolities as light hearts and, in addition, he suffered from insomnia, overwork, shortage of money, and the unquestionable, indubitable fact that he smoked too much. In recent months he'd cut his cigarettes down from two million a day to around five hundred thousand but he was well aware that it still wasn't half enough and the effort to do better left him edgy with nerves.

(4) DIJON

William Carlos Williams, *A Voyage to Pagany*

Towards the end of his travels through Pagany (Williams's word for Europe) in the 1920s, Dev explores Dijon with his sister and two American friends. They finish up at Ernest's gourmet restaurant.

All that day the four Americans wandered in the summer heat about Dijon, resting now over their drinks at some café or again seeing the curious façades of the twelfth century houses, built fortress strong, on what is to-day some back street; or again perusing, to shamefaced looks on the ladies' parts, some particularly gross praises in word and line to the perfections of one 'Louise' scrawled in crayon on the wall of a house on the rue de la Jouissance.

That evening they had cocktails in their rooms and then betook them as promised, to Ernest's place, found only after a sharp appetite-kindling walk of half an hour, round and about beyond the cathedral in the old city.

There was but one other party in the room, a strange party, as if at a family dinner a whore familiar with the *père de famille* should be invited to partake of it. The man himself was past middle age, but hearty. Their meal was nearly over when the Americans arrived. Bill asked Ernest about it. He said the gentleman was a doctor of the place and the little bright lady was his particular friend, to keep him going; the family knew it was she who kept him going and so she was permitted to be there.

And so the four Americans began to eat, and to drink *Richebourg, 1915, Chambertin* the same, *Musigny, Montrachet,* for two hours – until they could no more. Wow!

The science is exact. The grapes are not palatable; I told you that. Small and bitter. The soil must be poor, of a certain chemistry. They have tried them many places on earth but nowhere do they grow as here.

There was a map on the wall of the H. de la Poste at Beaune showing the famous vineyards. Here too the food was beyond compare: *Chablis, Corton.*

To Dijon, to Beaune must one go, said Dev to himself, from among all places 'in the world', to eat and to drink well.

(5) La Grande-Chartreuse
Matthew Arnold,
Stanzas from the Grande Chartreuse

Arnold visited the Grande-Chartreuse and its famous Carthusian monastery in September 1851 en route to Chambéry from Grenoble on his honeymoon. The visit inspired 'Stanzas from the Grande Chartreuse' published in Fraser's Magazine in 1855. These opening verses describe his approach to the monastery. The 'outbuilding' refers to the old infirmary outside the gate, which is now a museum dedicated to the history and lifestyle of the Carthusians. 'Courrerie' is presumably La Correrie.

Through Alpine meadows soft-suffused
With rain, where the thick crocus blows,
Past the dark forges long disused,
The mule-track from Saint Laurent goes.
The bridge is crossed, and slow we ride,
Through forest, up the mountain side.

The autumnal evening darkens round,
The wind is up, and drives the rain;
While, hark! far down, with strangled sound
Doth the Dead Guier's stream complain,
Where that wet smoke, among the woods,
Over his boiling cauldron broods.

Swift rush the spectral vapours white
Past limestone scars with ragged pines,
Showing – then blotting from our sight! –
Halt – through the cloud-drift something shines!
High in the valley, wet and drear,
The huts of Courrerie appear.

Strike leftward! cries our guide; and higher
Mounts up the stony forest-way.
At last the encircling trees retire;
Look! through the showery twilight grey
What pointed roofs are these advance?
A palace of the Kings of France?

Approach, for what we seek is here!
Alight, and sparely sup, and wait
For rest in this outbuilding near;
Then cross the sward and reach that gate.
Knock; pass the wicket! Thou art come
To the Carthusians' world-famed home.

(6) La Grande-Chartreuse

William Wordsworth, *The Prelude*

In The Prelude, Wordsworth recalls his tour in France, which he made with a fellow student when the country was still celebrating the 'glorious course' of the Revolution. They arrived on 13 July – the next day was the first anniversary of the fall of the Bastille, marked by a ceremony on the Champs de Mars in Paris at which Louis XVI pledged allegiance to the new constitution. Wordsworth and his friend, travelling southwards and caught up in the general spirit of celebration, became friendly with a group of delegates returning home from the festivities.

          In this blithe Company
We landed, took with them our evening Meal,
Guests welcome almost as the Angels were
To Abraham of old. The Supper done,
With flowing cups elate, and happy thoughts,
We rose at signal given, and form'd a ring
And, hand in hand, danced round and round the Board;
All hearts were open, every tongue was loud
With amity and glee; we bore a name
Honour'd in France, the name of Englishmen,
And hospitably did they give us Hail
As their forerunners in a glorious course,
And round, and round the board they danced again.
With this same Throng our voyage we pursu'd
At early dawn; the Monastery Bells
Made a sweet jingling in our youthful ears;
The rapid River flowing without noise,
And every Spire we saw among the rocks
Spake with a sense of peace, at intervals
Touching the heart amid the boisterous Crew
With which we were environ'd. Having parted
From this glad Rout, the Convent of Chartreuse
Received us two days afterwards, and there
We rested in an awful solitude;
Thence onward to the Country of the Swiss.

(7) Haute-Savoie: Peasant Life

John Berger, *Pig Earth*

Berger draws on his own experiences of living in a small peasant community in the Haute-Savoie to explore the culture and psychology of peasant life. Pig Earth includes three versions of the history of a character called Lucie Chabrol ('The Three Lives of Lucie Chabrol') – here, in the first version, the narrator, who has been away from the village and disconnected himself from the community, remembers his childhood with Lucie.

As a young child, two things were unusual about her. She remained very small. And as soon as she could crawl, and later walk, she had a habit of disappearing.

You lose her as easily as you lose a button, La Mélanie said.

I think of Lucie – for that is how she was christened – as a baby in her cradle. What is the difference between a baby and a small animal? An animal goes straight along its own path. A baby vacillates, rolling first to one side and then to the other. Either she's all smiles and gurgles, or a face all puckered up and bawling.

When she was six, Lucie was missing for a whole day. If I go out of the door now and take a few steps up the hillside to where the cows are grazing, I can see the track she took.

It leads to the skyline where the moon rises. In August when the cows are grazing up there, they are silhouetted as if against a great circular lantern. From there the path leads along the crest to a pass where there are some marmots, through a moraine of boulders the size of houses, along the edge of an escarpment, and finally down to the forest below.

In the evening Lucie came back with her hat full of mushrooms. Yet by that time, Marius à Brine had organised a search-party. I remember the men filling their lamps with paraffin.

When there wasn't any work to be done at home, Lucie went to school. The village teacher was called Masson. He used to read from the *Life of Voltaire* and the *curé* preached against this book in church. One thing impressed me about the *Life of Voltaire*. When there was famine, he distributed sacks of grain among the peasants at Ferney. Otherwise the *Life of Voltaire* belonged to that collection of books which we knew existed and which entailed a way of life we could not imagine. At what time of day did people read? we asked ourselves.

(8) Mer de Glace
Mary Shelley, *Frankenstein*

Wandering in his beloved Alps to ease his troubled soul, Franken-stein climbs to the Mer de Glace, where he finds himself confronted by his monster who, rejected and isolated, has left a trail of destruction in his wake. The Shelleys saw the Mer de Glace and other sights on a trip to Chamonix in 1816, and Mary's description is drawn from her recollections of the visit. 'Montanvert' is Montenvers.

It was nearly noon when I arrived at the top of the ascent. For some time I sat upon the rock that overlooks the sea of ice. A mist covered both that and the surrounding mountains. Presently a breeze dissipated the cloud, and I descended upon the glacier. The surface is very uneven, rising like the waves of a troubled sea, descending low, and interspersed by rifts that sink deep. The field of ice is almost a league in width, but I spent nearly two hours in crossing it. The opposite mountain is a bare perpendicular rock. From the side where I stood Montanvert was exactly opposite, at the distance of a league; and above it rose Mont Blanc, in awful majesty. I remained in a recess of the rock, gazing on this wonderful and stupendous scene. The sea, or rather the vast river of ice, wound among its dependent mountains, whose aerial summits hung over its recesses. Their icy and glittering peaks shone in the sunlight over the clouds. My heart, which was before sorrowful, now swelled with something like joy; I exclaimed – 'Wandering spirits, if indeed ye wander, and do not rest in your narrow beds, allow me this faint happiness, or take me, as your companion, away from the joys of life.'

As I said this, I suddenly beheld the figure of a man, at some distance, advancing towards me with superhuman speed. He bounded over the crevices in the ice, among which I had walked with caution; his stature, also, as he approached, seemed to exceed that of man. I was troubled: a mist came over my eyes, and I felt a faintness seize me; but I was quickly restored by the cold gale of the mountains. I perceived, as the shape came nearer (sight tremendous and abhorred?) that it was the wretch whom I had created. I trembled with rage and horror, resolving to wait his approach, and then close with him in mortal combat. He approached; his countenance bespoke bitter anguish, combined with disdain and malignity, while its unearthly ugliness rendered it almost too horrible for human eyes. But I scarcely observed this; rage and hatred had at first deprived me of utterance, and I recovered only to overwhelm him with words expressive of furious detestation and contempt.

'Devil,' I exclaimed, 'do you dare approach me? and do not you fear the fierce vengeance of my arm wreaked on your miserable head? Begone, vile insect! or rather, stay, that I may trample you to dust! and, oh! that I could, with the extinction of your miserable existence, restore those victims whom you have so diabolically murdered!'

(9) Mont Blanc

Percy Bysshe Shelley, *Mont Blanc*

These lines comprise the third section of Shelley's musing on the mountain. He saw Mont Blanc in July 1816 on a sightseeing trip with Mary, and composed the poem during their stay in Chamonix.

Some say that gleams of a remoter world
Visit the soul in sleep, – that death is slumber,
And that its shapes the busy thoughts outnumber
Of those who wake and live. – I look on high;
Has some unknown omnipotence unfurled
The veil of life and death? or do I lie
In dream, and does the mightier world of sleep
Spread far around and inaccessibly
Its circles? For the very spirit fails,
Driven like a homeless cloud from steep to steep
That vanishes among the viewless gales!
Far, far above, piercing the infinite sky,
Mont Blanc appears, – still, snowy, and serene –
Its subject mountains their unearthly forms
Pile around it, ice and rock; broad vales between
Of frozen floods, unfathomable deeps,
Blue as the overhanging heaven, that spread
And wind among the accumulated steeps;
A desert peopled by the storms alone,
Save when the eagle brings some hunter's bone,
And the wolf tracks her there – how hideously
Its shapes are heaped around! rude, bare, and high,
Ghastly, and scarred and riven. – Is this the scene
Where the old Earthquake-daemon taught her young
Ruin? Were these their toys? or did a sea
Of fire envelop once this silent snow?
None can reply – all seems eternal now.
The wilderness has a mysterious tongue
Which teaches awful doubt, or faith so mild,
So solemn, so serene, that man may be,
But for such faith, with nature reconciled;
Thou hast a voice, great Mountain, to repeal
Large codes of fraud and woe; not understood
By all, but which the wise, and great, and good
Interpret, or make felt, or deeply feel.

(10) MORVAN

Sylvie Germain, *Days of Anger*

Germain sets her third novel in a remote forest village in the Monts du Morvan, milking the isolation and mystery of the forest environment for her tale of sin and suffering, and merging the nature of the place with the emotions and passions of her characters.

Both he and she lived to be very old – the madness remained endlessly poised, and did not allow them time to die. They had completely confused death with their lives. And they both spent the duration of this long pause in their madness living in the same hamlet, perched on granite heights, in the shadow of the forests. One of them lived at the top of this small village, and the other at the bottom. The hamlet, called Oak-Wolf, was so tiny and so poor that there did not seem much sense in distinguishing a beginning and an end to it. Yet, short though the distance was between these two farms, it nevertheless represented a vast divide. Anything can occur in two different places, however close they might be. And depending on what happens there, either place may be isolated.

This village had no limits – it lay open to every wind, storm, snowfall and rainfall, and to every passion. The only boundaries were those of the forest, but these are moving boundaries, just as penetrable as they are intrusive – like the confines of the heart when madness encroaches upon love. The hamlet was not signposted. It was just a place whose name was known by word of mouth; a place whose force of being passed from one body to another, thriving in obscure glory in the flesh of its inhabitants.

Rarely did any stranger go up there. It was the people of Oak-Wolf that on Sundays and holidays, on market-days and when labour was being hired, came down into the nearest commune with a church, town hall, square, and bars. So rarely did any stranger venture up there that the villagers they descended on regarded these taciturn visitors as somewhat primitive beings, and the local priest even suspected that the Word of God had not quite managed to reach those semi-barbarians of the forests.

And yet it had travelled all the way up there, admittedly burdened by the mud along the paths – a mud steeped in the old beliefs, in ancient fears and obscure magic, and tangled with roots, branches and tree bark; wind-buffeted and rain-lashed, like the thick, dark, shadowy leaves.

(11) Saint-Sauveur-en-Puisaye

Colette, *My Mother's House*

Here, at the opening of her autobiographical narrative, Colette describes her childhood home, characteristically evoking the sensual impressions that linger in her memory. The house may still be seen (see introduction) – the rue de l'Hospice is now the rue Colette.

The house was large, topped by a lofty garret. The steep gradient of the street compelled the coach-houses, stables and poultry-house, the laundry and the dairy, to huddle on a lower level all round a closed courtyard.

By leaning over the garden wall, I could scratch with my finger the poultry-house roof. The Upper Garden overlooked the Lower Garden – a warm, confined enclosure reserved for the cultivation of aubergines and pimentos – where the smell of tomato leaves mingled in July with that of the apricots ripening on the walls. In the Upper Garden were two firs, a walnut-tree whose intolerant shade killed any flowers beneath it, some rose-bushes, a neglected lawn, and a dilapidated arbour. At the bottom, along the rue des Vignes, a boundary wall reinforced with a strong iron railing ought to have ensured the privacy of the two gardens, but I never knew those railings other than twisted and torn from their cement foundations, and grappling in mid-air with the invincible arms of a hundred-year-old wistaria.

In the rue de l'Hospice, a two-way flight of steps led up to the front door in the gloomy façade with its large bare windows. It was the typical burgher's house in an old village, but its dignity was upset a little by the steep gradient of the street, the stone steps being lopsided, ten on one side and six on the other.

A large solemn house, rather forbidding, with its shrill bell and its carriage-entrance with a huge bolt like an ancient dungeon, a house that smiled only on its garden side. The back, invisible to passers-by, was a sun-trap, swathed in a mantle of wistaria and bignonia too heavy for the trellis of worn iron-work, which sagged in the middle like a hammock and provided shade for the little flagged terrace and the threshold of the sitting-room.

Lives and works of extracted writers

ARNOLD, Matthew (1822–88). Arnold visited the **Grande-Chartreuse** in 1851 during his honeymoon travels on the continent. His poem 'Stanzas from the Grande Chartreuse', 1855 (Extract 5) was inspired by that visit and develops from a description of the romantic scenery through impressions of the ancient monastery to a reflection on the loss of faith and the isolation and spiritual paucity of his own age ('Take me, cowled forms, and fence me round,/Till I possess my soul again;/Till free my thoughts before me roll,/Not chafed by hourly false control'). On an earlier visit to France, in 1846, Arnold met George Sand (◊ Centre), whom he much admired (see his essay 'George Sand', 1877). He visited her château at **Nohant** and toured the region of Berri which she had made famous in her novels. Later in his life, in 1859, 1865, and 1869, he visited the country in the role of Foreign Assistant Commissioner to various commissions on education – and produced reports on *The Popular Education of France*, 1861, *A French Eton*, 1864, and *Schools and Universities on the Continent*, 1868. While in Paris, he took the opportunity to meet, among others, Mérimée, Renan, and Sainte-Beuve (on whom he published an essay in 1869).

Recommended biography: Park Honan, *Matthew Arnold: A Life*, Weidenfeld and Nicolson, London, 1981.

BERGER, John (1926–). Born and educated in London, Berger is an art historian, an essayist, a novelist and short-story writer, a journalist and a broadcaster. One of his special interests is the relationship between the writer and the reader, the artist and the public, the conception and the perception. This preoccupation is often apparent in his writing – it is often explicit as well as implicit, with clear expressions of the purpose behind his work and contextual background. Berger has lived and worked for many years in a small peasant village in the French Alps near **Taninges**, and he draws on his experiences there for *Pig Earth*, 1979, a collection of stories and poems which evoke and explore peasant life (Extract 7). Although the stories are vividly set against the specific landscape he knows, Berger has made it clear that 'Certain details apart, this village could exist in a number of countries across the world.' His concern is with the extinguishing of a way of life, the disappearance of the peasant class and the history and traditions that it carries with it. As he explains in his 'Historical Afterword' in *Pig Earth*, 'The remarkable continuity of peasant experience and the peasant view of the world, acquires, as it is threatened with extinction, an unprecedented and unexpected urgency. . . . The peasant suspicion of "progress", as it has finally been imposed by the global history of corporate capitalism and by the power of this history even over those seeking an alternative to it, is not altogether misplaced or groundless.' *Pig Earth* is the first of a three-part undertaking with the collective title *Into Their Labours* which traces the movement away from peasant society to the metropolis. The second part, *Once in Europa*, also set in Haute-Savoie, was published in 1989, and the third, *Lilac and Flag*, in 1991.

CHEVALLIER, Gabriel (1895–1969). Chevallier was born in **Lyon**, where he spent much of his life. He fought in the First World War and was decorated (Croix de Guerre and Chevalier de la Légion d'Honneur). After a variety of jobs (including art-teacher and commercial traveller), he turned to writing. Chevallier produced a considerable number of novels but his fame rests on one – *Clochemerle*, 1936 (*Clochemerle*, 1951). This affectionate comic novel celebrates the Beaujolais region, which Chevallier knew intimately, and at the same time mercilessly satirizes the social and political machinations of provincial small-town life. Set in the fictional but specifically located town of Clochemerle, which is described in minute detail, the novel tells of the squabbles, prejudices, pomposities and jealousies which arise around the mayor's decision to erect a public urinal. It is strong on local atmosphere and includes evocative descriptions of the Beaujolais countryside (Extract 1). The book was filmed in 1948 by Pierre Chenal, adapted for the screen by Chevallier himself. Several of his other novels have been translated into English.

COLETTE, Sidonie-Gabrielle (1873–1954). Colette was born in **Saint-Sauveur-en-Puisaye**. She spent her childhood there and attended the village school, her experiences forming the basis for *Claudine à l'école*, 1900 (*Claudine at School*, 1963). Her mother Sidonie was a major positive influence in her development and features in several of her works, especially the reminiscences of her childhood in *La Maison de Claudine*, 1922, and *Sido*, 1929 (*My Mother's House and Sido*, 1969 – Extract 11). In 1893 she married Henri Gauthier-Villars and moved to **Paris**. Gauthier-Villars had a nice line in getting other people to write novels for him and putting his name – or at least his pseudonym 'Willy' – on the covers. Colette soon became his (unpaid) literary slave and published six books under his name, including the first four Claudine novels, which met with enormous success. Willy's lack of scruples was not limited to the literary sphere – he was no great adherent to the notion of marital fidelity either. The marriage broke down completely in 1906, and Colette embarked on a period of bohemian independence, during which she performed in music-halls and developed a lesbian relationship with 'Missy', the Marquise de Morny. Among other novels, during this period she published (under the name Colette Willy) *La Vagabonde* , 1910 (*The Vagabond*, 1954), an impressive evocation of life backstage in the music halls of the *belle époque* and the story of a woman's struggle for independence. In 1913, Colette married Baron Henry de Jouvenel, with whom she had a daughter. The marriage lasted 12 years and during that time she continued to publish and to develop her reputation as a writer – most notably with *Chéri*, 1920 (*Chéri*, 1963). Her last marriage was in 1935 to Maurice de Goudeket, with whom she stayed until she died. Her later work includes memoirs of her life in Paris during the Second World War (Goudeket was Jewish) and the novel *Gigi*, 1944, which inadvertently gave the world Maurice Chevalier singing 'Thank Heaven for Little Girls' in the 1958 film version (songs by Lerner and Lowe, directed by Vincente Minelli).

Colette lived in **Paris** throughout her adult life and became one of the most loved and respected of its citizens. The most famous of her various addresses was her apartment in the **Palais-Royal** quadrangle, where she lived for 16 years and where she died on 3 August 1954. By that time, her complete works had been published (1948); she had been elected President of the Académie Goncourt (1949); and she had been named a Grand Officier of the Légion d'Honneur (1953). In 1954, Colette, once regarded as scandalous, became the first woman in France to be granted a state funeral.

Much of Colette's work has been translated into English. Her novels are typically concise, entertaining pieces which often evoke atmospherically the society of the *belle époque*. Her observations on sexual and emotional relationships are always acute, and her portrayals of women in search of an independent identity in a world dominated by hypocrisy and masculine values are especially powerful. The book highlighted here (see under Paris, Extract 9) – *Claudine à Paris*, 1901 (*Claudine in Paris*, 1958) – is the second in Colette's series of Claudine novels, charting the emotional and sexual adventures of its heroine, for which the novelist drew extensively from her own experience. The sensuality which motivates Colette is feminine and, not surprisingly in view of her own history, the egotism and sexuality of her male characters are treated with mistrust. *Claudine in Paris* charts the arrival of the 17-year-old Claudine in Paris from her country home in Burgundy where she spent her childhood. Written with characteristic life-affirming energy, the novel describes Claudine's early dislike of the city in contrast to her rural home, her initiation into Paris society, and her attraction to a much older man.

Recommended biography: Herbert Lottman, *Colette: A Life*, Minerva, London, 1991.

GERMAIN, SYLVIE (1954–   ). Ger-

main was born in **Châteauroux** (Indre). She studied at the Sorbonne,
graduating with a doctorate in philosophy. Between 1987 and 1993, she
taught philosophy to French students in
Prague. Since 1993, she has lived in
Paris. Germain has published several
novels, and a collection of short stories.
Most of her work is available in English
translation. Her writing is characterized
by a weaving of fantasy, mystery and
full-intensity human emotions into
narratives of considerable power and
depth. *Jours de colère*, 1989 (*Days of
Anger*, 1993) won the Prix Fémina in
1989. This is a claustrophobic novel of
jealousies and resentments, set in the
forests of the **Morvan**, redolent with
mystery and superstition. The main
characters are inhabitants of a small
remote village in the Jalles Forest (Extract 10). Germain evokes a strong
sense of place, working on the inter-
relationships between the physical environment and the events and emotions she describes. At the beginning of
the book, the murder of Catherine
Corvol by her husband is witnessed by
Ambroise Mauperthuis, who then uses
this knowledge to strip Corvol of his
possessions and his power, so making
him endure 'a punishment that human
justice, had it learned of his crime,
would not have imposed on him with
such cruelty.' The conflicts and passions of the novel emanate from this
action, the malevolence and bleak
savagery of which permeate the story.
Germain's style begs some comparisons
with that of the Chilean writer Isabel
Allende and there are echoes both of
the Magic Realism associated with writers like Allende and Gabriel García
Márquez and of the epic melodrama of
Allende's *The House of the Spirits*.

HEBDEN, Mark (1916–91). Mark
Hebden was a pseudonym of John Harris, who wrote detective and adventure
novels (he also wrote under the name
of Max Hennessy). Before he made his
living as a novelist, he had been a
sailor, an airman, a journalist, a travel

Sylvie Germain

courier, and a history teacher. He
proved himself also well able to turn his
hand to prose fiction – an efficient
spinner of detective tales, he created
Inspector Pel, a native Burgundian,
and wrote a number of novels built
around this character and set in Burgundy. Hebden is good on local colour
and manners, albeit from an Englishman's point of view. *Pel and the Predators*, 1984 (Extract 3), is typical – a
formulaic murder story considerably en-
livened by the atmospheric setting and
Hebden's tongue-in-cheek style. After
his death, Harris's daughter wrote
further Pel novels under the pseudonym
Juliet Hebden.

SHELLEY, Percy Bysshe (1792–1822),
and SHELLEY, Mary Wollstonecraft
(1797–1851). Shelley's poem 'Mont
Blanc' (Extract 9), a stirring evocation
of awesome power in a world dominated by unfathomable natural elements
and processes, was written while he was
staying in Switzerland in the summer of

1816, in the company of Mary Shelley (at that time still Mary Godwin) and Byron, whom he had met there for the first time. It was here also that Mary began to write *Frankenstein*, 1818. During their stay, the Shelleys visited **Chamonix** to see **Mont Blanc**. In this grand and desolate landscape, he found the inspiration for his poem and she a key setting for her novel – Mary has Frankenstein make a similar journey from Geneva to Chamonix which culminates in his dramatic confrontation with his monster on the **Mer de Glace** (Extract 8).

'Mont Blanc' was first published in *History of a Six Weeks' Tour*, 1817, the Shelleys' combined journal of their travels through France, Switzerland and Germany. See also the *Journals* of Mary Shelley for her account of the trip.

Recommended biographies: Claire Tomalin, *Shelley and His World*, Penguin, London and New York, 1992; Jane Dunn, *Moon in Eclipse: A Life of Mary Shelley*, Weidenfeld and Nicolson, London, 1978.

STENDHAL (1783–1842). Stendhal (real name Henri Beyle) was born in **Grenoble** on 23 January 1783. His mother died when he was only seven years old, and he spent the remainder of his childhood with his father and aunt, both of whom he detested – as he did Grenoble itself, which he saw as the epitome of narrow bourgeois provincialism. The extent of his detestation, as recounted in his unfinished autobiographical *Vie de Henry Brulard*, begun in 1835 (*The Life of Henry Brulard*, 1995), perhaps needs a pinch of salt, but he must nevertheless have been very happy to depart for **Paris** in 1799 to study at the École Polytechnique. In the event, his studies were set aside in favour of a job in the Ministry of War and, in 1800, he joined Napoleon's armies. In that year, his military service took him to Milan and he first experienced the country that was to fire his imagination and where he lived for

many years of his life. In 1802, Stendhal resigned his commission so that he could concentrate on training to be a writer (at this time his ambition was to be a playwright). He lived in Paris until 1806, reading extensively, attending theatre classes, and drawing up long lists of plays and poems that he intended to produce but which would never be written. In 1806 he rejoined the army, and served until 1814. He was involved in many of the major Napoleonic campaigns of the period. After the defeat of Napoleon, he lived in Milan until 1821, when he was expelled under suspicion of being a revolutionary. Between 1821 and 1830 he lived for the most part in Paris. At the end of 1830, he returned to Italy – to serve as French Consul at the port of Civitavecchia. He retained this position for the rest of his life, relieving the boredom of the small port with frequent trips to Rome and abroad, with a period of three years' leave in Paris, and by producing some of his best work. His health went into terminal decline after a cerebral haemorrhage in 1841 – he suffered a second stroke in a Paris street on 22 March 1842 and died early the following morning.

The epitaph on Stendhal's gravestone in the cemetery at **Montmartre** reads 'Arrigo Beyle, Milanese: scrisse, amo, visse' (Henri Beyle, Milanese: wrote, loved, lived). It seems a reasonable enough description of a man who felt more at home in Milan than in Paris, who left a literary legacy in a range of genres with two of the greatest novels in French literature as its centrepiece, who was obsessed with a wide variety of fulfilled and unfulfilled love affairs, and who had such energy and enthusiasm for life. Stendhal's writing includes biography and autobiography, critical and philosophical essays, journalism, art history, travel literature, and novels. His first published book came out in 1814 when he was living in Milan, but it was not until 1830, when he was 53, that *Le Rouge et le noir* appeared.

The idea for *Le Rouge et le noir*, 1830 (*Scarlet and Black*, 1953), is said to have originated in a real-life crime of passion, and the events leading up to it, reported in the *Gazette des Tribunaux* in 1827. The most popular interpretation of the title is that it refers to the alternative career paths of the military (scarlet) and the church (black). Set in the period of the Restoration (1814–30), the novel tells the story of Julien Sorel, a carpenter's son, and his determination to break through the confines of his social position. Without any advantages of birth or material wealth, only the church offers a way up the ladder. In the preceding era, under his hero Napoleon, he could have achieved glory through arms. Starting out with his emotions well contained by cunning hypocrisy and intrigue, his passion and sensibility increasingly break through, beginning with his cold seduction of Madame de Rênal, a provincial mayor's wife with whom he subsequently falls deeply in love. The narrative tracks Julien's 'progress' from a rural village, through a provincial town, **Besançon** (Extract 2), to the high society of **Paris**, mapping the stages of his futile battle against his destiny. Stendhal was interested in the motives behind the manners of his time – the social and political intrigues by which people sought to gain advantage and assert themselves. What he offers us in *Scarlet and Black* is an anatomy of French society in the Restoration period. Although writing at the time of the Romantics, Stendhal is assiduously 'realistic', focusing on normal speech patterns and on everyday lives and events, and minutely dissecting the psychology of his protagonist and other characters. The novel was too starkly realistic, bitter and ironically pessimistic for its time – although Balzac among others did realize its importance. Stendhal himself wrote that he would be successful later in the century ('J'aurai du succès vers 1880'). He was right.

Scarlet and Black illustrates what Stendhal called 'Beylisme' – the obsessive search for self-knowledge and self-fulfilment and the irrepressible energy that is generated in devotion to that obsession. This *égotisme* is justified on the ground that one can truly know only oneself. For Stendhal, our behaviour is dictated by our passions – our actions, whether good or bad, are driven by our self-interest and desire for happiness.

Stendhal's other masterpiece, *La Chartreuse de Parme*, 1839 (*The Charterhouse of Parma*, 1967), is set in his contemporary Italy and reflects his passion for Italian life and culture. Once again painting a broad satirical canvas of political and social culture, it centres around the life and loves of Fabrice del Dongo – unlike Sorel, a character who completely surrenders himself to his emotions.

Stendhal also produced some entertaining and personal travel literature, on both France and Italy. In 1838, he undertook a short tour in the south of France, which he wrote up in notebooks – these comprise in effect the draft of an entertaining and informative travel guide (a cross between subjective impressions and musings and travel-book facts) and have been translated as *Travels in the South of France*, 1971 (see under Languedoc–Roussillon, Extract 6). The book offers often amusing and always vividly evocative descriptions of the many places he visited – presenting us with an intriguing picture of life in southern France in the early 19th century. His *Mémoires d'un touriste*, 1838, is a book of travel impressions of France interlaced with political and social analysis.

Recommended biography: Jonathan Keates, *Stendhal*, Sinclair-Stevenson, London, 1994.

WILLIAMS, William Carlos (1883–1963). Poet, essayist and novelist Williams was born in Rutherford, New Jersey, where he lived all his life and where he practised as a paediatrician (nearby is the town of Paterson, the

William Carlos Williams

subject of Williams's wonderful and inventive epic poem *Paterson*, 1946–58). He did, however, spend a period abroad in his teens and in 1897 lived for a time in Paris. In the summer of 1923, Williams decided to take a year out from his medical practice – he and his wife spent around six months in New York, and then, in January 1924, left for Europe. During his tour of the continent, Williams travelled around France. He spent six weeks in **Paris**, where he renewed some old acquaintances, including Pound and McAlmon, and made many new ones, among them Joyce, Ford, Hemingway, and Man Ray. He also met the Surrealist Philippe Soupault, whose 1928 novel *Les Dernières Nuits de Paris* he translated (*Last Nights of Paris*, 1929). Williams did not on this occasion meet Gertrude Stein, but was introduced to her by McAlmon on his next and last trip to Europe in 1927 – Stein refers to the meeting in passing in *The Autobiography of Alice B. Toklas*.

Williams's travels during his 1924 tour provided the subject matter for his fictionalized travel book *A Voyage to Pagany*, 1928 ('Pagany' is Europe), which includes his responses to, among many other places, **Left Bank Paris**, **Carcassonne**, **Marseille**, the **Riviera**, and **Dijon** (Extract 4). The novel

tracks the progress of Dev, an American doctor on holiday in Europe, as he travels through France, Italy, Austria and Switzerland on a voyage of cultural and intellectual discovery. Williams/Dev finds himself overwhelmed by the foreignness of European culture, which he greets with delighted amazement – exclamations such as 'Wow' and 'Oh Boy' emphasizing both the American roots of the narrator and the inspirational nature of the journey. At the same time, there is a doctor's analytical eye at work, as in his description of the self-conscious customers of the **Dôme** in Paris – 'There was a certain type of international Dome face one might have detected in them all, a sort of wary face, a little on parade.' The revelatory experience of the European sojourn, and the distance it provides, are a means of renewing and informing the quest for a truly American culture, in which his own past and future are firmly rooted – 'So this is the beginning,' ends the novel. Significantly, as critic Harry Levin has pointed out, Williams's first publication on his return from his 'magnificent year' was *In the American Grain*, 1925, a collection of essays on aspects of American history.

For the strictly autobiographical version of Williams's 1924 trip, see the relevant pages of his *Autobiography*, 1951. See also Harry Levin's excellent introduction to the 1970 edition of *A Voyage to Pagany*.

Recommended biography: Mike Weaver offers critical analysis in the context of biographical information in *William Carlos Williams: The American Background*, Cambridge University Press, Cambridge, 1971.

WORDSWORTH, WILLIAM (1770–1850). In July 1790 Wordsworth, then studying at Cambridge, set off with a fellow student on a walking tour of the continent. They undertook a demanding and courageous, not to say physically gruelling tour – between mid July and late September, estimates biographer Stephen Gill, they travelled some three thousand miles, 'walking at least two thousand of them, many over mountainous terrain, at a rate of more than twenty, sometimes more than thirty miles a day.' They journeyed through France on their way to see the Alps in the midst of revolutionary celebrations, centred around the first anniversary of the storming of the Bastille. The excitement and energy of the country at this time – and Wordsworth's youthful elation at what seemed to be the progressive realization of popular hopes and ideals – are evocatively conveyed in Book VI of *The Prelude* (Extract 6), which relates his experiences and impressions during this tour. *The Prelude* was finished in 1805 but was substantially revised and eventually published posthumously. Originally conceived as a 'prelude' to *The Recluse*, a work Wordsworth never completed, the poem is subtitled *Growth of a Poet's Mind*, which reveals its intent. Through autobiography and psychological self-analysis, *The Prelude* traces Wordsworth's development as a poet, from his childhood, and offers insights into his character and thought.

In addition to Book VI, the sections of *The Prelude* which are of particular interest here are Books IX and X, describing his 'Residence in France'. Wordsworth lived in France from November 1791 to December 1792, experiencing the country in a more sinister phase of revolutionary development, and these sections, as well as including his impressions of the places he visited, concern his reactions to the French Revolution. As he recounts in Book X, he was in **Paris** in late 1792, when Robespierre was in the ascendancy, and in lines of foreboding presages his later disillusionment – 'Let me then relate that now/In some sort seeing with my proper eyes/That Liberty, and Life, and Death would soon/To the remotest corners of the land/Lie in the arbitrement of those who ruled/The capital City . . .' – for Wordsworth, the horrific aftermath of the 1789 Re-

volution came to represent a devastating collapse of the republican ideals that had inspired him ('Bliss was it in that dawn to be alive,/But to be young was very heaven . . .'). In *The Prelude* he portrays himself as increasingly torn between his ardent support for the Revolution itself, and for the right of the people to assert their will, and his fear and confusion at the vicious political manoeuvring and widespread violence that followed in its wake.

During his 'residence' in France, Wordsworth met a young French woman while staying at **Orléans**, and fell in love with her. Annette Vallon (1766–1841) was the daughter of a surgeon who lived at **Blois**, and Wordsworth spent much of his year in France in her company. She gave birth to a daughter shortly after he had left the country. Few details are known about their relationship at this time, or about its subsequent history (in *The Prelude* Wordsworth makes an oblique reference to the affair through the incongruous insertion into Book IX of the rather uninteresting poem 'Vaudracour and Julia', a tale of star-crossed lovers). Annette clearly hoped that Wordsworth would return to marry her, but he did not. Then war was declared between England and France in February 1793, making any visit impossible and separating Wordsworth from Annette and his French child until 1802. He returned to France in 1802 (he was by this time engaged to marry Mary Hutchinson). Accompanied by his sister Dorothy, he stayed for a month at **Calais** and met Annette and his daughter Caroline, then nine years old. It seems that friendly relations were maintained after this meeting until Annette's death. For the detailed story, in so far as it can be pieced together, see Émile Legouis, *William Wordsworth and Annette Vallon*, 1922, revised 1967.

Recommended biography: Stephen Gill, *William Wordsworth: A Life*, Oxford University Press, Oxford and New York, 1989.

Provence–Alpes–Côte d'Azur and Monaco

> 'In front of me, a wood of beautiful pines descends to the foot of the hill. In the far distance, the Lesser Alps raise their delicate crests. There is no sound. Only, sometimes near, sometimes far-away, the sound of a fife, a curlew in the lavender, mule-bells on the road . . . All the beauty of this Provençal countryside is born of the sun; it lives by light.'
>
> Alphonse Daudet, *Letters from My Windmill*

ALPES-DE-HAUTE-PROVENCE

Manosque. Birthplace of Jean Giono ◊. He was born at **1 rue Torte**, but was brought up at **14 rue Grande**. After his marriage in 1920, he moved into **No 8** on the same street. In 1929, he bought the house where he was to live for the rest of his life – Le Paraïs on the hillside of the **Mont d'Or**. The landscape and culture of the Provençal Alps feature prominently in Giono's work (Extract 10), with his recreation, in his own mythologized version of Provence, of mountain villages and peasant life.

Manosque was also the birthplace of the novelist Élémir Bourges (1852–1925).

ALPES-MARITIMES

Antibes/Cap d'Antibes. Jules Verne (1828–1905) stayed in a villa on the Cap d'Antibes (**Les Chênes Verts**) and is said to have been inspired by the surroundings to write *Vingt mille lieues sous les mers*, 1870 (*Twenty Thousand Leagues Under the Sea*, 1993).

Scott Fitzgerald ◊ and his wife Zelda stayed at the **Hôtel du Cap** in 1925 – it became the model for Gausse's hotel in *Tender is the Night*, 1934 (Extract 2). Nearby, the Fitzgeralds' friends, Gerald and Sara Murphy, owned what was one of the most luxurious villas on the Côte d'Azur – in *Tender is the Night*, the character of Dick Diver before his fall is based on Gerald Murphy and the terrace of the Divers' villa is modelled on the Murphys'. The Murphys were at the centre of a social circle which included artists, actors, writers, and other media celebrities (among the other writers they entertained were John Dos Passos, Hemingway, and Archibald Mac-Leish). The villa and its private beach became a focal point for the glittering cast of the wealthy and famous who came to the Côte d'Azur for sun and parties. The Murphys and their friends were among the first, aside from the locals, to stay on the south coast in the summer – until then it had been the

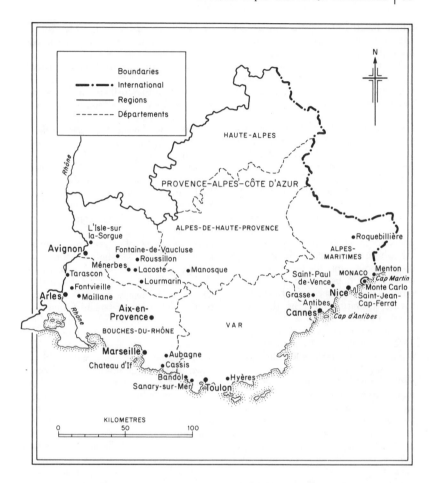

fashionable custom to move north during the hot months. In 1926, the Fitzgeralds spent most of the year in this dream-like environment, staying at **Juan-les-Pins**. In 1924, they had chosen **Saint-Raphaël**, and on their last visit, in 1929, they lived at **Cannes** (see below).

Graham Greene ◊ had an apartment in Antibes from 1966 to 1990.

Cannes. Prosper Mérimée (◊ Corsica) died in a house on the square named after him (at the corner of **rue Jean de Riouffe**) in 1870. He is buried in the **Protestant Cemetery**. Scott and Zelda

Fitzgerald (see above) took a villa in Cannes for the summer of 1929. In *Tender is the Night*, one of the protagonists, Rosemary, sits in a café on **La Croisette**, 'where the trees made a green twilight over the tables and an orchestra wooed an imaginary public of cosmopolites with the Nice Carnival Song and last year's American tune.' That, of course, was before apartment blocks, boutiques and traffic had changed the ambience.

Cap Martin. W.B. Yeats (1865–1939) came to the south of France for the winter of 1938–39 to try to recover his failing health. During his stay at Cap Martin he was taken seriously ill, and he died in his hotel here on 28 January 1939. He was originally buried at the village of **Roquebrune**, but his remains were transferred in 1948 to County Sligo in his native Ireland.

Grasse. André Gide (◊ Normandy) was fond of Grasse and nearby **Cabris** and spent time here towards the end of his life. In his *Journal* entry of 15 September 1941, he writes, 'One cannot imagine a more beautiful view than the one I enjoy, at any hour of the day, from the window of my room in the Grand Hotel. The town of Grasse opposite me dominated by the cathedral, whose tower breaks the line of the distant mountains, the harmonious disorder of the houses forming a series of terraces on the slope down to the deep ravine separating me from the town. While I am writing these lines the sun is finishing its course and, before disappearing behind the heights of Cabris, is pouring an ineffable golden light over the walls, the roofs, the whole town. A veil of rain has come to hide the mountainous background of the picture so that the cathedral tower, bathed in the last rays, now stands out against a bare sky, so it seems; on the left, another, smaller tower. The dinner hour struck some time ago and yet I cannot leave this sight.'

Grasse has long been famous for its perfume distilleries – see Patrick Süskind's ◊ *Das Parfüm*, 1985 (*Perfume*, 1986) for an imaginative and atmospheric portrayal of the town in the 18th century (Extract 3).

Lady Fortescue bought a property just outside Grasse, and recorded her experiences of Provençal life in her popular *Perfume from Provence*, 1935.

Menton. Robert Louis Stevenson (◊ Auvergne) stayed here in the winter of 1873–74 and wrote his essay 'Ordered South'. He met the Dowson family and spent some time entertaining their little boy, Ernest (◊ Brittany).

Aubrey Beardsley died in Menton of consumption in 1898 and is buried here.

The Spanish novelist Vicente Blasco Ibáñez (1867–1928) lived in what is now **avenue Blasco-Ibáñez** at the **Villa Fontana Rosa**. He died in Menton, but is buried in Valencia.

Katherine Mansfield (◊ Paris), suffering severely from tuberculosis, stayed here from January to April 1920, and returned later in the year for a longer period – she lived at the **Villa Isola Bella** in the **Garavan** *quartier* from September 1920 to May 1921 (it still stands). She took great comfort from the villa and gardens – 'the first real home of my own I've ever loved.' In a letter to John Middleton Murry of November 1920 she wrote, 'The wind of the last days has scattered almost the last of the fig leaves and now through those candle-shaped boughs I love so much there is a beautiful glimpse of the old town. Some fowls are making no end of a noise. I've just been for a walk on my small boulevard and looking down below at the houses all bright in the sun and housewives washing their linen in great tubs of glittering water and flinging it over the orange trees to dry. Perhaps all human activity is beautiful in the sunlight.'

The **Hôtel de Ville** in **rue de la République** boasts a Salle des Mariages decorated by Cocteau (see below) in 1957. More of his art is on display in the 17th century harbour bastion which houses the **Musée Cocteau** at the junction of the **promenade du Soleil** and **quai Napoléon III**.

Nice. Tobias Smollett ◊ stayed in Nice for some 18 months during his tour of France and Italy in 1763–65. He describes the town and its inhabitants at length in his sharp-tongued *Travels Through France and Italy*, 1766 (Extract 9). Smollett's rudeness about the inhabitants caused outrage and resentment among the locals in the 18th century – although his book was also, paradoxically, instrumental in promoting Nice as a resort for the English. Surprisingly enough, in view of his comments, there is a street named after him in the town, albeit with the wrong spelling – **rue Smolet**. The house in which he stayed is thought to have been **3 rue de la Terrasse**.

Graham Greene's 1982 *J'Accuse: The Dark Side of Nice* set out to publicize local government corruption and organized crime in Nice – see 'Lives and Works' for the story.

Roquebillière. Arthur Koestler (◊ Languedoc–Roussillon) spent an idyllic summer here with a girlfriend while war was brewing in 1939 ('All the sleepy, age-old mountain villages of the Maritime Alps north of the Riviera were now packed with soldiers – grumbling, drinking red wine, playing belotte, and bored.'). In the opening pages of his *Scum of the Earth*, 1941, there are evocative descriptions of the changing atmosphere in the village as war turned from threat to reality. 'We knew it was our last summer,' he writes, 'and everything around us assumed a dark, symbolical meaning. Yet it was still August, and the sun was still vigorous and bright and the figs went on ripening in our garden. We had never loved France so much as we loved it in those late August days; we had never been so achingly conscious of its sweetness and decay.'

Saint-Jean-Cap-Ferrat. Jean Cocteau (◊ Paris) was a frequent visitor to the Côte d'Azur. In his later years, he came here for extended stays at the **Villa Santo Sospir**, owned by his wealthy friend Madame Francine Weisweiller. In neighbouring **Villefranche**, the **Chapelle de St-Pierre** is decorated with frescoes by Cocteau (see also under Menton).

The **Villa Mauresque** on Cap Ferrat was the luxurious home of Somerset Maugham for many years. He moved into the house after it had been extensively renovated in 1928 and died here in 1965. When he was in residence, he was rarely without guests, who enjoyed the luxury of the villa and its grounds, impeccable room service, magnificent food, and spectacular scenery. Ian Fleming and Noël Coward were regulars – among the many and varied less frequent guests were Arnold Bennett, Churchill, Chagall, Cocteau, T.S. Eliot, Kipling, C.P. Snow, Evelyn Waugh, and Rebecca West. Apart from his extensive alterations to the house itself, Maugham had a tennis court and a marble swimming pool (sporting a sculpture by Bernini) installed in the gardens, and imported avocado trees from California to accompany the abundant cacti and palms. The Villa was sold to an American property speculator in 1968 who radically altered the house and divided the grounds into lots for development. The most recent owner has carried out extensive restoration work on the interior. Maugham's 'local' was the **Grand Hôtel du Cap Ferrat** which now boasts a **Somerset Maugham Piano Bar**.

Saint-Paul-de-Vence. James Baldwin (◊ Paris) came here in 1970 to recuperate after an illness. In 1971, at the urging of his friends Yves Montand and Simone Signoret, he rented and later bought a property on the **route de la Colle**, opposite the hotel **Le Hameau** where he stayed when he first came to the town. This remained his main home for the rest of his life – he died from cancer in 1987. Baldwin was a regular at the famous and expensive hotel-restaurant the **Colombe d'Or, place des Ormeaux** (where Signoret and Montand celebrated their wedding). Earlier, one evening in 1926, the outdoor diners at the Colombe d'Or included Scott and Zelda Fitzgerald and their friends the Murphys (see above, Cap d'Antibes). Among the other diners was the dancer Isadora Duncan, who invited Scott over to her table. It seems that the unbalanced Zelda was disturbed by the attention he was getting, or she was not getting, and on an impulse left her table and threw herself down a flight of stairs – she was not seriously injured but the action was an indication of the worsening mental condition that would play a major role in the Fitzgeralds' sad future.

MONACO

Monte Carlo. The café of the **Hôtel de Paris** became a gathering place for Cocteau, Diaghilev, Nijinsky, Picasso, Stravinsky, and others when they were involved in staging ballets at the small but richly funded theatre, the **Salle Garnier** in the neighbouring Casino.

In the last years of her life, Colette (◊ Burgundy) made several visits to the hotel with her husband Maurice de Goudeket. On one of them, there was a film being made in the hotel. Biographer Herbert Lottman (*Colette: A Life*, 1991) tells the story well – 'Goudeket remembered that as he maneuvered her wheelchair into the dining room between the cameras and their cables, Colette caught a glimpse of a pretty young actress standing in front of the lens, and she at once declared, "That's our Gigi for America." Goudeket looked up the young woman that very day and learned that she was Audrey Hepburn, a dancer who had not acted before. That autumn Hepburn was a sensational Gigi on the New York stage. "My love and gratitude to you always," she wrote to Colette after the Broadway opening.'

The **Casino** is a key setting in Graham Greene's ◊ short novel *Loser Takes All*, 1955 (Extract 7), and Somerset Maugham's short story 'The Facts of Life' (Extract 8). Virginia Woolf (1882–1941) took a peek at the gaming tables on one of her French holidays in May 1935. She was predictably disdainful, describing in her diary the players as 'a dingy sweaty rather sordid crew, with their faces all set & expressionless watching the gold bars sweeping this way and that in the middle . . . It was a blazing hot Sunday morning about 12, & this, we thought is the way our

culture spends its holidays. Vicious, dull & outside lurid.' Presumably Ms Woolf did not try her luck. The quotations are from Jan Morris's entertaining *Travels with Virginia Woolf*, 1993, which includes a brief chapter on France comprising mainly diary entries and morsels of correspondence. As Morris herself notes, 'Nobody was ever less of a travel writer, in the usual sense of the phrase, than Virginia Woolf.'

VAR

Bandol. Katherine Mansfield (◊ Paris) stayed here for several months in 1916 with John Middleton Murry. She wrote a piece called 'The Aloe', which later became 'Prelude', one of her finest short stories (*Bliss and Other Stories*, 1920).

Hyères. Robert Louis Stevenson (◊ Auvergne) lived in Hyères with his wife from spring 1883 to autumn 1884, when a cholera epidemic persuaded them to leave. While here, he wrote *A Child's Garden of Verses*, 1885, and *The Black Arrow*, 1888, and began work on *Kidnapped*, 1886.

Edith Wharton (1862–1937) had a winter home here from 1920. In the 1930s Aldous Huxley and his wife were frequent visitors from nearby **Sanary** where they were then living.

Earlier writers who spent time in Hyères include Swinburne and Tolstoy, both of whom stayed here during the 1860s.

Sanary-sur-Mer. Sybille Bedford ◊ lived here for some 14 years in the 1920s and 1930s, and describes the town and the surrounding region of coastal Provence in *Jigsaw*, 1989, her autobiographical novel. She also uses the area as the setting of her *A Compass Error*, 1968 (Extract 11). In 1973–74 Bedford published a two-volume biography of Aldous Huxley (1894–1963), who lived in Sanary in the 1930s.

Toulon. Ford Madox Ford (◊ Picardie) and his last companion Janice Biala took a villa at nearby **Cap Brun** in the 1930s. It became their main home until they were forced for financial reasons to leave France for the USA. Ford's affinity with Provence, and Ford himself, are celebrated by William Carlos Williams in his poem 'To Ford Madox Ford in Heaven', which affectionately remembers the writer in the context of Provence, his little earthly piece of heaven, painting him as a Falstaff-like lover of the good things of life: 'Provence, the fat assed Ford will never / again strain the chairs of your cafés / pull and pare for his dish your sacred garlic, / grunt and sweat and lick / his lips. . .'

Hemingway portrays the eccentric Englishman less sympathetically in *A Moveable Feast*, 1964, when he recounts an unwelcome encounter with the 'well clothed, up-ended hogshead' with his 'heavy, wheezing, ignoble presence' at the **Closerie des Lilas** in Paris – but then perhaps Hemingway's unfair and uncharitable account says more about Hemingway than it says about Ford. For Ford himself on Provence, see his *Provence*, 1934.

Toulon and its environs feature in Joseph Conrad's *The Rover*, 1923.

BOUCHES-DU-RHÔNE

Aix-en-Provence. Émile Zola (◊ Nord–Pas-de-Calais) spent his childhood and adolescence in Aix. He came here with his parents in 1843, when he was three, and left for Paris in 1858. In fact, he was brought up for the most part by his mother – Zola's father Francesco died when he was only seven. At first the family lived in the **impasse Sylvacane** and later, as financial circumstances grew harder after Francesco's death, moved out of the city to **Pont-de-Béraud**. Zola attended the Collège Bourbon (now the **Lycée Mignet**), where he met and began a long friendship with Paul Cézanne (1839–

1906). In his fiction, Aix provided the model for Plassans, an unpleasant provincial town (see, for example, *La Conquête de Plassans*, 1874; *The Conquest of Plassans*, 1994).

Blaise Cendrars (1887–1961) took refuge in Aix in the Second World War during the German Occupation. He lived in a small flat at **12 rue Clemenceau** (there is a plaque), where he stayed until 1948. In this becalmed period of 'hard exile', the traveller and adventurer found little to interest him other than reading and writing, both of which activities he undertook with productive enthusiasm. For Cendrars on Aix, see *L'Homme foudroyé*, 1945 (*The Astonished Man*, 1970). See also Robert Doisneau's photographs of Cendrars in Aix, taken in 1945.

Arles. More strongly associated with art than with literature, thanks to Van Gogh, the city nevertheless has something to offer the literary traveller. The **Muséon Arlaten**, dedicated to Provençal culture and tradition, was founded by Frédéric Mistral (see under Maillane) and inaugurated in 1909 with the help of the money he received when he won the Nobel Prize for Literature in 1904. A number of the explanatory labels are in his own handwriting. One of the rooms in the museum is now devoted to Mistral, and another to Le Félibrige (see under Avignon, Vaucluse). There is a statue of the poet in the nearby **place du Forum** – Mistral himself attended the unveiling.

Henry James (◊ Paris) visited Arles in 1882 and couldn't quite work out why he liked it: 'There are two shabby old inns at Arles, which compete closely for your custom. I mean by this that if you elect to go to the Hôtel du Forum, the Hôtel du Nord, which is placed exactly beside it (at a right angle) watches your arrival with ill-concealed disapproval; and if you take the chances of its neighbour, the Hôtel du Forum seems to glare at you invidiously from all its windows and doors. I forget which of these establishments I selected; whichever it was, I wished very much that it had been the other. The two stand together on the Place des Hommes, a little public square of Arles, which somehow quite misses its effect. As a city, indeed, Arles quite misses its effect in every way; and if it is a charming place, as I think it is, I can hardly tell the reason why.' (*A Little Tour in France*, 1885.)

Aubagne. Marcel Pagnol ◊ was born here in 1895 at **16 cours Barthélemy.** His *L'Eau des collines*, 1963 (*The Water of the Hills*, 1988), comprising *Jean de Florette* and *Manon des sources*, is set in a fictional village called 'Les Bastides Blanches' (Extract 14), which he locates close to Aubagne. His English translator, W. E. van Heyningen, points out that the village is closely based, topographically, on the real-life one of **La Treille,** up in the hills about 5 km away from Aubagne, where Pagnol spent holidays in his childhood. Not far from the village is the cemetery where Pagnol is buried, with, as van Heyningen says, many of the characters in his novel. The other fictional places in the story have also been roughly located by the translator, who usefully provides a map which is published in the current paperback edition (see Booklist). The **Syndicat d'Initiative d'Aubagne** on the esplanade De Gaulle organizes detailed itineraries for trips into the hills for those literary pilgrims who want to see the countryside and villages which Pagnol knew as a child, and which were his lasting inspiration – described in his autobiographies, used as settings for his fiction, and serving as locations for several of his films (including, for example, *Jofroi* and *Angèle*). There is a permanent exhibition at the Syndicat d'Initiative d'Aubagne of 'Le Petit Monde de Marcel Pagnol' with his characters represented by *santons*, the miniature figures with which Aubagne is associated.

Cassis. In 1927, Vanessa and Clive Bell acquired a house in this popular fishing port. Vanessa's sister, Virginia Woolf, and her husband Leonard, who had first stayed at Cassis in 1925, subsequently visited them here several times. As Jan Morris notes in her *Travels with Virginia Woolf*, 1993, they made the acquaintance of a Colonel Teed and his mistress – the Colonel owned the **Château de Fontcreuse** on the **Route de La Ciotat,** and the Woolfs later stayed in a small house on his estate called **La Bergère.** The Colonel substantially developed the vineyards of his estate and the Château now boasts some of the best wines of the tiny but respected Cassis district – you can therefore satisfy both literary and vinous curiosity by visiting the estate to test its produce. 'Our grand extravagance is wine, which the peasants sell,' wrote Virginia Woolf to Vita Sackville-West from Cassis in 1927, 'and Clive and Duncan fetch in great baskets, dressed in cotton clothes, with rope slippers . . .'.

Fontvieille. 'Between ourselves and things strange affinities exist.' Visiting friends at the **Château de Montaubon** in this Provençal village in 1860, Alphonse Daudet ◊ came upon four old stone windmills on a hillside overlooking the village. This place was to become for him a 'spiritual retreat', symbolized by his favourite windmill, the Moulin Avon, or Moulin Tissot as it was also known. Here, he no doubt conceived his ideas for the stories of *Lettres de mon moulin*, 1869 (*Letters from My Windmill*, 1978) – which, however, were written mainly in Paris. Although he tells us he thought about purchasing the Moulin Tissot, Daudet never lived here – but the mill and the hillside on which it stood have become his by 'spiritual adoption' to use the phrase of his biographer G. V. Dobie. In fact, what is now known as the **Moulin de Daudet** is not the Moulin Tissot, but one of the other mills on the hillside. It houses a museum dedicated to the author and, of course, still affords the magnificent view which

Daudet himself so admired (**Musée Alphonse Daudet**, avenue des Moulins, 13990 Fontvieille).

Maillane. 'What the poem is about is Provence – the seas and mountains of Provence; and above all, it is about the people of Provence, one people simple and free, bound together by their history, their customs, their legends, their landscapes, a people who, in the hour of their death, have found their great poet . . . So now, build your railways, plant your telegraph poles, expunge the language of Provence from your school books! Provence lives forever in *Mireille* and *Calendal.*' So writes Daudet in 'The Poet Mistral' (*Letters from My Windmill*), his short story in praise of his friend and fellow lover of Provence, Frédéric Mistral. Mistral (1830–1914) was born in the Mas du Juge, just outside Maillane. He is the most celebrated of Provençal poets and was a champion of the region's culture and language (he was a founder member and leader of Le Félibrige – see under Avignon). He wrote his verses in Provençal, translating them into French for wider readership. Despite his literary celebrity (he won the Nobel Prize for Literature in 1904), he lived his whole life in his native region, and his home was always here in Maillane. Mistral spent his childhood in the Mas – then, after his father's death, he moved into the centre of the village with his mother. They lived in a house which still stands and on the front of which Mistral engraved the image of a lizard and three lines of verse in Provençal: 'gai lesert, bèu toun soulèu/ l'ouro passa que trop lèu/e deman ploura belèu' ('joyous lizard, drink in your sunshine, time passes only too quickly and tomorrow, perhaps, it will rain'). When he was 46, he married a young woman from Burgundy and had a house built in the village opposite 'La Maison du Lézard'. Mistral lived in this house from 1876 until his death in 1914: his wife (who was only 19 when they married) lived another 30 years,

and this remained her home until she died. It is now a museum dedicated to the poet, and has been preserved very much as it was when Mistral lived in it – **La Maison Frédéric Mistral**, 11 rue Lamartine, 13910 Maillane. Exhibits include numerous documents, pictures and portraits (of, among others, his friends Daudet and Lamartine), furniture, books, and personal belongings – you can see his study, his library, his kitchen, and his bedroom. The statue of Mistral in the garden was erected some years after his death.

The poet is buried in the cemetery at Maillane. His tomb is modelled on the Pavillon de la Reine Jeanne at **Les Baux** – the seven-pointed star in the decoration was the symbol adopted by the founders of Le Félibrige.

Marseille. Marseille (often spelled Marseilles in English) and the nearby **Château d'If** are key settings in *Le Comte de Monte-Cristo*, 1845 (*The Count of Monte Cristo*, 1852) – see Extracts 4 and 5. If is a small island in the bay of Marseille. The Château was built in 1524 and later became a state prison – among its more famous real-life inmates was Mirabeau, imprisoned in 1774 for running up huge debts. The fictional associations are, however, the strongest – the Château d'If may be visited and the dungeons of Edmond Dantès and the Abbé Faria which play such an important part in the novel are the main attraction.

Marseille features too in the atmospheric and masterly opening chapter of Dickens's *Little Dorrit*, 1857, entitled 'Sun and Shadow'. 'Thirty years ago,' the novel begins, 'Marseilles lay burning in the sun, one day. A blazing sun upon a fierce August day was no greater rarity in southern France then, than at any other time, before or since. Everything in Marseilles, and about Marseilles, had stared at the fervid sky, and been stared at in return, until a staring habit had become universal there. Strangers were stared out of countenance by staring white houses, staring white walls, staring white streets, staring tracts of arid road, staring hills from which verdure was burnt away. The only things to be seen not fixedly staring and glaring were the vines drooping under their load of grapes. These did occasionally wink a little, as the hot air barely moved their faint leaves.'

Joseph Conrad (1857–1924) arrived in Marseille from Poland at the tender age of 17. He lived here for some three and a half years – although around 18 months of that time were spent on sea voyages, for it was during this period that he gained his first experiences of seamanship, developing his love for the sea that was to play such an important role in his life and fiction. When he was not on a long voyage, he was learning from the local seamen. He describes them in his autobiographical *A Personal Record*, 1912: 'Their sea-tanned faces, whiskered or shaved, lean or full, with the intent wrinkled eyes of the pilot-breed, and here and there a thin gold loop at the lobe of a hairy ear, bent over my sea-infancy . . . And I have been invited to sit in more than one tall, dark house of the old town at their hospitable board, had the *bouillabaisse* ladled out into a thick plate by their high-voiced broad-browed wives, talked to their daughters – thick-set girls, with pure profiles, glorious masses of black hair arranged with complicated art, dark eyes, and dazzlingly white teeth.'

Edmond Rostand, author of *Cyrano de Bergerac*, 1897, was born in 1868 at **No 14** in the street now named after him (**rue Edmond-Rostand**).

In spring 1891 Arthur Rimbaud (◊ Champagne–Ardenne) arrived in Marseille from Africa, in excruciating pain from a knee tumour. He had his right leg amputated at the **Hôpital de la Conception**. After a stay at his mother's home in the Ardennes, during which his health deteriorated, he made a forlorn attempt to return to Africa but ended up back in the same hospital, where he died in November 1891, aged 37.

Simone de Beauvoir (◊ Paris) spent a year here in 1931–32, teaching at the Lycée Montgrand. For her it was an unhappy year of solitude, as it enforced a separation from Sartre (◊ Paris). She created a considerable stir at the provincial school by sharing her radical political ideas and discussing Gide and Proust. Finding her colleagues uninteresting and unintellectual, she spent much of her spare time discovering the surrounding countryside in long solitary hikes and, to the horror of her colleagues at the Lycée, sitting in cafés and dining in restaurants unaccompanied.

The Senegalese novelist Sembène Ousmane ◊ worked as a docker in Marseille – *Le Docker noir*, 1956 (*Black Docker*, 1987) is set in the city and draws on the author's own experiences, vividly portraying life on the docks and in the African ghettos (Extract 6). Earlier, Jamaican-born Harlem Renaissance writer Claude McKay (1890–1948) had done light work on the docks during his stay in Marseille in 1926 – he used his experiences on the waterfront and in the working-class cafés in his novel *Banjo*, 1929.

Tarascon. The inhabitants of this small town on the Rhône between Arles and Avignon, which Daudet chose for the home of his comic hero Tartarin (Extract 13), were not best pleased at the time with the author's satirical portrait (albeit quite a gentle one) of their provincial life and their willingness to believe Tartarin's boastful stories. Henry James refers to this in his *A Little Tour in France*, 1884 – 'In the introduction which, for the new edition of his works, he has lately supplied to *Tartarin*, the author of this extravagant but kindly satire gives some account of the displeasure with which he has been visited by the ticklish Tarasconnais. Daudet relates that in his attempt to shed a humorous light upon the more erratic phases of the Provençal character, he selected Tarascon at a venture; not because the temperament of its natives is more vainglorious than that of their neighbours, or their rebellion against the "despotism of fact" more marked, but simply because he had to name a particular Provençal city . . . The Tarasconnais, however, declined to take the joke, and opened the vials of their wrath upon the mocking child of Nîmes, who would have been better employed, they doubtless thought, in showing up the infirmities of his own family.' Whatever the feelings at the time of the inhabitants of Tarascon, rancour has since turned to exploitation – you will find the **House of Tartarin** at 55 bis Boulevard Itam, with memorabilia, pictures from plays and films, and a waxwork model of Tartarin. The garden is planted with African flora and fauna to fit Daudet's description of it in the book. A real-life Tartarin can be seen in the processions of the Fêtes de la Tarasque held at the end of June.

Joseph Conrad

VAUCLUSE

Avignon. Petrarch (see below, Fontaine-de-Vaucluse) spent many years in exile in France, where his main homes were in Avignon, which he considered a hotbed of corruption and immorality, and his idyllic rural retreat of Vaucluse. In 1327, he first saw Laura in the church of Sainte-Claire d'Avignon, the site of which is now marked by a plaque at **22 rue du Roi René**.

Provençal poet Frédéric Mistral (see above, Maillane, Bouches-du-Rhône) came to school in Avignon in 1842. He attended the Collège Royal, now the **Lycée Frédéric Mistral**. He lodged, among other places, in a *pension* in **rue Pétramale** (there is a plaque), and later at the Hôtel Sixte-Isnard in the rue de l'Hôpital. Mistral began writing poetry during this period and his teacher, Joseph Roumanille (1818–1891), himself a poet writing in Provençal, recognized his pupil's outstanding talent and encouraged him to develop it. At the end of his schooling, which he com-

pleted at **Nîmes** and **Aix**, Mistral returned to his native village of Maillane to concentrate on his poetry. However, he frequently came to Avignon to visit his former teacher and in 1854, together with five other writers, they launched the Provençal literary movement Le Félibrige, which aimed to protect and raise awareness of Provençal history, culture and language, to produce a written grammar to standardize the language, and to campaign for the teaching of Provençal in schools. The movement was officially launched on 21 May 1854 at the nearby **Château de Font-Ségugne** at **Châteauneuf-de-Gadagne**, a favourite meeting place for the writers in 1852–55. From 1855, the main venue for the Félibres became the bookshop which Roumanille had opened in Avignon at 19 rue Saint-Agricol – where the **Librairie Roumanille** still exists.

Another of the founding members of Le Félibrige was the poet and dramatist Théodore Aubanel (1829–86), whose family printing business had been thriving in Avignon since 1744. Éditions

Aubanel is now in the **impasse Saint-Pierre**, and there is a small **Musée Théodore-Aubanel**.

Stéphane Mallarmé lived at **No 8 rue Portail Matheron** from 1869 to 1871 while teaching English at the *lycée*.

Avignon features as a key setting in Lawrence Durrell's ◊ *Avignon Quintet* (Extract 1). It also plays host to one of Europe's largest arts festivals every summer.

Fontaine-de-Vaucluse. The famous natural 'wonder' of the underground stream which comes out into the daylight through a great hole in a cliff to form an overflowing pool at its foot, with its dramatic setting in a narrow valley, brought the exiled Italian poet and humanist Petrarch (1304–74) here. Torn between spiritual cleanliness and the seductions of the world, he retreated to Vaucluse to nurse his idealizing devotion to 'Laura', whom he first saw in Avignon in 1327 and who inspired his love poetry. Since then, the natural phenomenon has been only part of the attraction – the links with the great, love-struck poet have long made this a place of pilgrimage for literary and other romantics. Chateaubriand, for example, records his visit in *Mémoires d'outre-tombe*, 1849–50 (*Memoirs*, 1961). Henry James, bewitched by the scenery and the phenomenon of the 'magical spring', and disgusted by the exploitative commercialism he found in the village (there is plenty here today), gives his impressions in *A Little Tour in France*, 1885. James concludes, 'The setting of the phenomenon struck me as so simple and so fine – the vast sad cliff, covered with the afternoon light, still and solid forever, while the liquid element rages and roars at its base – that I had no difficulty in understanding the celebrity of Vaucluse. I understood it, but I will not say that I understood Petrarch. He must have been very self-supporting, and Madonna Laura must indeed have been much to him . . . The only very definite conviction I

arrived at was that Vaucluse is indeed cockneyfied, but that I should have been a fool, all the same, not to come.'

Petrarch was thrilled and moved by the Fontaine-de-Vaucluse, and he found in it a perfect 'retreat'. Based in Avignon, and anxious to get away from that 'Babylon of vice', as he saw it, he spent much time here during his last years in France (between 1337 and 1353), living quietly in his house on the banks of the Sorgue in what was then a small rustic community, writing, tending his gardens, and visiting his friend the Bishop of Cavaillon in his summer residence, the now ruined château above the village.

In the village itself there is a monument to Petrarch, and, on the presumed site of Petrarch's home (destroyed by brigands in 1353), **Le Musée Iconographique et Bibliographique de Petrarque et de Laure** (Fontaine-de-Vaucluse, 84800 L'Isle-sur-la-Sorgue).

The nearby **Château de Saumane** was once owned by the de Sade family – one theory has it that Petrarch's perfect Laura was in fact Laure de Noves who married into the de Sades – and thus entered the ancestral history of the rather less than perfect Marquis.

L'Isle-sur-la-Sorgue. Birthplace of the poet René Char (1907–88). His poetry frequently reflects his attachment to the landscape and landmarks of his native region.

Lacoste. The ruined **château** on the hillside above this village was once the home of the Marquis de Sade (1740–1814). He first moved into the property, which had been acquired by the family in 1627, when he was 25 years old. He brought his mistress with him, whom he passed off as his wife, insisting that she be addressed as Madame la Marquise. He lived here also later in his life, eventually with the real Marquise. His idiosyncratic tastes and the stories and rumours that increasingly surrounded him made the place an object of fear and outrage for the local moral majority. In September 1792 the château was ransacked by revolutionaries and has never since been inhabited. The moody and brooding ruin is still in private ownership and is undergoing restoration work – but perhaps in this case an atmospheric ruin is more appropriate than a reconstruction.

Lourmarin. This attractive – and very touristy – village was the last home of Albert Camus (1913–60). He is buried in the cemetery here.

Ménerbes. Peter Mayle's *A Year in Provence*, 1989, has done wonders for the local tourist industries in the Lubéron, the undisputed charms of which it extols. Ménerbes, whose inhabitants are described in the book, is besieged by Mayle-inspired tourists in the summer.

Roussillon. In early 1942, Samuel Beckett (◊ Paris) and his partner Suzanne Deschevaux-Dumesnil arrived in this secluded village after a gruelling and secretive journey by foot of some

150 miles from Lyon. They fled from occupied Paris when the Resistance cell in which they had been involved was uncovered and broken up. They found safety from the Germans here in the unoccupied Vaucluse, living among the villagers and a motley group of refugees. As time went on, Beckett found the enforced isolation increasingly hard to take and during his stay in Roussillon suffered considerable mental anguish and depression. The liberating American soldiers first came to the village in August 1944, and Beckett and Suzanne finally got out of the Vaucluse in April 1945. During his time here, waiting, controlling his sanity as best he could, Beckett wrote *Watt* (published 1953), a novel concerned with communicative disintegration, and it is not difficult to see reflected in *En attendant Godot*, 1952 (*Waiting for Godot*, 1955) the boredom and frustration he experienced while waiting for the war to end, one way or another, in this rural haven that became a prison of the spirit as well as of the body.

BOOKLIST

For most of the extracted works, the original publisher in English can be found in 'Acknowledgments and Citations' at the end of the volume, as can the exact location of the extracts and the editions from which they are taken. The date in square brackets is that of the original publication of the work in its original language. For additional titles by the authors highlighted in this chapter and for recommended biographies, see 'Lives and Works'.

Beckett, Samuel, *Waiting for Godot* [1952], Faber and Faber, London, 1965/Grove Press, New York, 1954.

Beckett, Samuel, *Watt* [1953], John Calder, London, 1976/Grove Press, New York, 1970.

Bedford, Sybille, *A Compass Error* [1968], Virago, London, 1984/ NAL-Dutton, New York, 1985. **Extract 11.**

Bedford, Sybille, *Jigsaw: A Biographical Novel* [1989], Penguin, London and New York, 1990.

Bogarde, Dirk, *Jericho*, Penguin, London and New York, 1992. **Extract 12.**

Bruccoli, Matthew J., *Fitzgerald and Hemingway: A Dangerous Friendship*, André Deutsch, London, 1995.

Cendrars, Blaise, *The Astonished Man* [1945], N. Rootes, trans, Peter Owen, London, 1970.

Chateaubriand, François-René, *The Memoirs of Chateaubriand* [1849–50], Robert Baldick, trans, Penguin, London and New York, 1965. (Selections.)

Conrad, Joseph, *A Personal Record* [1912], Marlboro Press, Marlboro, VT, 1991.

Conrad, Joseph, *The Rover* [1923], Oxford University Press, Oxford and New York, 1992.

Daudet, Alphonse, *Letters from My Windmill* [1869], Frederick Davies, trans, Penguin, London and New York, 1978.

Daudet, Alphonse, *Tartarin of Tarascon* [1872] and *Tartarin on the Alps* [1885], Dent, London, 1969/Dutton, New York, 1969. **Extract 13.**

Dickens, Charles, *Little Dorrit* [1857], Penguin, London and New York, 1967.

Dumas, Alexandre, *The Count of Monte Cristo* [1845], David Coward, ed, Oxford University Press, Oxford, 1990/Bantam, New York, 1986. **Extracts 4 and 5.**

Durrell, Lawrence, *Caesar's Vast Ghost: Aspects of Provence* [1990], Faber and Faber, London, 1995.

Durrell, Lawrence, *Monsieur, or the Prince of Darkness* [1974], Faber and Faber, London, 1976/Viking Penguin, New York, 1984. **Extract 1.**

Durrell, Lawrence, *Spirit of Place: Letters and Essays on Travel*, Alan G. Thomas, ed, Faber and Faber, London, 1969.

Fitzgerald, F. Scott, *Tender is the Night* [1934], Penguin, London, 1955/Scribner, New York, 1985. **Extract 2.**

Fitzgerald, Zelda, *Collected Writings of Zelda Fitzgerald*, Abacus, London, 1993/Macmillan, New York, 1991.

Fitzgerald, Zelda, *Save Me the Waltz* [1932], Dutton, New York, 1968.

Ford, Ford Madox, *Provence* [1934], Ecco, Hopewell, NJ, 1992.

Fortescue, Lady, *Perfume from Provence* [1935], Black Swan, London, 1992/Hearst, New York, 1993.

Gide, André, *Journals 1889–1949*, Justin O'Brien, trans, Penguin, London and New York, 1967/ *The Journals of André Gide*, Justin O'Brien, trans, in 4 vols, Knopf, New York, 1947–51.

Giono, Jean, *Colline* [1929], Blackwell, Oxford, 1986.

Giono, Jean, *The Horseman on the Roof* [1952], J. Griffin, trans, Harvill, London, 1996. (Translation originally published as *The Hussar on the Roof*.)

Giono, Jean, *The Man Who Planted Trees* [1954], Peter Owen, London, 1989/Chelsea Green, Post Mills, VT, 1985. A new translation by Barbara Bray was published by Harvill, London, 1995. **Extract 10.**

Giono, Jean, *To the Slaughterhouse* [1931], N. Glass, trans, Peter Owen, London, 1969/Dufour, Chester Springs, PA, 1969.

Greene, Graham, *J'Accuse: The Dark Side of Nice*, Bodley Head, London, 1982.

Greene, Graham, *Loser Takes All* [1955], in *The Third Man and Loser Takes All*, William Heinemann and The Bodley Head, London, 1976/*Loser Takes All*, Viking Penguin, New York, 1989. **Extract 7.**

James, Henry, *A Little Tour in France* [1885], Penguin, London and New York, 1985.

Koestler, Arthur, *Scum of the Earth* [1941], Eland, London, 1991/Hippocrene, New York, 1991.

McKay, Claude, *Banjo* [1929], Harcourt Brace Jovanovich, Orlando, FL, 1970.

Mansfield, Katherine, *The Collected Stories of Katherine Mansfield*, Penguin, London and New York, 1981.

Mansfield, Katherine, *Katherine Mans-*

field's Letters to John Middleton Murry, Constable, London, 1951/ Knopf, New York, 1951.

Mayle, Peter, *A Year in Provence* [1989], Pan, London, 1990/Knopf, New York, 1990.

Maugham, W. Somerset, 'The Facts of Life' and 'The Three Fat Women of Antibes', in *Collected Short Stories*, Vol 1, Mandarin, London, 1990. **Extract 8.**

Maugham, W. Somerset, *The Razor's Edge* [1944], Penguin, London and New York, 1963.

Mistral, Frédéric, *Memoirs of Frédéric Mistral*, G. Wickes, trans, Alyscamps, Macclesfield, 1994/New Directions, New York, 1986.

Pagnol, Marcel, *My Father's Glory and My Mother's Castle* [1957], R. Barisse, trans, Picador, London, 1991/North Point Press, Berkeley, CA, 1991.

Pagnol, Marcel, *The Water of the Hills: Jean de Florette and Manon of the Springs* [1963], W.E. van Heyningen, trans, Picador, London, 1989/ *Jean de Florette and Manon of the Springs: Two Novels*, North Point Press, Berkeley, CA, 1988. **Extract 14.**

Petrarch, *Selections from the Canzoniere and Other Works*, Mark Musa, trans, Oxford University Press, Oxford and New York, 1985.

Petrarch, *The Sonnets of Petrarch*, Thomas G. Bergin, ed and trans, Heritage Press, New York, 1966. (Selections, bilingual.)

Sembène Ousmane, *Black Docker* [1956], Ros Schwartz, trans, Heinemann International, Oxford, 1987. **Extract 6.**

Smollett, Tobias, *Travels Through France and Italy* [1766], Oxford University Press, Oxford and New York, 1981. **Extract 9.**

Stevenson, Robert Louis, 'Ordered South', in *Travels with a Donkey in the Cévennes and Selected Travel Writings*, Oxford University Press, Oxford and New York, 1992.

Süskind, Patrick, *Perfume* [1985], John E. Woods, trans, Penguin, London, 1987/Knopf, New York, 1987. **Extract 3.**

Verne, Jules, *Twenty Thousand Leagues Under the Sea* [1870], H. Frith, trans, Everyman Library, Dent, London, 1993/Bantam, New York, 1985.

Williams, William Carlos, 'To Ford Madox Ford in Heaven', in *Penguin Modern Poets*, Vol 9 (Denise Levertov; Kenneth Rexroth; William Carlos Williams), Penguin, London, 1967/*Collected Poems* (2 vols), New Directions, New York, 1991.

Woolf, Virginia, *Travels with Virginia Woolf*, Jan Morris, ed, The Hogarth Press, London, 1993.

Zola, Émile, *The Conquest of Plassans* [1874], Alan Sutton, Gloucester, 1994.

Extracts

(1) AVIGNON

Lawrence Durrell, *Monsieur*

Returning to Avignon following the death of his beloved friend Piers, Bruce (the narrator) reflects on the town's significance in the 'three-cornered passion' of Piers, Sylvie and himself.

Confused messages waited for me at the hotel, but there was nothing to be done about them at this hour. I dozed on my bed until sunrise and then set out resolutely to find a coffee, traversing the old city with affection and distress, hearing my own sharp footsteps on the pavements, disembodied as a ghost. Avignon! Its shabby lights and sneaking cats were the same as ever; overturned dustbins, the glitter of fish scales, olive oil, broken glass, a dead scorpion. All the time we had been away on our travels round the world it had stayed pegged here at the confluence of its two green rivers. The past embalmed it, the present could not alter it. So many years of going away and coming back, of remembering and forgetting it. It had always waited for us, floating among its tenebrous monuments, the corpulence of its ragged bells, the putrescence of its squares.

And in a sense we had waited for it to reclaim us after every absence. It had been the most decisive part of our lives – the fall of Rob Sutcliffe, Sylvie's collapse, and now the suicide of Piers. Here it lay summer after summer, baking away in the sun, until its closely knitted roofs of weathered tile gave it the appearance of a piecrust fresh from the oven. It haunted one although it was rotten, fly-blown with expired dignities, almost deliquescent among its autumn river damps. There was not a corner of it that we did not love.

(2) CAP D'ANTIBES

F. Scott Fitzgerald, *Tender is the Night*

Fitzgerald introduces his readers to the Hôtel des Étrangers and to Rosemary, a key setting and a key character in his last complete and much revised novel. The book began its long gestation in 1925, when Fitzgerald himself was living on the Riviera. The original of Gausse's hotel is the exclusive Hôtel du Cap on Boulevard Kennedy.

On the pleasant shore of the French Riviera, about half way between Marseilles and the Italian border, stands a large, proud, rose-colored hotel. Deferential palms cool its flushed façade, and before it stretches a short dazzling beach. Lately it has become a summer resort of notable and fashionable people; a decade ago it was almost deserted after its English clientele went north in April. Now, many bungalows cluster near it, but when this story begins only the cupolas of a dozen old villas rotted like water lilies among the massed pines between Gausse's Hôtel des Étrangers and Cannes, five miles away.

The hotel and its bright tan prayer rug of a beach were one. In the early morning the distant image of Cannes, the pink and cream of old fortifications, the purple Alp that bounded Italy, were cast across the water and lay quavering in the ripples and rings sent up by seaplants through the clear shallows. Before eight a man came down to the beach in a blue bathrobe and with much preliminary application to his person of the chilly water, and much grunting and loud breathing, floundered a minute in the sea. When he had gone, beach and bay were quiet for an hour. Merchantmen crawled westward on the horizon; bus boys shouted in the hotel court; the dew dried upon the pines. In another hour the horns of motors began to blow down from the winding road along the low range of the Maures, which separates the littoral from true Provençal France.

A mile from the sea, where pines give way to dusty poplars, is an isolated railroad stop, whence one June morning in 1925 a victoria brought a woman and her daughter down to Gausse's Hotel. The mother's face was of a fading prettiness that would soon be patted with broken veins; her expression was both tranquil and aware in a pleasant way. However, one's eye moved on quickly to her daughter, who had magic in her pink palms and her cheeks lit to a lovely flame, like the thrilling flush of children after their cold baths in the evening. Her fine forehead sloped gently up to where her hair, bordering it like an armorial shield, burst into lovelocks and waves and curlicues of ash blonde and gold. Her eyes were bright, big, clear, wet, and shining, the color of her cheeks was real, breaking close to the surface from the strong young pump of her heart. Her body hovered delicately on the last edge of childhood – she was almost eighteen, nearly complete, but the dew was still on her.

(3) Grasse

Patrick Süskind, *Perfume*

The sinister, all-smelling Grenouille arrives in Grasse in his search for the perfect scent. Süskind's novel, set in the 18th century, powerfully evokes a town driven by commerce, hiding its wealth behind a mundane exterior.

He spent all that afternoon wandering about the town. It was unbelievably filthy, despite – or perhaps directly because of – all the water that gushed through the town in unchannelled rivulets and brooks, undermining the streets or flooding them with muck. In some neighbourhoods the houses stood so close together that only a yard-wide space was left for passageways and stairs, forcing pedestrians to jostle one another as they waded through the mire. And even in the squares and along the few broader streets, vehicles could hardly get out of each other's way.

Nevertheless, however filthy, cramped and slovenly, the town was bustling with the bustle of commerce. During his tour, Grenouille spotted no less than seven soapworks, a dozen master perfumers and glovers, countless small distilleries, pomade studios and spice shops, and finally some seven wholesalers in scents.

These were in fact merchants who completely controlled the wholesale supply of scent. One would hardly know it by their houses. The façades to the street looked modestly middle-class. But what was stored behind them, in warehouses and in gigantic cellars, in kegs of oil in stacks of finest lavender soaps, in demijohns of floral colognes, wines, alcohols, in bales of scented leather, in sacks and chests and crates stuffed with spices – Grenouille smelled out every detail through the thickest walls – these were riches beyond those of princes. And when he smelled his way more penetratingly through the prosaic shops and storerooms fronting the streets, he discovered that at the rear of these provincial family homes were buildings of the most luxurious sort. Around small but exquisite gardens, where oleander and palm trees flourished and fountains bordered by ornamental flowers leaped, extended the actual residential wings, usually built in a U-shape towards the south: on the upper floors, bedchambers drenched in sunlight, the walls covered with silk; on the ground floor wainscoted salons and dining rooms, sometimes with terraces built out into the open air, where, just as Baldini had said, people ate from porcelain with golden cutlery. The gentlemen who lived behind these modest façades reeked of gold and power, of carefully secured riches, and they reeked of it more strongly than anything else Grenouille had smelled thus far on his journey through the provinces.

(4) MARSEILLE

Alexandre Dumas, *The Count of Monte Cristo*

Dumas introduces us to Mercédès, the beautiful Catalane who loves and is loved by Edmond Dantès. Fernand, who appears in this scene, also loves her and his jealousy of Dantès leads him to become one of the conspirators. The Anse des Catalans, where the Catalan fishing community settled, was so isolated from the city at the time Dumas was writing (1840s) that its inhabitants hardly spoke French. Now its beach is one of the most popular around Marseille.

About a hundred paces from the spot where the two friends were, with their looks fixed on the distance, and their ears attentive, whilst they imbibed the sparkling wine of La Malgue, behind a bare, and torn, and weather-worn wall, was the small village of the Catalans.

One day a mysterious colony quitted Spain, and settled on the tongue of land on which it is to this day. It arrived from no one knew where, and spoke an unknown tongue. One of its chiefs, who understood Provençal, begged the commune of Marseilles to give them this bare and barren promontory, on which, like the sailors of ancient times, they had run their boats ashore. The request was granted, and three months afterwards, around the twelve or fifteen small vessels which had brought these gipsies of the sea, a small village sprang up.

This village, constructed in a singular and picturesque manner, half Moorish, half Spanish, is that which we behold at the present day inhabited by the descendants of those men who speak the language of their fathers. For three or four centuries they remained faithful to this little promontory, on which they had settled like a flight of sea-birds, without mixing with the Marseillaise population, intermarrying, and preserving their original customs and the costume of their mother country, as they have preserved its language.

Our readers will follow us along the only street of this little village, and enter with us into one of the houses, on the outside of which the sun had stamped that beautiful colour of the dead leaf peculiar to the buildings of the country, and within a coat of limewash, of that white tint which forms the only ornament of Spanish posadas.

A young and beautiful girl, with hair as black as jet, her eyes as velvety as the gazelle's, was leaning with her back against the wainscot, rubbing in her slender fingers, moulded after the antique, a bunch of heath-blossoms, the flowers of which she was picking off, and strewing on the floor; her arms bare to the elbow, embrowned, and resembling those of the Venus at Arles, moved with a kind of restless impatience, and she tapped the earth with her pliant and well-formed foot so as to display the pure and full shape of her well-turned leg, in its red cotton stocking with gray and blue clocks.

At three paces from her, seated in a chair which he balanced on two legs, leaning his elbow on an old worm-eaten table, was a tall young man of twenty or two-and-twenty, who was looking at her with an air in which vexation and uneasiness were mingled. He questioned her with his eyes, but the firm and steady gaze of the young girl controlled his look.

'You see, Mercédès,' said the young man, 'here is Easter come round again; tell me, is this the moment for a wedding?'

(5) MARSEILLE: CHÂTEAU D'IF

Alexandre Dumas, *The Count of Monte Cristo*

The victim of a cruel conspiracy, Edmond Dantès, still reeling from the shock of his arrest, is taken to the prison of the Château d'If. The Château, whose cells were also home to some famous real-life inmates, including Mirabeau and the 'Man in the Iron Mask', may be visited. The dismal dungeons where Dumas placed Dantès and the Abbé Faria are a main attraction.

Dantès made no resistance, he was like a man in a dream, he saw soldiers who stationed themselves on the sides, he felt himself forced up fresh stairs, he perceived he passed through a door, and the door closed behind him; but all this as mechanically as through a mist, nothing distinctly.

They halted for a minute, during which he strove to collect his thoughts; he looked around; he was in a court surrounded by high walls; he heard the measured tread of sentinels, and as they passed before the light he saw the barrels of their muskets shine.

They waited upwards of ten minutes. Captain Dantès could not escape, the gendarmes released him; they seemed awaiting orders. The orders arrived.

'Where is the prisoner?' said a voice.

'Here,' replied the gendarmes.

'Let him follow me; I am going to conduct him to his room.'

'Go!' said the gendarmes, pushing Dantès.

The prisoner followed his conductor, who led him into a room almost under ground, whose bare and reeking walls seemed as though impregnated with tears; a lamp placed on a stool illumined the apartment faintly, and showed Dantès the features of his conductor; an under-gaoler, ill-clothed, and of sullen appearance.

'Here is your chamber for to-night,' said he. 'It is late, and Monsieur le Gouverneur is asleep; to-morrow, perhaps, he may change you. In the meantime there is bread, water, and fresh straw, and that is all a prisoner can wish for. Good night!'

And before Dantès could open his mouth, – before he had noticed where the gaoler placed his bread or the water, – before he had glanced towards the corner where the straw was, the gaoler disappeared, taking with him the lamp.

Dantès was alone in darkness and in silence: cold as the shadows that he felt breathe on his burning forehead.

(6) MARSEILLE

Sembène Ousmane, *Black Docker*

Writer Diaw Falla scratches his living on the docks in Marseille in Ousmane's 1956 novel. The vivid descriptions of life in the city as a black immigrant and a docker are drawn from Ousmane's personal experiences.

He set off for work carrying his hook and his lunchbox. The autumnal grey sky promised a bright day. Men and women surged out of the neighbouring streets forming an endless procession along the avenues. Like Diaw, they were on their way to work. The older people walked slowly, the younger ones were more sprightly, chatting as they went. A rag-and-bone man was bowed under the weight of his load. A road-mender was spraying the tarmac. The dustcart collected the rubbish, the dustbins clanging noisily. In the place de la Joliette, there was a human tide. The quayside workers poured on to the esplanade by tram, bus and on foot. One side was lined with cafés and along the other was the goods station. Snack kiosks were wedged between the trees. People were calling and seeking each other out amid the chaos. The dockers were divided by a great misunderstanding: there were the veterans, who had been in the strike, men who knew their job, and who, to assert their rights, had unanimously voted to stop work. To thwart this decision, unemployed workers had been brought in.

They did not mingle, but clashed for no reason. They attacked each other with the testiness of wild animals, often at the slightest provocation. In every heart simmered an unhealthy passion looking for an outlet. Outwardly, they appeared to stick together, in work that sapped the vital strength from their muscles. In town, they discussed only the port and things related to it. Their language was crude: they heaped abuse on the supervisor, the employers and the foremen. The uncertainty of employment inflamed the abscess. It was always the same men who were hired, the same men who went home. The expressions on their faces reflected their inner discontent. Their skins were branded by the searing sun and dulled by the harsh weather which made deep furrows in their faces. Their hair was eaten away by bugs in the cereals. After years of this work, a man became a wreck, drained inside, nothing but an outer shell. Living in this hell, each year the docker takes another great stride towards his end. There were countless accidents. Mechanization had superseded their physical capacity, only a quarter of them toiled away maintaining the pace of the machines, replacing the output of the unemployed workers. It was the rivalry of bone against steel, a question of which was the stronger.

(7) Monte Carlo

Graham Greene, *Loser Takes All*

Cary and Bertram, in Monte Carlo to get married, anxiously await the arrival of Bertram's boss Mr Dreuther, who has promised to pay their bills. Greene wrote this short novel after spending a few weeks in Monte Carlo in 1955, where he stayed at the Hôtel de Paris and enjoyed the Casino.

'Like to go to the Casino? I asked Cary. 'We could spend, say, 1,000 francs now that everything's arranged.'

'Let's take a look at the port first and see if he's come.' We walked down the steps which reminded me of Montmartre except that everything was so creamy and clean and glittering and new, instead of grey and old and historic. Everywhere you were reminded of the Casino – the bookshops sold systems in envelopes, '2,500 francs a week guaranteed', the toyshops sold small roulette boards, the tobacconists sold ashtrays in the form of a wheel, and even in the women's shops there were scarves patterned with figures and *manqué* and *pair* and *impair* and *rouge* and *noir*.

There were a dozen yachts in the harbour, and three carried British flags, but none of them was Dreuther's *Seagull*. 'Wouldn't it be terrible if he'd forgotten?' Cary said.

'Miss Bullen would never let him forget. I expect he's unloading passengers at Nice. Anyway last night you wanted him to be late.'

'Yes, but this morning it feels scary. Perhaps we oughtn't to play the Casino – just in case.'

'We'll compromise,' I said. 'Three hundred francs. We can't leave Monaco without playing once.'

We hung around the *cuisine* for quite a while before we played. This was the serious time of day – there were no tourists and the *Salle Privée* was closed and only the veterans sat there. You had a feeling with all of them that their lunch depended on victory. It was a long, hard, dull employment for them – a cup of coffee and then to work till lunch-time – if their system was successful and they could afford the lunch. Once Cary laughed – I forget at what, and an old man and an old woman raised their heads from opposite sides of the table and stonily stared. They were offended by our frivolity: this was no game to them. Even if the system worked, what a toil went into earning the 2,500 francs a week. With their pads and their charts they left nothing to chance, and yet over and over again chance nipped in and shovelled away their tokens.

(8) MONTE CARLO
W. Somerset Maugham, *The Facts of Life*

Nicky Garnet, a young British tennis player in Monte Carlo for a tournament, starts to ignore his father's advice not to gamble, lend money or get involved with women.

He stood for a while looking at the losers' money being raked-in by the croupier and the money that was paid out to the winners. It was impossible to deny that it was thrilling. His friend was right, it did seem silly to leave Monte without putting something on the table just once. It would be an experience, and at his age you had to have all the experience you could get. He reflected that he hadn't promised his father not to gamble, he'd promised him not to forget his advice. It wasn't quite the same, was it? He took a hundred-franc note out of his pocket and rather shyly put it on number eighteen. He chose it because that was his age. With a wildly beating heart he watched the wheel turn; the little white ball whizzed about like a small demon of mischief; the wheel went round more slowly, the little white ball hesitated, it seemed about to stop, it went on again; Nicky could hardly believe his eyes when it fell into number eighteen. A lot of chips were passed over to him and his hands trembled as he took them. It seemed to amount to a lot of money. He was so confused that he never thought of putting anything on the following round; in fact he had no intention of playing any more, once was enough; and he was surprised when eighteen again came up. There was only one chip on it.

'By George, you've won again,' said a man who was standing near to him.

'Me? I hadn't got anything on.'

'Yes, you had. Your original stake. They always leave it on unless you ask for it back. Didn't you know?'

Another packet of chips was handed over to him. Nicky's head reeled. He counted his gains: seven thousand francs. A queer sense of power seized him; he felt wonderfully clever. This was the easiest way of making money that he had ever heard of. His frank, charming face was wreathed in smiles. His bright eyes met those of a woman standing by his side. She smiled.

(9) Nice

Tobias Smollett, *Travels Through France and Italy*

Writing in 1764, the pugnacious English novelist gives his advice on finding accommodation and domestic staff in Nice, where he stayed for eighteen months.

In the town of Nice, you will find no ready-furnished lodgings for a whole family. Just without one of the gates, there are two houses to be let, ready-furnished, for about five loui'dores per month. As for the country houses in this neighbourhood, they are damp in winter, and generally without chimnies; and in summer they are rendered uninhabitable by the heat and vermin. If you hire a tenement in Nice, you must take it for a year certain; and this will cost you about twenty pounds sterling. For this price, I have a ground floor paved with brick, consisting of a kitchen, two large halls, a couple of good rooms with chimnies, three large closets that serve for bed-chambers, and dressing rooms, a butler's room, and three apartments for servants, lumber or stores, to which we ascend by narrow stairs. I have likewise two small gardens, well stocked with oranges, lemons, peaches, figs, grapes, corinths, sallad, and pot-herbs. It is supplied with a draw-well of good water, and there is another in the vestibule of the house, which is cool, large and magnificent. You may hire furniture for such a tenement, for about two guineas a month: but I chose rather to buy what was necessary; and this cost me about sixty pounds. I suppose it will fetch me half the money when I leave the place. It is very difficult to find a tolerable cook at Nice. A common maid, who serves the people of the country, for three or four livres a month, will not live with an English family under eight or ten. They are all slovenly, slothful, and unconscionable cheats.

(10) Provençal Alps

Jean Giono, *The Man Who Planted Trees*

After the First World War, the narrator in Giono's short tale goes back to see the shepherd Elzéard Bouffier in the 'mountain heights quite unknown to tourists, in that ancient region where the Alps thrust down into Provence.' Uninterrupted by the war, Bouffier has been relentlessly pursuing his tree-planting.

He had pursued his plan, and beech trees as high as my shoulder, spreading out as far as the eye could reach, confirmed it. He showed me handsome clumps of birch planted five years before – that is, in 1915, when I had been fighting at Verdun. He had set them out in all the valleys where he had guessed – and rightly – that there was moisture almost at the surface of the ground. They were as delicate as young girls, and very well established.

Creation seemed to come about in a sort of chain reaction. He did not worry about it; he was determinedly pursuing his task in all its simplicity; but as we went back towards the village I saw water flowing in brooks that had been dry since the memory of man. This was the most impressive result of chain reaction that I had seen. These dry streams had once, long ago, run with water. Some of the dreary villages I mentioned before had been built on the sites of ancient Roman settlements, traces of which still remained; and archaeologists, exploring there, had found fishhooks where, in the twentieth century, cisterns were needed to assure a small supply of water.

The wind, too, scattered seeds. As the water reappeared, so there reappeared willows, rushes, meadows, gardens, flowers, and a certain purpose in being alive. But the transformation took place so gradually that it became part of the pattern without causing any astonishment. Hunters, climbing into the wilderness in pursuit of hares or wild boar, had of course noticed the sudden growth of little trees, but had attributed it to some natural caprice of the earth. That is why no one meddled with Elzéard Bouffier's work. If he had been detected he would have had opposition. He was undetectable. Who in the villages or in the administration could have dreamed of such perseverance in a magnificent generosity?

To have anything like a precise idea of this exceptional character one must not forget that he worked in total solitude: so total that, toward the end of his life, he lost the habit of speech. Or perhaps it was that he saw no need for it.

(11) PROVENCE: COAST

Sybille Bedford, *A Compass Error*

Flavia, living in coastal Provence between the wars, takes an early evening stroll down to the waterside in a port near Toulon, and has an intimation of the fragility of her pleasant and well ordered way of life.

She carried a book. She did not carry a bag. One of her trousers pockets held loose money, notes and coin, the other a comb, a clean handkerchief and an automatic pencil. She also carried on her the weekly letter from her tutor, a man in London whom she had not met, as a kind of talisman. At this hour Flavia had to hold on a bit to her morale; she became conscious of sticking to a part. Reading and swimming were things she had done and loved as long as she could remember. Now was something else.

The much painted waterfront of St-Jean had not become a car-park then. The boats in the harbour could be seen: fishing-boats and sailing-boats and some trawlers, and the line of pink-washed, blue-washed houses with four cafés almost in a row. People on the quay-side were doing things with ropes and baskets, clusters of men were standing huddled over that static game, there were plenty of people in those cafés, but there were no hordes.

Flavia bought herself a French newspaper at the kiosk and firmly made her way to a single café table. She ordered a Cinzano, watched the waiter slide a lump of ice into her glass and work the trigger of the soda syphon. The syphon spluttered, gurgled, shot dry air. The waiter shook it and produced another. Flavia thanked him, took a sip and unfolded *L'Oeuvre*. She read the opening of Madame Tabouis' column and looked up again, looked about her at the boats so quiet on the water, at the comings and goings, at the evening sky. She was conscious of not enjoying any of this as much as she might. In her mind she rolled over one of the phrases with which she used to amuse or scare herself as a child: The situation is fraught with perils.

Presently a man a couple of tables away caught her eye. He was middle-aged. '*Toujours seule?*' he called.

(12) PROVENCE: A VILLAGE

Dirk Bogarde, *Jericho*

Staying at the only hotel in a small (fictional) village in rural Provence, William Caldicott comes to terms with his decision to stay in France and take over the lease of his missing brother's house.

Eugène had suggested what I should eat and I had agreed and asked him to bring me a suitable wine. He did. I drank half, more than half actually, of the bottle but still felt grotty.

I thought that a decent claret would soothe, or set at ease, my restlessness, but it did not. So I went off to the bar and had a large brandy; that made it worse. Or made me worse. I rather think it stimulated more than soothed. I still felt uneasy, un-tired. Wretched. Of course, what I was doing really was trying to delay the moment when I would have to go up to my little room with its bleeding heart Jesus and the kittens and the lumpy bed. I would be stuck in there and forced to think things out. The best way to think things out would be to walk.

That is what I did. The little town was dead. No one moved. There were shaded lights here and there slitting through shutters, a cat ran across my path, a thin shadow. There was a light, fresh, clear wind. The fresh air of height, not low-lying air.

Now, where was I? I had been sent a key. Correct. I was presently in the deserted streets of a small French village. I had decided to take over the lease of my brother's house. For three years. My *missing* brother. Whom I had determined to try and find. Somehow.

So far those facts were clear.

My life in London, fixed permanently I'd always thought, was now at an end. I was facing a new start. Hence my irritation, my imbalance, my ragged feeling.

I found myself at the top of rue Émile Zola, the end nearest the square and the church which, at that exact moment, struck the half-hour. Ten-thirty. Across the square the signboard of the hotel suddenly went black as the lights were switched off. I stood alone on the cobbles, a little breeze riffled past, caught a paper wrapping on the street, danced it into a spiral, let it fall.

(13) TARASCON

Alphonse Daudet, *Tartarin of Tarascon*

The small Provençal town of Tarascon was made famous by Daudet's satirical portrait of its bourgeoisie and his larger-than-life creation of Tartarin, a lovable cross between Don Quixote and Sancho Panza. Fiction has become reality and the 'House of Tartarin' is at 55 bis Boulevard Itam. In this passage, from the first of the Tartarin novels, the would-be hero prepares for an evening stroll to his club.

Before starting, in the silence and obscurity of his study, he exercised himself for a while, warding off imaginary cuts and thrusts, lunging at the wall, and giving his muscles play; then he took his master-key and went through the garden leisurely; without hurrying mark you. 'Cool and calm – British courage, that is the sort, gentlemen.' At the garden end he opened the heavy iron door, violently and abruptly so that it should slam against the outer wall. If 'they' had been skulking behind it, you may wager they would have been jam. Unhappily, they were not there.

The way being open, out Tartarin would sally, quickly glancing to the right and left, ere banging the door to and fastening it smartly with double-locking. Then, on the way. Not so much as a cat upon the Avignon road – all the doors closed, and no lights in the casements. All was black, except for the parish lamps, well spaced apart, blinking in the river mist.

Calm and proud, Tartarin of Tarascon marched on in the night, ringing his heels with regularity, and sending sparks out of the paving-stones with the ferule of his stick. Whether in avenues, streets, or lanes, he took care to keep in the middle of the road – an excellent method of precaution, allowing one to see danger coming, and, above all, to avoid any droppings from windows, as happens after dark in Tarascon and the Old Town of Edinburgh. On seeing so much prudence in Tartarin, pray do not conclude that Tartarin had any fear – dear, no! he was only on his guard.

The best proof that Tartarin was not scared is, that instead of going to the club by the shortest cut, he went over the town by the longest and darkest way round, through a mass of vile, paltry alleys, at the mouth of which the Rhône could be seen ominously gleaming. The poor knight constantly hoped that, beyond the turn of one of these cut-throats' haunts, 'they' would leap from the shadow and fall on his back. I warrant you, 'they' would have been warmly received, though; but, alack! by reason of some nasty meanness of destiny, never indeed did Tartarin of Tarascon enjoy the luck to meet any ugly customers – not so much as a dog or a drunken man – nothing at all!

(14) La Treille

Marcel Pagnol, *The Water of the Hills*

Pagnol sets his memorable tale in and around a sharply visualized fictional Provençal village 'Les Bastides Blanches', which he locates near to his birthplace Aubagne and which is inspired by the real-life nearby village of La Treille where he spent summer holidays in his childhood. In this scene-setting passage, water, which plays such a major role in the story, is already highlighted as the focus and life-giving element of the village and the surrounding area.

Les Bastides Blanches was a village of a hundred and fifty inhabitants, perched on the prow of one of the last foothills of the Massif de l'Etoile, about ten kilometers from Aubagne. A dirt road led there on a slope so abrupt that from afar it appeared to be vertical; on the hillside beyond, nothing but a mule track left the village, with a number of footpaths leading off it to the sky.

About fifty rows of houses, whose whiteness remained only in the village's name, lined five or six streets that were neither paved nor tarred – streets that were narrow because of the sun and tortuous because of the mistral.

There was however a fairly long esplanade that dominated the valley on the west; it was supported by a rampart of trimmed stone a good ten meters high, finished off with a parapet under a row of ancient plane trees. This place was called the Boulevard, and the old people came there to sit and talk in the shade.

In the middle of the Boulevard a very wide flight of a dozen steps rose to the town square bordered by facades around a fountain with a stone shell attached to the middle. This was the origin of the village. Fifty years earlier, a summer resident from Marseille (two or three would come home during the hunting season) had left a small bag of gold coins to the community, and this had made it possible to conduct sparkling water from the only important spring in this part of the country to the square. It was then that the small farms scattered about the valleys and hillsides had been abandoned one by one, and the families had grouped themselves around the fountain, and the hamlet had become a village.

All day long one saw pitchers or jars under the jet of water and gossips listening to their rising music while they exchanged the news of the day.

Around the square there were a number of shops: the *bar-tabac*, the grocer, the baker, the butcher, and then the wide open workshop of the carpenter next door to the blacksmith, and at the end, the church; it was old, but not ancient, and its bell tower was hardly higher than the houses.

A small street left the square on the left to lead to another shaded esplanade that stretched out before the biggest building in the village.

This building was the town hall, as well as the meeting place of the Republican Club, the chief political activity of which was to organize the game of lotto and the *boules* contests. The *boules* tournaments took place on Sunday under the plane trees in both esplanades.

Lives and works of extracted writers

BEDFORD, Sybille (1911–). Bedford was born in Germany and brought up in England, France and Italy. As a journalist she has written widely on literature and travel, among other things, and also, as a law reporter, has covered major proceedings including the Auschwitz trials at Frankfurt, the *Lady Chatterley* obscenity case, and the trial of Jack Ruby. Her books have included travel literature and biography (of Aldous Huxley), and several novels. Bedford's experience of France relates primarily to coastal Provence around **Toulon**, where she lived in the 1920s and 1930s – see the 'France' section of her 'biographical novel' *Jigsaw: An Unsentimental Education*, 1989, for her vivid evocations and impressions of the region. In her novel *A Compass Error*, 1968 (Extract 11), set entirely in this area, Bedford tells the story of a young woman discovering her sexuality and the pain and complexities of human relations. Written with an intriguing unwillingness to paint any character in black or white, the novel unfolds its story of life-changing actions and decisions which in the end trap the protagonist, Flavia, who must learn to live with the effects of her actions. Drawn through an initial lesbian encounter with the sympathetic and bohemian Therese, Flavia moves on to a much more complex and threatening infatuation with Andrée who turns out to have a hidden agenda with shattering implications for Flavia and the lives of her mother and her mother's lover. The book is rich in local colour and uses its setting effectively as an appropriate environment for the social and sexual encounters which form the novel's core. The title refers to the consequences of bad decisions – 'The compass error that gets harder to correct every mile you go.'

BOGARDE, Sir Dirk (1921–). Bogarde (born Van den Bogaerde) is famous as an international film actor, at the quality end of the broad spectrum which that profession encompasses. However, in his later life he has become increasingly known for his considerable literary abilities, as demonstrated in his novels and volumes of autobiography. He lived in rural **Provence** for some 20 years and has written about his house and his life there in various parts of his six-volume autobiography – see especially *An Orderly Man*, 1983, and *A Short Walk from Harrods*, 1994. His novel *Jericho*, 1992, is set atmospherically in the region of France Bogarde knows so well (the place names are invented). William Caldicott, in the last throes of a disintegrating marriage in London, receives a letter from his brother James and the key to his house in a small village in Provence. James has mysteriously 'disappeared' and William goes out partly to find out what happened and also to see if he himself can find a new life in France. The characters are sharply observed, and the locale of a small Provençal town is vividly evoked (Extract 12), as are the changing seasons of Provence. Bogarde published a sequel to *Jericho* in 1994, entitled *A Period of Adjustment*, also set in the region.

In 1990, Bogarde was made a Commandeur de l'Ordre des Arts et des Lettres.

DAUDET, Alphonse (1840–97). Daudet was born in **Nîmes** in Languedoc on 13 May 1840, and spent his first nine years in this typically southern town, the sunny spirit of the Midi soaking indelibly into him. In 1949, his family moved to the industrial fogbound city of **Lyon**, which proved a depressing contrast. In 1856 Daudet was forced to take work as an usher at a college in **Alais** in the Cévennes, where he was mercilessly victimized by the students for his small stature, his short sight, and his youth. In 1857, this nightmare ended and Daudet left for Paris, where he worked as a journalist and, in 1858, published a collection of poems entitled *Les Amoureuses*, which gained him rapid acceptance in literary circles. After a few unsuccessful attempts to make his name as a playwright, he turned to prose fiction, and began on the writing career that was to bring him fame and fortune.

Daudet lived in **Paris** throughout his adult life, although he eventually also acquired a home in **Champrosay** in Essonne. He returned to the south only occasionally for visits – to, most significantly, his friend the poet Mistral at **Maillane** and to the Château de Montaubon at **Fontvieille**, where he found peace at the foot of a windmill which he made spiritually his own. The current 'Moulin de Daudet', housing the **Musée Alphonse Daudet** (see introduction), though, is one of the other windmills in Fontvieille. Alphonse Daudet died in Paris on 16 December 1897. The last 12 years of his life were plagued with unremitting pain, due to the gradual spread in his body of locomotor ataxy which emanated apparently from syphilis contracted during his early bohemian years in the city.

In his day, Daudet was immensely successful – at once respected by his literary peers (including Flaubert and Zola) and hugely popular with the wider public. His work splits broadly into two categories – stories of Paris and stories of the Midi. Although a considerable number of Daudet's novels are concerned with the Paris and Parisians he knew so well, these are now largely neglected, and it is for his novels and stories of the south for which he is best remembered. Bridging the two is *Numa Roumestan*, 1881 (*Numa Roumestan*, 1950), a novel in which Daudet grapples directly with the conflict that always haunted him – between his attrac-

tion for the passion and warmth of Provence and his love/hate for the urban sophistication of Paris. It is, however, his comic Tartarin novels and his evocative *Lettres de mon moulin*, 1869 (*Letters from My Windmill*, 1978) which are now most readily associated with his name. The *Letters* are, for the most part, short tales, both humorous and tragic, which vividly evoke rural Provençal life and landscape in the fluid and easy prose of a natural-born story-teller.

Daudet's larger-than-life anti-hero Tartarin from the small Provençal town of **Tarascon**, appears in three novels – *Tartarin de Tarascon*, 1872 (*Tartarin of Tarascon*, 1910); *Tartarin sur les Alpes*, 1885 (*Tartarin on the Alps*, 1910); and the much less successful *Port-Tarascon*, 1890. In *Tartarin de Tarascon* (Extract 13), Daudet introduces his protagonist, an amalgam of Don Quixote and Sancho Panza – a Provençal boaster and would-be hero whose reality is far removed from his fantasy. The story revolves around Tartarin's comical character and the outrageous adventures in which he entangles himself. Trapped by his boasting, he finds himself leaving home for a spell of big-game hunting in

Alphonse Daudet

Africa. Despite disastrous misadventures, he returns to Tarascon to find his reputation greatly enhanced by his absence and he resumes his tall tales immediately, turning his incompetence into heroism. The satirical portrayal of small-town Provence, as exemplified by the inhabitants of Tarascon, caused outrage among the real-life bourgeois Tarasconnais, although the town now wholeheartedly embraces the literary association it once despised (see introduction).

Recommended biography: G.V. Dobie, *Alphonse Daudet*, Thomas Nelson and Sons, London, 1949.

DUMAS, Alexandre (1802–70). Dumas *père* was born at **Villers-Cotterêts** in Picardie on 24 July 1802. His father had been a distinguished general in Napoleon's army, but he died poor when Alexandre was only three. Although his formal schooling had no great effect on him, Dumas read voraciously from an early age and this self-education continued as he worked his way through various clerical jobs, ending up in the household of the Duc d'Orléans, later King Louis-Philippe. His first significant literary success came with his play *Henri III et sa cour*, which was staged at the Comédie-Française in 1829. A high-gloss historical drama with plenty of action, written in prose and with no attention to the unities of the neo-classical theatre, the play brought Dumas to the forefront of the Romantic movement in the theatre and also foretold the huge popular appeal of his talent. He followed *Henri III* with more theatrical successes through the 1830s, many of them historical dramas, enhancing his reputation as the leader of the Romantic revolution, gaining him notoriety with the artistic establishment, and making him a literary and public celebrity.

His truly astonishing success, however, came when he turned his attention to the novel, applying to the genre his imaginative mix of history, romance and action with his fluid, energetic style and his flair for accessible narrative and convincing dialogue. His novels were originally published as *romans-feuilletons* – ie they were serialized in daily newspapers – and Dumas excelled in this art which demanded fast-moving plots and constant cliff-hanging sequences. Of his vast output, the two outstanding achievements are *Le Comte de Monte-Cristo*, 1845 (*The Count of Monte Cristo*, 1852) and *Les Trois Mousquetaires*, 1844 (*The Three Musketeers*, 1952). *The Count of Monte Cristo* is for some the greatest adventure novel ever written, with all the essential ingredients and more. It is also a mordant portrayal of the financiers and politicians who held such power in the **Paris** that Dumas knew, and a characteristically vivid evocation of the manners and morals of French society at the time. The enduring success of the book may be attributed to many things, but few would disagree that the character of Edmond Dantès, alias the Count of Monte Cristo, and the changes he undergoes through his cruel victimization and subsequent vengeance, are key factors. Significant settings include **Marseille** (Extract 4), Rome, and **Paris**, and, of course, the **Château d'If** where Dantès is imprisoned (Extract 5) and where some of the most memorable scenes take place.

The Three Musketeers is based on historical fact – although it was inspired by a 17th century historical novel entitled *Les Mémoires de d'Artagnan* which Dumas and his collaborator Auguste Maquet came across in the course of their researches. The result is an action-packed adventure novel, but it is interesting that many of the key events and characters have their basis in reality (Milady is an exception). There was, for example, a real d'Artagnan who came from Gascony and was a King's Musketeer. Researchers have also concluded that the originals for Athos, Porthos and Aramis were Musketeers from Gascony (the heroes' Gascon origins are frequently stressed). *The*

Three Musketeers remains an immensely entertaining book, not least because of its colourful key setting of 17th century Paris (the Musketeers all live in streets around the **Jardin du Luxembourg**).

Apart from novels and plays, among Dumas's numerous other publications are a 22-volume autobiography, *Mes Mémoires*, 1852–55, travel literature, and many children's stories.

Dumas achieved huge success in his own lifetime – he was a social and literary star on a scale rarely matched. With that success came great wealth, which presented the recipient with no problems when it came to spending it (see, for example, the story of his 'Château de Monte Cristo' under Île de France). His later life was plagued by financial problems, not because he was unable to earn money but because of his irrepressible prodigality. Alexandre Dumas died on 5 December 1870 in **Dieppe**, while staying with his son (the writer Alexandre Dumas *fils*). He was buried temporarily near Dieppe, but his son afterwards had the body removed to the cemetery at **Villers-Cotterêts**, where Dumas is now buried alongside his parents in the town of his birth. Despite the enormous wealth he had enjoyed, he died virtually penniless.

Recommended biography: Michael Ross, *Alexandre Dumas*, David and Charles, Newton Abbot, 1981.

DURRELL, Lawrence (1912–90). Novelist, poet and travel-writer Durrell lived for much of his life in the Mediterranean. He travelled widely, spending time in particular in Corfu, Athens, Alexandria (during the Second World War – the inspiration for his famous *Alexandria Quartet*), Rhodes, Argentina, Yugoslavia, and Cyprus. He finally settled in **Provence** in 1957 – for the last 33 years of his life, his home was in the village of **Sommières**, near Nîmes.

Durrell's delight in and fascination with Provençal landscape and culture find their way into the second of his two major sets of novels. *Monsieur, or*

the Prince of Darkness, 1974, is the opening book of the so-called *Avignon Quintet*, five connected, though not sequential novels, which Durrell wrote between 1974 and 1985 – he described them collectively as a 'quincunx'. The other titles are *Livia, or Buried Alive*, 1978, *Constance, or Solitary Practices*, 1982, *Sebastian, or Ruling Passions*, 1983, and *Quinx, or The Ripper's Tale*, 1985. There are many atmospheric passages on **Avignon** and the Provençal countryside, especially in the earlier books, but the settings range widely. The novel highlighted here, *Monsieur* (Extract 1), for example, includes significant portions set in Egypt and Venice. Characteristic of Durrell's work, *Monsieur* is complex narratively and thematically and readers may or may not find it worth the effort. Depending on taste, the style is rich and powerfully evocative or self-conscious and over-elaborate. Opening with the return of Bruce to Avignon following the unexplained death of his beloved friend Piers, the novel explores the inter-relations among a small group of characters, weaving into its narrative fabric a critique of the Western 'slavish belief in causality and determinism' through challenges to the characters' perceptions of each other and their reactions to the charismatic and manipulative Egyptian Akkad. Much of the action is recollected – fragments of the past shored against the wreck of a present in which, of the loving triangle at the centre of the book, the 'three-cornered passion' of Bruce, Piers and Sylvie, Piers is dead and Sylvie has suffered mental breakdown.

Those in search of Durrell's travel writing on France will find a selection in *Spirit of Place: Letters and Essays on Travel*, 1969. His *Caesar's Vast Ghost: Aspects of Provence*, published in 1990 just days before his death, is a mixture of personal memoir and reflection and evocative travelogue, with poems dotted about the text, and a selection of photographs (including one of his home in Sommières).

Durrell was also active in literary **Paris** in the 1930s. He became involved in the scene which centred around Henry Miller and Jack Kahane's Obelisk Press (specializing in books other publishers found too hot to handle). In 1935, Durrell, then in Corfu, wrote a letter to Miller congratulating him effusively on *Tropic of Cancer* ('I salute *Tropic* as the copy-book for my generation.'). It was the beginning of a lifelong friendship and, as the writers were rarely in the same place, of a voluminous and often inspirational correspondence – see *Lawrence Durrell and Henry Miller: A Private Correspondence*, edited by George Wickes, 1963. In the 1930s, Durrell was in Paris with his wife and visited Miller frequently. Durrell's novel *The Black Book*, 1938, was edited by Miller and published under the 'Villa Seurat Series' imprint (devised by Miller and the Durrells as a self-financing imprint of the Obelisk Press). Durrell not only paid the printing costs for his own book but also helped financially with the publication of Miller's *Max and the White Phagocytes*, 1938, and Anaïs Nin's *Winter of Artifice*, 1939.

FITZGERALD, F. Scott (1896–1940). The Fitzgeralds, Scott and Zelda, travelled and lived in Europe for substantial periods during the 1920s, but whether the continent was ever much more to them than a great place to party is open to doubt. In France, they lived in **Paris** and in the South – at **St Raphaël** in 1924, where Scott worked on his finest novel, *The Great Gatsby*, 1925; **Antibes** in 1925; **Juan-les-Pins** in 1926; and **Cannes** in 1929. Scott Fitzgerald was already a celebrity when he arrived – a highly successful, handsome and charming author, a hero of his 'Jazz Age' generation and married to the glamorous exhibitionist Zelda. High priests of the high life, they embarked on a restless, rootless round of big parties, big spending, wild antics, and very serious drinking. Their life in the sun, however, was short – their

wings melted swiftly in a self-destructive downward spiral. Zelda suffered a mental breakdown in 1930 (while they were staying in Paris), and spent the rest of her life in and out of mental institutions. Presumably from the emotional strain this caused plus his own alcoholism, Scott died young from a heart attack some ten years later while working in Hollywood. Zelda died in a fire in a mental hospital in 1948.

The extravagant lifestyle of the jet set on the **Riviera** forms the backdrop to *Tender is the Night* (Extract 2), first published in 1934 but subsequently revised several times and published in its current form in 1948. Fitzgerald had started to work on the book as early as 1925, while living on the Côte d'Azur – it was a project in which he had great faith and over which he laboured painfully. It never, however, achieved the critical or popular success that he felt it should. Perhaps it was worked over too many times. Perhaps it was the subject matter – the emotional problems of members of a wealthy, privileged set living in the luxury of the French Riviera – that was too remote from the mood of Depression America and alienating generally to readers based in the hard reality of the 1930s and 1940s. Opinions continue to vary on the merits of the novel, but few would deny the power of its portrayal of psychological disintegration and the sophistication of its style and structure (though perhaps not of its rather over-dramatic plot). Many of the key elements of Fitzgerald's own experience find their way into the story of Dick and Nicole Diver, a glamorous and wealthy couple, and their increasingly destructive relationship – Dick is the central figure, initially a charming and successful doctor who gradually sinks into alcoholism and despair. The reference points to Fitzgerald's own life, and in particular his relationship with Zelda, are many. Zelda Fitzgerald's novel *Save Me the Waltz*, 1932, in effect represents her version of the story, and is similarly replete with autobiographical elements.

During his stays in **Paris**, Fitzgerald met many members of the Anglo–American literary set, but wrote rather disparagingly of them in correspondence – for example, he comments in a letter of autumn 1925, 'I have met most of the American literary world here (the crowd that centers around Pound) and find them mostly junk-dealers; except a few like Hemingway who are doing rather more thinking and working than the young men around New York.' His meeting with Hemingway was perhaps the most significant thing that happened to Fitzgerald in Paris – and it was from this initial encounter that the two, with their contrasting personalities and writing styles, developed their famous and fluctuating friendship, during which they read, commented on, and influenced each other's work. In addition, Fitzgerald championed Hemingway when he was still relatively unknown, introducing him to Maxwell Perkins, his editor at Scribner's and paving the way for the publication by Scribner's of *The Sun Also Rises* – Perkins became the long-time editor and friend of both writers. For a detailed analysis of the relationship, see Matthew J. Bruccoli, *Fitzgerald and Hemingway: A Dangerous Friendship*, 1994.

For those in search of Fitzgerald on **Paris**, apart from the Paris-based scenes in *Tender is the Night*, his short story 'Babylon Revisited', is recommended (first published in 1931 and included in *The Crack-Up With Other Pieces and Stories*, 1965). In this affecting and resonant piece, a man revisits the city trying to pick up his life, but finds only change and lost opportunity. The Paris he knew has gone – much of the American colony has returned to America, the Ritz bar has 'gone back into France'. His own personal past, however, cannot be escaped – despite his rejection of his dissipated and alcoholic earlier life, it comes back to haunt him and to prevent him from being reunited with his daughter. The story encapsulates Fitzgerald's own re-

grets at the opportunities he squandered and the experiences he missed. His character, Charlie Wales, realizes that he had never participated in the real life of Paris – 'He had never eaten at a really cheap restaurant in Paris. Five-course dinner, four francs eighty, eighteen cents, wine included. For some odd reason he wished that he had. As they rolled on to the Left Bank and he felt its sudden provincialism, he thought, "I spoiled this city for myself. I didn't realize it, but the days came along one after another, and then two years were gone, and everything was gone, and I was gone."'

Recommended biography: Jeffrey Meyers, *Scott Fitzgerald*, Macmillan, London, 1994/HarperCollins, New York, 1994.

GIONO, Jean (1895–1970). Giono was born on 30 March 1895 in **Manosque**, where he remained throughout his childhood, and indeed where he lived virtually his whole life. He left the local school when he was 16 and found employment in the bank – where he continued to work until he was able to make enough money from his writing, interrupted only by his service in the infantry during the First World War. Giono's work celebrates his native Provence and the courage and integrity of peasant life. Tags like 'regionalist' are however misleading and diminishing – blending reality and fiction to create his own mythical Provence, Giono's novels are above all a song to individual strength and compassion in the face of ills perpetrated by social and political organization, evoking Provençal landscape and culture but also transforming it into a pantheistic world of his own invention. Despite his strongly held beliefs in the virtues of nature and natural living and his impassioned pacifism, Giono avoided involvement in any political movement – unsurprisingly in view of his deep suspicion of any kind of organized group. However, he was (unjustifiably) imprisoned out at the outbreak of the

Second World War in connection with anti-war pamphlets he had written, and again at the end of the War for collaboration. In 1953, he was awarded the Prix Monégasque for his overall literary achievement. In 1954, he was elected to the Académie Goncourt. He died on 9 October 1970 of heart disease.

Several of Giono's novels are available in translation. Among these, readers might first turn to *Colline*, 1929 (*Colline*, 1986), a strong example of his earlier work; *Le Grand Troupeau*, 1931 (*To the Slaughterhouse*, 1969), his novel of the First World War; and *Le Hussard sur le Toit*, 1952 (*The Horseman on the Roof*, 1996), one of a series of novels set in the 19th century and featuring his engaging hero Angelo Pardi, an idealistic and compassionate individualist (filmed in 1994 by Jean-Paul Rappeneau).

The work highlighted here, *The Man Who Planted Trees*, has a publishing history appropriate to its selfless hero. Rejected by the American editors for whom it had been written because it was fictional (they had asked for a brief piece on an 'unforgettable character' – Giono chose to invent one), the author donated the story, according to Norma

Graham Greene

L. Goodrich in her Afterword to the Peter Owen edition of the book, to 'all and sundry'. It was in fact picked up by *Vogue* in 1954 and published in its March issue of that year under the excruciating title 'The Man Who Planted Hope and Grew Happiness'. Subsequently published in book form in 1989, Giono's short and memorable fable attracted great attention, not least because of its relevance to the growing international interest in environmental issues and ecology. Giono, according to Goodrich, saw a parallel between the mission of the story and his own 'charitable' act in effectively giving it away: 'It is one of my stories of which I am the proudest. It does not bring me in one single penny and that it is why it has accomplished what it was written for.' Like much of his writing, *The Man Who Planted Trees* is inspired by Giono's love for his native region, the **Provençal Alps**. The story centres around the narrator's encounters with Elzéard Bouffier, a shepherd living in the remote *haux plateaux* who has decided to dedicate his life to planting trees. Over the years, while the rest of the world is torn by two world wars, his dedication transforms the landscape, brings fertility and hope, and enriches the life of the region. Giono focuses on the inner peace of Bouffier, the oneness of the man with his task, so that his story is at once a moving plea for afforestation and a portrayal of human compassion in heroic terms (Extract 10).

GREENE, Graham (1904–91). This most widely travelled of writers came as close as he ever got to 'settling down' when he bought an apartment in **Antibes** in 1966. Although he continued his globetrotting habits, it remained his home until 1990. Greene knew the south well, and his move to Antibes was partly motivated by his affair with Yvonne Cloetta, who lived with her husband in nearby **Juan-les-Pins** – she remained his close companion for the rest of his life. For many years, Greene lived in comfortable and uncontroversial privacy in Antibes. He was well respected in France, and in 1969 was made a Chevalier of the Légion d'Honneur. He brought controversy on himself, however, and for a time feared for his life, when, motivated by his outrage at the progress of the proceedings of a bitter divorce between Yvonne's daughter Martine and her husband, a property developer in **Nice**, he began to make accusations about local corruption and organized crime. In his discontent, Greene returned his insignia of the Légion d'Honneur, and in 1982 published his *J'Accuse: The Dark Side of Nice*, accusing the local government of widespread corruption, but focusing on the divorce case. Corruption was certainly there – the Mayor Jacques Médecin was later totally discredited and found guilty of the misuse of public funds – but Greene's personal campaign was not among his greatest moments. As biographer Michael Shelden pertinently comments, he 'was completely defeated on the legal front'. Martine's husband got the book banned in France and won his suit for libel against Greene and his publisher. Despite the attendant disruptive attention, and threats, that this affair brought to Greene's peace and solitude in Antibes, he continued to live there until 1990, when, in seriously declining health, he moved to Corseaux, near Vevey in Switzerland, and near also to the homes of his own daughter and Martine (Yvonne accompanied him). He died in hospital at Vevey on 3 April 1991.

For Greene on France, two short novels are recommended – *Loser Takes All*, 1955, and *The Tenth Man*, 1985. *Loser Takes All* (Extract 7) tells the story of a downtrodden and untrusting English accountant, Bertram, who goes to **Monte Carlo** with his fiancé Cary for his wedding and honeymoon at the expense of the head of his company who promises to join them and take care of everything. When his boss, Dreuther (a character based on Greene's friend the film producer Alexander Korda) fails to appear at the expected time,

money becomes a problem and Bertram resorts to working a system at the Casino. As he becomes increasingly obsessed with the system and increasingly rich, his relationship with Cary begins to break down and he faces some critical choices. The action takes place largely in the **Casino** and the **Hôtel de Paris**. Greene tells us in his Introduction that the story arose out of an enjoyable few weeks he himself spent at those luxurious and expensive locations. Like much of Greene's work, the story illuminates as it entertains, which it does very well – appropriately, *Loser Takes All* is among those works of fiction that Greene chose to describe as 'entertainments'. In his Introduction, he writes, 'So I disappeared to Monte Carlo for a few weeks to live luxuriously in the Hôtel de Paris (chargeable as an expense to income tax), to work long hours at the Casino tables (my losses I considered might be fairly chargeable too), and to write what I hoped would prove an amusing, agreeably sentimental *nouvelle* – something which neither my friends nor my enemies would expect.'

The Tenth Man is a concise and suspenseful story of deception with undertones of the impossibility of escaping personal destiny. The story begins in a prison in occupied France where the Germans are executing one man in every ten. The prisoners draw lots and a rich lawyer, Chavel, sells his 'short straw' to another prisoner who takes it in exchange for all Chavel's wealth and possessions. The rest of the book concerns Chavel's return to his old home, now occupied by the executed prisoner's sister and mother, and his attempts to build a life there with a fake identity, this time imprisoned in his own lies and deceit.

Recommended biographies: Norman Sherry's extensive but very readable *The Life of Graham Greene* has progressed to two volumes at the time of writing (Vol 1, 1904–1939; Vol 2, 1939–55) – the third and final one is awaited (published by Cape, London).

The shorter biography by Michael Shelden (*Graham Greene: The Man Within*, Minerva, London, 1995) covers Greene's whole life and offers a controversial, but thoroughly argued, analysis of his character.

MAUGHAM, W(illiam) Somerset (1874–1965). Maugham was born at the British Embassy in **Paris** and spoke French as his first language until the age of 10. Throughout his peripatetic life he made regular visits to the city. He lived in Paris for several months in 1905, and was one of a company of expatriate writers who frequented Le Chat Blanc, a café-restaurant in **rue d'Odessa**, Montparnasse. His companions at Le Chat Blanc included Arnold Bennett, Clive Bell and the poet and Satanist Aleister Crowley, who was the model for Oliver Haddo in Maugham's *The Magician*, 1908. Maugham returned to France with an ambulance unit in the First World War (before the brief career as a spy which provided him with material for the *Ashenden* stories, published in 1928). In 1926, he purchased the 'Villa Mauresque' on **Cap Ferrat**, finally moving into the house in 1928, when the extensive renovations had been completed. This was to be his home for the rest of his long life, although he continued to travel widely. Maugham died at Cap Ferrat on 16 December 1965, aged 92 – his ashes were flown to England for burial.

Maugham used the south of France as a locale for a number of his stories and novels. Among the former, 'The Facts of Life' (Extract 8) is a simple but beautifully constructed tale of how a naive young tennis player goes to **Monte Carlo** to play in a tournament, makes a killing at the casino and turns the tables on a cocotte who tries to fleece him. The narrator of 'The Facts of Life' is the father of the young man, and the story's charm lies in part in his frustration that his son has profited by completely ignoring his excellent advice not to gamble, lend money, or have anything to do with women.

Another story, 'The Three Fat Women of Antibes', is an amusing account of dieting on the Riviera. Both tales demonstrate Maugham's simple dictum that a short story should have a beginning, a middle and an end.

Among his longer works, *The Razor's Edge*, 1944, is a novel located mainly in France which includes an interesting description of the Riviera during the Great Depression – 'an estate agent told me that on the stretch of road that reaches from Toulon to the Italian border there were forty-eight thousand properties, large and small, to be sold.'

In part because of his homosexuality (he was acutely aware of the fate of Oscar Wilde), Maugham always found the French more congenial than the British, whose arrogance he thought insufferable: 'The British travelled a great deal on the Continent. They crowded the health resorts, Spa, Vichy, Homburg, Aix-les-Bains and Baden-Baden. In winter they went to the Riviera. They built themselves sumptuous villas at Cannes and Monte Carlo. Vast hotels were erected to accommodate them. They had plenty of money and spent it freely. They felt that they were a race apart and no sooner had they landed at Calais than it was borne in upon them that they were now among natives, not of course natives as were the Indians or the Chinese, but – natives.'

Recommended biography: Robert Calder, *Willie: The Life of W. Somerset Maugham*, Heinemann, London, 1989.

PAGNOL, Marcel (1895–1974). Pagnol was born in the Provençal town of **Aubagne** on 28 February 1895, auspiciously, given his subsequent career, in the year that the first cinematic film was shown. He was educated at the University of **Aix-en-Provence**, where he studied English, and he subsequently taught in various *lycées*, eventually obtaining a post at the Lycée Condorcet in **Paris**. Pagnol's early literary work was in the theatre – his best known play is his social satire *Topaze*, 1928, which has since been filmed several times (first and arguably best in 1933 by Louis Gasnier, with Pagnol's screenplay, later twice by Pagnol himself, and then in an unsuccessful English adaptation by Peter Sellers). In the 1930s, with the advent of talking films, Pagnol became keenly aware of the potential of cinema and turned his creative energies towards it. His work was both popular and critically acclaimed – in 1946 he became the first *cinéaste* to be elected to the Académie Française, a testimony to his critical reputation. Pagnol's work focuses on and is influenced by the language, culture and society of his native **Provence** – among his most famous films, some adapted from his plays, are his alternately moving and comic portrayals of life in **Marseille** in the trilogy *Marius*, 1931, *Fanny*, 1932, and *César*, 1936 (the first two written and supervised but not directed by Pagnol); his screen versions of fellow Provençal Jean Giono's *Jofroi*, 1934, *Angèle*, 1934, *Cigalon*, 1935, and *Regain*, 1937; and *La Femme du boulanger*, 1938. His later film work was less successful, but nevertheless continued to provide atmospheric evocations of Provence – as, for example, in his 1954 adaptation of Daudet's *Lettres de mon moulin*.

Pagnol's best work in his later life was in prose, notably in his two-part novel *L'Eau des collines* (see below) and his autobiographical work on his childhood in Provence, published in 1957 as *Souvenirs d'enfance* and comprising *La Gloire de mon père* and *Le Château de ma mère* (*My Father's Glory and My Mother's Castle*, 1991) – films of both books, directed by Yves Robert, were released in 1990.

L'Eau des collines, 1963 (*The Water of the Hills*, 1988) is a story set in rural Provence between the wars, and is richly evocative of the Provençal countryside and climate and offers a penetrating portrayal of a remote village community (Extract 14). The book comprises two novels, *Jean de Florette* and *Manon des sources* (*Manon of the Springs*), and tells an engrossing tale of deception and revenge. The Jean of the first part is an honest but naive town dweller who inherits property in the area and is destroyed by the scheming of the village elder and his nephew who want the land for their own purposes. They block the spring on which Jean's farm depends and effectively, by depriving him of water, the life force, drive him to his death as he strives desperately to keep his farm from falling into ruin. The second part, *Manon des sources*, is the story of his daughter, Manon, and how she finds a way to take revenge on the conspirators and on the whole village which played its role in her father's death through its tacit complicity with the deception. *L'Eau des collines* evolved from Pagnol's 1953 film *Manon des sources*. Perhaps reflecting this, and the author's general cinematic orientation, the novel is constructed in short chapters, like scenes in a film, and is keenly visualized. The story has resonance and depth – not least because of an essentially sympathetic portrayal of all the characters, including the two 'villains', and of a genuinely tragic twist at the end which makes the punishment of the main culprit complete indeed. The two novels were stunningly filmed in 1986 by Claude Berri.

SEMBÈNE OUSMANE (1923–). Born in Senegal, Sembène, despite his expulsion from school at the age of 14, has become one of the major figures in African Francophone literature and, through his work as a film director (eg *Xala*, 1974), a central influence in the evolution of African cinema. He lived in France in the 1950s, where he earned a living doing manual work, eventually becoming a docker in **Marseille**. He was a member of the French Communist Party and active in the dockers' trade union until his return to Senegal in 1960. His novels and short stories combine political commitment with outstanding literary abilities to produce powerful and involving illustrations of his perspectives on African culture and development – most notably in *Les Bouts de bois de Dieu*, 1960 (*God's Bits of Wood*, 1986). Most of his work is set in Africa, but his early novel of exploitation and racism, *Le Docker noir*, 1956 (*Black Docker*, 1987) is set in Marseille and draws heavily on his own experiences there (Extract 6). The hero is a writer who entrusts publication of his novel to a French woman in Paris who subsequently claims it for her own. He kills her in a struggle and is tried and imprisoned. Much of the novel tells the story leading to the killing. There are vivid portrayals of life in the black ghettos of Marseille, labour unrest and exploitation, and the poverty of the dockers. Sembène's dedication of *Black Docker* is a characteristically simple statement of a complex emotion, and a reminder of the background from which this great writer emerged: 'This book is dedicated to my mother,/ although she cannot read./Just knowing that she will run her/hands over it is enough to make me happy.'

SMOLLETT, Tobias (1721–71). The prolific Scottish-born author, editor and translator, and former surgeon, undertook a two-year trip to France and Italy between June 1763 and June 1765. Smollett was in declining health (he was suffering from consumption, and had also recently lost his only child), and the primary purpose of the trip was rest and a better climate. The literary outcome was *Travels Through France and Italy*, 1766. Although initially well received in Britain, the book caused a stir in France and brought its author much general opprobrium two years later with the publication of Sterne's (◊ Nord–Pas-de-Calais) immensely successful *A Sentimental Journey Through France and Italy*, 1768, in which he satirizes Smollett's hostile attitude and refers to him as 'Smelfungus' – 'the learned SMELFUNGUS travelled from Boulogne to Paris – from Paris to Rome – and so on – but he set out with the spleen and

jaundice, and every object he passed by was discoloured or distorted – He wrote an account of them, but 'twas nothing but the account of his miserable feelings.' Certainly, Smollett's caustic travelogue, full of arguments with landlords and many other trials and tribulations, is hardly bathed in the sweetness and light of tolerance and understanding. It is, however, highly entertaining, and by no means entirely negative. Written in epistolary form, it reveals an author who is interested in everything – commerce, lifestyle, fashion, food, taxation, economy – but who approaches it all with British insularity, combative and curmudgeonly throughout. The sections on **Boulogne**; **Paris**; **Lyon**; **Montpellier**; **Nîmes**; and **Villefranche** are especially worth reading, as are his extensive comments on **Nice** (Extract 9), where he was resident for some 18 months – his rudeness about the locals in *Travels* was received there with particular, and understandable, hostility and resentment.

Surprisingly enough, Smollett was no stranger to travel. In 1741 he had been to the West Indies as a navy surgeon's mate (he met his wife in Jamaica). He had also undertaken several trips to the continent before his 1763–65 visit – one of them, a trip to Paris in 1750, provided him with information for his novel *The Adventures of Peregrine Pickle*, 1751. And at the end of his life he lived in Italy (where he completed his masterpiece *The Expedition of Humphry Clinker*, 1771) – he died there and is buried in Leghorn, close to where he had made his final home. Thanks to *Travels*, though, Smollett is unlikely to lose his reputation as the archetypal crusty, suspicious, and complaining British traveller abroad.

Recommended biography: L.M. Knapp, *Tobias Smollett: Doctor of Men and Manners*, 1949.

SÜSKIND, Patrick (1949–). German novelist and playwright Süskind's *Das Parfüm*, 1985 (*Perfume*, 1986) is set in 18th century France with especially evocative scenes in **Paris** (see Paris, Extract 8) and **Grasse** (Extract 3), famous then and now as a major centre of the perfume industry. This black and bizarre story traces the life of Grenouille, the amoral anti-hero, from his extremely lowly beginnings through his apprenticeship to a master-perfumer to his complete manipulation of those around him. Grenouille perceives and manipulates the world through his extraordinary sense of smell. He strives for ultimate power through the perfect perfume which he distills from the essence of beautiful young virgins, whom he murders to capture their special human scents. A strange and memorable book which raises questions about our perceptions of truth and beauty and the nature of evil – evocative, comic and disturbing.

CORSICA

'The Corsican is grave and silent by nature. In the evening, a few figures appear to enjoy the cool air, but the strollers on the *corso* are nearly all foreigners. The islanders stay in front of their doors; each seems to be on the lookout, like a falcon in its nest.'

Prosper Mérimée, *Colomba*

HAUTE-CORSE

Bastia-Poretta airport. On 31 July 1944, the writer and aviator Antoine de Saint-Exupéry (1900–44) took off from here on a reconnaissance flight over the Mediterranean. The memorial stone recalls the fact that he did not return – shot down, in all probability, by an enemy plane.

Corte. James Boswell ◊ visited the city in 1765, when it was the capital of Corsica. One of the highlights of his *Journal of a Tour to Corsica*, 1768, is the account of his meetings in the castle (the 'Citadelle') with the hangman and three convicted criminals (Extract 3).

Île Rousse. A Corsican woman named Madame Dumont ran a cheap hotel in Paris in the 1940s and 1950s. The Hôtel Verneuil became for a time a centre for struggling American writers, among them James Baldwin (◊ Paris), whom she nursed through an illness brought on by a preference for cigarettes and alcohol over food. Later, in October 1956 shortly after a suicide attempt, Baldwin lived for some six months at Île Rousse, the home town of Madame Dumont, staying at the house of a friend.

CORSE-DU-SUD

Ajaccio. 'There is in Ajaccio a house which men still to be born will come in pilgrimage to see . . .'. The **Maison Bonaparte** (place Letizia), where Napoleon was born, was visited in 1840 by Gustave Flaubert (◊ Normandy) – his journal of his trip to Corsica was published in *Par les champs et par les grèves*, 1910.

Edward Lear ◊ visited the city in April 1868 and recorded his perceptions in *The Journal of a Landscape Painter in Corsica*, 1870 (Extract 1). See also *Granite Island*, 1971, for Dorothy Carrington's ◊ evocative description of her impressions as she approached the port on her first visit to Corsica in 1948 (Extract 6).

The Anglican Church on **avenue Général Leclerc**, now a dancing school, was built in the 1860s largely through the lobbying of Thomasina Campbell. Campbell was a Scottish woman who travelled throughout Corsica, despite the dangers of bandits and disease, and wrote of her experiences in

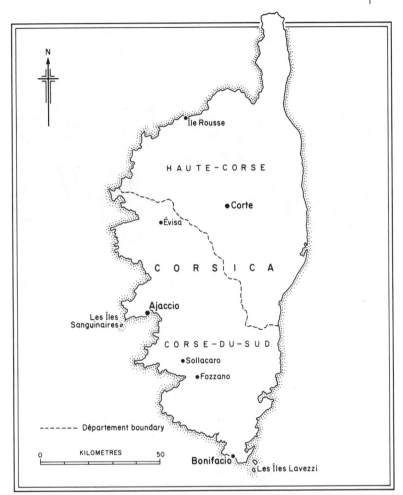

Southward Ho!, 1868. Nearby, there is a street named in her honour – **rue Miss Campbell**.

Bonifacio. Lear's artistic eye was much attracted by this picturesque town at the southern extremity of Corsica, with its dramatic setting, perched on cliffs that drop sheer down to the sea – see Extract 2.

Some say that Homer is describing Bonifacio in the *Odyssey* when he has Odysseus recount the adventure of the Greeks at the citadel of Lamos (Book X): 'There as we entered the glorious harbor, which a sky-towering / cliff encloses on either side, with no break anywhere, / and two projecting promontories facing each other / run out toward the mouth, and there is a narrow entrance . . .' (from the translation by Richmond Lattimore).

Évisa. This attractively sited village, high on a rocky spur, is now a popular destination for sea-bathing, skiing, and, especially, mountain-walking. Évisa as it was in the 19th century is described by Maupassant (◊ Normandy) in *Une Vie*, 1883 (*A Woman's Life*,

'Bonifacio' by Edward Lear

1965) – Extract 4. Although the action takes place mainly in Normandy, Corsica is an important and symbolic setting in the novel. The Corsican scenes show Maupassant at the height of his descriptive powers and provide memorably vivid evocations of the landscape and people.

Fozzano. This village was the model for the setting of Prosper Mérimée's ◊ novella *Colomba*, 1840 (*Carmen/ Colomba*, 1965). Although he names Colomba's home as Pietranera, a suburb of Bastia, diplomatically distancing his fiction from the reality which inspired it, it was in Fozzano that, in 1839, Mérimée met Madame Colomba Bartoli (*née* Carabelli) and it is Fozzano that you will recognize in his descriptions of Colomba's village (Extract 5). The real Colomba had been actively involved in a long-standing and bloody vendetta between the Carabellis and the Durazzos. She made a deep impression on Mérimée, who described her as 'a heroine who excels in the manufacture of cartridges and who is very skilled in despatching them to people who have the misfortune to displease her.' The feuding families lived in the 17th century houses-cum-fortresses you can still see in Fozzano. The graves of

Madame Bartoli and her son, who was killed in the vendetta, are in the village **chapel**. When Mérimée met Colomba she was 65 years old – her daughter Catherine, however, was dark and solemnly beautiful, and always wore black in mourning for her murdered brother (a habit followed by Colomba in the story) – the physical and psychological aspects of Mérimée's memorable heroine presumably owe something to both mother and daughter.

Les Îles Sanguinaires. Alphonse Daudet (◊ Provence) stayed in the Sanguinaires lighthouse in 1863, and describes the experience in *Lettres de mon moulin*, 1869 (*Letters from My Windmill*, 1978).

Les Îles Lavezzi. Also in *Letters from My Windmill* is a story based on the wreck of *La Sémillante*, a frigate bound for the Crimea which struck these rocks and sank in February 1855 – over 700 soldiers and sailors were drowned.

Sollacaro. Boswell ◊ came to this village in 1765 to meet the Corsican leader, Pasquale Paoli, as he records in his *Journal of a Tour to Corsica*. Boswell stayed here a week and the meeting marked the beginning of a lasting friendship between the two men. As he arrived, however, even the intrepid Boswell felt apprehensive – 'When I at last came in sight of Sollacaro, where Paoli was, I could not help being under considerable anxiety. My ideas of him had been greatly heightened by the conversations I had held with all sorts of people in the island, they having represented him to me as something above humanity. I had the strongest desire to see so exalted a character; but I feared I should be unable to give a proper account why I had presumed to trouble him with a visit, and that I should sink to nothing before him. I almost wished yet to go back without seeing him. These workings of sensibility employed my mind till I rode through the village, and came up to the house where he was lodged.' A plaque (near the post office) commemorates the event, describing Boswell as a 'British writer and friend of Corsica'.

Alexandre Dumas (◊ Provence) stayed briefly in Sollacaro in 1841, and subsequently wrote his romantic adventure Les Frères Corses, 1845 (The Corsican Brothers, 1983), which unfortunately is far from his best work.

BOOKLIST

For most of the extracted works, the original publisher in English can be found in 'Acknowledgments and Citations' at the end of the volume, as can the exact location of the extracts and the editions from which they are taken. The date in square brackets is that of the original publication of the work in its original language. For additional titles by the authors highlighted in this chapter and for recommended biographies, see 'Lives and Works'.

Boswell, James, The Journal of a Tour to Corsica [1768], In Print Publishing, Brighton, 1996. **Extract 3.**

Boswell, James, The Journals of James Boswell 1762–1795, selected and introduced by John Wain, Mandarin, London, 1992. (Includes a short extract from the Tour to Corsica and correspondence and journal entries on meetings with Rousseau and Voltaire.)

Campbell, Thomasina, Southward Ho!, Hatchard, London, 1868.

Carrington, Dorothy, The Dream-Hunters of Corsica [1995], Phoenix, London, 1996. **Extract 6.**

Carrington, Dorothy, Granite Island: A Portrait of Corsica [1971], Penguin, London and New York, 1984.

Daudet, Alphonse, Letters from My Windmill [1869], Frederick Davies, trans, Penguin, London and New York, 1978.

Dumas, Alexandre, The Corsican Brothers [1845], Buccaneer Books, Cutchogue, NY, 1983.

Homer, The Odyssey of Homer, Richmond Lattimore, trans, Harper and Row, New York, 1968.

Lear, Edward, The Journal of a Landscape Painter in Corsica [1870], in Edward Lear's Journals: A Selection, Herbert van Thal, ed, Arthur Barker, London, 1952. **Extracts 1 and 2.**

Maupassant, Guy de, A Woman's Life [1883], H.N.P. Sloman, trans, Penguin, London and New York, 1965. **Extract 4.**

Mérimée, Prosper, Carmen [1845] and Colomba [1840], Edward Marielle, trans, Penguin, London, 1965. **Extract 5.**

Mérimée, Prosper, Carmen and Other Stories, N. Jotcham, trans, Oxford University Press, Oxford, 1994. (Includes Mateo Falcone.)

Extracts

(1) Ajaccio

Edward Lear,
Journal of a Landscape Painter in Corsica

Newly arrived in Corsica in April 1868, Lear wanders around the town, and casts his painter's eye over its streets and its people. This extract is from his journal entry of 9 April 1868.

The day becomes finer; crossing the spacious place by the equestrian statue of the first Emperor Napoleon, I go down to the sea by a broad carriage-road, which, at its outset, is sheltered by a pleasant avenue of plane-trees, and afterwards leads on to the Capella de'Greci, and to the public cemetery which I had remarked in steaming up the gulf. I wander on – as is my way in coming to new places – in order that by seeing a little on all sides, the best sites for making characteristic drawings may be ascertained; along this shore there are so many beautiful bits, but chiefly about the small mortuary chapels, where cypress-trees and various shrubs flourish, and in the frequent combination of granite rocks with the sea and opposite gulf shore. Very few people seem about, though the city is so close by; the cut of the peasant-women's dress is much like that of the Ionians, the skirt full, with many small plaits or folds, the bodice and short jacket close-fitting – a graceful costume, but in nearly all cases of a dark hue, brown or purple, more usually black. The elder women – many of whose faces recall the portraits of Madame Mère – mostly wear a black handkerchief tied closely over the head; but the younger, who are not so frequently pretty as they are particularly graceful, wear two handkerchiefs, the one tied round the forehead and fastened behind the head (and of this kerchief only a portion of the front is seen), the other over the top of the head, fastened below the chin and falling on the back of the neck in a point like the head-dress represented in old Indian pictures. As for the men, they have a look as of porters or tradesmen out of work, carrying their hands in their pockets with what seems an idle and disconsolate air, and are in no wise picturesque or remarkable.

(2) BONIFACIO

Edward Lear,
Journal of a Landscape Painter in Corsica

Lear is much taken with the small fortified town of Bonifacio, with its medieval lanes, old buildings, and picturesque location. It provides him with plentiful opportunities for his artistic talents and on 22 April 1868 he finds himself a vantage point overlooking the city.

From this point there is a perfect view of this curious and interesting old Corsican city, and I know of no scene of the kind more strikingly beautiful. The exceedingly deep colour of the quiet narrow channel contrasts wondrously with the pale hues of the rocks and buildings, and the strange lonely character of the fort, and of the projecting cliffs rising perpendicularly from the water's edge, and striped with long ledges of singular form, is most impressive. A solitary cormorant flitting by is the only sign of life, and a complete silence adds to the charm of this wild spot, so full of memories of the sufferings of the Bonifacio people. I would gladly linger some days to explore more fully the position of this historic mediæval city, so unique in appearance and site. When the wind lashes this inland channel, how grandly the foaming waves must beat against the sides and hollows of these cliffs, wrinkled and worn by long buffeting!

While I am drawing, the stillness is broken by two boats, which, from the distant harbour come down the channel, those who are in them singing 'O pescator dell' onde'; at first the sound is feeble, but gradually swells into a loud chorus over the calm water and among the great caverns of the echoing cliffs. The boats steer for the cove near which I am sitting, and twenty individuals land on a ledge of rock just below me, where they place a barrel of wine and provisions, and prepare to pass the day. These are conscripts, chosen as soldiers only yesterday, and this their farewell fête before leaving their native Bonifacio, a place so peculiar in itself, and so remote from the outer world, that the attachment its inhabitants are said to bear towards it is easily understood.

(3) CORTE

James Boswell, *Journal of a Tour to Corsica*

In October 1765, before setting off to meet the Corsican leader, Pasquale Paoli, in Sollacaro, Boswell explores Corte, then the capital. Here, he meets some examples of the criminal class and learns how Corsica found its hangman.

I went up to the castle of Corte. The Commandant very civilly shewed me every part of it. As I wished to see all things in Corsica, I desired to see even the unhappy criminals. There were then three in the Castle; a man for the murder of his wife; a married lady who had hired one of her servants to strangle a woman of whom she was jealous; and the servant who had actually perpetrated this barbarous action. They were brought out from their cells, that I might talk with them. The murderer of his wife had a stupid hardened appearance, and told me he did it at the instigation of the devil. The servant was a poor despicable wretch. He had at first accused his mistress, but was afterwards prevailed with to deny his accusation, upon which he was put to the torture, by having lighted matches held between his fingers. This made him return to what he had formerly said, so as to be a strong evidence against his mistress. His hands were so miserably scorched, that he was a piteous object. I asked him why he had committed such a crime, he said, 'Perche era senza spirito. Because I was without understanding.' The lady seemed of a bold and resolute spirit. She spoke to me with great firmness, and denied her guilt, saying with a contemptuous smile, as she pointed to her servant, 'They can force that creature to say what they please.'

The hangman of Corsica was a great curiosity. Being held in the utmost detestation, he durst not live like another inhabitant of the island. He was obliged to take refuge in the castle, and there he was kept in a little corner turret, where he had just room for a miserable bed, and a little bit of fire to dress such victuals for himself as were sufficient to keep him alive; for nobody would have intercourse with him, but all turned their backs upon him. I went up and looked at him. And a more dirty, rueful spectacle I never beheld. He seemed sensible of his situation, and held down his head like an abhorred outcast.

It was a long time before they could get a hangman in Corsica, so that the punishment of the gallows was hardly known, all their criminals being shot. At last this creature whom I saw, who is a Sicilian, came with a message to Paoli. The General, who has a wonderful talent for physiognomy, on seeing the man said immediately to some of the people about him, 'Ecco il boia. Behold our hangman.' He gave orders to ask the man if he would accept of the office, and his answer was, 'My grandfather was a hangman, my father was a hangman. I have been a hangman myself, and am willing to continue so.' He was therefore immediately put into office, and the ignominious death dispensed by his hands hath had more effect than twenty executions by firearms.

It is remarkable that no Corsican would upon any account consent to be a hangman. Not the greatest criminals, who might have had their lives upon that condition. Even the wretch, who for a paltry hire, had strangled a woman, would rather submit to death, than do the same action, as the executioner of the law.

(4) Évisa

Guy de Maupassant, *A Woman's Life*

On their honeymoon in Corsica, a vivid and exotic contrast to their home region of Normandy, Jeanne and Julien visit Paoli Palabretti, a relative of their Corsican guide. He lives in the village of Évisa, high in the Val d'Ota.

Monsieur Palabretti hastened to obey and took them round the village, walking between the young couple. He dragged his feet and his words, coughing a good deal and repeating after every paroxysm: 'It's the cold air of the Val that gets me in the chest.'

He led them along a narrow path under the towering chestnuts and suddenly stopped, saying in his drawling voice: 'It was just here that my cousin, Jean Rinaldi, was murdered by Mathieu Lori. Look, I was there close to Jean, when Mathieu appeared ten yards away. "Jean," he shouted, "don't go to Albertacci, don't go there or I'll kill you; I swear I will." I seized Jean's arm: "Don't go there, Jean; he means what he says." It was all over a girl they were both after, Paulina Sinacoupi. But Jean shouted: "I'm going, Mathieu, and you won't stop me." Then Mathieu levelled his gun and before I could aim mine he fired. Jean leapt with both feet in the air like a child with a skipping-rope; yes, Monsieur, and he fell right on top of me, knocking my gun out of my hands, so that it rolled away as far as that tall chestnut over there. Jean had his mouth wide open but he didn't say a word; he was dead.'

The young pair listened in amazement to this calm eye-witness account of the crime and Jeanne asked: 'And what about the murderer?'

After a long fit of coughing Paoli Palabretti replied: 'Oh, he escaped to the mountains, but my brother got him the year after. You know my brother, of course, Philippi Palabretti, the bandit.'

Jeanne shivered: 'Your brother, a bandit?'

A flash of pride showed in the placid Corsican's glance: 'Yes, Madame; my brother had quite a reputation; he had shot six gendarmes. He died with Nicolas Morali, when they were cornered at Niolo, after six days' fighting, when they were nearly dead of starvation.'

And he added in a tone of resignation: 'It's the custom of the country,' in the tone in which he said: 'It's the cold air of the Val that gets me in the chest.'

(5) FOZZANO

Prosper Mérimée, *Colomba*

Although Mérimée nominally sets Colomba's home in Pietranera, a suburb of Bastia, the setting he describes is based on the village of Fozzano, about 90 km south of Ajaccio. In 1839 in Fozzano Mérimée met the women who inspired his tale of vengeance, with its beautiful and dangerous heroine. Here, he describes a village whose very development has been founded on hatred.

The village of Pietranera is laid out in a very haphazard fashion, like all the villages in Corsica; for to see a real street one has to go to Cargese, which was built by Monsieur de Marboeuf. The houses in Pietranera, scattered about at random without the slightest attempt at alignment, occupy the top of a small plateau, or rather a mountain ledge. Towards the middle of the village there stands a tall green oak, and near it there is a granite trough into which water is brought from a nearby spring through a wooden pipe. This monument of public utility was paid for jointly by the Della Rebbias and the Barricinis; but anybody who took this as an indication of a former period of friendship between the two families would be sorely mistaken. On the contrary, it is a product of their jealousy. At some time in the past, Colonel Della Rebbia sent the municipal council of his commune a small sum of money towards the erection of a fountain, and the layer Barricini hastened to make a similar donation: it is to this rivalry in generosity that Pietranera owes its water. Around the green oak and the fountain there is an open space known as the square, where idlers forgather in the evening. Sometimes they play cards there, and once a year, at carnival time, there is dancing. At opposite sides of the square there stand two buildings, higher than they are wide, made of granite and shale. These are the rival 'towers' of the Della Rebbias and the Barricinis. Their architecture is uniform, their height identical, and it can be seen that the rivalry between the two families has always continued without fortune deciding between them.

(6) THE MAQUIS

Dorothy Carrington, *Granite Island*

Carrington's fascinating physical, political, historical, and cultural exploration of Corsica begins with her first sight and scent of the island in 1948.

And so it happened that we found ourselves in early summer on a ship bound for Ajaccio, the Corsican capital. In the meantime I had read such books on Corsica as I could lay hands on: Mérimée's *Colomba*, a dramatic tale of blood vengeance; Boswell's exhilarating account of his visit to Pasquale Paoli, the Corsican leader who had freed his country from Genoese rule and given it a liberal constitution much in advance of his time. I had also read lives of

Napoleon that mentioned his obscure, frustrated youth in Ajaccio, and some travellers' reminiscences of rough journeys, fine landscapes, a proud, fierce hospitable people and bandits who were looked upon as heroes. We had arranged to meet Jean at the home of his uncle and aunt and see the statues and stay there awhile, after which my husband and Jean would return to England while I toured the rest of the island.

Details came into focus as we drew towards land: ridges, crests, chasms, promontories, the shadows of the mountains on the water; but few works of man, few houses or fields or roads. Only a lighthouse and an ancient watch-tower appeared on the Iles Sanguinaires, a chain of barren pyramidical islands flung out from the bay of Ajaccio like a bastion. It was then that we caught the scent of the maquis, borne out on a warm land breeze. This is the scent of all Corsica; bitter-sweet, akin to incense, heady, almost, as an anaesthetic after rain. The maquis is a dense jungle of aromatic evergreen plants and shrubs: arbutus, myrtle, cistus and lentisk, rosemary and lavender and thyme. It covers the land except where fields are cultivated and forests grow, and at present the forests are dwindling and the cultivated fields are few so that the maquis spreads over more than half the land. It may be useless except as a hideout for guerrillas and bandits, but it is a perpetual and potent enchantment; one sleeps and wakes with its fragrance which is like no other. Napoleon recalled it with nostalgia in St Helena when, humbled at last, he became like any Corsican ending his life in exile, his memories not of his palaces and triumphs but of the maquis-scent of childhood.

Lives and works of extracted writers

BOSWELL, James (1740–95). Boswell visited Corsica in 1765. Since 1763 he had been travelling in Europe on his 'Grand Tour' – among the highlights of which had been his meetings with Voltaire in France and Rousseau in Switzerland. It was Rousseau who had fired his imagination about Corsica and the Corsican cause and confirmed him in his intention to visit the country. In his *Du contrat social*, 1762 (*The Social Contract*, 1993), Rousseau had praised the Corsican government as progressive and enlightened compared to the decadent and corrupt administrations of the rest of Europe, and his conversation with Boswell on the subject had left the young man anxious to see for himself –

'I wished for something more than just the common course of what is called the tour of Europe; and Corsica occurred to me as a place which no body else had seen, and where I should find what was to be seen no where else, a people actually fighting for liberty.' At the time, Corsica was in revolt against the tyranny of the Genoese Republic, supported by France. The Corsican leader was Pasquale Paoli (1725–1807), a revolutionary idol for young intellectuals of the period.

Boswell's trip to Corsica lasted some 50 days. In that short time, driven by his journalistic instinct, he accumulated a wealth of impressions of the island, its people, its history, and its

James Boswell, dressed as a Corsican chief

leader. The tour was of considerable personal significance for him: he established a lifelong friendship with Paoli and developed a lasting commitment to the Corsican struggle for independence. He said in later years, 'I had got upon a rock in Corsica and jumped into the middle of life.'

When he returned to London, Boswell set about campaigning for the Corsican cause, acquired the nickname 'Mr Corsica Boswell', and became, at least to his friend Samuel Johnson's taste, a little wearing on the subject. Johnson wrote to him in April 1768, '. . . I wish you would empty your head of Corsica, which I think has filled it rather too long.' Boswell, however, was not to be shaken: 'But how can you bid me "empty my head of Corsica"? My noble-minded friend, do you not feel for an oppressed nation bravely struggling to be free? Consider fairly what is the case. The Corsicans never received any kindness from the Genoese. They

never agreed to be subject to them. They owe them nothing; and when reduced to an abject state of slavery, by force, shall they not rise in the great cause of liberty, and break the galling yoke? And shall not every liberal soul warm for them? Empty my head of Corsica! Empty it of honour, empty it of humanity, empty it of friendship, empty it of piety. No! while I live, Corsica and the cause of the brave islanders shall ever employ much of my attention . . .'.

Boswell's *An Account of Corsica* was published in February 1768. It comprised essentially two parts: a historical narrative on the country and *The Journal of a Tour to Corsica and Memoirs of Pascal Paoli*, the latter much more vivid, lively and original than the history which preceded it. 'Your History,' wrote Johnson to Boswell in September 1769, 'is like other histories, but your Journal is in a very high degree curious and delightful.' *The Journal of a Tour to Corsica* (Extract 3) is an entertaining, energetically written account of Boswell's impressions and experiences and of his meetings and conversations with Paoli.

Boswell followed events in Corsica with interest for the rest of his life and, as late as 1793, he made an unsuccessful bid for an official post when it became clear that Britain would annex the island. Corsica was annexed in 1794 by Britain at the behest of Paoli who had returned and was once again asserting its independence. However, France forced the British to give it up at the end of 1796. By then, Boswell was dead. The Corsican cause had remained for him an unrealized ideal, once a source of energizing optimism, later of disillusionment and disappointment.

Recommended biography: Iain Finlayson, *The Moth and the Candle: A Life of James Boswell*, Constable, London, 1990.

CARRINGTON, Dorothy. 'This book is based on the observations of a visit to

Corsica in 1948, interwoven with experiences and researches spaced through the next twenty years,' explains Carrington in her introductory note to the latest edition of *Granite Island: A Portrait of Corsica* (Extract 6), which first appeared in 1971. *Granite Island* is in fact an eloquent, scholarly, and engrossing examination of all aspects of Corsica and its people – its geography, its political and social history, and its culture and traditions, religious and secular. Combining personal commitment with rigorous research, and expressing the fruits of both with considerable literary ability, Carrington has produced a first-class 'travel book' which is also an essential source of reference for those seeking to understand Corsican culture and society.

At the end of *Granite Island*, she writes, '. . . for I already knew, by one of those decisions taken below consciousness, so as to seem like a judgment passed, an order received, that Corsica would be my lot.' Corsica indeed became her home and she has lived there for some 40 years, for long a recognized authority on the island. In 1986, she was made a Chevalier des Arts et des Lettres. In 1991, the University of Corsica awarded her a *doctorat honoris causa*.

Carrington's recent publications have included two other books relating to Corsica: *Napoleon and His Parents on the Threshold of History*, 1987, and *The Dream-Hunters of Corsica*, 1995, about the *mazzeri* – people who, according to an ancient Corsican belief, are both the harbingers and perpetrators, in a paranormal sense, of death.

LEAR, Edward (1812–88). Although still best known for his nonsense verse and limericks, the eccentric Victorian was also an inveterate traveller and an artist, specializing in pen and watercolour representations of landscape and wildlife. He published several entertaining travel books, illustrated with his own sketches. In 1868, he was living in **Cannes**, where he made the acquaintance of Prosper Mérimée ◊. Partly inspired by Mérimée's *Colomba*, he decided to undertake a tour of Corsica which, with its dramatic landscape, would offer many subjects for his canvas. He set off in April and returned in June – during his two-month tour of the island he made some 300 drawings. The literary fruit of the journey was *The Journal of a Landscape Painter in Corsica*, 1870 (Extracts 1 and 2), which comprises, in the form of daily journal entries, Lear's account of his experiences and impressions, presented with humour and much supporting annotation. His prose is fluent and easily readable and his perceptions are those of an artist sensitive to light and colour and of a traveller with a keen intellectual and emotional response to the local atmosphere and daily life of the many places he visits. The Corsican journal is currently, unfortunately, hard to find, but is well worth a trawl through the second-hand shops or library catalogues.

MAUPASSANT, Guy de. See under Normandy.

MÉRIMÉE, Prosper (1803–70). Mérimée was born and brought up in **Paris**. He studied law but never practised, turning instead to writing. His literary career began with two hoaxes – *Le Théâtre de Clara Gazul*, 1825, a collection of plays allegedly translated from the work of a Spanish actress (represented by Mérimée in a mantilla on the frontispiece of the first edition) and *La Guzla*, 1827, a volume of what were claimed to be Illyrian national songs. There followed further plays and a historical novel, *Chronique du règne du Charles IX*, 1829 (*A Chronicle of the Reign of Charles IX*, 1890), all published anonymously. However, it is for the short stories and novellas which he published over some 20 years (1829–50), mainly in literary journals, that Mérimée is now remembered. Despite his substantial output, literature was in reality a secondary occupation – in

1834 he was appointed Inspector General of Historic Monuments and in that capacity, working with Viollet-le-Duc, he travelled tirelessly throughout France and saved many churches and other monuments that are now cherished and admired (among them Sainte-Madeleine at Vézelay, the Abbaye de Thoronet, and Carcassonne). As a result of his professional explorations, he produced several volumes of travel literature, including one on Corsica – *Voyage en Corse*, 1840. He also published historical studies, and essays on and translations from Russian literature. Mérimée was not only a literary and cultural celebrity – under the Second Empire, he was a prominent figure at court and a member of the Sénat, through his close friendship with the Empress Eugénie whom he had known since she was a child. The last years of his life were marred by ill health. He died in **Cannes** in September 1870, where he is buried. Shortly after his death his library and belongings in his Parisian home were destroyed by fire – presumably the Commune resented his association with Napoleon III and Eugénie.

Mérimée's stories are notable for their economy of style, strong plotting, and for the objective and often ironic stance of the narrator which keeps sentimentality and melodrama out of these tales of passion and violence. By far his most famous publications are the two novellas – available in one volume in English translation – *Carmen*, 1845, which needs no further introduction, and *Colomba*, 1840. *Colomba*, set in Corsica, tells the story of a vendetta and the irresistible force of the ancient tradition of vengeance, represented by the formidable heroine Colomba. The book is rich in local colour and incidental information on Corsican culture and tradition. It is also a good story, expertly told, with a neat juxtaposition of the polite sophistication of the British tourists Colonel Nevil and his daughter with the customs of the Corsicans which emanate from fundamental passions and tensions. The book was inspired by Mérimée's meeting in **Fozzano** with a Madame Colomba Bartoli and her daughter during a visit to Corsica in 1839. Madame Bartoli had been involved in a vendetta for some 50 years and had lost her son in the process (see introduction).

Also set in Corsica is *Mateo Falcone*, published in the collection *Mosaïque*, 1833, and concerning a betrayal of family honour and its tragic consequences.

Languedoc–Roussillon; Midi–Pyrénées; Aquitaine; Poitou–Charentes

'Beyond a young womanhood with only a brief period of sexuality, beyond a marriage in which her husband understood her little, may have feared her, and surely abandoned her, Bertrande dreamed of a husband and lover who would come back, and be different. Then in the summer of 1556, a man presented himself to her as the long-lost Martin Guerre.'
Natalie Zemon Davis, *The Return of Martin Guerre*

LANGUEDOC–ROUSSILLON: GARD

Alès. It was here, in 1878, that Robert Louis Stevenson ◊ completed his challenging 12-day walking tour of the Cévennes – the range of low mountains which make up the south-eastern section of the Massif Central between the valleys of the Ardèche and the Hérault, and fall steeply down to Rhône basin. Stevenson, who had set out from **Le Monastier** in the Auvergne, with only his donkey Modestine for company, recorded his impressions and experiences in *Travels with a Donkey*, 1879 (Extract 4). With their changing landscape of forest and moorland, and valleys and gorges, the Cévennes are still much as they were in Stevenson's day. They remain remote and wild, and one of France's poorest areas. For romantics who want to follow in his footsteps through the rugged and dramatically varied mountain terrain, his route is well signposted (between **Le Puy** and **Alès**) and there are guest-houses and hotels rather better equipped to welcome weary travellers than the inns at which Stevenson sought food and shelter. The tourist information pack for Languedoc–Roussillon has details of packages and companies which hire out donkeys for the trek.

Nîmes. Alphonse Daudet (◊ Provence) was born at **20 Boulevard Gambetta**. At the opening of his semi-autobiographical novel *Le Petit Chose*, 1868, he describes Nîmes as 'a town in Languedoc where, as in every town in the Midi, you will find plenty of sun, a fair amount of dust, a Carmelite convent, and two or three Roman remains.'

Sommières. Lawrence Durrell (◊ Provence) lived in this secluded and picturesque village from 1957 until his

death in 1990. In his *Caesar's Vast Ghost: Aspects of Provence*, 1990, he attempts, through a combination of travel writing, memoir and reflection, to convey something of the spirit of the region that was his home for 33 years – 'to capture the poetic quiddity of this extraordinary cradle of romantic dissent without sentimentalizing it – for its romantic heart shelters a gorgeous brutality and extremism!' The book also includes poems and photographs (including several taken in and around Sommières).

Uzès. The name of Racine is in evidence (**Promenade Racine, Pavillon Racine**) because the playwright came to the town in 1661 (when he was 22) and stayed for about a year with his uncle, who was a canon here. The intention was that Racine would enter the priesthood, but nothing came of it and he left for a literary career in Paris. Another rather tenuous literary connection is highlighted in the **Musée Municipal** where you will find memorabilia of the Gide family – André Gide's father came from Uzès.

LANGUEDOC–ROUSSILLON: HÉRAULT

Montpellier. Rabelais (◊ Centre) studied medicine at the university's famous medical school – at the time one of the few European institutions allowed to practise anatomical dissection, then a new procedure. He enrolled in 1530, graduated quickly (which suggests he had studied previously in Paris), and by 1531 he was lecturing on Hippocrates and Galen. He returned to the university in the late 1530s to lecture again and to obtain his doctorate in medicine.

A young French painter named François-Xavier Fabre was in Florence at the time of the French Revolution and became a close friend there of the poet Vittorio Alfieri (1749–1803) and his mistress the Countess of Albany (formerly the wife of Bonnie Prince Charlie). Alfieri bequeathed his possessions, including his valuable library and art collection, to the Countess. She subsequently became Fabre's mistress and, on her death in 1824, he inherited both her and Alfieri's collections. These he donated in 1825 to his home town of Montpellier, and so the **Musée Fabre** was established. Some of the original paintings donated by Fabre (including a portrait of Alfieri) may still be seen in the museum, on **boulevard Bonne Nouvelle** – now one of the major museums of art outside Paris. The combined libraries of the Countess and Alfieri are housed in the adjacent **Gutenburg Médiathèque**, or, to use its former and more appealing name, the Hôtel Massilian – built in 1775 on the site of a mansion in which Molière's touring troupe gave performances in 1654 and 1655.

André Gide (◊ Normandy), who had briefly attended school in Montpellier in his childhood, came here in 1890 to meet Paul Valéry (◊ Île de France), who was then a student at the university, via a letter of introduction from their mutual friend, Pierre Louÿs (1870–1925). The oldest botanical garden in France, the **Jardin des Plantes**, was a favoured meeting place for them. In the Jardin, there is a memorial plaque to the stepdaughter of the English poet Edward Young (1683–1765)

– 'Placandis Narcissae Manibus' reads the plaque ('For the peace of the shade of Narcissa'). Narcissa is the character from Young's long poem *Night Thoughts on Life, Death and Immortality*, 1742–45, thought to represent his stepdaughter, whom he brought to the warmer climate of southern France in the hope that she would recover from her consumption – but she died here instead.

See Extract 6 for Stendhal's impressions of Montpellier, which he visited in 1838.

Pézenas. Molière came here with his company several times in the 1650s, and the **Musée de Vulliod-St-Germain** includes among its exhibits memorabilia of the dramatist and his connections with Pézenas. He is said to have performed in 1654 in the inner courtyard of the **Hôtel Alfonce**, 36 rue Conti.

Sète. Paul Valéry (◊ Île de France) was born in Sète in 1871. He is buried in the **Cimetière Marin**, which was the inspiration for his famous poem 'La Cimetière marin', 1920 ('The Graveyard by the Sea', in *Poems* – see Booklist), an elegiac meditation inspired by Valéry's recollection of this tranquil place of death in the presence of the life-affirming warmth of the sun, renewability of the sea and brilliant clarity of the sky. The nearby **Musée Paul Valéry** includes exhibits relating to his life and work as well as on the history of Sète, and also a collection of modern paintings.

LANGUEDOC–ROUSSILLON: AUDE

Carcassonne. See Extract 3 for Henry James's (◊ Paris) impression of this ancient fortified town. James was there in 1882, when much of the extensive restoration work had recently been completed (it began under the direction of Viollet-le-Duc in 1855 and continued through to the end of the century according to his plans).

LANGUEDOC–ROUSSILLON: PYRÉNÉES-ORIENTALES

Vernet. In the 1850s the spa of Vernet-les-Bains became a popular stopping place for English tourists in the Pyrénées. Anthony Trollope (◊ Auvergne) stayed here in 1859, and used it as a setting for his tragic short story 'La Mère Bauche', included in *Tales of All Countries*, 1861.

Arthur Koestler ◊ spent some time in a huge internment camp in Vernet at the outbreak of the Second World War. He recounts the experience in detail in *Scum of the Earth*, 1941 (Extract 7).

MIDI–PYRÉNÉES: ARIÈGE

Artigat. This village in the region around **Le Mas-d'Azil** was the home of Martin Guerre and the setting for the bizarre events which led to the famous 16th century trial of Arnaud de Tilh. Guerre, the son of a Gascon landowner, mysteriously disappeared in 1548 and was absent for 12 years. Someone who said he was Guerre returned to Artigat in 1556. He was accepted and welcomed by 'his' household and family. However, the family members, and the village community, became increasingly divided over whether this was indeed Martin Guerre or an opportunistic impostor. Guerre's wife, Bertrande, stood by him for a long time, but one of her sons, Pierre, became firmly convinced that he was lying, and eventually the evidence of his deceit became so strong that Bertrande rejected him and he was arrested. His guilt was proved beyond any doubt when Martin Guerre himself finally and dramatically reappeared during the trial in Toulouse. Arnaud de Tilh, who for four years had taken on another man's persona and acted as a good husband and an upstanding member of the community, was revealed as a con man *par*

excellence and condemned to death. The primary source for the story is the detailed report of the trial by the recorder – a Judge of the Court of Toulouse, Maître Jean de Coras. His account and commentary were published in Paris in 1565. This haunting and disturbing tale is the subject of Janet Lewis's ◊ novel *The Wife of Martin Guerre*, 1941 (Extract 1), which, as her title suggests, concentrates on the life of Guerre's wife and her psychological struggles as she comes to terms with the truth (in the novel Bertrande slowly becomes convinced that the man claiming to be her husband is an impostor and eventually gathers enough evidence against him for his deception to be revealed). The case has been given much attention in France with its inherent debate on the nature of identity and love. Montaigne among others has commented on it. For a fascinating and scholarly examination of the story in its historical context, see Natalie Zemon Davis, *The Return of Martin Guerre*, 1983. Davis also acted as consultant during the making of the 1982 film by Daniel Vigne *Le Retour de Martin Guerre* starring Gérard Depardieu and Nathalie Baye, which was shot in the Ariège.

MIDI–PYRÉNÉES: HAUTES-PYRÉNÉES

Lourdes. Zola's novel *Lourdes*, 1894 (*Lourdes*, 1993) remains the most impressive representation in literature of the crowds and spiritual frenzy at this religious shrine and the exploitative commercialism which surrounds it.

Tarbes. Théophile Gautier (1811–1872) was born at **23 rue de Brauhauban**. The innovative poet Jules Laforgue (1860–87), whose work had a significant influence on T.S. Eliot, was educated at the *lycée* here before his family moved to Paris in 1876. Tarbes is also the birthplace of novelist Christine de Rivoyre ◊.

AQUITAINE: PYRÉNÉES-ATLANTIQUES

Bayonne. Hemingway's (◊ Paris) group of rootless expatriates pass through Bayonne as they travel from Paris to Pamplona in *The Sun Also Rises*, 1926 (chapter 10): '. . . we stopped at the café on the square where we had eaten breakfast, and had a beer. It was hot, but the town had a cool, fresh, early-morning smell and it was pleasant sitting in the café. A breeze started to blow, and you could feel that the air came from the sea. There were pigeons out in the square, and the houses were a yellow, sun-baked colour, and I did not want to leave the café.'

Cambo-les-Bains. Playwright Edmond Rostand (1868–1918), suffering from tuberculosis, came here in November 1900 on the advice of his doctor. Then the rich and famous author of the enormously successful *Cyrano de Bergerac*, 1897 (*Cyrano de Bergerac*, 1993), he grew attracted to the region and in 1902 bought a substantial area of land on a wooded hillside above the spa. Here he designed and had built the palatial **Villa Arnaga**, and the vast and elaborate gardens which surround it. The whole was several years in construction – the Rostands finally moved into the villa in 1906. According to Rostand's son Maurice, it 'is not really a house: it is a great lyric poem composed by an extraordinary poet of the theatre.' Among the many guests who found their way to the villa were Henri Barbusse, Sarah Bernhardt, Jean Cocteau and Gabriele D'Annunzio. The villa is now **Le Musée Edmond Rostand** (route de Bayonne, 64250 Cambo-les-Bains), and you will find there exhibits relating to Rostand's life and work, to his family (his wife was the poet Rosemonde Gérard and his younger son the biologist Jean Rostand) and to Sarah Bernardt. Among the many documents on display are the costume designs for *Chantecler*, 1910 (*Chantecler*, 1987), which Rostand wrote while living at the villa. The museum is closed during the winter.

Hasparren. The poet and novelist Francis Jammes (1868–1938) lived here from 1921 until his death. He spent almost all his life in the south-west of France (before Hasparren he lived in **Orthez**, where he wrote much of his work), and it was this environment which inspired his poetry in celebration of nature and rural life. His house is now a small museum, with personal memorabilia and documentation on his life and work. Apart from the summer months, visits are by request – **Le Musée Francis Jammes**, 64240 Hasparren. Jammes is buried in the **cemetery** at Hasparren.

Hendaye. The novelist Pierre Loti (1850–1923) had a house in the **rue du Port** and visited Hendaye often. In June 1923, in seriously declining health, he came here from his home in Rochefort – and died a few days after his arrival.

The resort is a key location in Christine de Rivoyre's ◊ novel *Boy*, 1973 (*Boy*, 1974), set in the 1930s with the Spanish Civil War in progress over the border (Extract 5).

St-Jean-de-Luz. George Gissing took a house in the suburb of **Ciboure** in 1902. He died the following year at **St-Jean-Pied-de-Port** (see below), and was buried at St-Jean-de-Luz.

St-Jean-Pied-de-Port. The town, which has been part of France only since the Treaty of the Pyrenees, 1659, derives its name from the fact that it is located at the foot of the pass or *port* of Roncesvalles (Roncevaux) which climbs up, on the other side of the border, to the Puerto de Ibañeta. It was on this pass that Roland, Duke of the Marches of Brittany under Charlemagne, was killed in 778 in an ambush while retreating with the rearguard of

Charlemagne's army from Pamplona. He later became transmogrified into the great epic hero Roland in *Chanson de Roland* (*The Song of Roland*, 1937), the outstanding example of the *chansons de geste* ('songs of deeds' or 'songs of history' – epic verse narratives of heroism, often legendary but with some basis in historical fact). The earliest surviving manuscript of *Roland* is dated between 1130 and 1170 although the poem as we know it is thought to date back to before the end of the 11th century.

In 1903 the English novelist George Gissing (1857–1903) moved to St-Jean-Pied-de-Port with his French common-law wife Gabrielle Fleury. He was in failing health, and had moved inland from nearby St-Jean-de-Luz in the hope that the gentler climate would help him to recover. But he contracted pneumonia after a trip into the mountains and died within a few days, on 28 December 1903. His close friend H.G. Wells came out on hearing of his illness and was at his bedside when he died. The house in which Gissing stayed was the **Chalet Elgué**, in the adjacent hamlet of **Ispoure**.

MIDI-PYRÉNÉES: LOT

Saint-Cirq-Lapopie. This medieval village, sited on a height above the Lot Valley, captivated and inspired the Surrealist André Breton (1896–1966) in the later years of his life. He bought a house here in 1950 and visited it frequently until his death. In September 1966 he was taken ill during what was to prove his last visit – he died in Paris on the 28th. His house may be seen (though not visited) in **place du Carol**.

AQUITAINE: DORDOGNE

Saint-Michel-de-Montaigne. The great essayist and moralist Michel de Montaigne (1533–1592) was born and brought up in the **Château de Montaigne**. He inherited the property from his father in 1569, and in 1571, tired of public life and duties, he 'retired' here, intending to devote the rest of his life to books and contemplation. In the event, his last 20 years were much busier than he intended – including extensive travel (searching for a cure for his inherited complaint of stones which began to trouble him around 1580), his election to the position of Mayor of Bordeaux, and important diplomatic duties. Nevertheless, this was his true home and the place with which he is most strongly associated. It was here too that he died in 1592.

The original Château was destroyed by a fire in 1855 and was entirely rebuilt. There was, however, one very important survivor of the fire – the **tower** in which Montaigne housed his library and where he wrote many of his famous *Essais*. By his own account, he spent a great deal of time here, surrounded by his vast library. He describes it in Book III, chapter 3: 'My library is in the third story of a tower; on the first is my chapel, on the second a bedroom with antechambers, where I often lie to be alone; and above it there is a great wardrobe . . . My library is circular in shape, with no flat wall except that taken up by my table and chair; and, being rounded, it presents me with all my books at once, arranged about me on five tiers of shelves. From this room I have three open views, and its free space is sixteen paces across. In winter I am there less continually, for my house is perched on a hill, as its name implies, and there is no room more exposed to the winds than this. It is a little difficult of access and out of the way, but this I like, both for the benefit of the exercise and for its keeping people away from me. It is my throne, and I try to rule here absolutely, reserving this one corner from all society, conjugal, filial, and social.' ('On Three Kinds of Relationships', *Essays*, 1958, translated by J.M. Cohen.)

Montaigne's tower can be visited. Above the little entrance door is his family crest. Inside, the shells of the rooms and the winding staircase are as Montaigne knew them, but nothing now remains here of his books or his furniture (the furniture you see is not authentic). The imagination, however, is helped by one powerful reminder of the author who found solace and inspiration in this rough-hewn tower – on the beams of the library ceiling, Montaigne painted his favourite quotations in Latin and Greek and they can still be seen. (Château de Montaigne, Saint-Michel-de-Montaigne, 24230 Velines.)

AQUITAINE: GIRONDE

Bordeaux. Montaigne attended the Collège de la Guyenne. He later became Mayor of Bordeaux (1581–85). In the library in the former chapel of **Notre-Dame** there is the 1588 edition of his *Essais*, with the author's own annotations and corrections. In the **Musée d'Aquitaine**, 20 cours Pasteur you will find his tomb.

Montesquieu (see below under **Labrède**) studied and practised law in Bordeaux, where he was also a member of the local Académie. The above-mentioned library contains manuscripts of *Mes Pensées* and many of his letters. There is a bust of Montesquieu by Jean-Baptiste Lemoyne (1704–78) in the **Musée des Arts Décoratifs**, 39 rue Bouffard.

François Mauriac ◊ was born in the **rue du Pas-Saint-Georges**, and grew up in and around Bordeaux. The city and its surrounding countryside (the wine-growing regions or the claustrophobic pine forests of **Les Landes** – see Extract 2) are recurring settings for his novels, providing the backdrop to his stories of individuals struggling against the oppression and hypocrisy of provincial bourgeois life. There is a bust of the author in the **Jardin Public**. See also under **Saint-Macaire**, below.

In September 1913, Wilfred Owen (◊ Picardie) moved into a room at **95 rue Porte Dijeaux** – at the time, he was working in Bordeaux as an English teacher.

Other literary sons of Bordeaux were Jean Anouilh (1910–87) and Jacques Rivière (1886–1925).

Labrède. The **Château de Labrède** (or La Brède as it was known formerly) was the home of Charles de Secondat, baron de Montesquieu (1869–1755), the political philosopher, novelist, and contributor to the famous 18th century *Encyclopédie*, the bible of the Enlightenment. His home, still owned by his descendants, was aquired by the Montesquieu family in the 11th century and rebuilt in the 14th. Although the Château is not an especially impressive architectural monument in itself, its setting is outstandingly picturesque – it stands on an island of its own surrounded by a moat and a luxuriant park. It is open to visitors. Among the rooms on display are Montesquieu's bedroom/study, including such evocative memorabilia as his writing table, a stone in the fireplace worn down by his continually resting his foot on it, and the mirror on which he wrote 'Je réfléchis sans parler, ne parle pas sans réfléchir' ('I think without speaking, I don't speak without thinking'); and, most impressive, his library where he housed his stunning collection of 7000 volumes – many of which are still there. It was at Labrède that he wrote his epistolary novel *Les Lettres persanes*, 1721 (*Persian Letters*, 1973), and the work for which he is best remembered, *De l'esprit des lois*, 1748 (*The Spirit of the Laws*, 1989), his wide-ranging treatise which influenced the development of the American Constitution and which has a permanent place in the history of liberal thought.

Apart from his intellectual pursuits, Montesquieu was also the active proprietor of a successful wine estate (Graves is still produced here), and took great pride in the management and improvement of his property – it was he who directed the laying out of the park. Visitors to the Château will see that the home reflects the man – Montesquieu balanced intense intellectual activity with a commitment to the less cerebral pleasures of life. (Château de Labrède, route de Toulouse, 33650 Labrède.)

Saint-Macaire. Near to the village of **Saint-Maixant** is Malagar, the family property where François Mauriac spent part of his youth and which he inherited in 1927. He lived mainly in Paris, but always kept this home in his native region, overlooking the Garonne and with impressive views over the surrounding countryside. The property has been well preserved, with the interior as Mauriac knew it. House and grounds are now open to the public (for a limited period each year) – there is a small museum dedicated to the writer, with his furniture and personal memorabilia, and a library and research facilities. Biographer Robert Speaight in *François Mauriac: A Study of the Writer and the Man* recalls a visit to the property in 1974: 'A group of sixty English visitors were expected at Malagar; and when a cupboard of the old house was opened for me, and I saw the array of panama hats inside, it seemed as if I had only to step out onto the terrace, and there I should find Mauriac himself on the stone bench under the fig-tree, gazing out over the valley and the vines to the level horizon of the *Landes*.' He also highlights a remark by Mauriac that has considerable resonance for this literary guide: 'You can read the whole of humanity in some peasant of our country, and all the landscapes of the world in the horizons we have known as a child. The gift of the novelist consists in the power to show the universality of that narrow world where we were born, and where we have learnt to love and to suffer.' Malagar is used as a setting in *Destins*, 1927 (*Lines of Life*, 1958) and *Le Noeud de vipères*, 1932 (*The Knot of Vipers*, 1984). (Malagar, Saint-Maixant, 33490 Saint-Macare.)

POITOU–CHARENTES: CHARENTE

Champagne-Vigny. The Romantic novelist, poet and dramatist Alfred de Vigny (1797–1863) inherited the **Domaine du Maine-Giraud** here, about 20 km south of **Angoulême**, and it was to provide him in his later life with a much-valued retreat. After 1835, financial troubles and personal crises (including the death of his mother), combined with a dislike of the rivalries and struggles of life in Paris and the demands imposed by his wife's long-term invalidity, led him to come for long stays in his country manor house (on one occasion he lived here for three and a half years). He developed a considerable affection for the community, in which he was active and generous, and for the countryside of the Charente, his appreciation of which informed, for example, his famous poem 'La Maison du berger'.

Managing the property and caring for his wife during the day, Vigny spent his evenings writing in a small turret-room, producing here mainly letters and *pensées* – philosophical notes, personal reflections and drafts of unfinished works (the *pensées* were published as *Journal d'un poète*, 1867). But he also wrote some of his best poems at the Maine-Giraud – these, including 'La Maison du berger', were published in periodicals and subsequently in the posthumous collection *Les Destinées*, 1864.

The manor house in which Vigny lived is now part of a farm, and in a very different and less Romantic setting from the one he would have known. However, his secluded room in the turret remains intact, and there is also a museum in what used to be the dining room in the building opposite. The entrance door to the tower in which Vigny's room is located has a knocker modelled from his own hand – the one on the entrance door to the building opposite is modelled from his wife's hand. The *domaine* is private property and visits should be by appointment – Le Maine-Giraud, commune de Champagne-Vigny, 16250 Blanzac-Porcheresse.

In the town of Champagne-Vigny itself, there is another small museum dedicated to Alfred de Vigny in the **town hall**, in front of which there is a monument to him.

POITOU–CHARENTES: CHARENTE-MARITIME

Île d'Oléron. Pierre Loti (see below, under **Rochefort**) is buried in the garden of the house at **13 rue de la République.** He spent childhood summers here when it was owned by his aunts. The property eventually became his own and he sold it, but repurchased it in 1880. It may not be visited.

Rochefort. Birthplace of Jean Viaud, better known as the novelist Pierre Loti (1850–1923). Loti was born and brought up in the street now named after him, and it was his home throughout his life. He is known for his novels of romantic adventure, often set in oriental or tropical locations, drawing on his own experiences and travels as an officer in the navy, and for his travel literature. His best work, however, is generally considered to be *Pêcheur d'Islande*, 1886 (*Iceland Fisherman*, 1935), a novel focusing on the life of Breton fishermen who leave home for long periods to fish off the coast of Iceland. His house in Rochefort is now open to the public (**La Maison de Pierre Loti**, 141 rue Pierre-Loti, 17300 Rochefort). It looks quite ordinary from the outside, but don't be deceived – inside it is an amazing private palace of dreams and fantasies. Over the course of his life Loti, with the help of his substantial royalties, extended and transformed the house, adding secret doors and interconnecting corridors, collecting numerous strange and exotic artefacts, installing a small-scale mosque, and

creating many 'theme' rooms evoking his novels and his travels.

The nearby **Château de la Roche-Courbon** at **Saint-Porchaire** was a favourite haunt of Loti in his youth – he called it the 'Castle of the Sleeping Beauty' and renamed it Fontbruant in his fiction. It may be visited.

La Rochelle. Jean-Paul Sartre (◊ Paris) lived here with his mother and her new husband from 1917 to 1920 and attended the *lycée*. According to his recollections of his time at La Rochelle, Sartre considered that it was during his stay in this port that he first encountered everyday violence and where he began to develop political awareness – the boys were tough and fought often, collectively angry at having had their fathers stolen from them by the war, and there were Asian and African immigrants working in the factories and living in poverty. 'At La Rochelle I discovered something that was going to mark the rest of my life: the most profound relationships between men are based on violence.' (quoted by Annie Cohen-Solal in *Sartre: A Life*)

Georges Simenon (◊ Paris) moved into a 16th century country house called 'La Richardière' at nearby **Marsilly** in 1932. He and his wife lived there for three years – at least, they lived there for those periods when they were not on their frequent travels abroad. According to biographer Fenton Bresler, among the animals they kept at La Richardière were 'fifty or so large white turkeys, the biggest and most authoritative of which they called "Maigret" . . .' (*The Mystery of Georges Simenon*, 1983). They were forced to move when the lease expired, but took another house in the area at **Nieul-sur-Mer** in 1938 – they stayed until 1940 when the German occupation forced them to move on. Simenon was attracted by La Rochelle and the region around it and retained fond memories – on a later visit in 1966, he wrote in the visitor's book at the **Café de la Paix**, 'Au souvenir du temps le plus heureux de ma vie.'

BOOKLIST

For most of the extracted works, the original publisher in English can be found in 'Acknowledgments and Citations' at the end of the volume, as can the exact location of the extracts and the editions from which they are taken. The date in square brackets is that of the original publication of the work in its original language. For additional titles by the authors highlighted in this chapter and for recommended biographies, see 'Lives and Works'.

Davis, Natalie Zemon, *The Return of Martin Guerre*, Harvard University Press, Cambridge, MA, and London, 1983.

Durrell, Lawrence, *Caesar's Vast Ghost: Aspects of Provence* [1990], Faber and Faber, London, 1995.

Hemingway, Ernest, *The Sun Also Rises* [1926], Macmillan, New York, 1984. As *Fiesta*, Arrow, London, 1994.

James, Henry, *A Little Tour in France* [1885], Penguin, London and New York, 1985. **Extract 3.**

Koestler, Arthur, *Scum of the Earth* [1941], Eland, London, 1991/ Hippocrene, New York, 1991. **Extract 7.**

Lewis, Janet, *The Wife of Martin Guerre* [1941], Penguin, London and New York, 1984. **Extract 1.**

Mauriac, François, *The Desert of Love* [1925], Gerard Hopkins, trans, Penguin, London, 1989/Carroll and Graf, New York, 1989.

Mauriac, François, *The Frontenac Mystery* [1933], Gerard Hopkins, trans, Penguin, London, 1986.

Mauriac, François, *The Knot of Vipers* [1932], Penguin, London, 1985.

Mauriac, François, *Lines of Life* [1927], Penguin, London, 1958.

Mauriac, François, *Thérèse*, Gerard Hopkins, trans, Penguin, London and New York, 1975. (Includes the novels *Thérèse Desqueyroux* and *The End of the Night*, and the stories 'Thérèse at the Hotel' and 'Thérèse and the doctor'.) **Extract 2.**

Montaigne, Michel de *The Complete Works of Montaigne: Essays, Travel Journal, Letters*, Donald M. Frame, trans, Hamish Hamilton, London, 1958.

Montaigne, Michel de, *Complete Essays*, M.A. Screech, trans, Penguin, London and New York, 1993.

Montaigne, Michel de, *Essays*, J.M. Cohen, trans, Penguin, London, 1993. (Selections.)

Montesquieu, Baron de, *Persian Letters* [1721], L.J. Betts, trans, Penguin, London and New York, 1973.

Montesquieu, Baron de, *The Spirit of the Laws* [1748], Anne M. Cohler, trans, Cambridge University Press, Cambridge, 1989.

Rostand, Edmond, *Cyrano de Bergerac* [1897], E. Morgan, trans, Carcanet, Manchester, 1993/Bantam, New York, 1987.

Rivoyre, Christine de, *Boy* [1973], Eileen Ellenbogen, trans, Penguin, London, 1976. **Extract 5.**

Song of Roland, The, Dorothy L. Sayers, trans, Penguin, London and New York, 1937.

Stendhal, *Travels in the South of France*, Elisabeth Abbott, trans, Calder and Boyars, London, 1971/ Riverrun, New York, 1987. **Extract 6.**

Stevenson, Robert Louis, *The Cévennes Journal: Notes on a Journey through the French Highlands*, Gordon Golding, ed, Mainstream, Edinburgh, 1978.

Stevenson, Robert Louis, *Travels with a Donkey* [1879], in *Travels with a Donkey, An Inland Voyage, The Silverado Squatters*, Everyman, London, 1993. **Extract 4.**

Trollope, Anthony, 'La Mère Bauche', in *Tales of All Countries, First Series* [1861], Penguin, London and New York, 1993.

Valéry, Paul, *The Collected Works of Paul Valéry*, Jackson Matthews, ed, Vol 1, *Poems* and *On Poets and Poetry* (from *Cahiers*), Routledge and Kegan Paul, London, 1971/ Princeton University Press, Princeton, NJ, 1971 (bilingual with verse translations; includes 'La Cimetière marin').

Vigny, Alfred de, selected poems in *The Penguin of French Verse*, Brian Woledge, Geoffrey Brereton and Anthony Hartley, eds, Penguin, London and New York, 1975. (French verse with prose translations.)

Zola, Émile, *Lourdes* [1894], Alan Sutton, Gloucester, 1993.

Extracts

(1) Artigat

Janet Lewis, *The Wife of Martin Guerre*

To avoid a confrontation with his father over an incident on the farm, the young Martin Guerre takes leave of his wife, promising to return in a week. Punctuality was not his strong point: he came back twelve years later. The setting is sixteenth century Gascony.

She kissed him on both cheeks, feeling the warmth of the sun upon his flesh, caressing with her hand the short smooth beard, and then, in a brief premonition of disaster, held to his arm and would not let him go.

'Do not distress yourself,' he repeated tenderly. 'I shall be safe. I shall enjoy myself, moreover. And I shall see you in a week.'

So he went off. Once he turned to wave with a free, elated gesture, and then the shadows of the trees engulfed his figure. Bertrande returned to the farm, swinging the empty jug from a forefinger and thinking of the path which led down the valley beside the torrent falling and tumbling towards the Neste. Once she stepped aside to let pass a herd of swine being driven up into the oak forest to feed on acorns. She greeted the swineherd absently, thinking of Martin's journey, and how he would pass village after village, ford the cold streams, follow the narrow passes beside the Neste and eventually emerge into the greater valley of the Garonne, see the level fields, the walled cities, broad roads traversed by bands of merchants and armed men. The woods were still after the passage of the beasts – no insects and few birds. She wished that she might have gone with Martin. At the farm she found Sanxi, and was glad that she had not gone.

The afternoon passed as usual, but at suppertime, when Monsieur Guerre asked her where Martin was, and she answered, as had been arranged between them, 'I do not know,' she trembled beneath the cold grey gaze, penetrating and clear as a beam of light reflected from a wall of ice.

(2) BORDEAUX DISTRICT: LES LANDES

François Mauriac, *Thérèse Desqueyroux*

Pondering the idea that each individual must realize and accept his or her true self, Thérèse reveals the awfulness of her life with her husband Bernard in the stiflingly remote tiny settlement of 'Argelouse', in the area known as Les Landes.

'I shall not discuss with Bernard the rights and wrongs of such a moral doctrine: I'm even prepared to subscribe to his view that it doubtless contains much wretched sophistry. But he must understand, must make himself understand, just how a woman of my sort could be irritated by the life we led, just what she felt on those evenings in the dining-room at Argelouse when he was taking off his boots in the kitchen next door, and regaling me the while, in a rich local dialect, with talk of the day's happenings. I can see it all now: the captive birds struggling in the bag on the table, distending it with their movements, and Bernard eating slowly, relishing his recovered appetite, counting with loving care the "Fowler" drops, and saying, while he did so, "This is what is making me well." A great fire used to be burning on the hearth, and he had only to turn his chair to be able to stretch his slippered feet to the blaze. He would nod over *la Petite Gironde*. Sometimes he snored, but there were times too, when I scarcely heard him breathe. Old Madame Balion's clogs would sound on the kitchen flags, and she would appear with the candles. All around us was the silence: the silence of Argelouse! People who have never lived in that lost corner of the heath-country can have no idea what silence means. It stands like a wall about the house, and the house itself seems as though it were set solid in the dense mass of the forest, whence comes no sign of life, save occasionally the hooting of an owl. (At night I could almost believe that I heard the sob I was at such pains to stifle.)'

(3) CARCASSONNE

Henry James, *A Little Tour in France*

In 1882, the novelist Henry James visited the restored walled city of Carcassonne.

The image of a more crumbling Carcassonne rises in the mind, and there is no doubt that forty years ago the place was more affecting. On the other hand, as we see it today, it is a wonderful evocation; and if there is a great deal of new in the old, there is plenty of old in the new. The repaired crenellations, the inserted patches, of the walls of the outer circle sufficiently express this commixture. My walk brought me into full view of the Pyrenees, which, now that the sun had begun to sink and the shadows to grow long, had a wonderful violet glow. The platform at the base of the walls has a greater width on this side, and it made the scene more complete. Two or three old crones had crawled out of the Porte Narbonnaise, to examine the advancing visitor; and a very ancient peasant, lying there with his back against a tower, was tending half a dozen lean sheep. A poor man in a very old blouse, crippled and with crutches lying beside him, had been brought out and placed on a stool, where he enjoyed the afternoon as best he might. He looked so ill and so patient that I spoke to him; found that his legs were paralysed and he was quite helpless. He had formerly been seven years in the army, and had made the campaign of Mexico with Bazaine. Born in the old cité, he had come back there to end his days. It seemed strange, as he sat there, with those romantic walls behind him and the great picture of the Pyrenees in front, to think that he had been across the seas to the far-away new world, had made part of a famous expedition, and was now a cripple at the gate of the mediæval city where he had played as a child. All this struck me as a great deal of history for so modest a figure – a poor little figure that could only just unclose its palm for a small silver coin.

(4) Cévennes

R.L. Stevenson, *Travels with a Donkey*

Stevenson and his long-suffering donkey Modestine travel, as night falls, through remote country on the road to St Germain de Calberte. Stevenson undertook his walking tour in the Cévennes in September 1878.

We struck at last into a wide white high-road carpeted with noiseless dust. The night had come; the moon had been shining for a long while upon the opposite mountain; when on turning a corner my donkey and I issued ourselves into her light. I had emptied out my brandy at Florac, for I could bear the stuff no longer, and replaced it with some generous and scented Volnay; and now I drank to the moon's sacred majesty upon the road. It was but a couple of mouthfuls; yet I became thenceforth unconscious of my limbs, and my blood flowed with luxury. Even Modestine was inspired by this purified nocturnal sunshine, and bestirred her little hoofs to a livelier measure. The road wound and descended swiftly among masses of chestnuts. Hot dust rose from our feet and flowed away. Our two shadows – mine deformed by the knapsack, hers comically bestridden by the pack – now lay before us clearly outlined on the road, and now, as we turned a corner, went off into the ghostly distance, and sailed along the mountain like clouds. From time to time a warm wind rustled down the valley, and set all the chestnuts dangling their bunches of foliage and fruit; the ear was filled with whispering music, and the shadows danced in tune. And next moment the breeze had gone by, and in all the valley nothing moved except our travelling feet. On the opposite slope, the monstrous ribs and gullies of the mountain were faintly designed in the moonshine; and high overhead, in some lone house, there burned one lighted window, one square spark of red in the huge field of sad nocturnal colouring.

At a certain point, as I went downward, turning many acute angles, the moon disappeared behind the hill; and I pursued my way in great darkness, until another turning shot me without preparation into St Germain de Calberte. The place was asleep and silent, and buried in opaque night. Only from a single open door, some lamplight escaped upon the road to show me that I was come among men's habitations. The two last gossips of the evening, still talking by a garden wall, directed me to the inn. The landlady was getting her chicks to bed; the fire was already out, and had, not without grumbling, to be rekindled; half an hour later, and I must have gone supperless to roost.

(5) HENDAYE

Christine de Rivoyre, *Boy*

It is 14 July 1937 and the 12-year-old Hildegarde is forced by her father to go to church to 'pray for the godless revolutionaries' instead of to the beach. Rivoyre's novel of change and loss is set in the Basque region and is strong on local detail and atmosphere.

As for me, I put on my old yellow tobralco dress. It was in keeping with my frame of mind, I felt, and I never opened my mouth during the whole of the walk from the Villa Gure Geritza to the Chapel at Hendaye-Plage. Papa led the column, wearing a dark suit. Mama followed, hand-in-hand with Nadia. She was wearing a navy blue seersucker dress, with a straw boater. She never dresses up in Hendaye, except when Papa is there. Gisèle and I brought up the rear, dragging our feet. From time to time Papa would look round at us. 'What's the matter? Are you feeling ill? I see. In that case, you won't be going on the beach tomorrow either.' In response to this threat, we stepped out more briskly.

We walked beside the pier as far as the Deux Jumeaux. The tide was out and the people on the beach looked happy, and there were boys and girls of about my age, astride the swings and trapezes of the Seahorse Club. Some were swinging, some were sliding down the giant chute, others were running down to the sea. I could hear them shouting for joy. I thought: My God, how lucky they are. The light was so beautiful, it shimmered, and I thought: This is the loveliest day of the year and I am going to spend it in a tunnel. Papa never once looked towards the beach. He was interested in only one thing, the Revolution, which is now commemorated by a public holiday. He told us that, as far as he was concerned, the 14th of July was a day of mourning, and repeated for the umpteenth time that his grandmother Hildegarde, whenever she had occasion to set foot outside in the Rue David Johnston on the 14th of July, had always worn a crêpe veil. And he told us about the Château de Barèges, near Nantes, which was burnt down in 1793, and about the Bertauds de Barèges, who were stripped by an iniquitous law of their heritage and their rights. As we went past the Casino, he took the *Courrier Royal* out of his jacket pocket, and carried it in his outstretched hand, like a banner.

(6) MONTPELLIER

Stendhal, *Travels in the South of France*

In April 1838, Stendhal visited the town of Montpellier during a tour of the south, and was unimpressed by its cafés.

Toward one o'clock in Montpellier, I was taken to an inn on the Grande-Rue. This morning when I woke, I found that the only window in my room looked out on a street which may well be six feet wide. The house opposite has five stories.

I went out in search of a decent café, but found only pharmacies. To be sure, Montpellier is the home of doctors and, in consequence, of wealthy invalids. All the melancholy, tubercular Englishmen come here to die. At last I overcame my dislike of speaking to strangers and asked some men on the threshold of their shop to direct me to a good café and, in my search for a demi-tasse, I went to some that were truly incredible. Later on I realized that there was not one decent café in Montpellier.

I decided to put up at the hotel that was doing the most business. There, as I had not arrived by coach, a big, gaunt woman received me so coldly that my pride was stung. 'But what does it matter!' I said to myself and ordered my trunks sent up to a charming bedroom on the first floor with three windows looking out on the street and on a garden.

Through an indiscreet servant I learned the name of the fashionable café to which I hurried as fast as I could and, my desires being by this time unlimited, I asked for some hot water. In my pocket I had some excellent tea from Kiancha, which had never seen the sea, a present from charming Madame Boil . . . And again found myself in a repetition of the scene last year in Tours which may have bored the reader. All these towns in the interior of France are alike: the same rudeness, the same barbarous service. In the end I shall have to breakfast on chicory coffee and goat's milk, I think. The butter was not bad, though rather peculiar: it was white and it looked like hair pomade.

(7) VERNET

Arthur Koestler, *Scum of the Earth*

At the beginning of the Second World War, Koestler (a native of neutral Hungary) was interred by the French as an undesirable alien. Much of that time was spent in the prison camp in Vernet, near the Pyrenean frontier. A few weeks before his release (17 January 1940), he was put on latrine duty.

Our work consisted in collecting the latrine-bins of Section C and of the gendarmes' quarter outside the camp. Each squad was composed of twelve men and had to deal with about twenty bins. The contents of these twenty bins were collected in six bins, by means of decanting them into each other. As the handles of some of the bins were broken, they were difficult to manipulate, and it required a special technique to avoid the contents splashing over one's clothes. Each of the six full bins weighed from sixty to seventy pounds and was carried by two men across the camp to a narrow-gauge railway. The bins were loaded on to the trucks, and the trucks were pushed to the banks of the River Ariège, about half a mile outside the camp. The contents were emptied into a large open hole next to the river, the exhalations of which could be sensed in a circumference, varying with wind and weather, from a hundred yards to a mile. Then the empty bins were carried down a slope, slippery with ice or mud, to be scrubbed in the river. When the river was frozen we had first to break a hole in the ice. Then the bins were carried back up the slope to the trucks, the trucks pushed back to camp, the bins carried back to the latrines. The only protection against infections was to wash one's hands in cold water after work; the repeated epidemics of dysentery were an inevitable consequence of this sanitary system.

The operation was repeated twice a day. On the first two occasions I was sick; later I became accustomed to it. Sometimes Jacob, the jackdaw, made the journey to the river with us, perching on top of a latrine-bin and looking at the men who pushed the truck with glittering eyes full of black irony; sometimes Negro, the dog, accompanied us too; sometimes on the backward journey we sang the Song of the Latrine Squad, which combined a beautifully sad melody with an utterly unprintable text.

Lives and works of extracted writers

JAMES, Henry. See under Paris.

KOESTLER, Arthur (1905–83). The journalist, novelist, and essayist Koestler was based in **Paris** for several years in the 1930s. In August 1939 he was spending the summer in the Midi at **Roquebillière** with a girlfriend – a happy period rudely interrupted by the necessity to return to Paris with the outbreak of the war. His *Scum of the Earth*, 1941, begins with the end of that peaceful break in the Midi and the journey into the chaos of a country at war. The book was written in the first months of 1941 after Koestler had left occupied France for Britain. It is a vivid and analytical account of his experiences and observations in France as it adjusted to the outbreak of war and subsequently to German occupation. Koestler's own description of the book in his Preface of 1954 is a little harsh: 'The period character of the book is particularly evident in its political outlook. It is the romantically and naïvely Leftish outlook of the pink thirties.' Actually, this is not what stands out for the modern reader – rather it is Koestler's humane, intelligent and evocative portrayal of a country in a crisis of cultural disintegration and loss of national pride. In the early months of the war, he watches Paris 'turn grey': 'This town has always been thought of by her lovers as a person alive – not metaphorically, but as a psychological reality. Now they felt the beloved grow cold and stony in their arms; they watched the life fade out of her, inverted Pygmalions; and they walked in despair through her suddenly hostile avenues, as on tombstones.' There are glimpses of many parts of France at this period, and Koestler's journalistic eye often provides a description as good as any piece of photo-reportage – as, for example, in the passage in which he watches, from a café terrace in **Limoges**, the constant flow of refugees moving from north to south, describing the vast assortment of vehicles and the people and belongings crammed into them, 'all stewing together in a sort of surrealist *goulash*'. Although, as a Hungarian national, Koestler was from a neutral country, he was interred for a time by the French as an undesirable alien in the panic round-ups following the outbreak of war. Some of the most memorable writing, perhaps because it is laced with outrage, is in the section of the book describing this experience,

first in the **Roland Garros Stadium** in **Paris** and then in the huge internment camp at **Vernet** (Extract 7).

After the war, Koestler made a number of short trips to Paris, where he developed a close friendship with Albert Camus. In February 1949 he bought a house at **Fontaine-le-Port** on the Seine outside Paris, which remained his home until July 1952, when he moved to London.

Recommended biography: Iain Hamilton, *Koestler: A Biography*, Secker and Warburg, London, 1982.

LEWIS, Janet (1899–   ). The American poet and novelist Janet Lewis had visited France only briefly before writing *The Wife of Martin Guerre*, 1941 (see introduction, under Ariège, for details of the novel and the events on which it is based). Nevertheless, she achieves an atmospheric and finely detailed period setting (Extract 1) and successfully infuses her version of the story with the haunting strangeness it demands. In an Afterword in more recent editions of her book, she explains that she wrote it before reading the full account the trial of 'Martin Guerre' by Maître Jean de Coras – the authoritative and detailed source for the content of the judicial proceedings and the nature of the events that led up to them. 'Therefore,' admits Lewis, 'the story which I offer here differs somewhat from the story as I might wish to write it now.' *The Wife of Martin Guerre*, though, remains an engrossing and intelligent psychological study with skilful evocations of rural Gascony and life in a sixteenth-century French village.

Lewis's novel *The Ghost of Monsieur Scarron*, 1959, is set in the 17th century France of Louis XIV.

MAURIAC, FRANÇOIS (1885–1970). Mauriac was born in **Bordeaux** on 11 October 1885 into a wealthy Catholic middle-class family. In 1907, he moved to **Paris** to study but in 1909 turned his attention entirely to writing.

Before the First World War, he worked as a journalist and published volumes of poetry as well as his first prose fiction. In the 1920s, he established his literary reputation with several powerful short psychological novels, all set predominantly in his native region in the southwest and portraying the struggles of individuals against their oppressive and claustrophobic bourgeois environment – among these are *Le Désert de l'amour*, 1925 (*The Desert of Love*, 1984), which won the Grand Prix du Roman of the Académie Française, and *Thérèse Desqueyroux*, 1927 (see below). They also deal with a fundamental conflict that preoccupied Mauriac – that between religion and sensuality. Mauriac's biographer Robert Speaight quotes appropriately from a letter he wrote to André Gide: 'Our work can only be the image of that inconclusive struggle, of that trial in our heart, between God and the passion to which He subjects us, and which is nevertheless willed by him.' This struggle in Mauriac himself sent him spiralling down into a spiritual crisis at the end of the 1920s, which lasted until 1931. His novels after that date adopt a more positive approach and suggest that salvation can be compatible with revolt against the oppression and hypocrisy of bourgeois morality – as, for example, in *Le Noeud de vipères*, 1932 (*The Knot of Vipers*, 1984); the autobiographical *Le Mystère Frontenac*, 1933 (*The Frontenac Mystery*, 1952); and *La Fin de la nuit*, 1935 (*The End of the Night*, in *Thérèse*, 1947) – the book which prompted Sartre to accuse Mauriac of playing god in his narrative role, of making his characters behave as he thought they should rather than as he thought they would. Mauriac took the criticism to heart and responded to it in his future work.

In 1933, Mauriac was elected to the Académie Française. In 1952 he received the Nobel Prize for Literature. He wrote further novels towards the end of his life, and it is as a novelist that he is best remembered – but he was also an essayist, diarist, and playwright,

and a respected journalist. He died on 1 September 1970 in the apartment in Paris where he had lived for some 40 years. He also had a home in the Gironde which he had inherited from his family (see introduction).

The Thérèse stories, centred around his most famous character, comprise primarily the short novel *Thérèse Desqueyroux*, 1927, the short stories 'Thérèse chez le docteur' and 'Thérèse à l'hôtel' from *Plongées*, 1928, and the novel *Le Fin de la nuit*, all available in one volume in English translation under the title *Thérèse*, 1947. Set in the region around **Bordeaux** and in **Paris** the stories follow the fortunes of the eponymous heroine, through her life with her entirely unsuitable husband in a remote rural village in **Les Landes**, her attempt to murder him by slow poisoning, and the consequences of that action, to her life in Paris and her eventual death. In the main work, *Thérèse Desqueyroux*, Mauriac gives us a penetrating and sympathetic investigation of the psychology of this complex woman, who brings pain and tragedy into peoples' lives and yet at the same time craves love and understanding. He does this through a narrative which comprises largely the thoughts, emotions and memories of its subject. Like Flaubert in *Madame Bovary*, he stresses the heroine's frustration with provincial life (Extract 2) which is contrasted with the culture and sophistication of Paris, in this case represented by a young man, Jean Azévédo ('Jean Azévédo described Paris to me, and the friends he had there. I imagined a sort of realm in which the only law was "be thyself".') Although written from the standpoint of a committed Roman Catholic, the novel is far from simplistically moralistic – this analytical and psychological story is as subtle and complex as the character whose motivations and actions it anatomizes.

Recommended biography: Robert Speaight, *François Mauriac: A Study of the Writer and the Man*, Chatto and Windus, London, 1976.

RIVOYRE, Christine de (1921–). Born in **Tarbes** (Hautes-Pyrénées), Rivoyre studied in **Bordeaux** and **Paris**. She worked as a journalist on *Le Monde* from 1950 to 1955 and from 1955 to 1966 as Literary Editor of *Marie-Claire*. Since 1970, she has been a member of the panel of judges for the Prix de Médicis. Her own work has won various literary prizes, including, in 1984, the Prix Paul-Morand de l'Académie Française for her overall literary achievement.

Boy, 1973 (*Boy*, 1974) is set in the summer of 1937 near the Spanish border (especially in and around the coastal town of **Hendaye** – Extract 5). The Civil War rumbles on over the border, while a wealthy French family and its servants continue with their normal life and social assumptions, soon to be disrupted by both internal and external challenges to the old order. The focus of the book is the character of Monsieur Boy, the wealthy, hedonistic, extravagant and essentially tragic young man in whose character and fate the tensions at the heart of the novel are manifested. The story is told, until the final chapter, entirely through the subjective narrative of two characters, a young servant girl Suzon and the 12-year-old Hildegarde, one of the daughters of the house. The structural complexity that this involves in no way intrudes on the accessibility of the novel and the technique gives Rivoyre the opportunity to offer a sensitive and intimate portrayal of these two female characters while leaving Boy at one remove from the reader, appropriately distanced and ambiguous. For the final chapter, we are lent the eyes and mind of an older family servant, whose perceptions of the past and the present tie together the thematic strands while the central characters recede from our knowledge along with the pre-war world they have enjoyed.

Several of Rivoyre's other novels have also been translated into English, including *L'Alouette au miroir*, 1955 (*A Snare for the Heart*, 1960); *Les Sultans*, 1964 (*The Sultans*, 1967); and *Le Petit Matin*, 1968 (*Morning Twilight*, 1970).

STENDHAL. See under Rhône–Alpes.

STEVENSON, Robert Louis (1850–94). Born in Edinburgh, Stevenson suffered continuous ill health from a recurrent bronchial complaint (probably tuberculosis) and was frequently subject to sudden haemorrhages. He spent much of his life travelling in search of a climate that would suit him, and lived abroad for many years – in France, Switzerland, the USA, and Samoa, where he died.

France played a special part in Stevenson's life – he was much attracted to its literature and culture and its social freedom, which fitted his bohemian inclinations well. He spoke French fluently and felt at ease in the country. The places of particular significance to him included **Menton**, where he wintered in 1873–74, and wrote his essay 'Ordered South', 1874; the artists' villages of **Barbizon** and **Grez-sur-Loing** near **Fontainebleau**, which he loved and revisited several times – in **Grez** in 1876 Stevenson met and fell in love with the American Fanny Osbourne, who later became his wife; **Paris**, where Fanny had an apartment in **Montmartre** in the 1870s; **Saint-Marcel** near **Marseille** where he lived with her for a short time in 1882; and **Hyères** on the Riviera, where they lived from spring 1883 until the autumn of 1884.

In 1878, Stevenson undertook a gruelling 12-day walking tour in the **Cévennes**, starting at **Le Monastier**, near **Le Puy**, where he spent several weeks preparing for the trip. The adventure was undertaken primarily to provide him with material for a book, and he kept a daily diary to serve as his 'source material' – the diary was published in 1979 as *The Cévennes Journal: Notes of a Journey Through the French Highlands*, edited by J. Golding. In Le Monastier Stevenson bought a donkey to accompany him on the trip, whom he called Modestine – in *Travels with a Donkey in the Cévennes*, 1879 (Extract 4), she features prominently, not least because of his unkind treatment of her. The book is an evocative account of the arduous journey, by the end of which both Stevenson and the donkey were in a state of complete exhaustion. It tells of Stevenson's meetings with the locals in the remote mountain villages, his visits to inns, and to a monastery, and his experiences of sleeping rough in the forests and of struggling against the difficult terrain. He also writes enthu-

siastically about the protestant guerillas the Camisards, whose rebellion had broken out in 1702 at **Pont-de-Montvert**, and who resisted the French government for several years from their base in the forests of the Cévennes.

An earlier travel narrative, *An Inland Voyage*, 1878 (Stevenson's first published book), describes the much gentler experience of a canoe tour in Belgium and France which he undertook with a friend in 1876.

Recommended biography: Jenni Calder, *RLS: A Life*, Hamish Hamilton, London, 1980.

AUVERGNE; LIMOUSIN; CENTRE

> '. . . so in that moment all the flowers in our garden
> and in M Swann's park, and the water-lilies on the
> Vivonne and the good folk of the village and their
> little dwellings and the parish church and the whole
> of Combray and its surroundings, taking shape and
> solidity, sprang into being, town and gardens alike,
> from my cup of tea.'
>
> Marcel Proust, *Swann's Way*

AUVERGNE: HAUTE-LOIRE

Le Monastier. 'In a little place called
Le Monastier, in a pleasant highland
valley fifteen miles from Le Puy, I spent
about a month of fine days. Monastier
is notable for the making of lace, for
drunkenness, for freedom of language,
and for unparalleled political dissen-
sion.' So begins *Travels with a Donkey*,
1879 – Robert Louis Stevenson's story
of his arduous twelve-day walking tour
in the **Cévennes** (see Languedoc–
Roussillon, Extract 4). Stevenson set
out from Le Monastier, where he spent
several weeks preparing for the trip,
and where he bought his poor stubborn
and long-suffering donkey Modestine,
for '65 francs and a glass of brandy'.

Le Puy. Ruskin ◊ visited Le Puy on a
continental tour in 1840–41 and, as he
describes in his diary for 1840 (Extract
5), found it had much to offer his
geological, artistic and architectural interests.

Trollope ◊ was here in 1859 and used
the town, and the nearby **Château de
Polignac**, as the setting for his short
story 'The Château of Prince Polignac'
(Extract 6).

AUVERGNE: PUY-DE-DÔME

Châtelguyon. Guy de Maupassant (◊
Normandy) came to this watering-place
for his health and used it as the basis for
the spa he depicts in his novel *Mont-
Oriol*, 1887.

Pontgibaud. Madame de Lafayette
(1643–93), author of *La Princesse de
Clèves*, 1678 (*The Princess of Cleves*,
1950) was very much a Parisian, but
she moved to the Auvergne for several
years with her husband, who had various estates and houses in the region.
It was during this period that she gave
birth to her two sons. Despite the
beauty of the region, Madame de
Lafayette shared none of her husband's
taste for the countryside – and the
Comte de Lafayette's uncomfortable,
old-fashioned houses can only have
made her miss Paris all the more. Montaigne visited her at Pontgibaud in
1581 on his way home after the travels
recorded in his *Journal de voyage*, disco-

vered in 1770 and published in 1774 (*Travel Journal*, 1958). The essayist was not greatly impressed with the house: '. . . I went to greet Madame de La Fayette in passing, and I was half an hour in her parlor. This house has less beauty than reputation; the site of it is rather ugly than otherwise, the garden small, square, and the alleys in it raised a good four or five feet; the beds are at the bottom, with many fruit trees and few herbs in them, and the sides of these sunken beds are lined with freestone.'

LIMOUSIN: CREUSE

Aubusson. Birthplace of novelist Jules Sandeau (1811–83), now remembered primarily for his affair with George Sand ◊. She collaborated with him on the novel *Rose et blanche*, 1831, published under the pseudonym 'J. Sand', which she subsequently changed to 'G. Sand' for her own work. Sandeau was born in the street which has been named after him.

Boussac. The dramatically sited **Château** here is used as a key setting in George Sand's novel *Jeanne*, 1843. It may be visited, and among the rooms on exhibition is one in which Sand is said to have stayed (on the first floor).

LIMOUSIN: HAUTE-VIENNE

Bellac. Birthplace of playwright and novelist Jean Giraudoux (1882–1944). The house in which he was born has been converted into a museum (**Maison Natale de Jean Giraudoux**, 4 avenue Jean-Jaurès, 87300 Bellac). There is background information on his life and work, together with manuscripts, theatre posters, and personal memorabilia – and his son's collection of clocks from the Limousin region. There is also a monument in the town to Giraudoux, depicting him surrounded by some of his heroines.

CENTRE: INDRE

Chassignolles. '. . . the case was packed tight with seven letters, two of them in their small envelopes, the others showing traces of having been simply folded and sealed. In the late afternoon light coming through the door that I had left open behind me, I peered at them and found a date – 1862 – and then another. The copybook handwritings varied: I saw that the letters could not all be from one person, but the ink was faded and even a cursory glance through the soft wads of paper delicate as old skin showed that some of the French was very odd.' In 1972, the novelist, biographer and historian Gillian Tindall (1938–   ) bought a house in this village near **La Châtre**. She found a small box of letters which had been left untouched when the house had been cleared. All but one had been written in the early 1860s – they were addressed to Célestine, and were from suitors. The seventh letter was from Célestine's brother. From this meagre beginning, through a combination of impressive intuition, painstaking scholarly research which involved pouring over many official records and other primary and secondary sources, and conversations with members of the present-day local comunity of Chassignolles, Tindall proceeded to piece together a fascinating history of the village and its inhabitants over the last 150 years. Her *Célestine: Voices from a French Village*, 1995, is the result of her research and is as interesting for the process of discovery it narrates, and the intensity with which Tindall applies herself to her formidable detective work, as for the images it evokes of the village as it is now and as it was at various stages in its history. The book is an engrossing history of social change in rural France and a challenging investigation of the slender threads that connect us to the past – the letters, writes Tindall, 'have turned out more durable than the lives and endeavours they express.' Gillian Tindall has also written several novels set in France, and a study of relevance to the theme of this volume, *Countries of the Mind: the Meaning of Place to Writers*, 1991.

Gargilesse. In 1850, a friend of George Sand's ◊ son Maurice visited **Nohant** (see below) for the first time. This was the engraver Alexandre Manceau whom she appointed as her secretary and who not long afterwards became her lover in a relationship which was to prove both peaceful and lasting – it lasted in fact until Manceau's death in 1865. In 1857, Manceau bought and had fitted out for Sand a small house in this attractive village, which had captivated them both. She came here now and again between 1858 and 1864 to work in privacy, and to relax by walking in the countryside which she loved and knew well. The house has been converted into a small museum, displaying various personal effects of Sand and Maurice and a sizeable collection of documents (**Villa Algira**, Gargilesse-Dampierre, 36190 Orsennes). Sand writes of Gargilesse and what it meant to her in *Promenades autour d'un village*, 1859.

Nohant and environs. When her father died in 1808, Aurore Dupin came with her mother to the **Château de Nohant**, the property of Aurore's paternal grandmother. She spent her childhood here, brought up mainly by her grandmother, and subsequently inherited the Château when the old lady died in 1821. When she grew up, Aurore Dupin, after becoming Baronne Dudevant by a short-lived marriage, turned into George Sand ◊ and Nohant, where she did most of her writing, has become in consequence one of the most famous literary sites in France.

Until the 1848 Revolution, Sand divided her time between here and Paris – following her disillusionments with the progress of the Revolution,

she made Nohant her principal home and, from 1848 until her death in 1876, spent most of her time here, much loved for her devotion and good offices to the local community. Among the many friends she welcomed to Nohant were Balzac, Chopin (her lover for nine years), Delacroix (who was provided with a studio), Flaubert, Gautier, Liszt, and Turgenev and his companion the singer Pauline Viardot. A young and admiring English poet called Matthew Arnold (◊ Rhône–Alpes) paid a brief visit to Sand in 1846. His biographer Park Honan quotes from his essay 'George Sand', 1877: '. . . she touched politely, by a few questions and remarks upon England and things and persons English, – upon Oxford and Cambridge, Byron, Bulwer. As she spoke, her eyes, head, bearing, were all of them striking; but the main impression she made was . . . of *simplicity*, frank, cordial simplicity. After breakfast she led the way into the garden, asked me a few kind questions about myself and my plans, gathered a flower or two and gave them to me, shook hands heartily at the gate, and I saw her no more.'

The 'Château', which is in reality an elegant provincial middle-class house, may be visited (**La Maison de George Sand**, Château de Nohant, 36400 La Châtre). It retains much of its original ambience, containing various items of Sand's furniture and other belongings. Of special interest are the dining room, with the table laid for dinner as it would have been when Sand entertained her literary and artistic guests; the *salon*, with its collection of family portraits, including one of Sand aged 34 – among the furnishings in this room is the table which, according to Sand, was made from an old cherry tree that stood in the garden – 'a table that isn't much to look at, but a solid, faithful, honest table'; and the little room which had been her grandmother's *boudoir* and which for a time she made her study-bedroom because it offered the privacy and solitude she needed to work: 'I was then living in what had been my grandmother's boudoir, because it had only one door and could not be used as a thoroughfare under any pretext. This boudoir was so small that with my books, herbals, butterflies and pebbles (I was amusing myself with natural history, though without learning a thing), there was no room for a bed. A hammock answered to the purpose. For a desk I used a chiffonier, which I long shared with a cricket who had grown tame from watching me. He lived on my sealing wafers, which I made certain were always of the whitest, fearing lest he be poisoned.' (from *Histoire de ma vie*, 1854, translated by Dan Hofstadter in *My Life* – see Booklist). You can still see the rings on which she hung her hammock, and on the doorframe in this room are the marks she made to measure the growth of her children.

Among the other parts of the house open to visitors is the small theatre which Sand had built and where she staged amateur performances, mainly of her own plays. The stage remains set as it was for the last performance, given in 1864. Maurice Sand, George's artistic son (who was given lessons by Delacroix), added a theatre of his own – a puppet theatre, for which he wrote the plays and designed and carved the puppets, which were then dressed by his mother. The marionettes survive, and are on display. Also memorable is the room which George Sand made her own towards the end of her life in 1867, still with the wallpaper and furnishings which she chose for herself. She died in this room on 8 June 1876 – her grave is in the small family cemetery adjacent to the house.

Nohant has long been a destination for literary pilgrims. In 1907 Henry James and Edith Wharton paid a visit in the course of their motor tour through France. Wharton records the tour in *A Motor-Flight Through France*, 1908. She was especially taken with the puppet theatre.

Nohant and the surrounding towns, villages and landscape feature in many of Sand's novels, and her study of the traditions and culture of the peasant communities of the region then known as Berri infuses her stories with valuable anthropological and historical detail. Two tourist routes have been devised for those wishing to follow 'in the steps of George Sand' – one starts at **Châteauroux** and the other at **La Châtre**. Among the many places associated with her and her books is the **Château de Saint-Chartier**, the model for the château in *Les Maîtres sonneurs*, 1853 (*The Master Pipers*, 1994), the novel extracted here (Extract 4) – the real-life version is now home to an international festival of lute-players and master pipers which takes place every year over a weekend in July.

Of the museums in the area (see also **Gargilesse**, above), **Le Musée George-Sand et de la Vallée-Noire**, 71 rue Venose, La Châtre, housed in a 15th century château, has a section devoted to Sand as well as exhibits relating to two other writers associated with the region – the Belgian poet and novelist Jean de Boschère (1878–1957), who lived for a time at La Châtre, and Maurice Rollinat (1846–1903), noted for his part in the 19th century revival of the *ballade* in poetry. As a literary aside, it is worth noting that La Châtre was the birthplace of the writer Henri Latouche (real name Hyacinthe Thabaud de Latouche, 1785–1851), a friend of Sand – it was he who lent her his Paris home on quai Malaquais.

Several other of the local museums include exhibits of interest to those who want to know more about the regional traditions and culture so treasured by George Sand – for example, **Le Musée Bertrand**, 2 rue Descente-des-Cordeliers, Châteauroux, in addition to its collection of Napoleonic souvenirs, has displays evoking the history of the Berri region.

CENTRE: INDRE-ET-LOIRE

Chinon and environs. For the literary tourist, Chinon and its surrounding countryside and villages are dominated by the name and reputation of François Rabelais ◊. His father's town house was at **15 rue de Lamproie** in Chinon, but it has long since disappeared (there is a statue of Rabelais on **quai Jeanne d'Arc**). At nearby **Seuilly**, however, is **La Devinière**, the farmhouse where he is said to have been born and spent part of his childhood, and where there is now a small museum (**Le Musée Rabelais**, La Devinière, Seuilly, 37500 Chinon). Despite the uncertainty about whether or not it is the actual birthplace of the author, the house is a charming and atmospheric example of the period and the region. In the bedroom, the four-poster bed makes no pretence to be the one in which the author was born, but is genuinely local and of his time. The graffiti you can see near the window may have been the work of the adolescent Rabelais. The museum houses a motley collection of documents, and, among other things, illustrations of his books by various artists over the centuries (including a sketch by Matisse). In the cellars below the house, appropriately enough for this great singer of the vine, have been set out wine presses and various other vinous exhibits – if the sight makes you thirsty you can buy a large bottle of local red, brazenly labelled 'Gargantua', on your way out.

Of the five books which recount the outrageously comic adventures of Gargantua and Pantagruel, *Gargantua* is the one which owes the most to this house and its surroundings. The house itself was transmogrified into the residence of Grangousier. His enemy Picrichole is King of **Lerné**, to the west, and Picrichole's army is defeated near the **Abbey of Seuilly** (now used as a conference centre), where Rabelais himself may have been sent to school. The valley of **Négron**, in which the house is located, is the central site of the battle. Close to Chinon, on the banks of the Loire, Gargantua established his Thélème Abbey and its order of Thélèmites whose only rule was 'Do

what you will', 'because people who are free, well-born, and easy in honest company have a natural spur and instinct which drives them to virtuous deeds and deflects them from vice . . . For we always strive after things forbidden and covet what is denied us.'

For the more seriously Rabelaisian, or perhaps just the more serious, there are organized tours around Rabelais country – contact **Office de Tourisme**, 12 rue Voltaire, 37500 Chinon.

Loches. Birthplace of Alfred de Vigny (1797–1863). There is a statue of him in the **place de la Marne**.

Mettray. Jean Genet (◊ Brittany) was detained in the penitentiary colony here from September 1926 to March 1929. Genet's experiences at Mettray feature strongly in his novel *Le Miracle de la rose*, 1946 (*The Miracle of the Rose*, 1971).

La Riche. On the outskirts of **Tours** is the ruined priory of **Saint-Cosme**. Pierre de Ronsard (see below, under Loiret-Cher) succeeded his brother as Prior here. He received the benefices of this and the priory of Croixval (at **Trôo**) in 1565–66, and spent much of the last 20 years of his life, especially after the death of Charles IX in 1574, away from the court at these two priories. Saint-Cosme may be visited – the lodging where Ronsard stayed still exists and now houses a small museum, which includes information and exhibits on the history of the priory and the life of the poet. When Ronsard lived in the 15th century building, it had only two rooms – one on each floor, with an external staircase (which can still be seen) – but they have since been partitioned and there is an internal staircase dating from the 17th century. On the first floor was his bedroom and his study (the loggia). It was here that he died on 27 December 1585. He was buried in the church, and his remains were rediscovered during an archaeological excavation in 1933 – he was reinterred in

Honoré de Balzac, 1842

January 1934 in the same place under a new gravestone. Among the other evocative sights here is the restored refectory, dating from the 12th century. The small building which was added to the refectory in the 14th century, to serve partly as a kitchen and partly as accommodation for guests, now houses the library of the Société des Amis de Ronsard.

You can obtain an itinerary for a tour of buildings and places associated with Ronsard from the **Office de Tourisme**, 78 rue Bernard Palissy, Tours 37042.

Saché. The villages, châteaux and countryside of Balzac's ◊ native **Touraine** provided inspiration and settings for many of his novels. The Château in the attractive village of Saché, some 34 km south-west of **Tours**, was the home of Jean de Margonne, the lover of Mme de Balzac. Her son Honoré was always made welcome here and had a room on the top floor, to which he returned many times in his life, and where he wrote some of his most famous novels, including *Le Père Goriot*, 1834 (*Pere Goriot*, 1962) and *Le Lys dans la vallée*, 1835 (*The Lily in the Valley*, 1989), the latter set in the region and evoking vividly the quintessentially Romantic countryside of Touraine. Balzac's last visit here was in 1848, when he came to take refuge from the violence and horror of a Paris devastated by revolution.

In the château, not much changed since Balzac sat in his room and admired the surrounding woods and the winding Indre, is **Le Musée Balzac** (Château de Saché, 37190 Azay-le-Rideau). You can see the writer's room, preserved as it was when he used it, his bed, his writing accessories (including his coffee pot), and other personal effects. On the same floor are pictures, documents, proofs, and other exhibits evoking Balzac's life, work, and family and friends. The rooms are much as they were when M de Margonne lived there – even some of the original wallpaper has been uncovered and restored.

Saint-Cyr-sur-Loire. Here, just outside **Tours**, Anatole France (◊ Paris) spent the last 10 years of his life – it was the first time he had lived outside Paris. He moved into the property, **La Béchellerie**, in 1914 and gradually extended the grounds with additional purchases. He made major alterations to the manorhouse, which had had various inappropriate extensions and additions imposed on it by previous owners. France died here in October 1924. Inside and out, everything was carefully preserved by Lucien Psichari, France's grandson by his first marriage (whom the author took in after the death of his parents and who inherited the property – Psichari's father was the novelist Ernest Psichari who was killed on the Western Front. France moved to La Béchellerie from the Villa Saïd in Paris where he had lived happily for some 20 years, bringing with him his furniture, and even the fireplaces, from his old house, which had been demolished. His companion at this time was Emma Laprévote, former maid of the late Madame Arman de Caillavet (she of

the famous literary *salon* which France had long attended and with whom he had had a long-standing liaison). He eventually married her at the town hall of Saint-Cyr-sur-Loire in 1920. La Béchellerie is not open to visitors.

Tours. The city's most famous literary son is Balzac ◊, who was born here in 1799. The house in which he was born was destroyed by air raids in the Second World War, but his parents shortly afterwards moved to **53 rue Nationale** (then the rue d'Indre et Loire) which still stands. Henry James (◊ Paris) describes Tours in some detail at the beginning of his *A Little Tour in France*, 1885, and seeks out places described by Balzac in his novel *Le Curé de Tours*, 1832.

CENTRE: LOIR-ET-CHER

Blois. The poet Charles d'Orléans (1394–1465), nephew of Charles VI, returned to France in 1440 after his long imprisonment in England following the Battle of Agincourt. In about 1450 he settled in the **Château de Blois** and stayed here for most of the rest of his life. The Château became a literary and artistic centre – François Villon was a participant in one of Charles's poetry competitions (his contribution is included in the personal manuscript, still extant, which Charles kept of his own work and that of the other poets in his circle).

Wordsworth (◊ Rhône–Alpes) lived in Blois for part of his 'residence' in France in 1791–92 – it was the home town of Annette Vallon, by whom he had a daughter.

Couture-sur-Loir. Just outside this village is **Le Manoir de la Possonnière**, the birthplace and childhood home of France's greatest Renaissance poet and the leader of La Pléiade (see under Paris, Latin Quarter). The precise place of birth of Pierre de Ronsard (1524–85) was probably in one of the several buildings which used to stand beside the manor house and which no longer exist. Le Manoir itself, however, is well preserved. It was acquired and rebuilt by Ronsard's father at the beginning of the 16th century – you can still see the inscriptions with which he adorned the façade (in praise of reason and philosophy, love of life, fear of death, the all-seeing eye of God, etc) – part in Latin and part in French, reflecting the cultural transition taking place at the time. In his adult life, Ronsard revisited his first home frequently (it was inherited by his brother), and the natural beauty of the Loir Valley continued to provide inspiration for his odes and sonnets. The house may be visited, but opening times are limited so check in advance.

Ronsard was baptised in the **church** at Couture, and his parents were buried there – their tomb was vandalized during the Revolution, but you can still see their damaged effigies under the northwestern clock tower. Just outside Couture is the site of the **Île Verte** (signposted), a small island formed by the confluence of the Loir and the Braye where Ronsard wrote that he would like to buried – still a spot of moving natural beauty (he was in fact buried at the priory of Saint-Cosme – see above, under Indre-et-Loire). The **fontaine Bellerie**, however, another of the spots Ronsard most loved in his native countryside (see his ode 'À la Fontaine Bellerie' – 'O Fontaine Bellerie/Belle Fontaine chérie . . .'), is now no more than a farmyard pond and probably best left undiscovered. The **forêt de Gâtine**, to the south of Couture and near the priory of Croixval (one of the two priories he received in 1565–66), is also much reduced from the days when Ronsard used to wander under its trees. The process of reduction had begun even then and Ronsard expressed his distress with characteristic lyricism in his poem 'Contre les Bûcherons de la Forêt de Gastine' ('Against the woodcutters of Gastine Forest'), calling on the woodcutter to pause for thought: 'Ne vois-tu

pas le sang, lequel dégoutte à force/Des nymphes qui vivaient dessous la dure écorce?' ('Do you not see the blood, which drains freely from the nymphs who lived beneath the hard bark?'). See also his earlier ode 'À la Forêt de Gastine', in which he sings the praises of the forest's leafy solitude as a source of his poetic inspiration.

Talcy. The **Château de Talcy** dates from the 13th century, but was considerably modified and reconstructed by the Florentine banker Bernardo Salviati who acquired it in 1517. Herein lies the literary association – it was at the Château in 1545 that Ronsard met and fell in love with Salviati's daughter Cassandre – the Cassandre to whom he dedicated the sonnets of *Les Amours*, 1552. The Château may be visited, but is closed out of season.

Vendôme. Ronsard's residence here was in the **rue St-Jacques**, and the site is marked by a bust of the poet. In the **Parc Ronsard** is the impressive school building which once housed the **Collège des Oratoriens**, founded in the 17th century. Balzac was sent to the school when he was eight, and was a pupil here for some six years.

CENTRE: CHER

La Chapelle d'Angillon. Birthplace of Alain-Fournier ◊. There is a museum dedicated to his memory here (**Le Musée Permanent Alain-Fournier**).

Épineuil-le-Fleuriel. This is the village where Alain-Fournier spent his childhood, and which is the model for the fictional 'Sainte-Agathe' in *Le Grand Meaulnes*, 1913 (*Le Grand Meaulnes*, 1959). The village and surrounding area are redolent with echoes of the novel in place names, locations, etc. Of special interest is the **Musée-École d'Alain-Fournier**. This is the humble school-building where Fournier's father taught and where the family lived. It still functions as a school, but a small museum has been established which meticulously recreates the settings and atmosphere so memorably evoked in *Le Grand Meaulnes*. You can visit here the classroom where M Fournier (M Seurel in the novel) taught, and where Le Grand Meaulnes and François Seurel were students; the small kitchen where Mme Fournier prepared the evening meals watched by her son (as would François Seurel – see Extract 2); and the little attic room where Alain-Fournier slept as a child, and which is described in detail in the book: 'We slept in a big garrett, half bedroom, half attic. Other rooms provided for assistant masters had regular windows; no one knew why ours had only a dormer. The door scraped the floor and would not shut properly. When we went upstairs at night, shielding the candle from the draughts that pervaded the big house, we would try again to close the door and again have to give up the attempt. And all through the night we could feel, like a presence, the silence that overflowed the three lofts and came creeping into our room.' In the other attic rooms, exhibits include class photos, desks of the period, and similar memorabilia.

The village of Épineuil-le-Fleuriel, although now much more populous, has not changed much since the time of the novel and several names and places can be picked out as you walk along the streets. The neighbouring area also contains names which will ring bells – not least the town of **Meaulne** (without the 's'). **L'Association des Amis de Jacques Rivière et d'Alain-Fournier** (31 rue Arthur-Petit, 78220 Viroflay) organizes an annual tour (in French) retracing the steps of Le Grand Meaulnes.

CENTRE: LOIRET

Meung-sur-Loire. 'On the first Monday of April 1625, the market town of Meung, the birthplace of the author of

the *Roman de la Rose*, was in a wild state of excitement.' So begins *Les Trois Mousquetaires*, 1844 (*The Three Musketeers*, 1952), the opening scenes of which are set here. The town is indeed the birthplace of Jean de Meung (?– 1305), who continued *Le Roman de la Rose* which had been begun by Guillaume de Lorris earlier in the 13th century. The poet François Villon was imprisoned in the episcopal prison in Meung in 1461 (the reason is unknown, but Villon was no stranger to trouble). He refers to the incarceration ordered by the Bishop of Orléans – Thibault d'Aussingy – in the opening stanza of *Le Testament* ('The Last Will and Testament of François Villon' in *Poems* – see Booklist). He wrote his 'Epistre à ses amis' ('Epistle' in *Poems*) while in prison in Meung ('Will you leave poor Villon here?').

Orléans. Joan of Arc, Maid of Orléans, overshadows all other associations here, thanks to her relief of the city from English siege in 1429. However, Orléans was also the birthplace of dramatist, poet and essayist Charles Péguy (1873–1914). Perhaps not surprisingly, Joan finds a prominent place in his work, inspiring both his dramatic trilogy *Jeanne d'Arc*, 1897, and his long religious poem *Le Mystère de la charité de Jeanne d'Arc*, 1910 (*The Mystery of the Charity of Joan of Arc*, 1986). The **Centre Charles Péguy**, which includes an extensive collection of his manuscripts and correspondence, is at 11 rue du Tabour.

The **Musée des Beaux-Arts**, rue Louis-Roguet, includes work by Max Jacob (see below).

Saint-Benoît-sur-Loire. The restored Romanesque **church** here dates from the 11th century and is the sole survivor of the Benedictine abbey of Fleury (founded in the 7th century). Following his conversion to Christianity, the poet and painter Max Jacob (1876–1944) left Montmartre and came to Saint-Benoît for long periods of solitude, praying, and working on his poetry and his gouaches (paintings in opaque pigments). Attracted both by the peaceful surroundings and primarily by the solace and solitude offered by the ancient church, he first lived here from 1921 until 1928, when he returned to Paris. He moved permanently to Saint-Benoît in 1936 (to **63 rue Orléanaise**), but, being of Jewish origin, was arrested by the Germans during the war and incarcerated at Drancy, where he died from pneumonia. There is a plaque in the church, which reads 'Ici priait le poète Max Jacob'. He is buried in the **cemetery** at Saint-Benoît.

CENTRE: EURE-ET-LOIR

La Beauce. Rabelais provides an explanation of how this region got its name – Extract 1. With its vast agricultural plain, largely devoted to wheat, the Beauce provided an ideal setting for Zola's epic novel of an agricultural community, *La Terre*, 1887 (*The Earth*, 1980). In 1886 he visited **Châteaudun** and its surroundings. Near **Cloyes-sur-le-Loir** he found the village of **Romilly-sur-Aigre**, which became the model for the fictional community of Rognes in the novel – 'Of the little village of Rognes, built on the slope, there could be glimpsed only a few rooftops, huddled round the church whose tall steeple, of grey stone, provided a venerable haunt for families of rooks. And to the east, beyond the Loir where the chief town of the canton, Cloyes, lay concealed five miles away, the low hills of the Perche rose up in the distance, purple against the slate-grey sky. This was formerly the region of Dunois which nowadays formed part of the administrative district of Châteaudun: lying between Perche and the extreme edge of Beauce, its poor fertility had earned for it the title of the bad lands.'

Brou. 'And, in the sweeping of the wind, your ear/The passage of the Angels' wings will hear,/And on the lichen-crusted leads above/The rustle of the eternal rain of love.' You can see here the **church**, originally built in the 12th century, of Matthew Arnold's 'The Church of Brou', 1853. Although topographically inexact, placing the church in forested hills instead of on an open plain (Arnold based his description on an essay in French by Edgar Quinet), the poem is among his most successful. An admirer of the verses, Henry James tells of his visit to Brou in his *A Little Tour in France*, 1884, and how he was not put off by finding the church not quite where Arnold had led him to expect it – ' "So sleep, forever sleep, O princely pair!" I remembered that line of Matthew Arnold's and the stanza about the Duchess Margaret coming to watch the builders on her palfry white. Then there came to me something in regard to the moon shining on winter nights through the cold clere-story. The tone of the place at that hour was not at all lunar; it was cold and bright, but with the chill of an autumn morning; yet this, even with the fact of the unexpected remoteness of the church from the Jura added to it, did not prevent me from feeling that I looked at a monument in the production of which – or at least in the effect of which on the tourist mind of to-day – Matthew Arnold had been much concerned.'

Chartres. The **cathedral** is elaborately evoked in *La Cathédrale*, 1898 (*The Cathedral*, 1989), the third in the autobiographical series of four novels by J.-K. Huysmans (1848–1907) charting the spiritual progress of his protagonist Durtal. Henry Adams (1838–1918) also studies the cathedral in detail in his *Mont-Saint-Michel and Chartres*, 1904. 'For a first visit to Chartres,' he writes, 'choose some pleasant morning when the lights are soft, for one wants to be welcome, and the cathedral has moods, at times severe.' Fellow American and novelist Sherwood Anderson (1876–1941) spent several reflective days sitting with a friend in front of the church, watching life go on 'in the same tragic comic sweet way', musing on transience and continuity in the shade of the great building. In his autobiographical *A Story Teller's Story*, 1924, he writes, 'In the presence of the beautiful old church one was only more aware, all art could do no more than that – make people, like my friend and myself, more aware. An American girl put her face against the beautiful door of Chartres Cathedral and wept for her lost lover. What had been in the hearts of the workmen who once leaned over the same door carving it? They were fellows who had imaginations that flamed up. "Always wood for carvers to carve, always little flashing things to stir the souls of painters, always the tangle of human lives for the tale-tellers to mull over, dream over," I told myself.'

Illiers-Combray. In Proust's ◊ *À la recherche du temps perdu*, 1913–27 (*Remembrance of Things Past*, 1981), fictional Combray is the native town of the narrator Marcel's family, and the place where he spends his holidays as a child. His childhood days at Combray are evoked by the famous madeleine dipped in tea (Extract 3), through which the town, its streets and houses, its atmosphere, and its people come back to him in vivid detail. In Combray, Marcel stays at the house of his aunt Léonie, who is confined to her bedroom. In the surrounding countryside, he and his parents have two favourite walks, in different directions, which take on considerable symbolic significance for the narrator – 'Swann's way', in the direction of the estate at Tansonville (fictional) of Charles Swann and Odette and their daughter Gilberte; and the 'Guermantes way', in the direction of the château of the aristocratic Guermantes family.

Proust's places and people are intricately drawn from such a variety of real-life sources that it is difficult to be confident about specific Proustian con-

nections. However, there is no dispute that Combray is closely modelled on the real-life market town of Illiers near Chartres – so much so that in 1971, the centenary year of Proust's birth, fiction merged with reality when Illiers became Illiers-Combray. When he was a child, Proust came to Illiers several times with his parents at Easter and during the summer holidays. The family stayed in the house of his Aunt Amiot and her husband Jules, a successful tradesman, at 4 rue du Saint-Esprit, now **rue du Docteur-Proust**, the street since renamed in honour of his father. His visits ended when he suffered his first asthma attack at the age of nine – he returned in 1886 to attend his aunt's funeral, but the gardens and countryside he had played in as a child, with their abundance of asthma-inducing ingredients, were now closed to him.

Like tante Léonie in the novel, Proust's aunt was an invalid who lived mainly in her upstairs rooms. In Ernestine, the Amiots' cook, Proust found the principal inspiration for the character of Léonie's cook Françoise, with her memorable kitchen, full of wonders for the imaginative child. His memories of the house and its occupants, as well as many specific locations in the town of Illiers and its surroundings inspired his incomparably evocative descriptions in the opening 'Combray' chapter of *Du côté de chez Swann* (*Swann's Way*). Needless to say, little madeleine cakes are readily available from the local *boulangeries*.

In the 1970s La Société des Amis de Marcel Proust undertook extensive renovation of the house, and restored it according to the descriptions in *À la recherche*. Today's visitors to **La Maison de tante Léonie**, therefore, share the childhood memories of Marcel the narrator, rather than those of Marcel Proust – for it is the fiction that has shaped its present reality. As in the novel, the house has two entrances – the front door looking on to the rue du Docteur-Proust (rue Saint-Jacques in the book – 'monotonous and grey, with the three high sandstone steps before almost every one of its doors'), and the other at the end of the garden, accessible from **place Lemoine**. Through the latter Swann entered when he visited: Proust remembered in his creation of Léonie's house the garden gate with its little grill and the two contrasting bells of the Amiots – the loud jangling one which sounded automatically when one of the family entered and the visitors' bell – 'On those evenings when, as we sat in front of the house round the iron table beneath the big chestnut-tree, we heard, from the far end of the garden, not the shrill and assertive alarm bell which assailed and deafened with its ferruginous, interminable, frozen sound any member of the household who set it off on entering "without ringing", but the double tinkle, timid, oval, golden, of the visitors' bell, everyone would at once exclaim "A visitor! Who in the world can it be!" but they knew quite well that it could only be M. Swann.' In the house itself, you can see carefully recreated the kitchen of Françoise, laid out as described in the novel – 'overflowing with the offerings of the dairyman, the fruiterer, the greengrocer'; the dining room, where the 'big hanging lamp . . . well acquainted with my family and the dish of stewed beef, shed the same light as on every other evening'; the wooden staircase – 'That hateful staircase, up which I always went so sadly, gave out a smell of varnish which had, as it were, absorbed and crystallised the special quality of sorrow that I felt each evening . . .'; Léonie's bedroom, where she used to give Marcel the little shell-shaped madeleine cakes dipped in lime tea; and of course the room in which Marcel himself stayed, complete with its magic lantern – 'Someone had indeed had the happy idea of giving me, to distract me on evenings when I seemed abnormally wretched, a magic lantern, which used to be set on top of my lamp while we waited for dinner-time to come; and, after the fashion of the master-builders and glass-painters of the day, it substi-

tuted for the opaqueness of my walls an impalpable iridescence, supernatural phenomena of many colours, in whch legends were depicted as on a shifting and transitory window.' In the garden, the '*orangerie*' houses an exhibition of photographs by Paul Nadar of Proust's friends, relations, and acquaintances, many of whom were part-models for the characters of his novel – including Charles Haas, reputedly the principal model for Swann. The adjoining building, formerly l'épicerie Legué (Camus in the novel), has been turned into a **museum**, with photos, books, and various papers and documents recalling Proust's life.

Among the other Proustian connections of Illiers-Combray and its surroundings, far too numerous to mention here in their totality, are the following. **L'Église Saint-Jacques** becomes in the novel L'Église Saint-Hilaire – 'It was the steeple of Saint-Hilaire that shaped and crowned and consecrated every occupation, every hour of the day, every view in the town.' At **1 rue du Docteur-Proust** is the house once occupied by Mme Goupil, who appears under her own name in the novel and whose comings and goings tante Léonie watches from her window. The draper's shop of Jules Amiot was in the **market-place**. The fictional village of Méséglise is named after **Méréglise**, about 5 km out of Illiers (the 'Méséglise way' is the same as Swann's way, since to get there you had to pass Swann's estate). Tansonville is named after a small château about 3 km from Illiers. The *parc* of Tansonville was inspired by a garden owned by Jules Amiot, which he opened to the public, called the **Pré-Catelan** after the park in the Bois de Boulogne – it still exists in Illiers and may be visited. Among the models for the château of the Guermantes was the château at **Saint-Éman** – the walk from Illiers to Saint-Éman along the river recalls Proust's description of the 'Guermantes way'. (For a scholarly and extensive analysis of the relationship of Illiers and

its environs to Combray and its environs, see George Painter, *Marcel
Proust*.)

Le Musée Marcel-Proust and **La
Maison de tante Léonie** are at 4, rue du
Docteur Proust, 28120 Illiers-Combray.

BOOKLIST

*For most of the extracted works, the
original publisher in English can be found
in 'Acknowledgments and Citations' at
the end of the volume, as can the exact
location of the extracts and the editions
from which they are taken. The date in
square brackets is that of the original
publication of the work in its original
language. For additional titles by the authors highlighted in this chapter and for
recommended biographies, see 'Lives and
Works'.*

Adams, Henry, *Mont-Saint-Michel and
Chartres* [1904], Constable, Lon-
don, 1950/Viking Penguin, New
York, 1986.
Alain-Fournier, *Le Grand Meaulnes*
[1913], Frank Davison, trans, Pen-
guin, London and New York,
1966. **Extract 2.**
Anderson, Sherwood, *A Story Teller's
Story* [1924], Buccaneer Books,
Cutchogue, NY, 1990.
Arnold, Matthew, *The Poems of Matth-
ew Arnold*, Kenneth Allott, ed,
Longman, London, 1965.
Balzac, Honoré de, *The Lily in the
Valley* [1835], Carroll and Graf,
New York, 1989.
Dumas, Alexandre, *The Three Mus-
keteers* [1844], Lord Sudley, trans,
Penguin, London, 1982/Viking
Penguin, New York, 1982.
Flaubert–Sand: The Correspondence,
Francis Steegmuller and Barbara
Bray, trans, Harvill, London,
1993.
Genet, Jean, *The Miracle of the Rose*
[1946], B. Frechtman, trans, Pen-

guin, London, 1971/Grove Press,
New York, 1988.
Huysmans, J.-K., *The Cathedral*
[1898], David Blon, trans, De-
dalus, Sawtry, 1989.
Jacob, Max, *Double Life and Other
Pieces*, M. Bullock, trans, Oasis,
London, 1989.
Jacob, Max, *Hesitant Fire: Selected Pro-
se*, M. Black and M. Green, trans,
University of Nebraska Press,
1992.
James, Henry, *A Little Tour in France*
[1885], Penguin, London and New
York, 1985.
Montaigne, Michel de *The Complete
Works of Montaigne: Essays, Travel
Journal, Letters*, Donald M. Frame,
trans, Hamish Hamilton, London,
1958/Stanford University Press,
Stanford, CA, 1957.
Péguy, Charles, *The Mystery of the
Charity of Joan of Arc* [1910],
adapted by Jean-Paul Lucet, Jeffrey
Wainwright, trans, Carcanet,
Manchester, 1986.
Proust, Marcel, *Remembrance of Things
Past* [1913–1927], C.K. Scott
Moncrieff and Terence Kilmartin,
trans, Penguin, London and New
York, 1983. Vol 1 – *Swann's Way*
and *Within a Budding Grove*; Vol 2
– *The Guermantes Way* and *Cities of
the Plain*; Vol 3 – *The Captive*, *The
Fugitive*, and *Time Regained*. **Ex-
tract 3.**
Rabelais, François, *Gargantua and Pan-
tagruel* [1532–64], J.M. Cohen,
trans, Penguin, London and New
York, 1955. **Extract 1.**

Romance of the Rose, The, F. Horgan, trans, Oxford University Press, Oxford, 1994/L. Dahlberg, trans, Princeton University Press, Princeton, NJ, 1995.

Ronsard, Pierre de, *Songs and Sonnets of Pierre de Ronsard*, Hyperion, Westport, CT, 1985.

Ruskin, John, *The Diaries of John Ruskin, 1835–1847*, selected and edited by Joan Evans and John Howard Whitehouse, Oxford University Press, Oxford, 1956, p 87. **Extract 5.**

Sand, George, *The Devil's Pool and François the Waif* [1846 and 1850], Dent, London, undated.

Sand, George, *The Master Pipers* [1853], Rosemary Lloyd, trans, Oxford University Press, Oxford, 1994/Oxford University Press, New York, 1994. **Extract 4.**

Sand, George, *My Life*, Dan Hofstadter, ed and trans, Victor Gollancz, London, 1979. (Selections from *Histoire de ma vie*.)

Stevenson, Robert Louis, *Travels with a Donkey* [1879], in *Travels with a Donkey, An Inland Voyage, The Sil-*

verado Squatters, Everyman, London, 1993.

Tindall, Gillian, *Célestine: Voices from a French Village* [1995], Minerva, London, 1996/H. Holt, New York, 1996.

Tindall, Gillian, *Countries of the Mind: The Meaning of Place to Writers*, Hogarth Press, London, 1991/Northeastern University Press, Boston, MA, 1991.

Trollope, Anthony, 'The Château of Prince Polignac', in *Tales of All Countries, First Series* [1861], Penguin, London and New York, 1993. **Extract 6.**

Villon, François, *Poems*, Beram Saklatvala, trans, Everyman's Library, J.M. Dent, London, 1968. (Verse translations, partially with French originals.)

Wharton, Edith, *A Motor-Flight Through France* [1908], Picador, London, 1995/Northern Illinois University Press, Williston, IL, 1991.

Zola, Émile, *The Earth* [1887], Douglas Parmée, trans, Penguin, London and New York, 1980.

Extracts

(1) La Beauce

François Rabelais, *Gargantua and Pantagruel*

Rabelais explains for his readers the origins of La Beauce, now a region of vast prairies in the north west of the Département of Loiret.

The next day – after drinking as you will understand – they started on their way, Gargantua, his tutor Ponocrates, and his servants, together with the young page Eudemon; and as the weather was calm and temperate Grandgousier had dun-coloured boots made for his son; Babin calls them buskins.

So they passed joyfully along the highway, always in high spirits till they came above Orléans, at which place there was a great forest a hundred and five miles long and fifty-one miles wide, or thereabouts. This forest was horribly abundant and copiously swarming with ox-flies and hornets, so that it was an absolute brigands' lair for the poor mares, asses, and horses. But Gargantua's mare handsomely avenged all the outrages ever perpetrated there on the beasts of her kind, by a trick of which they had not the slightest inkling beforehand. As soon as they had entered this forest and the hornets had opened their attack she threw out her tail, and at her first skirmish swatted them so completely that she swept down the whole wood. Crossways and lengthways, here and there, this way and that, to front and to side, over and under, she swept down the trees as a mower does the grass, so that since that time there has been neither wood nor hornets, and the whole country has been reduced to a plain.

At the sight of this Gargantua felt very great delight. But the only boast he made was to say to his people: 'I find this fine.' (*Je trouve beau ce*); from which saying the country has ever afterwards been called La Beauce. But all they got for breakfast was empty air; in memory of which to this day the gentlemen of La Beauce break their fast on yawns, do very well by it, and spit the better for it.

(2) ÉPINEUIL-LE-FLEURIEL (CHER)

Alain-Fournier, *Le Grand Meaulnes*

Fournier bases his fictional village of Sainte-Agathe on Épineuil-le-Fleuriel, where he spent his childhood. The school in Sainte-Agathe is closely based on the school where his father taught and which was his home – it is still there and may be visited. The 'ailment' mentioned at the beginning of this extract was a weak knee.

The advent of Augustin Meaulnes, coinciding as it did with my recovery from this ailment, marked the beginning of a new life.

Before he came, when classes were over at four o'clock, an evening of solitude would stretch out before me. My father would carry the hot coals from the class-room stove to the dining-room fireplace; and one by one belated pupils would desert the chilling school-room where wisps of smoke still lingered. A few last games and capers out in the yard – then night. The two pupils whose turn it had been to sweep out the class-rooms would reach down their hooded capes from pegs under the playground roof and with their baskets hung over their arm race away, leaving the gate ajar . . .

Then, as long as a glimmer of daylight remained, I would go into the part of the building which comprised the Town Hall and sit tucked away in a corner of the Public Records office with its dead flies and flapping posters. I sat with a book on an old weighing-machine near a window overlooking the garden.

When night had set in, when the dogs in the neighbouring farmyard began to howl and a light showed through the window of our little kitchen I would go back. My mother was now seeing to preparations for supper. Mounting two or three steps of the stairway that led to the attic from the narrow kitchen, I would sit down without a word, my head pressed against the cold banisters, and watch her by the flickering light of a candle as she got her fire to draw.

But someone came and put an end to all these mild and childish pleasures. Someone blew out the candle which illumined for me the sweet natural face bent over the evening meal. Someone extinguished the lamp around which we had been a happy family group at night-time when my father had closed all the wooden shutters. And that someone was Augustin Meaulnes, whom in no time the other boys began to call *le grand Meaulnes*.

(3) ILLIERS-COMBRAY

Marcel Proust, *Swann's Way*

In the opening pages of this, the first volume of À la recherche du temps perdu, the novel's most famous incident occurs. The taste of a piece of madeleine cake dipped in tea brings to the narrator a flood of memories of his childhood in Combray, a fictional town closely based on real-life Illiers, now fused in name as well as memory with its Proustian counterpart and re-named Illiers-Combray.

And suddenly the memory revealed itself. The taste was that of the little piece of madeleine which on Sunday mornings at Combray (because on those mornings I did not go out before mass), when I used to say good morning to her in her bedroom, my aunt Léonie used to give me, dipping it first in her own cup of tea or tisane. The sight of the little madeleine had recalled nothing to my mind before I tasted it; perhaps because I had so often seen such things in the meantime, without tasting them, on the trays in pastry cooks' windows, that their image had dissociated itself from those Combray days to take its place among others more recent; perhaps because of those memories, so long abandoned and put out of mind, nothing now survived, everything was scattered; the shapes of things, including that of the little scallop-shell of pastry, so richly sensual under its severe, religious folds, were either obliterated or had been so long dormant as to have lost the power of expansion which would have allowed them to resume their place in my consciousness. But when from a long-distant past nothing subsists, after the people are dead, after the things are broken and scattered, taste and smell alone, more fragile but more enduring, more unsubstantial, more persistent, more faithful, remain poised for a long time, like souls, remembering, waiting, hoping, amid the ruins of all the rest; and bear unflinchingly, in the tiny and almost impalpable drop of their essence, the vast structure of recollection.

And as soon as I had recognized the taste of the piece of madeleine soaked in her decoction of lime-blossom which my aunt used to give me (although I did not yet know and must long postpone the discovery of why this memory made me so happy) immediately the old grey house upon the street, where her room was, rose up like a stage set to attach itself to the little pavilion opening on to the garden which had been built out behind it for my parents (the isolated segment which until that moment had been all that I could see); and with the house the town, from morning to night and all weathers, the Square where I used to be sent before lunch, the streets along which I used to run errands, the country roads we took when it was fine. And as in the game wherein the Japanese amuse themselves by filling a porcelain bowl with water and steeping in it little pieces of paper which until then are without character or form, but, the moment they become wet, stretch and twist and take on colour and distinctive shape, become flowers or houses or people, solid and recognisable, so in that moment all the flowers in our garden and in M. Swann's park, and the water-lilies on the Vivonne and the good folk of the village and their little dwellings and the parish church and the whole of Combray and its surroundings, taking shape and solidity, sprang into being, town and gardens alike, from my cup of tea.

(4) NOHANT

George Sand, *The Master Pipers*

> *The significance of folk-art, specifically music, in the life of rural France is a key theme of Sand's pastoral novel. Here, the (male) narrator describes the unexpected skill of Huriel, a mule-driver from the neighbouring Bourbonnais region who arrives unexpectedly at midsummer festivities in Nohant in Berri (Nohant was Sand's own home village).*

'Very well, Brulette!' I said with a sigh. 'It'll be as you want it. I'll do all in my power not to love you any more, just as you command, and, whatever happens, I'll be a good relative and a good friend to you, as it's my duty to be.'

She took my hand and, delighting in making her beaux run after her, she ran with me to the town square, where already the old people of the area had piled up logs and straw for the midsummer fire. Since she was the first to arrive, Brulette was asked to light the fire, and soon the flames rose up higher than the church door.

But we had no music to dance by, until Carnat's son, whose name was François, arrived with his bagpipes. He didn't have to be asked twice to help us out, for he, too, had a soft spot for Brulette, just like the rest of us.

We began dancing joyfully, but after a few minutes, everyone complained that the music was no good. François Carnat was still too much of a beginner, and we couldn't get into the rhythm. He didn't mind being teased, and kept going, happy to have a chance to practise, for I think it was the first time he played in public.

But that didn't suit anyone, and when we saw that the dance, instead of refreshing legs that were already weary, merely made them exhausted, there was talk of either going home or of the men going to finish off the evening in a tavern. Brulette and the other girls protested, calling us tipplers and louts; and we were in the middle of debating all this when suddenly a tall, good-looking chap appeared among us, before we'd even seen what direction he came from.

'Well then, boys and girls!' he called out, in a voice so loud it covered all the din we were making and was heard by every single one of us. 'Do you still want to dance? Well, cheer up. Here's a piper who's happened by, and who'll give you as much music as you like. What's more, he'll not even take any money from you for his services. Give me that,' he said to François Carnat, 'and listen to me. You may find it useful, for even if I'm not a musician by trade, I know a little more about it than you do.'

(5) LE PUY

John Ruskin, *Diary of 1840*

Ruskin spent a few days in Le Puy during his travels on the continent in 1840. Although not impressed with his accommodation ('abominable inn, all filth and lime dust'), he found much to please his artistic, architectural, and geological interest. At the time, the main industry in Le Puy was the manufacture of lace — hence the reference to lace on the locals' caps.

October 12th. LE PUY. Out sketching; got three capital subjects. Then up after dinner to basaltic beds above town, well formed, containing zircon in considerable quantity, well crystallized. The view glorious. Scrambled up a range of terraces of vineyard to the foot of the range; the crumbling basalt very slippery. Rolling grey clouds far over the east, with crests of rose colour shadowing the heaving hills; the town in full light, a little scattery in effect, but very bright. Chatted with some women and boys gathering their last grapes; one handsome boy playing very badly, but very merrily, on a kind of flageolet; the girls frank, and simple – a little, what we should call in England, bold, but it was mere manner. Much marvelling among them as to who we could be; guessed us for Parisians at first, then for Russians. We told them to try again, on which the youngest suggesting 'de la Normandie' raised a general laugh, so I suppose it was wit; on being told we were English, they came round to ask questions about the climate and country and manufactures, pointing to the lace on their caps as of their own making. Left them much delighted by the present of a franc; they said they would dance at our departure. The walls of the great road are chiefly made of basalt bricks, and the columns are put to every kind of use. They will carry the hill away in time. Curious picture in the Cathedral of eight gentlemen in red, on their knees, looking very fiercely out of the canvas; a ninth member of the family, naked, with an arrow stuck in his breast, and another in his back, taking the eighth affectionately round the neck and introducing him to a little grinning cherub, who is holding fast on by the cord of the window curtain, and kicking up his left leg in a manner much more energetic than decent, pointing at the same time over his shoulder and winking on the whole family; could not make it out. The architecture singularly mixed, but chiefly circular – Norman – with diamond ornament. The streets rich in effect, arched beneath, and dark with projecting roof. The place would take a month to sketch.

(6) Le Puy/Château de Polignac

Anthony Trollope, *The Château of Prince Polignac*

Trollope's humorous short story was written in France in 1859. The settings are Le Puy, which he describes in some detail, and the ruins of the 13–14th century Château de Polignac, about 5 km west of the town. Here, M Lacordaire takes the Englishwoman Mrs Thompson on a trip to the Château and prepares to pop the question.

And then they started. The road from Le Puy to Polignac is nearly all up hill; and a very steep hill it is, so that there was plenty of time for conversation. But the girls had it nearly all to themselves. Mimmy thought that she had never found M Lacordaire so stupid; and Lilian told her sister on the first safe opportunity that occurred, that it seemed very much as though they were all going to church.

'And do any of the Polignac people still live at this place?' asked Mrs Thompson, by way of making conversation; in answer to which M Lacordaire informed madame that the place was at present only a ruin; and then there was again silence till they found themselves under the rock, and were informed by the driver that the rest of the ascent must be made on foot.

The rock now stood abrupt and precipitous above their heads. It was larger in its circumference and with much larger space on its summit than those other volcanic rocks in and close to the town; but then at the same time it was higher from the ground, and quite as inaccessible except by the single path which led up to the château.

M Lacordaire, with conspicuous gallantry, first assisted Mrs Thompson from the carriage, and then handed down the two young ladies. No lady could have been so difficult to please as to complain of him, and yet Mrs Thompson thought that he was not as agreeable as usual. Those horrid boots and those horrid gloves gave him such an air of holiday finery that neither could he be at his ease wearing them, nor could she, in seeing them worn.

They were soon taken in hand by the poor woman whose privilege it was to show the ruins. For a little distance they walked up the path in single file; not that it was too narrow to accommodate two, but M Lacordaire's courage had not yet been screwed to a point which admitted of his offering his arm to the widow. For in France, it must be remembered, that this means more than it does in some other countries.

Mrs Thompson felt that all this was silly and useless. If they were not to be dear friends this coming out fêteing together, those boots and gloves and new hat were all very foolish; and if they were, the sooner that they understood each other the better. So Mrs Thompson, finding that the path was steep and the weather warm, stood still for a while leaning against the wall, with a look of considerable fatigue in her face.

'Will madame permit me the honour of offering her my arm?' said M Lacordaire. 'The road is so extraordinarily steep for madame to climb.'

Lives and works of extracted writers

ALAIN-FOURNIER (1886–1914). Alain-Fournier (real name Henri-Alban Fournier) was born in **La Chapelle d'Angillon** (Cher). He spent his childhood in the village of **Épineuil-le-Fleuriel**, which is the model for 'Sainte-Agathe' in *Le Grand Meaulnes* (see introduction). He finished his education in **Paris**, where he became a close friend of essayist and novelist Jacques Rivière (1886–1925), secretary and later director of the *Nouvelle Revue Française* (Rivière married Fournier's sister, Isabelle). His correspondence with Rivière between 1905 and 1914 has been published (selections are available in translation in *Towards the Lost Domain*, 1986). Fournier failed to get his *agrégation* – perhaps because he was distracted by writing, by his participation in Parisian literary circles (he was one of the many modern writers and artists who attended Paul Fort's weekly literary meetings at the **Closerie des Lilas**), and by his love for Yvonne de Quiévrecourt, a woman he met briefly and then did not see again until she was married (she was the model for Yvonne de Galais in *Le Grand Meaulnes*). Consequently, he spent some time in London in a clerical job and had turned to journalism in Paris by the outbreak of the First World War. Alain-Fournier was an early casualty of the conflict – he was killed in September 1914.

Le Grand Meaulnes, 1913 (*Le Grand Meaulnes*, 1959), first published in the *Nouvelle Revue Française*, is Fournier's great claim to fame. It is a haunting story of the passage from adolescence to adulthood of two schoolfriends, told in the sad, elegiac tones of one of the boys grown up. The novel plays with boys' love of mystery and magic, drawing its readers in and out of reality and making them experience the dreams and dis-appointments of its characters. At its core is the quest of Meaulnes to find again the 'lost domain' he accidentally stumbles on and the beautiful girl he falls in love with there. As the novel develops, and the boys grow up, they discover that there is a rational explanation for everything and inevitably happiness proves elusive and ideals are lost. This outstanding book is rich in its evocation of rural life and landscape (the changing seasons are always present, time is always seen to be passing). Fournier draws on many autobiographical details and memories of his own past in the villages and countryside of the **Cher** – no doubt the fact that he was remembering his childhood as he spun his tale explains something of its evocative power. The novel was filmed in 1967 as *The Wanderer*.

John Fowles, with whose *The Magus* there are some similarities, has paid homage to the lasting impact and influence of *Le Grand Meaulnes* – 'I learnt to value what I couldn't, over the years, forget. One such obstinate survivor was Alain-Fournier's *Le Grand Meaulnes*. A number of young thesis-writers have now told me they see no significant parallels between *Le Grand Meaulnes* and my own novel, *The Magus*. I must have severed the umbilical cord – the real connection requires such a metaphor – much more neatly than I supposed at the time; or perhaps modern academic criticism is blind to relationships that are far more emotional than structural.'

Recommended biography: W.J. Strachan's edition of Alain-Fournier's 'Letters from London', provides a useful biographical summary and translations of the novelist's correspondence with his family and friends, especially Rivière, during his period in London in 1905 – Alain-Fournier, *Towards the*

Lost Domain: Letters from London, 1905, W.J. Strachan, trans, Carcanet, Manchester, 1986.

BALZAC, Honoré de (1799–1850). Honoré Balzac (the 'de' was an affectation later introduced by his parents and adopted by Balzac himself) was born on 20 May 1799 in **Tours**. When he was eight, he was sent to the extremely demanding and authoritarian Collège des Oratoriens in **Vendôme**, where he was to stay for the next six years. In 1814, his parents took an apartment in **Paris** and Balzac became increasingly acquainted with the city that was to play so large a part in his life and in his life's work, *La Comédie humaine*. In 1816, his schooling over, he was apprenticed to a lawyer, but he soon decided against a career in the law and devoted himself instead to the idea of becoming a writer. In 1818, he was installed by his parents in a garret in Paris, where he spent two years trying to make his way in his chosen career. At this he was unsuccessful, producing nothing of note, and so he subsequently worked as a journalist and hack novelist, writing *genre* novels under pseudonyms. His first major success, with his novel *La Peau de chagrin*, did not come until 1831 (*Wild Ass's Skin*, 1977).

Following his initial failure as a writer, Balzac began on the first of a number of business ventures that were to prove financially disastrous and lead him more and more into debt. A publishing business failed. He started up a printing business, investing more, taking bigger and bigger risks, as that business also went down. Although some of his ideas were in principle sound, implementation was not his strong point and his failure left him in the heavy chains of debt – chains which were to help keep him at his desk, writing ferociously to ameliorate his insolvency. For posterity at least there was some good to come of this: his business failures ensured his staggering output and his enduring reputation.

Balzac's eccentric and punishing work habits have been much documented. He wrote for 10–14 hours every day – he would go to bed at 7 or 8 pm, instruct his servant to wake him at 12 or 1 am, put on his monk's robe made of white cashmere and begin what he called his 'monastic life', working through the night. He used prodigious amounts of strong black coffee to keep himself alert. He did much of his textual revision at proof stage, sending the printer an early draft and incurring huge correction charges and no doubt nervous breakdowns among the compositors with his extensive changes.

Balzac demonstrated a penchant for the older woman more than once – he had a number of liaisons with aristocratic ladies, with one of whom he had a child. His great love, however, was for the Russian countess Madame Hanska with whom he carried on a long and revealing correspondence. He married her near the end of his life in the Ukraine, where he had gone to get away from the revolutionary Paris of 1848 – they married at Berichev in March 1850. On the way back to France, Balzac was taken ill. He died on 18 August 1850, at his home in Paris.

The funeral attracted enormous attention and was a star-studded affair – Victor Hugo and Alexandre Dumas were among the pall bearers. Appropriately, the novelist was buried high up on a hill in **Père Lachaise**, ending up where his character Rastignac starts out on his 'assault' on Parisian society at the end of *Le Père Goriot* – 'Eugène, now alone, walked a few steps to the topmost part of the graveyard. He saw Paris, spread windingly along the two banks of the Seine. Lights were beginning to twinkle. His gaze fixed itself almost avidly on the space between the column in the Place Vendôme and the cupola of Les Invalides. There lived the world into which he had wished to penetrate. He fastened on the murmurous hive a look that seemed already to be sucking the honey from it, and uttered these words: "Now I'm ready for you." '

Touraine, especially **Saché** and the surrounding area, where he found refuge from his troubles, remained a region close to Balzac's heart and it features, as indeed do many other parts of France, in a number of his novels. Among those set in Touraine are *Le Curé de Tours*, 1832, and *Le Lys dans la vallée*, 1835 (*The Lily in the Valley*, 1989), the latter especially drawing on the countryside around Saché. For English readers, one of Balzac's best known works is *Eugénie Grandet*, 1833 (*Eugénie Grandet*, 1955), later to become part of *La Comédie humaine*, set in **Saumur** in neighbouring **Anjou** (see Pays de la Loire, Extract 19). This short and powerful novel revolves around the miserliness of the wealthy Monsieur Grandet and its consequences for his daughter, the eponymous heroine. Life in the small town of Saumur in the 19th century is vividly evoked.

Perhaps the most read of all Balzac's novels is *Le Père Goriot*, 1834 (*Pere Goriot*, 1962), a pessimistic portrait of selfishness, ingratitude and insincerity. Set in the Paris of the early 19th century (see Paris, Extract 12), the novel deals with the cynical machinations of Parisian high society as discovered through the eyes of the young and ambitious Eugène de Rastignac, who was to become one of the key characters in *La Comédie humaine*. Le Père Goriot of the title is a generous and devoted father who sacrifices everything for his ungrateful daughters.

It was during the writing of *Le Père Goriot* that Balzac came upon the idea for *La Comédie humaine*, famously declaring 'J'ai trouvé une idée merveilleuse. Je serai un homme de génie.'('I have had a wonderful idea. I will become a genius.') The *idée merveilleuse* was to link all his books to create a unified whole, with each novel effectively a chapter in the ultimate work. In furtherance of this, many of the characters, both primary and secondary, appear in various novels, some of the key ones, like Rastignac and the criminal Vautrin from *Le Père Goriot*, appearing very frequently at different stages of their lives – Rastignac, for example, shows up in some 23 books. Balzac's output was prolific and *La Comédie humaine* is a vast work (over 2000 characters in 91 books – 137 were planned), a great tapestry in literature of French society at the end of the 18th century and in the first half of the 19th (1789–1850). It is also an analysis of human frailty and motivation – with money as the driving force behind the many dangerous intrigues that run through the novels. In Balzac's world, wealth is power and the fuel of ambition. Subdividing his grand scheme into three major categories of 'Studies' (*Études philosophiques, Études analytiques*, and *Études de mœurs*, the largest category and itself split into subcategories comprising 'Scenes' from private, rural, provincial, political, and military life), Balzac's aim was to provide a systematic and all-embracing analysis of French society – Henry James wrote, 'Balzac, in the maturity of his vision, took in more human life than any one since Shakespeare, who has attempted to tell us stories about it.' (*A Little Tour in France.*)

Recommended biography: Graham Robb, *Balzac*, Picador, London, 1994.

PROUST, Marcel (1871–1922). Proust was born in **Auteuil**, then still a village outside Paris, on 10 July 1871. His parents were upper middle class: his father was a respected physician and his mother, with whom he developed an especially intimate and adoring relationship, was a woman of Jewish descent and of considerable intellect and culture. From the beginning, Proust was physically frail – he almost died at birth. In the spring of 1881, when he was nine, he had his first asthma attack. His formal education at the **Lycée Condorcet** was periodically interrupted by his ill health, but he passed his *baccalauréat* in arts in 1889 and won the *prix d'honneur* for his French

Marcel Proust

essays. After a year's military service at **Orléans** he was back in Paris studying law and political science at the Sorbonne. During the early 1890s, Proust was a regular at various literary *salons*, where he met, among others, Barbusse, Maupassant, and Anatole France. In these early days, he was still absorbing a wealth of information through his wide-ranging literary, artistic and musical interests that would later be put to such memorable use. Meanwhile, he published critical articles, personality portraits, stories, and poems – in various reviews and in the collection *Les Plaisirs et les jours*, 1896 (*Pleasures and Regrets*, 1986). He also worked on *Jean Santeuil*, a novel which he never completed and which was published in 1952 (*Jean Santeuil*, 1985). In his early thirties, Proust studied the work of Ruskin extensively, publishing various articles on him, and ultimately translating, with the help of his mother and his English friend Marie Nordlinger, *The Bible of Amiens* and *Sesame and Lilies* (*La Bible d'Amiens*, 1904, and *Sésame et les lys*, 1906).

Proust's health continued to deteriorate in the early 1900s, the real physical disability perhaps exacerbated by the chronic psychological problem of his reaction to his homosexuality and by the acute crisis of his mother's death in 1905. Gradually retiring from his active social life he became increasingly incapacitated – from around spring 1906 he developed what was to prove his lifelong habit of sleeping during the day and working, and sometimes going out, at night. He spent much of his time in bed, his windows tightly closed against both the noise of the boulevard and the asthma-inducing air. The walls of his Paris apartment were lined with cork for sound-proofing. In his late thirties, Proust began work on *À la recherche du temps perdu*, 1913–27 (*Remembrance of Things Past*, 1981/*In Search of Lost Time*, 1992). He continued to write and rewrite this immense novel for the rest of his life. Between 1914 and 1917 he became a virtual recluse, dedicating himself totally to his writing, even disconnecting his telephone to avoid interruptions.

The first volume of *À la recherche*, *Du côté de chez Swann* (*Swann's Way*), was published in 1913 to mediocre reviews. Over the years, however, it received increasing attention both in France and abroad. When the second volume, *À l'ombre des jeunes filles en fleurs* (*Within a Budding Grove*) – see under Paris, Extract 2 – was published in 1919 his reputation was considerable, and the award of the Prix Goncourt left his standing in no doubt. The year 1919 also saw the publication of *Pastiches et Mélanges*, a collection of pastiches (an art at which Proust excelled and which he uses in *À la recherche*), including his celebrated stylistic homage to Flaubert. In 1920, he was made Chevalier de la Légion d'honneur. Proust completed *À la recherche* in spring 1922, despite his considerable suffering – 'Tonight I wrote the words "The End" . . . now I can die.' He died at his home in Paris on 18 November 1922.

Before his death, two further volumes of his 3000-page novel were published – *Le Côté de Guermantes* (*The*

Guermantes Way) in 1920–21 and *Sodome et Gomorrhe* (*Cities of the Plain*) in 1921–22. The remaining three were published posthumously – *La Prisonnière* (*The Captive*, 1923; *Albertine disparue*, retitled *La Fugitive* (*The Fugitive*), 1925; and *Le Temps retrouvé* (*Time Regained*), 1927. *À la recherche du temps perdu* traces the development of the life of the narrator, Marcel, from childhood to maturity – a maturity crystallized in the climactic realization of his literary vocation with his decision to write the novel we have just read. The narrative is not linear but is in its structure a demonstration of one of the essential preoccupations of the book – the rediscovery of the past through random stimulations in the present, such as the famous tea-soaked Madeleine which at the beginning of the novel carries the narrator back to his childhood (Extract 3). The style recreates the psychological processes of memory – each finely tuned, winding, layered sentence a search in itself through sense, emotion, and intellect. The dominant tone of loss and the portrayal of the overwhelming destructiveness of time in the context of an individual's life are balanced by Proust's demonstration of the preservation of the past in memory, albeit not necessarily easily or rationally accessible, and by the ability of art to capture and conserve past experience. Within this framework, *À la recherche* ranges widely in its themes and subjects – including, among many other things, sexual relationships, both heterosexual and homosexual, the aesthetics of various art forms, the follies of contemporary society, the politics of class, and vividly evocative descriptions of Paris and various parts of provincial France. The canvas is vast and no brief summary can even begin to convey its scope.

For the most part, *À la recherche* is structured around specific, quite short phases of Marcel's life, which are associated with particular predominant settings – a major exception to the subjective narrative is the section 'Un amour de Swann' ('Swann in Love') which goes back to before Marcel's birth and which he tells in the third person. The settings are sometimes fictional and sometimes real – key fictional locations are based closely on real places: **Illiers**, for example, famously provided the model for Combray (see introduction and Extract 3), while Balbec (see under Normandy, Extract 3) is an amalgam of resorts which Proust himself had visited at various stages of his life, principally **Cabourg** in Normandy, but also significantly **Évian** in Haute-Savoie and **Beg-Meil** in Brittany. Many of the key characters too are based closely on people Proust knew – like the fictional settings, they are sometimes modelled on one individual, more often they are amalgams of several people. The fact that the fiction is close to the reality, but is quite clearly fiction, is important – *À la recherche* is a novel not an autobiography, and Marcel the narrator is not Marcel Proust even if his character is informed by Proust's experience. Diggers for the fool's gold of autobiographical interpretation lose the essence of the book and diminish it. In *Contre Sainte-Beuve*, published in 1954 and written in 1909 (*By Way of Sainte-Beuve*, 1958), Proust himself argues against the critical approach which interprets a literary work through the life of its writer.

Finally, a note on the English translations. The translation used for reference and extracts here is the 1981 one by Thomas Kilmartin, which revises the original English version by Scott Moncrieff – it is readily available in a three-volume paperback. This is based on the revised 1954 edition of the novel published under Gallimard's La Pléiade imprint. In 1989, La Pléiade completed the publication of a new definitive edition, taking into account the most recent research findings. A new translation by D.J. Enright, revising Kilmartin's text and including the changes of the 1989 edition, appeared in 1992 under the title *In Search of Lost Time*, a welcome literal rendition of

Proust's title. This latest translation is available in four volumes and is published, at time of writing, only in rather expensive hardback.

Recommended biography: George D. Painter, *Marcel Proust*, Penguin, London, 1990. See also Ronald Hayman, *Proust*, William Heinemann, London, 1990.

RABELAIS, François (?–1553). Very little is known for certain of the life of Rabelais. His father was a lawyer at **Chinon** and Rabelais is said to have been born (possibly in 1494) at nearby **Seuilly** at his father's country house, **La Devinière** (see introduction). In about 1510 Rabelais entered a Franciscan monastery at **Fontenay-le-Comte**. He stayed there until 1524, when he gained permission to join a more liberal Benedictine order at **Maillezais**, so finding release from the oppression of his Franciscan superiors – he had persisted in studying Greek, at that time actively discouraged in the light of a controversial biblical interpretation by Erasmus of the Greek text of St Luke. His monastic life seems to have ended around 1526, and he is thought then to have studied medicine in Paris. In 1531 Rabelais enrolled at the **University of Montpellier**. He lectured and published works on medicine during his spell at the university and subsequently, towards the end of 1532, he practised as a physician in **Lyon**. Around this time also he established an important friendship with Bishop Jean Du Bellay (uncle of the poet Joachim Du Bellay), with whom he travelled to Rome in 1534 and received a pardon from the Pope for leaving holy orders without permission. After spending some time as a secular priest at Du Bellay's abbey, Rabelais resumed his medical studies at Paris and later again at Montpellier, where he obtained a doctorate. In the early 1540s, he lived and worked in Piedmont (for the governor, Jean Du Bellay's brother Guillaume). He returned to Paris, but, with his books on the Sorbonne's 'censored' lists, he left

for Metz and then Rome, where he lived until 1549. In 1551, Rabelais was granted two benefices which must have brought him financial security, but he resigned these in 1553, the year he died.

The five-volume comic extravaganza for which Rabelais is famous is available in modern English translation as *Gargantua and Pantagruel*, 1955. The First Book was published in Lyon in 1532 as *Pantagruel, roi des Dipsodes* under the pen-name of Alcofribas Nasier (an anagram of François Rabelais). Despite censure from the theologians at the Sorbonne, the Second Book, *Gargantua*, the first in the narrative sequence, appeared in 1534. Rabelais, in the spirit so evident in his books, chose attack as his mode of defence – as he sets out in his Prologue to Gargantua (addressed to 'Most noble boozers and you my very esteemed and poxy friends'), there is behind his rumbustious tale 'an individual savour and abstruse teaching which will initiate you into certain very high sacraments and dread mysteries, concerning not only our religion, but also our public and private life.' *Gargantua* was also severely censured and condemned as obscene by those whose views it satirized. In 1546, the Third Book appeared – this too was condemned, on the grounds that it was heretical, despite royal approval by François 1er (encouraged by a dedication to his sister Marguerite de Navarre) and an absence of satire against theologians. In the same year the publisher Étienne Dolet was burned as a heretic. Rabelais himself left Paris and once again relied on the protection of Jean Du Bellay. In 1552 the Fourth Book was published (although the prologue and first 11 chapters had appeared separately four years earlier). It was condemned – it contained anti-papal satire which, at the time of writing, had seemed safe in the light of the new King Henry II's anti-papal policy: however, when the book appeared King and Pope had become reconciled. Whether or not

Rabelais resigned his two parishes because of this and whether or not he spent time in prison are matters of speculation. What is certain is that he died in Paris the following year. The Fifth Book was published posthumously and is considered by most scholars to be of dubious authenticity.

Presumably to some extent because the work was written over such a long timespan, there are great variations in treatment and in character portrayal in the different volumes. They describe the adventures of the giants Gargantua and his son Pantagruel (although in the Third Book Pantagruel seems generally to shrink to normal size) and subsequently of Pantagruel's servant, the roguish Panurge. Rabelais explores the human condition and rails against the laws, social customs, and institutions of his day through laughter. He uses his fantastic tales to set up debates about key issues of the time, drawing on his encyclopaedic knowledge, his vast vocabulary and his facility for parody and invention. Among his targets are war, the clerical establishment, fanaticism, and the education system. He is also, though, and arguably primarily, a great comic writer and is loved for his humanism and his unending celebration of eating and drinking and, in no kind of tension with that hedonism, of learning and the exchange of ideas.

Rabelais creates a cod mythology with which he offers explanations of the origins of places and peoples (see, for example, Extract 1) and much of his action is located in actual French towns and regions, often in his native **Touraine** (although everything is greatly exaggerated in the Rabelasian world, and hamlets become cities). The fictional events themselves may have their origins in fact. The wars between Grandgousier and King Picrochole, for example, have been identified as a representation of a long legal feud between Rabelais's father and another local landowner relating to some fishing and water rights on the Loire. It is not necessary to know this, however,

to enjoy the battle, and the real pleasure Rabelais offers us lies in his enormous verbal and comic energy. Readers of English literature will find reference points and the Rabelaisian influence in such writers as Swift, Sterne and James Joyce.

RUSKIN, John (1819–1900). The Victorian polymath Ruskin travelled widely on the continent throughout his life, especially in France, Italy, and Switzerland, relaxing, reflecting, sketching, and gathering impressions and information for works such as *The Seven Lamps of Architecture*, 1849, *The Stones of Venice*, 1851–53, and *The Bible of Amiens*, 1880. In France, Ruskin was attracted particularly to the cathedral towns, such as **Amiens** and **Rouen**, and to the French Alps – he first visited **Chamonix**, now a major Alpine tourist resort, in 1833 and was awestruck by the dramatic mountain landscape of the Mont Blanc massif. He went back to Chamonix many times and even considered buying a house there in the 1860s. Ruskin's diaries provide a good source of his travel impressions, revealing his wide-ranging artistic, architectural, religious, and scientific interests – see, for example, the piece on **Le Puy**, Extract 5.

Ruskin's publications found a significant French admirer in Marcel Proust, who studied his work in depth, published essays on it, and translated (with the assistance of his mother and his English friend Marie Nordlinger) *The Bible of Amiens* and *Sesame and Lilies*. George Painter discusses in detail the influence of Ruskin on Proust and his relevance to À *la Recherche* in his two-volume biography *Marcel Proust*, 1959 and 1965.

Recommended biography: John Dixon Hunt, *The Wider Sea: A Life of John Ruskin*, Dent, London, 1982.

SAND, George (1804–76). George Sand's real name was Aurore Dupin, Baronne Dudevant. She was born on 1 July 1804 in **Paris**. Her father, an officer in Napoleon's *Armée d'Italie*, died in a riding accident in 1808. After his death Aurore moved with her mother to her paternal grandmother's property, the **Château de Nohant**. She spent the best part of her childhood here, brought up mainly by her grandmother (her mother moved back to Paris), and it was to become her main home in her adult life (although until 1848 she divided her time between Nohant and Paris). Nohant was the place she most cherished, where she did much of her writing, and which she describes frequently in her novels. (Nohant is in what used to be Berri, now the region comprising the *départements* of Cher and Indre.) Between 1818 and 1821, Aurore attended an Augustinian convent in Paris – in 1921 her grandmother died and she inherited the property at Nohant. Her mother took her back to Paris, where she met and married Casimir Dudevant, an illegitimate but recognized son of the Baron Jean-François Dudevant. She lived with Dudevant at Nohant and had a son by him, but the marriage was unhappy and ended effectively in 1830, with legal separation following in 1836. She also gave birth to a daughter, probably fathered by one of her lovers. Sand's love life was marked by a series of often stormy, sometimes tumultuous affairs. Among her more famous lovers were Jules Sandeau (the novelist with whom she wrote *Rose et Blanche*, 1831, and from whom she derived her pseudonym), Alfred de Musset, and, for nine years, Frédéric Chopin. Her relationships often ended up in one form or another in her own novels, or in those of her lovers (for example, for her affair with Musset, see Sand's *Elle et lui*, 1859, and Musset's *La Confession d'un enfant du siècle*, 1836). Sand also became, in later life, a close friend and correspondent of Gustave Flaubert whom she met in 1857 (for their letters, see *Flaubert–Sand: The Correspondence*, Francis Steegmuller and Barbara Bray, trans, Harvill, London, 1993).

Sand's political sympathies were on

George Sand, dressed in men's clothing

the Left – and essentially feminist, despite (or 'as illustrated by', depending on how one interprets it) her own adoption of a male pseudonym and her famous habits of dressing as a man and smoking cigars. When the 1848 Revolution occurred, overthrowing the monarchy, she was active as a propagandist for the revolutionaries and published several political pamphlets. When the revolution began to turn in on itself, however, with the arrests of leading radicals, Sand became disillusioned and left Paris for Nohant, where she spent most of the rest of her life, writing, receiving her friends, staging amateur theatricals, managing the household, and becoming a much-loved pillar of the local community. She also experienced a long and untempestuous love affair with her young secretary Alexandre Manceau – it lasted from 1850 until 1865, when Manceau died. Sand herself lived another 10 years – she died from a painful intestinal illness just before her 72nd birthday on 8 June 1876.

George Sand's literary output was prolific. Her work includes novels, short stories, plays, travel writing, autobiography, highly intelligent and illuminating correspondence, and political essays and pamphlets. She is best known as a novelist, and even in that single genre her work ranges widely. In summary, her early novels explore social issues and sexual relationships from a woman's perspective – thus, for example, *Indiana*, 1832 (*Indiana*, 1994) is concerned with the oppressions of marriage, and *Valentine*, 1833 (*Valentine*, 1978), takes a similar subject with the additional consideration, to re-occur frequently, of relationships between people of different social classes. Her middle-period work is predominantly political, reflecting her hope and faith in the prospects for political and spiritual renewal. For example, *Le Compagnon du tour de France*, 1840 (*The Companion of the Tour of France*, 1993), is a novel about the aspirations and philosophies of politically aware workers of the time, telling the story of two young carpenters who fall in love with two young women of noble birth. *Le Meunier d'Angibault*, 1845 (*The Miller of Angibault*, 1995), is a tale of peasant life which works towards the foundation of a rural Utopia. It was in her later period, though, that Sand produced most of the novels for which she is now best known – novels which centre around and celebrate rural life and the traditions and values of peasant communities. Perhaps her most famous 'rustic novel' is *La Mare au diable*, 1846 (*The Devil's Pool*), a story of love and integrity overcoming shallowness and exploitation, with detailed information on traditional rural marriage customs supplied as an Appendix. The novel highlighted here, *Les Maîtres sonneurs*, 1853 (*The Master Pipers*, 1994) was written at Nohant with the disillusionments of the violent 1848 Revolution still fresh wounds in Sand's humanitarian spirit. Focusing on the gradual

evolution of understanding and tolerance between the conservative and self-contained Berri peasants and the free-spirited and adventurous woodcutters of Bourbonnais, the novel is an optimistic assertion of the values of love, equality in relationships, and solidarity. Sand vividly portrays, with a Romantic eye, the countryside she had known since her childhood and its peasant communities, traditions and, very significantly in this work, music (Extract 4). Typical of her rustic novels, *Les Maîtres sonneurs* is a Romantic pastoral idyll, with idealized central characters, but it is also an assertion of her socialist vision and her portrayal of a way of life that she perceived would soon disappear with the advance of industrialization. It would be a pity for the modern reader to be discouraged by the former and miss the latter.

Recommended biography: Curtis Gate, *George Sand: A Biography*, Hamish Hamilton, London, 1975. Selections from Sand's evocative and illuminating autobiography *Histoire de ma vie*, 1854, are available in English as *My Life*, Dan Hofstadter, ed and trans, Victor Gollancz, London, 1979.

TROLLOPE, Anthony (1815–82). Trollope's prolific literary career included some 47 novels and 42 short stories, as well as biographies and travel books. In his two short-story collections entitled *Tales of All Countries*, 1861 and 1863, he intended that each story would be 'redolent of some different country'. The stories rely heavily on Trollope's own observations – he was a great traveller, whether on a mission for the Post Office, in which he became a senior offical, or on holiday for his own pleasure, and the broad geographical coverage of the *Tales* reflects the extent of his travels. Trollope was, to use his own definition, a 'Hookite', travelling independently, 'on his own hook', not one of the 'Cookites', who had Thomas Cook make all the arrangements. The detailed and perceptive descriptions of his foreign settings reflect the keen interest and enthusiasm of the intelligent and open-minded traveller.

The short stories 'La Mère Bauche' and 'The Château of Prince Polignac' were written in 1859, while Trollope was on holiday in the **Pyrénées**. 'La Mère Bauche', set in **Vernet-les-Bains** (Pyrénées-Orientales), tells the story of a domineering mother and the tragic consequences when she persuades her son to give up the poor 'charity girl' who loves him. 'The Château of Prince Polignac' (Extract 6) is a happier tale of an Englishwoman living in **Le Puy** in the **Auvergne** and a Frenchman who proposes to her. The **Château de Polignac** to which he takes her on a sightseeing trip, and which she imagines will be a grand place, turns out to be a ruin,

and he himself turns out to be not quite all she had hoped.

Also set in France is Trollope's 1850 historical novel *La Vendée* based on the counter-Revolutionary rebellion which broke out in the **Vendée** in 1793, but this is arguably his least successful work and lacks the perceptiveness and immediacy characteristic of his books which derive from personal experience of the societies and places they describe.

Trollope's mother, the travel writer and novelist Frances Trollope (1780–1863), wrote the hugely successful *Paris and the Parisians*, 1835.

Recommended biography: N. John Hall, *Trollope: A Biography*, Clarendon Press, Oxford, 1991/Oxford University Press, New York, 1991.

PAYS DE LA LOIRE;
BRITTANY (BRETAGNE);
NORMANDY (BASSE-NORMANDIE
AND HAUTE-NORMANDIE)

'Her love expanded in that vast space before her.
It was filled with tumult at the vague hubbub that
arose. Then she poured it out again upon the squares
and promenades and streets; and that ancient
Norman city lay outspread before her eyes like an
enormous metropolis, a Babylon awaiting her.'

Gustave Flaubert, *Madame Bovary*

PAYS DE LA LOIRE: MAINE-ET-LOIRE

Liré. Birthplace of the Renaissance poet Joachim Du Bellay (c1522–60), a member of La Pléiade which centred around Ronsard (see under Centre, Loir-et-Cher). The ruins of the **Château de la Turmelière**, where he was born, are about 1500 m south of the small town of Liré. In the town centre, you will find an authentic and restored 16th century house at 18 rue du Grand-Logis which houses **Le Musée Joachim Du Bellay**, part of which is dedicated to the poet and part to local folklore and wine making.

Saumur. Setting for Balzac's *Eugénie Grandet*, which provides a vivid evocation of the town in the 19th century (Extract 19).

PAYS DE LA LOIRE: VENDÉE

The Vendée is famous for the counter-Revolutionary rebellion that broke out in 1793 and was finally crushed in 1795 (although the main 'war' was over by the end of 1793, guerilla fighting continued through 1794 and 1795). The traditional rural communities of the region, increasingly outraged by the anti-monarchical and anti-religious tendencies of the Revolution, and fired by the injustices of new land settlements, taxation and military requisitions, took arms in substantial numbers against the Revolutionary forces. The civil war that ensued was fierce and the quashing of the rebellion, in keeping with that violent period, was merciless and extrememly bloody. Victor Hugo's novel *Quatrevingt-Treize*, 1874 (*Ninety-Three*, 1988), vividly evokes the con-

flict and the horror and absurdity of war. The Vendée war is also the subject of Trollope's novel *La Vendée*, 1850 – unfortunately, and by the author's own admission, it is not a very good one.

Fontenay-le-Comte. Birthplace of the poet Nicolas Rapin (1538–1608). Rabelais (◊ Centre) entered the Franciscan monastery of Le-Puy-Saint-Martin in about 1510, leaving in 1524. The **Hôtel de Ville** now occupies the site. During the German occupation in the 1940s, Georges Simenon (◊ Paris) and his family took refuge here, in a large and luxurious apartment in the **Château de Terre-Neuve** overlooking the town.

Maillezais. Rabelais left the rigorous Franciscan regime of the abbey at Fontenay-le-Comte for the more liberal Benedictine environment of **Saint-Pierre-de-Maillezais**, the ruins of which may be seen. He spent much of his time here (probably 1524–26) travelling around the Poitou region with the Bishop Geoffroy d'Estissac, to whom he was secretary.

PAYS DE LA LOIRE: LOIRE-ATLANTIQUE

The landscape and people of this *département* (formerly Loire-Inférieure) are vividly evoked in Jean Rouaud's ◊

atmospheric *Les Champs d'honneur*, 1990 (*Fields of Glory*, 1992) – see Extract 10.

Le Croisic. Robert Browning (1812–89) was a frequent visitor to France and, from the 1860s onwards, would spend two to three months of almost every year in the country. In the 1860s he stayed in several remote Breton villages including Le Croisic (now in the Pays de la Loire *région*). A number of his poems relate to this area. For example, *Hervé Riel*, 1867, about a naval hero from Le Croisic, was written while Browning was staying in the village, and he later wrote *The Two Poets of Croisic*, 1878, a satiric comment on ambition and aspiration through the stories of two little-known poets associated with Le Croisic. Also reflecting his visits is the setting for *Fifine at the Fair*, 1872, in which Don Juan, walking with his wife in and around **Pornic**, is attracted by a gypsy girl at the village fair and led off into a series of complex reflections on the contrast between desire and love and on other fundamental aspects of personality and perception. The descriptions of the village and its surroundings provide departure points but also a background of physical reality for Don Juan's metaphysical explorations. In 'Gold Hair: A Story of Pornic', published in *Dramatis Personae*, 1864, Browning tells the story of a Breton girl thought to be virtuous and innocent but, after her death, revealed as a slave to avarice ('Had a spider found out the communion-cup,/Was a toad in the christening-font?').

Nantes. Jules Verne (1828–1905) was born in Nantes on 28 February 1828. The house in which he was born may be seen in the **Île Feydeau** at the corner of rue Olivier-de-Clisson and rue Kervégan. His parents later moved to houses in the **quai Jean-Bart** and **rue Jean-Jacques-Rousseau**. Verne spent his childhood and adolescence in the town, leaving for Paris in 1848. The family had a property in the south-west of Nantes, which they used as a holiday home in the summer – this is now a museum dedicated to the novelist (**3 rue de l'Hermitage**). You can see reconstructions of Verne's childhood bedroom, and his study in one of his Amiens homes. Other exhibits of interest include publicity posters, various personal mementoes, and models and illustrations of his stories.

In 1916 an influential encounter in the development of French Surrealism took place in Nantes when André Breton met the Dadaist writer Jacques-Pierre Vaché (1895–1919). Three years later, Vaché committed suicide in the Hôtel de France in place Graslin.

Le Pallet. Abélard (◊ Paris) was born here (about 19 km from Nantes) in 1079.

BRETAGNE: MORBIHAN

Belle-Île. See Helen Waddell's ◊ *Peter Abelard*, 1933, for an evocation of 12th century **Le Palais** (Extract 12). On the northern extremity of the island, at **Pointe des Poulains**, is an old fort which was once a summer residence of Sarah Bernhardt (1845–1923) and which has now shrunk to the function of clubhouse for the golf course.

Saint-Gildas-de-Rhuys. Abélard was abbot of the Benedictine abbey which gave its name to this peninsula on the southern coast of Brittany. After the disastrous consequences of his affair with Héloïse, Abélard moved from monastery to monastery in exile from Paris. He spent some six years in this wild country and was no friend of the pleasure-seeking monks who, rebelling against his austere rule, tried to poison him.

BRETAGNE: FINISTÈRE

Brest. The port is the atmospheric and nightmarish setting for Genet's ◊ dark

Jean Rouaud

novel *Querelle de Brest*, 1947 (*Querelle of Brest*, 1966) – Extract 1. Genet was here in the 1930s, before the city centre was destroyed in the Second World War. He joined an infantry regiment based in Brest (illicitly, as he had been disqualified from rejoining the army). As with many places he visited, he spent some time in the local prison before moving on.

Brest also serves as the setting for Prévert's war-clouded poem of loss and regret, 'Barbara' (included in *Selections from Paroles* – see Booklist).

Novelist and film-maker Alain Robbe-Grillet, founder and primary exponent of the Nouveau Roman, was born in Brest in August 1922. The first volume of his autobiography, *Le Miroir qui revient*, 1985 (*Ghosts in the Mirror*, 1988) includes Breton folklore and sexual-psychological exploration of his childhood among its mixed ingredients.

Jack Kerouac ◊ made a brief, cognac-fuelled visit to Brest in 1965 in search of his Breton ancestry. The trip is the subject of his short novel *Satori in Paris*, 1966 (Extract 2).

Pont-Aven. Ernest Dowson ◊ lived for six months in 1896 at the Hôtel Gloanec ('for a time at least my permanent home and address'). The picturesque town had for some years been popular with artists, poets and musicians (in 1888 Paul Gaugin established the 'School of Pont-Aven' here), and the Gloanec was the place to stay for those of an artistic turn of mind. Its location is indicated by a plaque in the **place Gaugin**. Dowson wrote 'Breton Afternoon' (Extract 13) while staying here, the poem of a willing exile, luxuriating in the peace and solitude of his temporary Breton home.

Quimper. Birthplace of the poet Max Jacob (1876–1944) – you can see a selection of his drawings and manuscripts at the **Musée des Beaux-Arts**, place Saint-Corentin. The museum also includes drawings by Cocteau.

BRETAGNE: CÔTES D'ARMOR (formerly Côtes-du-Nord)

Lancieux. The poet Robert Service (1874–1958), known for ballads inspired by the Gold Rush in the Yukon (like 'The Shooting of Dan McGrew') died at Lancieux, and is buried here.

Lannion. Birthplace of poet and novelist Charles Le Goffic (1863-1932). There is a statue in the **place Général Leclerc**.

The **Île Grande**, off the coast from Lannion, has a **rue Joseph-Conrad**. Conrad (1857–1924), looking for an isolated place to work, stayed here in April–September 1896, with his new wife Jessie. Among the pieces he produced while in Île Grande was his story 'The Idiots' (*Tales of Unrest*, 1898), a pessimistic tale of Breton peasant life.

Tréguier. This is the birthplace of the influential writer and thinker Ernest Renan (1823–92). His statue is in front of the **cathedral**, and the house in which he was born is now a museum –

Le Musée Ernest Renan is at 20 rue Renan (closed October–March). He spent the first 15 years of his life here and kept it as a holiday home until 1845. The house has been well preserved. Among the rooms which may be visited are the one where he slept and worked during his childhood and adolescence (including the desk he used for his school work), and a reconstruction of his study at the Collège de France. Exhibits include items of his furniture, personal memorabilia, manuscripts and documentation. Renan writes of his life at Tréguier in his *Souvenirs d'enfance et de jeunesse*, 1883.

BRETAGNE: ILLE-ET-VILAINE

Combourg. The **Château de Combourg**, originally built in the 11th century and developed in the 15th, was acquired by Chateaubriand's ◊ father in 1761 and became a place of considerable formative significance for the great Romantic writer ('It was in the woods of Combourg that I became what I am.'). He came here regularly for brief spells during his childhood, and lived permanently at the Château from 1784 to 1786 (between the ages of 16 and 18). He writes about it in detail in *Mémoires d'outre-tombe*, 1849–50 ('Memories from Beyond the Grave', translated as *The Memoirs of Chateaubriand*, 1961), evoking its silent, sombre and mysterious qualities – see Extract 4. His room (which is shown to visitors) was in the so-called 'Tour du Chat', an eerie and lonely lodging high in the supposedly haunted tower (the resident ghost, according to Chateaubriand, was reputed to be a count with a wooden leg who had been seen on the stairs of the tower – sometimes the wooden leg would take a walk itself, accompanied only by the black cat from which the tower took its name). His isolation and melancholy in this sprawling castle were increased by the lack of emotional as well as physical warmth – his father was cold and remote, and his mother taciturn, and Chateaubriand's life here, in this sad and beautiful environment, was one of solitude and reflection – it was here, he said, that he first experienced that *tristesse* that was to become 'my torment and my joy'. The grounds of the Château, and the Château itself, may be visited (but it is closed in winter). In addition to his bedroom in the Tour du Chat, you can see the furniture and other belongings that were in Chateaubriand's apartment in the rue du Bac in Paris (including the bed in which he died) and, although the park has been much reduced and some alterations were made to the Château when it was restored in the 19th century, the building looks and feels much as did when it played its part in the development of the great Romantic.

Dol-de-Bretagne. Chateaubriand went to school here from 1777 to 1781. The college he attended is now the **Notre Dame** boarding school in the rue Pierre Fluaux – there is a plaque.

Forêt de Paimpont. This 40 sq km forest is all that remains of the great woodland that covered a vast area of medieval Brittany and is strongly associated with Arthurian legend, as the Forêt de Brocéliande (by which name it is still also known). The present-day version may be only a fraction of the original, but it is still an atmospheric and haunting place, especially if you envisage it as the forest of Merlin, where he became the captive of the enchantress Vivien, the Lady of the Lake. There are a few key 'locations' from the stories dotted about the forest – among them, the **Val sans Retour**, near **Trehorenteuc**, where Morgan Le Fay trapped faithless lovers; the **Fontaine de Barenton**, near **Folle Pensée**, where Merlin first saw Vivien, with **Le Perron de Merlin** nearby – if you sprinkle a few drops of water on the stone, goes the legend, you will summon a rainstorm; and **Merlin's 'grave'**

near **Télhouet**. At the **Château de Comper-en-Brocéliande** (near **Concoret**), where Vivien is supposed to have been born, you will find the **Centre de l'Imaginaire Arthurien** which stages exhibitions and audio-visual presentations relating to the stories of Arthur and the Knights of the Round Table. It also organizes guided tours of the forest on request. Alternatively, the Syndicat d'Initiative at **Paimpont** has plans of various walks through the woods, highlighting points of interest for those with Arthurian inclinations.

The most famous of the medieval French poets and story-tellers who sourced their renderings of Arthurian stories from the Celtic legends and folklore known collectively as the *matière de Bretagne* was Chrétien de Troyes (12th century), and his romances are available in English translation.

John Fowles ◊ uses the Forêt de Paimpont as a setting in his compelling novella *The Ebony Tower*, 1974, with evocative descriptions of the forest and the region (Extract 8).

Saint-Malo. Chateaubriand was born here in 1768 while a great storm raged outside the hôtel where his mother gave birth – in the street now known as **rue de Chateaubriand** (he was born at present-day **No 3**, currently a part of the Hôtel de France). He was, he writes in his *Memoirs*, awakened from his first sleep by the noise of the storm, a fittingly tempestuous introduction to the world for the man who was to become for many the 'founding father' of Romanticism, whose melancholic vision and Romantic imagination would prove so lasting and influential. He spent his childhood in or near the port, with the seashore as playground and inspired by the stories of travellers and explorers who left from Saint-Malo for their great adventures. Chateaubriand himself departed from here in 1791 for his voyage to America, the first of his major voyages.

Long before he died, Chateaubriand made arrangements to be buried on the **Île du Grand Bé**, a small island just off the coast from Saint-Malo and accessible at low tide (be careful if the tide is coming in). Negotiations for the site of the tomb started as early as 1823 (he died in 1848) and were not concluded until 1836. It turned out, however, exactly as Chateaubriand had wished, and he lies there now, his tomb and its large granite cross facing out to the open sea. It quickly became an object of pilgrimage and early visitors included Hugo, Flaubert and Stendhal. Now the walk along the short causeway to the tomb is so popular that you may find it hard to achieve the requisite degree of Romantic isolation.

The **Musée d'Histoire de la Ville** in the Château in Saint-Malo includes a section dedicated to the 19th century which has several exhibits relating to Chateaubriand.

Vitré. In her letter to her daughter of 15 July 1671 Madame de Sévigné (1626–96) wrote, 'If I were to write down all my reveries for you I should always write you the longest letters in the world. But that is not very easy. So I content myself with what can be written and I dream whatever should be dreamed; I have the time and place for it. La Mousse has a fine little swelling on the teeth and the Abbé a little swelling on the knee, which leave me free in my avenue of trees to do what I please. And what I please means to walk up and down there in the evening until eight o'clock. My son has gone now and that leaves a silence, tranquillity and solitude that I don't think it is easy to find anywhere else.' (from *Selected Letters* translated by Leonard Tancock). South-east of Vitré is **Le Château des Rochers-Sévigné** (35500 Vitré). Madame de Sévigné became the owner of the Château through her short marriage to Henri, Baron and Marquis de Sévigné (who was killed in a duel seven years after the wedding). The Château became for her a place of retreat from the crowds and expense of her Paris life. She paid many visits to Les Rochers and around 250 of her famous letters were addressed from here or from Vitré. The Château, which is open to the public, is well preserved, and the exterior of the building and the grounds are much as Sévigné would have known them. Inside, among the rooms that may be visited is one which claims to be Sévigné's '*cabinet vert*', where she wrote and studied – in fact, the contents were moved here from the actual room which she favoured for the purpose when the Château was opened to the public. However, among the authentic contents are her portrait by Mignard and her bed, with its bedspread embroidered by her daughter, Madame de Grignan (see under Rhône–Alpes, Grignan). The octagonal chapel was installed in 1671 by Sévigné's uncle, the Abbé de Coulanges.

BASSE-NORMANDIE: MANCHE

Mont Saint-Michel. 'The church stands high on the summit of this granite rock, and on its west front is the platform, to which the tourist ought first to climb. From the edge of this platform, the eye plunges down, two-hundred and thirty-five feet, to the wide sands or the wider ocean, as the tides recede or advance, under an infinite sky, over a restless sea, which even we tourists can understand and feel without books or guides; but when we turn from the western view, and look at the church door, thirty or forty yards from the parapet where we stand, one needs to be eight centuries old to know what this mass of encrusted architecture meant to its builders, and even then one must still learn to feel it. The man who wanders into the twelfth century is lost, unless he can grow prematurely young.' The American writer and thinker Henry Adams (1838–1918) visited Normandy in sum-

mer 1895 and, as he puts it in his autobiographical *The Education of Henry Adams*, 1907, 'drifted back to Washington with a new sense of history'. In his critical work *Mont-Saint-Michel and Chartres*, 1904, from which the above passage is taken, Adams uses the two great architectural achievements of Saint-Michel and the cathedral at Chartres as spring-boards for his exploration of the spiritual 'unity' of the 12th and 13th centuries, in terms of the unified set of beliefs and responses to the world which informed art, religion and all other aspects of life. He compares this 'universe' to the 'multiverse' of the present, with its complex and dissonant variety (examined in *The Education of Henry Adams*).

BASSE-NORMANDIE: ORNE

La Ferté-Macé. E.E. Cummings ◊ was sent to a detention camp here in 1917. His experiences in the camp formed the basis for *The Enormous Room*, 1922 – Extract 7.

BASSE-NORMANDIE: CALVADOS

Cabourg. Marcel Proust (◊ Centre) first stayed in this seaside resort with his grandmother and later with his mother when he was in his teens. As an adult, he spent several summers in Cabourg between 1907 and 1914, the sea air providing some relief from his debilitating asthma. Proust knew various of the Normandy resorts quite well and the fictional Balbec, a key setting in *À la recherche du temps perdu*, 1913–1927 (*Remembrance of Things Past*, 1981), is drawn from his memories of such places as Cabourg, **Deauville**, **Houlgate** and **Honfleur**, as well as from Évian in Haute-Savoie and Beg-Meil in Brittany. Of these, Cabourg is one of the more dominant influences. The Proustian landmark here most worthy of note is the **Grand Hôtel**, the principal model for the eponymous hotel in Balbec – its provincial snobbishness gloriously crystallized in the character of its manager (Extract 3) – where the narrator stays and where he meets Saint-Loup and the Baron de Charlus. Proust himself stayed at the Grand Hôtel in Cabourg during his summer visits, renting several rooms at a time to avoid noise from neighbours, and keeping to his habit of sleeping during the day and working and venturing out at night. During his stay at the Grand in 1911, he finalized his draft of *Du côté de chez Swann* (*Swann's Way*), and secured the services of the hotel's shorthand-typist – she was an Englishwoman named Cecilia Hayward who apparently had a minimal grasp of French. She nevertheless became the person who first typed out what was to become the first volume of *À la recherche*, much of it dictated by the novelist from his rough draft. Proust last visited the Grand Hôtel in September 1914 – during the First World War it was requisitioned as a military hospital. The hotel today is much as it was during Proust's later stays (the Grand he knew as a child had been radically altered when he returned in 1907). In 1987, the owners undertook a reconstruction of his suite, complete with period furnishings – it may be seen whenever it is not occupied by a hotel guest. As for other places of Proustian interest, the Tourist Office in Cabourg, in association with La Société des Amis de Marcel Proust, organizes a tour along the Normandy coast between Cabourg and Honfleur which visits various landmarks in the area.

Deauville. Ford Madox Ford (◊ Picardie) died at Deauville in 1939. You will find his grave in the cemetery.

Honfleur. Baudelaire (◊ Paris) visited his elderly mother in her house here in what is now **rue Charles-Baudelaire**. He lived with her at Honfleur for several months in 1859, shortly after his father's death. The poet apparently was much taken with the town, as the

words on the plaque suggest: 'Honfleur a toujours été le plus cher de mes rêves' ('Honfleur has always been the dearest of my dreams').

La Roque-Baignard. André Gide's ◊ mother inherited the château here from her father, and the village was a regular summer holiday home during Gide's childhood. Later, when he himself inherited the château, he became mayor of the commune (1896–99). Gide used the village as a setting in two of his novels – *L'Immoraliste*, 1902 (*The Immoralist*, 1960) and *Isabelle*, 1911 (*La Symphonie Pastorale and Isabelle*, 1963).

HAUTE-NORMANDIE: EURE

Quillebeuf. This fishing port is the setting for *Emily L.* by Marguerite Duras ◊ (Extract 14).

HAUTE-NORMANDIE: SEINE-MARITIME

Croisset. At Croisset, on the banks of the Seine near Rouen, was the house where Flaubert ◊ lived for most of his life – and where he died in 1880. He did much of his writing here, in seclusion, appreciating the pleasant tranquillity of the gardens and the river. In the grounds, surrounded by lime trees, there was a pavilion, a summer house overlooking the Seine which Flaubert used for rest and contemplation. It was also favoured by his visitors – although he refused to entertain Louise Colet (the prototype for Madam Bovary) at Croisset, he did welcome many famous friends to the house, including Daudet, Maupassant, Turgenev, and Zola, and for them the pavilion would have been a place for conversation and relaxation. Flaubert was happy at Croisset, close to his mother, and later to his niece Caroline. The house, however, was sold by Caroline after his death and was demolished to make way for a factory – now there is a paper mill where it used to stand. Only the little pavilion remains, and it has been turned into a museum – **Le Pavillon Gustave-Flaubert**, 18 quai Gustave-Flaubert, 76830 Dieppedalle-Croisset. Predominantly, it is a haphazard collection of souvenirs of the writer which will move or leave you cold depending on your taste – for example, there is the handkerchief with which Flaubert mopped his brow before he died. As in the museum in Rouen (see below), there is a stuffed parrot – confounding Julian Barnes's ◊ Geoffrey Braithwaite as he struggles to identify the actual parrot which Flaubert had in front of him when he wrote 'Un coeur simple' ('A Simple Heart'). In Barnes's *Flaubert's Parrot*, 1984, Braithwaite visits the museum – '. . . the exhibits, carelessly laid out, catch your heart at random. Portraits, photographs, a clay bust; pipes, a tobacco jar, a letter opener; a toad-inkwell with a gaping mouth; the gold Buddha which stood on the writer's desk; a lock of hair, blonder, naturally, than in the photographs.'

In the **Town Hall** in Croisset you can see Flaubert's library – his volumes still shelved in the bookcases taken from his study.

Cuverville. This village was the home of André Gide ◊ for many years (Extract 5) – it serves as a setting in *La Porte étroite*, 1909 (*Strait is the Gate*, 1924). Gide is buried in the **Protestant cemetery**.

Dieppe. In the summer of 1895, Dieppe was the chosen resort of Beardsley, Symons, and others working on *The Savoy* – the literary journal which had a short life (eight issues in 1896) but considerable influence. Aubrey Beardsley (1872–98) stayed at nearby **Arques-la-Bataille**. Two years later, Ernest Dowson ◊, who had been one of the contributors to *The Savoy*, stayed at Arques for a few weeks. At the time Oscar Wilde (1854–1900), just released from prison, was living at **Berneval-sur-Mer** (devastated in the Second

World War) and writing *The Ballad of Reading Gaol*, 1898. Dowson and Wilde became good friends and visited each other frequently. In a letter of June 1897, Dowson wrote, 'Oscar came over & lunched with me the other day & carried me back with him to Berneval. His gorgeous spirits cheered me mightily. I was amused by the unconscious contrast between his present talk about his changed position & his notions of economy & his practise, which is perversely extravagant. He does not realize in the least that nobody except himself *could* manage to spend the money he does in a *petit trou de campagne*.'

Étretat. When she separated from her husband, Guy de Maupassant's ◊ mother lived with her two sons in a villa here. The small fishing village, which soon became a fashionable resort, was a much-loved home for Maupassant. He uses it as a setting in a number of his stories (see, for example, Extract 6). It was in Étretat that he attempted to rescue a drowning swimmer (picked up by a fishing boat before Maupassant got to him). The swimmer turned out to be Algernon Charles Swinburne (1837–1909), who was staying locally with a friend. As a result of his courageous attempt, Maupassant was invited to the house where Swinburne was staying, and found it to be full of strange and sometimes macabre objects – including a skinned hand, which was to turn up more than once in a story (most notably in 'La Main'). Later in his life, Maupassant had a house built in Étretat, which he called **La Guillette** – it still exists. He spent less and less time there as he grew older: the cold Normandy weather increasingly discomforted him in his declining health.

Fécamp. Probable birthplace of Maupassant (**rue sous-le-Bois**) – see below under **Tourville-sur-Arques**.

Le Havre. The town provides the setting for Maupassant's novel *Pierre et*

Jean, 1888 (*Pierre et Jean*, 1979), about the jealousy and rivalry between two brothers.

In the 1930s, Beauvoir (◊ Paris) and Sartre (◊ Paris) were teaching at provincial *lycées*, he here in Le Havre (at the **Lycée François-I**) and she in Rouen. They used to meet in Le Havre, preferring the liveliness and variety of the port to the more conventional and bourgeois character of Rouen. Beauvoir remembers the town (before the devastation of the Second World War), and especially its dock area, with affection in *La Force de l'âge*, 1960 (*The Prime of Life*, 1973) – Extract 9. Sartre used it as a model for 'Bouville' in *La Nausée*, 1939 (*Nausea*, 1965). Like his protagonist Roquentin in Bouville, Sartre lived in a cheap hotel in Le Havre near the railway station, overlooking the rail yard. 'This is my room,' Roquentin tells us at the beginning of the novel, 'which faces north-east. Down below is the rue des Mutilés and the shunting yard of the new station. From my window I can see the red and white flame of the Rendez-vous des Cheminots at the corner of the boulevard Victor-Noir. The Paris train has just come in. People are coming out of the old station and dispersing in the streets. I can hear footsteps and voices. A lot of people are waiting for the last tram. They must make a sad little group around the gas lamp under my window.' The rue Ancelot, running beneath Sartre's old classroom, was renamed **rue Jean-Paul Sartre** after his death – 'But,' writes his biographer Annie Cohen-Solal, 'according to the principal, the street sign has been regularly vandalized ever since.'

Raymond Queneau (◊ Paris) was born and brought up in Le Havre.

Rouen. In 1419, Rouen, then the capital of the duchy of Normandy, was besieged and captured by Henry V and it remained an English possession until 1449. In the closing scenes of *Henry V*, Shakespeare dramatizes the conquest and the subsequent political union of England and France through the marriage of Henry V to Catherine, the daughter of Charles VI (Extract 18).

The city must be thankful, at least from the point of view of its tourism industry, that its name is forever associated with the cruel trial, imprisonment and execution for heresy of the young Jeanne d'Arc (1412–31). The story of Joan's life and death has inspired many works of literature – among them, Voltaire's *La Pucelle*, 1755; Charles Péguy's *Jeanne d'Arc*, 1897 and *Le Mystère de la charité de Jeanne d'Arc*, 1909 (*The Mystery of the Charity of Joan of Arc*, 1986); George Bernard Shaw's *Saint Joan*, 1924; and Jean Anouilh's *L'Alouette*, 1953 (*The Lark*, 1987).

Pierre Corneille (1606–84) was born at **4 rue de la Pie**, now a museum, where he lived for much of his life. The house, however, has been extensively restored and not much remains of the original as Corneille would have known it. The 'authentic' parts are the cellar, the two party walls, a section of the façade at the back of the house, and the well (**La Maison de Corneille**, 4 rue de la Pie, 76310 Rouen). For his country house, see below, under **Petit-Couronne**.

John Evelyn ◊ stayed in Rouen in the 1640s and recorded his impressions in his diary (Extract 16).

Gustave Flaubert was born at the **Hôtel-Dieu**, a municipal hospital where his father was chief surgeon. He spent his childhood and youth here in the family apartment attached to the hospital. It now contains **Le Musée Flaubert et d'Histoire de la Médecine** (51 rue de Lecat, 76000 Rouen). The room in which Flaubert was born has been recreated and there are memorabilia, portraits, letters and documents, including manuscript pages from *Madame Bovary* (Extract 17). The fact that the museum is also dedicated to the horrors of 19th century medicine is entirely appropriate, for it was precisely in this atmosphere that the novelist grew up, he and his sister frequently making exploratory journeys into the wards and the hospital mortuary – many of the medical exhibits would no doubt have been familiar to him. The museum also contains a stuffed parrot, an item of importance in Flaubert's story 'Un coeur simple' ('A Simple Heart') and an object of Geoffrey Braithwaite's research in Julian Barnes's ◊ *Flaubert's Parrot*, 1984. Braithwaite visits and describes the museum early on in the novel, commenting on the juxtaposition of the literary and medical histories – 'The conjunction of these two museums seemed odd at first. It made sense when I remembered Lemot's famous cartoon of Flaubert dissecting Emma Bovary. It shows the novelist flourishing on the end of a large fork the dripping heart he has triumphantly torn from the heroine's body.' Those still not satiated after visiting this and the museum at **Crois-set** might take a look at the statue of the author in the **place des Carmes**, again brilliantly described by Julian Barnes (Extract 15). The **Cathedral**, which Flaubert loved, is the setting for a critical meeting between Emma Bovary and her lover Léon, who are trapped into a guided tour by a persistent and unsuspecting beadle, who takes them for innocent tourists. The one aspect of the Cathedral that Flaubert hated was the 19th century spire, and he cannot allow even his fictional characters to be subjected to it – pushed by the beadle to inspect it, 'Léon fled, for it seemed to him that his love, which for close on two hours had been immobilized like the stones around him in the church, was now about to vanish like smoke through that kind of truncated funnel, oblong cage or fretwork chimney, that perches so grotesquely on top of the Cathedral like an essay in the extravagant by some whimsical tinker.' Finally, if you want to pay your respects, the novelist is buried in the **Cimetière Monumental**, next to his close friend the poet and dramatist Louis Bouilhet (1822–69).

Rouen at the time of the Franco–Prussian war is vividly evoked in the opening scenes of Guy de Maupassant's 'Boule de Suif', his famous short story of the journey in a stagecoach from Rouen to Dieppe of a prostitute and several respectable Rouennais as they retreat from the Prussian advance.

Simone de Beauvoir taught at the **Lycée Jeanne d'Arc** here in the 1930s. She was not impressed with the city, finding it 'bourgeois and complacent', although it would later serve her as the partial setting, along with Paris, for her first novel *L'Invitée*, 1943 (*She Came to Stay*, 1975).

Pétit-Couronne. Here, a short distance from Rouen in what is now an industrial suburb, was the country home of Pierre Corneille. It was bought by his father in 1608. Corneille visited it regularly during his childhood and inherited it in 1639. The house is now a museum, evoking the life of the playwright and the ambience of a country house of the time. There are a few personal belongings on exhibition, including, at the door, Corneille's mounting block which he would have used regularly on his trips out to this country retreat from Rouen. Among the other exhibits are reconstructions of his study and of his thatched bakery (**La Maison des Champs de Pierre Corneille**, 62 rue Pierre-Corneille, 76650 Petit-Couronne).

Tourville-sur-Arques. Guy de Maupassant's parents rented the **Château de Miromesnil** for a time and according to local records this is where he was born. However, recent opinion tends to the conclusion that he was actually born in the rather less prestigious environment of **Fécamp**, where his mother's family lived.

Varengeville-sur-Mer. La Manoir **d'Ango**, adjacent to the village, was built in the 16th century, but has very 20th century literary connections. In the summer of 1927, Surrealists André Breton (1896–1966) and Louis Aragon (1897–1982) stayed here. Breton wrote a large part of *Nadja*, 1928 (*Nadja*, 1960) – there is a reference to La Manoir d'Ango and a photograph of it in the novel – while Aragon worked on his *Traité du style*, 1928 (*Treatise on Style*, 1991), assertively setting out the theoretical basis of his Surrealism.

Villequier. On 4 September 1843, Victor Hugo (◊ Paris) lost his daughter Léopoldine when she and her husband Charles Vacquerie were drowned in a boating accident at Villequier. Léopoldine was his favourite daughter, and she was only 19 when she died. The house in which the couple were staying has been converted into a museum – **Le Musée Victor Hugo**, rue Ernest-Binet, Villequier, 76490 Caudabec-en-Caux. There are numerous exhibits, including information on Hugo's work, personal memorabilia, a substantial collection of his drawings, correspondence, manuscripts, as well as sculptures and paintings, most notably the portrait of his daughter by Claude-Marie Dubufe which he especially treasured. There is also a reconstruction of a room from the young couple's house at Le Havre, where they lived. Léopoldine and her husband are buried in the small **cemetery** surrounding the church, along with Hugo's wife Adèle, another of his daughters (also Adèle) and members of the Vacquerie family. The devastatingly untimely loss of his daughter is the subject of some of the finest verses in Hugo's *Les Contemplations*, 1856.

Yvetot. Annie Ernaux ◊ grew up here and the town and its people are vividly evoked in her autobiographical novel *La Place*, 1983 (*Positions*, 1991) – Extract 20.

Maupassant went to school in a seminary in Yvetot in 1863–67.

BOOKLIST

For most of the extracted works, the original publisher in English can be found in 'Acknowledgments and Citations' at the end of the volume, as can the exact location of the extracts and the editions from which they are taken. The date in square brackets is that of the original publication of the work in its original language. For additional titles by the authors highlighted in this chapter and recommended biographies, see 'Lives and Works'.

Adams, Henry, *The Education of Henry Adams* [1907], Penguin, London and New York, 1995.

Adams, Henry, *Mont-Saint-Michel and Chartres* [1904], Constable, London, 1950/Viking Penguin, New York, 1986.

Anouilh, Jean, *The Lark* [1953], in *Five Plays*, Methuen, London, 1987.

Aragon, Louis, *Treatise on Style*, A. Water, trans, University of Nebraska Press, Lincoln, NE, 1991.

Balzac, Honoré de, *Eugénie Grandet* [1833], Marion Ayton Crawford, trans, Penguin, London and New York, 1955. **Extract 19.**

Barnes, Julian, *Cross Channel*, Cape, London, 1996/Knopf, New York, 1996.

Barnes, Julian, *Flaubert's Parrot* [1984], Picador, London, 1985/Vintage, New York, 1990. **Extract 15.**

Bates, H.E., *A Breath of French Air* [1959], Penguin, London, 1962.

Beauvoir, Simone de, *The Prime of Life* [1960], P. Green, trans, Penguin, London, 1973/Paragon House, New York, 1992. **Extract 9.**

Beauvoir, Simone de, *She Came to Stay* [1943], Y. Moyse and R. Senhouse, trans, Flamingo, London, 1984/W.W. Norton, New York, 1990.

Boyle, Kay, *Plagued by the Nightingale* [1931], Virago, London, 1981/ Viking Penguin, New York, 1990.

Breton, André, *Nadja* [1928], Richard Howard, trans, Grove Weidenfeld, New York, 1960.

Browning, Robert, *Dramatis Personae* [1864], Macdonald, London, 1975.

Chateaubriand, François-René, *The Memoirs of Chateaubriand* [1849–50], Robert Baldick, trans, Penguin, London and New York, 1965. (Selections.) **Extract 4.**

Chrétien de Troyes, *Arthurian Romances* [12th century], W.W. Comfort, trans, Everyman's Library, Dent, London, 1914/Dutton, New York, 1914.

Conrad, Joseph, *Tales of Unrest* [1898], Penguin, London and New York, 1977.

Cummings, E.E., *The Enormous Room* [1922], Liveright, New York and London, 1978. **Extract 7.**

Dowson, Ernest, 'Breton Afternooon' [1899], in *The Poems of Ernest Dowson*, Mark Longaker, ed, Oxford University Press, London, 1962/University of Pennsylvania Press, Philadelphia, PA, 1962. **Extract 13.**

Du Bellay, Joachim, *The Regrets* [1558], C.H. Sisson, trans, Carcanet, Manchester, 1984.

Duras, Marguerite, *Emily L.* [1987], Barbara Bray, trans, Flamingo, London, 1990/Pantheon, New York, 1989. **Extract 14.**

Ernaux, Annie, *Positions* [1983], Tanya Leslie, trans, Quartet, London, 1991/Seven Stories Press, New York, 1991. **Extract 20.**

Ernaux, Annie, *A Woman's Story* [1988], Tanya Leslie, trans, Quartet, London, 1990/Ballantine, New York, 1992.

Evelyn, John, *The Diary and Correspondence of John Evelyn*, William Bray, ed, Vol 1, George Bell and Sons, London, 1906. **Extract 16.**

Flaubert, Gustave, *Madame Bovary* [1856], Alan Russell, trans, Penguin, London and New York, 1950. **Extract 17.**

Flaubert, Gustave, *A Sentimental Education* [1869], Robert Baldick, trans, Penguin, London and New York, 1964.

Flaubert, Gustave, *Three Tales* [1877], Robert Baldick, trans, Penguin, London and New York, 1961.

Flaubert–Sand: The Correspondence, Francis Steegmuller and Barbara Bray, trans, Harvill, London, 1993.

Flaubert and Turgenev, A Friendship in Letters: The Complete Correspondence, Barbara Beaumont, ed and trans, The Athlone Press, London, 1985.

Fowles, John, *The Ebony Tower* [1974], Panther, London, 1975/ NAL-Dutton, New York, 1991. **Extract 8.**

Genet, Jean, *Querelle of Brest* [1947], Gregory Streatham, trans, Faber and Faber, London, 1990/*Querelle*, Grove Press, New York, 1975. **Extract 1.**

Gide, André, *The Immoralist* [1902], Dorothy Bussy, trans, Penguin, London and New York, 1960.

Gide, André, *Journals 1889–1949*, Justin O'Brien, trans, Penguin, London and New York, 1967. (Selections.) **Extract 5.**

Gide, André, *The Journals of André Gide*, Justin O'Brien, trans, in 4 vols, Knopf, New York, 1947–51.

Gide, André, *La Symphonie Pastorale & Isabelle* [1919, 1911], Dorothy Bussy, trans, Penguin, London, 1984.

Gide, André, *Strait is the Gate* [1909], Dorothy Bussy, trans, Penguin, London, 1969/Random House, New York, 1956.

Gracq, Julien, *A Dark Stranger* [1945],

W.J. Strachan, trans, Harvill, London, 1951.

Hugo, Victor, 'À Villequier', in *The Penguin Book of French Verse*, Brian Woledge, Geoffrey Brereton and Anthony Hartley, eds, Penguin, London and New York, 1975. (French verse with prose translations.)

Hugo, Victor, *Ninety-Three* [1874], Carroll and Graf, New York, 1988.

Kerouac, Jack, *Satori in Paris* [1966], Paladin, London, 1991/Grove Press, New York, 1988. **Extract 2.**

Loti, Pierre, *Iceland Fisherman* [1886], W.P. Baines, trans, Dent, London, 1961.

Maupassant, Guy de, *Pierre et Jean* [1888], L. Tancock, trans, Penguin, London and New York, 1979.

Maupassant, Guy de, *Selected Short Stories*, Roger Colet, trans, Penguin, London and New York, 1971. **Extract 6.**

Maupassant, Guy de, *A Woman's Life* [1883], H.N.P. Sloman, trans, Penguin, London and New York, 1965.

Péguy, Charles, *The Mystery of the Charity of Joan of Arc* [1910], adapted by Jean-Paul Lucet, Jeffrey Wainwright, trans, Carcanet, Manchester, 1986.

Prévert, Jacques, 'Barbara', in *Selections from Paroles*, Lawrence Ferlinghetti, trans, Penguin, London, 1965/City Lights, San Francisco, CA, 1990.

Proust, Marcel, *Remembrance of Things Past* [1913–1927], C.K. Scott Moncrieff and Terence Kilmartin, trans, Penguin, London and New York, 1983. Vol 1 – *Swann's Way* and *Within a Budding Grove*; Vol 2 – *The Guermantes Way* and *Cities of the Plain*; Vol 3 – *The Captive*, *The Fugitive*, and *Time Regained*. **Extract 3.**

Robbe-Grillet, Alain, *Ghosts in the Mirror* [1985], J.Levy, trans, John Calder, London, 1988/Grove Press, New York, 1989.

Roberts, Michèle, *Daughters of the House*, Virago, London, 1992/Avon, New York, 1994. **Extract 11.**

Roberts, Michèle, *A Piece of the Night*, The Womens Press, London, 1978.

Rouaud, Jean, *Fields of Glory* [1990], Ralph Manheim, trans, Harvill, London, 1992/Arcade, Berkeley, CA, 1992. **Extract 10.**

Rouaud, Jean, *Of Illustrious Men* [1993], Barbara Wright, trans, Harvill, London, 1995/Arcade, Berkeley, CA, 1995.

Sévigné, Madame de, *Selected Letters*, Leonard Tancock, trans, Penguin, London, 1982/Penguin, New York, 1982.

Sartre, Jean-Paul, *Nausea* [1939], Robert Baldick, trans, Penguin, London, 1965/Lloyd Alexander, trans, New Directions, New York, 1964.

Shakespeare, William, *King Henry the Fifth* [1598–99], in *Complete Works of Shakespeare*, Peter Alexander, ed, Collins, London, 1951. **Extract 18.**

Shaw, George Bernard, *Saint Joan* [1924], Penguin, London and New York, 1950.

Trollope, Anthony, *La Vendée* [1850], Oxford University Press, Oxford and New York, 1994.

Waddell, Helen, *Peter Abelard* [1933], Constable, London, 1987/Viking Penguin, New York, 1976. **Extract 12.**

Extracts

(1) BREST

Jean Genet, *Querelle of Brest*

Genet, in this scene-setting passage, describes with anticipation the end of the working day in the busy port of Brest, which provides an atmospheric setting for his dark tale of casual sex, murder and betrayal.

It rains sometimes in Brest during September. Wet weather makes the light linen clothes – open shirts and blue jeans – stick skin-tight to the muscular bodies of the men working in the port and arsenal. It happens, of course, that the weather is fine on certain evenings when the groups of masons, carpenters, and mechanics surge out from the shipyards. They are dog-tired. They walk along with dragging steps, and even if they lighten their gait the weight of their heavy tread only squelches with greater pressure into the puddles and the splash sends the drops bubbling up into the air all around them. Slow and ponderous, they move across the bows of the lighter, more rapid, hither-and-thither roving matelots out on the razzle, who are from that time on the chief adornment of the town. Brest will scintillate til daybreak with their dazzling antics, their incandescent gusts of laughter, their songs, their fun and skylarking, with their cat-calls and insults and wolf-whistles at the girls, their kisses, and the gaiety of their three rows of tape and their pom-poms.

The workmen are returning to their huts or lodgings. All through the long day they have toiled (your servicemen, soldiers or sailors, never have the feeling that they have toiled) in the multiple confusion of cooperative enterprise, dovetailing their respective ploys, each performing his allotted task towards the completion of a job which visibly unites them in close affinity. And now they are returning homewards. They are linked by an obscure comradeship – obscure to them – for it has an underlying tinge of hatred. Few of the men are married, and the wives of those few live some distance away. Towards six o'clock in the evening the workmen pass through the iron gates of the Dockyard and the Arsenal. They walk up in the direction of the railway-station where the canteens are, or down the road to Recouvrance where they have rented a cheap hotel. The majority are Italians, the rest Spaniards, with a sprinkling of Maltese and French.

It is among such an orgy of fatigue and relaxed limbs, such a debauch of male lassitude and slack muscles, that Sub-Lieutenant Seblon of *Le Vengeur* delights to saunter.

(2) Brest

Jack Kerouac, *Satori in Paris*

Nervous about wandering the streets of Brest in the small hours with no place to stay, Kerouac elicits the help of the local gendarmes, who take him to an inn on rue Victor Hugo.

A haggard guy like an Irishman comes out and tightens his bathrobe at the door, listens to the gendarmes, okay, leads me into the room next to the desk which I guess is where guys bring their girls for a quickie, unless I'm wrong and taking off again on joking about life – The bed is perfect with seventeen layers of blankets over sheets and I sleep for three hours and suddenly they're yelling and scrambling for breakfast again with shouts across courtyards, bing, bang, clatter of pots and shoes dropping on the second floor, cocks crowing, it's France and morning –

I gotta see it and anyway I cant sleep and where's my cognac!

I wash my teeth with my fingers at the little sink and rub my hair with my fingertips wishing I had my suitcase and step out in the inn like that looking for the toilet naturally. There's old innkeeper, actually a young guy thirty-five and a Breton, I forgot or omitted to ask his name, but he doesnt care how wildhaired I am and that the gendarmes had to find me a room, 'There's the toilet, first right.'

'La Poizette ah?' I yell.

He gives me the look that says 'Get in the toilet and shut up.'

When I come out I am trying to get to my sink in my room to comb my hair but he's already got breakfast coming for me in the diningroom where nobody is but us –

'Wait, comb my hair, get my cigarettes, and, ah, how about a beer first?'

'Wa? You crazy? Have your coffee first, your bread and butter.'

'Just a little beer.'

'A Wright, awright, just one – Sit here when you get back, I've got work to do in the kitchen.'

But this is all spoken that fast and even, but in Breton French which I dont have to make an effort like I do in Parisian French, to enunciate: just: 'Ey, weyondonc, pourquoi t'a peur que j'm'dégrise avec une 'tite bierre?' (Hey, come on, how come you're scared of me sobering up with a little beer?)

'On s'dégrise pas avec la bierre, Monsieur, mais avec le bon petit déjeuner.' (We dont sober up with beer, Monsieur, but with a nice breakfast.)

(3) CABOURG

Marcel Proust, *Within a Budding Grove*

In the second volume of À la recherche du temps perdu, the narrator Marcel, now in his teens, visits the fictional seaside resort of Balbec with his grandmother. Balbec, although derived from Proust's knowledge of various resorts, is principally based on Cabourg. The Grand Hôtel, again inspired by various of its type, owes much to its real-life counterpart in Cabourg.

But how much more were my sufferings increased when we had finally landed in the hall of the Grand Hotel at Balbec, and I stood there in front of the monumental staircase of imitation marble, while my grandmother, regardless of the growing hostility and contempt of the strangers among whom we were about to live, discussed 'terms' with the manager, a pot-bellied figure with a face and a voice alike covered with scars (left by the excision of countless pustules from the one, and from the other of the divers accents acquired from an alien ancestry and a cosmopolitan upbringing), a smart dinner-jacket, and the air of a psychologist who, whenever the 'omnibus' discharged a fresh load, invariably took the grandees for haggling skinflints and the flashy crooks for grandees! Forgetting, doubtless, that he himself was not drawing five hundred francs a month, he had a profound contempt for people to whom five hundred francs – or, as he preferred to put it, 'twenty-five louis' – was 'a lot of money,' and regarded them as belonging to a race of pariahs for whom the Grand Hotel was certainly not intended. It is true that even within its walls there were people who did not pay very much and yet had not forfeited the manager's esteem, provided that he was assured that they were watching their expenditure not from poverty so much as from avarice. For this could in no way lower their standing, since it is a vice and may consequently be found at every grade in the social hierarchy. Social position was the one thing by which the manager was impressed – social position, or rather the signs which seemed to him to imply that it was exalted, such as not taking one's hat off when one came into the hall, wearing knickerbockers or an overcoat with a waist, and taking a cigar with a band of purple and gold out of a crushed morocco case – to none of which advantages could I, alas, lay claim. He would also adorn his business conversation with choice expressions, to which, as a rule, he gave the wrong meaning.

(4) COMBOURG

François-René Chateaubriand, *Memoirs*

Chateaubriand's bedroom in the cold and lonesome Château de
Combourg was high up in the turret known as the 'Tour du Chat' –
it is still there and may be visited (see introduction). He stresses in
his memoirs the significance of his experience of living here in his
formative years.

The window of my keep opened on to the inner courtyard; in the daytime I
had a view of the battlements opposite, where hart's tongue flourished and a
wild plum-tree grew. A few martins, which in summer dived with shrill cries
into the holes in the walls, were my sole companions. At night I could see
only a few stars. When the moon was shining and sinking in the west, I knew
it by the beams which came through the diamond-shaped window-panes and
fell on my bed. Screech-owls, flitting from one tower to the next, passed time
and again between the moon and me, outlining on my curtains the mobile
shadow of their wings. Banished to the loneliest part of the château, at the
entrance to the galleries, I did not miss a single murmur of the darkness.
Sometimes the wind seemed to be running along light-footed; sometimes it
offered mournful plaints; all of a sudden my door was shaken violently, groans
came from the vaults, and then these sounds would die away, only to begin
once more. At four o'clock in the morning, the voice of the master of the
house, calling his valet at the entrance to the ancient cellars, echoed round
the château like the voice of the last phantom of the night. For me this voice
took the place of the sweet music with which Montaigne's father used to
awaken his son.

The Comte de Chateaubriand's unusual idea of making a child sleep by itself
at the top of a tower may have had its inconvenient side, but it turned out to
my advantage. This rough treatment left me with the courage of a man,
without robbing me of that lively imagination of which people nowadays try to
deprive the young. Instead of attempting to persuade me that ghosts did not
exist, my mother and father forced me to stand up to them.

(5) CUVERVILLE

André Gide, *Journals*

Writing in May 1906 from his Normandy home at Cuverville, Gide
captures a moment of pleasure, turns it over in his hands, reflects on
it, and allows the sensuous warmth, sights and smells of a spring day
to flood his senses, one perception leading to another.

Reached Cuverville yesterday. The weather is so beautiful that this day is
related to the happiest days of my childhood. I am writing this in the big room
above the kitchen, between the two open windows through which the sun's
warm joy surges in. Nothing but my tired reflection in the mirror hanging

above my table is an obstacle to the fullest development of my happiness. (I need to learn all over again, and methodically, how to be happy. This is a form of gymnastics, like exercise with dumbbells; it can be *achieved*.) My feet are in the sunlight, wearing green and blue list slippers. The warmth enters into me, rises within me like sap. In order to be utterly happy the only thing necessary is to refrain from comparing this moment with other moments of the past – which I often did not fully enjoy because I was comparing them with other moments of the future. This moment is no less full of delight than any other moment of the future or of the past. The grass of the lawn is deep like the grass in a churchyard. Each apple tree in the farmyard is a thick mass of blossoms. The whitewashed trunks prolong their whiteness right down to the ground. Every breath of air brings me some perfume, especially that of the wisteria, on the left, against the house, so loaded with blossoms that one can hear its bees from here. A bee has come into this room and won't leave. The light envelops each object as with honey.

(6) Étretat

Guy de Maupassant, *The Model*

For his immaculate short story about an ill-matched couple and the tragic consequences of their emotional mistakes, Maupassant chooses the setting of the coastal resort of Étretat, where he himself lived. For the modern reader the technique of this opening passage is cinematic – the author like a camera moving in gradually from the initial panoramic shot for a close-up of the couple whose story is about to be told.

Curved like a crescent moon, the little town of Étretat, with its white cliffs, its white shingle and its blue sea, was dozing in the sunshine of a bright July day. At the two horns of the crescent the two gates jutted out into the calm water, the smaller on the right like a dwarf foot, the larger on the left like a giant leg; and the needle, broad at the base and tapering upwards almost to the height of the cliff, pointed its sharp tip towards the sky.

On the beach a crowd of people were sitting along the water's edge watching the bathers. On the Casino terrace another crowd was sitting or walking about under the cloudless sky, resembling a colourful garden with the ladies' bright dresses and the red and blue parasols embroidered with large silk flowers. And on the promenade at the end of the terrace some other people, the quiet, sedate members of the community, were sauntering up and down, far away from the elegant throng.

A young man called Jean Summer, well known as a painter of note, was walking glumly beside an invalid chair in which a young woman, his wife, was sitting. A manservant was slowly pushing the bathchair along, and the crippled woman was gazing sadly at the gay skies, the gay sunshine and the gay crowds.

They neither spoke nor looked at one another.

'Let's stop a minute,' said the woman.

They stopped, and the painter sat down on a folding stool which the manservant opened out for him.

The people passing behind the silent, motionless couple looked at them pityingly. Their devotion had become a local legend: he had married her in spite of her infirmity, touched by her love, people said.

Not far away two young men were sitting on a capstan, chatting and idly looking out to sea.

'No, it isn't true,' one of them said. 'I tell you I know Jean Summer very well.'

'Then why did he marry her? For she *was* already crippled at the time, wasn't she?'

'Yes, she was. He married her . . . he married her . . . for the reason men always marry, because he was a fool.'

(7) La Ferté Macé

E.E. Cummings, *The Enormous Room*

Cummings's narrator 'C', newly arrived at the detention camp in the town of La Ferté-Macé (where Cummings was interred for three months in 1917), has his first experience of the lunch menu. Note: the current edition, from which this extract is taken, is typographically faithful to Cummings and therefore has no space before commas and other medial punctuation marks.

The din was perfectly terrific. It had a minutely large quality. Here and there,in a kind of sonal darkness,solid sincere unintelligible absurd wisps of profanity heavily flickered. Optically the phenomenon was equally remarkable:seated waggingly swaying corpse-like figures,swaggering,pounding with their little spoons,roaring hoarse unkempt. Evidently Monsieur le Surveillant had been forgotten. All at once the roar bulged unbearably. The roguish man,followed by the chef himself,entered with a suffering waddle,each of them bearing a huge bowl of steaming something. At least six people immediately rose,gesturing and imploring:'Ici' – 'Mais non, ici' – 'Mettez par ici' –

The bearers plumped their burdens carefully down,one at the head of the table and one in the middle. The men opposite the bowls stood up. Every man seized the empty plate in front of him and shoved it into his neighbor's hand;the plates moved toward the bowls,were filled amid uncouth protestations and accusations – 'Mettez plus que ça' – 'C'est pas juste, alors' – 'Donnez-moi encore des pommes' – 'Nom de Dieu, il n'y a pas assez' – 'Cohon, qu'est-ce qu'il veut?' – 'Shut up' – 'Gottverdummer' – and returned one by one. As each man received his own,he fell upon it with a sudden guzzle.

Eventually,in front of me,solemnly sat a faintly-smoking urine-coloured circular broth,in which soggily hung half-suspended slabs of raw potato. Following the example of my neighbors,I too addressed myself to La Soupe. I found her luke-warm, completely flavorless. I examined the hunk of bread. It was almost bluish in colour; in taste, mouldy, slightly sour. 'If you crumb some into the soup', remarked B, who had been studying my reactions from the corner of his eye, 'they both taste better.' I tried the experiment. It was a complete success. At least one felt as if one were getting nourishment. Between gulps I smelled the bread furtively. It smelled rather much like an old attic in which kites and other toys gradually are forgotten in a gentle darkness.

(8) Forêt de Paimpont

John Fowles, *The Ebony Tower*

Fowles's short story uses the Forêt de Paimpont, also known by its Arthurian name of Brocéliande, as a significant setting. Here, the young art critic David Williams is walking in the forest with the ageing artist Henry Breasley, about whom he is writing a book, and Breasley's two young female companions.

David was rather more noticing that all this could be used in his introduction. *Anyone who has had the good fortune to walk with the master, no, with Henry Breasley in his beloved forest of Paimpont, that still potent evocation . . .* the haze had gone, it was surprisingly warm, more like August than September, a peerless day; one couldn't actually write like that. But he was still basking – realizing his baptism of fire had been a blessing in disguise – in the old man's determined good graces. The importance, pervasive in mood if tenuous in the actual symbolism, of Breton medieval literature in the Coëtminais series was generally accepted now, though David had not been able to trace much public clarification from Breasley himself on the real extent of the influence. He had read the subject up cursorily before coming, but now he played a little ignorant; and discovered Breasley to be rather more learned and lettered than his briskly laconic manner at first sound suggested. The old man explained in his offhand way the sudden twelfth- and thirteenth-century mania for romantic legends, the mystery of island Britain ('sort of Wild Northern, what, knights for cowboys') filtering all over Europe *via* its French namesake; the sudden preoccupation with love and adventure and the magical, the importance of the once endless forest – of which the actual one they were walking in, Paimpont now, but the Brocéliande of the *lais* of Chrétien de Troyes, was an example – as the matrix for all these goings-on; the breaking out of the closed formal garden of other medieval art, the extraordinary yearning symbolized in these wandering horsemen and lost damsels and dragons and wizards, Tristan and Merlin and Lancelot . . .

'All damn' nonsense,' said Breasley. 'Just here and there, don't you know, David. What one needs. Suggestive. Stimulating, that's the word.' Then he went off on Marie de France and *Eliduc*. 'Damn' good tale. Read it several times. What's that old Swiss bamboozler's name. Jung, yes? His sort of stuff. Archetypal and all that.'

Ahead, the two girls turned off on a diagonal and narrower ride, more shady. Breasley and David followed some forty yards behind. The old man waved his stick.

'Those two gels now. Two gels in *Eliduc*.'

(9) LE HAVRE

Simone de Beauvoir, *The Prime of Life*

In the 1930s both Sartre and Beauvoir found themselves teaching at provincial lycées in Normandy, he at Le Havre and she at Rouen. Le Havre was their preferred meeting place.

We generally met in Le Havre, which struck us as being a more cheerful place than Rouen. I loved the old docks, and the *quais* with their sailors' dives and disreputable hotels, and the narrow houses, their slate roofs pulled down over their eyes: one façade was plastered from top to bottom with sea shells. The most attractive street in this area was the Rue des Galions, all lighted up at night with its multicoloured signs – the Chat Noir, the Lanterne Rouge, the Moulin Rose, the Étoile Violette. Everyone in Le Havre knew it. Between two brothels, each guarded by a tough pimp, was that renowned restaurant, La Grosse Tonne; we went there occasionally to sample the *sole normande* and *soufflé au calvados*. Most of the time we ate in the big Brasserie Paillette, a quiet and commonplace establishment. We spent hours on end in the Café Guillaume Tell, where Sartre often settled down to write; with its red plush banquettes and plate-glass bay windows it was a very comfortable sort of place. The people with whom we rubbed elbows in the streets and public squares were a more animated and motley crowd than the good folk of Rouen. The reason for this was that Le Havre was a big port, where people from all parts of the world mingled. A lot of big business was handled there by up-to-date methods; the inhabitants lived in the present instead of burying themselves in the shadows of the past. When it was fine weather we sat out on the veranda of a little bistro near the beach, called Les Mouettes. I would eat plums in brandy and gaze at the green and choppy sea, far away in the middle distance. We strolled down the broad central boulevards, climbed up to Sainte-Adresse, and wandered through lanes high above the city, lined with wealthy villas. In Rouen there were always walls to block my vision; here one's eye could travel to the horizon, and a fresh wind blew in my face from the uttermost parts of the earth. Two or three times we took a boat across to Honfleur. This little slate-built port, where the past seemed to have survived in all its freshness, we found a charming place.

(10) LOIRE-ATLANTIQUE

Jean Rouaud, *Fields of Glory*

Rouaud's novel, through intimate character portaits of members of a family living in a small town in the département of the Lower Loire (now Loire-Atlantique), records the passing of a way of life with the ravages of the First World War. His facility for writing sharply descriptive prose laced with gentle irony and subtle psychology is readily apparent in this short passage on the region's damp climate.

In the Lower Loire, rain is a life companion. It gives the region, which is otherwise rather nondescript, a characteristic style. Clouds charged with ocean mist plunge into the Loire estuary near Saint-Nazare, follow the river upstream, and like an endless bucket chain empty their excess humidity on the Nantes area. The actual amount of water cannot bear comparison with the monsoon rains, but is distributed so evenly over the whole year that in the minds of casual visitors, who are not always favoured with a break in the clouds, the region's reputation for cloud and rain is soon established. It is hard to undeceive them, even by pointing out the legendary mildness of the climate – witness the mimosa in the hinterland and, here and there in the gardens of leading citizens, a dog-eared palm tree – because the statistics on precipitation and hours of sunshine speak for themselves. Undeniably it's a damp climate, but in the end you get used to it. Under a persistent drizzle you swear in all seriousness that it's not raining. Wearers of glasses wipe the rain off them twenty times a day without thinking, get used to walking behind a constellation of droplets that diffract and break up the landscape, creating a gigantic kaleidoscope in which, unable to take bearings, they let themselves be guided by memory. But at nightfall, when a gentle rain descends on the town and the neon signs come on, inscribing their luminous calligraphy on the blue-black night, those little dancing stars that glitter before your eyes, those blue, red, green and yellow sparks that splatter your glasses, suggest the *son et lumière* at Versailles. And how dull the original seems by comparison when you take off your glasses.

(11) NORMANDIE: COUNTRYSIDE

Michèle Roberts, *Daughters of the House*

Thérèse, one of the two protagonists in Roberts's novel, returns to the village of her childhood after 20 years' absence. The village of Blémont-la-Fontaine is fictional.

The bus plunged along the banks of the Seine. Thérèse remembered strings of ancient houses, black and cream displays of timbering, plaster, thatch. The great flat river sliding between cliffs. A calm green emptiness which turned in spring to a pink carnival of flowering orchards. How many new houses there were now, how very tidy and rebuilt everything seemed. *Restored*, that was the word one used. *Corrected. Freshened.*

She felt peculiar. It was her clothes, she decided. Her knees exposed by the skirt of her dress riding up when she sat down. Her legs, nude in fawn nylons. Her general sense of skimpy coverings, of being too visible. In the bus she was a focus for others' glances, however casual, and she resented it.

When at Caudebec a couple of Algerian men got on to the bus Thérèse stared at them. Black people didn't live in the green Norman countryside. Surely they all lived in ghettoes on the outskirts of cities.

Mutters from the other passengers reached her.

A bad lot, I'm afraid, always looking for trouble.

Far too many of them coming in.

Thérèse turned her head aside and gazed out of the window. Billboards hoisted posters in Gothic lettering that advertised ancient inns, traditional cider and Calvados, authentic butter and cheese. Grandmother's this and that, everything from pine furniture to apricot jam. The signs all pointed somewhere else: over there; that's the real thing. Then the bus jolted round a sharp corner with a blare of its horn and they swept into Blémont's little main street.

The bus-stop, just as in the old days, was the area of pavement outside the *Mairie*. This florid building was now painted salmon pink, no longer the faded grey that Thérèse remembered. She shrugged, watching the bus depart, backside of blue glass farting exhaust. She stooped to pick up her bags.

(12) LE PALAIS

Helen Waddell, *Peter Abelard*

Abelard arrives in his native Brittany from Paris to see Heloise at Le Palais, where he has taken her for her safety and where she has given birth to their son. Waddell effectively contrasts the wildness and fertility of Brittany with the scholasticism of Abelard's life in the cloisters of Notre Dame.

They had been faggoting here, he saw, but had not finished staking them: the faggots lay here and there as they had been tied, strangely black against the quick green of the grass, and growing among them as though the sunlight had spilled itself, the primroses lay in drifts. He reined in the mare that he might look at it. Something older stirred in him than the movement of his heart at the sight of his ancient roof-tree. He saw the faggots, dead in spring, with their promise of winter fires: the eternal rhythm of the seasons spoke to his blood: he saw the succession of life and death, and the hearth that gave life unto the world.

So when as it seemed to him his eyes were opened and he saw her, it was with no surprise, with hardly a quicker beat of his pulse. How should she not be here, that was the stillness in the heart of flame, the beauty of all beauty? She had been kneeling, gathering primroses, and now moved out from the stack of faggots that had hidden her, but he had no thought for that, nor how it was that at first the valley had held all the promise of the earth but this, and then had flowered in her. She stood there, holding up her long green gown to make a lap for the flowers, her head bowed, gravely pondering. Have you gathered enough, O Beloved, for the woodland rides of the world? For in that green lap lies the seed of mortal beauty, the sap of ancient trees, the white flower of the thorn.

For a long moment, silence kept the valley. Then the mare, impatient to be home, pawed the soft ground and tossed her head with a jingling of the bit. At the sharp sound in that quiet place, Heloise raised her head, and saw a strange horseman on the track beside the stream. The light was in her eyes. She put up her hand to shade them, but in that moment he had leapt to the ground and was striding towards her, his cloak streaming behind him in the old remembered gesture. She did not move to meet him, because she could not: but as he came nearer he cried aloud, not to greet her, but at the glory that was in her face.

(13) PONT-AVEN

Ernest Dowson, *Breton Afternoon*

Dowson sheds his elegant fin-de-siècle melancholic light on the rural peacefulness of the Breton countryside, as he takes time out from his cares and woes. The poem was first published in the volume Decorations *in 1899. It was written in Pont-Aven, where Dowson was living in 1896.*

Here, where the breath of the scented-gorse floats through the sun-stained air
On a steep hill-side, on a grassy ledge, I have lain hours long and heard
Only the faint breeze pass in a whisper like a prayer,
And the river ripple by and the distant call of a bird.

On the lone hill-side, in the gold sunshine, I will hush me and repose,
And the world fades into a dream and a spell is cast on me;
And what was all the strife about, for the myrtle or the rose,
And why have I wept for a white girl's paleness passing ivory!

Out of the tumult of angry tongues, in a land alone, apart,
In a perfumed dream-land set betwixt the bounds of life and death,
Here will I lie while the clouds fly by and delve an hole where my heart
May sleep deep down with the gorse above and red, red earth beneath.

Sleep and be quiet for an afternoon, till the rose-white angelus
Softly steals my way from the village under the hill:
Mother of God, O Misericord, look down in pity on us,
The weak and blind who stand in our light and wreak ourselves such ill.

(14) Quillebeuf

Marguerite Duras, *Emily L.*

This short and intriguing novel is set in the decaying fishing port of Quillebeuf. Throughout the book, the narrator and her partner remain in the café of the Hôtel de la Marine, leaving it only through memory and imagination, while Duras proceeds to explore the process of creating fiction from reality.

We'd driven to Quillebeuf, as we often did that summer.

We got there at the usual time, late afternoon. As usual we went for a stroll beside the white rail that runs along the quayside from the church at the entrance to the harbor to the disued path that leads out of it, probably to the forest of Brotonne.

We look at the tanker port on the other side of the river, and at the tall cliffs of Le Havre in the distance, and at the sky. Then at the red ferry crossing and the people being taken across the river. And all the time, frail and white, fencing off the water, there's the rail.

We go and sit on the terrace outside the Hôtel de la Marine, in the middle of the square, opposite the ramp leading onto the ferry.

The tables are in the shadow of the hotel buildings. The air is still. There's no wind.

I look at you. You're looking at the place. The heat. The flat waters of the river. The summer. And then you look past all that. With your hands, your beautiful white hands, clasped under your chin, you look without seeing. Without moving, you ask me what's the matter. I answer as usual. Nothing's the matter. I'm just looking at you.

You don't move at first, then from where I'm sitting I can see a smile in your eyes. You say, 'You like this place. One day it'll all be in a book – the square, the heat, the river.'

I don't answer. I don't know. I tell you I don't know in advance, or only very rarely.

(15) Rouen

Julian Barnes, *Flaubert's Parrot*

In these opening paragraphs of the novel, Barnes's troubled narrator, Geoffrey Braithwaite, contemplates Flaubert's statue in Rouen and reveals his concern for detail – a concern which he hopes will lead him to some of the answers he seeks.

Six North Africans were playing boule beneath Flaubert's statue. Clean cracks sounded over the grumble of jammed traffic. With a final, ironic caress from the fingertips, a brown hand dispatched a silver globe. It landed, hopped heavily, and curved in a slow scatter of hard dust. The thrower remained a stylish, temporary statue: knees not quite unbent, and the right hand ecstatically spread. I noticed a furled white shirt, a bare forearm and a blob on the back of the wrist. Not a watch, as I first thought, or a tattoo, but a coloured transfer: the face of a political sage much admired in the desert.

Let me start with the statue: the one above, the permanent, unstylish one, the one crying cupreous tears, the floppy-tied, square-waistcoated, baggy-trousered, straggle-moustached, wary, aloof bequeathed image of the man. Flaubert doesn't return the gaze. He stares south from the place des Carmes towards the Cathedral, out over the city he despised, and which in turn has largely ignored him. The head is defensively high: only the pigeons can see the full extent of the writer's baldness.

This statue isn't the original one. The Germans took the first Flaubert away in 1941, along with the railings and the door-knockers. Perhaps he was processed into cap-badges. For a decade or so, the pedestal was empty. Then a Mayor of Rouen who was keen on statues rediscovered the original plaster cast – made by a Russian called Leopold Bernstamm – and the city council approved the making of a new image. Rouen bought itself a proper metal statue in 93 per cent copper and 7 per cent tin: the founders, Rudier of Châtillon-sous-Bagneux, assert that such an alloy is guarantee against corrosion. Two other towns, Trouville and Barentin, contributed to the project and received stone statues. These have worn less well. At Trouville Flaubert's upper thigh has had to be patched, and bits of his moustache have fallen off: structural wires poke out like twigs from a concrete stub on his upper lip.

(16) ROUEN

John Evelyn, *Diary*

This extract is from Evelyn's diary entry of 18 March 1644. He had stayed previously in Rouen during his tour of France in 1643–44.

I lay at the White Cross in Rouen, which is a very large city, on the Seine, having two smaller rivers besides, called the Aubette and the Robec. There stand yet the ruins of a magnificent bridge of stone, now supplied by one of the boats only, to which come up vessels of considerable burthen. The other side of the water consists of meadows, and there have the Reformed a Church.

The Cathedral Nôtre Dame was built, as they acknowledge, by the English; some English words graven in Gothic characters upon the front seem to confirm it. The towers and whole church are full of carving. It has three steeples, with a pyramid; in one of these I saw the famous bell so much talked of, thirteen feet in height, thirty-two round, the diameter eleven, weighing 40,000 pounds.

In the Chapel d'Amboise, built by a Cardinal of that name, lies his body, with several fair monuments. The choir has behind it a great dragon painted on the wall, which they say had done much harm to the inhabitants, till vanquished by St. Romain, their Archbishop; for which there is an annual procession. It was now near Easter, and many images were exposed with scenes and stories representing the Passion; made up of little puppets, to which there was great resort and devotion, with offerings. Before the church is a fair palace. St. Ouen is another goodly church and an abbey with fine gardens. Here the King hath lodgings, when he makes his progress through these parts. The structure, where the Court of Parliament is kept, is very magnificent, containing very fair halls and chambers, especially La Chambre Dorée. The town-house is also well built, and so are some gentlemen's houses; but most part of the rest are of timber, like our merchants' in London, in the wooden part of the city.

(17) ROUEN

Gustave Flaubert, *Madame Bovary*

The coach from Yonville carries Emma Bovary on her weekly escape from her small-town life to the bustle and energy of Rouen, where she surreptitiously meets her lover Léon, the sights, sounds and smells of the city providing her with the intoxication she needs for her romantic adventure.

That mass of life down there gave her a dizzy feeling. Her heart swelled, as though those hundred and twenty thousand throbbing hearts had sent up to her all at once the fumes of the passions she imagined to be theirs. Her love expanded in that vast space before her. It was filled with tumult at the vague hubbub that arose. Then she poured it out again upon the squares and promenades and streets; and that ancient Norman city lay outspread beneath her eyes like an enormous metropolis, a Babylon awaiting her. She leaned out of the window, holding on with both hands, and sniffed the breeze. The three horses were galloping along, the pebbles grinding in the mud, the coach rocking, Hivert hailing the traffic from afar, while the good citizens who had been spending the night at the Bois-Guillaume peacefully descended the hill in their little family carriages.

They stopped at the city gates. Emma unbuckled her overshoes, put on a fresh pair of gloves, rearranged her shawl, and twenty yards farther on stepped out of the *Hirondelle*.

The town was waking. Shop fronts were being polished by assistants in caps, and at the street corners women with baskets at their hips uttered occasional resonant cries. She slipped along the wall, her eyes on the ground, smiling for joy beneath her lowered black veil.

To avoid the main streets, where she might be seen, Emma plunged into dark alley-ways, and emerged, wet with perspiration, at the lower end of the Rue Nationale, close by the fountain. This is the district of the theatres, bars and brothels. Often a cart would pass by loaded with rickety stage scenery. Aproned waiters scattered sand over the pavement, between the tubs of evergreen. She walked amid a smell of absinthe, cigars and oysters.

She turned a corner and recognized his crimped hair curling out beneath his hat.

Léon continued along the pavement. She followed him to the hotel. He climbed the stairs. He opened the door. He went in. . . . What an embrace! And after kisses, such a flood of words, as they recounted the troubles of the week, their misgivings, their anxiety about the letters. But it was all over now, and they gazed at one another with voluptuous laughter and tender endearments on their lips.

(18) ROUEN

William Shakespeare, *Henry V*

Following his bloody success at Agincourt in 1415, Henry re-invaded France in 1417, eventually capturing the capital of the duchy of Normandy in 1419 (it remained under English rule until 1449). This was followed by the marriage of Henry to Catherine, daughter of the French King Charles VI – under the marriage treaty Henry became heir to the French crown. Shakespeare's imagined courtship of 'Kate' by Henry plays with the idea of the rough English soldier-king in the polished French court and produces this famous romantically unromantic proposal.

Marry, if you would put me to verses or to dance for your sake, Kate, why you undid me; for the one I have neither words nor measure, and for the other I have no strength in measure, yet a reasonable measure in strength. If I could win a lady at leap-frog, or by vaulting into my saddle with my armour on my back, under the correction of bragging be it spoken, I should quickly leap into a wife. Or if I might buffet for my love, or bound my horse for her favours, I could lay on like a butcher, and sit like a jack-an-apes, never off. But, before God, Kate, I cannot look greenly, nor gasp out my eloquence, nor I have no cunning in protestation; only downright oaths, which I never use till urg'd, nor ever break for urging. If thou canst love a fellow of this temper, Kate, whose face is not worth sun-burning, that never looks in his glass for love of anything he sees there, let thine eye be thy cook. I speak to thee plain soldier. If thou canst love me for this, take me; if not, to say to thee that I shall die is true – but for thy love, by the lord, no; yet I love thee too. And while thou liv'st, dear Kate, take a fellow of plain and uncoined constancy; for he perforce must do thee right, because he hath not the gift to woo in other places; for these fellows of infinite tongue, that can rhyme themselves into ladies' favours, they do always reason themselves out again. What! a speaker is but a prater: a rhyme is but a ballad. A good leg will fall; a straight back will stoop; a black beard will turn white; a curl'd pate will grow bald; a fair face will whither; a full eye will wax hollow. But a good heart, Kate, is the sun and the moon; or, rather, the sun, and not the moon – for it shines bright and never changes, but keeps his course truly. If thou would have such a one, take me; and take me, take a soldier; take a soldier, take a king. And what say'st thou, then, to my love? Speak, my fair, and fairly, I pray thee.

(19) SAUMUR

Honoré de Balzac, *Eugénie Grandet*

*The small town of Saumur, the centre of the Anjou wine trade, is
the setting for Balzac's famous novel of miserliness and its consequences. Introducing his readers to Saumur, Balzac is at pains to relate
everything to money, which is to play such a major role in the
ensuing story.*

You will see a dealer in barrel staves sitting at his door twiddling his thumbs as
he gossips with a neighbour: to all appearances he possesses nothing more than
some rickety bottle racks and two or three bundles of laths, yet his
well-stocked timber-yard on the quay supplies all the coopers in Anjou. He
knows, to a stave, how many casks he can *do* for you, if the vintage is good. A
few scorching days make his fortune. A spell of rainy weather ruins him. In a
single morning the price of a puncheon may rise to eleven francs or fall to six.

Here, as in Touraine, the business done in the district is dependent on the
weather's vagaries. Vinegrowers, land-owners, timber-merchants, coopers,
innkeepers, lightermen are all on the watch for a ray of sunshine. They go to
be in a state of dread, fearing they may hear next morning that there has been
a frost in the night. They dread rain, and wind and drought as well: they would
like the weather arranged to suit them, and humidity, warmth, and cloud laid
on according to their requirements. There is a perpetual dual in progress
between celestial forces and terrestrial interests. Faces lengthen or deck
themselves with smiles as the barometer falls or rises. You may hear the words
'This is golden weather!' passed from mouth to mouth, or the remark 'It's
raining gold louis!' exchanged between neighbours, from one end to the other
of this street, the Old High Street of Saumur; and everyone knows to a sou just
how much profit a sunbeam or a timely shower is bringing him, and is mentally
engaged in setting down figures accordingly on the credit side of his ledger.
After about twelve o'clock on a Saturday in the summer you will not be able to
do a sou's worth of business with these fine businessmen. Each of them has his
vineyard, his own little bit of land, and goes there for the week-end.

(20) YVETOT

Annie Ernaux, *Positions*

Shortly after the end of the Second World War, the narrator's parents in Ernaux's autobiographical novel take over a small café and grocery store in Yvetot ('Y———'), a town in the centre of the Caux region. The 'positions' of the title (like 'La Place' in the French), are positions in society, the defining boundaries of class which isolate or alienate one section of a community from another, a daughter from her father . . .

It was a café for regulars, habitual drinkers who dropped in before or after work and whose place was sacred: gangs from the building sites, as well as a few customers whose *position* meant they could have chosen a less proletarian establishment: a retired naval officer and an inspector from the national health service. In other words, *humble* people. The Sunday clientele was different, with whole families rolling in for an aperitif around eleven, lemonade for the children. In the afternoon it was then men from the old people's home who had been allowed until six. They were a merry, noisy lot and enjoyed singing popular songs. Occasionally, when they'd had one too many, they had to sober up on a blanket in one of the outhouses before being fit to be sent back to the nuns. Going to their Sunday local was like visiting the family. My father was aware of the social role he played by offering a temple of freedom and rejoicing to those who, as he put it, 'had not always been like that', although he couldn't exactly say why they had turned that way. Obviously, for those who had never set foot in the café, it was just a 'boozer' where one drank oneself silly. The girls employed by the underwear factory next door would turn up after work to celebrate birthdays, weddings and departures. From the shop they bought packets of sponge fingers which they dipped into *vin mousseux*, bursting into peals of laughter, bent double over the café tables.

As I write, I try to steer a middle course between rehabilitating a lifestyle generally considered to be inferior, and denouncing the feelings of estrangement it brings with it. This was the way we lived and so of course we were happy although we realized the humiliating limitations of our class. (We knew full well that 'it wasn't quite good enough at our place'.) Consequently I would like to convey both the happiness and the alienation we felt. Instead, it seems that I am constantly wavering between the two.

Lives and works of extracted writers

BALZAC, Honoré de. See Centre.

BARNES, Julian (1946–). English novelist Barnes has said in interviews that he was astonished at the enormous international success of *Flaubert's Parrot*, 1984 (Extract 15), the novel that made him the first English writer to win the prestigious Prix Médicis. He presumably thought that the esoteric subject matter, experimental narrative, and the interweaving of literary criticism with the story would make it a book for minority tastes – thus modestly ignoring the lucidity of style and thought and the perfectly pitched humour which make this a hugely impressive and at the same time readily accessible book. The parrot of the title is the stuffed one, named Loulou, in

Julian Barnes

Flaubert's story 'Un coeur simple' (see under Flaubert, below). The book, set largely in **Rouen** and **Croisset**, is narrated by Geoffrey Braithwaite, a doctor who is an amateur researcher. The core of his investigation is to discover the 'real' stuffed parrot which was the inspiration behind Loulou in Flaubert's tale. Reality, as you might expect, remains elusive. The book contains many interesting anecdotal notes about Flaubert's life, but it becomes increasingly clear to the reader that the narrative is filtered through the subjective perspective of Dr Braithwaite, whose own experiences and crises, in particular the suicide of his wife, are the parallel subject of this skilful, multi-layered and amusing novel.

Also of interest to readers of this guide will be *Metroland*, 1980, part of which is set in **Paris** amid the student unrest of 1968, and *Cross Channel*, 1996, a set of short stories which explore aspects of the English relationship to France and the French.

Barnes himself has significant cross-Channel appeal – his work is highly regarded in France. In addition to the Prix Médicis for *Flaubert's Parrot*, he was awarded the Prix Fémina in 1992 for *Talking It Over*, 1991, and in 1995 he became an Officier de l'Ordre des Arts et des Lettres.

BEAUVOIR, Simone de. See under Paris.

CHATEAUBRIAND, François-René (1768–1848). Chateaubriand, for many the 'founding father' of Romanticism, was born in **Saint-Malo** on 4 September 1768 into a Breton noble family. He spent his youth in Brittany – among his most formative experiences were his two years (1784–86) at the **Château de Combourg**, which proved fertile territory for the development of Chateaubriand's melancholic Romantic imagination (see introduction and Extract 4). He left Combourg to join the army, was presented at Court, and at the same time began to mix in literary circles. When the French Revolution came, Chateaubriand witnessed its early stages, including the fall of the Bastille, and, while sympathizing with its aims, became increasingly disgusted with its violence and direction. In June 1971, he set sail for a voyage of exploration to America: his exotic tale *Atala*, 1801 (*Atala and René*, 1952), which brought him literary fame, and his prose epic *Les Natchez*, 1826 (*The Natchez: an Indian Tale*, 1827), draw on his experiences and impressions.

Learning of the fall of the monarchy, Chateaubriand returned to France in 1792. Fighting with the Royalist Armée des Émigrés, he was wounded, honourably discharged and left for England, where he stayed for several years. He was back in France in 1800 and shortly afterwards published *Le Génie du christianisme*, 1802 (*The Genius of Christianity*, 1856), which, chiming well with the restoration of Roman Catholicism as the official religion of France, brought him into favour with Napoleon. There followed a spell in Rome as First Secretary to the French Ambassador, and further adventurous travels – this time in Greece and the Middle East. In 1807, Chateaubriand, increasingly critical of Napoleon's regime, was forced to leave Paris and took a property called La Vallée-aux-Loups in **Châtenay** (see under Île de France), where he stayed for some ten years. Here, he wrote, among other things, his epic *Les Martyrs*, 1809 (*The Martyrs*, 1859), and the *Itinéraire de Paris à Jerusalem*, 1811. Most importantly, he did substantial work on his *Mémoires d'outre-tombe*, 1849–50 (*Memoirs*, 1961) which he was to continue writing for the next 40 years.

Under the restored monarchy of Louis XVIII, Chateaubriand sustained his involvement in political life, moving in and out of favour, and eventually forced to sell La Vallée-aux-Loups because of a financial crisis deepened by a loss of position. Back in favour, he later served as ambassador in both Berlin and London, and, as minister of foreign affairs in 1823, he was influential in the French policy of intervention in Spain. He was also briefly, under Charles X, ambassador to Rome. Following the July Revolution in 1830 and the taking of the throne by Louis-Philippe, Chateaubriand resigned all his remaining official appointments in support of the deposed monarch Charles, of whom he had himself been severely critical.

In the later part of his life, he devoted himself to writing. His great consolation was Juliette Récamier, whom he visited daily in the **rue du Bac** in **Paris**. He gave a series of readings from his *Memoirs* at her prestigious literary *salon*. Never in love with his wife, Chateaubriand had had a large number of 'madams', as she came to call them. Récamier, however, was the 'Arch-Madam', the great love of his life and very influential in helping him complete what is now regarded as his greatest work.

The *Memoirs* were finished in 1847. Chateaubriand died in 1848 (he did not see their publication), and was buried, as he had long planned, on the little **Île du Grand Bé**, just off the coast from Saint-Malo (see introduction).

Chateaubriand's *Memoirs* (Extract 4) constitute a vivid examination not only of his own personal development and experiences, from early childhood to old age, but also of the period in which he lived, from the Ancien Régime to the July Monarchy (there are portraits of the kings, politicians – Mirabeau, Danton, Talleyrand – and, especially, of Napoleon). The early part of the book, about the author's childhood and adolescence in Brittany, is particularly memorable. Shot through with his melancholic vision, richly lyrical in style, testimony to his belief in the power of the passions and the imagination, the *Memoirs* present us with a highly personalized account of the varied and remarkable life of one of the most influential figures in French literary history.

Recommended biography: George Painter, *Chateaubriand: A Biography*, Chatto and Windus, London, 1977 (3 vols).

CUMMINGS, E.E. (1894–1962). Edward Estlin Cummings arrived in France in 1917, having signed up for service in the Norton-Harjes Ambulance Service. After a few happy weeks discovering Paris, he took up his duties. His wartime experiences were to provide him with the raw material for his first book.

Cummings's remarkable *The Enormous Room*, 1922 (Extract 7), is an autobiographical novel based on his internment in a detention camp at **La Ferté-Macé** in September–December 1917. He served as an ambulance driver in a *Section Sanitaire* on the Somme at **Germaine**, near **St Quentin**. He and his friend William Slater Brown, an American college student, spent more time with the French than their fellow Americans and were not on good terms with the rest of the Section, especially with a Mr Anderson, its head. Brown was arrested because of rather too frank letters he wrote to friends in America about the low morale of the French troops and various other items of gossip from the French soldiers he associated with – Cummings was arrested for no better ostensible reason than that he was Brown's friend, although Anderson's dislike of him was clearly not immaterial. As a consequence of this, he was transported to the detention camp at La Ferté-Macé and his experiences there form the basis of *The Enormous Room*. As would be expected from the experimental painter and poet, the book is unique as war memoirs go. Written in a variety of styles, with narrative allusions to Bunyan's *Pilgrim's Progress*, many French words and phrases in the normal flow of the text, full of humour and light irony, both realistic and surrealistic (as befits the story it relates), the novel has the energy and excitement of a kind of a merry adventure – 'C' and 'B' frequently declare how glad they are to be in the prison camp rather than in the company of the detested Mr Anderson and, despite its brutal and oppressive regime, the camp is some kind of oasis from the chaos of war. The gruesome reality and the injustices of internment are subdued by the soaring individualism of the narrator and the many fellow inmates whose characters he sets out in larger-than-life detail. At another level, the camp and its regime are equivalent to national governments and the oppression, prejudices, and injustices they perpetrate on their citizens, the 'inmates'. *The Enormous Room* was much praised on its first publication, although Cummings himself was unhappy with changes to his style and various omissions. These were improved, at least to some extent, in subsequent editions. The current (1978) edition is to be praised for its inclusion of the full text, Cummings's original and characteristic punctuation, and a selection of the author's own illustrations.

Cummings was released in December 1917 and went back to the USA. He returned to Europe in 1921 with his friend Dos Passos, and stayed for two and a half years, travelling widely but based in **Paris**. The city excited and attracted him and he records his impressions and experiences in poetry, drawings and letters. It was here that he met Ezra Pound, with whom he developed a lifelong friendship. Cummings revisited Paris a number of times in the 1930s–60s, but never lived there permanently again.

Recommended biography: Richard S. Kennedy, *Dreams in the Mirror: A Biography of E.E. Cummings*, Liveright, New York, 1980.

DOWSON, Ernest (1867–1900). Thanks largely to the emphasis of early commentaries, Dowson has become the archetype of the melancholic and self-destructive poet, personifying *fin-de-siècle* languour and decadence. Although reports of his decadence may have been greatly exaggerated, there is no doubt that the world weariness and melodic sadness of his verse speak to kindred spirits here at the end of the 20th century, as perhaps does his sense of rootlessness and alienation. Never really comfortable in his home country, Dowson felt a special affinity with France and its culture. In his short, peripatetic life, he spent much time there, glad to be away from what he considered the hypocrisy and insularity of the British. His first trips to France were as a young child with his father. On one of them, in 1873, his father became friendly with Robert Louis Stevenson when they stayed at the same hotel in **Menton** – Stevenson wrote in a letter home, 'I have made myself indispensable to the Dowsons' little boy (aet. 6), a popularity that brings with it its own fatigues, as you may fancy.' When he became old enough to travel alone, Dowson frequently visited France for extended stays, first visiting Brittany, the region with which he is most closely associated, in 1890.

In 1894, his father died – he had suffered from seriously declining health due to tuberculosis and he may have committed suicide. Six months after his death, Dowson's mother, depressed and in financial difficulty, also died – this time certainly by suicide. Ernest Dowson subsequently led a wandering existence, struggling against poverty and doing his best to make a living from literary journalism, translation, and his own poems and short stories. He translated works by a number of major French authors, including Zola, Balzac, Voltaire, and Verlaine (whom he met in London and later re-encountered in Paris).

In the summer of 1895 he was frequently in **Dieppe**, where Aubrey Beardsley, Arthur Symons and others had gathered – at that time *The Savoy*

magazine, of which eight issues appeared in 1896, was in the development stage, and Dowson was drawn into the circle as a contributor. Towards the end of 1895, he lived in **Paris** for some three months until moving to **Pont-Aven** in Brittany, which became his home for six months. Dowson wrote several poems reflecting his attraction to Britanny – his biographer Mark Longaker quotes his friend Edgar Jepson on this: 'I think he was happiest in the remote Breton villages whither he now and again withdrew himself, and from which he wrote his most delightful letters. They used to give me the impression that the world went well with him there – as well, at any rate, as it could ever go with him.' 'Breton Afternoon' (Extract 13), included in *Decorations*, 1899, is a gently melancholic escape into the natural world from what Dowson elsewhere famously called 'the weeping and the laughter'.

In 1897, Dowson was back in France at **Arques-la-Bataille** near **Dieppe**. Oscar Wilde had recently been released from prison and was living at nearby **Berneval-sur-Mer** – Wilde and Dowson became good friends and met frequently during this period. For the last three months of 1897, Dowson lived in Paris again – and he made what was to be his last visit to the city in 1899. He was planning to leave London for Paris in 1900 when his constantly declining health put an end to his plans and finally to his life. He died on 23 February 1900 – he was only 32 years old. Wilde wrote of him in a letter just after he had learned of his death, 'Poor wounded wonderful fellow that he was, a tragic reproduction of all tragic poetry, like a symbol, or a scene. I hope bay leaves will be laid on his tomb, and rue, and myrtle too, for he knew what love is.'

Recommended biography: Mark Longaker, *Ernest Dowson*, University of Pennsylvania Press, Philadelphia, PA, 1945, rev 1967. There are also excellent and concise biographical essays in Desmond Flower and Henry Maas, *The*

Letters of Ernest Dowson, Cassell, London, 1967.

DURAS, Marguerite (1914–96). Duras (real name Marguerite Donnadieu) was born on 4 April 1914 at Giadinh in Indo–China. She attended the *lycée* at Saigon and stayed in Indo–China until 1932, when she left to study in **Paris**. Her childhood was not an easy one – with her mother struggling against increasing financial crisis to bring up three children (her father died when she was very young). Her experiences in Indo–China feature strongly in her work – most famously in her autobiographical novel *L'Amant*, 1984 (*The Lover*, 1985). Duras lived for many years in Paris in the **rue St Benoît** (6th) and she was a familiar figure in the local cafés and the rue de Buci street market, yet another worthy addition to the literary associations of that most literary of *quartiers*.

Duras was a prolific writer and her work is consistently intelligent, sensitive, and innovative. She made major contributions to the novel, to cinema, and to the theatre, especially through her experimentation with narrative, and she received fitting recognition for her work in all three media. Her highest literary award was the Prix Goncourt which she received for *The Lover* in 1984. For her work in the theatre, she was awarded the Grand Prix du Théâtre de l'Académie Française in 1983. Her narratively and stylistically innovative film *India Song*, 1975, won her the Grand Prix de l'Académie du Cinéma – although her most famous contribution to film was her screenplay for *Hiroshima mon amour*, 1959, directed by Alain Resnais.

Typically, Duras takes as her subject the essential isolation of human beings from each other – demonstrated in the ephemeral attempts at harmony and understanding of lovers, a coming together and a moving apart. Themes of emotional anguish are conveyed in a paradoxically restrained and remote style, as if the control of expression is the only 'order' which controls the chaos – the impact is always immediate and powerful, with all the ambiguity and complexity of her subject conveyed in simple and direct language.

The example chosen here, *Emily L.*, 1987 (*Emily L.*, 1989) is an engrossing hall of mirrors of a novel which may be seen on one level as a portrayal of the author's perceptions of the process of writing fiction. What we read is a story about how the book we are reading was conceived, which itself may be fictional or real. The 'present' setting is entirely in the café of the Hôtel de la Marine in **Quilleboeuf**, a decaying Norman fishing port (Extract 14). A French couple, of whom the narrator, a writer, is one, become increasingly interested in a British couple who are also in the café. Much of the narrative is about the history of the strangers, but, the reader assumes, this is in fact the imagination of the narrator at work. Although superficially the main subjects of the narrative, the British couple merely offer the narrator/novelist an opportunity to explore, through the story they inspire, her own current concerns and preoccupations. *Emily L.* is written in the sparse, semi-poetic prose that Duras uses so effectively in her incisive examinations of personal relationships, each perception encapsulated, encased in its own haiku-clear sentence/ moment ('I look at you. You're looking at the place. The heat. The flat waters of the river. The summer. And then you look past all that.') As with all her work, it merits reading and re-reading.

ERNAUX, Annie (1940–). Ernaux was born on 1 September 1940 in **Lillebonne** and brought up in **Yvetot**. She studied at **Rouen University**, and qualified as a secondary school teacher. She taught literature in **Bonneville**, **Annecy** and **Pontoise** until 1977, when she joined the Centre National d'Enseignement à Distance. She now lives in the Paris region.

Ernaux published her first book in 1974 and has since become one of the foremost modern French novelists. Much of her work is set in her native Normandy and influenced by her working class origins there. Her early novels in particular deal with major feminist issues – for example, the subjugation of a woman's identity in marriage and motherhood, and the trials of a young woman undergoing an abortion. Her most successful writing to date has been that which explores familial and social relationships through intensely personal (though tightly controlled) narratives which combine autobiographical elements and social comment within a novelistic framework. This is the case in her best known work, *La Place*, 1983 (*Positions*, 1991), which draws on her childhood and working-class family background (Extract 20). This short novel, which won the Prix Renaudot in 1984, is a moving evocation of her father, written in short episodic passages – rather like a photo album in prose. Essentially it is about a daughter, now an educated middle-class married woman and a teacher, re-connecting herself to her 'roots' and her father through a reconstruction of his character and background. A labourer and then owner of a café and grocery shop in the small town of 'Y_____' (**Yvetot**), he strove to provide his daughter with the opportunity for a better life which necessarily involved her moving from the social milieu or 'position' in which he himself was locked. This theme of the separation or distancing of children from parents through divisions of class adds universality to the power of the personal memoir. The novel is consciously restrained in its style and tone – the narrator explains in the early pages of the book, 'I realize now that a novel is out of the question. If I wish to tell the story of a life governed by necessity, I have no right to adopt an artistic approach, or attempt to produce something "moving" or "gripping". I shall collate my father's words, tastes and mannerisms, as well as the main events of his life. In short, all the external evidence of his existence, an

existence which I too shared.' It is precisely the unsentimental clarity of the writing that makes the pictures it evokes so vivid, and its portrayal of the father, infused with respect and affection, so moving. *La Place* also provides us with evocations of rural and smalltown Normandy over the years from the First World War through to the 1960s.

Une femme, 1988 (*A Woman's Story*, 1990), in a similar vein to *La Place*, was written shortly after the death of Ernaux's mother, and is an evocation of her life with an exploration of the relationship between mother and daughter.

EVELYN, John (1620–1706). Evelyn is best known as one of the great English diarists. He kept his *Memoirs or Diary* (first published in 1818) for most of his long life. Like the writings of Pepys, with whom he was friendly, it constitutes a fascinating record of his life and times, although Evelyn's work is much less personal and much more sober than that of Pepys. Evelyn was a man of considerable learning (he was a member of the Royal Society) and his interests were many and varied (including, for example, gardening and air pollution, on both of which subjects he published books). He travelled widely on the Continent, especially in the 1840s, and his diary entries on his experiences (Extract 16 and Paris, Extracts 13 and 41) reveal him to have been an observant and intelligent traveller. His appreciation and understanding of what he saw and the people he met were no doubt aided by his ability to speak French, Italian and Spanish. He also translated a number of specialist books from French (on such subjects as architecture and gardening).

FLAUBERT, Gustave (1821–80). Flaubert was born on 12 December 1821 in the Hôtel-Dieu, a municipal hospital, in **Rouen**. His father was chief surgeon and his mother the daughter of a physician. Flaubert became interested in literature when he was very young and pursued this interest during his education in Rouen, writing short stories, a play and a novel (entitled *L'Éducation sentimentale* but not otherwise related to his famous work of the same name). In 1841, he began studying law in Paris, but he abandoned these studies in 1844 after suffering a severe nervous attack, which may have been epilepsy. His family moved shortly afterwards to a house on the banks of the Seine not far from Rouen, at **Croisset** – the house where Flaubert lived for most of his life (although he also kept apartments in **Paris**). In 1846 in Paris, Flaubert met the poet and novelist Louise Colet, with whom he had a stormy, on-off relationship for the next nine years and whom he kept at a distance despite much ardent correspondence. Colet was later to inspire, unflatteringly for her, the character of Emma Bovary.

In 1851, after an extended visit to Egypt and the Middle East with his friend the writer, journalist and photographer Maxime du Camp (1822–94) – a stay in a warmer climate had been advised by his doctors in light of his deteriorating physical condition – Flaubert began work on *Madame Bovary*. He worked slowly, with constant revision of his text, and in seclusion. It took him five years to write the novel, which was published in April 1856 in serial form with cuts to which the author objected. Before publication of *Bovary* in its final form, Flaubert was tried for producing a morally offensive book – he was acquitted in February 1857 and the novel was published in April. With it came fame (although many of the critics were hostile – Baudelaire was a notable exception) and Flaubert became part of the literary world of Paris, meeting among many others Victor Hugo whom he greatly admired, and developing correspondence with various writers and artists, especially after scoring further literary success with the publication of his exotic historical novel *Salammbô*, 1862

(*Salammbo*, 1977). In 1863, he met Turgenev (1818–83) with whom he developed a close friendship – their correspondence is published in English in *A Friendship in Letters – Flaubert and Turgenev: the Complete Correspondence*, 1985. Another famous correspondent and friend was George Sand (◊ Centre) – although their literary views differed considerably, they kept up their correspondence until Sand's death in 1876 (see *Flaubert–Sand: The Correspondence*, 1993).

The reception of *L'Éducation sentimentale*, published in 1869 (*A Sentimental Education*, 1964), disappointed Flaubert and this, combined with the collapse of the Second Empire in 1870, the deaths of friends and of his mother, and the onset of financial problems (caused by the need to rescue a relative from ruin), made the early 1870s a bleak period. In the last years of his life, however, Flaubert saw a revival of his fortunes, with the successful publication of *Trois contes*, 1877 (*Three Tales*, 1961), encouraging support from younger writers, and a modest pension which was arranged for him by his friends. He died suddenly from a stroke in May 1880, leaving behind him an unfinished novel, *Bouvard et Pécuchet*, which was published in 1881 (*Bouvard and Pécuchet*, 1976).

Flaubert's working method was characterized by massive research and painstaking self-correction ('. . . this one inn-scene will take me three months' he wrote to Colet while working on *Bovary*). He spent much of his time secluded at his Croisset home, and cultivated a reputation as a misanthropist (although he had many close friends during his life). He hated stupidity (*la bêtise*) in all its forms, and, especially, held bourgeois values and morals in venomous contempt. This is apparent in his masterpiece, *Madame Bovary*, 1857 (*Madame Bovary*, 1950) – Extract 17. The novel is a searing condemnation of provincial, bourgeois lifestyle and attitudes. Emma Bovary entertains the most romantic dreams but her reality could not be further removed – a completely unsuitable marriage to an honest but boring doctor, two adulterous relationships which fail to sustain the flames of passion ('Emma had rediscovered in adultery all the banality of marriage') and which end in her rejection, and a slide into debt. Reality continually disappoints and ultimately destroys her. Flaubert tells the story from the position of a dispassionate narrator, neither condemning nor defending his protagonists. Emma and Charles Bovary seem, whatever their personal failings, merely the victims of a wider social *malaise* which is at once the catalyst of their misfortunes and the value system which ultimately condemns them to their fate. Much of the action is set in a provincial town in the vicinity of **Rouen**, which Flaubert calls 'Yonville'. His portrayal of this town and its inhabitants, especially the glib and superficially intellectual Monsieur Homais, is central to the novel which above all conveys with depressing conviction the power and durability of bourgeois morality and materialism.

In *A Sentimental Education*, Flaubert evokes the **Paris** of the recent past, exploring with characteristic cynicism the social and political conflicts of the turbulent 1840s and early 1850s (Flaubert himself was in Paris in February 1848 when the Revolution broke out). Against this background the novel traces the attempts of Frédéric Moreau, a student from the provinces, to make his way in Parisian society.

Of particular interest to readers of this literary guide will be Flaubert's story 'Un coeur simple' ('A Simple Heart'), in *Three Tales*. Said to have been the author's response to George Sand's discomfort with his cynicism (and by some cynical critics to be ironic in intent), this is a moving portrayal of a servant-girl who gradually loses everything and everyone she loves and is left only with fragments of her past for comfort – including the stuffed parrot which plays another significant literary role in Julian Barnes's ◊ *Flaubert's Par-*

rot. 'A Simple Heart' is set realistically in the Normandy of Flaubert's childhood with many autobiographical details in the settings (which include **Pont-l'Évêque** and **Trouville**) and characters.

Recommended biography: Francis Steegmuller, *Flaubert and Madame Bovary*, Hamish Hamilton, London, 1958.

FOWLES, John (1926–). English novelist Fowles graduated in French from Oxford University, where, he says, he read 'omniverously though much more out of ignorance than intelligence'. Among the aspects of French literature and culture that especially interested him were the writings of Marie de France (12th century), to whose *Lais* he attributes, in the introduction to his translation of the tale of 'Eliduc' from that work, the 'mood' of his novella *The Ebony Tower*. The *Lais* were named after the Breton songs commemorating great events (the Arthurian stories are the best known), and, with their part fabulous, part realistic Breton settings, re-tell tales from Celtic folklore, focusing principally on the plights of thwarted lovers. In Fowles's words, 'Marie grafted her own knowledge of the world on the old material. . . . Effectively she introduced a totally new element into European literature. It was composed not least of sexual honesty and a very feminine awareness of how people really behaved – and how behaviour and moral problems can be expressed through things like dialogue and action.' His translation of 'Eliduc' is published in the stories collectively entitled *The Ebony Tower*, 1974.

Appropriately, in light of this, *The Ebony Tower* itself is set in Britanny (Extract 8). As in his novel *The Magus*, 1966, its central character is placed in a milieu which challenges his assumptions and leads him to question his own life. David Williams is a middle-class English intellectual, an art critic and painter who visits the old artist Henry Breasley about whom he is writing a book. Breasley's unconventional lifestyle and the two young women who live with him, aided by the setting of the forest of **Paimpont**, redolent with Arthurian legend and ancient wildness, lead Williams to recognize that his established views and values are singularly inconsequential and vulnerable. Fowles skilfully weaves the atmosphere of this part of Brittany into the narrative of his tale, using its mythical associations to set off the powerless conventionality of his protagonist.

GENET, Jean (1910–86). Genet was born on 19 December 1910 in **Paris**. In 1911, his single mother handed him over to a foundling home and he was placed with foster parents in the village of **Alligny-en-Morvan**. His education ended when he was 12 and he was sent to an apprenticeship in Paris from which he promptly ran away, setting the precedent for a series of offences which culminated in his detention in the agricultural penitentiary colony in **Mettray** near Tours from September 1926 to March 1929 – featured in *Le Miracle de la rose*, 1946 (*The Miracle of the Rose*, 1971). After a spell in the army, ending in desertion, Genet was in and out of prison many times for theft, vagrancy and other crimes, at home and abroad. His literary career began in the 1940s. Arrested yet again, this time for stealing books, he wrote a poem in the Parisian prison of **Fresnes** and self-published it in September 1942. Among its readers was Jean Cocteau (◊ Paris). Genet was introduced to Cocteau in 1943 and showed him the manuscript of his novel *Notre-Dame-des-fleurs*, 1944 (*Our Lady of the Flowers*, 1964), which he had recently completed. Cocteau arranged for it to be published – anonymously, because it was too hot for a publisher to put a name on it. This novel and *The Miracle of the Rose* (concerning the adoration of boys in the Mettray prison of a murderer awaiting execution) secured Genet's reputation as a writer of originality and significance. In 1943, an expensive defence lawyer secured by Cocteau saved Genet from a possible life sentence for repeated offences. In 1949, Cocteau and Sartre organized a petition which led to a complete pardon – he was saved in effect by his achievements and potential as a writer. Genet was befriended by Sartre and Beauvoir, who saw in him an embodiment of the Existentialist hero, and, in Sartre's words, a 'true literary genius'. Sartre's *Saint Genet, comédien et martyr* (*Saint Genet: Actor and Martyr*, 1983), an extensive psychoanalytical assessment of the character and motivation of Genet, was published in 1952. This literary sanctification and definition left its subject with some crisis of identity – the moral and social rebel trapped in his own notoriety, stuck and wriggling on a pin. However, he resurfaced later in the 1950s as an innovative and, of course, controversial playwright. From the 1960s, Genet spent much of his time supporting political causes, including the American Civil Rights movement, the Black Panthers, the Palestinian Liberation Organization and, most controversially, the German Baader-Meinhof terrorist group. He died, apparently from a fall, on 15 April 1986 in Jack's, a cheap Parisian hotel, while suffering from terminal cancer. He was buried, in accordance with his wishes, in Morocco.

In addition to the novels mentioned above, Genet also published his autobiographical *Journal du voleur*, 1948 (*The Thief's Journal*, 1971); *Pompes funèbres* (*Funeral Rites*, 1969); and *Querelle de Brest*, 1947 (*Querelle of Brest*, 1966). His fiction draws heavily on his experiences of vagrancy, theft, homosexuality, prostitution, and incarceration to depict a world in which traditional values and morals have no meaning. In the theatre, these experiences were directed into innovative scripts with more overtly political themes. Characterized by representations of violence and abuse through a stylized theatricality, Genet's plays are disturbing and aggressive, challenging their audience with striking visions of cruelty and corruption: *Les Bonnes*, 1947 (*The Maids*, 1989), *Le Balcon* (*The Balcony*, 1991), and *Les Nègres*, 1958 (*The Blacks*, 1960) are outstanding examples.

Querelle of Brest (Extract 1) is a dark novel of casual sex (mainly between men) and casual murder set almost entirely in **Brest**. The port provides a murky background for the murky tale and there are atmospheric descriptions of misty nights and low-life streets. The novel rejects – or, more accurately, does not recognize – accepted social values, refusing to make any kind of judgement about the crimes and betrayals of its central character, challenging the reader, torn between fascination and repulsion, to make his or her own judgement if he or she must. Like the Existential protagonists of Sartre and Camus, Querelle 'defines himself by his actions', to adapt one of Sartre's own stock phrases. The novel was filmed as *Querelle* by Fassbinder in 1982.

In *La Force de l'âge*, 1960 (*The Prime of Life*, 1973), Simone de Beauvoir describes her and Sartre's first meeting with Genet at the **Flore**, when Genet came over to their table – ' "You Sartre?", he inquired brusquely. With his close-cropped hair and thin, tight lips and suspicious, rather aggressive expression, he struck us as a pretty hard case. He sat down, but stayed only a moment. But he came back on other occasions, and we saw a good deal of each other. Hard he certainly was; an outcast from the day he was born, he had no reason to respect the society that had rejected him. But his eyes could still smile, and a child's astonishment lingered about his lips.'

Recommended biography: Edmund White, *Genet*, Picador, London, 1994.

GIDE, André (1869–1951). 'The humanist of our age', as E.M. Forster described him, was born in **Paris** on 22 November 1869. An only child, he was raised in a strict Protestant household.

André Gide on his travels – an autographed photograph sent to his friend Sylvia Beach

From the age of 11, after the death of his father, he was brought up by his devoted but over-protective mother and he led an unsettled childhood with a much disrupted formal education. After the rigorously Protestant and conventionally bourgeois environment of his youth, Gide's travels in North Africa in the mid-1890s allowed him to give rein to his homosexual desires and to revel in the pleasure of escape and indulgence. His marriage in 1895 to his cousin Madelaine, for whom he had developed an intense 'spiritual' love from the age of 13, served as a restraining counterbalance to the wilder side of his nature. The marriage lasted some 43 years, until Madelaine's death, and, despite the fact that the relationship was often distressingly strained and uncommunicative, Gide remained devoted to her. For much of his life, Gide's home was at **Cuverville**, at the property Madelaine inherited from her father, in the Normandy he had known as a child (his mother had property in **La Roque-Baignard**). He died in Paris in February 1951 and was buried at Cuverville.

In his writing, Gide explores his own inner conflicts – the novels are not strictly autobiographical, often demonstrating a lack of restraint which the author did not permit himself in his own life, but they certainly explore aspects of Gide's own personality and experience, and characteristically debate the conflict between a given morality and individual freedom. *Les Nourritures terrestres*, 1897 (*Fruits of the Earth*, 1949), is a lyrical hymn to self-fulfilment, written in the euphoria engendered by his travels in North Africa and his recovery from life-threatening tuberculosis. At the time of its publication it made little impact, either with its subject matter or its experimental structure and high lyricism. After the First World War, however, it became almost a manifesto for young intellectuals – to the extent that Gide felt obliged to add a cautionary note, reminding his enthusiasts that the book was intended to 'teach you to care more for yourself than for it, and then more for all the rest than for yourself.' In *L'Immoraliste*, 1902 (*The Immoralist*, 1960), the narrator causes the death of his wife in his pursuit of his 'inner self'; in *La Porte étroite*, 1909 (*Strait is the Gate*, 1924), by contrast, the story is of a tragedy caused by the renunciation of sexual passion in favour of religious fulfilment. For Gide, his only 'true' novel (in the sense that it was panoramic in scope and complex in its structure) was *Les Faux-Monnayeurs*, 1926 (*The Counterfeiters*, 1966), set in Paris in the early 20th century and concerning essentially the repetitive inability of successive generations to distinguish reality from illusion, the individualism and originality of the younger constantly suppressed by the guile or blind incompetence of the elder.

Apart from these and his other novels, Gide's literary activity ranged over drama, essays, criticism, translation. He also played the prominent role in the foundation of the prestigious literary review, the *Nouvelle Revue Française*. But his intellectual pursuits were not purely literary – he wrote several works of analysis on political, social and cultural issues; for example, his attacks on colonialism – such as *Voyage au Congo*, 1927 (*Travels in the Congo*, 1962) – and his defence of homosexuality in *Corydon*, 1924 (*Corydon*, 1978) which attracted much controversy. For many, though, his most enduring work is his frank and compelling autobigraphy *Si le grain ne meurt*, 1926 (*If It Die*, 1950), dealing with his early life, from birth to marriage, and written with some 20 years of hindsight, and his enormously impressive *Journal*, which he kept from 1885, when he was 16, until 1949. The *Journal*, full of Gide's experiences and inner debates, his aestheticism (Extract 5), and his wide-ranging reflections on life and art (his own and other people's), as well as major issues of his day, is above all a record of the development of one of the century's great intellectuals and testimony to what he most sought – his individual integrity. A selection is readily available in translation (*Journals 1889–1949*, 1967).

André Gide was awarded the Nobel Prize for Literature in 1947, at the age of 78.

Recommended biography: There are useful biographies by George Painter and Enid Starkie, both published in the 1950s, but by far the most insightful work on Gide is by Gide.

KEROUAC, Jack (1922–69). Jean Louis Kéroack (a mutation, apparently, of the original 'Kérouac') was born in Massachusetts to French–Canadian parents. His lifelong interest in exploring the origins of his name and his Breton and Canadian ancestry, of making some firm link with his past, took him on a brief trip to **Brest** by way of **Paris** in 1965. He planned a substantial trip which would also take in Cornwall, the Netherlands and Germany. In the event, he ran out of money and grew homesick for Florida within 10 days. He did, however, in a permanent drunken haze, make it to Paris and Brest – in Brest he even managed to meet a member of the Lebris family, who were related to the Kérouacs, and was entertained by him at his luxurious home and refuelled with his expensive cognac. The literary outcome of the trip was the short autobiographical novel *Satori in Paris*, 1966 (Extract 2), a picaresque, drunken, inspirational passage through the streets and bars of Paris and Brest, with assorted encounters along the way. What constitutes the 'satori' (a Zen word for 'enlightenment' – in Kerouac's words, '"sudden illumination", "sudden awakening", or simply "kick in the eye"') is open to interpretation, and the novel is essentially an exploration of its origin. 'Somewhere during my ten days in Paris (and Brittany)', he writes, 'I received an illumination of some kind that seems to've changed me again.' The satori probably is the cumulative effect of the series of friendly encounters the narrator experiences amid the general, and anticipated, rejection of his shabbiness and drunkenness – the connections he makes with strangers illuminate the significance of compassion. At the beginning of the novel he explains, 'This book'll say, in effect, have pity on us all, and dont get mad at me for writing at all.'

Recommended biography: Gerald Nicosia, *Memory Babe: A Critical Biography of Jack Kerouac*, Grove Press, New York, 1983.

MAUPASSANT, Guy de (1850–93). Maupassant was born on 5 August 1850 in Normandy – there is some dispute over his actual birthplace (see introduction). His parents separated when he was a child and Guy and his brother lived with their mother at **Étretat**, which provides a setting for a number of his stories (Extract 6). Maupassant was educated in a *lycée* in Paris, a seminary at **Yvetot**, which he hated, and at the *lycée* in **Rouen**. He began studying law in **Paris**, but his studies were interrupted by his service in the Franco–Prussian war (an experience which was to find its way into various of his stories, most notably 'Boule de Suif'). After the war a financial crisis in the family forced Maupassant to look for employment instead of resuming his studies – he found it in the naval ministry and continued to work as a civil servant until 1882, by which time he was making a more than comfortable living from his writing. In the late 1870s in Paris, Maupassant became a regular visitor to Flaubert's Sunday gatherings in **rue Murillo**. Flaubert, who had been a close friend of his mother, already knew Maupassant from Normandy and now took him under his wing, recognizing his talent and acting as a literary father figure, effectively 'training' him in the craft of writing. Maupassant's early work included a volume of poems and several plays – and he later published travel literature – but it was a short story that made him famous. In 1880, his much-loved 'Boule de Suif' was published in *Les Soirées de Médan*, a collection of six stories by members of the Naturalist group of writers who met regularly at Zola's country house in Médan. Maupassant became a celebrity almost overnight and from that point his reputation grew and he was enormously successful. His lifestyle was correspondingly extravagant – he moved into a luxurious apartment in Paris, mixed in high society, travelled widely, and entertained an astonishing number of mistresses. His health, however, was in terminal decline. Although in appearance he was sturdy and robust, and although he enjoyed sports and outdoor activities, he was far from fit. The first signs of syphilis had been discerned in 1877. This disease, combined with his dissolute lifestyle, overwork, and his nervous and depressive tendencies, led Maupassant early to his grave. In 1892, seriously ill and unable to write any longer, he attempted suicide. He died in an asylum on 6 March 1893, insane and suffering from general paralysis, in great mental and physical distress.

Maupassant produced 16 volumes of short stories. The majority centre around rural and small-town life in Normandy or Parisian society, from the lower middle class to the rich and privileged. They are notable for their clarity of style – no doubt helped by the influence of Flaubert – and their often remarkable concision in structure and expression, filling very few pages and yet carrying penetration, depth and roundness. They range greatly in genre, from comic through satirical to tragic, from slice-of-life to horror and fantasy. Maupassant's preoccupation is with fallibility and hypocrisy, and the world he portrays overall is one governed by selfishness, manifested in the cruelty of human beings to one another – a truly pessimistic vision.

He also published six novels. The first of these, *Une Vie*, 1883 (*A Woman's Life*, 1965), is a story of disillusionment and hopeless love. Set largely in a wet and suitably bleak **Normandy**, the novel tells the story of Jeanne and the persistent defeat of her hopes and dreams as her life develops. Starting out impressionable, trusting and vulnerable, Jeanne experiences a series of misfortunes and is destined to be a victim: her romantic hopes for her marriage are dashed as her husband becomes increasingly miserly and abusive; her son, whom she spoils in unrelenting devotion, turns out to be a wastrel; her local priests are respectively cynical and cruel; she discovers her mother was unfaithful to her father; and so on. In this moving and deeply pessimistic novel, **Corsica** is used to symbolize the romance and colour that elude Jeanne for all her life except for the short and precious period of escape she spends on the island. There for her honeymoon, the country fires her with its passion and wildness, and Maupassant excels in vivid descriptions of the

Corsican landscape and life (see Corsica, Extract 4) so that they linger in the reader's memory as they linger in the memory of his protagonist.

Maupassant's other novels are: *Bel-Ami*, 1885 (*Bel-Ami*, 1975), a mordant story of Parisian newspaper life; *Mont-Oriol*, 1887, set in a spa in the **Auvergne**; *Pierre et Jean*, 1888 (*Pierre et Jean*, 1979), a novel of brotherly conflict set in **Le Havre**; *Fort comme la mort*, 1889, concerning the love of an old man for a young girl; and *Notre coeur*, 1890 (*Notre Coeur*, 1933), set among the Parisian high society of the *salons* and concerning the hopeless love of a young man for a sophisticated young widow.

Recommended biography: Francis Steegmuller, *Maupassant*, Collins, London, 1950.

PROUST, Marcel. See under Centre.

ROBERTS, Michèle (1949–). Born to a French mother and English father, Roberts has published novels, short stories, and poetry. She has been a prominent and accomplished exponent of recent British feminist writing, and has, in addition to her own contributions, been instrumental in the promotion of other women writers through her editorial role in several collections of feminist prose and poetry.

Her novel *Daughters of the House*, 1992 (Extract 11), set in **Normandy**, tells the story of two cousins, Léonie and Thérèse, growing up after the war, their childhood experiences, perceptions and imaginings, and their accidental discovery of a dark village secret. Despite Léonie's attempts to shut out the past, the return of Thérèse some 20 years later forces her to revisit the truths she had locked away. To deny your past, the novel seems to say, is to deny yourself. The story is atmospherically told, and the life and culture of a Normandy village are skilfully evoked (the village described is fictional).

The earlier and strongly feminist *A Piece of the Night*, 1978, focuses on the growth of the heroine through lesbianism and female relationships. Set in Normandy and London, it concerns, like *Daughters of the House*, the return of a woman to the home of her childhood after many years away.

Roberts's 1984 novel *The Wild Girl* uses **Provence** as its setting.

ROUAUD, JEAN (1952–   ). Rouaud was 38 when his first novel, *Les Champs d'honneur*, 1990 (*Fields of Glory*, 1992), won the Prix Goncourt – it was the first time in 40 years that the Goncourt had been awarded to a first novel. Until then, he had had a varied career, working as a nightwatchman, a stagehand, a teacher of philosophy, and, at the time he won the Goncourt, a newspaper seller in Paris. *Fields of Glory* (Extract 10) is certainly an impressive start. Written in strikingly lucid prose, and with a light, often humorous touch, it is in substance a series of finely wrought character portraits – snapshots from the varied lives of several members from several generations of a middle-class family living in the *département* of **Loire-Atlantique** (where Rouaud himself was born). Nostalgic and intimate, and at the same time cool and rational, the dominant concern of the story is the shadow that hangs over it – the First World War which emerges in its full horror in the closing chapters. Rouaud skilfully weaves together his book's apparently episodic sketches into a tapestry of the impacts of war on France and its people.

Rouaud's second novel, *Des Hommes illustres*, 1993, has also been translated (*Of Illustrious Men*, 1995), and concerns a son's exploration of the life of his father, a commercial traveller struggling to earn a living in the towns and villages of Brittany.

WADDELL, Helen (1889–1965). The medievalist Helen Waddell was born in Tokyo and educated in Belfast. She spent two years in **Paris** in the 1920s, on a travelling fellowship from Oxford University, researching for her book on *The Wandering Scholars*, 1927, at the Bibiliothèque Nationale. Her time in the city provided her with a keen sense of the medieval Paris in which Peter Abélard's (◊ Paris) story unfolded – a story which had increasingly preoccupied her for many years. Her novel *Peter Abelard*, 1933 (Extract 12), tells the tale of Abélard and Héloïse with the scrupulous attention to detail and knowledge of the intellectual and social climate of 12th century France that one would expect from a distinguished medievalist. Perhaps surprisingly, Waddell's novel is also very readable and carries emotional involvement in its tragic story together with a vivid evocation of the medieval environment, in particular in **Paris** and **Brittany**, the key settings. On its publication the book was critically acclaimed and rapidly became a bestseller (it had nine reprintings in its first year). For the reader, it has the conviction of an author truly dedicated to her tale – writing to her sister when the novel was almost finished, Waddell commented 'Queer, but I feel as if the best thing I've ever written, or ever will write, is now over. I've always known that that chapter of the discovery of God would be the hardest to do, and that if I made it insincere or sentimental it would be worse than useless. Now it's done, and I can't ever write anything like it again, because it seems to have used up all the knowledge I have. And I felt for so long that once *Abelard* was written the thing for which I was born would be done. Not that I'm in any mood to say the *Nunc Dimittis*. But just it's queer.'

Waddell planned a second volume which would be called *Héloïse* and would tell the story 'as Héloïse saw it'. Unfortunately, she never managed to put her plan into action – 'I do not know when it will be written. *Peter Abelard* took seven years.'

Recommended biography: Monica Blackett, *The Mark of the Maker: A Portrait of Helen Wadell*, Constable, London, 1973.

ÎLE-DE-FRANCE

> 'Mallarmé showed me the valley, which the early
> heat of summer was turning to gold. *"Look!"* he said.
> "It's the first cymbal clash of autumn over the earth."
> When autumn came, he was no longer there.'
> Paul Valéry, 'Last Visit to Mallarmé'

VAL D'OISE

Montmorency. In April 1756, Jean-Jacques Rousseau (1712–78) left Paris and accepted the invitation of Madame d'Épinay, who owned the **Château de la Chevrette**, to live in a small house on her estate ('L'Ermitage') which she had had built on the edge of the forest. The isolated house and its peaceful environment suited Rousseau perfectly, but unfortunately the arrangement was to prove short-lived: tensions developed between Madame d'Épinay and Rousseau, especially after he had met and developed an unrequited passion for her cousin Sophie d'Houdetot. He left amid the public collapse of his friendship with Madame d'Épinay, in December 1757. L'Ermitage is now part of a clinic (**10 rue de l'Ermitage**), and is marked with a plaque.

On 15 December 1757, Rousseau moved into a modest house with a garden in nearby **Mont-Louis**, and he stayed here until 1762 – for the peripatetic philosopher, a considerable length of time. The years he spent at Mont-Louis were highly productive – the period saw the publication of *Lettre à d'Alembert*, 1758, *Julie ou la Nouvelle Héloïse*, 1761 (*Julie or the New Eloise*,

1987), *Du contrat social*, 1762 (*The Social Contract*, 1993), and *Émile*, 1762 (*Emile*, 1991). As he records in Volume 10 of *Les Confessions*, written 1764–70 (*The Confessions*, 1970), this was among the happier periods of his life – he had the privacy he craved away from the high society of Paris, and at the same time he made new friends, especially the Maréchal and Maréchale de Luxembourg (who helped him with much needed renovations to the house). He was forced reluctantly to leave Mont-Louis in June 1762 and make for Switzerland – *Émile* and its author had been condemned by the Parlement de Paris for offending religious orthodoxy.

The house has been well conserved and may be visited. On the ground floor are the kitchen and Thérèse Levasseur's room (he had begun a liaison with Levasseur in 1745 and the relationship continued throughout his life). In Rousseau's bedroom is furniture from L'Ermitage – including his bed and the table on which he wrote *La Nouvelle Héloïse* – and his candlesticks with glass surrounds to protect the flames when he worked outside. In an extension added since Rousseau's time is a museum devoted to his life and works. The garden is much as the writer would have known it, as is the little

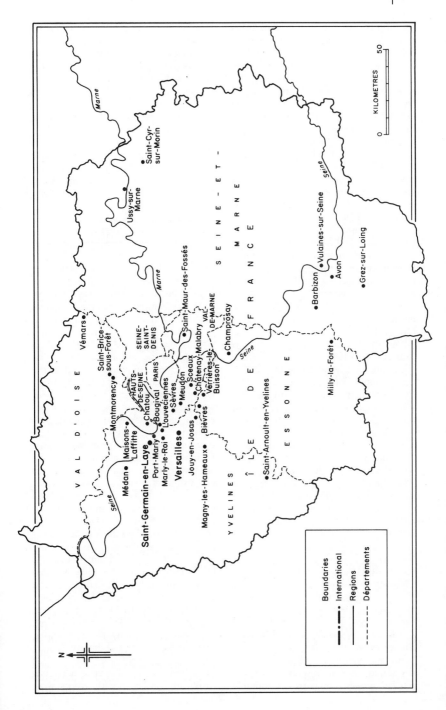

pavilion (referred to as '*le donjon*' in *Les Confessions*) – a place which he especially liked and where, in February 1758, 'without shelter from the wind and the snow and without any fire other than the one in my heart, I wrote, over a period of three weeks, my *Lettre à d'Alembert* on the theatre.' The fireplace which you now see in *le donjon* was added in 1759 thanks to the good offices of the Luxembourgs. A neighbouring house has been turned into Le Centre de Documentation sur Jean-Jacques Rousseau et le XVIIIe Siècle, and together the two houses now comprise the **Musée et Centre Jean-Jacques Rousseau**, 5 rue Jean-Jacques Rousseau, 95160 Montmorency.

One other literary connection for Montmorency – the Polish Romantic poet Adam Mickiewicz (1798–1855) is buried in the **cemetery** here.

Saint-Brice-sous-Forêt. Edith Wharton (1862–1937) moved out to this village in 1919 from her apartment in central Paris where she had lived since 1907. She bought an estate here called the Pavillon Colombe, and it became her permanent home. Among the young admirers who came to see her in the 1920s was Scott Fitzgerald, who, according to one version of the story, was nervous about meeting the venerable Mrs Wharton and got through a bottle of wine on the short trip from Paris. His alcohol-inspired attempts at frivolous flattery and informality were met with stony and uncomprehending formality on the part of his unamused hostess.

Vémars. François Mauriac (◊ Aquitaine) is buried here. The **Château de la Motte** was the home of his wife's family, where he hid during his days in the Resistance in the Second World War, and which served as the country house of the Mauriacs while they were living in Paris. Mauriac's visits to Vémars became more frequent as he grew older, its gentler climate comparing favourably

to that of the Gironde, where he retained his own family home (see under Aquitaine). The Château now serves as the **town hall**, but a small museum has been established which comprises a reconstruction of Mauriac's study, with personal memorabilia, his typewriter, books, etc, and numerous photographs, some taken at Vémars in 1952 following the announcement of his Nobel Prize. The Château de la Motte, with its **Musée François-Mauriac** is at 5 rue Léon-Bouchard, 95470 Vémars. Visits to the museum are by appointment only.

YVELINES

Bougival. Ivan Sergeevich Turgenev (1818–83) spent much of his life in France, largely because it was the home of the celebrated opera singer Pauline Viardot. He had first met her in Saint Petersburg in 1843, when she was already married, and instantly fell in love. From the late 1840s onwards he spent as much time as he could in the company of the Viardots, and eventually a curious *ménage à trois* developed, with Louis Viardot and Turgenev becoming close friends and Turgenev remaining devoted to Pauline – although their relationship was probably, at least for most of the time, platonic. In 1863–70 Turgenev accompanied the Viardots when they left France to live in Baden-Baden, and when they returned he moved into their house in rue de Douai in Paris (the house no longer exists). In 1874, Turgenev and the Viardots jointly bought '**Les Frènes**', an Italianate villa, at Bougival and Turgenev built for himself a cross between a Swiss chalet and a Russian *datcha* in the grounds. The two houses became their summer home until Louis Viardot and Turgenev died in 1883, and they were visited here by many writers (among them Maupassant and Henry James) and other celebrities of the period. (Turgenev was by this time a famous writer in France and his works were readily available in translation – in Paris in the 1870s he associated especially with Daudet, Flaubert, Edmond de Goncourt, Maupassant and Zola). Suffering from cancer, Turgenev died in his chalet on 3 September 1883. Louis Viardot had died a few months earlier. Pauline, who was 20 years younger than her husband, lived until 1910, her 90th year.

Both houses still exist and have been extensively restored. A museum was opened to the public in Turgenev's chalet in 1983, the centenary of his death. It displays memorabilia and substantial information about his life and works, his relationship with the Viardots, and his time in France (particularly his friendships with contemporary French writers). Of special interest are the room in which he died and his study – the decor and contents of which have been carefully reconstructed from contemporary accounts with furniture resembling the writer's own. **Le Musée Ivan-Tourgueniev** is at Les Frênes, 16 rue Ivan-Tourgueniev, 78280 Bougival. Limited opening times – unless visiting on a Sunday, it is necessary to make an appointment in advance.

Louveciennes. Anaïs Nin (◊ Paris) and her husband Hugo Guiler bought a house here in 1930, which remained their main home until they left France at the end of the decade – although they spent most winters in Parisian apartments. The house, dilapidated when they bought it, was soon decorated and furnished as befitted Nin's taste for the exotic – the principal colours were turquoise, apricot and peach, there was an Arabian lamp above the entrance, a zodiac chart graced the library wall, a crystal fishbowl with glass fish stood on the mantel of the Moroccan tiled fireplace, and so on. Henry Miller was a frequent visitor here – it was at Louveciennes that he first met Nin in autumn 1931, introduced by a mutual friend. A selection of Nin's diary entries relating to her relationships with Miller and his then

wife June Mansfield Smith, and her encounters with them at Louveciennes, is available in *Henry and June*, 1987 – see also Volume 1, 1966, of her *Journals* (1931–1934), and Philip Kaufman's 1990 film *Henry and June*.

The house in which she lived, at **2 bis rue Monbuisson**, has been the subject of some local contovery. In 1995 the Louveciennes Project of the Anaïs Nin Institute attempted to buy the house, now fallen into considerable disrepair in private ownership, but the elderly owner was having none of it. In 1996, the property was sold privately. In light of rumours that the house was to be demolished, a new preservation campaign was launched with a view to restoring it and converting it into a museum devoted to expatriate writers. Once again, there has been, at time of writing, little local interest. Rumours regarding the demolition were strongly denied by the Deputy Mayor, who insisted that the new owners had bought the house on condition they carry out restoration work. There was no willingness, however, to commit local government funds. Newspaper articles quoted Deputy Mayor Danielle Gaudillat – 'For us to buy it and turn it into a museum, no way. The house has no architectural value, and Anaïs Nin wasn't even a French writer.' It seems that Nin's house is having as much trouble surviving as a literary landmark as Nin herself had getting her books published.

Maisons-Laffitte. Birthplace of Jean Cocteau ◊. His childhood was spent here and at his parents' other home in the centre of Paris.

Marly-le-Roi. At **1 bis, rue Champflour** is the house in which Alexandre Dumas *fils* (1824–95) and his family lived in the later part of the writer's life and where Dumas died. The property had been left to him by the previous owner, a close friend of Dumas *père*.

Médan. In May 1878, Émile Zola (◊ Nord) bought a country property here with earnings from the huge success of his novel *L'Assommoir*, 1877 (*L'Assommoir*, 1970), and proceeded over the years to extend his estate and the house to considerably more luxurious proportions, adding the two unmatching and bizarrely inappropriate towers which you see on either side of the orginal building, now dwarfed by their presence. Zola lived at Médan for the greater part of each year until his death in 1902 (apart from his period of exile in 1898–99 during the Dreyfus Affair), spending the colder months in Paris. He wrote many of his best known novels here, including *Nana*, 1880 (*Nana*, 1972), *La Terre*, 1887 (*The Earth*, 1980), and *Germinal*, 1885 (*Germinal*, 1954). Among the friends who visited him at Médan were Daudet, Edmond de Goncourt, Vallès, and, until 1885, Cézanne. Most famously, it was a regular gathering place for the group of writers who at the time were seen as the leading lights of the Naturalist movement in literature – Zola and his then 'disciples' Maupassant, Huysmans, Céard, Alexis, and Hennique. In 1880 the group published a collection of stories entitled *Les Soirées de Médan*, which included Guy de Maupassant's celebrated 'Boule de suif'.

It was here also that Zola met the woman who would become his long-term mistress. In spring 1888 his wife Alexandrine engaged a young woman at Médan to help with sewing and mending. Zola, some 27 years her senior, was instantly attracted to Jeanne Rozerot. They became lovers and by the autumn of the same year he had installed her in a flat in Paris – she had two children by him in 1889 and 1891. In 1893, by which time his wife had learned of the relationship, Zola acquired a property for Jeanne and the children in nearby **Cheverchemont** – from his study, with the help of binoculars, he could see the house and garden. Later, he arranged for them to move to **Verneuil** and cycled there every day to visit them.

On Sunday, 28 September 1902, Zola and Alexandrine left Médan to spend the winter in Paris. On their first night back in their city apartment, Zola died from carbon monoxide poisoning – whether the blocked chimney that caused it was an accident or a deliberate act of violence against the leading Dreyfusard is an open question. The following year, Zola's friends came to Médan on the first Sunday in October, to honour his memory and this tradition has continued ever since, with an annual pilgimage to his former home.

Since 1985 part of the house has been turned into a museum dedicated to Zola and his works. For many years previously, however, it had been used as a hospital for children and subsequently as a nursing school – besides, some of the grounds had been sold off after Zola's death by his wife. Consequently it has undergone considerable change both inside and out, although some of the rooms retain aspects of their original decor. Fortunately, Zola became a keen photographer and the photographs on display in his huge study and in the billiard room, for example, show us both the decor and contents of the rooms as they were when they were his domain. There are many of his photos on display in the museum, among them pictures of Maupassant and the other authors of *Les Soirées de Médan*. The exhibits also include various items of furniture belonging to the family, personal memorabilia of the novelist, and, among others, documents and correspondence relating to his role in the Dreyfus Affair.

La Maison de Zola is at 26 rue Pasteur, Médan, 78670 Villennes-sur-Seine. Opening times are limited – contact the Tourist Office in **St-Germain-en-Laye**, which, incidentally, organizes a literary tour of the region.

Port-Marly. In 1844 Alexandre Dumas (◊ Provence) bought some land with the intention of building a small summer retreat here on the sloping banks of the Seine. His plans, however, developed like one of his novels – growing rapidly more and more expansive and romantic. Simply spending more money whenever a construction problem or a new idea arose, Dumas watched over the whole building and landscaping process and the fantastic plans were, surprisingly enough, turned into reality. The house-warming party was held in July 1847 with no less than 600 guests.

The façade of the **Château de Monte Cristo**, as Dumas christened it, was designed roughly in the Renaissance style. The windows, apparently, recall those of his birthplace at **Villers-Cotterêts**. Above them are the profiles of his literary heroes (Homer, Sophocles, Shakespeare, Goethe, Byron, Hugo . . .) – 'my personal Panthéon'. His own profile is above the front door. Inside, on the first floor, is the apartment Dumas had designed for his own use – a sumptuous Moorish fantasy in which the Count of Monte Cristo himself would feel completely at home. It was decorated by two Tunisian artists whom Dumas enountered on his travels in North Africa and whom, with the permission of the Bey of Tunis, he brought back with him to France expressly for the purpose. In the grounds of the Château he constructed a lake, with a small island in the middle of it, on which he built the small chalet, overlooking the main house, which he called the 'Château d'If' Here he had his study. On the stones of the Chalet are engraved the titles of his works, or as many as he could fit on – an appropriate testimony to his prolific achievement.

The Château was permanently 'open house' for friends, writers in peril, hangers on and scroungers, and, with the constant hospitality and an inevitably large retinue of servants, continued to soak up money as it had done from its conception. The debtors became ever more numerous and demanding. The property was seized in 1850 and Dumas lost it and everything in it.

In the 1970s the Château de Monte Cristo and the Château d'If narrowly escaped demolition, but were rescued by public opinion and the pressure of the Société des Amis d'Alexandre Dumas. They have been extensively restored, with help, for the restoration of the sumptuous interior, from the King of Morocco, and a small museum has been established (**Le Château de Monte Cristo**, 1 avenue Kennedy, 78560 Port-Marly). Opening times are limited – check in advance.

Port-Royal-des-Champs. The convent of Port-Royal-des-Champs, founded in 1204, earned a special place in the religious and cultural history of France in the 17th century, when it became a major centre of Jansenism. The nearby Ferme des Granges, a dependency of the convent, was occupied by *solitaires*, mainly lay men from various walks of life who chose a life of restraint and seclusion. They established the respected 'Petites Écoles' for boys, and a building dedicated to this purpose was constucted by the *solitaires* themselves next to the farm in around 1652. Among those who received part of their education here was Jean Racine (1639–99). Blaise Pascal (1623–62) was a frequent visitor to the Port-Royal and wrote here some of his *Lettres provinciales*, 1656–57 (*The Provincial Letters*, 1967), championing the Jansenists against Jesuit attack – his sister became a nun at the convent. In 1709, Jesuit hostility led to the expulsion of the nuns from Port-Royal and shortly afterwards the convent was destroyed by order of Louis XIV. Its significant and dramatic history provided the inspiration for Sainte-Beuve's five-volume *Port-Royal* (1840–59). Racine himself wrote a history of it – *Abrégé de l'histoire de Port-Royal*, written 1698, published in full 1747.

Naturally, there is not much to see of the original convent – however the building put up by the *solitaires* survived (because by the time the religious buildings were razed it had been converted to agricultural use for the farm). It is now the **Musée National des Granges de Port-Royal** (Magny-les-Hameaux, 78470 Saint-Rémy-lès-Chevreuse). The museum, with busts of Pascal and Racine at the entrance, is devoted to the history of Jansenism and especially to that of Port-Royal. The room in which Racine stayed and studied may still be seen.

Saint-Arnoult-en-Yvelines. In 1951, the great Surrealist and Communist writer Louis Aragon (1897–1982) bought the **Moulin de Villeneuve**, a large country property developed from an old water mill and set in picturesque and spacious grounds on the banks of the river Rémarde. Aragon bought the estate in the name of Elsa Triolet (1896–1970), the Russian-born writer who had been his companion since 1928, so that she could have her own 'corner of France'. When Triolet died in 1970, Aragon arranged for her to be buried in the gardens. Because it reminded him too much of Elsa, Aragon rarely stayed in the house after her death, but was buried next to her when he himself died in 1982 – their grave is within sight of the house shaded by two large beech trees of which Elsa was especially fond. Aragon bequeathed the house and its contents to the state. After a long period of neglect, it was extensively restored (including the water mill, which was not working in Aragon's time) and finally opened to the public in 1995.

The rooms which may be visited are very much as they were when Triolet and Aragon lived in them – with their original furnishings and decor, and, most importantly, the two writers' vast collection of books which dominates every room. Among the rooms on display are their respective studies – it was here at the Moulin that Aragon worked on one of the highlights of his later period, *La Semaine sainte*, 1958 (*Holy Week*, 1961).

Le Moulin de Villeneuve, Route de Villeneuve, 78730 Saint-Arnoult-en-

Yvelines, is in the care of La Fondation Elsa Triolet-Louis Aragon. At time of writing, it is open every day except Monday.

Saint-Germain-en-Laye. The **Pavillon Henri-IV** was converted into apartments for rent and a restaurant in 1836. In 1844, Alexandre Dumas *père* (◊ Provence), plagued by admirers and scroungers in Paris and in search of a country home where he could work in relative peace, came upon the Pavillon, and rented a section of the building. Among the works he wrote here were *La Reine Margot*, 1845 (*Queen Margot*, 1994), and *Vingt ans après*, 1845 (*Twenty Years After*, 1993).

Versailles. The *moraliste* Jean de La Bruyère (1645–96) lived at **22 rue des Réservoirs**, and died there.

53 avenue de Paris was the home of the poet and essayist Robert de Montesquiou (1855–1921), said to have been the model both for Charlus in Proust's *À la recherche du temps perdu*, 1913–27 (*Remembrance of Things Past*, 1981) and Des Esseintes in Huysmans's *À rebours*, 1884 (*Against Nature*, 1966).

Nancy Mitford (◊ Paris), whose *The Sun King*, 1966, about Louis XIV at Versailles, was enormously successful, spent the last years of her life at **4 rue d'Artois**. In 1967, she moved here from her Paris apartment, where she had lived for 20 years. She died in the house in 1973 – after suffering for four years from a rare and extremely painful form of Hodgkinson's Disease.

For a contemporary view of life in the **Château de Versailles** at the time of Louis XIV, and in the early years of the reign of Louis XV, see the *Mémoires* of the Duc de Saint-Simon (1675–1755). The *Mémoires*, much admired by Proust, were completed near the end of Saint-Simon's life, but he had been preparing and researching them over many years – making copious notes on his daily observations of the public and private goings-on in the court and combining these with primary source material from the earlier journal of the Marquis de Dangeau (1638–1720), along with numerous other records and documentation. The letters of Madame de Sévigné (1626–96) also contain accounts of scandals and other aspects of court life. Voltaire (who was at Versailles in 1744 during his brief time as a court poet) published *Le Siècle de Louis XIV* in 1751 (rev. 1756 and 1768) – a history of the characters and politics, coloured with his personal vision of the development of civilization (*The Age of Louis 14th*, 1961).

The room of most literary interest for those undertaking a tour of the Château is the **Grand Cabinet**, where Racine's *Esther*, 1689, and *Athalie*, 1691, were performed in the presence of Louis XIV. Earlier, in 1663, Molière's *L'Impromptu de Versailles* was staged for the King at Versailles – the support and protection of Louis XIV was of considerable significance in the continuation of Molière's controversial career. There are portraits of both dramatists, along with other writers of the time, in Room 8 of the **17th Century gallery**.

ESSONNE

Bièvres and Jouy-en-Josas. In the late summers of 1834 and 1835, Victor Hugo (◊ Paris) and his family came to stay with his friend Bertin (editor of the *Journal des débats*) at the **Château des Roches**. At the same time, he installed his mistress Juliette Drouet nearby in a house in the village of **Les Metz**, in the municipality of **Jouy-en-Josas** (Yvelines). Almost every day they met at an old chestnut tree about halfway between the two places – the tree's hollow trunk was a useful place for her to leave her messages and for him to leave his letters and poems. The château at Bièvres has since been rebuilt, although its gardens remain intact, but the house at Les Metz still stands and is identified by a plaque (10 rue Victor-Hugo,

78350 Jouy-en-Josas). Neither can be visited.

Champrosay. In 1868, Alphonse Daudet (◊ Provence) and his wife rented a house in this village near **Draveil**. The house, in which they spent three successive summers, stands at what is now **11 rue Alphonse-Daudet** (it cannot be visited) – it had previously been the home of the artist Eugène Delacroix (1798–1863). Julia Daudet's family, the Allards, had a villa in Champrosay and, after 1872, the Daudets lived there whenever they were in the village, until, in 1886, they bought a large house nearby (**33 rue Alphonse-Daudet**). Champrosay continued to be their country home until Daudet's death in 1897. Among their regular visitors was Edmond de Goncourt, who became ill and died here in July 1896.

Milly-la-Forêt. Jean Cocteau (◊ Paris) bought a house here on the edge of the Forêt de Fontainebleau in 1947. He died at Milly on 11 October 1963 and is buried in the **cemetery**. His frescoes of plants may be seen in the 12th century **chapel**.

Verrières-le-Buisson. In 1966, following the death of his two sons in a car accident in 1961 and his second divorce in 1965, the writer, art critic and politician André Malraux (1901–76) established a relationship with the novelist and poet Louise de Vilmorin (1902–69). Her home was the **Château de Verrières**, 4 rue d'Estienne d'Orves. Malraux lived partially here until 1969, when he moved in permanently – his political career ended with the fall of de Gaulle's government, in which he had been minister for cultural affairs. Unfortunately, Vilmorin died the same year, adding to a long list of personal bereavements for Malraux – she is buried in the grounds of the Château. Malraux remained here until his own death in 1976. He was buried in the cemetery at Verrières, but in 1996 it was announced that his remains would be moved to the Panthéon on the 20th anniversary of his death (23 November 1996). (The Château de Verrières cannot be visited.)

SEINE-ET-MARNE

Avon. Katherine Mansfield (◊ Paris) came here in October 1922, in the terminal stages of her long suffering from tuberculosis. She ended her days at the 'Institute for the Harmonious Development of Man' of George Gurdjieff, who directed a community of 'disciples' essentially on the principle that emotional, physical, and intellectual balance could be restored through a regime of hard work, discomfort, and strict routines and discipline. The Institute was sited at the neighbouring estate of **Le Prieuré des Basses-Loges**. She died there in January 1923 and is buried in the **cemetery** at Avon.

Barbizon. Robert Louis Stevenson (◊ Languedoc–Roussillon) made several visits to this village near **Fontainebleau** in the 1870s. He first came in 1875, by which time the painters of the Barbizon School (Millet, Corot, Théodore Rousseau, etc) had largely disappeared – however, it was still a thriving artists' colony (it continues to be a resort favoured by artists) and Stevenson was much attracted to the bohemian, multinational society it offered. On a visit to another Fontainebleau village, **Grez-sur-Loing**, Stevenson met Fanny Osbourne, who later became his wife.

Saint-Cyr-sur-Morin. The adventure novelist Mac Orlan (Pierre Dumarchey, 1882–1970) lived at what is now **La Maison Mac Orlan** (in the *hameau* of **Archet**) from 1924 until his death. It was here that he wrote *Le Quai des brumes*, 1927, the novel so memorably filmed by Marcel Carné in 1938. In accordance with Mac Orlan's wishes, the house must now be occupied by a practising writer and at time of writing

it is not open to the public. This may change, depending on the decision of future residents.

Ussy-sur-Marne. Ussy became Samuel Beckett's (◊ Paris) second home in the 1950s. He bought a plot of land here and had a small house designed and built, using his earnings from the success of *Waiting for Godot* – he later called it 'the house that *Godot* built'. It became an essential refuge for the retiring Beckett, and he spent long periods at the house, working in solitude, away from the many demands for his attention that distracted him in Paris.

Vulaines-sur-Seine. In 1874, the poet Stéphane Mallarmé (1842–98), father of the Symbolists, found a small house in the hamlet of **Valvins** beside the Seine here in the forest of Fontainebleau. He rented the first floor, accessible from outside by a stone staircase, and it became his regular summer home (he was an English teacher by profession). Mallarmé grew increasingly attached to the house and its environment, walking along the bank and boating on the river (see Extract 2, by Valéry) – its leafy calm must have provided him with the peace he needed for the composition of his intricate and complex verse. In the last decade of his life he spent more and more time here and in 1897 made it his permanent home. He died in his study in September 1898, and was buried in the neigbouring village of **Samoreau** (his grave is in the cemetery there). Friends who attended the funeral included Jarry, Renoir, Rodin, and Valéry. Valéry ◊ later wrote of his last visit to Mallarmé – 'I saw Stéphane Mallarmé for the last time on July 14, 1898, at Valvins. When luncheon was over, he took me to his "workroom", which was four paces long and two paces wide. The window looked out at the Seine and the forest through the foliage gashed with sunlight, and the least tremors of the sparkling river were faintly echoed on the walls.' Later, they walked in the fields near the house. 'Mallarmé showed me the valley, which the early heat of summer was turning to gold. "*Look!*" he said. "It's the first cymbal clash of autumn over the earth." When autumn came, he was no longer there.' (from the essay 'Dernière Visite à Mallarmé', 1923, translated as 'Last Visit to Mallarmé', in *Collected Works*, Vol 8).

The house is now a museum dedicated to the poet (**La Maison de Mallarmé**, 3 quai Mallarmé, 77870 Vulaines-sur-Seine), which atmospherically evokes Mallarmé's lifestyle. Among other things, you can see his study, and items of furniture from his Parisian apartment where he held his famous *Mardis*, the prestigious Tuesday afternoon literary gatherings which were attended by many leading literary figures of the time.

VAL-DE-MARNE

Saint-Maur-des-Fossés. Raymond Radiguet ◊ was born here in 1903, at **30 bis avenue des Rochers**. The river and its banks, the pleasures of which he experienced in his childhood and early adolescence, resurface as an atmospheric setting in *Le Diable au corps*, 1923 (*Devil in the Flesh*, 1969) – Extract 1.

HAUTS-DE-SEINE

Châtenay-Malabry. Chateaubriand (◊ Brittany) moved here in 1807, encouraged by Napoleon, to whose regime he had become increasingly hostile, to put some distance between himself and Paris. He bought **La Vallée aux Loups** and proceeded to redesign both house and grounds. The park which he created became especially dear to him – he planted a great variety of trees which reminded him of his travels and the many different countries he had visited. Several, and in particular a rare and magnificent magnolia, were, according to Chateaubriand's wife, contributed by the Empress Joséphine. La Vallée-aux-

Loups was Chateaubriand's home for 10 years and he wrote several books here, including, among others, the record of his travels to the Orient, *Itinéraire de Paris à Jerusalem*, 1811, and *Les Martyrs*, 1809. He also began his famous autobiography, *Mémoires d'outre-tombe*, 1849–50 (*The Memoirs of Chateaubriand*, 1961), in which he refers to the work he had done on the house and his life here.

In 1816, under the Second Bourbon Restoration, Chateaubriand published a pamphlet which included some criticism of the government and this led to a fall from grace and loss of position, and precipitated a financial crisis that eventually forced him to sell La Vallée-aux-Loups, where he had hoped to spend the rest of his life. It was bought in 1818 by a colleague, Mathieu de Montmorency. Chateaubriand's connection with the house, though, was not quite over – in 1826, Madame Récamier (whom Chateaubriand visited daily in Paris in his later years and with whom he was in love) took a few months' refuge here from her famous *salon* and copied out the manuscript of the first three volumes of *Mémoires d'outre-tombe* – her 'manuscript of 1826' has been a crucial source for current editions of the work.

A later 19th century owner made changes to the house, altering to an extent Chateaubriand's design. In 1914, it was bought by a doctor who opened a rest home (Paul Léautaud died here in 1956), but he also established La Vallée-aux-Loups as the headquarters of La Société Chateaubriand, formed in 1929, so paving the way for it to be preserved as a monument to its famous owner. The last purchaser was the *département* of Hauts-de-Seine, and under its management La Vallée-aux-Loups was restored and opened to the public in 1987. It houses a library dedicated to the Romantic period, hosts various cultural events (among them performances of works by Romantic composers every May), and includes a museum evoking Chateaubriand's life and times. The grounds are magnificent, especially in autumn. Chateaubriand sometimes wrote in the summerhouse in the park, known as the 'Tour de Velléda' – it reputedly also served as a clandestine meeting place for the writer and his mistresses, until his wife, presumably suspicious, had a chapel installed on the first floor.

Of this home for which he developed a great affection, Chateaubriand wrote, 'La Vallée-aux-Loups, of all the things that have escaped me, is the only one I regret.' **La Vallée-aux-Loups, Maison-Musée Chateaubriand** is at 87 rue Chateaubriand, 92290 Châtenay-Malabry.

Chatou. Here Renoir painted *Le Déjeuner des Canotiers* at the restaurant Fournaise. Chatou and the other villages on the banks of the Seine were favourite destinations in the later 19th century for week-enders looking for lazing and liaisons on the river and they also became fashionable among writers and artists. Maupassant, who rented an apartment in Chatou for a time, describes in 'Yvette' the floating cabaret 'La Grenouillère', which was moored next to an island in the river, and was made famous in paintings by Renoir and Monet: 'An immense roofed vessel, moored to the bank, was laden with a mass of women and men, sitting and drinking at tables, or else standing, shouting, singing, bawling, dancing, capering about to the sound of a grumbling piano, out of tune and tinny as a saucepan. Big red-headed, red-lipped girls were walking about, flaunting themselves in both directions with the dual temptation of their busts and their behinds, catching everyone's eye, half-drunk and foul-mouthed. Others were dancing distractedly with half-naked young men in linen trousers and cotton vests and with jockey-caps on their heads. And from all this activity rose a smell of sweat and face powder, vapours from the perfumery and the armpit. The drinkers around the tables were swallowing white, red, yellow, and green concoctions, and were shouting, yelling for no reason, giving in to a violent need to make a racket, to an animal urge to fill their ears and heads with noise. Every other second a swimmer stood on the roof and jumped into the water, throwing up a shower over the nearest customers, who screamed like savages.'

Maupassant also sets another of his best stories, 'Une Partie de campagne', in this area (the story so evocatively filmed by Jean Renoir in 1936). Pierre Cogny, in his introduction to *Le Maison Tellier et autres contes* (Flammarion, 1980), remarks that the inn in which Maupassant stayed in nearby **Bezons** was the model for the inn in 'Une Partie de campagne'.

Meudon. After his father's death, Sartre (◊ Paris) spent his early childhood here at the home of his mother's parents. This period is the subject of his autobiographical *Les Mots*, 1964 (*Words*, 1964).

Granted amnesty in 1951, Céline (◊ Paris) returned to France from Denmark and settled in Meudon for the last 10 years of his life. He practised as a doctor and wrote several novels here before his death in July 1961. Two admiring Americans, William Burroughs and Allen Ginsberg, visited him in Meudon in July 1958. Restoration work has been done on the house **(route des Gardes)** which was extensively damaged by fire in 1969 – it cannot be visited.

Sceaux. The current **Château de Sceaux** dates from the 19th century. Its predecessor, a luxurious 17th century version, was once the home of Louise de Bourbon, Duchesse du Maine (1676–1753), whose court here was a famous social and cultural centre. Her many visitors included Voltaire and Madame du Châtelet, Madame du Deffand, and Fontenelle. The Château now houses the **Musée de l'Île de France**. Florian (1755–94), best known for his *Fables*, 1792, is buried in the old **churchyard** of Sceaux.

Sèvres. Balzac (♢ Centre) dreamed of being a rich and successful businessman – an unrealized ambition which drove him further and further into debt through the failure of his various schemes. One of these was **Les Jardies**, a weaver's property which he bought at Sèvres with borrowed money in 1837, at a time when his financial problems were especially severe (he had had to leave Paris to escape his creditors). He subsequently bought other pieces of neighbouring land, characteristically responding to his financial crisis by enlarging it. Balzac himself then moved into temporary lodging which he rented in the name of his brother-in-law while work on his grand scheme began. First, he had a curious tall and narrow Swiss-chalet style house built for himself, three rooms on top of each other with an external ladder the only access to the two upper floors of the three-storey building. The internal decoration was grand, but purely imaginary – Balzac had to be content with charcoal notes on the walls heralding the arrival of dreamed-of luxuries – 'Here a ceiling painted by Eugène Delacroix', 'Here a tapestry by Aubusson', etc. As his friend the novelist and journalist Léon Gozlan (1803–66) reported in *Balzac en pantoufles*, 1856, these projects never advanced beyond the charcoal inscriptions on bare plaster walls, a sad testament to the gap between the aspiration and the reality. The house never really became a 'home' – 'If he lived, thought and worked there', said Gozlan, 'he

never actually dwelt there. He camped rather than set up home.'

For the steeply inclined land around the house, rendering cultivation virtually impracticable, Balzac had even more adventurous plans. Here he would grow vegetables, develop a dairy farm to serve the neighbourhood, produce his own wine, and grow vast quantities of pineapples so cornering the market in that exotic fruit, which he would sell from a shop on the boulevard Montmartre (he spent a day looking for a suitable premises with Théophile Gautier, the façade and shop sign already clear in his mind). The project was short-lived and never approached completion – Balzac was forced by creditors to quit the property at the end of 1840, leaving numerous debts behind him, at the butcher, the laundry, etc, etc, and it was sold the following year. In his two years here he had been briefly imprisoned by the Rural National Guard for avoiding service, and frequently harassed by creditors.

Nothing of Balzac's dream house remains, and almost all the surrounding land was sold and developed long ago. All that is left today of Les Jardies is the humble little house of the weaver, which was subsequently purchased and extended by the republican Léon Gambetta, who died there in 1882 and to whom it became a shrine. The ground floor is now the **Musée Gambetta, Villa Les Jardies**, 14 rue Gambetta, 92310 Sèvres.

Les Jardies is located in the suburb of **Ville d'Avray**, which was, incidentally, where writer, actor, singer and jazzman Boris Vian (1920–59) was born.

BOOKLIST

For most of the extracted works, the original publisher in English can be found in 'Acknowledgments and Citations' at the end of the volume, as can the exact location of the extracts and the editions from which they are taken. The date in square brackets is that of the original publication of the work in its original language. For additional titles by the authors highlighted in this chapter and recommended biographies, see 'Lives and Works'.

Chateaubriand, François-René, *The Memoirs of Chateaubriand* [1849–50], Robert Baldick, trans, Penguin, London and New York, 1965. (Selections.)

Flaubert and Turgenev, A Friendship in Letters: The Complete Correspondence, Barbara Beaumont, ed and trans, The Athlone Press, London, 1985.

Huysmans, J.-K., *Against Nature* [1884], R. Baldick, trans, Penguin, London and New York, 1966.

Maupassant, Guy de, *A Day in the Country and Other Stories*, D. Coward, trans, Oxford University Press, Oxford and New York, 1990.

Mitford, Nancy, *The Sun King*, Hamish Hamilton, London, 1966.

Nin, Anaïs, *Henry and June*, Penguin, London, 1990/Harcourt Brace, Orlando, FL, 1990.

Nin, Anaïs, *Journals, 1931–34*, Peter Owen, London, 1966.

Nin, Anaïs, *Journals, 1934–1939*, Peter Owen, London, 1967.

Pascal, Blaise, *The Provincial Letters* [1656–57], A.J. Krailsheimer, trans, Penguin, London, 1967/Viking Penguin, New York, 1995.

Proust, Marcel, *Remembrance of Things Past* [1913–27], C.K. Scott Moncrieff and Terence Kilmartin, trans, Penguin, London and New York, 1983. Vol 1 – *Swann's Way* and *Within a Budding Grove*; Vol 2 – *The Guermantes Way* and *Cities of the Plain*; Vol 3 – *The Captive, The Fugitive*, and *Time Regained*.

Radiguet, Raymond, *The Devil in the Flesh* [1923], A.M. Sheridan Smith, trans, Marion Boyars, London, 1982. **Extract 1.**

Rousseau, Jean-Jacques, *The Confessions*, J.M. Cohen, trans, Penguin, London, 1970/Viking Penguin, New York, 1995.

Rousseau, Jean-Jacques, *Julie or the New Eloise* [1761], J.H. McDowell, trans, Penn State University Press, University Park, PA, 1987.

Sartre, Jean-Paul, *Words* [1964], Irene Clephane, trans, Penguin, London, 1964/Bernard Frechtman, trans, Vintage, New York, 1981.

Sévigné, Madame de, *Selected Letters*, Leonard Tancock, trans, Penguin, London, 1982/Penguin, New York, 1982.

Valéry, Paul, 'Valvins' [1898], David Paul, trans, in *The Collected Works of Paul Valéry*, Jackson Matthews, ed, Vol 1, *Poems* and *On Poets and Poetry* (from *Cahiers*), Routledge and Kegan Paul, London, 1971/Princeton University Press, Princeton, NJ, 1971 (bilingual with verse translations) **Extract 2**; Vol 8, *Leonardo, Poe, Mallarmé*, essays, selections from *Cahiers*, and letters, Malcolm Cowley and James R. Lawler, trans, Routledge and Kegan Paul, London, 1972/Princeton University Press, Princeton, NJ, 1972.

Voltaire, *The Age of Louis 14th* [1768], P. Pollack, trans, Dent, London, 1961.

Extracts

(1) THE MARNE

Raymond Radiguet, *The Devil in the Flesh*

The love affair between Radiguet's 16-year-old narrator and Marthe Lacombe, the young wife of a soldier (Jacques), takes place during the First World War in the countryside close to Paris on the banks of the Marne. In the summer evenings, they go down to the river and take out a rowing boat.

Love wishes to share its happiness. A woman who is cool by nature becomes demonstrative, kisses you in the nape of the neck and invents innumerable tricks to distract you if you happen to be writing a letter. I never wanted to kiss Marthe so much as when her attention was taken up by something else; or to touch her hair and undo it as when she was pinning it up. In the boat I would throw myself upon her and smother her with kisses to make her let go of the oars and let the boat lose its way among the herbs and the white and yellow water-lilies. She saw this as a sign of uncontrollable passion, whereas I was really in the grip of this powerful urge to disturb her. We would then moor the boat behind some tall tufts of grass. The danger of being seen or of capsizing the boat made our sport all the more pleasurable.

Nor did I complain of the hostility of the landlord and his wife who made my presence in Marthe's rooms so difficult.

My obsessive desire to possess Marthe as Jacques had never been able to, to kiss some part of her skin after making her swear that no other lips but mine had touched it, was really only a kind of profligacy. But did I admit it? All love has a youth, a maturity and an old age. Was I already at that final stage when love no longer satisfied me unless accompanied each time by some new trick? For if my pleasure was based on habit, it thrived on the thousand and one slight changes it imposed on habit. It is not primarily by increasing the doses, which would soon become lethal, that an addict finds ecstasy, but in the rhythm he invents, either by changing the times, or by employing various deceptions to confuse the organism.

I loved that left bank of the Marne so much that I used to cross over on to the other side, which was so very different, in order to contemplate the side I loved. The right bank is more harsh. It is occupied by farmers and market-gardeners, whereas mine is left to idlers. We moored the boat to a tree and went and lay in the corn. The field shivered in the evening breeze. Our selfish desire succeeded in forgetting prejudice, sacrificing the corn to the comfort of our love as it had sacrificed Jacques.

(2) VALVINS

Paul Valéry, *Valvins*

This was one of 23 poems presented to Stéphane Mallarmé by his friends in 1897 (it was first published in 1898). Valvins is the village in the forest of Fontainbleau where Mallarmé spent many summers and where he enjoyed boating on the Seine. In content, form, and language, Valéry pays homage to Mallarmé, the father of the Symbolist movement. The poem was originally in the form of a sonnet (an octave and a sestet), and the rhyming scheme has been lost in the translation.

Should you seek to untangle the forest that cools you
Blissful, you melt into the leaves, suppose you are
In the fluid and for all time literary yawl
Trailing numbers of suns, burningly poised

On the whiteness of its flanks caressed by
The emotive Seine, or adumbrating the sung afternoon,
As the giant wood immerses a long tress
And blends your sail with the essence of summer.

But ever close to you, surrendered by the silence
To the miscellaneous cries of all the raw azure,
The ghost of a scattered page of a non-existent

Book quivers suggesting an errant sail
Upon the powdery skin of the virid river
Amid the long gaze of the half-opened Seine.

Lives and works of extracted writers

RADIGUET, Raymond (1903–23). Radiguet was born near Paris on 18 June 1903, in **Saint-Maur-des-Fossés** (Seine-et-Marne), close to the banks of the Marne – an environment which was to figure atmospherically in *Le Diable au corps* (Extract 1). By the age of 15, he was mixing in the post-war avant-garde literary and artistic circles of Paris, meeting, among others, Max Jacob, Blaise Cendrars, and André Breton. When he met Jean Cocteau in 1919 he had already had poems published in the avant-garde magazine *Sic*, and also by Tristan Tzara in *Dada* and André Breton in *Littérature*. His relationship with Cocteau proved crucial in his prodigious literary development, and their friendship developed rapidly. Radiguet's biographer Margaret Crosland comments, 'Apart from his family, whom he genuinely loved, he probably never cared for anyone . . . Obviously he responded to Cocteau as a friend,

Paul Valéry at Shakespeare and Company in Paris

probably as a lover, but for his work he needed most of all the older man's guidance, his gift for talent-spotting and for acting as go-between with editors and publishers.' Whether or not she is right in her speculations about Radiguet's feelings, it is certainly true that Cocteau was a crucial influence in directing and harnessing his wild-child talent, while at the same time providing him with unfettered access to the exciting and intoxicating world of the avant-garde in which the older man was a prime mover. With the stardom and wealth that accompanied the huge success of *Le Diable au corps*, Radiguet began to distance himself to an extent from Cocteau (remarking rather cruelly that he did not want to be known in his middle age as 'Madame Cocteau'), and to turn his sexual attentions increasingly towards women. His taste of fortune and fame was, however, very short. He contracted typhoid and died in December 1923, the year in which the novel which preserves his name was published.

Le Diable au corps, 1923 (*The Devil in the Flesh*, 1968) was written, astonishingly, between the author's 16th and 18th years. Set in a village in the countryside close to Paris in the final year of the First World War, it is a psychological analysis of the passionate relationship between a young man of 16 and a young married woman of 19, whose husband is at the front. The novel is notable for the clarity of the author's understanding and communication of the motivations behind the actions of his adolescent protagonist, through whose eyes the story unfolds. Primarily, this is an examination of sexual love, with its pain and joy and its manipulative impulses – the last especially portrayed with disarming honesty and insight. It is also a reflection of the great social upheaval caused by the war (as, for example, portrayed also in Ford Madox Ford's *Parade's End*) – it is the war which allows this love affair to happen, which heightens the desire to live in the present, with the old established order of things and the associated sexual morality disrupted and fundamentally challenged. The story was filmed in 1947 by Claude Autant-Lara.

Radiguet's only other novel, published posthumously thanks to Cocteau, is *Le Bal du comte d'Orgel*, 1924 (*Count d'Orgel's Ball*, 1953) which he wrote when he was 18 – the 'ball' of the title is based on the celebrated fancy-dress balls given by the Comte de Beaumont in Paris in the 1920s. Writing to his US editor in 1924, Scott Fitzgerald recommmended it – '. . . and though I'm only half through it I'd get an opinion on it if I were you. It's cosmopolitan rather than French and

my instinct tells me that in a good translation it might make an enormous hit in America, where everyone is yearning for Paris. Do look it up and get at least one opinion on it. The preface is by the dadaist Jean Cocteau but the book is not dada at all.'

Recommended biography: Margaret Crosland, *Raymond Radiguet: A Biographical Study with Selections from His Work*, Peter Owen, London, 1976.

VALÉRY, PAUL (1871–1945). One of the key figures of 20th century French literature and thought, Valéry was born in the fishing port of **Sète** on the French Mediterranean. He studied law in **Montpellier** and, after 1894, lived in **Paris**. In 1897 he joined the War Office, where he worked until 1900, when he took a job at Agence Havas (the news agency). He worked at Havas until 1922, which was also the year of publication of his best known collection of poems, *Charmes*. After that, he devoted himself to his writing and to the various prestigious positions that were bestowed upon him – including President of the PEN Club, election to the Académie Française, President of Intellectual Co-operation at the League of Nations, and Professor of Poetics at the Collège de France (a chair especially created for him). He died in July 1945 and, after a state funeral in Paris, was buried in the graveyard at **Sète** which had provided the setting and inspiration for his famous poem 'La Cimetière marin'.

As a young man, Valéry was friendly with the novelist and Symbolist poet Pierre Louÿs (1870–1925) – through Louÿs he met two enormously influential writers with whom he was to develop lasting friendships: André Gide and Stéphane Mallarmé. Mallarmé in particular (see Extract 2) was a key influence in Valéry's development of his own highly crafted and formally constrained verse – although he abandoned poetry completely between 1892 and 1912, rejecting it as an emotively literary language which required too great a compromise of the intellect. When he returned to poetry it was to revise his previous work, at the urging of Gide and the publisher Gaston Gallimard. However, he did not stop there – he went on to write, over some four years, the long verse monologue 'La Jeune Parque', an image-rich exploration within a single consciousness of the tension between the need for rational clarity and the pull of emotion and sensuality. As in much of Valéry's poetry, the careful, intellectually distanced, technically brilliant composer produces, almost paradoxically, a musical and colourful verse of great linguistic sensuality – the poetry itself crystallizing the poet's constant concern with the relationship between the sometimes coordinated (as in love) and sometimes conflicting energies of the intellect and the emotions. *Charmes* followed in 1922, comprising poems written between 1913 and 1922, and including 'La Cimetière marin', 1920 ('The Graveyard by the Sea', in *Poems* – see Booklist).

Valéry also wrote many critical, philosophical and biographical essays (in translation see, for example, Volume 8 of the *Collected Works*, which includes pieces on Leonardo da Vinci, Mallarmé, and Poe); Socratic-style dialogues on, for example, the aesthetics of dance and of architecture; an unfinished play, *Mon Faust*; and the famous *La Soirée avec Monsieur Teste*, 1896 (*Monsieur Teste*, 1951), the closest he came to a novel and the first of several works featuring the monstrous character Teste, who is a kind of manifestation of the intellect turned in on itself, observing itself observing what goes on around it and analysing the feelings and sensations experienced by the body it inhabits.

Some years after his death, between 1957 and 1961, Valéry's *Cahiers*, or notebooks, were first published. Now translated into many languages, these were the private journals that he kept over some 50 years, writing entries daily, jotting down anything from brief personal thoughts and reflections to substantial analysis of intellectual processes over a wide range of contexts (mathematics and religion, for instance), to philosophical discussion of the nature of poetry. *Cahiers* established Valéry's reputation as a great thinker as much as a great poet and essayist.

PARIS

> 'Until you have wasted time in a city you cannot
> pretend to know it well. The soul of a big city is not
> to be grasped so easily; in order to make contact with
> it, you have to have been bored, you have to have
> suffered a bit in those places that contain it. Anyone
> can get hold of a guide and tick off all the
> monuments, but within the very confines of Paris
> there is another city as difficult of access as
> Timbuktu once was.'
>
> Julien Green, *Paris*

The Left Bank

LATIN QUARTER AND ENVIRONS

Les événements de mai. The Events of May 1968, which centred around the student areas of the Left Bank, blazed spectacularly for only a brief time, but have a lasting symbolism that far outweighs their actual impact on social and political reality. As in other Western countries at the end of the 1960s, the student movement in France had been growing in militancy. Protest marches, largely about Vietnam, had been increasing in size and frequency. There were additional reasons for student unrest here, emanating from an intransigent hierarchy in the education system which took no account of the changing needs and culture of its student population. The situation became increasingly intense day by day in 1968, until, on 10 May, the Sorbonne was occupied by police and leading student activists were imprisoned. That night, the barricades went up and street fighting broke out. In the days that followed, the marches, strikes and occupations of buildings spread from Paris to the provinces and from the university world to industry, with workers and students suddenly brought together in a physical and ideological revolution against the oppressions of a conservative hierarchical establishment. 'The collective hallucination,' writes Mavis Gallant in *Paris Notebooks*, 'was that life can change quite suddenly, and for the better.' The 'revolution' spread like fire – many people not normally politically active were caught up in the spirit of it; it escalated at an astonishing pace; brought Paris and other parts of the country to a standstill; tripped over itself; began to disintegrate into factions within a few days; burned itself out by the end of the month. It had not changed the world, but it did have some impact on the national political scene: on the Right, de Gaulle's resignation the following year reflected the break-down of his dominant hold over the country for which the Events were at least in part responsible, and on the Left the traditional main party, the Parti Communiste Français, which had not supported the students, became increasingly marginalized in favour of the Parti Socialiste and one François Mitterrand who took over its leadership in 1971. In the wider context, the Events in some ways symbolize the soaring hopes and ideals of the youth movement of the 1960s, as well as their vulnerability and transience.

For a stunning piece of eye-witness reportage of the Events, so vivid the tear gas gets in your eyes, turn to Mavis Gallant's ◊ 'The Events in May: A Paris Notebook' (Extract 11), first published in the *New Yorker* in 1968 and included in her *Paris Notebooks*, 1988. Lawrence Ferlinghetti's ◊ novel *Love in the Days of Rage*, 1988 (Extract 10) is set against the background of the Events and includes his reflections on their significance. James Jones's *The Merry Month of May*, 1971, concerns the conflicts and crises in an American family during the riots. Julian Barnes's *Metroland*, 1980, is also set, partially, in student Paris 1968.

Rue de la Bûcherie (5th). Simone de Beauvoir ◊ lived in a crumbling apartment at No 11 from October 1948 to August 1955. Prolific 18th century writer Restif (or Rétif) de la Bretonne (1734–1806) lived, and also died, at No 16 (formerly No 27). His bizarre and unsettling nocturnal observations on the streets of Paris are recorded in the sketches of *Les Nuits de Paris ou le spectateur nocturne*, 1788–94, which includes, among many other things, a memorable account of the body-snatching habits of medical students in this *quartier*. At No 37, facing Notre-Dame, is **Shakespeare and Company** – see below under **rue de l'Odéon** (Odéon–Saint-Germain-des-Prés–Invalides).

Rue du Cardinal-Lemoine (5th). In 1870 Verlaine ◊ married Mathilde Mauté and they moved into a fourth-floor apartment at No 2, with a balcony overloooking the Seine. It was here that Verlaine had his brief taste of normality in the form of a happy married life. It did not last long – drunkenness, violent fits of temper, and Rimbaud soon took over. The novelist and poet Valéry Larbaud (1881–1957) had an apartment at No 71. In 1921 he lent it rent-free to his friends James and Nora Joyce, who made it their home for several months. No 74 was the address of a dance-hall, or *bal musette* called the 'Bal du Printemps'. In 1924 it became one of the gathering places of the ex-pat literary/artistic set. Ford Madox Ford (◊ Picardie) and his companion Stella Bowen hired the place every Friday night and threw parties which were attended by anybody who was anybody. Jean Rhys ◊, with whom Ford had an affair, and Hemingway ◊ were among the regulars. Hemingway, who also lived for a time in an apartment in the same building, sets an early scene of *The Sun Also Rises*, 1927, in a *bal musette*, which he locates in nearby rue de la Montagne-Saint-Geneviève, based on the Friday night parties in the Bal du Printemps. In addition to those in *The Sun Also Rises*, he provides atmospheric descriptions of the *quartier* in 'The Snows of Kilimanjaro', 1936 (Extract 6), and *A Moveable Feast*, 1964.

Place de la Contrescarpe (5th). A plaque at No 1 indicates the site of the Pomme de Pin tavern. In fact the ancient tavern was sited at the corner of rue Mouffetard and rue Blainville. Rabelais refers to it, and in the 16th century it was a meeting place for the poets of La Pléiade – the highly influential group led by Ronsard which aimed to establish a new poetic language for France by reference to classical and Italian influences, and which introduced innovations in versification, content, and theory (the function of poetry and the role of the poet) across the whole range of poetic expression and form.

Rue Descartes (5th). Paul Verlaine died at **No 39** in 1896. During the last years of his life he lived exclusively in the Latin Quarter, identifying with its bohemian and artistic milieux, and moving from one squalid apartment to another. When he was not in hospital, he spent much of his time in the literary cafés in and around the **boulevard Saint-Michel**. Despite his poverty, ill health, eccentricity and alcoholism, Verlaine continued to welcome his literary friends to his seedy homes. In his cramped room at what was then the Hôtel des Nations, **216 rue Saint-Jacques**, he even reinstated his literary Wednesday *soirées*.

Rue Lhomond (5th). In Balzac's *Le Père Goriot*, the lodging house of Mme Vauquer (Eugène Rastignac's first home in Paris) is located in the rue Neuve-Sainte-Geneviève (Extract 12) – now called the rue Lhomond.

Boulevard de l'Hôpital (5th and 13th). 'The Hôpital, Father! My beautiful Manon, my own beloved, thrown into that place like the filthiest harlot!' In 1654 **La Saltpêtrière** (near the **métro Saint-Marcel**), which had originally been used as an arsenal, became a place of confinement for the poor – soon afterwards it also became a prison for 'women of ill repute', in reality not only prostitutes but also unwanted wives incarcerated on the accusations of their husbands. The Hôpital, as it was then simply known, features prominently in Prévost's *Manon Lescaut*, 1731 (*Manon Lescaut*, 1949), when the eponymous pleasure-loving heroine is imprisoned there and the love-obsessed chevalier Des Grieux sets about rescuing her. La Saltpêtrière is now one of the main Paris hospitals, and a section of it, with an old courtyard, is called Manon Lescaut (it cannot be visited).

Rue Linné (5th). Georges Perec ◊ lived in a mezzanine apartment at **No 13** from 1974 until his death in 1982. It

was here that he wrote his remarkable *La Vie mode d'emploi*, 1978 (*Life: A User's Manual*, 1987).

Rue Mouffetard (5th). See Extract 22 for Kay Boyle's ◊ vivid and atmospheric description of the street.

Square Paul-Painlevé (5th). The statue of Montaigne, just off **rue de Cluny**, is a 1988 copy of the original, which reputedly suffered worn-out feet from rubbing by successive generations of students for luck in their exams.

Rue du Pot-de-Fer (5th). George Orwell ◊ arrived in Paris in spring 1928 and moved into a cheap hotel at **No 6**, where he stayed until he left for London in December 1929. He calls the street 'rue du Coq d'Or' in *Down and Out in Paris and London*, 1933, and describes it evocatively, if exaggerating its slumminess, in the opening chapter.

Rue Saint-Jacques (5th). The 'outlaw' medieval poet François Villon (c 1431– ?) lived in this street, then the true heart of the Latin Quarter, in his student days. His home, under the patronage of the wealthy Guillaume de Villon (whose name he adopted – he was born François de Montcorbier), was in the cloister of the church of Saint-Benoît-le-Bientourné on the corner of rue Saint-Jacques and rue des Écoles (the site of which is now occupied by part of the Sorbonne), where Guillaume was chaplain. It was here that Villon became involved in the brawl which led to his fatal stabbing of a priest in 1455 – an event which, combined with his involvement in a burglary of the Collège de Navarre in 1456, led to several years' absence from the inns and bawdy-houses of his beloved Paris. It seems he returned only for a short time – in 1462 he was arrested in connection with a street riot and condemned to hang. He was pardoned in 1463 but forced into exile from Paris and virtually nothing is known of his subsequent life.

English poet Ernest Dowson (◊ Brittany) lived in a hotel at **No 214** for some three months at the end of 1895. Money was always a problem for Dowson and he had to move on to the less financially demanding environment of Brittany. In a letter of October 1895 from rue Saint-Jacques he wrote, 'The rooms are cheap enough & one can eat cheap enough but it is impossible to live in Paris without sitting in cafés & they mount up.' He stayed here again for the last three months of 1897.

In 1910, the Swiss-born poet and novelist Blaise Cendrars (1887–1961), then still known by his real name of Frédéric Sauser, rented a room at **No 216**. An earlier resident had been Paul Verlaine, who had had a tiny apartment here – it was one of his many addresses as he wandered from room to room in the *quartier* in the final sad years of his life.

Place Saint-Michel (5th/6th). Apollinaire ◊ gave his first reading at the café called **Le Départ** on the corner of place Saint-Michel and quai Saint-Michel, the cellar of which was then a venue for weekly 'Soirées' sponsored by the poetry magazine *La Plume*. There, he met, among many others, Alfred Jarry (1873–1907), author of *Ubu roi*, who was instrumental in cultivating Apollinaire's reputation as an eccentric bohemian and joker.

Rue Saint-André-des-Arts (6th). E.E. Cummings (◊ Normandy) took rooms in a cheap hotel at **No 46** when he lived in Paris in the early 1920s.

Rue du Sommerard (5th). Before he moved to the rue Saint-André-des-Arts, Cummings lived in a hotel at **No 13** in 1921.

Quai de la Tournelle (5th). In 1582, a tavern called **La Tour d'Argent** opened at **No 15**. With its pleasant situation by the river and its celebrated culinary treatments of heron, swan, crane, eel, etc, it rapidly became a favourite haunt of the gastronomically inclined rich and famous. It has continued in that tradition ever since. The present Tour d'Argent dates from 1814, when the original restaurant was renovated following the devastation of the Revolution. In terms of its reputation, however, nothing changed and literary diners in the 19th century included Alexandre Dumas *père*, Victor Hugo, and, in the happier moments of their tumultuous relationship, George Sand and Alfred de Musset. Later, in the time of the Third Republic, names of famous regulars crept into the menu ('potage Anatole France', for example). There is now a small museum in La Tour, with memories of its great dishes and illustrious guests – but you will need a fat wallet, because it is open only to clients of the restaurant.

MONTPARNASSE AND ENVIRONS

Rue d'Assas (6th). August Strindberg (1849–1912) stayed at **No 62**, then the Pension Orfila, in 1895–96. It was during his time in Paris, following the breakdown of his second marriage, that Strindberg experienced the intense personal crisis which he describes in *Inferno*, 1898 (*Inferno*, 1979). The narrator in Miller's *Tropic of Cancer*, 1934, visits the building, reflects 'on the meaning of that inferno which Strindberg had so mercilessly depicted', and works out 'why it is that Paris attracts the tortured, the hallucinated, the great maniacs of love.'

Rue Cassini (14th). Balzac (◊ Centre) lived at **No 1** (the house no longer exists) from 1830 to 1834, his longest stay in any of his Paris homes. Alain-Fournier (◊ Centre) lived at **No 2** from 1910 to 1914, and wrote *Le Grand Meaulnes*, 1913 (*Le Grand Meaulnes*, 1966) there.

Rue du Château (14th). This street has its place in literary history thanks to

Jacques Prévert ◊ who shared a house here with Marcel Duhamel and Yves Tanguy in the late 1920s. The 'Groupe de la rue du Château', visited by many Surrealists of the time, had its headquarters at No 54, in a house which no longer exists.

Rue Delambre (14th). From 1924 to 1932, No 4 was home to the 'Black Manikin' bookshop and press of Edward Titus, husband of Helena Rubenstein. Titus published, in 1929, the first Paris edition of Lawrence's *Lady Chatterley's Lover*. He also took over the literary and artistic magazine *This Quarter* and ran it to critical acclaim until he closed the press in 1932. At No 10 was the 'Dingo American Bar and Restaurant', and it was here, in April 1925, that Scott Fitzgerald (◊ Côte d'Azur) first met Ernest Hemingway ◊.

Avenue de Denfert-Rochereau (14th). No 92 was the Infirmerie Marie-Thérèse, a charitable foundation offering shelter to priests and noblewomen who had been ruined by the Revolution. It was opened on the initiative of Madame de Chateaubriand, who also managed it. Chateaubriand (◊ Brittany) acquired a neighbouring property (currently No 88) where he and his wife lived from 1826 to 1838.

Place Denfert-Rochereau (14th). Jean Rhys ◊ describes the square and the surrounding streets atmospherically in *Quartet*, 1928 (Extract 21).

Rue de Dombasle (15th). Arthur Koestler (◊ Languedoc–Roussillon) had a seventh-floor apartment at No 10. He was living here when the Second World War began and he was arrested as an 'undesirable alien' – see *Scum of the Earth*, 1941, for his eye-witness record of how Paris changed in the early months of the war.

Boulevard Edgar-Quinet (14th and 15th). Sartre ◊ moved into an apartment in the rather ugly block at No 29

in 1973. He was in declining health and virtually blind. The apartment was larger than his previous one in the **boulevard Raspail**, and, although on the 10th storey, well served by lifts. Sartre was increasingly unable to live by himself and was constantly looked after here by Simone de Beauvoir and various of the other women in his life. His biographer Annie Cohen-Solal quotes him as saying, 'I no longer like it here. This is where I no longer work.' Nevertheless, the apartment became the venue for numerous meetings relating to Sartre's continuing active involvement in political and literary life.

Rue des Favorites (15th). Samuel Beckett ◊ lived in an apartment at No 6 from 1939 to 1960, when he and his partner Suzanne Deschevaux-Dumesnil moved to a larger flat in a modern block in the **boulevard Saint-Jacques** (14th), where Beckett's study overlooked the exercise yard of the Santé prison.

Place Léon-Paul-Fargue (7th and 15th). Léon-Paul Fargue (1876–1947) died on 24 November 1947 in an apartment on the square which is now named after him – a plaque marks the spot. Born in central Paris, Fargue is remembered for his urban verse and especially for his prose impressions and memoirs of the city, and some of its literary inhabitants, in *Le Piéton de Paris*, 1939.

Rue de Fleurus (6th). Gertrude Stein ◊ lived at No 27 from 1903 to 1938, in an apartment which she shared after 1909 with her constant companion Alice B. Toklas, and in which she entertained many of the leading artists and expatriate writers in Paris. Before the First World War, her *salon* was a primary gathering place for modern painters – among whom Picasso was her closest friend. In the 1920s and 1930s this was *the* address in Paris for American and British writers – the list of those who visited her here is enormous. In *A Moveable Feast*, 1964, Heming-

Jean-Paul Sartre and Simone de Beauvoir at La Coupole

way, a once regular visitor with whom she fell out, remembers her legendary art collection – 'It was like one of the best rooms in the finest museum except there was a big fireplace and it was warm and comfortable and they gave you good things to eat and tea and natural distilled liqueurs made from purple plums, yellow plums or wild rasperries. These were fragrant, colourless alcohols served from cut-glass carafes in small glasses and whether they were *questsche*, *mirabelle* or *frambroise* they all tasted like the fruits they came from, converted into a controlled fire on your tongue that warmed you and loosened it.' Stein's fascinatingly and subjectively anecdotal *The Autobiography of Alice B. Toklas*, 1933 (Extract 19), paints an evocative portrait of life at 27 rue de Fleurus.

Boulevard du Montparnasse (6th and 14th). Although it had long had literary associations and residents, Montparnasse truly came into its own when it took over from Montmartre as the heart of literary and artistic Paris just before the First World War, when luminaries such as Apollinaire and Picasso descended to its cafés. The large establishments which then became gathering places for both French and ex-pat artists and writers are the key literary landmarks along the boulevard, although most are now landmarks in name only. **La Rotonde**, was favoured, before 1917, by Lenin and Trotsky as well as by Apollinaire and his friends. In an apartment in the same building (**No 103**), above the café, Simone de Beauvoir was born in 1908. In the 1920s, the **Dôme**, now much changed, was a focal point for the English and American expatriate community, but it is for its associations with Beauvoir and Sartre that it is primarily remembered. It was their main meeting place before the Flore (see under Saint-Germain). In *La Force de l'âge*, 1960 (*The Prime of Life*, 1973), Beauvoir explains, 'We had set up our GHQ, as it were, in the Dôme. On those mornings when I was not in the *lycée* I used to have breakfast there. I never worked in my hotel room, but preferred one of the booths at the far end of the café. All around me were German refugees, reading the papers or playing chess, and other foreigners, of all nationalities, conducting passionate arguments in low voices. The murmur of their conversation did not bother me: to sit facing a blank sheet of paper all alone is an austere experience, whereas here I could always glance up and reassure myself that humanity existed.' At the bar of **La Coupole**, also favoured by Beauvoir and Sartre, and recently restored, Louis Aragon met Elsa Triolet in 1928. The then noisy and boisterous **Le Select** was, like the Dôme, a favourite ex-pat gathering place – the names of these cafés crop up frequently in the work of English and American writers of the 1920s and 1930s, and the tendency continued in the post-war period of the 1940s and 1950s, as for example in James Baldwin's *Giovanni's Room*, 1956 (Extract 24) – although by then the centre of literary and intellectual life had shifted decisively to the streets and cafés of Saint-Germain-des-Prés.

Of all Parisian literary cafés, the **Closerie des Lilas** (No 171) is among the most famous, and, unlike the other renowned cafés of boulevard Montparnasse, retains something of its special ambience. In the mind of the English or American literary tourist it is now primarily associated with Ernest Hemingway, who describes it in *A Moveable Feast*, 1964, as 'one of the best cafés in Paris'. He preferred its clientele to the more star-studded casts of the Dôme and the Rotonde and appreciated its comfort – 'It was warm inside in the winter and in the spring and fall it was very fine outside with the tables under the shade of the trees on the side where the statue of Marshal Ney was, and the square, regular tables under the big awnings along the boulevard.' He wrote much of *The Sun Also Rises* here, standing at the bar (a plaque marks the spot) in between his encounters with literary acquaintances – mainly fellow expatriates but among them Blaise Cendrars, who, he says, was the only poet who came to the Closerie des Lilas, 'with his broken boxer's face and his pinned-up empty sleeve, rolling a cigarette with his one good hand.' (Cendrars had lost his arm in 1915 in the Battle for the Marne.) Earlier, when it was a much more modest establishment (it changed after the First World War from a *guinguette* to a bar and restaurant), the Closerie had numbered among its regulars Baudelaire, Verlaine, Strindberg, Wilde, and Paul Fort. George du Maurier mentions it in *Trilby*, 1894, as a place 'to see the students dance the cancan, or try and dance it yourself, which is not so easy as it seems'. In 1912, Fort organized weekly literary evenings here which attracted huge audiences (including, among many others, Jarry, Alain-Fournier, Apollinaire, Carco, and Claudel). A little later, Dadaists and Surrealists like Tzara, Breton, and Soupault added their names to the Closerie's history. One of its rowdiest evenings occurred during a banquet in 1925 when the Surrealists clashed with more conservative patrons over the issue of patriotism and went into overdrive, yelling 'À bas la France!' and generally causing a riot (Soupault distinguished himself by swinging from a chandelier and throwing plates). In the 1930s it was a favourite café of Beauvoir and Sartre. In 1980, Françoise Sagan saw Sartre for the first time in some 20 years. She took him, now blind and at the end of his life (he died that year), to dinner at the Closerie: 'I went to fetch him in the Boulevard Edgar-Quinet – I never pass by there now without feeling a pang of grief. We went to La Closerie des Lilas. I held him by the hand to prevent him from falling, and I was so intimidated I could not speak without stammering. I think we made the oddest pair in French literary history, and the maîtres d'hôtel fluttered about us like frightened crows.' (from *With Fondest Regards* – see Booklist).

Rue du Montparnasse (6th). The poet and critic Charles-Augustin Sainte-Beuve (1804–69) lived at **No 11** from 1850 until his death.

Rue Notre-Dame-des-Champs (6th). Ezra Pound ◊ and his wife Dorothy Shakespear moved into a studio on the ground floor of **70 bis** in December 1921. Pound was a key figure in literary circles during his stay in Paris (he left in 1924) and his apartment became a well known venue for expatriate writers – Joyce, Hemingway (who gave Pound boxing lessons, as he recounts in *A Moveable Feast*), Wyndham Lewis, Ford Madox Ford, and many others visited him here. The appearance of the apartment was characteristically eccentric – most of the furniture was hand-made by Pound himself, from boards and canvas fastened together with hammer and nails and painted brightly. Ford remembered one of the chairs – 'It was enormous, compounded of balks of white pine, and had a slung canvas seat so large that, once you sat down, there you lay until someone pulled you out.' Texan short-story writer Katherine Anne Porter (1890–1980) rented the same apartment in 1934, and lived here until she went back home in 1936. Hemingway ◊ and his first wife Hadley moved into an apartment at **No 113** in January 1924. Victor Hugo ◊ and Charles-Augustine Sainte-Beuve, who were then close friends, lived in houses in the street in the late 1820s – but both buildings have since been demolished.

Boulevard Raspail (6th, 7th and 14th). The statue of Balzac by Rodin, near the junction with boulevard du Montparnasse, caused enormous controversy at the time it was commissioned – completed in 1898, it was not until 1939, long after the sculptor's death, that it was finally erected here. Sartre ◊ moved into a small studio apartment at **No 222** in the 1960s, returning towards the end of his life to his earlier stamping ground of Montparnasse – he had been driven out of his apartment in Saint-Germain-des-Prés by terrorist attacks.

Rue Saint-Romain (6th). Djuna Barnes ◊ lived with her lover Thelma Wood in a fifth-floor apartment at **No 9** in the late 1920s.

Rue Schoelcher (14th). In August 1955, Simone de Beauvoir moved into a large studio apartment on the ground floor of **No 11 bis**, where she lived until her death in 1986. It was the first flat she had owned in Paris and she had been able to buy it with the money earned by *Les Mandarins*, 1954 (*The Mandarins*, 1957) which had won the Prix Goncourt. She called it 'the place that Goncourt bought'. Only a couple of métro stops away from her birthplace, the flat overlooked the cememtery of Montparnasse, where she was to be buried, under the same tombstone as Jean-Paul Sartre. An earlier occupant of the apartment had been Anaïs Nin ◊, who moved in with her then husband Hugo Guiler in August 1925. They also rented a small room on the top floor of the building, which Nin used for writing.

Rue de la Tombe-Issoire (14th). 'I began to explore Villa Seurat. It is a charming street. The houses are all small, and various colours of stucco. Most of them have studio windows. Some are private and some are divided into apartments . . . Trees grow in the backyards, and sometimes in the front. The street is cobblestone and as the sidewalk is so narrow, one often walks in the middle. I found a studio there for Henry. It is on the top floor. A big studio room, with skylight windows, and a small bedroom with a balcony. The kitchen is very small, inside of a closet. But the studio is joyous and light. Henry is tremendously excited about the idea of living there.' (Anaïs Nin, *Journal* entry for June 1934.) Off rue de la Tombe-Issoire, at No 101, is the **Villa Seurat**, a private cul-de-sac designed for sculptors and artists, which was opened in 1926. In the early 1930s, Henry Miller ◊ stayed for a short time in the apartment of a friend at **No 18**, but in 1934 Anaïs Nin ◊ found him a studio apartment in the same building and rented it for him. Nin notes in her *Journal* entry for September 1934 that she found a picture of a former resident, Antonin Artaud (another of her friends/lovers) while helping Miller clean out the apartment – 'His cheeks looked hollow, his eyes visionary and fanatical. Antonin Artaud had always refused to give photographs of himself because he feared voodoo curses (*envoûtements*, as he said) and believed that harm could come to him if some demonic person stuck pins into the portrait.' Auspiciously, the first edition of *Tropic of Cancer* was published by Jack Kahane's Obelisk Press on the very day Miller moved in to his Villa Seurat apartment. It delighted him and he lived here from 1934 until he left the city in 1939. Among his regular visitors later in the decade was Lawrence Durrell (◊ Provence), with whom he developed a lifelong friendship (see *Lawrence Durrell and Henry Miller: A Private Correspondence*, 1963). In 1937, Miller became editor of the 'Villa Seurat Series', attached to the Obelisk Press – books by Nin (*Winter of Artifice*), Durrell (*The Black Book*) and Miller himself (*Max and the White Phagocytes*) were published under its imprint.

Rue de Vaugirard (15th). In *Mes Parents*, 1986 (*My Parents*, 1993), Hervé Guibert describes scenes from his life at **No 293** (Extract 42).

ODÉON–SAINT-GERMAIN-DES-PRÉS–INVALIDES

Rue de l'Abbé Grégoire (6th). American novelist James Fenimore Cooper (1789–1851) moved into an apartment at **No 12** when he first came to Paris in July 1826. It was here that he first met Sir Walter Scott, who visited him shortly after he moved in. Cooper lived in Paris for several years and his recollections of his time in the city are included in *A Residence in France*, part of the 4-volume *Gleanings in Europe*, 1837–38.

Rue de l'Ancienne Comédie (6th). The street owes its name to the Comédie Française, which was on the site of **No 14** from 1689 to 1770. Across the road, the **Café Procope**, dating from 1684 and one of the first cafés to open in Paris, was guaranteed a roaring trade. It rapidly became a watering hole for actors, writers and critics. Its literary clientele in the 18th century included Beaumarchais, Diderot, Rousseau and Voltaire. Later, the Procope was frequented by Balzac, Gautier, Longfellow, Musset, George Sand, Verlaine, and Wilde, among many others. After closing earlier this century, the Procope reopened in 1952. Further restoration work was done in the 1980s.

Rue du Bac (7th). Nos 118–120 are the **Hôtel de Clermont-Tonnerre** – Chateaubriand (◊ Brittany) had an apartment here on the ground floor from 1838 until his death. Earlier, in 1815–18, he had lodged at **No 46**.

Rue de Bellechasse (7th). Alphonse Daudet (◊ Provence) lived at **No 31** (where there is a plaque) from 1885 until 1897, the year he died (see below, **rue de l'Université**).

Rue des Beaux-Arts (6th). Prosper Mérimée (◊ Corsica) lived for a time at

No 10. In April 1900 Oscar Wilde took a room at No 13, which was then the modest Hôtel d'Alsace. He became bedridden in October of that year – 'My wallpaper and I are fighting a duel to the death. One or the other of us has to go.' He died in his room here on 30 November 1900. Thomas Wolfe (1900–38) stayed at the Hôtel d'Alsace in 1925 during a European tour. He drew on his experiences in Paris and other parts of France for the European scenes of his autobiographical novel *Of Time and the River*, 1935.

Rue Bonaparte (6th). In October 1946, Jean-Paul Sartre ◊ moved into a small apartment at No 42, on the corner of rue Bonaparte and place Saint-Germain, occupying a room which served him as both study and bedroom. His balcony, above the **Café Bonaparte**, overlooked the square. Sartre stayed here for 16 years, near to the **Café de Flore** which became his headquarters, eventually moving out in 1962 after two terrorist bomb attacks (he was targeted because of his sympathetic campaigning for the Algerian cause).

Rue Cassette (6th). Alfred Jarry (1873–1907), creator of Ubu, lived at No 20, and died there. Francis Steegmuller, in *Apollinaire: Poet Among the Painters*, quotes Apollinaire's description of his visit to Jarry's apartment. Jarry, reports Apollinaire, had cut the storeys of his house in two, feeling that the ceilings were too high. The house thus had 15 storeys while remaining the same size as its neighbours – 'it is but a reduction of a skyscraper' concludes Apollinaire. 'For that matter,' he adds, 'reductions, abounded in Alfred Jarry's abode . . . Jarry was quite comfortable standing up, but I was taller than he, and had to bend. The bed was but a reduction of a bed – a pallet: low beds were the fashion, Jarry told me. The writing table was but the reduction of a table: Jarry wrote on the floor, stretched out on his stomach. The furnishing

was but the reduction of furnishing, consisting solely of the bed. On the wall hung the reduction of a picture. It was a portrait of Jarry, most of which he had burned, leaving only the head, which made him look like a certain lithograph of Balzac that I know . . .'.

Rue Christine (6th). In 1938, Gertrude Stein ◊ and Alice B. Toklas moved to an apartment at No 5 when the lease on their famous **rue de Fleurus** home ran out. During the war, Stein left her great art collection here unattended, until her return after the liberation. Just before the Germans left Paris in 1944 several members of the Gestapo raided the flat – the theft and destruction of the paintings was narrowly avoided by the intervention of a neighbour who called the police. Stein continued to live here and receive admirers until her death in 1946 – Toklas stayed until 1964.

Rue Dupuytren (6th). No 8 was the first home of Shakespeare and Company (see below under **rue de l'Odéon**).

Rue Edmond-Valentin (7th). James and Nora Joyce rented an apartment at No 7 from 1934 to 1939.

Eiffel Tower. Completed in 1889, this now universal symbol of Paris had many enemies at the time of its construction. A group of prominent artists and writers were vociferous in their opposition – among them Maupassant, who sometimes lunched in the Tower restaurant because it was the only place in Paris from which you couldn't see it; Verlaine, who took long diversions to keep out of its way; and Huysmans, who described it as a hollow candlestick. Younger writers, however, tended to see it as a symbol of modernity, and it gradually made more friends than enemies, many of those who were initially against it eventually submitting to its audacious charm. It has found its way into poetry, prose, theatre and film many times since – Apollinaire, Aragon, Cocteau, and Cendrars are among the writers who have praised its modernity and elegance. For a fascinating examination of the symbolic and metaphorical significance of the Tower, turn to *La Tour Eiffel*, 1964, by Roland Barthes (*The Eiffel Tower and Other Mythologies*, 1980). Among the Tower's fictional tourists is Raymond Queneau's ◊ Zazie, who is more confused than impressed (Extract 7).

Rue Férou (6th). Hemingway ◊ and Pauline Pfeiffer took an apartment at **No 6** in March 1927.

Rue de Furstenberg (6th). No 6 is **Le Musée Eugène-Delacroix.** This was the home of the great Romantic painter (1798–1863) for the last six years of his life. His admirer Baudelaire visited him here, as did George Sand.

Rue Gît-le-Coeur (6th). In the late 1950s and early 1960s an extremely cheap and rundown establishment, nameless and in the bottom of the 13 categories used to classify French hotels, became the 'Beat Hotel'. Residents included Allen Ginsberg, Gregory Corso, and William Burroughs, who, with help from Ginsberg and others, finally got *The Naked Lunch* finished here (it was published in Paris in 1959). The Beat Hotel was at **No 9** – it closed in 1963 and another hotel now takes its place.

Rue de Grenelle (7th). Alfred de Musset (1810–57) lived at **No 59** from 1824 to 1840. **No 102** was the home of Madame de Staël (1766–1817) in 1800 – later, in 1855, Robert (1812–89) and Elizabeth Barrett Browning (1806–61) took an apartment here but did not stay long because they found their 'abominable quarters' cramped and cold.

Rue Guénégaud (6th). 'At the end of the rue Guénégaud, as you come up from the river, you find the Passage du Pont-Neuf, a sort of narrow, dark corridor connecting rue Mazarine and rue de

Seine. This passage is thirty yards long and two in width at the most; it is paved with yellowish flagstones, worn and loose, which always exude a damp, pungent smell, and it is covered with a flat, glazed roofing black with grime.' So begins *Thérèse Raquin*, 1867 (*Thérèse Raquin*, 1962), with Zola quickly establishing the mood and setting for his dark and compelling tale of a murder and the haunting guilt which destroys its perpetrators. Between 1930 and 1934, **No 15** rue Guénégaud was home to Nancy Cunard's Hours Press. In 1930 Samuel Beckett entered his poem *Whoroscope* in a poetry competition organized by the Press, posting it through the door of No 15 in the small hours of the night on which the competition closed, having written it in less than 24 hours. It won, Beckett was awarded the prize of £10, and Nancy Cunard subsequently published it, giving the Hours Press the lasting honour of having produced Beckett's first separately published work.

Rue Hautefeuille (6th). Baudelaire ◊ was born at the house that was then No 13. A plaque at present-day **No 15** marks the spot.

Boulevard des Invalides (7th). The poet Charles-Marie Leconte de Lisle (1818–94) lived in a small apartment on the fifth floor of **No 8**, and this became an important address for the Parnassians, of whom he was the acknowledged leader. 'Le Parnasse' was a Second-Empire literary countermovement to Romanticism, Realism and Naturalism which strove in theory for a more objective, 'scientific', approach to poetry through the repression of the artist's personality and attention to formal rigour – to some extent preparing the way for Symbolist poetics. The main players in the group met here every week on Saturday evenings. Parnassian poet Catulle Mendès described the apartment as 'not luxurious but always clean and perfectly arranged, like a well written stanza.'

The young Anatole France was a frequent participant, as were Mallarmé and Verlaine. **No 52**, the Hôtel Masseran, was the home of Comte Étienne de Beaumont whose annual fancy dress balls in the 1920s were among the most famous of social events. Raymond Radiguet (◊ Île de France) attended two of them and they provided the inspiration for the ball of his *Le Bal du comte d'Orgel*, 1924 (*Count d'Orgel's Ball*, 1953).

Rue Jacob (6th). This street was Colette's (◊ Burgundy) first address in Paris. Newly married to the unscrupulous Willy, she moved into his bachelor flat and shortly afterwards to a fourth-floor apartment, between two courtyards, with one of the rooms overlooking **rue Visconti**. Colette makes this Claudine's first home in Paris and describes the apartment and her/Claudine's first reactions to the street and the city in *Claudine à Paris*, 1901 (*Claudine in Paris*, 1958) – see Extract 9. Mérimée (◊ Corsica) lived in a house on the site of **No 18** in 1848. **No 20** was bought by the wealthy American Natalie Clifford Barney (1876–1972) in 1909 and she lived there until she died. Barney's weekly literary *salons* were famous, especially in the 1920s, among both French and expatriate writers. She was also for many years a central figure in lesbian culture in Paris – Djuna Barnes ◊ caricatures Barney and her home in *Ladies Almanack*, 1928.

Jardin du Luxembourg. Wandering around the Luxembourg you will encounter (in stone) Baudelaire, Flaubert, Heredia, Murger, Sainte-Beuve, Sand, Madame de Ségur, Stendhal, and Verlaine. See Extract 14 for Shusha Guppy's ◊ fond memories of the garden and its friendly literary ghosts, and Extract 13 for English diarist John Evelyn's ◊ impressions when he visited the Luxembourg in 1644.

Place Laurent Prache (6th). The memorial to Apollinaire by his friend Picasso was unveiled in 1959.

Rue de Lille (7th). Prosper Mérimée lived at **No 52** for the last 18 years of his life. Shortly after his death in Cannes in September 1870, his apartment here was set on fire and his library and belongings were destroyed – the arson was perpetrated by the Commune, presumably in reaction to Mérimée's close relationship during the Second Empire with Eugénie and Napoleon III.

Quai Malaquais (6th). George Sand (◊ Centre) moved into **No 19** in 1832 and stayed until 1836. The place suited her well – at that time, she later wrote, it was secluded and shaded by the trees in the surrounding gardens in which the 'blackbirds sang and the sparrows twittered', reminding her of her beloved countryside at Nohant. Among her famous lovers was Mérimée, whom she received here – and it was here also that she set up house with Musset. In the same house some eight years after Sand left, Anatole France ◊ was born in 1844. His father ran a bookshop on the premises, called the 'Librairie de France'. Shortly after France's birth, the family and the shop moved to **No 15**, where he spent the first nine years of his life. The bookshop was an old-fashioned *librairie à chaise* – with chairs spread around the shop to encourage people to linger – and was a popular meeting place for local writers and intellectuals. It specialized in books relating to the French Revolution – no doubt planting the seed for France's greatest work, *Les Dieux ont soif*, 1912 (*The Gods Will Have Blood*, 1979) – Extract 31. In 1853, the lease ran out and the shop moved to nearby **Quai Voltaire**.

Rue de Médicis (6th). 'I was born on November 22nd, 1869. My parents at that time lived in the Rue de Médicis in an apartment on the fourth floor which they left a few years later and of which I have kept no recollection. Stay though, I do remember the balcony, or rather what could be seen from the balcony – the bird's-eye view of the

Place with its ornamental piece of water and fountain; or rather, to be still more exact, I remember the paper dragons which my father used to cut out for me and which we launched into the air from the balcony; I remember their floating away in the wind over the fountain in the Place below and being carried away as far as the Luxembourg Gardens, where they used sometimes to catch in the top branches of the horse-chestnut trees.' André Gide (◊ Normandy), *Si le grain ne meurt*, 1926 (*If It Die*, 1950). Gide was born at No 19, which is today **No 2 place Edmond-Rostand**.

Rue Monsieur (7th). Nancy Mitford ◊ moved into the ground floor apartment at **No 7** in 1947, and lived here for some 20 years.

Rue Monsieur-le-Prince (6th). Richard Wright (1908–60) moved to Paris in 1947 and stayed for the rest of his life – he took an apartment at **No 14** in 1948 which became his home for the next 11 years. Wright, a celebrated writer since the publication of *Native Son* in 1940, was made an honorary citizen of Paris shortly after he arrived. Henry Wadsworth Longfellow (1807–82) took lodgings at **No 49** in June 1826 while studying at the Sorbonne. He later moved to **rue Racine**. A plaque at **No 60** claims that Balzac bought his coffee and candles here. Given his consumption of both, he must have been a valued customer.

Rue de l'Odéon (6th). In the 1920s and 1930s this street was a major literary centre for French, British and American writers – thanks to the admirable efforts of Sylvia Beach (1887–1962) and Adrienne Monnier (1892–1955). Monnier opened her Maison des Amis du Livre at **No 7** in 1915. The bookshop and its associated library service concentrated on French avant-garde writing and on translations of American and British fiction, and Monnier published a review, *Le Navire*

d'argent, which carried translations of work by Hemingway, E.E. Cummings, and T.S. Eliot among many others. The bookshop was also a *salon*, and regulars who gave readings at Monnier's weekly gatherings included Breton, Gide, Valéry, Fargue, Claudel, and Léautaud. Sylvia Beach opened Shakespeare and Company in November 1919 in **rue Dupuytren**. In July 1921 she moved her English-language library and bookshop to **No 12** rue de l'Odéon, opposite Adrienne Monnier's shop – she also moved in with Monnier, with whom she lived at **No 18** until 1937. While Beach was still in the rue Dupuytren, James Joyce (1882–1941) had turned up at her shop, disconsolate because, following the obscenity trial, he was unable to publish *Ulysses* in the UK or USA. Beach proposed to him that she publish it herself, which she did – in English with a French typesetter and an unconscionable number of proof corrections. It was the beginning of a long friendship between Beach and Joyce which lasted till his death in 1941. The first edition of *Ulysses* was published in 1922 under the imprint of Shakespeare and Company and launched in the Maison des Amis du Livre – symbolizing the crucial role of these two women in supporting and promoting new writing and bringing together many of the leading figures in French, British and American literature between the wars.

Sylvia Beach was generous and hospitable to the writers who came to her shop. Apart from Joyce, among her earliest regulars were Archibald MacLeish, Pound, Sherwood Anderson, Robert McAlmon (who used it as a club and mailing address), and Hemingway (a favourite of both Monnier and Beach), who would spend hours reading in a back room. In *A Moveable Feast*, published posthumously in 1964, Hemingway remembers the shop on the rue de l'Odéon – 'On a cold windswept street, this was a warm cheerful place with a big stove in winter, tables and shelves of books, new books in the

Sylvia Beach (left) and Adrienne Monnier at Shakespeare and Company

window, and photographs on the wall of famous writers both dead and living.' Of Beach he said, 'No one that I ever knew was nicer to me.' Later regulars, in the 1930s, included Henry Miller, Anaïs Nin, and Lawrence Durrell. But the list of friends and visitors is enormous – between 1919 and the closure of the shop during the German occupation, Shakespeare and Company was a vital destination for any British or American writer living in Paris or passing through.

Both the original shops have now gone. However, Shakespeare and Company has risen from the ashes – Sylvia's mantle was taken up in 1951 by George

Whitman, reputedly the great-grandson of Walt, who bought an old grocery store on **rue de la Bûcherie** in the Fifth and turned it into a bookstore called Librairie Mistral. He continued the tradition established by Sylvia Beach of literary hospitality and support to writers, and the shop has long been a literary institution, an informal gathering place, a shelter from the cold for penniless novelists and poets, and a venue for readings and lectures. Whitman renamed the shop Shakespeare and Company in 1964 in Sylvia's honour. It is a wonderful, shambolic place, packed to bursting with old and new books in English and, at time of writing in 1996, is still presided over by Whitman. Among the more famous regulars at the re-incarnated Shakespeare and Company have been the leading Beat poets, Lawrence Ferlinghetti, Gregory Corso, and Allen Ginsberg.

For further reading on Beach and Monnier, see *Sylvia Beach and the Lost Generation*, 1985, by Noel Riley Fitch; Sylvia Beach's *Shakespeare & Co*, 1959; and Adrienne Monnier's *Rue de l'Odéon*, published posthumously in 1960.

Quai d'Orsay (7th). Playwright and novelist Jean Giraudoux (1882–1944) died at **No 89**, probably from poisoning, while Paris was still under German occupation. At the corner of the quai d'Orsay, near the **Pont de l'Alma**, is the entrance to the **sewers (Égouts)**, part of which may be visited, and which Hugo so memorably and symbolically describes in *Les Misérables*, 1862 (*Les Misérables*, 1976) – see Extract 27.

Rue Racine (6th). Longfellow stayed at **No 5**, at that time a *pension de famille*, when he was a student at the Sorbonne in the 1820s.

Square Robiac (7th). James Joyce lived at **No 2** in this small square (off **rue de Grenelle**) with his wife Nora from 1925 to 1931 – they stayed here longer than in any of their other Paris homes.

Place Saint-André-des-Arts (6th). See Extract 26 for Sartre's evocative description of this little square and **rue Danton** at the time of the German occupation.

Rue Saint-Dominique (7th). In 1750, the Marquise Du Deffand (1697–1780), who corresponded with Horace Walpole over some 15 years, opened her literary *salon* at **Nos 10–12**, opposite the square in front of the **Église Sainte-Clotilde**. It became a favourite and fashionable meeting place for the *encyclopédistes* and other new writers and thinkers (the so-called *philosophes*) of the Enlightenment (including d'Alembert, Diderot and Montesquieu), rivalling the *salon* of Madame Geoffrin in **rue Saint-Honoré** (see under Châtelet–Louvre–Bois de Boulogne). In 1764, her protégée Julie de Lespinasse (1732–76) opened her own *salon* at **No 6**, 'stealing' many of Du Deffand's regulars but creating something very much her own, which became an extremely influential debating forum, attracting prominent politicians and writers and philosophers from overseas (including Hume) as well as the local celebrities. Jean d'Alembert (1717–83), who by then was Secrétaire Perpétuel of the Académie Française, deserted Du Deffand for Lespinasse – and she features, along with d'Alembert, to whom she was devoted, as one of the three speakers in Diderot's *Le Rêve de d'Alembert*, 1769 (*D'Alembert's Dream*, 1966).

Boulevard Saint-Germain (5th, 6th and 7th). The most famous of the literary cafés of Saint-Germain is the **Café de Flore**, established in 1890. Ironically, considering its now renowned associations with the left-wing intelligentsia, at the turn of the century the Flore was the meeting place for the founders of the unpleasantly right-wing Action Française which was formed in 1899 – here Maurras, Barrès and colleagues wrote their articles and discussed their ideas. The café, however, has since become famously and probably indelibly associated with Simone de Beauvoir and Jean-Paul Sartre, for whom it was a combination of living area, office, and reception room. They adopted it during the Second World War, moving away from the Dôme in Montparnasse because, among other reasons, their old favourite was now frequented by Germans. Beauvoir explains the importance to them of the Flore and describes their life there in detail in *La Force de l'âge*, 1960 (*The Prime of Life*, 1973) – see Extract 34. She is also amusing on the relationship of the Flore and the neighbouring **Deux Magots** – '. . . if a couple of Flore regulars happened to meet in the Deux

James Joyce

Magots, then mutual recognition would be acknowledged by a smile and a nod. This very seldom, in fact, happened; between the two establishments an invisible but impenetrable barrier appeared to exist. If a customer at the Flore, whether male or female, was deceiving his or her accredited partner, any illicit meetings would take place at the Deux Magots, or so the legend ran.' Other regulars who, like Beauvoir and Sartre, had their special tables, included Breton and Prévert.

Among the ex-pats, Djuna Barnes, who lived nearby, was a regular in the 1920s, often sitting alone. She first met Joyce here, later interviewing him at the Deux Magots. In the 1950s James Baldwin ◊ was frequently to be found in the upper room writing to the accompaniment of coffee in the afternoon

which turned to alcohol as the day went on. The Flore continued for many years to be a gathering place for writers and intellectuals – today its reputation enables it to charge high prices and it is patronized mainly by tourists and Parisians with more money than sense. It does, however, retain its ambience and is worth at least one very expensive cup of coffee.

The **Deux Magots**, which opened in 1875 (current decor dates from 1914), is equally pricey and if anything even more popular with tourists. Early patrons included Mallarmé, Rimbaud and Verlaine. In 1933 it established its own literary prize – the first recipient was Raymond Queneau. Sharing the Surrealists and Existentialists with the Flore in the 1940s and 1950s, the Deux Magots also became a regular meeting place for black writers Richard Wright, Chester Himes and James Baldwin. On arriving in Paris in 1948, Baldwin was taken straight to the café where his welcoming party included Wright and Sartre. Djuna Barnes interviewed Joyce for *Vanity Fair* at the café soon after her arrival in Paris in the early 1920s.

Across the road from the Flore and the Deux Magots is **Brasserie Lipp**, founded in 1880 by an Alascien named Leonard Lipp, which has long attracted a mixed clientele of writers, actors, and politicians (among whom was Mitterrand). Literary regulars have included Apollinaire, who lived nearby (see below), the poet Léon-Paul Fargue, Gide, and, of course, Sartre.

The **Mabillon**, a little further down on the same side as the Flore and Deux Magots, was the favourite hang-out of Lawrence Ferlinghetti ◊ when he lived in Paris in 1948–50. The nearby picturesque **Rhumerie martiniquaise**, recently refurbished, opened its doors in 1931 and quickly attracted artists and writers in the mood for a little Caribbean dreaming – Léon-Paul Fargue, Man Ray, and Antonin Artaud were among those who appreciated its atmosphere.

Djuna Barnes moved into an apartment at **No 173** in 1921 and stayed, with her lover Thelma Wood, until 1927.

In 1912, when his affair with Marie Laurencin had ended, Apollinaire ◊ moved back across the Pont Mirabeau (see under Auteuil) to the centre of Paris and took a small top-floor flat at **No 202** which was to become his home until his death here in November 1918. Surrealist leader André Breton remembered the apartment affectionately, remarking, '. . . you had to pick your way around the furniture loaded with numerous African or Polynesian fetishes mixed up with strange objects and the shelves on which the stacks of books with the yellow covers of the time "looked like pats of butter", as he so appropriately put it.' He also recalled that the walls of the apartment were lined with paintings, including pieces by Picasso, Derain and Chirico. Paul Léautaud, in his *Journal Littéraire* entry of 11 November, tells of a little piece of irony connected with Apollinaire's death (he died on 9 November). On that day, the Armistice was signed and crowds flooded the streets around the little flat where the poet lay dead. The people shouted 'Down with Guillaume! Down with Guillaume!'. They meant Kaiser Wilhelm. Gertrude Stein in *The Autobiography of Alice B. Toklas* wrongly has Apollinaire dying on the day of the Armistice, and records that he heard such shouts while he was still alive, believing it to be him they were shouting at. Of his death, Stein writes 'The death of Guillaume Apollinaire at this time made a very serious difference to all his friends apart from their sorrow at his death. It was the moment just after the war when many things had changed and people naturally fell apart. Guillaume would have been a bond of union, he always had a quality of keeping people together, and now that he was gone everybody ceased to be friends.'

Place Saint-Germain-des-Prés (6th). For a discourse on the difficulties of contemplating the ancient church with the time and respect it deserves in contemporary Paris, see Milan Kundera's ◊ *Immortality*, 1991 (Extract 35).

Place Saint-Sulpice (6th). The church of Saint-Sulpice was much admired by J.-K. Huysmans. It features especially in his novel *Là-bas*, 1891 (*Là-Bas: Down There*, 1993). Georges Perec spent three days in place Saint-Sulpice, much of the time in the **Café de la Mairie**, and recorded every detail of what he saw in his as yet untranslated *Tentative d'épuisement d'un lieu parisien*, 1975 – a curiously compulsive and atmospheric catalogue of everyday events and passings-by. The Café de la Mairie also features prominently in Djuna Barnes's novel *Nightwood*, 1936 (Extract 37).

Rue de Seine (6th). At **No 60** is the **Hôtel de la Louisiane**, which has been home for many writers, French and expatriate. Simone de Beauvoir and Jean-Paul Sartre both had rooms here towards the end of the Second World War. Of the various modest hotels in which Beauvoir stayed (she and Sartre preferred to live in (different) hotel rooms rather than set up their own 'homes'), the Louisiane was among her favourites. She remarks in *La Force de l'âge*, 1960 (*The Prime of Life*, 1973), 'My room contained a divan, several bookshelves, a large and massive table, and a poster on the wall representing an English Lifeguardsman. The day I arrived, Sartre upset a bottle of ink over the moquette carpet, with the result that the proprietess instantly removed it; but the parquet flooring suited me as well as any carpet would have . . . None of my previous retreats had come so close to being the apartment of my dreams, and I felt like staying there for the rest of my life.'

Rue de Savoie (6th). Blaise Cendrars (1887–1961) rented an attic apartment at **No 4** with his wife Féla in 1912.

Rue de Sèvres (6th, 7th, 15th). The novelist J.-K. Huysmans (1848–1907) lived in a fifth floor apartment at **No 11** from 1874 to 1899. The 'Abbaye aux Bois' was located at **No 16** and it was here that Mme Récamier (1777–1849) lived from 1819 until her death. Visitors to her prestigious literary *salon* included Balzac, Lamartine, Musset, and Stendhal. Her most frequent visitor, though, was Chateaubriand who came here almost daily in his later years to read extracts from his *Mémoires d'outre-tombe*, 1849–50 (*The Memoirs of Chateaubriand*, 1965). **Rue Récamier** recalls her presence.

Rue Suger (6th). Huysmans was born at **No 9**.

Rue de Tournon (6th). Balzac (◊ Centre) lived at **No 2** from 1827 to 1830 –

later, from 1874 to 1881, André Gide (◊ Normandy) spent formative years here (he was six years old in 1874). Lamartine (1790–1869) lived for a time at **No 4**, as did Ernest Renan (1823–92). After selling his bookshop in 1866, Anatole France's ◊ father took a small apartment on the fourth floor of **No 5** – France, then in his twenties, lived with his parents here. Alphonse Daudet (◊ Provence) moved into shabby quarters at **No 7**, the Hôtel du Sénat, when he first came to Paris in 1857. At the corner of rue de Tournon and rue de Vaugirard was the Hôtel Foyot where Raymond Radiguet (◊ Île de France) took rooms following the success of *Le Diable au corps* in 1923 (*Devil in the Flesh*, 1969). He did not stay long – he fell ill with typhoid and died here the same year at the age of 20.

The **Café de Tournon**, near the rue de Vaugirard, was a centre for British and American writers in the 1950s. It was a favourite meeting place for Richard Wright and his circle (which included for a time James Baldwin). It was also the virtual headquarters of *The Paris Review*, the famous literary journal originally conceived by the novelists Peter Mattheissen and Harold Humes and launched in 1953, under the editorial management of George Plimpton. The *Review*'s offices were in nearby **rue Garancière**, but the Tournon rapidly became the main gathering place for its editorial board and many of its existing and potential contributors. (Plimpton returned to the USA in 1956, and has run the *Review* from New York ever since, though retaining a Paris-based editor). The café was also a regular venue for the group involved in *Merlin*, the short-lived but important literary review dedicated to experimental writing and founded in 1952 by the Scottish writer Alexander Trocchi and American Jane Lougee. The English poet Christopher Logue, then living in Paris in bohemian poverty, was a key member of the *Merlin* group and a regular at the Tournon.

Rue de l'Université (7th). T.S. Eliot (1888–1965) stayed in a *pension* at No 9 on his first visit to Paris in 1910. The Joyces stayed in the same hotel in 1920, the year they arrived in Paris, and subsequently for short periods in 1921 and 1922. No 41 was the last of Daudet's many Parisian homes. He died here on 16 December 1897, after he had only recently moved from **rue de Bellechasse**, forced by his illness to take an apartment where there was only one flight of stairs to negotiate.

Rue de Varenne (7th). Edith Wharton (1862–1937) moved into a luxurious apartment at No 53 in 1909 – she had earlier stayed at No 58, across the road, in an apartment sublet by her friend George Vanderbilt. 'My years of Paris life were spent entirely in the rue de Varenne – rich years, crowded and happy years,' reads the plaque at No 53. She was visited here by her friend Henry James ◊, by whose work she was much influenced. Of Wharton's novels, only two are set entirely in France – the short *Madame de Treyes*, 1907, set in Paris, and *The Reef*, 1912, which centres around a group of characters in a French château – both stories point up contrasts between American and European social codes and cultural traditions. The same theme, a favourite for Wharton as it was for James, pervades one of her best works, *The Custom of the Country*, · 1913, partially set in Paris. In 1907, James stayed several weeks in her apartment, and accompanied her and her husband on a tour to the south (recorded in Wharton's *A Motor-Flight Through France*, 1908). It was the penultimate of James's many visits to Paris – in 1908 he returned briefly for the last time. After 1919, Wharton lived just outside Paris at a country estate in the village of Saint-Brice-sous-Forêt (Val d'Oise).

Rue de Vaugirard (6th). Samuel Beckett ◊ wrote *Dream of Fair to Middling Women* (Extract 30) in 1932, while living at the **Hôtel Trianon**, just off boulevard Saint-Michel. Ford Madox Ford (◊ Picardie) had an apartment at No 32. Madame de Lafayette (1634–93) lived at No 50 from 1655 until her death. Best known as the author of *La Princesse de Clèves*, 1678 (*The Princess of Cleves*, 1950), her work had an enormous influence on the development of the French novel. She was a central figure in Parisian literary circles and her *salon* here was attended by the major aristocratic intellectuals of the period, including her close friends Madame de Sévigné and the Duc de La Rochefoucauld. Scott and Zelda Fitzgerald (◊ Provence) lived at No 58 for five months in 1928 and for part of their stay in Paris in 1929. Ferlinghetti ◊ had a run-down apartment at No 89 in 1948–50.

Rue de Verneuil (7th). In 1948–49 James Baldwin ◊ lived in this street. At that time, it was something of a centre for a group of penniless Americans, mainly writers, thanks to the free-wheeling bohemian charms of a run-down hotel, the **Hôtel Verneuil** at No 29. The Corsican landlady took a liking to Baldwin, nursed him through an illness, and he later spent six months in her home town in Corsica at the house of a friend.

Rue Visconti (6th). At No 17, Balzac established his ill-fated printing business in 1827. Jean Racine (1639–99) spent the last seven years of his life, and died, in a house on the site of No 24.

Quai Voltaire (7th). The bookshop of Anatole France's father moved to No 9 in 1853 from **quai Malaquais** and the family lived above it for the next 13 years. Baudelaire lived at No 19 in 1856–58, and Oscar Wilde had a suite of rooms on the second floor here in 1883. From 1841 to 1849 Alfred de Musset (1810–57) lived at No 25, which later was home to the novelist and dramatist Henry de Montherlant (1868–1971). The quai now takes the name of Voltaire because he died in 1778 at **No 27**, where he was staying with the Marquis de Villette. **No 29** was once the home of Marie de Flavigny, Comtesse d'Agoult (1805–76), who wrote under the pseudonym Daniel Stern (her best known work is the novel *Nélida*, 1845). She moved here in 1839 when her celebrated affair with Liszt came to an end – her regular visitors included Alfred de Vigny, Eugène Sue, and Sainte-Beuve.

The Islands

ÎLE DE LA CITÉ

Place Dauphine (1st). This leafy little triangular refuge amid the official buildings of the Île makes a number of appearances in fiction. Simenon's Maigret, for instance, comes here for food and reflection from his office in nearby **quai des Orfèvres**; Évariste Gamelin, the protagonist of Anatole France's *Les Dieux ont soif*, 1912 (*The Gods Will Have Blood*, 1979), has his home in the square; and in his Surrealist semi-autobiographical novel *Nadja*, 1928 (*Nadja*, 1960), André Breton dines here in the fading light with the mysterious Nadja (self-styled 'Nadja because in Russian it's the beginning of the word hope, and because it's only the beginning'). He writes, 'Place Dauphine is certainly one of the most profoundly secluded places I know of, one of the worst wastelands in Paris. Whenever I happen to be there, I feel the desire to go somewhere else gradually ebbing out of me, I have to struggle against myself to get free from a gentle, over-insistent, and, finally, crushing embrace. Besides, I lived for some time in a hotel near this square, the City Hotel, where the comings and goings at all hours, for anyone not satisfied with oversimplified solutions, are suspect.' In her memoirs, *La nostalgie n'est plus ce qu'elle était*, 1976 (*Nostalgia Isn't What It Used To Be*, 1978), Simone Signoret (1921–85) describes

place Dauphine evocatively – she lived here with Yves Montand.

Quai aux Fleurs (4th) – **No 9**, built in 1849, is thought to be on the site of the home of Canon Fulbert, the vengeful uncle of Héloïse, where Abélard ◊ lodged and the lovers pursued their famous love affair. There are medallions in the street doors representing the lovers. Other researchers have suggested that the site is now marked by nearby **10 rue Chanoinesse**. Novelist and poet Francis Carco (1886–1958) had an apartment at **No 13** which he lent to Katherine Mansfield ◊, with whom he had an affair. She stayed here, alone, in 1915, and perhaps had it in mind in her story 'Feuille d'Album' (Extract 28).

Rue Massillon (4th). A plaque on the corner of rue Massillon and rue Chanoinesse indicates the site of the house in which the Renaissance poet Joachim Du Bellay (c1522–60) died.

Notre-Dame. The cathedral was virtually saved from crumbling into ruin by the impact of Hugo's ◊ stirring novel *Notre Dame de Paris – 1482*, 1831 (*Notre Dame de Paris*, 1993). His detailed and atmospheric descriptions of Notre-Dame in the 15th century stirred public awareness of the city's medieval history and architecture, resulting in the establishment of a Commission of Historic Monuments and in significant restoration work on the cathedral itself. Rather less sensitive to its splendours was Rabelais's Gargantua, who sat on the towers to escape the intrusively curious Parisians, urinated a 'piss-flood' on the crowds below, and pinched the bells to hang on his horse's collar. Some of the spectators who had survived the flood declared that they had been drenched in sport, *par ris* – hence, according to Rabelais, the name 'Paris'. In Henry James's *The Ambassadors*, 1903, Lambert Strether takes momentary refuge in the cathedral from life's complications (Extract 23).

ÎLE SAINT-LOUIS

Quai d'Anjou. The house at **No 17** is the Hôtel de Lauzun, also known as the Hôtel de Pimodan. Built in the 1650s it was the home of the Duc de Lauzon in the 1680s and of the Marquis de Pimodan around a century later. In the 19th century, it became a favourite residence for literary and artistic bohemians. Baudelaire lived on the top floor in 1843–45. His biographer Joanna Richardson evokes the unconventionality of its residents by quoting Baudelaire's facetious response to a complaint from his landlord about the noise: 'I give you my word that nothing extraordinary happens here. I chop wood in the salon, I drag my mistress along the floor by her hair. That is common practice, and you have no right to interfere.' It was in the Hôtel de Pimodan (as it was known at that time) that Théophile Gautier first met Baudelaire. It was also here that the Club des Haschischins held its monthly meetings in the apartment of Fernand Boissard, a wealthy young painter and man of letters. The 'Hashish Eaters' included among others Gautier (who himself rented an apartment in the Hôtel in 1848), Nerval and Balzac, and probably also Baudelaire. The combination of the hashish and the splendour of the decoration on the walls and ceilings of the Hôtel must have been heady indeed. The mansion may be visited, but the opening hours are very limited. If you are lucky enough to have the opportunity, it is well worth seeing – the decoration is well preserved and quite remarkable.

Cramped quarters at **No 29** were the scene of much Anglo–American publishing activity in the 1920s. It was here that William Bird had the shop of his Three Mountains Press. Robert McAlmon joined forces with Bird and the offices became the base also for his Contact Press. To these two independent avant-garde publishers was added the weighty presence of Ford Madox Ford (◊ Picardie), to whom Bird offered such space as there was (a narrow gallery) when Ford launched the *Transatlantic Review* in 1924.

Quai de Béthune (4th). Francis Carco lived at **No 18** from 1949 until his death in 1958.

Quai Bourbon (4th). In his novel *L'Oeuvre*, 1886 (*The Masterpiece*, 1986), Zola locates the studio of his protagonist, the artist Claude Lantier at the corner of quai Bourbon and rue Le Regrattier.

Quai d'Orléans (4th). **No 6** houses the Polish Library of Paris, founded in 1838. The great Polish Romantic poet Adam Mickiewicz (1798–1855) was its first librarian. Mickiewicz was professor of Slavic literature at the **Collège de France** from 1840 to 1844. The library now has a room dedicated to Chopin, and in the same building there is **Le Musée Mickiewicz**, with memorabilia of the poet and his time.

Rue Le Regrattier (4th). Baudelaire installed Jeanne Duval, his 'Black Venus', in the house which still stands at **No 6**. The street was then more colourfully and perhaps appropriately known as rue de la Femme-sans-Tête. In the 1920s, the exciting and enterprising Nancy Cunard lived at **No 1** – it was here that Louis Aragon first met her and, for a time, fell in love with her. Cunard's Hours Press published Aragon's ingenious verse translation of Lewis Carroll's nonsense epic *The Hunting of the Snark – La Chasse au Snark*, 1929.

Rue Saint-Louis-en-l'Île (4th). The **Hôtel Lambert**, at **No 2**, dates from the 1640s and was for a time the property of Voltaire (1694–1778) and his companion Madame du Châtelet (1706–49), but whether they actually lived here is a matter of debate. From the 1840s and for much of the 20th century, the Hôtel Lambert was owned by the Czartoryski family and was a centre for Polish life and culture in Paris.

The Right Bank

BOIS DE BOULOGNE– AUTEUIL–PASSY

Rue Boileau (16th). So-named because the poet Nicolas Boileau (1636–1711) lived in the street. He owned a vast property on the site of what is now the **hameau Boileau**.

Bois de Boulogne. The primary literary connection of the Bois is with Proust, who describes its landscape and the fashionable society it then attracted in detail in À *la recherche du temps perdu*, 1913–27 – see especially the first volume, *Du côté de chez Swann* (*Swann's Way*) – Extract 2. In *Aurélien*, 1944, Louis Aragon, wrote, like Proust, of the need to see and be seen in the Bois – 'Everybody looked as if they were there for something, but they didn't really know what.' It was part of the ritual, he says, 'to give the impression that one had come in haste, passing by, going somewhere else, or coming from somewhere else, because one had promised someone, as a favour . . .'. Françoise Sagan ◊ paints a lonelier picture of the park as a moody setting for emotional games in her acutely observed *Aimez-vous Brahms . . .*, 1959 (*Aimez-Vous Brahms . . .*, 1962) – Extract 3.

Rue Gros (16th). Apollinaire ◊ moved out here from Montmartre to be closer to his lover Marie Laurencin. He subsequently found rooms in **rue La Fontaine**, where Laurencin herself lived. The nearby **Pont Mirabeau**, over which he crossed the Seine into Auteuil, became the poignant setting for his famous poem 'Le Pont Mirabeau' which he composed following the break-up of the relationship.

Rue Hamelin (16th). Marcel Proust (◊ Centre), forced by rebuilding work out of his boulevard Haussmann home, moved into a small fifth-floor apartment at **No 44** in October 1919. He died here in November 1922. The building has since been converted into a hotel and the apartment in which Proust spent his last three years has long gone.

Rue La Fontaine (16th). Proust was born in a house on the site of **No 96** in July 1871, which was the home of his uncle. His parents had moved temporarily out to a peaceful house in Auteuil to avoid the dangers of central Paris during the Commune.

Boulevard de Montmorency (16th). In 1868, Edmond (1822–96) and Jules (1830–70) de Goncourt moved out of central Paris into Auteuil. They made their new home at **No 67** (then No 53). Jules became increasingly ill with syphilis shortly afterwards and died here in 1870. Edmond, however, continued to live in the house until his own death in 1896. It was here that he established his famous literary *salon*, the Sunday afternoon meetings in 'Le Grenier', to which he welcomed many literary stars of the period, including Daudet, Flaubert, Maupassant, and Zola. In the celebrated *Journal*, a rich and amusing source of information, anecdote and gossip about many key literary figures of the period, the Goncourts describe the day they acquired the house (entry of 4 August 1868): 'We stood on the stone steps of the house in Auteuil we so much desired to own. The sun was still shining, and the lawn and the leaves of the shrubs were glittering under the rain of the garden hose. "Eighty-two thousand five hundred francs," said my brother; and our hearts pounded in our breasts. "I'll write to you tomorrow," the proprietor said; "probably I shall accept the offer." "Eighty-three thousand and an immediate answer?" The proprietor thought it over five eternal minutes and then let fall drearily, "Done!" We left, absolutely intoxicated.' The house cannot be visited. It is now the property of the Académie Goncourt, which awards the Prix Goncourt, the most prestigious literary prize in France, and which was founded with money from Edmond's will.

Rue de Passy (16th). Paul Claudel (1868–1955) had an apartment at **No 80**. In his *Journal* entry of 15 May 1925, Gide records a visit of the previous evening: 'I go through two rooms, the second of which is rather large, and find myself in a third one, still larger, which he uses as a bedroom and workroom. Open army couch in a corner; a low book-case goes around two sides of the room; many objects, brought back from the Far East, decorate it. . . . He is enormous and short; he looks like Ubu. We sit down in two armchairs. He completely fills his. Mine, a sort of chaise-longue, has such a low back that to be comfortable in it I should have to get too far away from Claudel. I give up and lean forward. In the presence of Claudel I am aware only of what I lack; he dominates me; he overhangs me; he has more base and surface, more health, money, genius, power, children, faith, etc, than I. I think only of obeying without a word.' (Translation from *Journals 1889–1949* – see Booklist.)

Rue Paul-Valéry (16th). Valéry (◊ Île de France) lived at **No 40**, and died here on 20 July 1945.

Rue Pergolèse (16th). Scott and Zelda Fitzgerald (◊ Provence) had their last Paris apartment at **No 10** in 1930. It was while they were staying here that Zelda's mental breakdown finally occurred.

Rue Raynouard (16th). In 1841, Balzac (◊ Centre) found a refuge from his creditors in the suburban village of Passy, where he stayed until 1847. He moved into **No 47** (it was then 19 rue Basse). He took the house under the name of Mlle Breugnol-Desreaux, in fact Mme Breugnol, his housekeeper-mistress. Unusual, picturesque and secluded, it provided an ideal shelter for him – the main entrance is below street level and there is another entrance, or exit, on the **rue Berton** (which still retains the character of the rural village). There was also a network of cellars under the street which the author could use to escape down to the river (a section of these now houses **Le Musée du Vin**, the entrance to which is in the nearby **Square Charles Dickens**). Balzac applied himself relentlessly to his writing, producing here some of his most important work (including *La Cousine Bette*, 1846 and *Le Cousin Pons*, 1847). Writing to Mme Hanska in 1845, he explained that each day he worked from midnight till 8 am, took a quarter of an hour for breakfast, worked until 5 pm, had dinner and went to bed early to be awoken again at midnight.

The 'upside down house', as Nerval described it, is now **La Maison de Balzac** and the whole building at 47 rue Raynouard is devoted to the writer's life and work. There are detailed exhibitions and a library and documentation centre. For those in search of memorabilia, the study is the core attraction with, among other things, the novelist's armchair and his indispensable *cafetière*, bearing his initials. From the study window you can see **rue Berton** and **17 rue d'Ankara**, now the Turkish Embassy, which was the residence of the Princesse de Lamballe and later the private clinic of Dr Émile Blanche, who treated Gérard de Nerval and Guy de Maupassant. Maupassant died here in 1893.

Rue de Siam (16th). George Gissing (1857–1903) and his French common-law wife Gabrielle Fleury lived at **No 13** in 1899.

Boulevard Suchet (16th). P.G. Wodehouse (◊ Picardie) spent the last years of the Second World War in Paris and had an apartment at **No 36** in 1945–

46. Colette ◊ lived at **No 69** from 1917 to 1927.

Avenue des Sycomores (16th). No 38 was the home of André Gide (◊ Normandy) – he had the house built for him by the architect Louis Bonnier.

Avenue Théophile-Gautier (16th). François Mauriac (◊ Aquitaine) lived at **No 38** for the last 40 years of his life.

Avenue Victor-Hugo (16th). Hugo ◊ died in a house on the site of **No 124** (at the time it was avenue d'Eyleau). The room in which he died is reconstructed in **La Maison de Victor Hugo** in **place des Vosges.** Lamartine died in 1869 near the square named after him (the house no longer exists).

Rue des Vignes (16th). James Joyce took an apartment at **No 34** in 1939. It was the last of the Joyces' many homes in Paris since their arrival in 1920. They left at the end of 1939 with the onset of the war. Just over a year later, in January 1941, Joyce died in Zurich from a perforated ulcer.

ÉTOILE–LOUVRE–CHÂTELET

Place André-Malraux (1st). The **Comédie-Française**, or the Théâtre Français, founded by Louis XIV, has had its home here since the end of the 18th century, although the building has been much changed since the company first moved in. Literary travellers will want to see the various statues and busts of actors and writers on display, including Dumas *fils*, George Sand, and Voltaire (the famous statue by Houdon). You can also see the chair on which Molière was sitting in 1673 when he collapsed during a performance of, ironically, *Le Malade imaginaire* – he died the same evening.

Rue des Acacias (17th). At the end of Sebastian Faulks's moving and atmos-

pheric novel of 1930s France, *The Girl at the Lion d'Or*, 1989, the resilient heroine Anne resurfaces from despair in this street with the modest prospect of a job behind the bar in one of its 'huddled cafés'. She notes ironically that there is a street with the same name in Janvilliers, the fictional but vividly evoked provincial coastal town which provides the principal setting for this story of isolation and frustrated love.

Rue d'Anjou (8th). Cocteau ◊ had an apartment at **No 10.** Benjamin Constant (1767–1830), author of *Adolphe*, 1816 (*Adolphe*, 1994), died at **No 29.**

Rue d'Argenteuil (1st). Pierre Corneille (1606–84) died in a house on the site of **No 6**, on which there is a plaque. He is buried in the nearby church of Saint-Roch (see **rue Saint-Honoré**).

Rue d'Artois (8th). Alfred de Vigny (1797–1863) died at **No 6.**

Rue de Balzac (8th). The street whose name now celebrates the author is the one in which he died in 1850. Balzac (◊ Centre) lived at what was then No 14 rue Fortunée – **No 22** occupies the site. Despite his enormous debts, he managed to fit out what was to be his last Paris address with luxurious furniture. He was attracted to the apartment because of its privacy – most of its windows were concealed by the walls of the courtyard, there was an 'escape' route into an adjoining church, useful if one happened to be harassed by creditors, and there was a secret apartment which was ideal for the harbouring of his 'mysterious foreigner', Mme Hanska. On 17 August 1850, Victor Hugo paid his last visit to the dying writer (Balzac died the next day) – 'His face was purple, almost black, leaning to the right, unshaven, his grey hair cut short; his eye was open and staring. I saw him in profile and, seen thus, he looked like Napoleon. . . . An unbearable stench rose from the bed. I lifted the blanket and took Balzac's hand. It was covered with sweat. I pressed it, but he did not return the pressure.' (Quoted by Graham Robb in *Balzac*.)

Rue de Castiglione (1st). George Orwell's ◊ graphic descriptions of the kitchens of elegant restaurants and hotels in *Down and Out in Paris and London*, 1933 (Extract 25) derive from personal experience. In the autumn of 1929 he was employed as a *plongeur* in the kitchens of the **Hôtel Lotti** (No 7). American journalist Janet Flanner (1892–1978) wrote an occasional 'Letter from Paris' for the *New Yorker* over many years and also published books arising from her life in Paris (*An American in Paris*, 1940; *Paris Journal*, 1965 and 1971). She moved into a room at the **Hôtel Continental** (now the Inter-Continental) in 1949 and lived there for 20 years.

Avenue des Champs-Élysées (8th). Charles Dickens (◊ Boulogne) took rooms at **No 49** in 1855 – 'Each room has but one window in it, but we have no fewer than six rooms (besides the back ones) looking on the Champs Elysées, with the wonderful life perpetually flowing up and down.' Robert (1812–89) and Elizabeth Barrett Browning (1806–61) stayed in an apartment at **No 138** in 1851.

Place de la Concorde (8th). See Extract 5 for Prévert's image of deprivation and rejection in this spacious, now traffic-filled square with its symbolism of national unity and reconciliation. It also serves as the setting for a key scene in Nancy Mitford's *The Blessing*, 1951 (Extract 4).

Rue Coquillière (1st). At the end of the street, as it leads into the gardens of Les Halles, is the magnificent 16th century **Église de Saint-Eustache**. Its 'literary' events have included the baptism of Molière in 1622 and the funeral of La Fontaine in 1695. In 1673, Molière was buried in the cemetery here, but only after several days of great controversy. The vicar at first refused to permit a man of the acting profession, especially Molière who was no friend of the clerical establishment, to be buried on consecrated ground. After interventions from the King and the involvement of the Archbishop, it was eventually agreed that Molière should be buried here, but without ceremony. In the event, as befits one of France's greatest dramatists, this was ignored and there was a full-scale funeral attended by hundreds of Molière's friends and supporters. At the beginning of the 18th century his remains – or at least what were presumed to be his remains – were transferred to **Père Lachaise**.

Rue de Courcelles (8th and 17th). Dickens took an apartment at **No 38** (then 48) in 1846. Marcel Proust (◊ Centre) lived at **No 45** from 1900 to 1906 in a spacious and luxuriously furnished apartment which reflected the social and professional success of his father. Dr Proust died in 1903 and his wife followed him two years later – in 1906 Marcel moved to **boulevard Haussmann**. Colette (◊ Burgundy), with her then husband 'Willy' (Henri Gauthier-Villars), settled into a studio apartment at **No 93** in 1903 – they later, thanks to the success of the early Claudine novels, published under Willy's name, moved to a town house at **177 bis**, taking the first floor. Henri Barbusse (◊ Picardie) lived at **No 105**.

Rue Fortuny (17th). Edmond Rostand (1868–1918) lived at **No 2** in the 1890s and wrote *Cyrano de Bergerac*, 1897 (*Cyrano de Bergerac*, 1993).

Avenue Franklin D. Roosevelt (8th). Somerset Maugham (◊ Provence) spent his childhood at **No 25** until 1884, when, both his parents having died, he left for England.

Les Halles (1st). For a vivid evocation of the *quartier* and its people when it was home to the central markets of Paris, see Zola's *Le Ventre de Paris*, 1873 (*The Belly of Paris*, 1996). Patrick Süskind (◊ Provence) offers an imaginative portrayal of it in the 18th century in *Das Parfüm*, 1985 (*Perfume*, 1986) – Extract 8.

Boulevard Haussmann (8th). Proust lived at **No 102** from 1906 to 1919. The bedroom of his first-floor apartment overlooked the boulevard, but he kept both shutters and windows closed, to keep out the noise and the asthma-inducing pollen from the chestnut trees and dust from the street. The curtains were always drawn, because Proust slept during the day, and the air was forever thick with the smell of his medications. In 1910 he had the walls lined with cork to make it sound-proof. Much of *À la recherche du temps perdu*, 1913–27, was written in this fuggy, strangely panelled room, Proust often writing in bed and increasingly reclusive as his health declined and his great project progressed. In 1919 the building was sold to a banker, M Varin-Bernier, who started rebuilding work and Proust, to his great discomfort, was forced to leave. 102 boulevard Haussmann is now owned by Banque SNVB, which took over the Varin-Bernier bank. In partnership with La Société des Amis de Marcel Proust, SNVB has undertaken a reconstruction of Proust's bedroom and opened it to the public. Only the fireplace is authentic – Proust's original cork was sold off for making into bottle corks when he left and his furniture and personal belongings are in the **Musée Carnavalet**. Nevertheless, the site is real and the reconstruction atmospheric. Visiting times are restricted – check with **Banque SNVB**, 102 boulevard Haussmann, 75008 Paris; tel 44 90 40 63.

Avenue Hoche (8th). At **No 12** was the home of Madame Arman de Caillavet, hostess of one of the last of the famous Parisian salons. Her regular visitors included Maupassant, Proust, and Anatole France (with whom she had a long-lasting affair).

Rue Jean-Jacques-Rousseau (1st). So named because Rousseau lived on the street from 1770 to 1778 with Thérèse Levasseur, who by that time had become Madame Rousseau. It was then rue Plâtrière and they lived in a house on the site of the current **No 52**.

Musée du Louvre (1st). William Hazlitt (1778–1830) came here to copy paintings for four months in the winter of 1802–03, and seems to have spent more time in the Louvre than the rest of Paris – 'Here, for four months together, I strolled and studied, and daily heard the warning sound – *"Quatre heures passées, il faut fermer, Citoyens"* . . .'. In his captivating collection of musings and memories, *Paris*, 1983 (*Paris*, 1991), novelist and diarist Julien Green (1900–) writes of a visit to the Louvre – 'At the Louvre. Claude (we call him "the Lorrainer") with his peach-coloured skies, his joyful light. Of all painters, none has so wonderfully suggested what the Lost Land might be, the Elsewhere that will forever haunt mankind. Through the large windows that overlook the river I gazed out at Paris in the rain, a sight of which I never tire. Then the sun began to shine through the raindrops and the city took on the indefinable air of the distances in one of the paintings behind me.' Green, born in Paris of American parents, has spent most of his life there, has long written exclusively in French, and is a member of the Académie Française – *Paris* is a charming exploration of his enduring love for his city.

Boulevard Malesherbes (8th and 17th). **No 9** was the home of Marcel Proust from 1871, the year of his birth, until 1900 – the Prousts occupied a large first-floor apartment at the back of the house. In 1866, Dumas *père* (◊ Provence), impoverished by his own profligacy, moved into the last of his various Paris homes – a fourth-floor apartment at **No 107**. Chad in James's *The Ambassadors*, 1903, has an apartment on this street. James himself lived in nearby **rue Cambon** (then rue de Luxembourg) in 1875–76.

Rue de Mathurins (8th). No 40 was the last Parisian home of Madame de Staël (1766–1817) – she died here on 14 July 1817.

Rue du Mont-Thabor (1st). Alfred de Musset died at **No 6** in 1857.

Rue Murillo (8th). From 1869 to 1875, Gustave Flaubert (◊ Normandy) kept an apartment here, overlooking **parc Monceau**. During his brief stays in Paris, he paused from his writing on Sundays to entertain his friends. These Sunday gatherings were attended by, among many others, Daudet, Huysmans, Maupassant, and Turgenev.

Palais Royal (1st). Cocteau ◊ moved into **36 rue Montpensier** in 1940 and kept the apartment until his death in 1963. His friend Colette (◊ Burgundy) lived at **9 rue de Beaujolais**. She took a small flat here in the late 1920s, but it was not until 1938 that she finally moved into the apartment that was to become associated with her, where she received the great and the good, and where she stayed until her death in 1954.

For all its varied history, from rowdy Paris night-spot full of gambling houses and cafés to its present sedate tranquillity, one of the strangest sights in the Palais Royal must have been that of Gérard de Nerval (◊ Picardie) in the 1850s, walking, as was his habit, a pet lobster on a blue-ribbon leash. He liked lobsters, he explained to his friend Théophile Gautier, because they were quiet, serious, and knew the secrets of the sea. And they did not bark.

Rue de Richelieu (1st and 2nd). Playwright Marie-Joseph Chénier (1764–1811) lived for a time at **No 12** and

also at **No 18**. Denis Diderot (1713–84) died at **No 39**. In the last few months of his life, Molière (Jean-Baptiste Poquelin, 1622–73) lived in a house on the site of **No 40**. On the corner of rue de Richelieu and rue Molière is the **Fontaine Molière**, dating from 1844. **No 56** was where, in her Hôtel de Nevers, the Marquise de Lambert (1647–1733) opened her *salon* in 1710. It became extremely influential – attendees included Montesquieu and Marivaux, and it was said that the approval of the Marquise was an essential requirement for all aspiring members of the Académie Française. The main entrance to the **Bibliothèque Nationale** is at No 58. For lovers of the macabre, in his *Guide des Cimitières de Paris*, 1990, Marcel Le Clere notes that the plinth of the statue of Voltaire in the entrance hall contains the great man's heart.

Rue de Rivoli (1st). Galignani's famous English bookshop at **No 224** has been here since 1855. The **Hôtel Meurice** at No 228, a centre for the German forces of occupation in the Second World War, was in the 19th century especially popular with British tourists. Among its more famous guests were Thackeray, who recommended it in his *Paris Sketch Book*, Dickens, and Wilkie Collins.

Rue de Rome (8th). Stéphane Mallarmé (1842–98) lived at **No 89** and it was here that he held his famous *Mardis* – the literary Tuesday afternoon gatherings that helped to cement his considerable influence on the development of 20th century French poetry. Among his regular visitors were Claudel and Valéry. The *Mardis* also attracted writers from overseas, among them George Moore and Oscar Wilde.

Rue du faubourg Saint-Honoré (8th). Coco Chanel's town house was at **No 29**. Jean Cocteau was among the young writers who visited her here (Chanel designed the costumes for various of his plays and films). **No 39** has been the British Embassy since 1825. William Makepeace Thackeray (1811–63), who lived in Paris from 1834 to 1837, married Isabella Shawe here in 1836. *The Paris Sketch Book*, 1840, a collection of essays and stories, was his first full-length book. Somerset Maugham was born at the Embassy in 1847 – his father, a solicitor, was keen to ensure that he would not be affected by legislation then under consideration that anyone born on French soil could be conscripted into the army. The Embassy and its society are the subject of Nancy Mitford's satirical *Don't Tell Alfred*, 1960. In November 1875, Flaubert moved into an apartment at **No 240** – he had been forced to move from his **rue Murillo** apartment by a financial crisis, caused by his niece's husband, into this more modest accommodation (owned by his niece). He continued, however, to hold his famous Sunday afternoons whenever he was in Paris. It was here that Henry James met Flaubert in 1876.

Rue Saint-Honoré (1st and 8th). Georges Perec ◊ lived in an attic flat at **No 203** in his student days – an experience which finds its way into his novel *Un Homme qui dort*, 1967 (*A Man Asleep*, 1991) – see Extract 36. Pierre Corneille is buried in the church of **Saint-Roch** at **No 296**. At **No 374** was the extremely influential *salon* of Marie-Thérèse Geoffrin (1699–1777) which became in 1750 the primary meeting place for the *encyclopédistes* and the new writers and thinkers (the *philosophes*) of the Enlightenment – it also attracted musicians and artists. Among her visitors were Diderot, Fontenelle, Montesquieu, Voltaire and, from overseas, Hume, Mozart, and Walpole.

Square Saint-Jacques (4th). There is a memorial in this little square near **place de Châtelet** to Gérard de Nerval (◊ Picardie), who died nearby. In the small hours of the freezing cold night of 26 January 1855, Nerval made his way to a dive he knew in rue de la Vieille Lanterne, a gloomy cul-de-sac in what was then a highly disreputable *quartier*. It was two o'clock in the morning and he was refused entry to his intended shelter from the cold. At daybreak, he was found hanged – presumably he had committed suicide. The street in which Nerval died no longer exists – on its site is the **Théâtre de la Ville**. There is a plaque inside the Theatre – the exact spot where Nerval's body was found has been identified as that now occupied by the prompt-box.

Rue de Tilsitt (8th). Scott and Zelda Fitzgerald (◊ Provence) took an apartment at **No 14** in 1925.

Jardin des Tuileries (1st). See Extract 41 for John Evelyn's (◊ Normandy) impressions of the gardens in 1664.

Place Vendôme (1st). From 1917, towards the end of his life, Marcel Proust became a familiar figure at the Ritz, resurfacing from his reclusive lifestyle as his great novel drew to its close. He would dine here with friends several times a week, in a private room, and then gossip with the waiters about the goings-on in the hotel, gathering fuel for his fiction. He was dining here on 27 July 1917, as a guest of his friend the princesse Soutzo (Cocteau was also one of the party), when there was a huge German air-raid on Paris. Proust watched it from a balcony and used the experience in *Le Temps retrouvé* (*Time Regained*), for the scene in which the narrator and Saint-Loup talk about air raids. The Ritz now boasts a **suite de Marcel Proust**. Between the wars, the **Ritz Bar** was a regular haunt of Hemingway and Fitzgerald, as well as the favoured watering place of well-heeled British writers like Somerset Maugham. In 1944, Hemingway, who was among the first liberating Americans to enter Paris, promptly took a suite at the hotel and liberated the cellars (see under 'Lives and Works').

While staying here after the war Hemingway received many visitors – among them the young J.D. Salinger (1919–), then a sergeant in the Counter Intelligence Corps.

MADELAINE–OPÉRA–BOURSE (GRANDS BOULEVARDS)

Passage de Choiseul (2nd). Céline's mother ran a shop here at the turn of the century, selling old lace and antiques, and the novelist spent his childhood in the *quartier*, which was then a centre for the *petite bourgeoisie*. The passage is mutated in *Mort à crédit*, 1936 (*Death on the Installment Plan*, 1966) into the nightmarishly grim passage des Bérésinas. Earlier, in the 1860s, Anatole France had worked here in the shop of the young publisher Alphonse Lemerre.

Rue Danielle-Casanova (1st and 2nd). In this street, then known as rue Neuve-des-Petits-Champs, Stendhal (◊ Rhône–Alpes) died at No 22 in 1842. It was the house of his cousin Romain Colomb, who brought him here after he had collapsed from a stroke in nearby **rue des Capucines**.

Rue Daunou (2nd). At No 5 is the famous **Harry's Bar**, rich in literary associations. Harry's was opened in 1923 by Scottish-born Harry MacElhone, said to have mixed the first Bloody Mary to cure Hemingway's hangovers. It initially attracted mainly American writers, publishers and intellectuals. In addition to Hemingway, among its original regular clientele were Scott Fitzgerald, Kay Boyle, Ezra Pound, and Robert McAlmon. In 1958, Harry died and his son Andy took over. Andy made efforts to draw in Parisian regulars as well as the traditional expatriate customers – and added Prévert, Sartre and Beauvoir to the bar's literary history. Publisher John Calder remarks in his obituary of Andy

MacElhone (*The Guardian*, 30 September 1996) that the meeting of American and British writers with Sartre and Beauvoir in Harry's led to many of them being published in *Les Temps modernes*. Andy was succeeded by his son Duncan, who now runs the bar, keeping Harry's firmly in the family. Calder also mentions in his obituary article Harry MacElhone's ingenious method of ensuring that his non-French customers didn't get lost – he provided cards with the address written as 'Sank Roo Doe Noo' so that cab drivers could understand their instructions.

Rue du Faubourg-Montmartre (9th). Isidore Ducasse, who wrote under the pseudonym Comte de Lautréamont (1846–70), died at **No 7** in November 1870 at the age of 24. If you walk through to the courtyard you will see, opposite the entrance to the restaurant **Chartier**, a small plaque displaying a suitable quotation from his work – 'Qui ouvre la porte de ma chambre funéraire? J'avais dit que personne n'entrât. Qui que vous soyez, éloignez-vous.' ('Who opens the door of my funeral chamber? I had said that nobody should enter it. Whoever you are, go away.') Little is known of the mysterious author of the strange and nightmarish prose-poems, the six *Chants de Maldoror*, 1874 (*Maldoror*, 1947), later much praised by the Surrealists. It is known, however, that he lived at various addresses in this *quartier*, aspects of which become absorbed into his hallucinatory world (including **rue Vivienne** where he lived for a time). For another nightmarish vision of the street, see Henry Miller's *Tropic of Cancer*, 1934 (Extract 17).

Boulevard Montmartre (2nd). At **No 11** is the entrance to the **passage des Panoramas**, which opened in 1800. Here, at the stage door of the Théâtre des Variétés, Zola's (◊ Nord) comte Muffat waits for Nana. 'From then on, the Count kept watch at the stage-door itself, though he did not like this part of the passage, where he was afraid of being recognized. It was at the junction of the Galerie des Variétés and the Galerie Saint-Marc, a shady-looking corner full of obscure little shops – a shoemaker's without any customers, a few dusty furniture shops, and a smoky, somnolent reading-room whose shaded lamps cast sleepy green light all evening. There was never anybody in this corner but well-dressed, patient gentlemen prowling around among the drunken scene-shifters and ragged chorus-girls who always congregate about stage-doors.' (*Nana*, 1880; *Nana*, 1972.) The passage and the theatre itself are described in detail in the novel – see especially chapter 7 for the passage des Panoramas and chapter 1 for the theatre. A waxwork version of Zola, together with those of a number of other literary celebrities, can be seen at **No 10**, the **Musée Grevin**.

Rue Saint-Joseph (2nd). Zola was born at **No 10**.

MONTMARTRE AND ENVIRONS

Rue d'Amsterdam (9th). Baudelaire ◊ had an apartment at **No 22** in 1860. Dumas *père* (◊ Provence) lived at **No 79** in 1843.

Place Blanche (9th). The cafés in and around place Blanche were frequented by the Surrealists between the wars (including Aragon, Arp, Breton, Char, Dali, Ernst, Éluard, Miró and Tzara, among many others). Participant Marcel Jean remembers the meetings in his introduction to the *Collected French Writings* of Jean Arp – '. . .but when I think of prewar Place Blanche, I remember gatherings not devoid of either gaiety or boredom, a "school of poetry" if you will – as uncomplementary as these terms may appear – often passionate and contradictory, a true magnetic field in which André Breton, like a

magnet, exerted a singular power of attraction and repulsion.'

Rue de Bruxelles (9th). Zola (◊ Nord) died at **No 21 bis** in September 1902 from carbon monoxide – the result of a blocked chimney. The verdict was accidental death but the possibility that the incident was connected with his central role in the Dreyfus Affair has left lingering doubts.

Rue de Calais (9th). Arnold Bennett (1867–1931) lived in an apartment at **No 4** from 1903 to 1906 – at the time he was writing *The Old Wives' Tale*, 1908, part of which is set in Paris.

Rue Chaptal (9th). Behind the iron gates of **No 16** is a piece of the early 19th century. This remarkably preserved Italianate villa was built in 1830, just five years after the rue Chaptal itself was created. It was bought in July of that year by the artist Ary Scheffer (1795–1858), who welcomed many literary and artistic friends and acquaintances to the house, some to have their portraits painted, others simply as guests – among them were the Brownings, Delacroix, Liszt, Chopin, Sand, Lamartine, Turgenev, Dickens, and the philosopher Ernest Renan, who married Scheffer's niece. It is now **Le Musée de la Vie Romantique**, and, set back as it is from the street by a tree-lined alley leading into a courtyard, it provides an unexpected and charming rural ambience in which to enjoy its well presented and evocative exhibits. The museum, comprising the main house, the two artist's studios which Scheffer had built on either side of the courtyard, and a *jardin d'hiver* which was added at the end of the 19th century, is in large part dedicated to George Sand and many of the people in her life. It includes personal belongings and memorabilia – among the more curious are plaster casts of Chopin's left hand and of Sand's right arm and hand (which shows slight deformities caused by the strain of prolific writing). There are also items of furniture from her house at Nohant, meticulously exhibited in a reconstructed *salon* of the period, and many portraits. In other rooms, the museum shows paintings from the Scheffer–Renan collection and stages temporary exhibitions relating to the Romantic period. Highly recommended, Le Musée de la Vie Romantique is a rare example of a museum which conveys as much through its ambience as it does through its contents and documentation.

Place de Clichy (9th/17th). 'We were walking to the Place Clichy, Fred, Henry and I. Henry makes me aware of the street, of people. He is smelling the street, observing. He shows me the whore with the wooden stump who stands near the Gaumont Palace. He shows me the narrow streets winding up, lined with small hotels, and the whores standing by the doorways, under red lights.' So writes Anaïs Nin in her *Journal* entry for April 1932. Henry Miller ◊ lived in the working-class *quartier* of Clichy in 1932–33, sharing an apartment with his friend Alfred Perlès – a period which provided him with the inspiration for *Quiet Days in Clichy*, 1956. 'On a grey day in Paris,' he writes, 'I often found myself walking towards the Place Clichy in Montmartre. From Clichy to Aubervilliers there is a long string of cafés, restaurants, theatres, cinemas, haberdashers, hotels and bordels. It is the broadway of Paris corresponding to that little stretch between 42nd and 53rd Streets. Broadway is fast, dizzying, dazzling, and no place to sit down. Montmartre is sluggish, lazy, indifferent, somewhat shabby and seedy-looking, not glamorous so much as seductive, not scintillating but glowing with a smouldering flame.'

Rue Fontaine (9th). André Breton (1896–1966) lived at **No 42** for many years in a studio apartment which became a key meeting and debating place for Surrealists – as did the cafés in the nearby **place Blanche**.

Rue Gabrielle (18th). Poet and sculptor Jean Arp (1887–1966) lived at **No 1** in 1914.

Rue Girardon (18th). The peripatetic Gérard de Nerval (◊ Picardie) lived in **allée des Brouillards** in 1846, just off this street, in the not inaptly named 'Château des Brouillards', originally built by the poet Jean-Jacques Lefranc, Marquis de Pompignan (1709–84) and later the abode of vagabonds, anarchists and other shady characters. Another literary resident was the Naturalist novelist and short-story writer Paul Alexis (1847–1901).

Rue de la Goutte d'Or (18th). The symbolically rich name of the street is also the name by which this poor, multinational immigrants' *quartier* is known (it is now being redeveloped). In Michel Tournier's (1924–) novel *La Goutte d'or*, 1985 (*The Golden Droplet*, 1987), about the experiences of a boy from North Africa who comes to Paris as an immigrant worker, the title refers both to the *quartier* and to a treasured jewel which becomes the protagonist's good-luck charm. The *quartier* is also the setting for a more famous work – Zola's story of the suffering and oppression of working-class life, *L'Assommoir*, 1877 (*L'Assommoir*, 1970).

Rue Joseph de Maistre (18th). Genet (◊ Brittany) lived on and off at **No 12** in 1939–40. His room overlooked the **Cimetière du Nord**, as did the garret apartment of his transvestite character Divine in *Notre-Dame-des-fleurs*, 1944 (*Our Lady of the Flowers*, 1964) – he gives Divine an address in nearby **rue Caulaincourt**.

Rue Moncey (9th). Guy de Maupassant (◊ Provence) lived at **No 2** when he first moved to Paris in 1869, in a small room in a house owned by his father. He left in 1876 for a larger apartment nearby at **17 rue Clauzel** where things were much livelier – all his neighbours were prostitutes (note it was No 17 – the plaque on No 19 is wrong).

Rue Nollet (17th). Harlem Renaissance poet and novelist Langston Hughes (1902–67) lived at **No 15** in 1924. His Montmartre days are recalled in his autobiography *The Big Sea*, 1940.

Square d'Orléans (9th). This attractive square in the *quartier* known as 'La Nouvelle-Athènes' was once home to George Sand (◊ Centre) and Frédéric Chopin – they moved here in 1842 from **rue Pigalle**, he to **No 9** and she to **No 5**. Sand left in 1847, when her affair with Chopin ended – he stayed on another two years.

Rue de Ravignan (18th). The impecunious poet and painter Max Jacob (1876–1944) lived in a poor and gloomy apartment at **No 7** from 1901 to 1914 – it was here that he experienced his first vision of Christ that set him on the road to his conversion to Christianity. In 1914, he moved to **17 rue Gabrielle**, nearby.

Boulevard Rochechouart (9th/18th). 'Nous cherchons fortune/autour du Chat Noir/Au clair de la lune/à Montmartre, le soir,' sang Aristide Bruant. **No 84** was the café-cabaret Le Chat Noir, which opened in 1881 and became a huge success. The club, with its famously rude patron Rodolphe Salis, and its satirical and bawdy singers and comic poets, rapidly became popular in literary and artistic circles – Daudet, Hugo, Verlaine and Zola were among the many who were entertained here in its early days. There were mock 'literary' evenings on Fridays and Saturdays, headed up by the humorist Alphonse Allais (1854–1905), a regular contributor to the weekly *Le Chat noir*, from which the club took its name. As the cabaret's reputation grew, it was increasingly instrumental in attracting tourists and would-be bohemians to Montmartre. By 1885 it had become so popular that Salis had to move it to

larger premises – it closed in 1897, by which time he had made his fortune. **No 84** was taken over by the singer-songwriter Aristide Bruant (1851–1925), he of the scarlet scarf and black hat in the famous Toulouse-Lautrec poster, who had performed regularly at Le Chat Noir – he opened his own club Le Mirliton, attracting huge crowds of the *bourgeoisie* eager for a little Montmartre adventure.

Rue Saint-Georges (9th). Henry Murger (1822–61), author of *Scènes de la vie de bohème* (source of Puccini's *La Bohème*), was born at **No 19**. The Goncourt brothers lived at **No 43** from 1849 to 1868 before moving out to **Auteuil**.

Rue des Saules (18th). Au Lapin Agile, the little cottage at **No 4**, started life in 1860 as the Cabaret des Assassins. It was bought in 1903 by Aristide Bruant (see **boulevard Rochechouart**), who put its management in the hands of his friend Frédérique Gérard (Frédé). Thanks to Frédé it became a great success with artists and writers in the early years of the century – among those who enjoyed the informal and bohemian atmosphere were Apollinaire, Picasso, Max Jacob, André Salmon, Mac Orlan, and the novelist of bohemian Montmartre and Pigalle, Francis Carco (1886–1958). The Lapin Agile still operates as a cabaret club, but the tourist clientele is rather different from the night owls who made it famous. Perhaps it is best viewed from the outside – externally, it is much as it was in its heyday, and evokes images of a Montmartre long gone.

Cité Véron (18th). Jacques Prévert ◊ lived here from 1955. Writing in *A Girl in Paris*, 1991, Shusha Guppy ◊ recalls a visit to him in the 1950s: 'Jacques opened the door dressed in grey trousers and a pale blue pullover – the shade of his eyes – soaked cigarette butt at the corner of his mouth, which he took out to greet me and once inside used to

Au Lapin Agile, 1872

start up another cigarette. He led me to his study, a large light room opening on to a flat terrace. From it you could see the motionless red sails of the Moulin Rouge silhouetted against the grey wintry sky . . .'

HÔTEL DE VILLE–TEMPLE– MARAIS–BASTILLE

Boulevard Beaumarchais (4th). Nos 2–20 are on the site of a splendid mansion and gardens which were the home of the playwright Pierre-Augustin Caron de Beaumarchais (1732–99), author of *Le Barbier de Séville*, 1775 (*The Barber of Seville*, 1964) and *Le Mariage de Figaro*, 1784 (*The Marriage of Figaro*, 1964), from whom the boulevard takes its name.

Rue de Lesdiguières (4th). Balzac (◊ Centre) moved out of his parents' home in **rue du Temple** in 1819 to live in a poor garret here for two years, striving to make his way as a writer. The building in which he lived no longer exists.

Rue Pavée (4th). Alphonse Daudet (◊ Provence) lived for some ten years at **No 24**, the Hôtel Lamoignon (now the Bibliothèque Historique de la Ville de Paris). He and his wife felt a strong affinity for the Marais and when they moved from here in 1876 it was to nearby **place des Vosges**.

Rue du Parc-Royal (3rd). Théophile Gautier (1811–72) lived at **No 4** from 1822 to 1831.

Boulevard Richard-Lenoir (11th). Simenon locates the home of Maigret on this boulevard (see under **place des Vosges**).

Rue du faubourg Saint-Antoine (11th). The *quartier* of which this street is the main artery, running from place de la Bastille to place de la Nation, was a working-class district which featured prominently in the revolutions of 1789 and 1848 – and many among those who stormed the Bastille were from this area. Its dark, narrow streets and gloomy taverns are described in two great novels of the Revolution: Hugo's

Les Misérables and Dickens's *A Tale of Two Cities* (Extract 32).

Rue Saint-Antoine (4th). No 62, now occupied by the Caisse Nationale des Monuments Historiques, is the **Hôtel de Sully**, dating from the 1620s. In the 1720s a physically mild but psychologically humiliating assault took place on Voltaire just outside it. He had quarrelled with a nobleman, the chevalier de Rohan, who had three servants attack the young Voltaire with sticks as he was leaving the hôtel, where he had dined with the duc de Sully. To add to the indignity, Rohan watched in amusement from the other side of the street, shouting instructions to his servants. Not long afterwards, the enraged Voltaire was given a short spell in the Bastille, probably primarily to prevent him from exacting a disproportionate revenge on his assailant – he was carrying pistols when he was arrested.

Cour Saint-François (12th). This sad little cul-de-sac off **rue Moreau** was home to Verlaine ◊ in 1885–86. In a seedy hotel populated by pimps and prostitutes, he lived in a damp tiny room on the ground floor, while his widowed mother occupied an apartment on the first floor. She fell ill with pneumonia in January 1886 and died here. Verlaine, himself suffering from a bout of ill health which rendered him unable to walk, could not be taken up the stairs to see her – the staircase was too narrow for a stretcher. It was also too narrow for the coffin, which had to be lowered from a window.

Rue de Sévigné. The **Musée de Carnavalet** is at **No 23**. Now a fascinating museum devoted to the history of Paris, it was the Parisian home of Madame de Sévigné (1626–96) from 1677 until 1694 – there is a room dedicated to her in the museum, which includes her portrait by Nanteuil. Other exhibits of literary interest include a reconstruction of the bedroom from Paul Léautaud's (1872–1956) ramshackle

house at Fontenay-aux-Roses, just outside Paris, where he lived for the last half of his life. In his very eccentric old age, he continued writing here, by candlelight with a quill pen, his acerbic and extraordinary *Journal littéraire 1893–1956*, 1956–66, surrounded by his two dozen cats and the old furniture they had all but scratched to destruction. Next to this, and in complete contrast, is a reconstruction of the room where Proust slept and worked, with its ambience of tired elegance. The bedroom of poet and novelist Anna de Noailles (1876–1933) is also on display.

Rue de Sully (4th). At No 1 is the **Bibliothèque de l'Arsenal**. In 1824, the novelist Charles Nodier (1780–1844) became Librarian here and established his important *salon* which was for a time the primary meeting place of the Romantic movement. Regulars included Balzac, Dumas *père*, Hugo, Lamartine, Musset, Nerval, and Vigny.

Boulevard du Temple (3rd). Flaubert (◊ Normandy) had an apartment at No 42 from 1856 to 1869.

Rue du Temple (3rd). In his *Les Mystères de Paris*, 1842–43 (*The Mysteries of Paris*, 1988), Eugène Sue (1804–57) located his famous concierge M. Pipelet at No 17, and describes in some detail the less than salubrious character of the house and the *quartier* at the beginning of the 19th century. Balzac lived in this street, probably at No 124 (sources differ on the number) in his parents' home before moving to his garret in **rue de Lesdiguières** to try his hand at earning a living by writing.

Rue des Tournelles (3rd). No 56 was the last home of the famous courtesan, the cultured and very fashionable Ninon de Lenclos (c1620–1705). She was prominent in intellectual and literary circles and her *salon* was among the most popular of the day. Her visitors included Molière, La Fontaine, La

Rochefoucauld, and Madame de Lafayette.

Rue de Turenne (3rd). The burlesque poet, novelist and playwright Paul Scarron (1610–60) lived at **No 56** (on the corner of rue de Turenne and rue Villehardouin) from 1654 until his death. He lived here with his young wife, who was later to become Madame de Maintenon, second wife of Louis XIV.

Crébillon *père* (1674–1762), the playwright, moved into the house in 1741 and lived here until he died.

Rue Vieille du Temple (3rd). Beaumarchais lived for a time at **No 47**, the Hôtel des Ambassadeurs de Hollande. It was here that he wrote *The Marriage of Figaro*.

Place des Vosges (3rd and 4th). Madame de Sévigné was born at **No 1**, where she spent the first ten years of her life.

Victor Hugo ◊ lived in a huge apartment on the second floor of **No 6** from 1832 to 1848, when place des Vosges was still known as place Royale. Hugo was by then a literary, political and social celebrity and he received many famous visitors here before leaving the apartment when the *quartier* was besieged by revolutionaries. He decorated his home according to his rather Gothic tastes – the walls of his reception room hung with a red damask, and the antique furnishings and ornaments exotic and curious. Charles Dickens visited Hugo here and recorded his impressions in a letter of 24 January 1847: 'We were at Victor Hugo's house last Sunday week, a most extraordinary place, looking like an old curiosity shop, or the property room of some gloomy, vast, old theatre. I was much struck by Hugo himself, who looks like a genius as he is, every inch of him, and is very interesting and satisfactory from head to foot. His wife is a handsome woman with black flashing eyes, who looks as if she might poison his break-

fast any morning when the humour seized her. There is also a charming ditto daughter of fifteen or sixteen, with ditto eyes, and hardly any drapery above the waist, whom I should suspect of carrying a sharp poignard in her stays, but for her not appearing to wear any. Sitting among old armour and old tapestry, and old coffers, and grim old chairs and tables, and old canopies of state from old palaces, and old golden lions going to play at skittles with ponderous old golden balls, they made a most romantic show, and looked liked a chapter out of one of his own books.'

Since 1903, the hôtel has been a museum dedicated to Hugo's life and work. The many exhibits in **La Maison de Victor Hugo** include his pen and ink drawings, personal memorabilia, and furniture which he designed himself. Among the sculptures and paintings are a bust of Hugo by Rodin, portraits of his wife Adèle and his mistress Juliette Drouet, and a depiction of the riotous first night of his Romantic verse drama *Hernani*. There are also reconstructions of rooms from other places – the dining room at Guernsey, Juliette Drouet's 'Chinese room', which Hugo designed in the home he provided for her at Guernsey, and the room in which he died in his last Paris apartment (which no longer exists).

Place des Vosges has had other famous literary residents. Théophile Gautier lived on the second floor at **No 8** in 1831–34, as did Alphonse Daudet in the 1870s. Georges Simenon ◊ lived in the 1920s in a small flat at **No 21**, later, as he became more successful, moving into a larger and more luxurious apartment in the same building. In some of the Maigret novels Simenon locates the home of his famous detective in place des Vosges, while in many others he is said to live in **boulevard Richard-Lenoir** (11th). Maigret kindly explains away this apparent inconsistency in the amusing *Les Mémoires de Maigret*, 1950 (*Maigret's Memoirs*, 1964). The apartment on boulevard

Richard-Lenoir, it seems, needed extensive building work – 'Simenon was just off to Africa, where he was to spend nearly a year. "Why don't you move into my flat in the Place des Vosges until the job's finished?" And so it happened that we went to live there, at No 21 to be exact, without encouraging the reproach of disloyalty to our dear old Boulevard.'

Ernest Hemingway with Sylvia Beach in front of Shakespeare and Company, 1928 (Hemingway's bandage was the consequence of a domestic accident)

LITERARY GRAVES

Authors are listed alphabetically under each cemetery. A number in brackets after the name indicates the division of the cemetery in which the grave is located.

BAGNEUX
44 avenue Marx-Dormoy, Montrouge
Francis Carco
Jules Laforgue

BATIGNOLLES
8 rue Saint-Just (17th) (Métro – Porte-de-Clichy)
André Breton (31st)
Blaise Cendrars (7th)
Paul Verlaine (11th)

MONTMARTRE
Entrance – avenue Rachel (18th) (Métro – Place-Clichy)
Pierre-Simon Ballanche (30th)
Louise Colet (33rd)
Marceline Desbordes-Valmore (26th)
Alexandre Dumas *fils* (21st)
Georges Feydeau (30th)
Théophile Gautier (3rd)
Delphine Gay (12th)
Émile de Girardin (12th)
Edmond and Jules de Goncourt (13th)
Heinrich Heine (27th)
Marcel Jouhandeau (30th)
Eugène Labiche (17th)
Henri Meilhac (21st)
Henry Murger (5th)
Juliette Récamier (30th)
Ernest Renan (22nd)
Stendhal (30th)
François Truffaut (21st)
Alfred de Vigny (13th)
Émile Zola (bust only – he was originally buried here but his remains were subsequently transferred to the Panthéon)

MONTPARNASSE
Entrance – boulevard Edgar-Quinet (14th) (Métro – Raspail)
Raymond Aron (24th)
Charles Baudelaire (6th) (his step-father, Jacques Aupick, is also buried here)
Simone de Beauvoir (20th)
Samuel Beckett (12th)
Paul Bourget (26th)
François Coppée (9th)
Julio Cortázar (3rd)
Robert Desnos (15th)
Marguerite Duras (21st)
Léon-Paul Fargue (18th)
Joris-Karl Huysmans (2nd)
Eugène Ionesco (6th)
Pierre-Jean Jouve (3rd)
Joseph Kessel (28th)
Maurice Leblanc (10th)
Pierre Louÿs (26th)
Guy de Maupassant (26th)
Catulle Mendès (22nd)
Hégésippe Moreau (2nd)
Edgar Quinet (11th)
Charles-Augustin Sainte-Beuve (17th)
Jules Sandeau (9th)
Jean-Paul Sartre (20th)
Georges Schehadé (11th)
Pierre Seghers (7th)
Tristan Tzara (8th)
César Vallejo (12th)
Vercors (29th)

NEUILLY
Ancien Cimetière, rue Victor-Noir (Métro – Pont-de-Neuilly)
Anatole France (1st)

PASSY
*2 rue du Commandant-Schloesing
(16th) (Métro – Trocadéro)*
Jean Giraudoux

PÈRE LACHAISE
*Main entrance – boulevard de
Ménilmontant (20th) (Métro –
Père-Lachaise)*
Abélard and Héloïse (7th)
Comtesse d'Agoult, aka Daniel
Stern (54th)
Guillaume Apollinaire (86th)
Miguel Asturias (10th)
Honoré de Balzac (48th)
Henri Barbusse (97th)
Pierre-Augustin Caron de
Beaumarchais (28th)
Jacques-Henri Bernardin de Saint-
Pierre (11th)
Sarah Bernhardt (44th)
Anthelme Brillat-Savarin (28th)
Marie-Joseph Chénier (8th)
Colette (4th)
Benjamin Constant (29th)
Alphonse Daudet (26th)
Paul Éluard (97th)
Jean de La Fontaine (25th)
Louis-Sébastien Mercier (11th)
Elisa Mercoeur (17th)
Jules Michelet (52nd)
Molière (25th)
Jim Morrison (6th)
Alfred de Musset (4th)
Gérard de Nerval (49th)
Anna de Noailles (28th)
Charles Nodier (49th)
Marcel Proust (85th)
Raymond Radiguet (56th)
Henri de Régnier (86th)
Jules Romains (3rd)
Jean-François, Marquis de Saint-
Lambert (11th)
Simone Signoret (44th)
Getrude Stein and Alice B. Toklas
(94th)
Sully-Prudhomme (44th)
Jules Vallès (66th)

Comte de Villiers de l'Isle-Adam
(79th)
Oscar Wilde (89th)
Richard Wright (Colombarium)

CHURCHES
*Saint-Étienne-du-Mont, place Sainte-
Geneviève (5th) (Métro –
Luxembourg/Cardinal-Lemoine)*
Blaise Pascal
Jean Racine (epitaph in chapel by
Boileau)
*Saint-Germain-des-Prés, place Saint-
Germain (6th) (Metro – St-
Germain-des-Prés)*
Nicolas Boileau
René Descartes
*Saint-Gervais-et-Saint-Protais, 2 rue
François-Miron (4th) (Métro –
Hôtel-de-Ville/Saint-Paul)*
Crébillon *père*
Paul Scarron
*Saint-Roch, 296 rue Saint-Honoré
(1st) (Métro – Tuileries)*
Pierre Corneille
Denis Diderot (but there is no
plaque for him)
*Saint-Sulpice, place Saint-Sulpice (6th)
(Métro – St-Sulpice)*
Madame de Lafayette
Montesquieu

THE PANTHÉON
*Place du Panthéon (5th) (Métro –
Luxembourg/Cardinal-Lemoine)*
Victor Hugo
André Malraux
Jean-Jacques Rousseau
Voltaire
Émile Zola
There are also monuments at the
Panthéon to Diderot and the
encyclopédistes and Rousseau, and
commemorative plaques to
Saint-Exupéry and to writers
killed in the First World War
(including Alain-Fournier and
Charles Péguy)

BOOKLIST

For most of the extracted works, the original publisher in English can be found in 'Acknowledgments and Citations' at the end of the volume, as can the exact location of the extracts and the editions from which they are taken. The date in square brackets is that of the original publication of the work in its original language. For additional titles by the authors highlighted in this chapter and for recommended biographies, see 'Lives and Works'.

Abelard and Heloise: Their Lives, Their Loves, Their Letters, Donald E. Ericson, ed, Bennet-Edwards, New York, 1990.

Abélard, Peter, *Petrus Abaelardus and Heloise: Letters*, B. Radice, trans, Penguin, London and New York, 1974.

Apollinaire, Guillaume, *Alcools* [1913], University of California Press, Berkeley, CA, 1992. (Bilingual with verse translations.)

Apollinaire, Guillaume, *Calligrammes: Poems of Peace and War (1913–1916)* [1918], University of California Press, Berkeley, CA, 1991. (Bilingual with verse translations.) **Extract 33** from 'A Phantom of the Clouds' in *Calligrammes* translated by J. Edmondson.

Apollinaire, Guillaume, *The Selected Writings of Guillaume Apollinaire*, Roger Shattuck, trans, New Directions, New York, 1971.

Aragon, Louis, *Paris Peasant* [1926], Exact Change, Boston, MA, 1993.

Arp, Jean, *Collected French Writings*, Marcel Jean, ed, Joachim Neugroschel, trans, Calder and Boyars, London, 1974/as *Arp on Arp*, Viking Press, New York, 1972.

Baldwin, James, *Giovanni's Room* [1956], Penguin, London, 1990/ Viking Penguin, London, 1990. **Extract 20.**

Baldwin, James, *Notes of a Native Son* [1955], Corgi, London, 1969/ Beacon, Boston, MA, 1990.

Balzac, Honoré de, *Cousin Bette* [1846], Marion Ayton Crawford, trans, Penguin, London and New York, 1965.

Balzac, Honoré de, *Cousin Pons* [1847], H.J. Hunt, trans, Penguin, London and New York, 1968.

Balzac, Honoré de, *Pere Goriot* [1834], M. A. Crawford, trans, Penguin, London, 1969/Henry Reed, trans, New American Library, New York, 1962. **Extract 12.**

Barnes, Djuna, *Ladies Almanack* [1928], Harper and Row, New York, 1972.

Barnes, Djuna, *Nightwood* [1936], Faber and Faber, London, 1985/New Directions, New York, 1946. **Extract 37.**

Barnes, Julian, *Metroland* [1980], Picador, London, 1992/Random House, New York, 1992.

Barthes, Roland, *The Eiffel Tower and Other Mythologies*, Farrar, Straus and Giroux, New York, 1980.

Baudelaire, Charles, *The Flowers of Evil* [1857], J. McGowan, trans, Oxford University Press, Oxford and New York, 1993. (Bilingual, with verse translations.)

Baudelaire, Charles, 'Morning Twilight' [in *Les Fleurs du Mal*, 1861], Laurence Kitchin, trans, in *Baudelaire's Paris*, Forest Books, London, 1990. (Bilingual with verse translations, also includes single poems by Nerval and Verlaine.) **Extract 24.**

Baudelaire, Charles, *Paris Spleen*, New Directions, New York, 1970.

Beach, Sylvia, *Shakespeare & Co* [1959], University of Nebraska Press, Lincoln, NB, 1980.

Beauvoir, Simone de, *Force of Circumstance* [1963], R. Howard, trans, Penguin, London, 1975.

Beauvoir, Simone de, *Letters to Sartre*, Quintin Hoare, sel and trans, Vintage, London, 1992.

Beauvoir, Simone de, *The Mandarins* [1954], L. Friedman, trans, Flamingo, London, 1984/W.W. Norton, New York, 1991.

Beauvoir, Simone de, *Memoirs of a Dutiful Daughter* [1958], J. Kirkup, trans, Penguin, London, 1963/HarperCollins, New York, 1974.

Beauvoir, Simone de, *The Prime of Life* [1960], P. Green, trans, Penguin, London, 1973/Paragon House, New York, 1992. **Extract 34.**

Beckett, Samuel, *Dream of Fair to Middling Women* [written 1932], Calder, London 1993/Riverrun, New York, 1993. **Extract 30.**

Bennett, Arnold, *Journal* [1932–33], in *Collected Works*, Vol 38, Ayer, Salem, NH, 1976.

Bennett, Arnold, *The Old Wives' Tale* [1908], Oxford University Press, Oxford and New York, 1995.

Benstock, Shari, *Women of the Left Bank: Paris 1900–1940*, Virago, London, 1987/University of Texas Press, Austin, TX, 1986.

Boyle, Kay, and Robert McAlmon, *Being Geniuses Together: 1920–1930* [1968], North Point Press, Berkeley, CA, 1984.

Boyle, Kay, *My Next Bride* [1934], Virago, London, 1986/Viking Penguin, New York, 1986. **Extract 22.**

Breton, André, *Nadja* [1928], Richard Howard, trans, Grove Weidenfeld, New York, 1960.

Cardinal, Marie, *Devotion and Disorder* [1987], K. Montin, trans, The Women's Press, London, 1991.

Cardinal, Marie, *The Words to Say It* [1975], Pat Goodheart, trans, The Women's Press, London, 1984/Van Vector and Goodheart, Cambridge, MA, 1985. **Extract 1.**

Céline, Louis-Ferdinand, *Journey to the End of the Night* [1932], Ralph Manheim, trans, Calder, London, 1991/New Directions, New York, 1983. **Extract 29.**

Céline, Louis-Ferdinand, *Death on the Installment Plan* [1936], Ralph Manheim, trans, New Directions, New York, 1971. As *Death on Credit*, Ralph Manheim, trans, Calder, London, 1989.

Cocteau, Jean, *Les Enfants Terribles* [1929], Rosamond Lehmann, trans, Penguin, London and New York, 1961. **Extract 16.**

Cocteau, Jean, *Tempest of Stars*, Jeremy Reed, trans, Enitharmon, London, 1992. (Selected poems, bilingual verse translations.)

Colette, *Claudine in Paris* [1901], Antonia White, trans, Penguin, London, 1990/Ballantine, New York, NY, 1982. **Extract 9.**

Colette, *The Claudine Novels*, Antonia White, trans, Penguin, London, 1987.

Colette, *The Vagabond* [1910], Enid Mcleod, trans, Penguin, London, 1990/Ballantine, New York, 1982.

Constant, Benjamin, *Adolphe* [1816], E.P. Courtney, trans, Blackwell, London, 1994.

Cooper, James Fenimore, *Gleanings in Europe: France* [1837–38], State University of New York Press, NY, 1983.

Dickens, Charles, *Dickens in France*, In Print Publishing, Brighton, 1996. (Selected non-fiction and correspondence.)

Dickens, Charles, *A Tale of Two Cities* [1859], Penguin, London and New York, 1970. **Extract 32.**

Diderot, Denis, *Rameau's Nephew* [1804] and *D'Alembert's Dream* [1769], Leonard Tancock, trans, Penguin, London and New York, 1966.

Du Maurier, George, *Trilby* [1895], Penguin, London, 1994/Dover, New York, 1995.

Evelyn, John, *The Diary and Correspondence of John Evelyn*, William Bray, ed, Vol 1, George Bell and Sons, London, 1906. **Extracts 13 and 41.**

Fabre, Michel, *From Harlem to Paris: Black American Writers in France, 1840–1980*, University of Illinois Press, Urbana and Chicago, IL, 1991.

Faulks, Sebastian, *The Girl at the Lion d'Or* [1989], Vintage, London, 1990.

Ferlinghetti, Lawrence, *Her*, New Directions, New York, 1960.

Ferlinghetti, Lawrence, *Love in the Days of Rage* [1988], Minerva, London, 1990/NAL–Dutton, New York, 1990. **Extract 10.**

Fitch, Noel Riley, *Sylvia Beach and the Lost Generation*, Penguin, London, 1985/Viking Penguin, New York, 1985.

Fitzgerald, F. Scott, 'Babylon Revisited' [1931], in *The Crack-Up With Other Pieces and Stories*, Penguin, London, 1965/*Babylon Revisited and Other Stories*, Scribner, New York, 1988.

Flanner, Janet, *Paris Journal, 1944–1955*, and *Paris Journal, 1956–1965*, Harcourt Brace Jovanovich, Orlando, FL, 1988.

Ford, Hugh, *Published in Paris: American and British Writers, Printers, and Publishers in Paris, 1920–1939*, Pushcart, Yonkers, NY, 1975.

France, Anatole, *The Gods Will Have Blood* [1912], Frederick Davies, trans, Penguin, London, 1979/Viking Penguin, New York, 1995. **Extract 31.**

Gallant, Mavis, *Paris Notebooks*, Hamish Hamilton, London, 1989/Viking Penguin, New York, 1989. **Extract 11.**

Genet, Jean, *Our Lady of the Flowers* [1944], B. Frechtman, trans, Faber and Faber, London, 1964/Grove Press, New York, 1987.

Gide, André, *If It Die* [1926], Dorothy Bussy, trans, Penguin, London and New York, 1977.

Gide, André, *Journals 1889–1949*, Justin O'Brien, trans, Penguin, London and New York, 1967. (Selections.)

Goncourt, Edmond and Jules, *The Goncourt Journals 1851–1870*, Lewis Galentière, trans, Cassell, London, 1937. (Selected and annotated.)

Green, Julien, *Paris* [1983], J.A. Underwood, trans, Marion Boyars, London and New York, 1993.

Gridley, Roy E., *The Brownings and France*, Athlone, London, 1982.

Guibert, Hervé, *My Parents* [1986], Liz Heron, trans, Serpent's Tail, London, 1993. **Extract 42.**

Guibert, Hervé, *To the Friend Who Did Not Save My Life* [1990], James Kirkup, trans, Quartet, London, 1995/Macmillan, New York, 1991.

Guppy, Shusha, *A Girl in Paris* [1990], Minerva, London, 1991. **Extract 14.**

Hemingway, Ernest, *A Moveable Feast* [1964], Arrow, London, 1994/Scribner, New York, 1987.

Hemingway, Ernest, *The Snows of Kilimanjaro and Other Stories*, Grafton, London, 1977/Scribner, New York, 1987. **Extract 6.**

Hemingway, Ernest, *The Sun Also Rises* [1926], Scribner, New York, 1984. As *Fiesta*, Arrow, London, 1994.

Hughes, Langston, *The Big Sea* [1940], Serpent's Tail, London, 1987.

Hugo, Victor, *The Last Day of a Condemned Man* [1829], G. Woollen, trans, Oxford University Press, Oxford, 1992.

Hugo, Victor, *Les Misérables* [1862], Norman Denny, trans, Penguin, London, 1982/C.E. Wilbur, trans, Random House, New York, 1980. **Extract 27.**

Hugo, Victor, *Notre Dame de Paris* [1831], A.J. Krailsheimer, trans, Oxford University Press, Oxford and New York, 1993. Also as *The Hunchback of Notre Dame*, J. Sturrock, trans, Penguin, London and New York, 1978.

Huysmans, J.-K., *Là-Bas: Down There* [1891], Robert Irwin, trans, Dedalus, Sawtry, 1993.

James, Henry, *The Ambassadors* [1903], Penguin, London and New York, 1986. **Extract 23.**

James, Henry, *The American* [1877], Norton, New York, 1978.

James, Henry, *Autobiography*, W.H. Allen, London, 1956. (Includes *A Small Boy and Others* and *Notes of a Son and Brother*.)

Jones, James, *The Merry Month of May*, Dell, New York, 1971.

Koestler, Arthur, *Scum of the Earth* [1941], Eland, London, 1991/Hippocrene Books, New York, NY, 1991.

Kundera, Milan, *Immortality* [1991, English edition], Peter Kussi, trans, Faber and Faber, London and Boston, 1992. **Extract 35.**

Lafayette, Madame de, *The Princesse de Clèves* [1678], Nancy Mitford, trans (rev L. Tancock), Penguin, London and New York, 1978.

Lautréamont, Comte de, *Maldoror* [1874], New Directions, New York, 1947.

Lautréamont, Comte de, *Maldoror and Poems*, P. Knight, trans, Penguin, London, 1978/Viking Penguin, New York, 1988.

Littlewood, Ian, *Paris: A Literary Companion*, John Murray, London, 1987.

Mansfield, Katherine, *The Collected Stories of Katherine Mansfield*, Penguin, London and New York, 1981. **Extract 28.**

Melly, George, *Paris and the Surrealists*, Thames and Hudson, London and New York, 1991.

Miller, Henry, *Quiet Days in Clichy* [1956], New English Library, London, 1983/Grove Press, New York, 1987.

Miller, Henry, *Tropic of Cancer* [1934], Panther, London, 1965/Grove Press, New York, 1987. **Extract 17.**

Mitford, Nancy, *The Blessing* [1951], Penguin, London, 1957/Carroll and Graf, New York, 1989. **Extract 4.**

Modiano, Patrick, *Honeymoon* [1990], Barbara Wright, trans, Harvill, London, 1992/Godine, New York, 1994. **Extract 40.**

Modiano, Patrick, *A Trace of Malice* [1988], A. Bell, trans, Ellis, London, 1995.

Morton, Brian N., *Americans in Paris*, Quill, New York, 1986.

Nin, Anaïs, *The Four-Chambered Heart* [1950], Virago, London, 1992/Ohio University Press, Athens, OH, 1959. **Extract 38.**

Nin, Anaïs, *Henry and June*, Penguin, London, 1990/Harcourt Brace, Orlando, FL, 1990.

Nin, Anaïs, *Journals, 1931–34*, Peter Owen, London, 1966/*The Diary of Anaïs Nin 1931–1934*, Harcourt Brace, Orlando, FL, 1966.

Nin, Anaïs, *Journals, 1934–1939*, Peter Owen, London, 1967/*The Diary of Anaïs Nin 1934–1939*, Harcourt Brace, Orlando, FL, 1967.

Orwell, George, *Down and Out in Paris and London* [1933], Penguin, London, 1975/Harcourt Brace, Orlando, FL, 1972. **Extract 25.**

Perec, Georges, *Life: A User's Manual* [1978], David Bellos, trans, Harvill, London, 1987/Godine, New York, 1988.

Perec, Georges, *Things: A Story of the Sixties* [1965] and *A Man Asleep* [1967], Andrew Leak, trans, Harvill, London, 1991/Godine, Boston, MA, 1990. **Extract 36.**

Pound, Ezra, *Selected Poems*, Faber and Faber, London, 1948/New Directions, New York, 1957. **Extract 15.**

Prévert, Jacques, *Selections from Paroles*, Lawrence Ferlinghetti, trans, Penguin, London, 1965/City Lights, San Francisco, CA, 1990. **Extract 5.**

Prévost, L'Abbé, *Manon Lescaut* [1731], Leonard Tancock, trans, Penguin, London, 1949/Viking Penguin, New York, 1988.

Proust, Marcel, *Remembrance of Things Past* [1913–1927], C.K. Scott

Moncrieff and Terence Kilmartin, trans, Penguin, London and New York, 1983. Vol 1 – *Swann's Way* and *Within a Budding Grove*; Vol 2 – *The Guermantes Way* and *Cities of the Plain*; Vol 3 – *The Captive, The Fugitive*, and *Time Regained*. **Extract 2.**

Queneau, Raymond, *Zazie in the Metro* [1959], Barbara Wright, trans, John Calder, London, 1982/ Riverrun Press, New York, 1982. **Extract 7.**

Rabelais, François, *Gargantua and Pantagruel* [1532–64], J.M. Cohen, trans, Penguin, London and New York, 1955.

Radiguet, Raymond, *Count D'Orgel's Ball* [1924], V. Schiff, trans, Marion Boyars, London, 1953/A. Cancogni, trans, Eridanos, New York, 1989.

Rhys, Jean, *Good Morning, Midnight* [1939], Penguin, London, 1969/ Harper and Row, New York, 1970.

Rhys, Jean, *Quartet* [1928], Penguin, London and New York, 1973. **Extract 21.**

Rhys, Jean, *Tigers Are Better-Looking*, Penguin, London and New York, 1972. (Includes selected stories from *The Left Bank*.)

Sagan, Françoise, *Aimez-Vous Brahms . . .* [1959], Peter Wiles, trans, Penguin, London and New York, 1962. **Extract 3.**

Sagan, Françoise, *Bonjour Tristesse* [1953], Irene Ash, trans, Penguin, London, 1958/NAL–Dutton, New York, 1983.

Sagan, Françoise, *A Certain Smile* [1956], Irene Ash, trans, Penguin, London and New York, 1960.

Sagan, Françoise, *The Leash* [1989], Christine Donougher, trans, Allsion and Busby, London, 1991.

Sagan, Françoise, *With Fondest Regards* [1984], Christine Donougher, trans, W.H. Allen, London, 1986/ NAL–Dutton, New York, 1985.

Sartre, Jean-Paul, *Iron in the Soul* [1949], Gerard Hopkins, trans, Penguin, London, 1985/also translated as *Troubled Sleep*, Vintage, New York, 1973. **Extract 26.**

Sawyer-Lauçanno, Christopher, *The Continual Pilgrimage: American Writers in Paris, 1944–1960*, Bloomsbury, London, 1992.

Signoret, Simone, *Nostalgia Isn't What It Used To Be* [1976], Weidenfeld, London, 1978.

Simenon, Georges, *Maigret's Memoirs* [1950], Jean Stewart, trans, Penguin, London, 1965/Harcourt Brace Jovanovich, Orlando, FL, 1985.

Simenon, Georges, *Maigret and the Saturday Caller* [1962], Tony White, trans, Penguin, London and New York, 1964. **Extract 18.**

Simenon, Georges, *Maigret Victorious: A Sixth Omnibus*, Hamish Hamilton, London, 1975 (includes *Maigret's Memoirs* and *Maigret and the Saturday Caller*).

Stein, Gertrude, *The Autobiography of Alice B. Toklas* [1933], Penguin, London and New York, 1966. **Extract 19.**

Stein, Gertrude, *Paris France: Personal Recollections* [1940], Peter Owen, London, 1995.

Strindberg, August, *Inferno and From an Occult Diary*, M. Sandbach, trans, Penguin, London and New York, 1979.

Sue, Eugène, *The Mysteries of Paris* [1842-43], Dedalus, Sawtry, 1988.

Süskind, Patrick, *Perfume* [1985], John E. Woods, trans, Penguin, London, 1987/Knopf, New York, 1987. **Extract 8.**

Thackeray, William Makepiece, *The Paris Sketch Book* [1840], Smith, Elder & Co, London, 1898.

Tournier, Michel, *The Golden Droplet* [1985], Barbara Wright, trans, Collins, London, 1987/Doubleday, New York, 1987.

Verlaine, Paul, *Selected Poems*, C.F. MacIntyre, trans, University of California Press, Berkeley, CA, 1948. **Extract 39.**

Waddell, Helen, *Peter Abelard* [1933], Constable, London, 1987/Viking Penguin, New York, 1976.

Wharton, Edith, *The Custom of the Country* [1913], Penguin, London, 1987/Macmillan, New York, 1976.

Wharton, Edith, *Madame de Treymes* [1907], Penguin, London, 1995/ *Madame de Treymes and Others*, Macmillan, New York, 1981.

Williams, William Carlos, *A Voyage to Pagany* [1928], New Directions, New York, 1970.

Wolfe, Thomas, *Of Time and the River* [1935], Macmillan, New York, 1976.

Zola, Émile, *L'Assommoir* [1877], Leonard Tancock, trans, Penguin, London and New York, 1970.

Zola, Émile, *The Beast in Man* (UK)/*La Bête Humaine* (US) [1890], L. Tancock, trans, Penguin, London and New York, 1977.

Zola, Émile, *The Belly of Paris* [1873], Ernest Alfred Vizetelly, trans, Sun & Moon Press, Los Angeles, CA, 1996.

Zola, Émile, *The Masterpiece* [1886], Alan Sutton, Gloucester, 1986/ University of Michigan Press, Ann Arbor, MI, 1968.

Zola, Émile, *Nana* [1880], George Holden, trans, Penguin, London, 1972.

Zola, Émile, *Thérèse Raquin* [1867], Leonard Tancock, trans, Penguin, London, 1962/Penguin, New York, 1962.

Extracts

(1) Alésia

Marie Cardinal, *The Words to Say It*

The cul-de-sac where Cardinal's narrator goes for her sessions of psychoanalysis is in the Alésia district of Paris (14th). In this extract, well into her long period of psychoanalysis, she is still unable to cope with everyday hassles but each experience leads to the opening of a new file in her memory.

One day, before going to the dead-end street, I had stopped my rusty, battered old jalopy in a clearly marked no-parking area. Only an errand to do, a package to pick up, I wouldn't be there for more than two minutes. It should be said that my car constituted a tolerable expenditure in my budget only so long as I had no repairs to make or fines to pay. So I took good care of it and tried to avoid any infraction.

I run, I pick up the package at full speed, I come back and see a policeman calmly writing out a parking ticket. I go up to him, my heart in my mouth. 'It was for my job. I've not been here five minutes.'

'License and registration, please.'

I hand him my papers, and at the same time start to cry like a baby. A crying jag, sobs, gulps, impossible to stop myself. The policeman gives me back my papers with the look of someone who refuses to be taken in. I bawl even harder.

'Will you pay the fine now or later?'

'Later.'

'OK, move on! That'll help you learn not to leave your car just anywhere.'

I get to the doctor's in a deplorable state. I stretch out on the couch, my face swollen with tears, sucking down mucus, because, of course, I forgot to bring a handkerchief, my throat painfully irritated, hard as a rock.

I started to tell my little story – the no parking area, the street to be crossed, the package to pick up, just a few seconds, and yet there is a policeman already there with his book of parking tickets. I complain of being broke, . . . of always being the scapegoat . . . of being unable to get people to love me, of not having a good personality, . . . of not being attractive physically. My mother was always saying to me, 'You are as ugly a louse.' 'Your eyes are like the holes in a blanket.' 'Your posture is bad, your feet are too big, fortunately you have pretty ears . . .'

My throat constricts and makes me suffer more. I have the impression that I can no longer swallow my saliva, it's difficult to breathe. I'm choking . . . I'm two or three years old, I am in the playroom of my childhood with my brother.

(2) Bois de Boulogne

Marcel Proust, *Swann's Way*

In this first volume of À la recherche du temps perdu, Proust's narrator Marcel describes an autumn walk through the Bois on his way to Versailles. The Bois de Boulogne is one of Marcel's favoured Parisian haunts – among the many memorable felicities of Proust's novel are the intricate and astonishingly evocative descriptions of its scenic charms and of its contemporary function as a gathering place for fashionable society.

That sense of the complexity of the Bois de Boulogne which makes it an artificial place and, in the zoological or mythological sense of the word, a Garden, came to me again this year as I crossed it on my way to Trianon, on one of those mornings early in November when, in Paris, if we stay indoors, being so near and yet excluded from the transformation scene of autumn, which is drawing so rapidly to a close without our witnessing it, we feel a veritable fever of yearning for the fallen leaves that can go so far as to keep us awake at night. Into my closed room they had been drifting already for a month, summoned there by my desire to see them, slipping between my thoughts and the object, whatever it might be, upon which I was trying to concentrate them, whirling in front of me like those brown spots that sometimes, whatever we may be looking at, will seem to be dancing or swimming before our eyes. And on that morning, no longer hearing the splash of the rain as on the preceding days, seeing the smile of fine weather at the corners of my drawn curtains, as at the corners of closed lips betraying the secret of their happiness, I had felt that I might be able to look at those yellow leaves with the light shining through them, in their supreme beauty; and being no more able to restrain myself from going to see the trees than, in my childhood days, when the wind howled in the chimney, I had been able to resist the longing to visit the sea, I had risen and left the house to go to Trianon via the Bois de Boulogne. It was the hour and the season in which the Bois seems, perhaps, most multiform, not only because it is the most subdivided, but because it is subdivided in a different way. Even in the unwooded parts, where the horizon is large, here and there against the background of a dark and distant mass of trees, now leafless or still keeping their summer foliage unchanged, a double row of orange-red chestnuts seemed, as in a picture just begun, to be the only thing painted so far by an artist who had not yet laid any colour on the rest, and to be offering their cloister, in full daylight, for the casual exercise of the human figures that would be added to the picture later on.

(3) BOIS DE BOULOGNE

Françoise Sagan, *Aimez-Vous Brahms . . .*

Love hurts, as Simon discovers in Sagan's typically sharp and perceptive novel about the choice faced by Paule, a 39-year-old career woman, between the romantic and much younger Simon and the less than romantic Roger, her lover for six years. In this passage, hope, youth, warmth are, like the lake in the Bois, victims of a chill in the air.

The lake in the Bois de Boulogne stretched icily before them under a cheerless sun; a hardy oarsman – one of those strange men one daily sees trying to preserve a figure which no one could possibly care about, so characterless is their appearance – was making a lone effort to resurrect the summer, his oar sending up an occasional spray of water, silvery, sparkling, and almost inopportune, so sadly did winter proclaim itself among the frozen shapes of the trees. She watched him tussling down in the boat, his brow puckered with determination. He would row round the island and come back exhausted and pleased with himself: she found a touch of symbolism in this short, obdurate, daily pull. Simon, beside her, was silent. He was waiting. She turned to him and smiled. He looked at her without returning her smile. The Paule for whom he had driven right across a province the night before (a Paule not merely available but naked and vanquished in his mind like the road he had driven along) had nothing in common with the tranquil Paule (she had been barely pleased to see him) who drowsed beside him on an iron bench in trite surroundings. He was disappointed and, misinterpreting his disappointment, he thought he did not love her any more. That obsessed week in the country, in that dreary house, had been a perfect example of the absurdities into which his imagination could lead him. Yet he could not repress this aching desire within him, this dizziness at the very thought of tilting her weary head against the back of the bench, thereby bruising the nape of her neck, and of lowering his lips on to those serene full lips from which had flowed, for two hours now, a stream of gracious, pacifying words which he had no wish to hear. She had written: 'Come back soon.' And more than his longing for these words he rued his delight in receiving them, his ridiculous feeling of joy, his confidence. He preferred having been unhappy for a worthwhile reason to being happy for a poor one. He told her so, and her eyes swung away from the oarsman to settle on him.

'*Mon petit Simon*, everyone feels that way: it's perfectly natural.'

(4) PLACE DE LA CONCORDE

Nancy Mitford, *The Blessing*

> *Sigi, the small but machiavellian son of Charles-Edouard and Grace, shows his extraordinary determination when he achieves his ambition of 'riding' the Marly horses. The horses mark the entrance to the Avenue des Champs-Élysées.*

The next day, after luncheon, Charles-Edouard and Sigi set out to walk to the Jockey Club, both feeling the need for a little fresh air after their various excesses of the previous night. They crossed the Place de la Concorde as only Frenchmen can, that is to say they sauntered through the traffic, chatting away, looking neither to right nor to left and assuming that the vehicles whizzing by would miss them, even if only by inches. (A miss is as good as a mile might be taken as their motto by French pedestrians.) The skirts of their coats were sometimes blown up by passing motors, but they were, in fact, missed, and reached the other side in safety. . . .

Some workmen were engaged upon Coustou's horses. The right-hand one was being cleaned and the other, with the arm of its groom over its back, still had a long ladder poised against the stone mane.

'Papa! Can I?'

Charles-Edouard looked round. There was nobody very near them, and no policeman nearer than the Concorde bridge.

'Do you know the words?'

'Yes. You'll hear, when I'm up there.'

'On your honour, Sigi?'

'*Honneur*,' he cried, taking off his coat, '*à la Grande Armée!*'

He nipped up the ladder and, clambering with the agility of a monkey on to the horse's back, began to chant: '*A la voix du vainqueur d'Austerlitz l'empire d'Allemagne tombe. La confédération du Rhin commence. Les royaumes de Wurtembourg et de Bavière sont crées. Venise se réunit a la couronne de fer, et l'Italie toute entière se range sous les lois de son libérateur. Honneur à la Grande Armée.*'

The motors in the Champs Elysées and Place de la Concorde began to draw into the side and stop while their occupants got out to have a better view of the charming sight.

'It must be for the cinema,' they said to each other. '*C'est trop joli.*'

And indeed the little boy, with his blue trousers, yellow jersey, and mop of bright black hair on the white horse, outlined against a dappled sky, made a fascinating picture. Charles-Edouard laughed out loud as he looked. Then, as several whistling policemen arrived on the spot, he decided to allow Sigismond to deal alone with the situation as it developed. He hailed a taxi and went home.

(5) Place de la Concorde

Jacques Prévert, *La Belle Saison*

Prévert managed to combine simplicity with subtlety and significance, and his accessibility made him an immensely popular poet. This short poem, here translated by Lawrence Ferlinghetti, is included in Prévert's anthology, Paroles. 'La Belle Saison' refers to the 'summer months', and, like the final line, gives added or alternative meaning to the opening words.

> Starved lost frozen
> Alone without a cent
> A girl of sixteen
> Standing still
> Place de la Concorde
> At noon August Fifteenth

(6) Place de la Contrescarpe

Ernest Hemingway, *The Snows of Kilimanjaro*

As he lies dying in Africa, the protagonist in Hemingway's short story remembers his past life in Paris, recalling all the stories he meant to write and now never will. Hemingway lived in rue Cardinal Lemoine when he first came to Paris and the area described here was well known to him. Like Hemingway, the narrator believes he had a room in the building in which Verlaine died. However, Hemingway's writing room was in rue Mouffetard and Verlaine died in nearby rue Descartes.

Around that *Place* there were two kinds; the drunkards and the sportifs. The drunkards killed their poverty that way; the sportifs took it out in exercise. They were the descendants of the Communards and it was no struggle for them to know their politics. They knew who had shot their fathers, their relatives, their brothers, and their friends when the Versailles troops came in and took the town after the Commune and executed anyone they could catch with calloused hands, or who wore a cap, or carried any other sign he was a working man. And in that poverty, and in that quarter across the street from a Boucherie Chevaline and a wine co-operative he had written the start of all he was to do. There never was another part of Paris that he loved like that, the sprawling trees, the old white plastered houses painted brown below, the long green of the autobus in that round square, the purple flower dye upon the paving, the sudden drop down the hill of the rue Cardinal Lemoine to the River, and the other way the narrow crowded world of the rue Mouffetard. The street that ran up toward the Panthéon and the other that he always took with the bicycle, the only asphalted street in all that quarter, smooth under the tires, with the high narrow houses and the cheap tall hotel where Paul Verlaine had died. There were only two rooms in the apartments where they lived and he had a room on the top floor of that hotel that cost him sixty francs a month where he did his writing, and from it he could see the roofs and chimney pots and all the hills of Paris.

(7) EIFFEL TOWER
Raymond Queneau, *Zazie in the Metro*

> *Zazie, on her first trip to Paris from the provinces and thwarted by a strike in her great ambition to ride the métro, surveys Paris from the Eiffel Tower. Her inexpert guides, uncle Gabriel and taxi driver Charles, point out the landmarks and Zazie discovers once again that things are not necessarily what they seem.*

'Ah, Paris,' cried Gabriel with greedy enthusiasm. 'Hey, Zazie,' he added abruptly, pointing at something a long way away, 'look!! the metro!!!'
'The metro?' said she.
She frowned.
'The elevated, of course,' said Gabriel blissfully.
Before Zazie had had time to bellyache he iksclaimed again:
'And that! over there!! look!!! The Panthéon!!!!'
'Tisn't the Panthéon,' said Charles, 'it's the Invalides.'
'You're not going to start all over again,' said Zazie.
'Oh go on,' cried Gabriel, 'so that isn't the Panthéon?'
'No, it's the Invalides,' replied Charles.
Gabriel turned in his direction and looked him in the cornea of the eyes: 'Are you sure about that,' he asks him, 'are you really so sure as all that?'
Charles didn't answer.
'What is there that you're absolutely sure about?' Gabriel insisted.
'I've got it,' Charles then roars, 'that thing there, tisn't the Invalides it's the Sacré-Coeur.'
'And you I suppose,' says Gabriel jovially, 'wouldn't by any chance be the sacred cow?'
'Little humorists your age,' says Zazie, 'give me the willies.'

After which they observed the orama in silence, then Zazie investigated what was going on some 300 metres below as the plumb line falls.

'Tisn't as high as all that,' Zazie remarked.

'All the same,' said Charles, 'you can only just make out the people.'

'Yes,' said Gabriel, sniffing, 'you can hardly see them but you can smell them just the same.'

'Less than in the metro,' said Charles.

'You never go in it,' said Gabriel. 'Nor do I, for that matter.'

Wishing to avoid this painful subject, Zazie said to her uncle:

'You aren't looking. Lean over, it's funny, you know.'

Gabriel made an attempt to cast an eye into the depths.

'Hell,' said he, retreating, 'it makes me giddy.'

He mopped his brow and gave off an aroma.

'Personally,' he adds, 'I'm going down. If you haven't had enough I'll wait for you on the ground floor.'

(8) LES HALLES
Patrick Süskind, *Perfume*

In the streets of 18th century Paris the young Grenouille glories in the smells that surround him. In this extract, he flares his extraordinary nostrils in the great market of Les Halles.

When he had smelled his fill of the thick gruel of the streets, he would go to airier terrain, where the odours were thinner, mixing with the wind as they unfurled, much as perfume does – to the market of Les Halles, for instance, where the odours of the day lived on into the evening, invisibly but ever so distinctly, as if the vendors still swarmed among the crowd, as if the baskets still stood there stuffed full of vegetables and eggs, or the casks full of wine and vinegar, the sacks with their spices and potatoes and flour, the crates of nails and screws, the meat tables, the tables full of cloth and dishes and shoe soles and all the hundreds of other things sold there during the day . . . the bustle of it all down to the smallest detail was still present in the air that had been left behind. Grenouille saw the whole market smelling, if it can be put that way. And he smelled it more precisely than many people could see it, for his perception was perception after the fact and thus of a higher order: an essence, a spirit of what had been, something undisturbed by the everyday accidents of the moment, like noise, glare or the nauseating press of living human beings.

(9) Rue Jacob

Colette, *Claudine in Paris*

The young Claudine, ill since her move from the country to Paris, is not overly impressed by the sights and sounds of the city she perceives from her father's apartment in rue Jacob (6th) – the street where Colette herself spent her early days in Paris.

I've begun to get interested in the noises in the courtyard. A big, depressing courtyard; at the far end of it, the backside of a black house. In the courtyard itself, the anonymous little buildings with tiled roofs . . . tiles like the ones you see in the country. A low dark door opens, I'm told, on the Rue Visconti. I've never seen anyone walking across this courtyard but workmen in blouses and sad, bare-headed women whose busts sag down towards their hips at every step in the way peculiar to worn-out drudges. A child plays there silently, invariably all by himself. I think he belongs to the concierge of this sinister block of flats. On the ground floor of our home – if I dare call it 'home', this square house full of people whom I don't know and instinctively dislike – a dirty servant-girl in a Breton coif punishes a poor little dog every morning. No doubt it misbehaves during the night in the kitchen, but oh how it yelps and it cries! Let that girl just wait till I'm well, she shall perish by my hand and no other! Lastly, every Thursday, a barrel-organ grinds out shocking love-songs from ten to eleven, and every Friday a pauper (they say a pauper here and not 'an unfortunate' as they do in Montigny), a real classic pauper with a white beard comes and declaims pathetically: 'Ladies and gentleman . . . remember . . . a pore unfortunate! . . . Can't hardly see at all! . . . He looks to your kind 'eartedness! . . . Ladies and gentlemen, please! (one, two, three . . .) . . . *if* you p-p-please!' All this in a little minor sing-song that ends up in the major. I make Mélie throw this venerable old man four sous out of the window; she grumbles and says that I spoil beggars.

(10) Left Bank, 1968

Lawrence Ferlinghetti, *Love in the Days of Rage*

Ferlinghetti's love story is set against the vivid background of the events of May 1968. Here he evokes both the euphoria of revolution and the accompanying disillusionment at its fragmentation.

On the thirteenth of May the general strike hit the city, with tens of thousands of students marching arm in arm with workers to the Place de la République, and if the Bastille had still been standing it would have been taken again, for now Paris was burning, the sweet, acrid smell of tear gas everywhere, scenes of desolation up and down the boulevards like battle scenes in the Liberation of Paris 1945, troops of helmeted police charging the massed demonstrators behind barricades of flaming cars. And at the end of the second week in May there was a great march to occupy the Theater of France at the Odéon, with famous poets, playwrights, professors, and editors side by side marching with the students up from the Métro Odéon, where they had met underground; so then at the Odéon another revolutionary free commune sprang into existence with day-and-night sessions on every conceivable subject from dope to free sex to de Gaulle and back again. But, elsewhere, what the Marxists called 'recuperation' had already set in, with the unions already stealing the ball away from the original student movement, and the Communist Party beginning to play its opportunist and reactionary role, preventing any real revolution by supporting existing organizations and law-and-order, as it did in every incipient revolution around the world in the sixties. This revolution would be *confiscated* from the students, as happened at the Renault plant, to which the students marched only to find that the unions had locked them out, and the communist unions especially distanced themselves more and more from the students, for the CP hated them because old fart Marx and his ideas had been severely rejected by the student movement, which was anarchist and Trotskyist and visionary, and the CP never really understood the students at all, for their romanticism was closer to Jean-Jacques Rousseau than to Marx. Still, the Odéon held out as the ongoing symbol of the original spirit of 'sixty-eight, the *agora*, the people's tribune where the young spirit spoke and sang.

(11) LEFT BANK, 1968

Mavis Gallant, *Paris Notebooks*

Canadian writer Gallant was unintentionally in the midst of the 'Events' of May 1968 – she lived on the Left Bank at the time. The following extract from her compelling journal of the period is part of her entry for 13 May, when the strikes, demonstrations and riots were in full swing.

On the Boulevard du Montparnasse, not a traffic policeman in sight. Students (I suppose they are) direct traffic. From about the Rue de Montparnasse on, considerable crowd collected on pavements. Reach intersection Saint-Michel-Montparnasse a little after five: Marchers pouring by, red flags, black flags. On a pole near me are a poster sign for the Gothic exhibition at the Louvre and a French flag. Demonstrator, young man, shinnies up, rips off the flag, lets it drop. I burst out, *'Ce n'est pas élégant!'* Am given some funny looks, but no one answers. Man in crowd picks flag up off the pavement, hangs it over the poster. In the middle of the road, small island for pedestrians. Make my way over to the traffic island between a wave of Anarchists and a ripple of North Vietnam supporters. Stand on step of traffic island, which means standing with one foot in front of the other, heel to toe, and hang on to *borne* with arm straight back from the shoulder. Remain in this position, with only minor shifts, until a quarter to nine. I can see straight down the Boulevard Saint-Michel. Nothing but people, a river running uphill. Red flags, black flags, flag of old Spanish Republic, flags I can't identify. Mixture of students and workers. ORTF (Office de Radiodiffusion-Télévision Française, the state-owned radio-TV organization), led by the critic Max-Pol Fouchet, who gets a hand. Hospital personnel, lawyers (small group), film stars – recognize Jean-Pierre Cassel, Michel Piccoli. Recognize film directors – all the New Wave, except for those still in Cannes. Helicopter overhead, the same helicopter that hovers over all demonstrations, making a count. I am joined by a nurse from the Pitié Hospital. Tells me she is on night duty but wanted to see this anyway. Confirms rumor that one student had a hand amputated, denies rumor about 'secret' deaths (ie, student deaths kept secret under police pressure) – says impossible to camouflage a death in a hospital. Tells me one or two things about the police. Confirms what I'd heard, but she is a calm girl and does not add imaginary trimmings. Truth quite enough. Yes, they continued to beat the wounded who were lying on stretchers. True that they would not let anyone be taken to hospital until they had checked that person's identity, no matter how serious the injury. We are joined by a *lycée* professor, woman of about forty, who has marched as far as Denfert-Rochereau and come back as a spectator. She holds a sign on a stick – 'À BAS LA REPRÉSSION POLICIÈRE', in rather wobbly capitals. Holds stick upside down and leans on it. Says she had been a Gaullist all her life until last Friday.

(12) Rue Lhomond

Honoré de Balzac, *Pere Goriot*

> *Demonstrating his sense of the significance of place, Balzac introduces his readers to the lodging house of Madame Vauquer, where Eugène de Rastignac first stays in Paris and which contrasts so vividly with the high-society lifestyle he covets. The rue Neuve-Sainte-Geneviève is now rue Lhomond (5th) – at the time Balzac was writing this area of Paris was obscure and squalid.*

The house which Madame Vauquer lets out as lodgings is her own property. It stands in the lower part of the Rue Neuve-Sainte-Geneviève, at the point where the ground drops to the Rue de l'Arbalète. Carriages rarely attempt this steep rough slope, so that comparative silence reigns in all the streets huddled between the Military Hospital and the Panthéon. The somber colors reflected from the cupolas of these two buildings darken the entire atmosphere of the place and impart a yellow tinge to the air. Here the pavements are dry, there is neither mud nor water in the gutters, grass grows along the walls. The spirits of the most carefree visitor droop with those of the passersby; the sound of a carriage is an event; the houses are sunk in gloom, the garden walls look like prisons. A Parisian losing his way here would see nothing but lodging houses and institutions, penury or boredom, old age declining into death, bright youth pressed into drudgery. In the whole of Paris there is no district more hideous; and none, we must add, more unknown. The Rue Neuve-Sainte-Geneviève in particular is like a bronze picture frame. It is the only frame suited to our story, for which the reader's mind must be prepared by dark colors and solemn thoughts: he must be made to feel like the traveler going down into the catacombs, the daylight fading step by step, the drone of the guide becoming steadily hollower. A true comparison! Who is to decide which is the grimmer sight: withered hearts, or empty skulls?

(13) Jardin du Luxembourg

John Evelyn, *Diary*

This description of the pleasures of the Luxembourg is from Evelyn's diary entry of 1 April 1644.

In sum, nothing is wanted to render this palace and gardens perfectly beautiful and magnificent; nor is it one of the least diversions to see the number of persons of quality, citizens and strangers, who frequent it, and to whom all access is freely permitted, so that you shall see some walks and retirements full of gallants and ladies; in others, melancholy friars; in others, studious scholars; in others, jolly citizens, some sitting or lying on the grass, others running and jumping; some playing at bowls and ball, others dancing and singing; and all this without the least disturbance, by reason of the largeness of the place.

(14) Jardin du Luxembourg

Shusha Guppy, *A Girl in Paris*

Guppy, a Persian student in Paris in the 1950s, describes one of her favourite Left Bank memories.

The Alliance Française was on boulevard Raspail, and I could walk to it in twenty minutes by taking a short-cut through the Luxembourg Gardens. Every morning I set off at 8.30, entered the garden by the main door on the boulevard, walked down the wide central alley, then took a diagonal route along the chestnut avenues and emerged near my destination. Sometimes on the way back I would change my itinerary to explore various parts of the park, walk past the Children's Corner and its merry-go-round, the English Garden, linger by the pond or sit awhile by the Médicis Fountain. I had seen postcards of the Luxembourg Gardens in Persia, old ones in which the women had long dresses, large hats and parasols, and the men frock coats, top-hats and canes – and new ones sent by friends. I had glimpsed them in French movies, and I had read about them in novels. I visualized Cosette, in *Les Misérables*, sitting on a bench, Gavroche skipping along merrily, his *képi* rakishly tilted back, poets like Victor Hugo, Vigny, Verlaine, Musset sauntering along the shaded paths with their Muses, real or invisible. I imagined their ghosts forever haunting the darker corners, the breeze whispering their poems, their statues coming to life at night to roam about the moonlit flowerbeds and lawns.

I remembered all this as I walked that first cloudy November morning. The gardens were empty, except for a few students hurrying towards various

Faculties in the area. Here and there an early-rising park attendant half-heartedly swept the last decaying leaves and shovelled them into his wheelbarrow. The trees were already denuded, their branches charcoal drawings against the milky sky. In the months that followed I walked through the gardens daily and witnessed their changes, reflecting each season and Nature's cycle of death and resurrection. Soon the first snows covered the ground and turned the naked branches into crystalline coral sprays; later it melted away, unveiling the snowdrops and crocuses on the ground and the buds on the trees. Then one day suddenly it was summer and ablaze with flowers . . .

Later I visited other parks, both in Paris and around it. Many, like Versailles, are far grander and more beautiful, but whenever I am in Paris it is to the Luxembourg Gardens that I am drawn by some invisible melancholy thread of memory.

(15) THE MÉTRO

Ezra Pound, *In a Station of the Metro*

This Imagist piece was originally published in the collection Lustra in 1916. Perhaps not quite appropriate to the well lighted and tiled Métro stations of the 1990s, it nevertheless retains its emotive power.

The apparition of these faces in the crowd;
Petals on a wet, black bough.

(16) CITÉ MONTHIERS

Jean Cocteau, *Les Enfants Terribles*

Cocteau opens his strange story with a description of Cité Monthiers, an alley in the 9th where he himself played as a schoolboy. The secret rites of the schoolchildren and their deliberate alienation from the adult world foretell the isolation and internecine relationships of the four adolescent protagonists which are to be the focus of the novel.

That portion of old Paris known as the Cité Monthiers is bounded on the one side by the rue de Clichy, on the other by the rue d'Amsterdam. Should you choose to approach it from the rue de Clichy, you would come to a pair of wrought iron gates: but if you were to come by way of the rue d'Amsterdam, you would reach another entrance, open day and night, and giving access, first to a block of tenements, and then to the courtyard proper, an oblong court containing a row of small private dwellings secretively disposed beneath the flat towering walls of the main structure. Clearly these little houses must be the abode of artists. The windows are blind, covered with photographers' drapes, but it is comparatively easy to guess what they conceal: rooms chock-a-block with weapons and lengths of brocade, with canvases depicting basketfuls of cats, or the families of Bolivian diplomats. Here dwells the Master, illustrious, unacknowledged, well-nigh prostrated by the weight of his public honours and commissions, with all this dumb provincial stronghold to seal him from disturbance.

Twice a day, however, at half past ten in the morning and four o'clock in the afternoon, the silence is shattered by a sound of tumult. The doors of the little Lycée Condorcet, opposite number 72b rue d'Amsterdam, open, and a horde of schoolboys emerges to occupy the Cité and set up their headquarters. Thus it has re-assumed a sort of medieval character – something in the nature of a Court of Love, a Wonder Fair, an Athletes' Stadium, a Stamp Exchange; also a gangsters' tribune cum place of public execution; also a breeding-ground for rags – rags to be hatched out finally in class, after long incubation, before the incredulous eyes of the authorities. Terrors they are, these lads, and no mistake – the terrors of the Fifth. A year from now, having become the Fourth, they will have shaken the dust of the rue d'Amsterdam from their shoes and swaggered into the rue Caumartin with their four books bound with a strap and a square of felt in lieu of a satchel.

But now they are in the Fifth, where the tenebrous instincts of childhood still predominate: animal, vegetable instincts, almost indefinable because they operate in regions below conscious memory, and vanish without trace, like some of childhood's griefs; and also because children stop talking when grown-ups draw nigh. They stop talking, they take on the aspect of beings of a different order of creation – conjuring themselves at will an instantaneous coat of bristles or assuming the bland passivity of some form of plant life. Their rites are obscure, inexorably secret; calling, we know, for infinite cunning, for ordeal by fear and torture; requiring victims, summary executions, human sacrifices.

(17) RUE DU FAUBOURG MONTMARTRE

Henry Miller, *Tropic of Cancer*

Miller's narrator in this autobiographical novel describes the Rue du Faubourg Montmartre as he saw it in the 1930s.

And I know what a devil's street is the Faubourg Montmartre with its brass plates and rubber goods, the lights twinkling all night and sex running through the street like a sewer. To walk from the Rue Lafayette to the boulevard is like running the gauntlet; they attach themselves to you like barnacles, they eat into you like ants, they coax, wheedle, cajole, implore, beseech, they try it out in German, English, Spanish, they show you their torn hearts and their busted shoes, and long after you've chopped the tentacles away, long after the fizz and sizzle has died out, the fragrance of the *lavabo* clings to your nostrils – it is the odor of the *Parfum de Danse* whose effectiveness is guaranteed only for a distance of twenty centimeters. One could piss away a whole lifetime in that little stretch between the boulevard and the Rue Lafayette. Every bar is alive, throbbing, the dice loaded; the cashiers are perched like vultures on their high stools and the money they handle has a human stink to it. There is no equivalent in the Banque de France for the blood money that passes currency here, the money that glistens with human sweat, that passes like a forest fire from hand to hand and leaves behind it a smoke and stench. A man who can walk through the Faubourg Montmartre at night without panting or sweating, without a prayer or a curse on his lips, a man like that has no balls, and if he has, then he ought to be castrated.

(18) MONTMARTRE

Georges Simenon, *Maigret and the Saturday Caller*

Maigret walks down to the Place des Abbesses after a visit to Madame Planchon (whose husband has told Maigret he intends to murder her) in the rue Tholozé. As in so much of his writing, Simenon reveals his intimate knowledge of the quartier he describes.

Planchon's wife had not asked him to take off his coat, so Maigret had remained nearly an hour that way in the overheated house. Out now in the fine drizzle, which seemed to be composed of invisible ice-crystals, the coldness gripped him. Ever since his Sunday walk in the same district, he had felt that he was starting a cold, and this was what gave him the idea, instead of going down the Rue Lepic to find a taxi in the Place Blanche, of turning left towards the Place des Abbesses.

This was where the decorator had telephoned him from on the Monday evening. It was the last time they had been in touch.

The Place des Abbesses, with its Métro station, the Théâtre de l'Atelier, which looked like a toy or a stage set, and its bistros and small shops, seemed to the Inspector far more the genuine working-class Montmartre than the Place du Tertre, which had become a tourist trap, and he remembered that when he had first discovered it, shortly after his arrival in Paris, one chilly morning in spring sunshine, he had felt he had been transported into a picture by Utrillo.

It was swarming with ordinary people, people from the surrounding areas, coming and going, like a big town on market day, and it was also as if there were some family link between them, as if in some village.

He knew, from experience, that some of the older people had never in fact set foot outside the area and that there were still shops that had been handed down from father to son for several generations.

He looked through the windows of several bistros before he noticed, on a tobacco counter, a small cash register which seemed new.

Remembering the noises he had heard during his conversation with Planchon, he went in.

It was nice and warm inside, with a homely smell of wine and cooking. The tables, seven or eight at the most, were covered with paper table-cloths, and a slate announced that there were sausages and mash for lunch.

Two builders in overalls were already eating at the far end. The proprietress, dressed in black, was sitting at a desk against a background of cigarettes, cigars and lottery tickets.

A waiter, his sleeves rolled up to the elbows and wearing a blue apron, was serving wine and apéritifs at the counter.

There were about ten people drinking and they all turned to look at him. There was a fairly long silence before they started talking again.

'A hot rum,' he ordered.

(19) MONTMARTRE

Gertrude Stein,
The Autobiography of Alice B. Toklas

In 1907, Gertrude Stein and Alice B. Toklas visit a young painter called Picasso in Montmartre. The wooden building referred to was the 'Bateau Lavoir' on place Émile-Goudeau, in which many now-famous artists rented space. It burned down in 1970.

Gertrude Stein and I about ten days later went to Montmartre, I for the first time. I have never ceased to love it. We go there every now and then and I always have the same tender expectant feeling that I had then. It is a place where you were always standing and sometimes waiting, not for anything to happen, but just standing. The inhabitants of Montmartre did not sit much, they mostly stood which was just as well as the chairs, the dining room chairs of France, did not tempt one to sit. So I went to Montmartre and I began my apprenticeship of standing. We first went to see Picasso and then we went to see Fernande. Picasso now never likes to go to Montmartre, he does not like to think about it much less talk about it. Even to Gertrude Stein he is hesitant about talking of it, there were things that at that time cut deeply into his spanish pride and the end of his Montmartre life was bitterness and disillusion, and there is nothing more bitter than spanish disillusion.

But at this time he was in and of Montmartre and lived in the rue Ravignan.

We went to the Odéon and there got into an omnibus, that is we mounted on top of an omnibus, the nice old horse-pulled omnibuses that went pretty quickly and steadily across Paris and up the hill to the Place Blanche. There we got out and climbed a steep street lined with shops with things to eat, the rue Lepic, and then turning we went around a corner and climbed even more steeply in fact almost straight up and came to the rue Ravignan, now Place Emile-Gondeau but otherwise unchanged, with its steps leading up to the little flat square with its few but tender little trees, a man carpentering in the corner of it, the last time I was there not very long ago there was still a man carpentering in a corner of it, and a little café just before you went up the steps where they all used to eat, it is still there, and to the left the low wooden building of studios that is still there.

(20) Montparnasse

James Baldwin, *Giovanni's Room*

Preparing to end his gay relationship with Giovanni, and anxious to reassert for himself his attraction to women, Baldwin's troubled narrator goes to Montparnasse in search of solace and sex.

I felt elated yet, as I walked down Raspail toward the cafes of Montparnasse, I could not fail to remember that Hella and I had walked here, Giovanni and I had walked here. And with each step, the face that glowed insistently before me was not her face, but his. I was beginning to wonder how he would take my news. I did not think he would fight me but I was afraid of what I would see in his face. I was afraid of the pain I would see there. But even this was not my real fear. My real fear was buried and was driving me to Montparnasse. I wanted to find a girl, any girl at all.

But the terraces seemed oddly deserted. I walked along slowly, on both sides of the street, looking at the tables. I saw no one I knew. I walked down as far as the *Closerie des Lilas* and I had a solitary drink there. I read my letters again. I thought of finding Giovanni at once and telling him I was leaving him but I knew he would not yet have opened the bar and he might be almost anywhere in Paris at this hour. I walked slowly back up the boulevard. Then I saw a couple of girls, French whores, but they were not very attractive. I told myself that I could do better than *that*. I got to the *Select* and sat down. I watched the people pass, and I drank. No one I knew appeared on the boulevard for the longest while.

The person who appeared, and whom I did not know very well, was a girl named Sue, blonde and rather puffy, with the quality, in spite of the fact that she was not pretty, of the girls who are selected each year to Miss Rheingold. She wore her curly blonde hair cut very short, she had small breasts and a big behind, and, in order, no doubt, to indicate to the world how little she cared for appearance or sensuality, she almost always wore tight blue jeans. I think she came from Philadelphia and her family was very rich. Sometimes, when she was drunk, she reviled them, and, sometimes, drunk in another way, she extolled their virtues of thrift and fidelity. I was both dismayed and relieved to see her. The moment she appeared I began, mentally, to take off all her clothes.

'Sit down,' I said. 'Have a drink.'

(21) MONTPARNASSE

Jean Rhys, *Quartet*

Marya, the protagonist of this concise and atmospheric novel, walks the streets and sits in the cafés that Rhys herself knew well. The Lion de Belfort is on place Denfert-Rochereau. The avenue d'Orléans is now avenue du Leclerc.

It was a foggy afternoon, with a cold sharpness in the air. Outside, the street lamps were lit. 'It might be London,' thought Marya. The Boulevard Arago, like everything else, seemed unreal, fantastic, but also extraordinarily familiar, and she was trying to account for this mysterious impression of familiarity.

She felt cold when she reached the Avenue d'Orléans and walked into a bar for some hot coffee. The place was empty save for a big man who was sitting opposite drinking a demi of dark beer. He stared at Marya steadily and heavily as he drank, and when she took Stephan's letter and reread it he thought: 'Doubtless a rendezvous.'

'My lawyer didn't know his métier. Instead of defending me he told the court that I knew six languages. A stupid affair at Brussels was referred to. This did me in quite . . .'

A stupid affair at Brussels. But when she tried to think this out her tired brain would only conjure up disconnected remembrances of Brussels: waiters in white jackets bearing aloft tall, slim glasses of beer, the Paris trains clanking into the dark station, the sun on the red-striped umbrellas in the flower market, the green trees of the Avenue Louise.

She sat there, smoking cigarette after cigarette, long after the large man had disappeared. Every time that the door of the café swung open to admit a customer she saw the crimson lights of the tobacco shop opposite and the crimson reflection on the asphalt and she began to picture the endless labyrinth of the Paris streets, glistening hardly, crowded with hurrying people. But now she thought of them without fear, rather with a strange excitement.

'What's the use of worrying about things?' she asked herself. I don't care. I'm sick of being sad.'

She came out of the café and stood for several minutes looking at the Lion de Belfort fair – the booths, the swings, the crowds of people jostling each other in a white glare of light to the gay, metallic music of the merry-go-rounds.

(22) Rue Mouffetard

Kay Boyle, *My Next Bride*

*Victoria, a young American woman learning life the hard way in
1930s Paris, is taken by Antony Lister, a charismatic and
unpredictable artist who has told her he loves her, to the busy Rue
Mouffetard in the Latin Quarter so that he can buy a new set of
clothes, get rid of his expensive suit and thus, he hopes, shed his old
life for a new one.*

The rue Mouffetard ran down as if going to the sea, cobbled like a village
street, and even at ten at night it was alive with lights in the shop-windows
and thronged with people moving up and down it, buying the food for Sunday
and carrying their full market *filets* home. If you walked in the middle, the
places on either side were close enough to touch, with their crocks and their
china set out on the sidewalk, their ropes and their serpents of sausage hanging
in festoons, their winter apples and pears nesting in brittle, glassy straw, their
eggs by the dozens tasteless and cold as billiard balls; here was the stench of
honest people's flesh and food, and refuse in the gutters so profuse and richly
intermingled that it was like a south wind blowing. The meat in the butcher
shops stood unbleeding on the marble slabs (having been packed in Argen-
tine), the smooth columns of butter were cut by wires thinner than a hair, and
overhead the working-men's coats and trousers and aprons flapped for sale,
lifeless as hung men jerking by their gullets.

'Whenever you see me, let me know,' said Antony. He was holding her arm
fast in the bend of his arm. Across the narrow avenue of night which ran
between the houses beat the banners and pennants of clothing in a grotesque
mimicry of taken life on the air.

'I like it here,' Victoria said, and they went down the rue Mouffetard
together. All about, as if they were swimming in it, was the uneven diverse
melody of these voices of the others, these people without leisure who walked
on the dry, summery cobbles on Saturday night without complaint. 'Maybe
New Orleans is like this,' Victoria said, watching the people pause and dawdle
and meander. They were not gay, but the women's heads were bare to
February and they were slow enough in their choosing for this to be a summer
evening in a southern town. Around the corner, bleak with winter, Paris was
hiding in the dark.

(23) NOTRE-DAME

Henry James, *The Ambassadors*

James's protagonist Lambert Strether seeks refuge from his struggles with himself and the complications of his role as an 'ambassador' in the cool shade of Notre-Dame.

He was aware of having no errand in such a place but the desire not to be, for the hour, in certain other places; a sense of safety, of simplification, which each time he yielded to it he amused himself by thinking of as a private concession to cowardice. The great church had no altar for his worship, no direct voice for his soul; but it was none the less soothing even to sanctity; for he could feel while there what he couldn't elsewhere, that he was a plain tired man taking the holiday he had earned. He was tired, but he wasn't plain – that was the pity and the trouble of it; he was able, however, to drop his problem at the door very much as if it had been the copper piece that he deposited, on the threshold, in the receptacle of the inveterate blind beggar. He trod the long dim nave, sat in the splendid choir, paused before the clustered chapels of the east end, and the mighty monument laid upon him its spell. He might have been a student under the charm of a museum – which was exactly what, in a foreign town, in the afternoon of life, he would have liked to be free to be. This form of sacrifice did at any rate for the occasion as well as another; it made him quite sufficiently understand how, within the precinct, for the real refugee, the things of the world could fall into abeyance. That was the cowardice, probably – to dodge them, to beg the question, not to deal with it in the hard outer light; but his own oblivions were too brief, too vain, to hurt anyone but himself, and he had a vague and fanciful kindness for certain persons whom he met, figures of mystery and anxiety, and whom, with observation for his pastime, he ranked as those who were fleeing from justice. Justice was outside, in the hard light, and injustice too; but one was as absent as the other from the air of the long aisles and the brightness of the many altars.

(24) PARIS: DAYBREAK

Charles Baudelaire, from *Morning Twilight*

'Morning Twilight' is in the 'Tableaux Parisiens' section of Les Fleurs du Mal, published in 1861. The poet sees his city under attack from industrialization, poverty and overcrowding and here portrays the dawning of a new day as if waking into a nightmare.

Smoke went up here and there as homely fires were fed
Women of pleasure, dull and bleary eyed,
Slept in a stupor, gross lips gaping wide.
Poor, shrunken women bent rheumatic arms,
Blew on infusions, blew upon their palms.

It was the hour when cold and landlord's gain
Persecute women in pre-natal pain.
Far off, like sobs cut short by frothing blood,
A cock's crow ripped apart the misty flood.
The fog drenched all the buildings like a sea,
Moribund rejects of society
Hiccuped their last death rattles, out of sight.
Dissolute men reached home, disrupted in the night.

Shivering dawn, attired in rose and green
Moved slow across the Seine's deserted scene.
Dismal, laborious, blinking through the murk,
Old Paris grabbed his tools and set to work.

(25) PARIS: DISHWASHING

George Orwell, *Down and Out in Paris and London*

Orwell describes his experiences as a plongeur (washer-up) in a new restaurant in rue du Commerce in 1929. Despite the appalling squalor and inefficiency in the kitchen, the restaurant was, according to Orwell, quite successful.

The cook's working hours were from eight in the morning till midnight, and mine from seven in the morning till half past twelve the next morning – seventeen and a half hours, almost without a break. We never had time to sit down till five in the afternoon, and even then there was no seat except the top of the dustbin. Boris, who lived near by and had not to catch the last Métro home, worked from eight in the morning till two the next morning – eighteen hours a day, seven days a week. Such hours, though not usual, are nothing extraordinary in Paris.

Life settled at once into a routine that made the Hôtel X seem like a holiday. Every morning at six I drove myself out of bed, did not shave, sometimes washed, hurried up to the Place d'Italie and fought for a place on the Métro. By seven I was in the desolation of the cold, filthy kitchen, with the potato skins and bones and fishtails littered on the floor, and a pile of plates, stuck together in their grease, waiting from overnight. I could not start on the plates yet, because the water was cold, and I had to fetch milk and make coffee, for the others arrived at eight and expected to find coffee ready. Also, there were always several copper saucepans to clean. Those copper saucepans are the bane of a *plongeur's* life. They have to be scoured with sand and bunches of chain, ten minutes to each one, and then polished on the outside with Brasso. Fortunately, the art of making them has been lost and they are gradually vanishing from French kitchens, though one can still buy them second-hand.

When I had begun on the plates the cook would take me away from the plates to begin skinning onions, and when I had begun on the onions the *patron* would arrive and send me out to buy cabbages. When I came back with the cabbages the *patron's* wife would tell me to go to some shop half a mile away and buy a pot of rouge; by the time I came back there would be more vegetables waiting, and the plates were still not done. In this way our incompetence piled one job on another throughout the day, everything in arrears.

(26) Paris, 1940

Jean-Paul Sartre, *Iron in the Soul*

Sartre effectively conveys the sense of change and loss that accompanied the fall of Paris to the Germans. The familiar has become unfamiliar, the life energy of the city has drained away.

Nobody on the Boulevard Saint-Germain: in the Rue Danton, nobody. The iron shutters had not even been lowered. The windows glittered. The proprietors had just removed the handles from the doors – and gone. It was Sunday. For the last three days it had been Sunday. The whole week now, in Paris, consisted of one day, a ready-made, colourless sort of day, rather stiffer than usual, rather more synthetic, over-marked by silence, and already filled by a secretly working rot. Daniel approached a large shop (knitted goods and textiles); the multicoloured balls of wool, arranged in pyramids, were in the process of turning yellow. They smelt of old age. In the establishment next door a display of baby-linen and ladies' blouses was fading rapidly. White dust was accumulating, like flour, upon the shelves. The plate-glass was stained with long white streaks. Daniel thought – 'The windows are weeping.' Behind them all was festival. Flies were buzzing in their millions. Sunday. When the Parisians returned they would find their dead city motionless beneath the weight of a stagnant Sunday. *If they return!* Daniel gave free reign to that irresistible desire to laugh which had been with him all morning as he stalked the streets. *If they return.*

The tiny square of Saint-André-des-Arts lay abandoned in the sunlight, lifeless. Black night reigned in the heart of noon. The sun was a fake; a magnesium flare concealing darkness. In a split second it would go out. He pressed his face to one of the big windows of the Brasserie Alsacienne. I lunched here with Mathieu. That had been in February, when Mathieu was on leave. It had been swarming with heroes and angels. After a while he managed to distinguish in the darkness of the interior a number of ambiguous blotches, mushrooms growing in a cellar. They were paper napkins. Where are the heroes? Where are the angels? There were still two iron chairs on the terrace: Daniel took one of them by its back, carried it to the edge of the pavement, and sat down, a gentleman of leisure beneath the military sky, in a white glare that was alive with childhood memories. At his back he could feel the magnetic pressure of silence. He looked at the empty bridge, at the padlocked book-boxes on the quay, at the clock-face that had no hands. 'They should have knocked all this about a bit,' he thought: 'dropped a few bombs, just to make us realize what was what.' A shadow slipped past the Prefecture of Police on the further bank of the Seine, as though on a moving roadway. Paris was not, strictly speaking, empty. It was peopled by little broken scraps of time that sprang here and there to life, to be almost immediately absorbed again into this radiance of eternity. 'The city is hollow' – thought Daniel.

(27) Paris: Sewers

Victor Hugo, *Les Misérables*

In one of his many entertaining digressions, in this case as a preamble to his hero Jean Valjean's flight through the sewers of Paris, Hugo sees the sewers as both metaphor for the dark underside of the city's life and the place where truth is stripped of all pretension and laid bare.

The sewer, in ancient Paris, is the resting-place of all failure and all effort. To political economy it is a detritus, and to social philosophy a residue. It is the conscience of the town where all things converge and clash. There is darkness here, but no secrets. Everything has its true or at least its definitive form. There is this to be said for the muck-heap, that it does not lie. Innocence dwells in it. The mask of Basil is there, the cardboard and the strings, accented with honest filth; and beside it, the false nose of Scapin. Every foulness of civilization, fallen into disuse, sinks into that ditch of truth wherein ends the huge social down-slide, to be swallowed, but to spread. It is a vast confusion. No false appearance, no white-washing, is possible; filth strips off its shirt in utter starkness, all illusions and mirages scattered, nothing left except what is, showing the ugly face of what ends. Reality and disappearance: here, a bottleneck proclaims drunkenness, a basket-handle tells of home life; and there the apple-core that had literary opinions again becomes an apple-core. The face on the coin turns frankly green, the spittle of Caiaphas encounters the vomit of Falstaff, the gold piece from the gaming house rattles against the nail from which the suicide hung, a livid foetus is wrapped in the spangles which last Shrove Tuesday danced at the Opéra, a wig which passed judgement on men wallows near the decay which was the skirt of Margoton. It is more than fraternity, it is close intimacy. That which was painted is besmeared. The last veil is stripped away. A sewer is a cynic. It says everything.

(28) PARIS: A STUDIO APARTMENT

Katherine Mansfield, *Feuille d'Album*

*The enigmatic young artist at the centre of this short story leads a
quiet life in his Paris atelier.*

He lived at the top of a tall mournful building overlooking the river. One of
those buildings that look so romantic on rainy nights and moonlight nights,
when the shutters are shut, and the heavy door, and the sign advertising 'a
little apartment to let immediately' gleams forlorn beyond words. One of those
buildings that smell so unromantic all the year round, and where the concierge
lives in a glass cage on the ground floor, wrapped up in a filthy shawl, stirring
something in a saucepan and ladling out tit-bits to the swollen old dog lolling
on a bead cushion . . . Perched up in the air the studio had a wonderful view.
The two big windows faced the water; he could see the boats and the barges
swinging up and down, and the fringe of an island planted with trees, like a
round bouquet. The side window looked across to another house, shabbier and
still smaller, and down below there was a flower market. You could see the
tops of huge umbrellas, with frills of bright flowers escaping from them, booths
covered with striped awning where they sold plants in boxes and clumps of wet
gleaming palms in terracotta jars. Among the flowers the old women scuttled
from side to side, like crabs. Really there was no need for him to go out. If he
sat at the window until his white beard fell over the sill he still would have
found something to draw . . .

How surprised those tender women would have been if they had managed to
force the door. For he kept his studio as neat as a pin. Everything was arranged
to form a pattern, a little 'still life' as it were – the saucepans with their lids on
the wall behind the gas stove, the bowl of eggs, milk-jug and teapot on the
shelf, the books and the lamp with the crinkly paper shade on the table. An
Indian curtain that had a fringe of red leopards marching round it covered his
bed by day, and on the wall beside the bed on a level with your eyes when you
were lying down there was a small neatly printed notice: GET UP AT ONCE.

(29) PARIS: SUBURBS

Louis-Ferdinand Céline,
Journey to the End of the Night

*Through his narrator Bardamu, Céline presents a characteristically
splenetic view of life in a poor dismal suburb, no doubt like
Courbevoie where he was born, and the numbing effects of poverty,
laced with his unique brand of black humour.*

Everybody coughed in my street. It keeps you busy. To see the sun you have to
climb up to Sacré-Coeur at least, because of the smoke.

From up there you get a beautiful view; then you realize that way down at
the bottom of the plain it's us and the houses we live in. But if you try to pick

out any particular place, everything you see is so ugly, so uniformly ugly, that you can't find it.

Still further down it's always the Seine, winding from bridge to bridge like an elongated blob of phlegm.

When you live in Rancy you don't even realize how sad you've become. You simply stop feeling like doing anything much. What with scrimping and going without this and that, you stop wanting anything.

For months I borrowed money right and left. The people were so poor and so suspicious in my neighborhood that they couldn't make up their minds to send for me before dark, though I was the cheapest doctor imaginable. I spent nights and nights crossing little moonless courtyards in quest of ten or fifteen francs.

In the morning there was such a beating of carpets the whole street sounded like one big drum.

One morning I met Bébert on the sidewalk; his aunt, the concierge, was out shopping, and he was holding down the lodge for her. He was raising a cloud from the sidewalk with a broom.

Anybody who didn't raise dust at seven o'clock in the morning in those parts would get himself known all up and down the street, as an out-and-out pig. Carpet-beating was a sign of cleanliness, good housekeeping. Nothing more was needed. Your breath could stink all it liked, no matter. Bébert swallowed all the dust he raised in addition to what was sent down from the upper floors. Still, a few spots of sunlight reached the street, but like inside a church, pale, muffled, mystic.

Bébert had seen me coming, I was the neighborhood doctor who lived near the bus stop. Bébert had the greenish look of an apple that would never get ripe. He was scratching himself, and watching him made me want to scratch too. The fact is I had fleas myself, I'd caught them from patients during the night. They like to jump on your overcoat, because its the warmest and dampest place available. You learn that in medical school.

Bébert abandoned his carpet to come and say good morning. From every window they watched us talking.

If you've got to love something, you'll be taking less of a chance with children than with grownups, you'll at least have the excuse of hoping they won't turn out as crummy as the rest of us. How are you to know?

(30) Père Lachaise

Samuel Beckett, *Dream of Fair to Middling Women*

A slim reference to the Père Lachaise cemetery admittedly, but Beckett never stays in the same place for longer than a sentence in this humorous, allusive and high-energy novel, written at the Trianon Hotel in rue de Vaugirard in 1932.

But Liebert and the Syra-Cusa were a cursed nuisance. How can we bring ourselves to speak of Liebert? Oh he was a miserable man. He was a persecution. He would come in in the morning, at the first weals of dawn, and drag the bedclothes off the innocent Belacqua. What did he want? That is what is so hard to understand. Nothing would do him but to elucidate Valéry. He declaimed Valerian abominations of his own.

'He is the illegitimate cretin' said Belacqua, worn out, behind his back one fine day to the scandalised Lucien, 'of Mrs Beeton and Philippus Bombastus von Hohenheim.'

Lucien recoiled. Because every one that knew the man thought he was wonderful. He appeared one night with a portable gramophone and put on the . . . the Kleine Nachtmusik and then Tristan and *insisted on turning out the light.* That was the end of that. Belacqua could not be expected to see him any more after that. But ill will was a thing that Liebert could not bear. Malevolent he could not bear to be. So when he went to England he quoted Belacqua as his bosom butty, ami unique and all the rest. And he picked up a slick English universitaire (hockey and Verlaine) in the provinces somewhere, she was a she-woman to her finger-tips, and by heaven he had to marry her. Belacqua laffed and laffed. He remembered how Liebert used to visit Musset in the Père Lachaise and sitting by the tomb make notes for a meditation and then come home in the bus and pull out photographs of the current pucelle who was so wonderful (elle est adorable, oh elle est formidable, oh elle est tout à fait sidérante) and who drove him so crazy and had such a powerful effect on him and gave him such a lift. He detailed the powerful effect, he set forth the lift, with piscatorial pantomime. A truly miserable man.

(31) Pont Neuf

Anatole France, *The Gods Will Have Blood*

France's novel of the Revolution starts in spring 1793 and ends with the downfall of Robespierre. Its central story concerns Évariste Gamelin, a young artist whose ideals lead him to become an icy instrument of the Terror. France achieves a vivid evocation of Paris in the grips of Revolutionary fanaticism where people still carry on with their everyday lives.

There the glazier's wife informed Gamelin that Desmahis was not in, which did not greatly surprise the artist since he knew his friend's dissipated, vagabond nature and never ceased to marvel that a man with so little perseverance was able to produce so many engravings so finely done. Gamelin decided to wait for a while. The glazier's wife offered him a chair. She was in a bad temper and grumbled about the poor state of business despite everybody saying that the Revolution, by breaking windows, was making the fortune of glaziers.

Night began to fall: giving up waiting, Gamelin took his leave. Whilst crossing the Pont-Neuf, he saw coming back along the Quai des Morfondus, carrying torches and driving back the crowds, a mounted detachment of the national guard escorting, with a clattering of their sabres, a cart in which a

man was being driven slowly to the guillotine – a man nobody knew, some
ci-devant aristocrat, the first to be condemned by the Revolutionary Tribunal.
He could be glimpsed now and then between the Guards' hats, seated facing
the rear of the cart, his hands tied behind his back, his bare head swaying. The
executioner was standing beside him, leaning against the rail of the cart. The
passers-by, who had now formed a large crowd of onlookers, were telling each
other he was probably one of those who had been trying to starve people, and
they stood watching indifferently. As he came closer, Gamelin suddenly
recognized Desmahis amongst them. He was trying to push his way through
the crowd to run across the Quai in front of the procession. Gamelin called out
and grasped him by the shoulder; Desmahis turned his head.

He was a young sturdily built, handsome man. At the Academy of Arts they
had used to say that Desmahis possessed the head of Bacchus and the body of
Hercules. His friends had called him 'Barbaroux' on account of his resembl-
ance to that deputy of the people.

'Wait,' Gamelin said. 'I've something important to say to you.'

'Don't bother me now!' Desmahis replied roughly.

And, watching for an opportunity to cross quickly, he muttered over his
shoulder:

'I was following a girl, a marvellous creature, in a straw hat, a milliner's
assistant, fair hair right down her back: this damned cart got in the way . . .
She'll be at the other end of the bridge by now.'

Gamelin tried again to hold him back, swearing that the matter was of great
importance.

But Desmahis had already slipped across in between horses, guards, sabres
and torches, and was in fast pursuit of the young girl from the milliner's shop.

(32) FAUBOURG SAINT ANTOINE
Charles Dickens, *A Tale of Two Cities*

*The destitute inhabitants of the working-class area of the Faubourg
Saint Antoine provided many participants in the street mobs of the
Revolution. It is a key setting in Dickens's novel (the location of the
wine shop of Monsieur Defarges). In this passage, the Revolution is
waiting to happen.*

A narrow winding street, full of offence and stench, with other narrow
winding streets diverging, all peopled by rags and nightcaps, and all smelling
of rags and nightcaps, and all visible things with a brooding look upon them
that looked ill. In the hunted air of the people there was yet some wild-beast
thought of the possibility of turning at bay. Depressed and slinking though
they were, eyes of fire were not wanting among them; nor compressed lips,
white with what they suppressed; nor foreheads knitted into the likeness of the
gallows-rope they mused about enduring, or inflicting. The trade signs (and
they were almost as many as the shops) were, all, grim illustrations of Want.
The butcher and the porkman painted up, only the leanest scrags of meat; the

baker, the coarsest of meagre loaves. The people rudely pictured as drinking in the wine shops, croaked over their scanty measures of thin wine and beer, and were gloweringly confidential together. Nothing was represented in a flourishing condition, save tools and weapons; but, the cutler's knives and axes were sharp and bright, the smith's hammers were heavy, and the gunmaker's stock was murderous. The crippling stones of the pavement, with their many little reservoirs of mud and water, had no footways, but broke off abruptly at the doors. The kennel, to make amends, ran down the middle of the street – when it ran at all: which was only after heavy rains, and then it ran, by many eccentric fits, into the houses. Across the streets, at wide intervals, one clumsy lamp was slung by a rope and pulley; at night, when the lamplighter had let these down, and lighted, and hoisted them again, a feeble grove of dim wicks swung in a sickly manner overhead, as if they were at sea. Indeed they were at sea, and the ship and crew were in peril of tempest.

For, the time was to come, when the gaunt scarecrows of that region should have watched the lamplighter, in their idleness and hunger, so long, as to conceive the idea of improving on his method, and hauling up men by those ropes and pulleys, to flare upon the darkness of their condition. But, the time was not come yet; and every wind that blew over France shook the rags of the scarecrows in vain, for the birds, fine of song and feather, took no warning.

(33) Boulevard Saint-Germain

Guillaume Apollinaire,
from *A Phantom of the Clouds*

These opening stanzas set the scene for Apollinaire's resonant free-verse poem which translates the acute and vivid evocation of a street performance into musings upon the passing of youth, and the spirit of the new century. At the time the poem was written, Apollinaire lived in a top-floor flat in Saint-Germain.

It was the eve of July 14th
About four in the afternoon
I went down into the street to see the acrobats

These performers in the open air
Are beginning to be rare in Paris
In my youth we saw many more than today
Almost all have left for the provinces

I took the boulevard Saint-Germain
And on a small square between Saint-Germain-des-Prés and the statue of
    Danton
I came upon the acrobats
A crowd encircled them silent and resigned to waiting
I found a space in the circle where I could see everything

Formidable weights
Belgian cities lifted to arm's length by a Russian worker from Longwy
Black and hollow dumb-bells with frozen rivers for their shafts
Fingers rolling a cigarette as bitter and delicious as life

(34) Saint-Germain: Café de Flore

Simone de Beauvoir, *The Prime of Life*

*Beauvoir and Sartre first made the Café de Flore their second home
and office at the end of the 1930s, and it has ever since been
associated with them and their friends. Even before they adopted it,
it was already an established gathering place for writers, film-
makers, and other assorted intellectuals. In the second volume of her
autobiography Beauvoir highlights its importance in her life. In this
extract, the time is the 1940s and Paris is under German
occupation.*

Little by little, as the morning passed, the room would fill up, till by apéritif
time it was packed. You would see Picasso there, smiling at Dora Marr, who
had her big dog with her on the lead; Léon-Paul Fargue would be sitting
quietly in a corner, and Jacques Prévert holding forth to a circle of
acquaintances; while a noisy discussion would always be going on at the
cinéastes table – they had been there almost daily since 1939. Here and there
in this mob you might find one or two old gentlemen who were local residents.
I remember one such, who was afflicted with a disease of the prostate, and
wore some kind of apparatus that bulged inside one of his trouser legs. There
was another, known as 'the Marquis' or 'the Gaullist', who used to play
dominoes with two young girl friends of his, whom, it was said, he maintained
in fine style. He was a stoop-shouldered man, with down-thrust head and
drooping moustachios; he would murmur in Jean's or Pascal's ear the news
items he had just heard on the latest BBC broadcast, and these would be
promptly passed on from table to table. Throughout all this the two journalists
still sat there and brooded, out loud, upon the possibility of exterminating the
Jews.

I would return to my hotel for lunch, after which, unless I had a class at the
lycée, I resumed my table at the Flore. I went out for dinner, and then returned
again till closing time. It always gave me a thrill of pleasure at night to walk in
out of the icy darkness and find myself in this warm, well-lit, snug retreat, with
its charming blue-and-red wallpaper. Frequently the entire 'family' was to be
found at the Flore, but with its members, according to our principles of
behaviour, scattered in every corner of the room. For instance, Sartre might
be chatting with Wanda at one table, Lise and Bourla at another, and Olga
and I sitting together at a third. Yet Sartre and I were the only two who turned
up regularly every night. 'When they die,' Bourla remarked of us, faintly
irritated, 'you'll have to dig them a grave under the floor.'

(35) Saint-Germain-des-Prés

Milan Kundera, *Immortality*

In this extract from Kundera's discursive novel, car-hater Professor Avenarius explains his viewpoint over dinner with the author/ narrator. They have just been comparing two women by drawing diagrams of arrows to indicate the relationship between body and mind.

'I prefer Laura,' Avenarius replied firmly, adding: 'Above all, however, I prefer jogging at night. Do you like the church of Saint-Germain-des-Prés?'

I nodded.

'Yet you've never really seen it.'

'I don't understand,' I said.

'I was recently walking down the Rue de Rennes towards the boulevard and I counted how many times I was able to look at the church without being bumped into by a hurrying passer-by or nearly run over by a car. I counted seven very short glances, which cost me a bruised left arm because an impatient young man struck me with his elbow. I was allowed an eighth glance when I stopped in front of the church door and lifted my head. But I only saw the façade, in a highly distorted fish-eye perspective. From such fleeting and deformed views my mind had put together some sort of rough representation that has no more in common with that church than Laura does with my drawing of two arrows. The church of Saint-Germain-des-Prés has disappeared and all the churches in towns have disappeared in the same way, like the moon when it enters an eclipse. The cars that fill the streets have narrowed the pavements, which are crowded with pedestrians. If they want to look at each other, they see cars in the background, if they want to look at the building across the street they see cars in the foreground; there isn't a single angle of view from which cars will not be visible, from the back, in front, on both sides. Their omnipresent noise corrodes every moment of contemplation like an acid. Cars have made the former beauty of cities invisible. I am not like those stupid moralists who are incensed that ten thousand people are killed each year on the highways. At least there are that many fewer drivers. But I protest that cars have led to the eclipse of cathedrals.'

After a moment of silence, Professor Avenarius said: 'I feel like ordering some cheese.'

(36) Rue Saint-Honoré

Georges Perec, *A Man Asleep*

Perec's brilliant short novel about a young man in deep depression is written entirely in the second person singular. You are living in a 'cupboard-like garret which never loses your smell' on rue Saint-Honoré . . .

. . . thus begins and ends your kingdom, perfectly encircled by the hosts of ever-present noises – some friendly, some hostile – which are now all that keep you attached to the world: the dripping tap on the landing, the noises from your neighbour's room, his throat-clearing, the drawers which he opens and closes, his coughing fits, the whistling of his kettle, the noises of the Rue Saint-Honoré, the incessant rumble of the city. From far away, the siren of a fire engine seems to be heading straight for you, then moving away, then drawing closer again. At the junction of Rue Saint-Honoré and Rue des Pyramides the measured succession of car noises, braking, stopping, pulling away, accelerating, imparts a rhythm to time almost as surely as the tirelessly dripping tap or the bells of Saint-Roch.

Your alarm-clock has been showing five-fifteen for a long time now. It stopped, probably when you were out, and you haven't bothered to wind it up again. Time no longer penetrates into the silence of your room, it is all around, a permanent medium, even more present and obsessive than the hands of a clock that you could choose not to look at, and yet slightly warped, out of true, somehow suspect: time passes, but you never know what time it is, the chimes of Saint-Roch do not distinguish the quarter-hours from the halves, or the three-quarters, the traffic-lights at the junction of Rue Saint-Honoré and Rue des Pyramides do not change every minute, the tap does not drip every second. It is ten o'clock, or perhaps eleven, for how can you be sure that you heard correctly, it's late, it's early, the sun rises, night falls, the sounds never quite cease altogether, time never stops completely, even it is now reduced to the merely imperceptible: a hairline crack in the wall of silence, the forgotten murmur of the drip-feed, almost indistinguishable from the beats of your heart.

(37) Place Saint-Sulpice

Djuna Barnes, *Nightwood*

Barnes wrote her haunting and poetic novel in Paris in the 1930s. She uses the place Saint-Sulpice and its café as the stamping ground for the doctor, a central and unifying character of the book.

Close to the church of St Sulpice, around the corner in the *rue Servandoni*, lived the doctor. His small slouching figure was a feature of the *Place*. To the proprietor of the *Café de la Mairie du VIe* he was almost a son. This relatively small square, through which tram lines ran in several directions, bounded on one side by the church and on the other by the court, was the doctor's 'city'. What he could not find here to answer to his needs, could be found in the narrow streets that ran into it. Here he had been seen ordering details for funerals in the *parlour* with its black broad-cloth curtains and mounted pictures of hearses; buying holy pictures and *petits Jésus* in the *boutique* displaying vestments and flowering candles. He had shouted down at least one judge in the *Mairie du Luxembourg* after a dozen cigars had failed to bring about his ends.

He walked, pathetic and alone, among the pasteboard booths of the *Foire St Germain* when for a time its imitation castles squatted in the square. He was seen coming at a smart pace down the left side of the church to go into Mass; bathing in the holy water stoup as if he were its single and beholden bird, pushing aside weary French maids and local tradespeople with the impatience of a soul in physical distress.

Sometimes, late at night, before turning into the *Café de la Mairie du VI*, he would be observed staring up at the huge towers of the church which rose into the sky, unlovely but reassuring, running a thick warm finger around his throat, where, in spite of its custom, his hair surprised him, lifting along his back and creeping up over his collar. Standing small and insubordinate, he would watch the basins of the fountain loosing their skirts of water in a ragged and flowing hem, sometimes crying to a man's departing shadow: 'Aren't you the beauty!'

(38) THE SEINE

Anaïs Nin, *The Four-Chambered Heart*

The lovers Rango and Djuna have a house-boat on the Seine, as did Nin herself, which becomes the setting for their passionate affair. Here Nin explains one of the seasonal inconveniences of life on the river, characteristically delighting in its unconventionality.

The Seine River began to swell from the rains, and to rise high above the watermark painted on the stones in the Middle Ages. It covered the quays at first with a thin layer of water, and the hobos quartered under the bridge had to move to their country homes under the trees. Then it lapped the foot of the stairway, ascended one step, and then another, and at last settled on the eighth, deep enough to drown a man.

The barges stationed there rose with it; the barge dwellers had to lower their rowboats and row to shore, climb up a rope ladder to the wall, climb over the wall to the firm ground. Strollers loved to watch this ritual, like a gentle invasion of the city by the barges' population.

At night the ceremony was perilous, and rowing back and forth from the barges was not without difficulties. As the river swelled, the currents became violent. The smiling Seine showed a more ominous aspect of its character.

The rope ladder was ancient, and some of its solidity undermined by time. Rango's chivalrous behaviour was suited to the circumstances; he helped

Djuna climb over the wall without showing too much of the scalloped sea-shell edge of her petticoat to the curious bystanders; he then carried her into the rowboat, and rowed with vigor. He stood up at first and with a pole pushed the boat away from the shore, as it had a tendency to be pushed by the current against the stairway, then another current would absorb it in the opposite direction, and he had to fight to avoid sailing down the Seine.

His pants rolled up, his strong dark legs bare, his hair wild in the wind, his muscular arms taut, he smiled with enjoyment of his power, and Djuna lay back and allowed herself to be rescued each time anew, or to be rowed like a great lady of Venice.

(39) The Seine

Paul Verlaine, from *Parisian Nocturne*

'Nocturne Parisien' appeared in Verlaine's first volume of poetry, Poèmes saturniens, published in 1866. In the lines that precede this extract the poet has waxed lyrical on the grandeur and history of rivers such as the Tiber and the Nile – here he contemplates the 'gloomy' Seine as night falls on the city, searching for the essence of its mysterious attraction.

– You, Seine, have nothing. Two quays, and that's all,
two dirty quays with musty old bookstalls
littered from end to end, and a low crowd
make rings in the water, fishing with line and rod.
Yes, but when the evening has thinned out the loungers,
stupified with drowsiness and hunger,
and sunset reddens the sky with freckles, then
how it fetches the dreamers forth from lair and den,
to lean on the Pont de la Cité and dream,
heart and hair to the wind, near Notre-Dame!
Pursued by the night-breeze, the cloud-banks fly, copper-red,
through the silent azure sky.
Pressing a rosy kiss on the king's brow
by the west door, the dying sun sinks low.
The swallow flees the shadow of the night,
and here the bat comes, staggering in her flight.
The noise dies down. Vaguely before long
one hears the city hum its evening song,
that fawns on its tyrants and gnaws its sufferers;
this is the dawn of crimes, thefts, and amours.

(40) BOULEVARD SOULT

Patrick Modiano, *Honeymoon*

*Gone to ground in the outlying areas of Paris, and searching for
Ingrid and Rigaud, a couple from his past, Jean walks down the
Boulevard Soult in the 12th. Modiano himself was born in the
outskirts of the Paris and the 'nowhere land' character of these
suburbs has a lasting symbolism for him.*

Just now, before I went back to the hotel, I was surprised to see that the façade
of the former Colonial Museum and the fountains in the square were
illuminated. Two tourist coaches were parked at the start of the Boulevard
Soult. Did the zoo stay open at night just before the fourteenth of July? What
on earth could bring visitors to this district at nine in the evening?

I wondered whether Annette would be entertaining all our friends next
week, as we did every year on the fourteenth of July, on our big terrace in the
Cité Veron. I was almost sure she would: she would need people round her,
because of my disappearance. And Cavanaugh would certainly encourage her
not to give up this custom.

I walked along the Boulevard Soult. The apartment blocks were silhouetted
against the light. Occasionally there was a big patch of sunlight on one of their
façades. I noticed some too, from time to time, on the pavements. These
contrasts of light and shade in the setting sun, this heat and this deserted
boulevard . . . Casablanca. Yes, I was walking down one of those broad
avenues in Casablanca. Night fell. The din of the televisions reached me
through the open windows. Once again, it was Paris. I went into a phone box
and looked in the book for the name: Rigaud. A whole column of Rigauds
with their Christian names. But I couldn't remember his.

And yet I felt certain that Rigaud was still alive, somewhere in one of these
suburban districts. How many men and women who you imagine are dead or
have disappeared live in these apartment blocks that mark the outskirts of
Paris . . . I had already spotted two or three, at the Porte Dorée, with a
reflection of the past on their face. They could tell you a long story, but they
will remain silent to the end, and they are completely indifferent to the fact
that the world has forgotten them.

(41) TUILERIES

John Evelyn, *Diary*

*Evelyn was a keen and observant traveller. In late 1663 and early
1664 he spent several weeks in Paris. This extract is taken from his
diary entry of 8 February 1664.*

I finished this day with a walk in the great garden of the Tuileries, rarely
contrived for privacy, shade or company, by groves, plantations of tall trees,
especially that in the middle, being of elms, the other of mulberries; and that

labyrinth of cypresses; not omitting the noble hedges of pomegranates, fountains, fish-ponds, and an aviary; but, above all, the artificial echo, redoubling the words so distinctly; and, as it is never without some fair nymph singing to its grateful returns; standing at one of the focuses, which is under a tree, or little cabinet of hedges, the voice seems to descend from the clouds; at another, as if it was underground. This being at the bottom of the garden, we were let into another, which being kept with all imaginable accurateness as to the orangery, precious shrubs, and rare fruits, seemed a Paradise. From a terrace in this place we saw so many coaches, as one would hardly think could be maintained in the whole city, going, late as it was in the year, towards the course, which is a place adjoining, of near an English mile long, planted with four rows of trees, making a large circle in the middle. This course is walled about, near breast high, with squared freestone, and has a stately arch at the entrance, with sculpture and statues about it, built by Mary di Medicis. Here it is that the gallants and ladies of the Court take the air and divert themselves, as with us in Hyde Park, the circle being capable of containing a hundred coaches to turn commodiously, and the larger of the plantations for five or six coaches a-breast.

Returning through the Tuileries, we saw a building in which are kept wild beasts for the King's pleasure, a bear, a wolf, a wild boar, a leopard, &c.

(42) Rue de Vaugirard

Hervé Guibert, *My Parents*

The narrator in Guibert's autobiographical novel, now living away from home in Paris, moves into a new apartment in the 15th. Reflecting on fragments of his past, he explores the contradictions and ambiguities in his developing relationship with his parents as he asserts his own life and identity.

After a year I leave the room in rue des Entrepreneurs. My mother has found a one-room flat to let in a block they've just finished at 293, rue de Vaugirard, very near where my great-aunts live. I think it's September when I move, or June perhaps; it's a lovely day, at their insistence my parents did the moving and have gone to have a rest, and I'm left on my own in the flat that's been invaded by my mother's all-embracing words of advice about upkeep and her notes giving me detailed instructions about the water and electricity meters, about needing to defrost the fridge regularly, about the use of certain cleaning products. The sliding door of my window onto the balcony is wide open; I'm on the sixth floor and it becomes only too obvious that all my mother's notes, like arrows, merely point to this void where I should throw myself, to put a sarcastic end to their whole plan. I close the window and tear up the notes. My friend Bertrand comes to see me, we drop some acid and start twirling round the empty, barely-furnished room to the waltz tempo of a sad old Bowie number, 'The Little Drummer Boy'.

I lost my watch a few months ago, that Lip watch from my first communion that I'm so fond of; I think the strap broke and it slipped off my wrist. Every now and then when my mother's in Paris on a visit she still comes to do my housework, she's got keys and we arrange it so that she does it while I'm out. One day when I get home I find set side by side on the table my watch and, upright, a little red and white plastic dildo that I'd long since forgotten about and which must have slipped down between the mattress and the wall. And all my mother did was write this little note: 'Darling rabbit, I'm delighted to have found your watch, I give you a kiss on the tip of your nose.' Now there at last is a charming story.

Lives and works of extracted writers

ABÉLARD, Pierre (Peter) (1079–1142). Born near **Nantes**, Abélard studied in Paris and became one of the greatest scholars of his age. In his late thirties, when he was a famous logician and teaching in Paris, he met and fell in love with Héloïse (1101–64), an intelligent and educated young woman, who was the niece of Fulbert, a canon of **Notre-Dame**, in whose house Abélard lodged rent-free in exchange for tutoring her (a ruse which, as Abélard later explained, allowed him enormous freedom to pursue the love affair). Their affair flourished, Héloïse gave birth to a son, and, at Abélard's insistence, they were secretly married. Fulbert, however, was not to be reconciled, and thinking that Abélard had forced Héloïse into a nunnery and reneged on the marriage took his revenge by arranging for the scholar to be attacked and castrated. After that, the lovers were separated. Abélard became a monk wandering from monastery to monastery. He spent six years as Abbot at **St-Gildas-de-Rhuys** in Brittany, where the hedonistic monks rebelled against his strict and scholastic rule and tried to poison him. He was also accused of heresy. He did, however, eventually return to Paris and resume his teaching. He spent the last years of his life at the famous Benedictine monastery of **Cluny** (Burgundy) under the protection of its renowned abbott Peter the Venerable (1092–1156). Héloïse remained passionately in love with Abélard, but spent the rest of her life, at his instigation, in a nunnery – becoming the Abbess of the Abbaye du Paraclete, founded for her by Abélard in 1123, which stood near **Nogent-sur-Seine**. In death, Abélard and Heloïse were reunited there in the crypt until their tomb was destroyed in 1792 – after that, their remains were moved to Paris and officially re-interred on 6 November 1817 in **Père Lachaise**, where they are the senior citizens and much visited, their once secret affair now famous in many countries and many languages.

Some of Abélard's scholastic works survive, but the most famous 'literature' associated with his name is the moving correspondence, generally thought to be genuine, between himself and Héloïse which dates from the 1130s (*The Letters of Héloïse and Abélard*). The whole story from Abélard's point of view is told in his *Historia calamitatum* (*The Story of My Misfortunes*, 1958), which provides a frank and moving account of the tragic events. This tale of star-crossed lovers has inspired more than one writer to add to its chances of immortality. Jean de Meung, for instance, produced a rendering of the letters. Alexander Pope provided his version of the story in 'Eloisa to Abelard'. Twentieth century examples are George Augustus Moore's novel *Heloïse and Abelard*, 1921, and the medievalist Helen Waddell's best-selling *Peter Abelard*, 1933 (see under Brittany, Extract 12).

APOLLINAIRE, Guillaume (1880–1918). Apollinaire (real name Wilhelm de Kostrowitsky) was born in Rome on 26 August 1880, illegitimately. He was educated in **Monte Carlo**, then in **Cannes**, and finally at the *lycée* in **Nice**. At 18, he became tutor to the daughter of a German viscountess – a position which enabled him to travel extensively in Europe and to continue the literary and scholarly reading which he had pursued in his schooldays. During this period he met Annie Playden, an English governess, the first of several great loves which were to be fertile sources of inspiration in his verse. In 1902, Apollinaire moved to Paris, and found work in a bank.

In Paris, he quickly became involved in avant-garde literary circles and met many young writers and artists of the time (including Picasso, Paul Fort, and Alfred Jarry). Among these was the painter Marie Laurencin with whom he was to embark on an intense and stormy affair, the breaking up of which inspired his famous poem 'Le Pont Mirabeau', a linguistically and thematically intricate piece which defies translation even into literal prose (there are, however, brave attempts at verse translations in the *Random House* anthology and *Selected Writings* – see Booklist).

As well as founding a short-lived literary review, *Le Festin d'Esope* (he later, with friends, started the more successful *Les Soirées de Paris*), Apollinaire threw himself into a wide variety of literary activities, including erotica publishing, art journalism, and reviews of new fiction. In 1911 he became a

regular columnist on the *Mercure de France*, purveying skilful and amusing anecdotal literary and artistic gossip. In the same year, his now considerable reputation took on a new and unexpected dimension. Probably because of his unconventional background, coupled with his avant-garde activities, he was briefly incarcerated, without foundation, for involvement in the headline-grabbing theft of the *Mona Lisa* from the Louvre.

By the time the First World War was declared, however, Apollinaire was acknowledged as a leading and influential figure of the avant-garde. He fought in the trenches near **Verdun**, receiving the Croix de Guerre, and returning to Paris with a head wound sustained in March 1916. In 1918, he married Jacqueline Kolb, a French bourgeoise, rather a contrast to his normal bohemian society. The shadow of the war, however, still hovered. Apollinaire died in Paris on 9 November 1918 from influenza complicated by pneumonia, combined with the weakening effects of his wound and the operations it entailed.

Apollinaire is remembered chiefly for the poems in his two major collections – *Alcools, Poèmes 1989–1913*, 1913 (*Alcools*, 1992), praised by Camus as one of the most astonishing works of French poetry ever produced, and *Calligrammes, Poèmes de la Paix et de la Guerre (1913–1916)*, 1918 (*Calligrammes: Poems of Peace and War*, 1992). He shows himself at once a master of short lyrical poems and an innovator in structure and imagery. His work is characterized by a tension between clarity and enigma – intricacies and ambivalences often lurking beneath the apparently luminous surface. This is true, for example, in two of his best known poems. In 'Le Pont Mirabeau', the poet's reflections on lost love develop into intricate imagery which weaves the physical with the ethereal. In the free-verse 'Un Fantôme de Nuées' ('A Phantom of the Clouds'), a naturalistic scene of a street performance by acrobats (Extract 33) develops into a meditation on the contrast between the continuity of human society and the isolation of the individual in his ephemeral passage through existence. The realistic expression of the early stanzas of the poem has, by the close, given way to startlingly surrealistic imagery ('And the organist hid his face in his hands/With fingers like the descendants of his destiny/Tiny foetuses which emerged from his beard'). *Calligrammes* includes poems written in the trenches as well as the pictorial poems which give the collection its title (like 'Il Pleut', which represents falling drops of water typographically).

Although subsequently criticized by the Surrealist leaders Breton and Aragon as too hidebound by literary conventions, Apollinaire is rightly considered an enormously influential figure in the development of modern French poetry in the early years of the 20th century and in paving the way for the Surrealist movement (he is, indeed, said by some to have coined the word *surréaliste*, using it to describe one of his plays).

Aside from his two major poetry collections, among Apollinaire's publications are *Les Peintres cubistes*, 1913, an attempt to present the aesthetic principles of Cubism in words; two novels, *Le Poète assassiné*, 1916 (*The Poet Assassinated*, 1985), and *La Femme assise*, 1920; several plays; and *L'Hérésiarque et Cie*, 1910 (*The Wandering Jew and Other Stories*, 1967), a collection of short stories. His first published volume of poetry, *Le Bestiaire, ou Cortège d'Orphée*, 1911 (translations in *Selected Writings*, 1971), included illustrations by Fauvist-influenced artist Raoul Dufy (1877–1953).

Recommended biography: Francis Steegmuller, *Apollinaire: Poet Among the Painters*, Penguin, London and New York, 1986.

BALDWIN, James (1924–87). The African–American novelist, short-story writer, playwright and essayist Baldwin first arrived in Paris in 1948. The years he lived there (1948–54 and 1955–57) were, according to Baldwin himself, crucial in providing him with the environment and analytical distance he needed to discover his own identity and formulate his literary responses to racism and the social and psychological struggles of his contemporary African–Americans. Like many other expatriate writers, Baldwin appreciated the 'anonymity' that Paris offered its visitors – in his essay 'A Question of Identity', 1951, he writes 'Neither does the Parisian exhibit the faintest personal interest, or curiosity, concerning the life, or habits of any stranger [. . .] It is this arrogant indifference on the part of the Parisian, with its unpredictable effects on the traveler, which makes so splendid the Paris air, to say nothing whatever of the exhilarating effect it has on the Paris scene.'

During these years in Paris, for most of which he was in severe financial hardship, Baldwin met and associated with many expatriate writers, including fellow African–American novelists Richard Wright (with whom Baldwin fell out over his essays on Wright's work) and Chester Himes. He also frequented the bars and nightclubs of the Paris gay world, which provided him with the milieu for *Giovanni's Room*, 1956 – the second of the two novels Baldwin worked on and published during his Paris years (the first, which quickly established his reputation as the successor to Richard Wright, was *Go Tell It on the Mountain*, 1953).

Giovanni's Room (Extract 20) concerns a man who represses and attempts to reject his homosexuality with disastrous consequences for himself and those involved with him. Set in Paris in the 1950s, it tells the story of a young American, David, and his relationship with Giovanni, an Italian working in a gay bar who falls passionately in love with him. David, by contrast, does not allow himself to regard the relationship as more than casual and instead pursues his heterosexual relationship with Hella, his American fiancé. He discovers too late that with her he was only looking for an escape route from his real sexuality and his true identity. Baldwin is good on the street life of Paris and paints a vivid picture of the bohemian and gay worlds of the city at the time.

Later in his life, Baldwin returned often to Paris. In 1971, France became once again his main home. He rented and subsequently bought a property in **St-Paul-de-Vence** near Nice, where he lived until his death from cancer in December 1987, his long-time heavy drinking and smoking finally taking their toll.

For Baldwin on Paris, apart from *Giovanni's Room*, it is worth also turning to several of the essays included in *Notes of a Native Son*, 1955 ('A Question of Identity', 'Equal in Paris', and 'Encounter on the Seine').

Recommended biography: David Leeming, *James Baldwin: A Biography*, Penguin, London and New York, 1995.

BALZAC, Honoré de. See under Centre.

BARNES, Djuna (1892–1982). American novelist, short-story writer, and journalist Barnes spent much of the 1920s and 1930s in Paris. She returned permanently to the USA at the end of 1939 where she lived out the last 40 years of her life in a small flat in Greenwich Village, New York.

She first came to Paris in 1921, a high-earning journalist for American magazines, on an assignment for *McCall's*. She was especially known for her pieces on famous names – Barnes was an early, and often mordantly witty, practitioner of the celebrity interview. One of her most successful was with James Joyce, whose work she admired and whose influence is apparent in *Nightwood*. The interview, published in *Vanity Fair* in 1922, took place in Paris over several meetings at the **Deux Magots** (see both *Interviews*, 1985, and the section on Joyce in her

article 'Vagaries Malicieux', originally published in 1924 and reissued as *Vagaries Malicieux*, 1974). The respect must have been mutual, for Joyce presented her with a signed proof copy of *Ulysses* in February 1922 – in desperate need of money Barnes sold it 30 years later to Harvard University for $125.00.

In Paris, Barnes became a prominent figure in the American colony. In 1928, she privately published the *Ladies Almanack* (reissued by Harper and Row in 1972), 'written and illustrated by a Lady of Fashion', which obscurely and bawdily caricatured various women of the artistic and literary Left Bank – most notably her friend the celebrated hostess and high priestess of lesbian culture in 1920s Paris, Natalie Clifford Barney, and the famous *New Yorker* journalist Janet Flanner (Genêt).

The longer Barnes stayed in Europe, the weaker her contacts with New York editors became, and in her later years in Paris, and subsequently, she was increasingly dependent on the generosity of wealthy friends such as Natalie Barney and Peggy Guggenheim for support. She also became locked, in the 1930s, into a vicious circle of depression (she attempted suicide in a London hotel in 1939), ill health, and alcoholism (a habit she finally kicked in 1950). She left Paris at the end of 1939, in bad mental and physical condition, and returned to Europe only once in the rest of her life.

Barnes remains an essentially private and enigmatic figure – although the extensively researched and sensitively written biography by Phillip Herring sheds much light – and responses to her supposed personality disorder are as varied as responses to her work. Her reputation as a writer rests primarily with one book, a unique and strange novel that has provoked opinions ranging from admiration to contempt ever since its first publication. The autobiographical motivation for *Nightwood*, 1936, was the break-up of Barnes's long affair with Thelma Wood, with whom she had lived in Paris for several years (the character of Robin is inspired by Wood), and the narrative is fuelled by Barnes's passion for her life in Paris in the 1920s, her happiest time, and her reactions to the people she knew there. A 'difficult' novel that rewards the effort, *Nightwood* is written in an intensely poetic style. Often darkly humorous, it creates and explores a gallery of characters all of whom are locked into suffering which derives both from within their own characters and from the ways in which they interact with others. Many of the encounters and conversations which form the 'action' of the novel take place in the cafés and streets of Paris (Extract 37). Eccentric and arresting, *Nightwood* is memorable not least for its originality of expression ('Her eyes flowed in tears that never reached the surface.'; 'She defiled the very meaning of personality in her passion to be a person.'). The first American edition of the book (1937) included a preface by T.S. Eliot in which he endorsed the novel for its 'great achievement of a style, the beauty of its phrasing, the brilliance of wit and characterization, and a quality of horror and doom very nearly related to that of Elizabethan tragedy.'

Recommended biography: Phillip Herring, *Djuna: The Life and Work of Djuna Barnes*, Viking Penguin, New York, 1995.

BAUDELAIRE, Charles (1821–67). Baudelaire was born in Paris. His elderly father died when he was six and his much younger mother subsequently married Commandant Jacques Aupick, later Colonel Aupick, whose military career took him for some four years to **Lyon**, where Baudelaire was educated at the Collège Royal. He then attended the Collège Louis-Le-Grand in Paris. In 1839, he was expelled for indiscipline and determined, to the horror of his military step-father, to pursue a literary career. As well as making acquaintances in literary and artistic circles, Baudelaire revealed a taste for dissipa-

tion – to the extent that the Aupicks shipped him off on a trip to India in an attempt to change his lifestyle. He left the ship at Mauritius, returning to Paris in 1842: the trip had certainly not left him more conventional. In 1843 he moved into the **Hôtel Pimodan** or **Hôtel de Lauzun** on the **Île St Louis**, then a splendidly bohemian home of artists and intellectuals walking on the wild side (see introduction). It was around this time that he met the mulatto woman known as Jeanne Duval who was to inspire some of the most memorable poems of *Les Fleurs du Mal* (for example, 'Le Balcon'). Smoking opium and hashish, visiting prostitutes, spending money on the promiscuous and profligate Duval, and leading a generally extravagant lifestyle, Baudelaire managed to get through a large part of his inheritance within two years. In 1844 he was limited by a *conseil judiciaire* arranged by his family to a regular allowance and this left him struggling for money, moving from one poor apartment to another – poverty was to afflict him throughout his life. In the meantime he had made the acquaintance of the beautiful Apollonie Sabatier (known as *La Présidente*, the addressee of Théophile Gautier's sexually explicit account of erotic experiences in Italy, *Lettre à la Présidente*). She was sculpted, painted, admired and much visited by a circle of bohemian writers and artists of the time. Baudelaire developed an idolizing passion for her and she became the inspiration for a cycle of poems in *Les Fleurs du Mal*, as did the other key woman in his life, the actress Marie Daubrun, with whom he supposedly had a liaison in 1854–55.

Les Fleurs du Mal was published in June 1857 – it was seized in July and Baudelaire was fined for offences against public morality (at the same time receiving praise from Hugo and Flaubert, himself recently prosecuted for committing the same offence in *Madame Bovary*). Six poems were banned and the second edition appeared without them, and with new poems added, in 1861. Baudelaire's financial resources continued to decline and his living conditions became increasingly squalid. He moved to Brussels in the vain hope of making a living by lecturing. In 1866 he became terminally ill with paralysis and aphasia and was taken back to Paris, where he died on 31 August 1867, only 46 years old, never receiving in his lifetime the general acclaim as a poet of genius that is now instantly associated with his name.

Les Fleurs du Mal, 1857 (*The Flowers of Evil*, 1993) is a collection of individual poems which, said Baudelaire, could be fully appreciated only in the context of the connecting framework within which he presented them. The original 1857 edition contained 100 poems arranged in five sections – 'Spleen et Idéal'; 'Fleurs du Mal'; 'Révolte'; 'Le Vin'; and 'La Mort'. In the revised 1861 edition, a new section, 'Tableaux parisiens', was added to the structure, and the number of poems increased to 126. The poetry of *Les Fleurs du Mal* veers from lyrical celebrations of spiritual love to viciously ironic attacks on greed and corruption. The key struggle is between the search for the ideal (through, for example, art, eroticism, drugs, revolt against the political and moral establishment) and the despairing disgust and squalid isolation that Baudelaire characterized as 'Spleen', that evil sun which always rises to melt the wings of aspiration. *Les Fleurs du Mal* contains many elements of Romanticism (such as the poet's isolation, the Gothic portrayal of poverty and sin, the longing for an escape from the horrors of modern reality), but it also heralds Symbolist modernity with its evocative mingling of sounds, scents, and colours (see the poem 'Correspondances' on this), linguistically distilling the senses into a raw-nerve analysis of the poet's response to his world, working through the power of particular images and words. In the context of this literary guide, Baudelaire's at once fascinated and horrified response to the urban experience of his contemporary Paris is especially evocative and powerful (see Extract 24).

Aside from *Les Fleurs du Mal*, Baudelaire also published a number of short prose pieces, often called 'prose poems', in various journals. These were collected after his death as *Petits poèmes en prose*, 1869, later to be given Baudelaire's own title of *Le Spleen de Paris*. He also published literary and art criticism, and translations of Edgar Allan Poe, to whose work he was much attracted, and parts of De Quincey's *Confessions of an Opium Eater*.

Recommended biography: Joanna Richardson, *Baudelaire*, John Murray, London, 1994.

BEAUVOIR, Simone de (1908–86). For a writer who is now and probably forever identified with the famous Left Bank cafés around Saint-Germain and Montparnasse, Beauvoir's birthplace could hardly have been more appropriate. She was born on 9 January 1908 in an apartment above the café **La Rotonde** on **boulevard Montparnasse**. She trained for a career as a teacher, ending up at the Sorbonne where she studied for her *agrégation* in philosophy and met Jean-Paul Sartre ◊ with whom she was to remain in a close and unconventional 'open' relationship until his death in 1980 (living separately from one another, each free to experience other relationships, rejecting the ideas of marriage and family). Beauvoir taught outside Paris before the Second World War, but returned to take a teaching post in the capital in 1938. After the war, she devoted herself to writing. As well as producing fiction and autobiography, Beauvoir was prominent in the Existentialist movement and did path-breaking work on the oppression of women. Politically she was on the left and active. She was a Communist sympathizer in the 1940s. Increasingly attracted to Marxism, she visited China and the USSR with Sartre in the 1950s and wrote enthusiastically about Communist China. She campaigned against the French actions in the Algerian war. In the 'revolution' of May 1968 she joined the Maoist students and helped to distribute banned literature on the streets. After 1968, she became involved and influential in the feminist movement. In 1986 Beauvoir was diagnosed as suffering from severe complications resulting from cirrhotic damage – she died on 14 April, and was buried next to Sartre in the cemetery at **Montparnasse**, opposite her last home, under a mutual gravestone.

Beauvoir published several novels. *L'Invitée*, appeared in 1943 (*She Came to Stay*, 1975), and was followed by *Le Sang des autres*, 1945 (*The Blood of Others*, 1964), *Tous les hommes sont mortels*, 1946 (*All Men Are Mortal*, 1992), *Les Mandarins*, 1954 (*The Mandarins*, 1957), *Les Belles Images*, 1966 (*Les Belles Images*, 1968) and the short-story volume *La Femme rompue*, 1968 (*The Woman Destroyed*, 1969). Another collection of short stories, written much earlier, was published in 1979 under the title *Quand prime le spirituel* (*When Things of the Spirit Come First*, 1982).

Les Mandarins won the Prix Goncourt of 1954, and is perhaps Beauvoir's greatest achievement in fiction. Set in post-liberation Paris, the novel is concerned with the political and moral dilemmas of left-wing intellectuals in the post-war period. Beauvoir employs an intriguing interwoven dual narrative – partly in the first person by Anne, a psychotherapist, and partly in the third person from the perspective of Henri, a writer/journalist. Characteristically, she parallels the 'external', wider debate with an 'internal' struggle based around sexual relations, in which her leading characters must make difficult personal decisions.

In 1958, Beauvoir published the first of her four-volume autobiography, a remarkably lucid, entertaining, intellectually challenging and historically fascinating work. The four volumes are all available in translation: *Mémoires d'une jeune fille rangée*, 1958 (*Memoirs of a Dutiful Daughter*, 1963); *La Force de l'âge*, 1960 (*The Prime of Life*, 1973); *La Force des choses*, 1963 (*Force of Circumstance*, 1975); and *Tout compte fait*, 1972 (*All Said and Done*, 1974). For readers of this guide, *The Prime of Life* (Extract 34) is especially recommended. Covering the 1930s and 1940s up to the end of the war, it provides a compelling mix of ingredients – Beauvoir's own account of her personal and literary development, and of the essential importance to her of her relationship with Sartre; her illustrious friends and acquaintances (among them Prévert, Picasso, Genet); an eyewitness account of Paris as war approached and of the city under occupation; and a keenly observed portrait of political and cultural trends in France at the time. In terms of places, Paris dominates, but in this period Beauvoir also spent several years teaching in *lycées* first in **Marseille** and later in **Rouen** ('the town centre, as far as I was concerned, always remained the station'), while Sartre was teaching in **Le Havre** (Normandy, Extract 9), and her experiences in these as well as various other parts of France are recounted.

Of Beauvoir's philosophical, political and other essayistic writing, her famous and enormously influential *Le Deuxième Sexe*, 1949 (*The Second Sex*, 1953) is pre-eminent. An extensive demonstration of the oppression of women, at the heart of the book is the notion that 'on ne naît pas femme, on le devient' ('you are not born a woman, you become one'). At the time of its publication, *The Second Sex* shocked many readers with, for example, its depiction of the roles of wife and mother as instruments of oppression – it was not until the upsurge of the feminist movement in the late 1960s that Beauvoir was widely recognized as a heroine of feminism.

The publication of Beauvoir's letters to Sartre in 1990 (*Letters to Sartre*, 1991) revealed a rather different, more vulnerable and sexually conventional side to her character, and caused considerable controversy.

Recommended biography: Deirdre Bair, *Simone de Beauvoir: A Biography*, Jonathan Cape, London, 1990.

BECKETT, Samuel (1906–89). Beckett first left his native Ireland for Paris in 1928, when he was 22 years old. At Trinity College Dublin he had read English, French and Italian, and he came to Paris as a *lecteur d'anglais* at the École Normale Supérieure. During this first period in the city he met James Joyce, whom he admired, and with whom he established a lasting friendship, in the course of which he did much research and other work for Joyce. Beckett published his first story in 1929 in *Transition*, the Paris-based review dedicated to experimental art and literature, and in 1930 his long poem *Whoroscope* won the poetry competition organized by Nancy Cunard's Hours Press – she subsequently printed it, making it Beckett's first separately published work. In the same year, Beckett returned to Dublin. After a brief spell of lecturing in French at Trinity, and a subsequent rootless period of some five years which he spent in Germany, France, Ireland and London (during which he published poetry in various reviews, and worked on and off as a reviewer and translator), he finally settled permanently in Paris. At the end of the 1930s he met Suzanne Deschevaux-Dumesnil, with whom he would live for around 40 years. It was at this time also that he began to write predominantly in French – thus shedding the cultural baggage carried by his native language. Among his major works originally written in French are the plays *En attendant Godot*, 1952 (*Waiting for Godot*, 1955) and *Fin de partie*, 1957 (*Endgame*, 1958), and the trilogy of novels *Molloy*, 1951 (*Molloy*, 1955), *Malone meurt*, 1951 (*Malone Dies*, 1958), and *L'Innomable*, 1953 (*The Unnamable*, 1959). Beckett was in Paris during the German occupation and remained there for as long as he could. He joined the Resistance in October 1940 – he later dismissed his activities as 'Boy Scout stuff', but then he was invariably modest and dismissive about all his achievements. Eventually things became too dangerous in Paris, and, after some hair-raising escapes from the Gestapo, Beckett and Suzanne fled south to the village of **Roussillon** in the Vaucluse – they spent the next two and a half years there until the war ended. At Roussillon, Beckett wrote his third novel *Watt*, published in 1953 – the last one he wrote in English. After the war, he received the Croix de Guerre and the Médaille de la Résistance.

Fame came in 1953 with the first performances in Paris of *En attendant Godot*. Beckett had turned to plays as a temporary relief from the arduous work of novel writing, but ironically it was his work in the theatre that brought him world renown and with which he is now primarily associated, although it is his remarkable prose fiction no less than his tragicomic and technically startling dramatizations of the funny and horrifying human condition that place him at the forefront of 20th century literary achievement. In appropriate recognition of that achievement, Beckett received the Nobel Prize for Literature in 1969. In the 1980s his health deteriorated, and in 1988 he was moved to a nursing home, severely incapacitated. Suzanne died in the summer of that year and Beckett followed her in December.

The novel extracted here, *Dream of Fair to Middling Women* (Extract 30), was written in 1932 when Beckett was only 26, and shows in embryonic form many of the themes and concerns that would infuse his more famous novels and plays. It remained unpublished until 1992, after the author's death. It is a picaresque tale, with autobiographical elements, of a young man's travels and loves in various European cities, including (of course) Paris and Dublin. Shot through with experiment, humour and Beckett's passion for words and languages, the book reads like a rush of adrenalin, and couples constant asides on the process of writing a novel with its obscure narrative ('the only unity in this story is involuntary unity'). Eoin O'Brien, in his foreword to the first edition, recalls interestingly that Beckett referred to *Dream* as 'the chest into which I threw my wild thoughts'.

Recommended biographies: Deirdre Bair, *Samuel Beckett: A Biography*, Vintage, London, 1990; James Knowlson *Damned to Fame: the Life of Samuel Beckett*, Bloomsbury, London, 1996.

BOYLE, Kay (1903–94). American writer Boyle spent some 20 years in France, most of them in Paris. When she was 19, she met and married a French exchange student in Cincinnati. She came to Europe with him in 1923 – her novel *Plagued by the Nightingale*, 1931, draws on her experience of living with his family in **Britanny** – but the relationship broke down and Boyle became involved with the poet Ernest Walsh, who co-founded and edited the literary magazine *This Quarter*. She had a child by Walsh, but he died of consumption before it was born – her novel *Year Before Last*, 1932, relates in part to this period of her life. In 1928, she moved permanently to Paris and stayed until the Second World War, finally returning to the USA in 1941. During the 1930s Boyle became an active and prominent member of the expatriate literary scene.

My Next Bride, 1934 (Extract 22), is also a novel with autobiographical elements. It concerns a young American woman, Victoria John, who comes to Paris in the early 1930s to get a job and paint. She takes a room in **Neuilly** where she becomes involved in a 'utopian' colony run by an American self-styled artist called Sorrel. A core theme is the increasing revelation of the squalor and hypocrisy that lie behind the attractively bohemian veneer. Sorrel is closely based on Raymond Duncan, Isadora Duncan's brother, who ran a colony in Neuilly in the 1920s. Boyle met him at a tea party, became involved in his enterprise, and was manipulated and exploited by him much in the way that Sorrel manipulates and exploits Victoria in the novel. Other events and characters also derive from Boyle's own experiences. The book moves slowly, and its fascination is not in the pace of events but in the skilful exposure of the conflictual psychology of a young, self-confessed 'puritan' American woman living in 1930s Paris and experiencing harsh reality in the form of, among things, poverty, overwork, unwanted pregnancy, and disenchantment. The reality shocks accumulate until she matures, breaks free of the colony, and finds true friendship and trust. Incidentally, the novel is dedicated to 'Caresse' – this is Caresse Crosby, who with her husband Harry founded the Black Sun press in Paris and for whom Boyle translated Raymond Radiguet's *Le Diable au corps*, 1923, and Surrealist René Crevel's *Babylone*, 1927.

Over her long career, Boyle published novels, short stories, poetry, autobiography, and essays on political and social issues. In addition to the titles already mentioned, of particular interest to readers of this guide will be *Primer for Combat*, 1942, which portrays France under German occupation, and her edition of Robert McAlmon's *Being Geniuses Together*, originally published in 1938 and comprising his personal record of life in expatriate literary/artistic circles in Paris in the 1920s. Boyle's edition, published in 1968, includes additional chapters providing her own recollections of the period.

CARDINAL, Marie (1929–). Cardinal was born on 9 March 1929 in Algiers. She was educated in Algiers and Paris, graduating from the Sorbonne. After teaching in French *lycées* abroad, she became, in 1962, a professional writer. Her first novel, *Écoutez la mer*, 1962, won the Prix International du Premier Roman. Since then, she has published around a dozen books, many of them unfortunately awaiting translation into English. Often semi-autobiographical, her novels explore personal insecurities and intimate relationships with uncompromising incisiveness. Her most famous work, *Les Mots pour le dire*, 1975 (*The Words to Say It*, 1984), subtitled 'an autobiographical novel', tells the story of a woman's discovery through psychoanalysis of the reasons behind a traumatic psychosomatic disorder and of her coming to terms with her body – and consequently with her whole self. Told in first-person narrative, the novel reconstructs the experience of discovery by constantly interrelating the present and the past (Extract 1) and following in its structure the pattern of the narrator's development through her sessions of psychoanalysis. Cardinal succeeds in conveying a sense of awesome honesty – that everything she sets down is the raw truth – a rare achievement in an autobiography, let alone a novel. *The Words to Say It* won the Prix Littré in 1976 and is available in an excellent English translation.

Also available in translation is *Les Grands désordres*, 1987 (*Devotion and Disorder*, 1991) a novel about heroin addiction in the context of the relationship between a mother and daughter.

CÉLINE, Louis-Ferdinand (1894–1961). Céline (real name Louis-Ferdinand Destouches) was born on 27 May 1894 in the industrial Parisian suburb of **Courbevoie**. His father was an insurance clerk, and his mother ran a shop selling old lace and antiques in the **passage de Choiseul** near the Bourse – the family moved there shortly after Céline's birth. In 1913 Céline volunteered for service in a cavalry regiment and saw action in the early months of the First World War – he was wounded, decorated, and invalided out. After spending time in London and West Africa, he studied medicine

at the University of Rennes and qualified as a doctor in 1924. There were further spells of working abroad (in Geneva and Detroit) before he set up a private practice in **Clichy**, subsequently moving to the municipal clinic there. At the age of 38, he published his first novel – *Le Voyage au bout de la nuit*, 1932 (*Journey to the End of the Night*, 1983), winning the Prix Renaudot and scoring a huge success. He followed it in 1936 with *Mort à crédit* (*Death on the Installment Plan*, 1971), which alienated many who had been enthusiastic about the first novel with its bleak vision and what they considered its obscenity. In the years immediately before the Second World War, Céline published several political pamphlets which revealed him as an antisemitic holding views on the extreme right – his antisemitism was enormously damaging to his reputation and for many years evaluation of his considerable literary merit was avoided or clouded by its shadow. In 1944 he fled Paris with his wife to take refuge in Denmark. Their wanderings in Germany before they were allowed into Denmark form the basis of the trilogy of novels *D'un château l'autre*, 1957 (*Castle to Castle*, 1976), *Nord*, 1960 (*North*, 1972), and *Rigodon*, 1969 (*Rigadoon*, 1975). Céline was arrested and imprisoned on arriving in Denmark on collaboration charges (he stayed in prison for over a year). He was granted amnesty and returned to France in 1951. He settled soon afterwards in the Parisian suburb of **Meudon** where he again set up in practice as a doctor and embarked on a very productive last ten years of writing which included several more novels and his *Entretiens avec le professeur Y*, 1955 (*Interviews with Professor Y*, 1986), which provides much information on his approach to the novel and to language, and on his working methods. Céline died on 1 July 1961 at Meudon – on the same day as Ernest Hemingway.

Journey to the End of the Night carried with it the shock of the new, both in style and content. Its challenge to conventional cultural codes and the accepted literary language opened up, along with Queneau's ◊ work, new avenues for the modern French novel. The story is told in the style of an autobiography by one Bardamu, who, like Céline himself, practises as a doctor in a poor and decaying suburb of Paris (the fictional La Garenne-Rancy, which, suggests translator Ralph Manheim, seems to be roughly in the area where the actual **La Garenne-Columbes** is situated). In this spleen-blast of a novel (Extract 29), we follow Bardamu's experiences in the trenches, in First World War Paris, in French colonial Africa, in New York, and, most memorably, in the poverty-rotten Parisian suburb of Rancy (*rance* means 'rancid'). Céline's world is a dark pit of exploitation and machination – there are only abusers and abused. The novel is written with such fire in the belly and such dark humour that it is an easy and compulsive read despite its bleak and apparently nihilistic standpoint. In its original French, it is written in, shockingly for its time, Parisian street slang, full of obscenities and linguistic brutalities, and with Céline's idiosyncratic punctuation – a style ideally suited to the sordid and abusive world it portrays with great, paradoxically invigorating, energy. Céline's portrayal of the seedy suburb where Bardamu works and of other parts of Paris are atmospheric and clearly derive from his intimate knowledge of the city (look especially for his wonderful scene of late-evening fishing in the Seine as the *bouquinistes* close down). Despite that knowledge, he is not over-fussy about geographical accuracy, and he also often mixes in fictional places with real ones.

Recommended biography: Patrick McCarthy, *Céline: A Critical Biography*, Allen Lane, London, 1975.

COCTEAU, Jean (1889–1963). Cocteau was born in the suburban town of **Maisons-Laffitte** on 5 July 1889. He hit the ground running and sustained his startling artistic and intellectual energy throughout his life. When he was 15, an intelligent but unruly pupil at school in Paris, he ran away to **Marseille**, and stayed there, according to his own account, for a year, living under a false identity in the brothel-crowded streets of the Vieux Port. It was in Marseille, says Cocteau, that he first saw opium smoking – although it was not until he was in his thirties that he acquired the opium habit in earnest (following the death of Radiguet, ◊ Ile de France, with whom he was in love).

Cocteau became a leading light in the literary and artistic avant-garde between the wars, resolutely modernist and provocative. Despite his participation in a wide variety of artistic activities – poetry, prose fiction, theatre, film, art, and ballet – he always insisted that he was primarily a poet and that all his artistic endeavours emanated from his poetic core (he referred to his novels as 'Poésie de Roman', his plays as 'Poésie de Théâtre', etc). He published several volumes of poetry – *Tempest of Stars*, 1992, provides a good selection in translation. In the theatre, he ranged from tragedy in *La Machine infernale*, 1934 (*The Infernal Machine*, 1936) to farcical ballet in *Le Boeuf sur le toit*, 1920. He collaborated with, among others, Dufy, Diaghilev, Picasso, and Stranvinsky. Cocteau, however, is now more readily remembered for his work in prose and in film. His cinematic work was both innovative and influential, at its best perhaps in *Orphée* (*Orpheus*), 1950, a multi-layered allegory characteristically working through myth and fantasy to convey a reality founded in Cocteau's own experience and in *La Belle et la Bête* (*Beauty and the Beast*), 1946, a visually striking psycho-analytical interpretation of the famous fairy tale. His novels include *Thomas l'Imposteur*, 1923 (*Thomas the Impostor*, 1957), *Le Grand Écart*, 1923 (*The Miscreant*, 1986), and the peak of his prose fiction, *Les Enfants terribles*, 1929 (*Les Enfants Terribles*, 1955).

Les Enfants terribles (Extract 16) is a strange and compelling tale which portrays four young people who live an isolated life in a world of their own making, their inter-relationships the foundations on which it depends. A picture of alienated youth, it found a place in the hearts of contemporary and future adolescents and to an extent predicted the self-assertion and intellectual revolt of post-war generations. The novel was written very quickly, driven by creative adrenalin mixed with opium. However, Cocteau told Gertrude Stein that he had been 'carrying the book' since 1913 and biographer Francis Steegmuller points out that it comprises a range of sharply remembered experiences and scenes from Cocteau's own life – certainly there is a sense that something is being exorcised or at least released in this disturbing and tragic tale. Like the drawings which illustrate the book, the style is stark and simple, in powerful contrast to the strangeness and complexity of the characters and events it portrays. Cocteau himself adapted the novel for the screen and the film was directed by Jean-Pierre Melville (*Les Enfants terribles*, 1950).

For most of his life, Cocteau lived in Paris – for his last 23 years, he had an apartment in the **Palais-Royal**. He had another home at **Milly-la-Forêt**, on the outskirts of the Forêt de Fontainebleau, where he died on 11 October 1963. He is buried in the cemetery there.

Recommended biography: Francis Steegmuller, *Cocteau: A Biography*, Constable, London, 1986/David R. Godine, Boston, MA, 1986.

COLETTE. See under Burgundy.

DICKENS, Charles. See under Pas-de-Calais.

EVELYN, John. See under Normandy.

FERLINGHETTI, Lawrence (1920–). Poet, novelist, painter and publisher Ferlinghetti first experienced France on active service off the coast of Normandy in 1944. He was back, however, in 1948, as a postgraduate student at the Sorbonne (he obtained his doctorate in 1950). Like many writers in the 1940s and 1950s, Ferlinghetti was attracted to Paris by its pre-war literary scene and the great American ex-pat writers it had nourished. But for him the formative influence of the city in his artistic development was far more than mere wishful thinking and slavish imitation of illustrious predecessors. Ferlinghetti felt a strong affinity with Paris and its culture and it was here that he started to write his first collection of poetry (*Pictures of the Gone World*, 1955), and his first novel, *Her*, which was eventually published in 1960. *Her*, influenced in particular by Djuna Barnes's *Nightwood* which Ferlinghetti admired, explores, through the roaming narrative of an interior voice, a young American in Paris searching for his own identity ('looking for himself'), expressed as his search for a woman with whom he is obsessed – an autobiographical analysis, to an extent, of the importance of Paris to Ferlinghetti's own personal and artistic development.

Among the friends Ferlinghetti made in Paris was George Whitman, and it was Whitman's bookstore, later to be named Shakespeare & Company after Sylvia Beach's famous original, that inspired Ferlinghetti to set up his City Lights bookstore in San Francisco in 1953. Like Whitman's shop, it would become a centre for writers and artists. Under the City Lights publishing imprint, many new French and other European writers have been translated and made available to an American readership. One of its early publications was Ferlinghetti's own superb translations of selections from Prévert's *Paroles* (Extract 5).

Love in the Days of Rage, 1988 (Extract 10), is a short novel set against the background of The Events of May 1968. It tells of the love affair between two 'outsiders' in Paris – a young radical-minded American artist,

Annie, and a middle-aged Portuguese banker, Julian (formerly an anarchist). Gradually drawn into and affected by the Events, their relationship becomes interwoven with the dialectics and dynamics of the 'revolution' that seems to be in progress. The book is also about Ferlinghetti's own love of Paris – and his sensual descriptions of the city invite comparison with Henry Miller ('The night was warm, and there was something in the air that excited her, a sensual joy, in the deceptively still evening, a *douceur* that she had only known in Paris, under the grey roofs or out in gardens like Luxembourg, where even the stone statues seemed to have a sensual softness. There was no other city she knew that had this strange erotic quality in its gardens and its streets, in the very air itself, a sensual mystery that enveloped everything.') This personal exploration of the essence of Paris (Ferlinghetti is especially good on the significance of its contrasting artistic and bourgeois cultures) and reflection on May 68 is intriguingly constructed and evokes the city and the Events with a poet's eye and imagery.

Recommended biography: Barry Silesky, *Ferlinghetti: An Artist in His Time*, Warner, New York, 1990.

FRANCE, Anatole (1844–1924). France (real name Jacques-Anatole-François Thibault) was born in Paris on 16 April 1844. The house in which he was born, on **quai Malaquais,** was home also to his father's bookshop. After an upbringing surrounded by books and writers, France found work with publishing houses. His own early writing comprised largely reviews and essays of literary criticism. He also, in 1873 and 1876 respectively, published a volume of poetry and a poetic drama, which reflected his associations as a young man with the Parnassian movement, a Second-Empire literary counter-movement to Romanticism, Realism and Naturalism, which strove in theory for a more objective, 'scientific', approach to poetry through the repres-

sion of the artist's personality and formal rigour. From 1876 to 1890, France was a librarian at the Sénat, a post which left him with ample time to write. He contributed regularly to journals and newspapers and in 1888 achieved the prestigious position of Literary Editor of *Le Temps* (an influential daily paper which lasted from 1861 to 1942 and whose place was taken by *Le Monde*). Four volumes of critical essays written for *Le Temps* were published as *La Vie littéraire*, 1888–92 (*On Life and Letters*, 1924). France was also publishing short stories and novels: his first major success came with his novel *Le Crime de Sylvestre Bonnard*, 1881 (*The Crime of Sylvestre Bonnard*, 1948). From then on, his reputation grew and he became one of the most renowned literary and intellectual figures in France. In 1897 he was elected to the Académie Française, but not without controversy – he was no friend of the religious and political establishment. France was often witheringly critical in his writing and identified increasingly with the political left as he grew older. During the Dreyfus affair, he demonstrated his humanity and sense of justice by speaking out in favour of the misjudged Jewish officer, putting the cause above the risk of losing friends and popularity. In 1921 he received the Nobel Prize for Literature. By then, he had moved out of Paris and was living in **Saint-Cyr-sur-Loire** just outside Tours. He spent the last 10 years of his life there, living with and eventually marrying the former maid of Madame Arman de Caillavet (hostess of one of the last famous Parisian *salons*, with whom he had had a long liaison). He died at Saint-Cyr-sur-Loire on 12 October 1924.

France's novels and stories range from evocative and largely autobiographical works evoking his childhood – *Le Livre de mon ami*, 1885, *Pierre Nozière*, 1899, *Le Petit Pierre*, 1919, and *La Vie en fleur*, 1922 – to the fierce political satire of his four-novel *Histoire contemporaine*, 1897–1901, or his satirical allegory on human progress, *L'Île des pingouins*, 1908 (*Penguin Island*, 1995). His greatest achievement was the book he published at the age of 68. *Les Dieux ont soif*, 1912 (*The Gods Will Have Blood*, 1979) is one of the finest novels about the French Revolution and a terrifying study in fanaticism (Extract 31). The protagonist is Évariste Gamelin, a young and idealistic artist who gradually loses whatever humane impulses he started out with as he rises to the role of magistrate on the Revolutionary Tribunal and becomes an instrument of the Terror. In this book it is not so much power as unfettered idealism which corrupts – and France's reasoned and humanitarian condemnation of Gamelin gives his period-specific story its timeless universality. At the same time, the novel provides a vivid evocation of Paris in the 15 months preceding the downfall of Robespierre – a city plagued by fanaticism, greed and fear, its old symbols torn down and its new heroes, like Marat and Robespierre, rising and falling in the tidal wave of blood that followed the Revolution. In this environment the man of reason, the intellectual humanitarian Brotteaux in France's novel (the fictional counterpart of France himself), cannot survive and falls because of his very inability to lose his sense of balance.

Recommended biography: David Tylden-Wright, *Anatole France*, Collins, London, 1967.

GALLANT, MAVIS (1922–). Gallant, a Canadian-born writer and critic, emigrated to France in 1950 and made her home in Paris. She has been a regular contributor to the *New Yorker*, and, as a book reviewer, to the *New York Times*. In addition to her journalism and essays, Gallant has published novels and short stories. The book highlighted here, *Paris Notebooks*, 1988, is a selection of her non-fiction writing, focusing on her views on French literature and culture and including both essays and book reviews.

Among the highlights are her remarkable eye-witness account of The Events of May 1968 (Extract 11), and a fascinating essay on the famous Gabrielle Russier case of the late 1960s, whose protagonists lived in **Marseille** – a case which gripped France and left the nation wrestling with a guilty conscience (an under-age youth had an affair with an older woman who was pilloried and imprisoned and subsequently suffered mental collapse and committed suicide).

GUIBERT, Hervé (1955–91). Born in Paris, Guibert was a photographer, journalist (he was for a time photography correspondent for *Le Monde*), critic, and, most importantly, a novelist. He published around 20 books in his brief life, including short stories, novels, and *photo-romans* (Guibert was influential in the development of this genre in the 1980s, experimenting with and exploring the relationship between text and image). The common thread in his work is its autobiographical orientation and this becomes especially significant in his later novels, which reflect his own slow death from AIDS and explore the psychology of a young man dying. For example, in *À l'ami qui ne m'as pas sauvé la vie*, 1990 (*To the Friend Who Did Not Save My Life*, 1995), Guibert undertakes an uncompromising examination of the disease and attitudes to its treatment in the context of a young man's account of the death by AIDS of his friend Musil, a character based on the philosopher Michel Foucault. *Le Protocole compassionnel*, 1991 (*The Compassion Protocol*, 1995) contains, as Guibert put it, 'the same people' as the previous novel: 'Hervé Guibert, a writer suffering from AIDS, his companions, the community of the sick and their carers.' In this book, the story revolves around the relationship between a beautiful woman doctor and the narrator, a young man in a deteriorating, old man's body. Guibert died on 27 December 1991 from an AIDS-related illness –

two weeks earlier he had, like the fictional sufferer in *To the Friend Who Did Not Save My Life*, tried to kill himself. Always controversial, and always driven by creative energy, Guibert made a video of his final days which was subsequently shown on French television. He is buried on the Isle of Elba.

To an extent, Guibert's contribution to the development of awareness about AIDS and compassion towards AIDS sufferers (*To the Friend Who Did Not Save My Life* sold over 130 000 copies in the year of its publication) has overshadowed his other literary achievements. The book highlighted here comes from an earlier period. *Mes Parents*, 1986 (*My Parents*, 1993) is an autobiographical novel about the narrator's development through childhood to adolescence. It is a self-analytical exploration of his changing relationship to his parents, and the development of his homosexuality. Comparable in its ruthless honesty to Marie Cardinal's more powerful *The Words to Say It*, Guibert's novel is structured in short episodic 'memories' of the narrator, of life with his family in Paris and **La Rochelle**, and on various holidays, and eventually of his own new-found independence in Paris (Extract 42). Through these fragments of the past he reveals and illuminates his private impulses and responses, and the ambiguity and complexity of his feelings about his parents (the passages concerning his mother's cancer are especially effective in this respect).

The posthumously published *Des Aveugles*, 1995 (*Blindsight*, 1995) is a departure from Guibert's autobiographical fiction and offers a remarkable and innovative exploration of the world of the blind.

GUPPY, SHUSHA. Guppy is a journalist and singer. *A Girl in Paris*, 1991 (Extract 14), is the second volume of her memoirs, following on from *The Blindfold Horse: Memories of a Persian Childhood*, 1988. It is an account of Guppy's formative experiences in Paris in the 1950s. Arriving as a student from her native Persia, she gradually became involved in the cultural and political life of the Left Bank and met many writers, artists and musicians. Her straightforward account of her meetings and impressions offers numerous intriguing glimpses of what it was like to be part of the Left Bank scene in the 1950s and her anecdotes about encounters with, among others, Camus, Aragon, Sartre, Prévert (who befriended her), Beckett, and Christopher Logue are always entertaining and sometimes illuminating.

HEMINGWAY, Ernest (1899–1961). Hemingway was in Paris briefly in May 1918, on his way to serve in an ambulance unit on the Italian front (where he was badly wounded by shrapnel). He returned with his first wife Hadley to join the growing expatriate community in December 1921, and lived in the city on and off until March 1928, when he returned to the USA with his second wife, Pauline Pfiefer. When he arrived he was earning his living as a journalist, travelling widely and writing features for the *Toronto Star Weekly*. In Paris, encouraged in particular by Ezra Pound and Gertrude Stein, he made the transition from journalism to literature and did much of his finest work during his famous days here – which, as is clear from *A Moveable Feast*, 1964, stayed with him all his life.

Hemingway was an assertive and engaging personality and made numerous literary friends in Paris. A very few – Sylvia Beach, Ezra Pound, and James Joyce most notably – retained his good opinion, but most, and many of those who, like Stein ◊, Scott Fitzgerald (◊ Provence) and Ford Madox Ford (◊ Picardie), had given him support and advice, ended up receiving the sharp end of his pen (one, Robert McAlmon, also got the sharp end of his fist). The friendship and subsequent fall-out with Gertrude Stein is especially well known and is enshrined in the respective put-downs in their highly entertaining and evocative, but factually unreliable memoirs – Stein's *The Autobiography of Alice B. Toklas*, 1933, and Hemingway's *A Moveable Feast*.

A *Moveable Feast* was, with the exception of the chapter about Ford Madox Ford, written in Cuba and the USA between 1957 and 1960 and published posthumously – Hemingway revisited Paris while working on the book to make sure that his topographical details were accurate. It offers a vivid set of recollections of people and places, but it was written outside its time, with emotions and memories shaped by later turns in relationships and events. There are engaging accounts of his favourite café, the **Closerie des Lilas**, and of Sylvia Beach and Shakespeare and Company. There are also fond memories of Pound and Joyce and passages of heartfelt devotion to the city itself – 'There is never any ending to Paris and the memory of each person who has lived in it differs from that of any other. We always returned to it no matter who we were or how it was changed or with what difficulties, or ease, it could be reached.' But *A Moveable Feast* also contains some treacherous writing which comes from the darker side of Hemingway's nature – there are, for example, inaccurate and damagingly unfair portrayals of Fitzgerald and Ford, a bitchy piece on Stein, and a startlingly vicious attack on Wyndham Lewis. *A Moveable Feast* is essentially autobiographical fiction – taken as such, it is revealing both as a perspective on literary life in Paris among the so-called 'lost generation' of the 1920s, and as a sometimes sad record of aspects of its writer's own complex personality – on the one hand, his generosity and genuine enthusiasm for life, and, on the other, his egocentred hostility and self-aggrandizing defensiveness.

After 1928, Hemingway never lived in Paris again, although he returned several times, most notably in 1944. In keeping with his love of macho heroics,

he had joined the US army as a foreign correspondent (as a means of getting involved in the fighting) and was among the first American soldiers to enter Paris – Sylvia Beach tells how he helped to clear her street of snipers when he came to see her in the **rue de l'Odéon** shortly after his arrival. His main part in the liberation, though, seems to have been the liberation of the **Ritz**, one of his old haunts, where he promptly took a suite and ordered 50 martinis for himself and his company.

In his fiction, Hemingway's finest writing on Paris is to be found in his masterly short story 'The Snows of Kilimanjaro', 1936, about a novelist dying in Africa, remembering all the stories he might have written in flashbacks to an earlier life in Paris. Hemingway draws vividly on his own experiences of the city (see Extract 6, on the area where he lived in his early years there). He does this also in the early Paris-based chapters of *The Sun Also Rises*, 1926 (published in Britain as *Fiesta*), which contain precisely detailed and atmospheric evocations of the city and its life. This disillusioned novel of the lost generation, with the hard-boiled economy of style and toughness of attitude which became Hemingway's hallmarks, tells of the exploits and relationships of a group of wandering expatriates who journey from Paris to the fiesta at Pamplona. In his *Love and Death in the American Novel*, 1966, Leslie Fielder suggests that Paris stands for 'the world of women and work, for "civilization" with all its moral complexity . . . The mountains of Spain, on the other hand, represent the West, a world of male companions and sport, and anti-civilization, simple and joyous . . .'. The same contrast is apparent in 'The Snows of Kilimanjaro', where Africa substitutes for Spain and Paris is the setting for the narrator's confrontation with his past. Certainly Hemingway himself adds weight to this analysis when he writes in *A Moveable Feast*, 'But Paris was a very old city and we were young and nothing was simple there, not even poverty, nor sudden money, nor the moonlight, nor right and wrong nor the breathing of someone who lay beside you in the moonlight.'

Hemingway received the Nobel Prize for Literature in 1954.

Recommended biography: Jeffrey Meyers, *Hemingway: A Biography*, Macmillan, London, 1985.

HUGO, Victor-Marie (1802–85). The great Romantic writer was born on 26 February 1802 in **Besançon**. His father served in Napoleon's Republican army and rose to the rank of general – his duties took the family to Corsica, Italy and Spain. Hugo's mother resented the constant disruptions to family life and she separated from her husband in 1812, returning to Paris with Victor and his two brothers. Hugo began his prodigious literary career very young – he was writing stories and tragedies when he was 13, and had drafted his first novel and won a prize for poetry before his 17th birthday. In 1819, at the age of 17, he founded a literary journal together with his brothers which ran until 1821. By the late 1820s he was already a major figure in French literature and his *salon* was the key meeting place for Romantic artists and

Victor Hugo

writers. His *Odes et ballades*, 1826, were praised by the writer and critic Sainte-Beuve (1804–69) who became his close friend during an especially creative period – Sainte-Beuve also fell in love with Hugo's wife, and later became bitterly hostile. In 1829, the poetry collection *Les Orientales* appeared, demonstrating Hugo's impressive facility and inventiveness over a range of verse forms.

Hugo's humanist approach to life and his growing Republican sympathies (he had previously taken a Royalist road) were now manifesting themselves, in addition to his literary genius: his first great example of art with a social conscience came with the novel *Le Dernier Jour d'un condamné à mort*, 1829 (*The Last Day of a Condemned Man*, 1992), an impassioned outcry against the death penalty. His play *Hernani*, 1830, a Romantic verse drama which defied classical conventions, produced a riot at its first performance, in keeping with the best traditions of avant-garde theatre – fighting broke out at the beginning of the first performance between Hugo's friends and the supporters of classicism. In 1831, his great, brooding novel *Notre Dame de Paris – 1482* (*Notre Dame de Paris*, 1993) was published, set in 15th century Paris and including such an impressively detailed and erudite depiction of the cathedral that the book influenced the public perception of the city's architecture and led to the establishment of a Commission of Historic Monuments. The novel was an instant and immense success and enhanced even further Hugo's gigantic reputation. In 1837 he was nominated to the Légion d'Honneur. In 1841, he became a member of the Académie Française.

Hugo's creativity took a downturn in the 1840s with the failure of his play *Les Burgraves*, 1843, and the personal tragedy of his daughter's death in a boating accident. Following the collapse of the July Monarchy in 1848, he was elected to the Assemblée Constituante and re-elected to the Assemblée

Législative that succeeded it. He made speeches in support of laudable social issues, such as free education and freedom of the press, but these had little effect in the conservative Assemblée. When Louis-Napoléon executed his *coup d'état* in 1851, Hugo, who had shown open opposition to the future emperor's government, went into exile for some 20 years, for most of which he lived in Guernsey. Several volumes of verse followed, including the satirical *Les Châtiments*, 1853, written shortly after his exile and expressing his outrage at the actions of Louis-Napoléon, and the contrasting lyrical and visionary *Les Contemplations*, 1856, arguably the pinnacle of his poetic achievements. Among the other works he completed in exile was his prose masterpiece, *Les Misérables*. Even after his exile was over, he returned to Guernsey to write another impressive novel, *Quatrevingt-Treize*, 1874 (*Ninety-Three*, 1988), dealing with the civil war in the **Vendée**.

Hugo returned to France in 1870, after the emperor's abdication, to find he had grown in popularity to almost legendary proportions. He continued to hold political positions, but had little influence. However, through his faithful battling on behalf of humanitarian and libertarian causes, and his outstanding literary genius, he maintained his status as a national hero. When he died on 22 May 1885, numerous prominent politicians and literary and theatrical celebrities came to pay their respects. The state funeral was an internationally famous event. Hugo, in a pauper's coffin at his own request, lay in state under the Arc de Triomphe and was then taken across the city to the **Panthéon** to be buried. Some two million people attended.

Les Misérables, 1862 (*Les Misérables*, 1976) is a combination of thrilling narrative, memorable character portraits, social and political comment, and long digressions on historical events and social issues – most notably a memorable description of the battle of Waterloo and a symbolic and dark discourse on the Paris sewers (Extract 27), which become the setting for one of the most dramatic episodes in the book. The *misérables* of the title are the oppressed, the poor, the unfortunates of life, the victims of fate and circumstance, but above all the victims of social and political injustice. The connecting thread of the narrative, which begins in 1815, is the life of Jean Valjean, who perhaps represents Everyman. When the action begins, Valjean, a released convict, steals from a bishop who has helped him when no one else would give him shelter. The novel, however, tells the story of the reassertion of his conscience and his humanity and we follow him through the many stages of his regeneration, seeing that despite his misfortunes he is free to make his own moral choices. In the vast canvas of this rich and colourful book, Hugo gives us many vivid characters, from the prostitute Fantine and her daughter Cosette, whom Valjean 'adopts', to the street-urchin Gavroche (killed in the riots of 1832 which Hugo vividly evokes), to the sinister and driven inspector Javert, whose pursuit of Valjean is the source of much of the book's excitement. The many digressions and authorial interpolations are a reminder that the action that engrosses us takes place in the wider sweep of social and political history and serve to comment on the injustices so perpetrated. In terms of its settings, *Les Misérables* is most memorable for its evocation of central Paris in the first half of the 19th century, before Haussmann changed it forever. However, much of the significant action in the early part of the novel takes place in Montreuil-sur-Mer, now **Montreuil** (see Pas-de-Calais, Extract 8). *Les Misérables* has been filmed, serialized for television, and even adapted for the stage as a musical, which has enjoyed enormous success.

Recommended biography: Joanna Richardson, *Victor Hugo*, Weidenfeld and Nicolson, London, 1976.

JAMES, Henry (1843–1916). James's father, a writer on religious, social and literary topics, provided his sons with a distinctly and deliberately cosmopolitan upbringing in America and Europe – determined that they should not affiliate strongly with one particular culture until they were able to make their own choices. Henry James was born in New York City, and educated in New York, London, Paris and Geneva. No doubt the 'detached' nature of his upbringing encouraged James's early positioning of himself as an 'observer' of life – a position reflected in the remote narrative stance that runs through his fiction. On the other hand, he quickly identified his own spiritual affiliation with Europe – preferring what he saw as its cultural depth and artistically nurturing environment to the creatively constraining and culturally arid America of his experience. The reactions of Americans confronted by Europeans or European culture constitute a recurring theme in James's novels and short stories.

James settled permanently in Europe in 1875. He lived most of his life in London (he became a British citizen in 1915), but made frequent visits to the Continent. He visited many parts of France, but it was Paris that most attracted him and that remained throughout his life a fascinating and rewarding destination. He first saw the city as a child in 1844, and made his last visit there in 1908. Of his many stays and visits, the most significant was the year he lived in Paris in 1875–76, before he made his home in London, supplementing his income by writing articles on life in France for the New York *Tribune*. It was during this stay that he first met Turgenev, who subsequently introduced him to Flaubert. Attending from time to time Flaubert's Sunday *salon*, James also met Daudet, Edmond de Goncourt, Zola and, later, Maupassant. In a much later visit, in 1907, he stayed for several weeks with Edith Wharton at her Paris apartment – James and the Whartons

undertook a motor tour to the south of France, which Wharton describes in her *A Motor-Flight Through France*, 1908.

James uses Paris as the setting for one of his greatest novels – *The Ambassadors*, 1903. The novel focuses on the story of Lambert Strether, a gentle-mannered middle-aged American editor, who is sent by his fiancé Mrs Newsome, a formidably strict and conventional Massachusetts widow, to bring back her son Chad, who seems more inclined to remain in Paris than to return to his New England home. Portraying a variety of American responses to the unconventionality and colour of life in Paris, *The Ambassadors* is more importantly a remarkably sensitive and intricate depiction of the gradual shifting in Strether's attitudes and perceptions as he develops his understanding of the attractions of Paris and of the relationship between Chad and the charming comtesse de Vionnet (the subject of a rude awakening in Strether towards the end of the novel in an outstanding passage which marries visual with psychological perception). Although there are exceptions (eg Extract 23), and although Chad's apartment, for example, is in a real Paris street (**boulevard Malesherbes**), there are few descriptions of the city in the novel – rather, the spirit of Paris dominates the book, as it dominates the characters.

For other of James's works which feature Paris as a setting, see in particular his novel *The American*, 1877, in which a wealthy American businessman 'takes on' Paris and attempts to become part of its aristocracy; and his masterly short story 'Madame de Mauves', 1874, concerning the marriage of an American woman to a French count and the responses of the central character, a young American, to his love for her – a story in which the constraints of national conventions and morality impinge on the capacity to embrace life. James's recollections of his early years in Paris can be found in his autobiographical *A Small Boy and Others*, 1913, and *Notes of a Son and Brother*, 1914.

For James on elsewhere in France, turn to his *A Little Tour in France*, 1885, a travel narrative based on a tour he undertook in October 1882. An intelligent and perceptive traveller, he constantly relates what he sees to literature and history. Starting at **Tours**, the birthplace of Balzac, he explores many towns and châteaux of provincial France – among others, **Arles**, **Nantes**, **La Rochelle**, **Poitiers**, **Bordeaux**, **Carcassone** (see Languedoc–Roussillon, Extract 3), **Montpellier**, **Avignon**, **Beaune**, and **Dijon**. James spoke fluent French, and travelled with confidence, striking up conversations, making acquaintances, and generally remaining uncontaminated by the coyness and defensiveness in the face of the foreign that so often plague British and American travel writing.

Recommended biography: Leon Edel, *Henry James: A Life*, Collins, London, 1985.

KUNDERA, Milan (1929–). After the Russian invasion of his native Czechoslovakia in 1968, Kundera found life increasingly hard – his books were proscribed, and he lost his job and his Communist Party membership in 1970. In 1975 he travelled to France to take up the position of visiting lecturer at the University of Haute-Bretagne in **Rennes**, where he stayed until 1979. In 1980 he moved to Paris to teach at the École des Hautes Études en Sciences Sociales, and has lived in the city ever since. He became a French national in 1981. Kundera is an Officier des Arts et des Lettres and has won many prizes for his work, including the Prix Médicis Étranger (1973) and the Prix de la Critique of the Académie Française for his *L'Art du roman*, 1987 (*The Art of the Novel*, 1988).

Immortality, 1991 (Extract 35), is a discursive, playful novel which moves in and out of periods and stories, the narrator constantly 'intruding' with his own comments and views, part character and part commentator. Set in Paris, the book focuses primarily on the discussion of ideas, with characters and events quite deliberately subjugated to that central purpose. If the novel has a central theme, which it may not, it is probably the dilemma we face in squaring our egocentricity with our mortality, and of defining for ourselves what is 'significant' in the context of that driving tension ('A man longs to be immortal . . .'). There are, however, a great many subjects presented for consideration within this framing theme, with attendant ironies and paradoxes to provoke and stimulate some and induce a headache in others. Kundera is skilful in seducing and teasing his readers through his whimsical argument, his apparently unstructured structure, and his silken style.

Like much of his work, *Immortality* was written in Czech (as *Nesmrtelnost*) but first published in French. His 1995 novel *Le Lenteur* (*Slowness*, 1996) was, however, written in French. Working with two timeframes (contemporary and 18th century) in the same setting of a French château, the novel sees Kundera exploring further the discursive and speculative possibilities of the form at the expense of character and plot.

MANSFIELD, Katherine (1888–1923). Mansfield was born in New Zealand. In her short and turbulent life, plagued after 1917 by worsening and debilitating tuberculosis, she experienced much and travelled widely, latterly in search of climates suited to her failing health. In 1909 she married. Pregnant by another man, she left her husband days after the wedding, later giving birth to a still-born baby in Bavaria. In 1911, in London, she met the literary editor, writer and critic John Middleton Murry (1889–1957) with whom she had a deep but often emotionally draining relationship which lasted until her death (they eventually married in 1918). Among their friends were D.H. and Frieda Lawrence – Mansfield is thought to have been a significant inspiration for the character of Gudrun in Lawrence's *Women in Love*, 1920.

Of the various places Mansfield visited and lived in, France seems to have been where she felt most at home. She retained a great attraction to Paris throughout her life and stayed in the city many times. In December 1913 she and Murry even moved to Paris intending to make it their home, but they stayed only for a few months – Murry, at that time in dire financial straits, found a job back in London and anyway did not share Mansfield's ever-growing passion for France. On an earlier trip, in 1912, Murry had introduced Mansfield to the novelist Francis Carco, who was acting as Paris correspondent for the modernist literary journal *Rhythm*, which he edited. She later had an affair with Carco – in 1915 she crossed to France despite the war, making a dangerous journey into a war zone to meet him. They had a brief sexual fling, and the adventure provided the inspiration for her story 'An Indiscreet Journey' (*Something Childish and Other Stories*, 1924). Carco, according to Mansfield herself, was also part of the inspiration for the character of Duquette in 'Je Ne Parle Pas Français' (*Bliss and Other Stories*, 1920). Mansfield last saw Paris in 1922, when she came for specialist treatment by a doctor who claimed to have a cure for tuberculosis. When the treatment proved unsuccessful, she moved to **Avon** near **Fontainebleau**, where she spent her last days at the rather dubious Institute for the Harmonious Development of Man run by George Gurdjieff. Already in the terminal stages of her illness, she arrived at Avon in October 1922 and died there on 9 January the following year.

The other part of France with which Mansfield is now readily associated is the **Riviera**, where she stayed several times towards the end of her life, hoping that the climate would ease her illness. In January 1916, she and Murry took a villa in **Bandol** and lived there until the spring. Later, she lived in **Menton** from January to April 1920 and again from September 1920 to May 1921, mostly by herself. See her story 'The Doves' Nest' for a poignant vignette of the life of lonely women in a villa on the Riviera (*The Doves' Nest and Other Stories*, 1923).

Mansfield's stories offer us glimpses of other people's lives. Variously pathetic, humorous, charming, satiric, her keenly observed portraits of people alone and of people together are memorable for the characters they create – sometimes brought to life with depth and complexity in very few pages. 'Feuille d'Album' (*Bliss and Other Stories*, 1920) – Extract 28 – is typical. Set in Paris, it concerns a shy, impenetrable young artist who responds to no-one except a girl who lives across the street, with whom he falls in love, despite never having spoken to her. (The chat-up line with which the story closes is one to savour.) The concision and clarity of Mansfield's style may convey a superficial impression of simplicity, but the best examples of her work, like the pieces mentioned here, demand a range of responses, both intellectual and emotional, which broadens with each re-reading.

Recommended biography: Claire Tomalin, *Katherine Mansfield: A Secret Life*, Penguin, London, 1988.

MILLER, Henry (1891–1980). (See also the entry on Lawrence Durrell under Provence.) Miller lived in Paris from 1930 to 1939, and it was here that he wrote his most famous novels and dedicated himself seriously to writing. He spent his early months in the city penniless and close to starving, sleeping in friends' apartments and dependent on their generosity for money and food ('I have no money, no resources, no hopes. I am the happiest man alive,' exclaims the narrator of *Tropic of Cancer*). For most of his life, and for the whole of his time in Paris, Miller was either destitute or very close to it. The 1930s were, nevertheless, a time of considerable fulfilment and creativity. A key actor in this respect was Anaïs Nin, whom he met in 1932 and with whom he later had an affair. Nin befriended Miller, put him up frequently at her house in **Louveciennes** just outside Paris, advised him on his writing and pushed him to apply himself to it in earnest, found and rented for him an apartment in the **Villa Seurat** in Montmartre, and financed the printing of the Paris edition of *Tropic of Cancer*. The sexual, emotional and intellectual relationship between Miller and Nin was a crucial one in the development of both writers – see, for example, the biographies of Miller and Nin by, respectively, Mary Dearborn and Deirdre Bair; *Henry and June*, 1987 (a selection from Nin's journals); and Philip Kaufman's 1990 film *Henry and June*, based on Nin's journals ('June' is Miller's second wife June Mansfield Smith).

Tropic of Cancer was Miller's first published novel. It appeared in Paris in 1934, published by Jack Kahane's Obelisk Press (in association with which Miller and Durrell later set up the 'Villa Seurat Series'). The book, like its successors, was banned everywhere else – the first US edition of *Cancer* came off the presses in 1961. The novel is fictionalized autobiography – a high-energy episodic narration of the thoughts and adventures, most memorably the sexual adventures, of an impoverished American writer living in Paris and writing his novel of rebellion – 'a gob of spit in the face of Art, a kick in the pants to God, Man, Destiny, Time, Love, Beauty', a hymn to the physicality and immediacy of life. An affirmative novel of ideas, eroticism, alcohol, and passion, *Tropic of Cancer* is also about Miller's love affair with Paris. He conveys his feelings for the city with the language of sexual passion – 'Paris hadn't been good to him, any more than it had to me, or to anybody, for that matter, but when you've suffered and endured things here it's then

that Paris takes hold of you, grabs you by the balls, you might say, like some lovesick bitch who'd rather die than let you get out of her hands.' It is essentially Miller's relationship with Paris that gives the novel its life and inspires its best passages (Extract 17).

Among the other books Miller published in Paris in the 1930s were *Tropic of Capricorn*, 1939, a more clearly autobiographical novel focusing on his earlier life in the USA, and *Black Spring*, 1936, comprising short pieces arising from his experiences in both the USA and Paris.

Quiet Days in Clichy was published much later, in 1956 (it was largely written in the early 1940s and revised before publication). It is more nostalgic in tone than the earlier novels, harking back to Miller's early days in Paris (hardly quiet ones). Like Hemingway in *A Moveable Feast*, Miller portrays a young artist struggling with poverty and yet living free and feeling right in a city which seems to welcome and cherish such wanderers and their adventures. As he had written in *Tropic of Cancer*, 'I understood then why it is that Paris attracts the tortured, the hallucinated, the great maniacs of love. I understood why it is that here, at the very hub of the wheel, one can embrace the most fantastic, the most impossible theories, without finding them in the least strange; it is here that one reads again the books of his youth and then enigmas take on new meanings, one for every white hair.'

Feminist commentators have been understandably critical of Miller's focus on male-driven eroticism and his portrayal of women as subservient to that over-riding obsession. He was one of the authors singled out for special attention by Kate Millett in her seminal *Sexual Politics*, 1970.

The Second World War forced Miller to leave Paris in 1939 – he visited his friends the Durrells in Corfu and then, at the end of the year, sailed for the USA where he lived for the rest of his life.

Recommended biography: Mary V. Dearborn, *The Happiest Man Alive: A Biography of Henry Miller,* HarperCollins, London, 1991.

MITFORD, Nancy (1904–73). Mitford was born into the English aristocracy, one of six daughters of the second Lord Redesdale. She was never, however, much attached to England. She visited Paris during a cultural tour of Europe in 1922, and was instantly attracted to the city – for the rest of her life she was a dedicated Francophile. She moved to Paris permanently in 1947, and lived in the same apartment in the **7th** for 20 years. In 1967, she took a house at **Versailles**, where she died on 30 June 1973, after suffering for four years from cancer. Shortly before she died, in 1972, she was awarded the Légion d'Honneur.

Mitford's attraction to France and its history and culture is apparent in much of her writing. One of her most successful novels, *The Blessing,* 1951 (Extract 4), is the story of a middle-class English woman, Grace, who marries a French aristocrat and experiences the difficulties and conflicts that arise through the contrast in their respective cultures and societies, both at his country home in **Provence** and more especially in Paris. The troubles of married life prove too much for Grace and she returns to England only to find that she increasingly misses France and her husband. The 'blessing' of the title is their small son Sigi, whose machinations are aimed at keeping his parents apart. The novel contrasts life in Britain and France, to the distinct advantage of the latter.

The Blessing was the second of three novels which feature the same family and various other common characters. The first, *The Pursuit of Love,* 1945, tells the story, principally, of the life and loves of Linda Radlett, daughter of an English aristocrat, brought up (as was Mitford) in the Cotswolds, frustrated in two marriages, experiencing real love and happiness in Paris, and finally separated from her real-life dream by the onset of war. The third, *Don't Tell Alfred,* 1960, is set in and around the British Embassy in Paris and plays wittily with caricatures of Englishness and with the traditional competitiveness between the British and French.

Mitford also translated *La Princesse de Clèves* and André Roussin's comic play *La Petite Hutte* (*The Little Hut*), and wrote several biographies relating to French history – her *Madame de Pompadour,* 1954, was popular and entertaining if not especially thorough historically; *Voltaire in Love,* 1957, tells the story of Voltaire's relationship with Madame Du Châtelet; and the bestselling and much-praised *The Sun King,* 1966 – even de Gaulle liked it – is a sumptuously illustrated account of Louis XIV and Versailles.

Recommended biography: Selina Hastings, *Nancy Mitford,* Hamish Hamilton, London, 1985.

MODIANO, Patrick (1945–). Modiano was born on 30 July 1945 in the outskirts of Paris at **Boulogne-sur-**

Patrick Modiano

Seine. He was educated in **Annecy** and Paris. His first three novels – *La Place de l'Étoile*, 1968, *La Ronde de nuit*, 1969 (*Night Rounds*, 1972), and *Les Boulevards de ceinture*, 1972 (*Ring Roads*, 1974) – are concerned primarily with the experience of and responses to the German occupation, especially as they relate to individual and collective psychology and sense of identity. His collaboration with Louis Malle on the screenplay of *Lacombe Lucien*, 1974, also reflects his fascination with this subject. While not directly concerned with the occupation, his later novels continue core themes set up in his initial trilogy. Modiano characteristically tells stories of a search to uncover the past, of people dislocated from their roots searching for a sense of belonging or for lost connections. Favourite settings for these quests are the suburbs of Paris, obscure in-between places where it is easy to lose and be lost (Extract 40).

Les Boulevards de ceinture won the Grand Prix du Roman de l'Académie Française and Modiano received the Prix Goncourt for *Rue des boutiques obscures*, 1978 (*Missing Person*, 1980). He remains, however, relatively ignored by English readers although a number of his books have been translated. Among those not already mentioned are *Quartier perdu*, 1984 (*A Trace of Malice*, 1988) and his excellent *Voyage de noces*, 1990 (*Honeymoon*, 1992).

Honeymoon (Extract 40) bears Modiano's hallmarks – the mingling of the past with the present, especially the past of wartime France, and precise settings, particularly in various parts of Paris (although there are also important scenes in this book in **Juan-Les-Pins** in Provence). The novel tells the story of Jean, who opts out of his life and goes to ground, symbolically, in the limbo-land of the periphery, the outskirts of Paris. He winds up living in hotels in these districts and searching for traces of a couple whom he first met in the south during the war and whose story is told in parallel with his own, as part of his own ('The past and the present merge in my mind through a phenomenon of superimposition.'). Place, and the memory of place, are central to the novel – they are the anchors which hold us in our sense of order and continuity. Without them there is emptiness and confusion, and yet, says Jean, visiting a street from his past and confronted with change, 'Circumstances and settings are of no importance. One day this sense of emptiness and remorse submerges you. Then, like a tide it ebbs and disappears. But in the end it returns in force . . .'.

NIN, Anaïs (1903–77). (See also under Miller, above.) Nin was born in **Neuilly** to Spanish–Cuban parents. She spent her early childhood in various parts of Europe until her parents separated, when, aged 11, she went with her mother to New York where she grew up. In 1923 she married a banker named Hugo Guiler. Guiler received a Paris posting, and at the end of 1924 Nin accompanied him to France, where she was to live for the next 15 years. She spent much of her time in Paris, although from 1930 she and Hugo had their main home in **Louveciennes**, a suburban village on the Seine. She left France in 1939 and after that lived mainly in the USA.

Paris in the 1920s and 1930s provided Nin with an environment in which she could give full expression to her bohemian and convention-flouting inclinations. Her sexual adventures were many – including affairs with, among others, Miller, Artaud, her analysts, a half-Scottish/half-Peruvian Communist named Gonzalo Moré, and, if her journal is to be believed, a brief but intense incestuous affair with her father.

Nin's motivations and personality remain enigmatic, despite the existence of her extensive *Journals* – she began her lifelong habit of diary writing when she was 11 – which are now well known for the intimacy and minute detail of their sexual and psychological content. Nin, however, continually and obsessively revised and reworked the diaries and whether particular episodes are fact or fantasy has long been the subject of rather futile academic debate. Bearing in mind their extremely subjective perspective, the volumes covering the 1930s (the first two volumes to be published) are nevertheless of interest for their view of the period and for Nin's versions of her various and complicated relationships – in particular, her affair and friendship with Henry Miller.

Nin also wrote novels, literary criticism, short stories, and erotica, but her work is generally dismissed as minor – ironically her greatest commercial success was *Delta of Venus*, 1968, a re-issue of earlier pornographic writing, which she herself considered of little value.

The novel highlighted here, *The Four-Chambered Heart*, 1950, centres around the relationship between Rango, a Spanish guitarist playing in Paris cafés and Djuna, who finds in him the 'free spirit' which allows her to release her own passionate nature and experience intense emotion and desire. The relationship is complicated, however, by Rango's invalid wife, Zora, and the interest of the novel derives from the emotional complexities and tensions among the three characters. Rango and Djuna spend most of their time together in a houseboat on the Seine (Nin herself lived in one towards the end of her stay in Paris). The boat-home is a symbolically apt setting for the affair – defying convention and providing a shell-like isolation from the everyday life of the city all around. The book has its moments (eg Extract 38), but it is hard to find literary merit in the overblown style ('But the black sun of his jealousy eclipsed the Mediterranean sun, churned the sea's turquoise gentleness.'); unbelievable dialogue ('I must be a mermaid, Rango. I have no fear of depths and a great fear of shallow living.'); and Nin's apparent need to bestow every emotion with the signifi-

cance of a natural disaster. The self-consciousness extends even to the names of her characters – John, Jane and Mary would presumably have been too prosaic, so we have Rango, Djuna, and Zora.

Much of Nin's work was self-published and she did not receive any significant kind of acclaim until the 1960s and 1970s, when she was re-evaluated in the light of the feminist movement. It is indeed her subject matter and approach that make it hard now to evaluate Nin's work objectively. She was unquestionably adventurous and morally challenging for her time, both in her own life and in her writing. Her focus on themes of eroticism and self-exploration from the woman's point of view brought her finally into the literary limelight in her later years. Pioneer, prophet for the feminist movement, neglected talent, literary poseur, pornographic shock-merchant? Take your choice.

Recommended biography: Deirdre Bair, *Anaïs Nin: A Biography*, Bloomsbury, London, 1995.

ORWELL, George (1903–50). Orwell, real name Eric Arthur Blair, returned to Europe from service with the Indian Imperial Police in Burma in 1927. Shortly afterwards, in the spring of 1928, he took a decision to go to Paris and write. He lived in a cheap hotel in the **Latin Quarter** until December 1929, when he went back to London. Orwell was a modest and restrained character and, as far as his biographers can ascertain from scant information on this period of his life, had little if any contact with the expatriate, or French, literary groups that were in full swing at the time. He seems to have led a relatively solitary life and worked on short stories and novels that never saw the light of publication – not a very fruitful period, then, although he was later anxious to emphasize, in his Preface to the French edition of *Down and Out in Paris and London* (*La Vache enragée*), that he felt no hostility to the

Georges Perec

city and had happy memories of his time here. In the autumn of 1929, Orwell ran out of money – a process hastened by a theft in his hotel room. It was between this occurrence and his departure in December that he was forced to take work as a hotel washer-up and porter – and this period of two to three months at the end of his Paris adventure provided the subject matter for the Parisian section of *Down and Out in Paris and London*, 1933 (Extract 25).

Those interested in assessing the extent to which *Down and Out* is literal autobiography will find interesting analyses in the biographies by Bernard Crick and Michael Shelden. In sum-

mary, while the book does not attempt to portray events in the order in which they happened and while some of the characters are representative rather than particular, *Down and Out* is fundamentally an accurate portrayal of Orwell's experience and observations. In the first chapter he comments, 'Poverty is what I am writing about.' No-one would argue with that. *Down and Out* is an exploration of urban life at the bottom of the pile. The narrator tells of his slummy accommodation; his search for employment; and his work as a *plongeur* (washer-up) in 'Hotel X' (Orwell actually worked at the luxury **Hotel Lotti** near place Vendôme), and subsequently in a new Russian restaurant in **rue du Commerce** in the 15th. His story of poverty, exploitation, and appallingly squalid working conditions in outwardly respectable and expensive establishments should not be read before dinner. Orwell's own conclusions on his experience are: 'Still I can point to one or two things I have definitely learned by being hard up. I shall never again think that all tramps are drunken scoundrels, nor expect a beggar to be grateful when I give him a penny, nor be surprised if men out of work lack energy, nor subscribe to the Salvation Army, nor pawn my clothes, nor refuse a handbill, nor enjoy a meal at a smart restaurant. That is a beginning.'

Orwell wrote little else on his life in Paris. He did draw on it, however, for his essay 'How the Poor Die', 1946, in which he recalls his two weeks ('several weeks' according to the essay) in the **Hôpital Cochin** in spring of 1929, when he was taken ill with a bout of pneumonia.

Recommended biography: Bernard Crick, *George Orwell: A Life*, Secker and Warburg, London, 1980.

PEREC, Georges (1936–82). Perec was born in Paris on 7 March 1936. His parents were Polish Jews, both of whom died during the war – his father in combat in 1940 and his mother at Auschwitz in 1943. Georges went to stay with his aunt and uncle as a refugee in **Villard-de-Lans** (Rhône–Alpes) – memories of his childhood there and of the war years play a part in the autobiographical sections of his *W ou le Souvenir d'enfance*, 1975 (*W or the Memory of Childhood*, 1995). After the war, he was educated at a boarding school in **Étampes** and at the Lycée Claude-Bernard in Paris. He attended the Sorbonne but dropped out of his courses, intent on becoming a writer and furthering his own education through reading and involvement in literary and intellectual circles. In 1962 he obtained the post of librarian in a medical research laboratory in Paris.

Before that, he had done two years' military service in the parachute regiment, worked briefly as a market researcher, and spent a year in Tunisia. Perec kept his post at the laboratory until 1979. In 1981, he was writer-in-residence at the University of Queensland, Australia – he had arranged to spend 53 days there working on a novel entitled *53 Jours*, which he left unfinished and which was published posthumously in 1989 (*53 Days*, 1992). In February 1982, cancer was diagnosed and it proved inoperable – he died in March, a few days before his 46th birthday.

Perec is among the century's most original and consistently challenging writers. His first novel, *Les Choses: Une histoire des années soixantes*, 1965 (*Things: A Story of the Sixties*, 1991) is a witty and satirical commentary on the power of advertising and consumerism in the post-war boom of the late fifties and sixties. It won the Prix Renaudot in 1965 and was an immediate success. Focusing on a young Parisian couple, Perec portrays the conflict between their desire for freedom and independence and their desire to be rich enough to buy stylish clothes, furniture, and other material attractions, in the irresistible pursuit of which they make life-changing decisions. 'Things' become the source of motivation and ambition. Deliberately echoing Flaubert's *L'Éducation sentimentale* in its simple and objective style, the novel sustains the remoteness of the narrator, offering an ironically observed portrayal of a society in the midst of change and confusion, in which Paris is a little like a huge candy store – and if you can't afford the candy you can only look at the jars.

Perec adopted a very different style for each book he wrote, and his subsequent novel, *Un Homme qui dort*, 1967 (*A Man Asleep*, 1991) is written entirely in the second person singular (the informal *tu* in the French) – the literary equivalent of the cinema's 'subjective camera', in which audience and narrator become one and in which the viewer or reader becomes intimately drawn into the action (Extract 36). The subject is a young man in deep depression who increasingly alienates himself from the world around him, secluding himself in his tiny apartment, wandering the streets of Paris alone, and sitting alone in bars and cafés watching as life goes on around him. As the novel closes, he begins to re-awaken from his 'sleep' of alienation with the realization that 'indifference is futile' and that no-one except himself is perpetuating his predicament. Perec places his engrossing short novel in the context of various other works of alienation and dysfunction through allusions and references to, for example, Kafka's *Metamorphosis*, Herman Melville's short story 'Bartleby', and Joyce's *A Portrait of the Artist as a Young Man*. *A Man Asleep* was made into a film in 1974 by Perec himself with Bernard Queysanne.

In the light of Perec's fascination with form, style, language and words (he supplied the crossword puzzles to *Le Point* magazine for six years), it is not surprising that he became a member of the OULIPO group of writers – Ouvroir de Littérature Potentielle, a movement which flourished in the 1960s and 1970s and which was based around the notion that creation and innovation in literature were best nurtured if stylistic, linguistic or structural constraints were imposed. There were many intriguing variations of these – in relation to Perec, his *La Disparition*, 1969 (*A Void*, 1995) is an appropriate example – a novel in which the letter 'e' is absent.

Perhaps Perec's greatest achievement is *La Vie mode d'emploi*, 1978 (*Life: A User's Manual*, 1987), a vast canvas of humanity, paradoxically set in one night in an apartment block in Paris, with the 99 chapters extending stories and lives from what is going on simultaneously in each of the rooms. The novel won the Prix Médicis in 1978.

Recommended biography: David Belloc, *Georges Perec: A Life in Words*, Harvill, London, 1993.

POUND, Ezra (1885–1972). Pound left the USA for Europe in 1909. He was based in London until 1920, although he made frequent visits to the continent. In April 1921, after spending three months in the south of France at **Saint-Raphaël**, he moved to Paris with his English wife Dorothy Shakespear. Pound's stay in the city was relatively short – he left in 1924, but spent much of 1923 travelling in Italy – and yet while he was here he was at the centre of expatriate literary life. He must certainly have been hard to miss – he sported a moustache and goatee and a high-standing shock of wiry hair, and took to sporting a velvet cap and old-fashioned necktie that made him look like a Latin Quarter artist c1840.

When Pound moved to Paris he was already well known in literary circles as the founder of the Imagist school of poetry. Imagism is characterized by short poems which concentrate on cadence rather than the regularity of metre and aim for precise and clear 'concrete' images, avoiding the abstract or symbolic. The approach is heavily influenced by such Japanese forms as the haiku which aim to convey a thought or emotion through a short, vivid and immediate image – see, for example, his two-line poem 'In a Station of the Metro' (*Lustra*, 1916), Extract 15. 'The natural object,' said Pound, 'is always the adequate symbol'.

Pound's energy, likeable eccentricity, and sincere generosity to younger writers brought him many friends and admirers. His apartment on **rue Notre-Dame-des-Champs** rivalled for a time that of Gertrude Stein on **rue du Fleurus** as the literary centre of the Anglo–American colony – although, as Hemingway remembered, Pound's apartment was 'as poor as Gertrude Stein's studio was rich' (he made most of his own furniture from crates, boards and canvas, which must have contrasted bizarrely with the careful elegance of Stein's home). Stein and Pound did meet, they but did not get

Ezra Pound at Shakespeare and Company

on – perhaps each saw in the other the danger of competition.

Among the writers whom Pound helped while he was in Paris were Joyce, whom he had previously encouraged to move to the city, T.S. Eliot, whose *The Waste Land* he edited during this period, and Hemingway, who gave him boxing lessons in exchange for literary advice. In *A Moveable Feast*, 1964, Hemingway remembered Pound with affection as 'the most generous writer I have ever known and the most disinterested. He helped poets, painters, sculptors and prose writers that he believed in and he would help anyone whether he believed in them or not if they were in trouble.' Pound also played a part in raising funds for Ford Madox Ford's (◊ Picardie) *Transatlantic Review*. As for his own writings, it was around this time that he began to focus exclusively, at least in terms of his creative work, on the *Cantos*, the first of which had been published in 1919 – the collected version finally appeared in 1970. (Among the many esoteric and wide-ranging cultural interests that make up this fascinating but confusingly allusive and often impenetrable poetry are Provençal songs and troubadour ballads, which also inform the pieces in *Provença*, published in 1910.) However, Pound did also write, while in Paris, an experimental opera, *Le Testament de Villon*, which was finally staged in 1926 before a première audience which included, as well as himself, a number of literary friends – Joyce, Eliot, and Hemingway, among others.

In 1924, Pound moved his base to Italy, where, as the Second World War approached, he sank into the obsession with unsavoury right wing politics which cast a long dark shadow over his reputation, signalled his mental instability, and began his slow and tragic decline. His last visit to Paris was in 1965, at the age of 80. He saw a production of Beckett's *Endgame*, and remarked to his companion 'C'est moi dans la poubelle' ('That's me in the dustbin').

Recommended biography: Humphrey Carpenter, *A Serious Character: The Life of Ezra Pound*, Faber and Faber, London and Boston, 1988.

PRÉVERT, Jacques (1900–77). Prévert was born on 4 February 1900 in **Neuilly-sur-Seine**. In the late 1920s he was peripherally involved in the Surrealist movement, along with his friends Marcel Duhamel and Yves Tanguy, whom he had met during his military service and with whom he shared a house in Paris in the **rue du Château** in Montparnasse – the 'Groupe de la rue du Château' welcomed many Surrealist artists and writers of the time. Between 1932 and 1936, Prévert was active in the left-wing agit-prop Groupe Octobre, for which he wrote political sketches. He first achieved major success as a screenwriter, and made a significant contribution to the development of French cinema in the 1930s and 1940s. His most famous credits are for Marcel Carné's *Quai des brumes*, 1938, and *Les Enfants du Paradis*, 1945, and Jean Renoir's *Le Crime de monsieur Lange*, 1935. It was not until relatively late in his writing career, in 1946 with the publication of *Paroles*, that Prévert became famous for the poetry with which he is now instantly associated.

Prévert has the privilege, from the English reader's point of view, of having been translated by Lawrence Ferlinghetti, whose verse translations are among the very few truly enjoyable and rewarding renderings in English of French poetry that this writer has come across. Ferlinghetti's *Prévert: Selections from Paroles*, 1965, includes translations of around half the poems that were published in *Paroles*. Prévert's collection appeared soon after the end of the Second World War and the poems often reflect this either directly or indirectly in their mood of dissent and protest (Extract 5). Perhaps because of that mood, Prévert's work in *Paroles* found a new following in the 1960s, when Ferlinghetti's selection was published and protest singer Joan Baez included his 'Song in the Blood' on her poetry album *Baptism*. While not always finding critical favour, perhaps because his poetry was insufficiently obscure, Prévert enjoyed an enormous readership with *Paroles*, which broke through the barriers of the usual poetry 'market' with its accessibility, its witty wordplay, and its focus on everyday language and issues. The British 'Merseybeat' poets Roger McGough, Adrian Henri and Brian Patten achieved this in the UK in the late 1960s, with a similar combination of protest, lyricism and jokes and puns. Thematically, his work is driven by an anti-establishment humanitarianism and an acute perception of the nuances of personal relationships. Stylistically, his poems work through an intelligent use of accessible language and a dazzlingly good ear for the rhythms of natural speech. Many of Prévert's poems were set to music by Joseph Kosma and sung, most famously, by Juliette Gréco and Yves Montand.

PROUST, Marcel. See under Centre.

QUENEAU, Raymond (1903–76). Queneau was born in **Le Havre**, where he spent his childhood. He studied philosophy at the Sorbonne, graduating in 1925. In the late 1920s he associated with Prévert ◊ and the 'Groupe de la rue du Château' – and, like Prévert, contributed for a short time to the Surrealist movement. Also in the late 1920s he did military service with the Zouaves in Morocco – an experience which is reflected in his novel *Odile*, 1937 (*Odile*, 1992). He worked for many years in journalism and publishing, and was the first general editor of the prestigious *Encyclopédie de la Pléiade*, which was launched in 1956. He was a member of the Société Mathémathique de France, and was elected to the Académie Goncourt in 1951. In 1960, together with the mathematician François Le Lionnais, Queneau founded OULIPO, a move-

ment which based itself around the imposition of formal constraints, and which produced works of remarkable ingenuity and inventiveness, notably by Queneau himself and Georges Perec ◊. One of Queneau's most intriguing pieces is *Cent mille milliards de poèmes*, 1961, comprising 10 sonnets with lines which can be interchanged (the rhyme scheme and grammatical structure being identical) – the number of poems that could be generated is revealed in the title (100 000 000 000 000).

Queneau has published novels, poetry, short stories, and essays – although he might have objected to those categorizations, arguing that there were no 'essential differences' between his novels and his poetry. One of his major concerns was what he saw as the stagnation of literary language and its increasing irrelevance to the reality of spoken French. His stylistic experimentation is motivated by the search for a means of reproducing in literature the energy and immediacy of the way people speak. Fortunately for his readers, this is far from a purely intellectual exercise for Queneau, and his writing is infused with a humanitarian, comic and ironic commentary on urban, predominantly working-class, life.

Zazie dans le métro, 1959 (*Zazie in the Metro*, 1982) is Queneau's most lighthearted, and his only best-selling work. This comic novel tells the story of Zazie, a precocious young girl from the provinces on her first visit to Paris. Thwarted in her ambition to ride the métro, which is closed because of a strike, she spends her time in confused sight-seeing (Extract 7) and strange encounters – a foul-mouthed Alice in an urban Wonderland. The English translation by Barbara Wright bravely attempts to recreate the abundant wordplay and inventive 'néo-français' (Queneau's term) derived from street slang. Readers will find in *Zazie* similarities not only to *Alice in Wonderland* (Queneau's favourite book) but also to the work of Joyce and Beckett. Thematically, this high-energy comic novel has at its heart the very uncertain relationship of appearance to reality (is that dome the Panthéon or the Invalides? is female impersonator uncle George actually a homosexual? is the man Zazie meets near the flea market a sex maniac or a policeman?) and Zazie's experience of 'growing up' through a series of adventures and encounters which demonstrate precisely that uncertainty ('Did you see the métro?' 'No.' 'What *have* you done then?' 'I've aged.'). Louis Malle made a film of the novel (*Zazie dans le métro*, 1960), appropriately employing techniques from the New Wave box of tricks, jump cuts and all, in an attempt to translate Queneau's literary innovations and eccentricities into cinematic language.

RHYS, Jean (1890–1979). Rhys (Ella Gwendolen Rees Williams) was born in Dominica, where she grew up. She moved to Britain in 1907. She saw Paris for the first time in autumn 1919, living there until early 1920, and it became her home for most of the period between 1922 and 1927, when she returned permanently to the UK. Although her personal life in Paris was full of trouble, Rhys remembered the city as the place she loved most – in her old age she wrote, 'I have been very faithful to it and never really loved any other city.' Unlike many of her expatriate contemporaries, Rhys did not come to Paris to be a writer and mingle in literary society – she had married a Dutch author and journalist who was then based in the city. It was here, however, that she first saw her work published, and her life in Paris was to provide the material for many of her novels and stories. The key character in this context was Ford Madox Ford (◊ Picardie) who was introduced to Rhys in 1924, read drafts of some her stories, recognized her talent, encouraged her to write for publication, gave her editorial advice and help, published her work in his *Transatlantic Review*, and wrote the preface to her first collection of stories *The Left Bank: Sketches and Studies of Present-Day Bohemian Paris*, 1927.

Through Ford Rhys associated with the literary crowd in the Left Bank cafés and restaurants, and was a regular at his weekly parties in the *bal musette* fictionalized by Hemingway in *The Sun Also Rises*. Shy and reticent, she seems not, however, to have developed any significant friendship with writers other than Ford himself. That friendship took a turn for the worse when Rhys and Ford became lovers (Rhys had moved in with Ford and his wife Stella Bowen when her husband had been jailed and then deported). The unfortunate affair ended in 1926 with Ford's rejection of her, and her novel *Quartet*, 1928 (originally published as *Postures*), may be seen as Rhys's fictional representation of the entanglement. In it, a young woman becomes manipulated by an older man Heidler, and the novel's themes of sexual passion, rejection, isolation, and violence arise from Rhys's depiction of their relationship – themes which would reoccur frequently in her later work. The novel, atmospherically set amid the cafés and cheap hotels of a wintry and melancholic **Montparnasse** (Extract 21), focuses on the psychology of the protagonist Marya's responses, perceptions and dilemmas. With its crisp and economic style and its frank portrayal of the sexual and emotional reactions of a young woman, it begs comparison with the work of Françoise Sagan ◊, which would appear some 25 years later – although Rhys portrays a more sordid end of the spectrum than is characteristic for Sagan.

Among Rhys's other fiction arising from her Parisian experiences are *After Leaving Mr Mackenzie*, 1930, set in London and Paris, a bleak story of emotional loss and desolation and the associated mental crisis, and *Good Morning, Midnight*, 1939, which follows the fortunes of a middle-aged woman alone in Paris looking for ways to ease her solitude.

After a flurry of writing during and

after her Paris years, Rhys went into a long period of obscurity – so much so that it was assumed more than once that she had died. Fame and due recognition came to her late in life – 'too late' as she often said in her old age. After a 1958 radio broadcast of *Good Morning, Midnight* she regained public attention, and 1966 saw the appearance of her best known novel, *Wide Sargasso Sea*, the first she had published since 1939. Thanks to her late glory, almost all of her books came back into print in the 1970s and are now readily available. In 1981, too late for Rhys to see it, the film of *Quartet* was released, directed by James Ivory and produced by Ismail Merchant, with Isabelle Adjani in the leading role.

Recommended biography: Carole Angier, *Jean Rhys*, Penguin, London and New York, 1992. (Includes a detailed analysis of the relationship between Rhys's life and fiction.)

SAGAN, Françoise (1935–). Sagan (real name Françoise Quoirez) was born in **Cajarc** (Lot) on 21 June 1935. She was educated in Paris, where her parents lived (her father was a wealthy industrialist). Now famous as a prolific writer of novels, plays, essays and short stories, and long a 'media personality' in France with her espousal of left-wing causes, her jet-set lifestyle, and her passion for gambling and fast cars (an enduring one despite a serious accident in 1957), Sagan scored a major success with her first book, *Bonjour tristesse*, 1953 (*Bonjour Tristesse*, 1954), which she wrote when she was 18. She wrote it after failing her examinations at the Sorbonne and dropping out. The book became a best seller, was very hip (and of course shocking for some) because of its frank portrayal of an adolescent woman's emotions and sexuality, and it won the Prix des Critiques. The story of a young woman's reaction against the intention of her promiscuous father to commit to a relationship and marry, and the tragic consequences of her intervention, sets the tone for much of

Sagan's subsequent work. The novel is short, written in a crisp, direct style (which translates well into English) with a highly intelligent and perceptive portrayal of social and sexual relationships. Characteristically, too, it is bitter-sweet – Sagan combines cynicism with sympathy and tenderness for the travails of her characters.

Un certain sourire, 1956 (*A Certain Smile*, 1956) is another high point, dealing with an affair between a young woman and a much older married man and her discovery of the pleasure and pain involved in a 'serious' relationship. *Aimez-vous Brahms . . .*, 1959 (*Aimez-vous Brahms*, 1960 – Extract 3) is, again and typically, an examination of the psychology of sexual relationships. It tells the story of Paule, a 39-year-old professional, and her choice between two lovers – one a young and romantic admirer who falls in love with her at first sight and the other her complacent and unfaithful lover of six years who offers not romance but familiarity and some kind of point to the efforts she has put into the relationship. As always, Sagan is sharp and perceptive about the motivations and thoughts of her male as well as her female characters. Among her later novels, *La Femme fardée*, 1981 (*The Painted Lady*, 1984) stands out – it is an ambitious attempt to broaden her canvas (but it is not set in France); as does *La Laisse*, 1989 (*The Leash*, 1991), set in Paris – a caustic portrayal of the attempts of a pampered husband to break out of his life of spoon-fed luxury.

Her essays are also well worth reading – especially her autobiographical *Avec mon meilleur souvenir*, 1984 (*With Fondest Regards*, 1986), which includes pieces, among others, on Jean-Paul Sartre, speed, gambling, Saint-Tropez, Orson Welles, and jazz singer Billie Holiday who told Sagan in a Paris nightclub, a few months before she died in hospital with two policemen at her side, 'De toute manière, darling, I am going to die very soon in New York, between two cops.'

SARTRE, Jean-Paul (1905–80). Sartre was born on 21 June 1905 in Paris. In 1906 his father died and his mother took him to **Meudon**, where they lived in her parents' home until 1911. Apart from three years in **La Rochelle**, where his mother moved after she remarried and where Sartre attended the *lycée*, and a brief period in **Le Havre** as a philosophy teacher at the *lycée* there, he lived almost all his life in Paris. He attended the École Normale Supérieure from 1924 to 1929, during which time he met Simone de Beauvoir ◊ who was to become his lifelong companion. He achieved first place in his *agrégation* – second place went to Beauvoir. In the 1930s he published his first significant philosophical works and his first novel, *La Nausée*, 1939 (*Nausea*, 1965). He was called up in 1939 and was subsequently captured by the Germans. During his time in the army (a not very arduous assignment in a meteorological unit) and as a captive, he kept a diary which was published in 1983 as *Carnets de la drôle de guerre* (*The War Diaries*, 1984); he worked on his famous philosophical treatise *L'Être et le néant*, 1943 (*Being and Nothingness*, 1956); he began *L'Âge de raison*, 1945 (*The Age of Reason*, 1987); he wrote and directed his first play in the prison camp; and he also produced voluminous correspondence (for his letters to Beauvoir at this time see *Quiet Moments in a War*, 1993). He escaped in 1941 and resumed his job as a teacher, but he also became associated with the Resistance movement, and developed an increasing commitment to the political left. In 1945 Sartre founded *Les Temps Modernes*, a multidisciplinary journal promoting and debating leftist ideology and thought, primarily in the contexts of, though by no means limited to, politics and literature – although it continued after Sartre's death in 1980, the journal reached its peak in the 1950s when it became a central focus for political and cultural debate. In the 1950s and 1960s, Sartre became increasingly preoccupied with political issues. After the Soviet invasion of Hungary, he turned his attention away from his hope for a Western *rapprochement* with the USSR to French policies and action in Algeria. He strongly supported the student movement in May 1968, and, in 1970, became editor-in-chief of the Maoist journal *La Cause du peuple*. In 1971, together with a group of colleagues, he set up a revolutionary press agency called Libération, a project which developed, in 1973, into the launch of the daily *Libération*, now still representing the left, though much changed, and one of France's major newspapers. Sartre's identification with left wing and radical causes continued up to his death, despite declining health and, from 1973, blindness. Among his last major concerns were the Israeli–Palestinian conflict and the plight of the Vietnamese boat people. He died on 15 April 1980. At his funeral, over 50 000 people followed his coffin through Paris, past his old haunts. He might have died a member of the Légion d'Honneur and the holder of the Nobel Prize for Literature, 1964 – but he had declined both.

Philosopher, novelist, short-story writer, playwright, biographer, autobiographer, diarist, critic, and political polemicist, Jean-Paul Sartre remains, despite his detractors, an enormously influential figure in the intellectual and literary history of the 20th century. His development of Existentialist thought – which revolves essentially around the struggle of the individual's consciousness with the 'outside world', or the set of imposed circumstances in which it finds itself, and with other individual consciousnesses – runs through his work and is set out in different aspects in his philosophical texts, notably *Being and Nothingness* and *Critique de la raison dialectique*, 1960 (*The Critique of Dialectical Reason*, 1976). His explorations of Existentialism encouraged innovation in the other genres in which he worked. Among his biographies (whose subjects included Baudelaire and Flaubert), there is his devastating psychoanalytical examination of Jean Genet, his role, and his work in *Saint Genet, comédien et martyr*, 1952 (*Saint Genet, Actor and Martyr*, 1963). His autobiographical *Les Mots*, 1963 (*Words*, 1964) is a self-analytical and meticulously written evocation of his early years. His plays are essentially dramatizations of his philosophical and political concerns, which sometimes make for surprisingly compulsive theatre – as, for example, does *Huis Clos*, 1944 (*No Exit*, 1948), in which three characters interact to mutual disadvantage in the hell to which they have been condemned – a *salon* in which they have to stay together forever. Among Sartre's novels, *Nausea* is perhaps the most famous – in it he attempts to represent in fiction his Existentialist vision. It tells the story of Antoine Roquentin, who becomes increasingly alienated by the absurd and contingent nature of the world around him and the novel portrays him in an increasing state of Existential angst, physically manifested as nausea. Through his character Sartre explores questions of individual identity and the search for significance, and in so doing presents a picture of alienation from and hostility to the established order of things, the old assumptions, which was to become the essence of the Left Bank protest movement which centred around the cafés of Saint-Germain-des-Prés in the 1940s and 1950s, and which defined itself as Existentialist.

The novel highlighted here, *La Mort dans l'âme*, 1949 (*Iron in the Soul*, 1950) is the third volume in the projected 4-volume set *Les Chemins de la liberté* (*The Roads to Freedom*) – the fourth volume never appeared. The first two novels in the series are *L'Âge de raison*, 1945 (*The Age of Reason*, 1961) and *Le Sursis*, 1945 (*The Reprieve*, 1963). *Iron in the Soul* is set in the occupied France of 1940 (Extract 26) and portrays a diverse set of characters and places in a state of flux, with choices to make and loyalties to decide. The breakdown of the known order (represented in the novel by the fall of Paris, the heart of French culture) is an ideal context for Sartre to explore his Existential themes and he shows his characters working out their own destinies – the central character of *The Roads to Freedom*, Mathieu Delarue, moves in the course of the novels from a commitment to his own individual freedom through to, in *Iron in the Soul*, involvement in the conflict and solidarity with his colleagues. A mixture of action and political/philosophical polemic, the novel is both a dramatic portrayal of a country in crisis and a demonstration of Sartre's ideas and politics at the time.

Recommended biography: Annie Cohen-Solal, *Sartre: A Life*, Minerva, London, 1991/Pantheon, New York, 1987.

SIMENON, Georges (1903–89). Simenon was born in Liège, Belgium, on 12 February 1903. He began to write at the age of 16, working as a reporter on the *Gazette de Liège*. When he was 22, he moved to Paris. His early time there was spent in poverty, but he soon rose to fame and fortune through his astonishingly prolific output of short stories and novels. At the peak of his literary production, he was writing 80 pages a day, producing a short novel in three days. At the same he was generating numerous short stories for magazines (often eight in a day, according to Simenon himself); sometimes several would be published in the same issue of a magazine, each under a different pseudonym (in fact, Simenon published his hundreds of novels under around 20 pseudonyms – but still over 200 were signed in his own name). The money he earned from his writing allowed him to indulge his obsession for travel, which he did extensively. His other famous obsession was sex, which, he claimed in a 1977 interview, he had had with 10 000 women (he later explained that 8000 of these had been prostitutes). In keeping with his restless spirit, Simenon lived in various parts of France, and for a time in the USA, but he finally settled in Switzerland in 1957. In 1972, he suddenly gave up creative writing, as if he had overcome an addiction, or expelled a demon – he even changed his passport description from 'novelist' to 'no profession'. After that, he restricted his writing to auto-biography, of which he produced some 12 volumes. He died at his home in Lausanne, Switzerland, on 4 September 1989.

Simenon's most famous literary crea-tion is Commissaire Maigret, who appears in over 80 novels, and whose adventures have been much filmed and televised since the first Maigret novel, *Pietr-le-Letton*, appeared in 1931 (*Maig-ret and the Enigmatic Lett*, 1963). Although by no means all of them are set in Paris, Simenon's Maigret stories are perhaps especially memorable for their portrait of life in the cafés and bars of the poorer *quartiers* of the capit-al. The author is a roving camera paus-ing and focusing here and there on a life or a story from the teeming mass of lives and stories that the city contains. In the genre of detective fiction, Sime-non is distinctive for his concentration on the psychology of his main character (and on the psychology of crime) – the whodunnit and what-happens-next in-terests in effect take second place to the thoughts and intuitive responses of Maigret and the motivations of the unfortunates whose paths he crosses. In the novel highlighted here, **Mont-martre** is a key setting. *Maigret et le client du samedi*, 1962 (*Maigret and the Saturday Caller*, 1964) starts with the curious occurrence of a man coming to Maigret to confess that he is about to murder his wife and her lover. Typical-ly, this is a sad tale of suffering, selfish-ness and greed set atmospherically and with specific local detail in the Paris Simenon knew so well (Extract 18).

Recommended biography: Patrick Marn-ham, *The Man Who Wasn't Maigret: A Portrait of Georges Simenon*, Blooms-bury, London, 1992.

STEIN, Gertrude (1874–1946). Stein arrived in Paris in 1903, and moved into her brother Leo's apartment at **27 rue de Fleurus**, next to the Jardin du Luxembourg. This was her home until 1938, and where she held her famous *salons* from the early 1900s to the 1930s. Alice B. Toklas moved in in 1909, as Stein's secretary, and became her lifelong companion. In 1914, Leo moved out – they later became so estranged that Stein denied his exist-ence.

In the years before the First World War, the visitors to the rue de Fleurus were primarily artists and buyers of art – Leo and Gertrude's *salon* was a centre for the discussion and promotion of modern painting (Gertrude was an ar-dent supporter of Cubism). Among the regular guests were Matisse and Picasso, who became a close friend of Stein for many years. The walls of the apartment were lined with what became a legen-dary art collection, with paintings by

Gertrude Stein

Picasso, Gaugin, Cézanne, Renoir, and Matisse among many others.

After the war, the artistic circle drifted away from Paris, to be replaced by young American writers who came to or stayed in France, attracted by the literary and social culture of Paris (and the very favourable exchange rate), and alienated from their home country with its traditional value system which they rejected, with no idea, however, of what to put in its place. Stein gave them a name when she told Hemingway, 'You are all a lost generation.' Her now predominantly literary *salons* again became renowned, and she received in her apartment at one time or another almost all the notable British and American writers of the avant-garde who lived in or passed through Paris in the 1920s and 1930s – getting an introduction to Miss Stein was on the agenda of most of them. A significant exception to her vast literary acquaintance was James Joyce, whose reputation as the greatest and most innovative writer of the time she seemed to resent, perhaps because her own experimental writing was, by comparison, barely noticed.

Stein's own work has, on the whole, continued to find only a very small public, although elements of her consciously naïve and unadorned style influenced some of the younger writers she encouraged, among them Hemingway and Sherwood Anderson. Her experimental use of repetition and minimal punctuation can render her style difficult and obscure, and the eccentricity of some her undertakings – like her enormous *The Making of Americans*, published by Robert McAlmon's small press in Paris in 1925 – made it hard for even adventurous publishers to see a market, although she did publish a number of short pieces in reviews such as *Transition*. Stein resorted to private publication in the 1930s when she and Toklas set up their own press, Plain Editions, which Stein financed by selling two of her Picassos. Several of her titles appeared under its imprint – the

first Plain title was her novel *Lucy Church Amiably*, 1930, a typically idiosyncratic celebration of the countryside around Stein's summer home at **Bilignin**, just outside **Belley**.

It was not until the publication of *The Autobiography of Alice B. Toklas* (Extract 19) in 1933 that Stein achieved a wide readership. Unlike her previous work – although retaining elements, to great effect, of her characteristic style – it is an instantly accessible, fast-moving, and very humorous collection of anecdotes about her life in the rue de Fleurus and the various people she met there, from Picasso to Hemingway. Although it is Stein's memoir, it is written entirely in the style, and from the perspective of Alice B. Toklas. Like Hemingway's ◊ *A Moveable Feast*, it is a highly subjective memoir and needs a pinch of salt – a number of the people who appear in it (Matisse, Tzara, Braque, among others) published their combined objections in the February 1935 issue of *Transition*. Hemingway himself responded to his portrayal by writing critically of Stein in *A Moveable Feast*. Nevertheless, the picture it paints is no doubt *essentially* true, and *The Autobiography* remains one of the best and most entertaining insights into artistic and literary Paris from the turn of the century to the end of the 1920s.

In 1938, Stein was forced to give up the lease on the rue de Fleurus apartment and she and Alice moved into a new home on **rue Christine**. During the war they remained in France, living at their other home at Bilignin – an experience which inspired *Wars I Have Seen*, 1945, which deals with her life in rural France in wartime and the arrival of the liberating Americans in autumn 1944 (her play *Yes Is For a Very Young Man*, 1946, was drawn from this memoir); and *Brewsie and Willie*, 1946, a novel which works through conversations in American slang among a group of American GIs in France to convey their thoughts about going home. Stein and Toklas returned to Paris in 1944, where Gertrude died of stomach cancer in 1946. Alice continued to live at their apartment until 1964 (she died in 1967). They are buried under the same tombstone in **Père Lachaise**.

Among Stein's other work is *Paris France*, 1940, a short book of personal reminiscences and reflections, highlighting what attracted her so much to the French lifestyle. See also Alice B. Toklas's *What Is Remembered*, 1963, and *The Alice B. Toklas Cook Book*, 1954, combining recipes with memories. *Gertrude Stein Remembered*, 1994, compiled by Linda Simon, collects pieces on Stein by, among others, Sylvia Beach, Sherwood Anderson, Robert McAlmon, and Thornton Wilder.

Recommended biography: Janet Hobhouse, *Everybody Who Was Anybody: A Biography of Gertrude Stein*, Arena, London, 1975.

SÜSKIND, Patrick. See under Provence.

VERLAINE, Paul (1844–96). Verlaine began his turbulent life in **Metz**, where he was born into a middle-class family on 30 March 1844. He was educated in Paris at the Lycée Condorcet. He began to study law at university but, already distracted by the temptations of literature, café-life and alcohol, he was far from a dedicated student. In 1864 his father, despairing of his son's academic prospects, found him employment as a clerk in an insurance company and subsequently at the Hôtel de Ville. These undemanding positions left Verlaine with plenty of time to spend in the society of young writers and artists, and he became associated with the group of poets centred around *Le Parnasse contemporain* – a series of three volumes of poetry, published in instalments, which appeared in 1866, 1871, and 1876, and in which some of Verlaine's own work appeared. The Parnassian movement in French poetry comprised essentially a rejection of what it saw as the outdated and indulgent self expression and formal indiscipline of

Romanticism (as represented, for example, by the work of Lamartine) – instead, Les Parnassiens sought greater objectivity and technical perfection. To an extent they paved the way for Symbolism – it was with this theoretical impetus that poets such as Baudelaire, Mallarmé and Verlaine developed their various and far-reaching innovations in style and content.

In Verlaine's early collection *Poèmes saturniens*, 1866, the Parnassian influence is strong – but the most memorable poems in the volume, such as 'Nocturne Parisien' (Extract 39), already show characteristics of the stunning evocations of mood and sensation that lie at the heart of his best work. His second published volume, *Fêtes galantes*, 1869, again in the Parnassian vein, features carefully composed word-pictures, with references to the stylized pastorals of Fragonard, Watteau, etc – as, for example, in the famous 'Clair de lune'.

In 1869, Verlaine met and fell in love with 16-year-old Mathilde Mauté, and they married in 1870. The poems of *La Bonne Chanson*, 1870, celebrate this period and reveal his (sadly unrealized) aspirations for married life. Mauté was ill suited to Verlaine's tempestuous, emotion-driven personality – they were married long enough to have a child, but the relationship disintegrated rapidly and was legally ended in 1874. Its chances of success were not helped by Verlaine's increasing drunkenness, which developed considerably during his service in the Garde Nationale in 1870–71, and during his unemployment following the collapse of the Commune of 1871 (for which he had worked briefly in the press censorship department).

It was in 1871 that Verlaine received some verses from the adolescent and extremely unruly Arthur Rimbaud (◊ Champagne–Ardenne), whom he invited to Paris. And so began their famous and stormy affair. Verlaine, obsessed with Rimbaud, left his home and family in 1872. The two poets led a wandering, dissolute life, staying for a time in London and Brussels. From this period emerged the poems of *Romans sans paroles*, 1874, which fluctuate in mood from the joy of the open road to abject misery and bitter regret. The affair, marked by a series of drunken arguments, ended abruptly when Verlaine shot and wounded Rimbaud in Brussels in July 1873 – he spent the next two years in prison at Mons. The relationship between Verlaine and Rimbaud is the subject of British playwright Christopher Hampton's *Total Eclipse*, 1968.

During his incarceration, Verlaine turned back to the Catholic faith into which he had been born. The poems of *Sagesse*, 1880–81, reflect his 'conversion' and penitence. For the rest of his life, he would punctuate his habitual debauchery with periodic attacks of guilt.

On his release from prison, Verlaine went to England, where he spent almost two years as a schoolteacher. He continued teaching when he returned to France in 1877, and in **Rethel** in the Ardennes he met and befriended Lucien Létinois, a pupil at the Collège Notre-Dame. With Létinois, he tried but failed to earn his living as a farmer in the Ardennes, returned to England and finally came full circle back to Paris, where his '*fils adoptif*' died of typhoid. The collection *Amour*, 1888, includes many poems inspired by Létinois.

In 1883–85 Verlaine tried rural life again, but the attempt came to an end when he was imprisoned for attacking his mother, who was keeping house for him. After this episode, Verlaine lived in Paris for the rest of his life, in poverty and reliant on the help of his friends and public institutions for his survival.

Despite his penury, alcoholism, and increasing ill health, Verlaine spent his last years a respected literary figure, and a key reference point for the Symbolists. Apart from the growing reputation of his poetry, he had gained prominence with his *Les Poètes maudits*, 1884, a short critical study aiming to bring attention to six poets whom Verlaine thought neglected – including Mallarmé, Rimbaud, and 'Pauvre Lelian' (an anagram of his own name). His poem 'Art poétique', published in the volume *Jadis et naguère*, 1885, was another important contribution to the poetic debate of the time, and constitutes a concise summary of Verlaine's own poetic values and aims. In it, he emphasizes the importance of rhythm and 'musicality' ('De la musique avant toute chose'), advises against grandiloquence and verbosity, and against over-rigidity of rhyme and form – the stress is on fluidity and subtlety, on nuance and shades of tone and meaning, and on the cautious freedom of *vers libéré*, as opposed to the more radical *vers libre* which Verlaine did not espouse.

At its best, Verlaine's verse is unsurpassed in its ability to evoke shades of mood and nuances of mood-driven perception. These it achieves through quite remarkable precision and control in the choice of rhythm and language – all the more captivating for the contrast with the messy and out-of-control life from which they emerged.

Recommended biography: Joanna Richardson, *Paul Verlaine*, Weidenfeld and Nicolson, London, 1971.

ACKNOWLEDGMENTS AND CITATIONS

The author and publisher are very grateful to the many literary agents, publishers, authors, translators, and other individuals who have given their permission for the use of extracts and photographs, supplied photographs, or helped in the location of copyright holders. Every effort has been made to identify and contact the appropriate copyright owners or their representatives. The publisher would welcome any further information.

EXTRACTS

Nord–Pas-de-Calais; Picardie; Champagne–Ardenne; Alsace–Lorraine: (1) Julien Gracq, *A Balcony in the Forest*, Richard Howard, trans, Harvill, London, 1992, pp 10–11. First published in Great Britain by Hutchinson and Co 1960, in a new edition by Harvill 1996. © Librairie José Corti 1958. English translation © George Braziller, Inc 1959. By permission of The Harvill Press. (2) Elizabeth Bowen, *The House in Paris*, Penguin, London, 1976, pp 144–145. Copyright 1935 and renewed 1963 by Elizabeth Bowen. By permission of Alfred A. Knopf, Inc. (3) Charles Dickens, 'Our French Watering Place', in *The Uncommercial Traveller and Reprinted Pieces*, Oxford University Press, Oxford, 1958, pp 402–403. (4) Laurence Sterne, *A Sentimental Journey Through France and Italy*, Penguin, London, 1986, pp 36–37. (5) Arthur Rimbaud, 'By the Bandstand', in *Rimbaud: Poems*, Everyman's Library Pocket Poets, London, 1994, pp 25–26. Originally published in *Arthur Rimbaud: Complete Works*, translated by Paul Schmidt. Copyright © 1967, 1970, 1971, 1972, 1975 by Paul Schmidt. By permission of Harper-Collins Publishers, Inc. (6) P.G. Wodehouse, *French Leave*, The Popular Book Club, London, 1957, pp 64–65. First published by Herbert Jenkins. By permission of Random House UK Ltd and A.P. Watt Ltd on behalf of The Trustees of the Wodehouse Trust. (7) Gérard de Nerval, *Sylvie*, in *Aurélia, followed by Sylvie*, Kendall Lappin, trans, Asylum Arts, Santa Maria, CA, 1993, pp 127–128. *Sylvie* translation copyright © 1993 Kendall Lappin. (8) Victor Hugo, *Les Misérables*, Norman Denny, trans, Penguin, London, 1982, pp 177–178. Introduction by Norman Denny. This translation first published by The Folio Society in 1976. Translation copyright © 1976 The Folio Society.

By permission of The Folio Society. (9) Émile Zola, *Germinal*, Leonard Tancock, trans, Penguin, London, 1954, pp 78–79. Copyright © Leonard Tancock 1954. By permission of Penguin Books Ltd. (10) Claude Simon, *The Flanders Road*, Richard Howard, trans, John Calder, London, 1985, p 231. Copyright © 1960 Les Éditions de Minuit. Translation copyright © 1961, 1985 George Braziller, Inc. By permission of The Calder Educational Trust, London, and Riverrun Press, New York. (11) Johann Wolfgang von Goethe, *Truth and Fantasy*, Eithne Wilkins and Ernst Kaiser, trans, Weidenfeld and Nicolson, London, 1949, pp 130–131. (12) Ford Madox Ford, *Parade's End, Volume 2: No More Parades*, Sphere, London, 1969, pp 53–54. By permission of David Higham Associates. (13) Robert Graves, *Goodbye To All That*, Penguin, London, 1960, pp 175–176. Copyright © Robert Graves, 1929, 1957. By permission of Carcanet Press Ltd. (14) Wilfred Owen, 'Anthem for Doomed Youth', *The Collected Poems of Wilfred Owen*, C. Day Lewis, ed, Chatto and Windus, London, 1963, p 44. (15) Siegfried Sassoon, *Memoirs of an Infantry Officer*, Faber and Faber, London, 1930, pp 28–29. By permission of Faber and Faber Ltd and George Sassoon. (16) Henri Barbusse, *Under Fire*, Fitzwater Wray, trans, Everyman's Library, J.M. Dent, London, 1929, pp 148–149. (17) Erich Maria Remarque, *All Quiet on the Western Front*, Triad Granada, London, 1977, pp 186–187. Translation copyright © Putnam and Co Ltd. **Burgundy; Franche-Comté; Rhône–Alpes:** Gabriel Chevallier, *Clochemerle*, Jocelyn Godefroi, trans, Penguin, London, 1971, pp 16–17. Copyright © Gabriel Chevallier, 1936. By permission of Reed Books. (2) Stendhal, *Scarlet and Black*, Margaret R. B. Shaw, trans, Penguin,

London, 1953, pp 177–178. Copyright © 1953 by Margaret R.B. Shaw. By permission of Penguin Books Ltd. (3) Mark Hebden, *Pel and the Predators*, Futura, London, 1985, pp 2–3. Copyright © 1984 by Mark Hebden. First published in Great Britain in 1984 by Hamish Hamilton Ltd. (4) William Carlos Williams, *A Voyage to Pagany*, New Directions, New York, 1970, pp 237–238. Copyright © 1938, 1970 by New Directions Publishing Corp. By permission of New Directions Publishing Corp. (5) Matthew Arnold, 'Stanzas from the Grande Chartreuse', in *The Poems of Matthew Arnold*, Kenneth Allott, ed, Longman, London, 1965. (6) William Wordsworth, *The Prelude*, Oxford University Press, Oxford and New York, 1970, p 96. (7) John Berger, *Pig Earth*, Writers and Readers Publishing Cooperative, London, 1979, pp 106–107. Copyright © John Berger 1979. Published in the USA by Pantheon Boooks. By permission of Pantheon Books, a division of Random House, Inc. (8) Mary Shelley, *Frankenstein*, Oxford University Press, Oxford, 1980, pp 98–99. (9) Percy Bysshe Shelley, 'Mont Blanc', in *Poetical Works*, Thomas Hutchinson, ed, with corrections by G.M. Matthews, Oxford University Press, Oxford and New York, 1970, p 533. (10) Sylvie Germain, *Days of Anger*, Christine Donougher, trans, Dedalus, Sawtry, 1993, p 14. *Jours de colère* copyright © Éditions Gallimard. English translation copyright © Christine Donougher 1993. By permission of Dedalus Books and David R. Godine, Publisher, Inc. (11) Colette, *My Mother's House and Sido*, Una Vincenzo Troubridge and Enid McLeod, trans, Penguin, London, 1966, pp 23–24. Translation copyright 1953 by Martin Secker and Warburg Ltd. By permission of Reed Books. **Provence–Alpes–Côte d'Azur and Monaco:** (1) Lawrence Durrell, *Monsieur, or The Prince of Darkness*, Faber and Faber, London, 1976, p 15. Copyright © Lawrence Durrell, 1974. By permission of Faber and Faber Ltd. (2) F. Scott Fitzgerald, *Tender Is the Night*, Scribner, New York, 1985, pp 17–18. By permission of Scribner, a Division of Simon & Schuster. Copyright 1933, 1934 by Charles Scribner's Sons. Copyright renewed © 1961, 1962 by Frances Scott Fitzgerald Lanahan. (3) Patrick Süskind, *Perfume: The Story of a Murderer*, John E. Woods, trans, Hamish Hamilton, London, 1986, pp 122–123. First published as *Das Parfüm* by Diogenes Verlag AG, Zurich, 1985. Copyright © Diogenes Verlag AG, 1985. Translation copyright © John E. Woods 1986. By permission of Penguin Books Ltd. (4) Alexandre Dumas, *The Count of Monte Cristo*, World's Classics, Oxford University Press, Oxford, 1990, pp 15–16. (5) *Ibid*, pp 66–67. (6) Sembène Ousmane, *Black Docker*, Ros Schwartz, trans, Heinemann, Oxford, 1987, pp 69–70. *Le Docker noir* © Présence Africaine, Paris, 1973. Translation copyright © Ros Schwartz 1986. By permission of Heinemann Educational, Oxford, and La Société Nouvelle Présence Africaine. (7) Graham Greene, *Loser Takes All*, in *The Third Man and Loser Takes All*, William Heinemann and The Bodley Head, London, 1976, pp 152–153. By permission of David Higham Associates. (8) W. Somerset Maugham, 'The Facts of Life', in *Collected Short Stories*, Mandarin, London, 1990, pp 251–252. Copyright © by The Royal Literary Fund. By permission of Reed Books and A.P. Watt Ltd on behalf of The Royal Literary Fund. (9) Tobias Smollett, *Travels Through France and Italy*, World's Classics, Oxford University Press, Oxford, 1981, pp 151–152. (10) Jean Giono, *The Man Who Planted Trees*, Peter Owen, London, 1989, pp 25–26. Copyright © 1985 by Chelsea Green Publishing Company. Originally published in *Vogue* under the title 'The Man Who Planted Hope and Grew Happiness'. Copyright ©1954 (renewed in 1982) by The Condé Nast Publications, Inc. By permission of Peter Owen Ltd. (11) Sybille Bedford, *A Compass Error*, Virago, London, 1984, pp 24–25. Copyright © Sybille Bedford 1968. By permission of HarperCollins Publishers Ltd. (12) Dirk Bogarde, *Jericho*, Penguin, London, 1992, pp 100–101. Copyright © Motley Films Ltd, 1992. By permission of Penguin Books Ltd and the Peters, Fraser and Dunlop Group Ltd. (13) Alphonse Daudet, *Tartarin of Tarascon*, Everyman's Library, J.M. Dent, London, and Dutton, New York, 1969, p 11. (14) Marcel Pagnol, *The Water of the Hills*, W.E. van Heyningen, trans, Picador, London, 1989, pp 3–4. Copyright © Marcel Pagnol, 1962. English translation copyright © 1988 by W.E. van Heyningen. By permission of André Deutsch Ltd. **Corsica:** (1) Edward Lear, *Journal of a Landscape Painter in Corsica*, in *Edward Lear's Journals: A Selection*, Herbert van Thal, ed, Arthur Barker, London, 1952, pp 135–136. (2) *Ibid*, p 183. (3) James Boswell, *The Journal of a Tour to Corsica*, In Print Publishing, Brighton, 1996, pp 34–36. (4) Guy de Maupassant, *A Woman's Life*, H.N.P. Sloman, trans, Penguin, London, 1965, pp 61–62. Copyright © H.N.P. Sloman, 1965. By permission of Penguin Books Ltd. (5) Prosper Mérimée, *Colomba*, in *Carmen/Colomba*, Edward Marielle, trans, Penguin, London, 1965, pp 148–149. Copyright © Edward Marielle, 1965. By permission of Penguin Books Ltd. (6) Dorothy Carrington, *Granite Island: A Portrait of Corsica*, Penguin, London, 1984, p 2. Copyright © Dorothy Carrington, 1971. By permission of A.M. Heath & Company Ltd. **Languedoc–Roussillon; Midi–Pyrénées; Aquitaine; Poitou–Charentes:** (1) Janet Lewis, *The Wife of Martin Guerre*, Penguin, London, 1977, p 24. Copyright © Janet Lewis, 1941. (2) François Mauriac, *Thérèse Desqueyroux*, in *Thérèse*, Gerard Hopkins, trans, Penguin, London, 1959, pp 63–64. Translation copyright © Eyre Methuen Ltd, 1972. (3) Henry James, *A Little Tour in*

France, Penguin, London, 1985, pp 137–138. (4) Robert Louis Stevenson, *Travels With a Donkey*, in *Travels With a Donkey, An Inland Voyage*, The *Silverado Squatters*, Everyman, London, 1993, pp 205–206. (5) Christine de Rivoyre, *Boy*, Eileen Ellenbogen, trans, Penguin, London, 1976, pp 100–101. Copyright © Éditions Grasset & Fasquelle, 1973. Translation copyright © Hamish Hamilton Ltd, 1974. By permission of Penguin Books Ltd. (6) Stendhal, *Travels in the South of France*, Elisabeth Abbott, trans, Calder and Boyars, London, 1971, pp 171–172. Copyright © Elisabeth Abbott, 1970. By permission of The Calder Educational Trust and Riverrun Press, New York. (7) Arthur Koestler, *Scum of the Earth*, Eland, London, 1991, pp 136–137. By permission of the Peters Fraser and Dunlop Group Ltd. **Auvergne, Limousin, Centre:** (1) *Gargantua and Pantagruel*, J.M. Cohen, trans, Penguin, London, 1955, pp 73–74. Copyright © J.M. Cohen, 1955. By permission of Penguin Books Ltd. (2) Alain-Fournier, *Le Grand Meaulnes*, Frank Davison, trans, Penguin, London, 1966, pp 17–18. Translation copyright © Oxford University Press 1959. By permission of Oxford University Press. (3) Marcel Proust, *Remembrance of Things Past*, C.K. Scott Moncrieff and Terence Kilmartin, trans, Penguin, London, 1983, Vol 1, pp 50–51. Translation copyright © by Random House, Inc. By permission of Random House, Inc and Random House UK Ltd. (4) George Sand, *The Master Pipers*, Rosemary Lloyd, trans, World's Classics, Oxford University Press, Oxford and New York, 1994, pp 74–75. Copyright © Rosemary Lloyd 1994. By permission of Oxford University Press. (5) John Ruskin, *The Diaries of John Ruskin*, selected and edited by Joan Evans and John Howard Whitehouse, Oxford University Press, Oxford, 1956, p 87. (6) Anthony Trollope, 'The Château of Prince Polignac', in *Anthony Trollope: The Collected Shorter Fiction*, Julian Thompson, ed, Robinson, London, 1992, pp 115–116. **Pays de la Loire; Brittany; Normandy:** (1) Jean Genet, *Querelle of Brest*, Gregory Streatham, trans, Faber and Faber, London, 1973, p 10. Copyright © Jean Genet, 1953. Translation copyright © Anthony Blond Ltd, 1966. By permission of Faber and Faber Ltd. (2) Jack Kerouac, *Satori in Paris*, Paladin, London, 1991, pp 73–74. Copyright © Jack Kerouac 1966. (3) Marcel Proust, *Remembrance of Things Past*, C.K. Scott Moncrieff and Terence Kilmartin, trans, Penguin, London, 1983, Vol 1, pp 712–713. Translation copyright © by Random House, Inc. By permission of Random House, Inc and Random House UK Ltd. (4) François-René Chateaubriand, *The Memoirs of Chateaubriand*, Robert Baldick, trans, Penguin, London, 1965, p 84. Translation copyright © Hamish Hamilton, 1961. (5) André Gide, *Journals 1889–1949*, Justin O'Brien, selected and trans, Penguin, London,

1967, pp 109–110. Copyright 1947 by Alfred A. Knopf, Inc. By permission of Alfred A. Knopf, Inc. (6) Guy de Maupassant, 'The Model', in *Selected Short Stories*, Roger Colet, trans, Penguin, London, 1971, pp 243–244. Copyright © Roger Colet, 1971. By permission of Penguin Books Ltd. (7) E.E. Cummings, *The Enormous Room*, Liveright, New York and London, 1978, pp 67–68. A typescript edition, with drawings by the author, edited by George James Firmage. Copyright 1922, 1950, © 1978 by the Trustees for the E.E. Cummings Trust. Copyright © 1978 by George James Firmage. By permission of Liveright Publishing Corporation. (8) John Fowles, 'The Ebony Tower', in *The Ebony Tower*, Panther, London, 1974, p 58. Copyright © 1974 by John Fowles. By permission of Sheil Land Associates Ltd on behalf of John Fowles. (9) Simone de Beauvoir, *The Prime of Life*, Peter Green, trans, Penguin, London, 1965, p 202. *La Force de l'âge* first published in France,1960. Copyright © Librairie Gallimard, 1960. Translation copyright © The World Publishing Company, 1962. By permission of Penguin Books Ltd. (10) Jean Rouaud, *Fields of Glory*, Ralph Manheim, trans, Harvill, London, 1992, pp 9–10. First published in France by Les Éditions de Minuit in 1990, in Great Britain by Harvill in 1992. Copyright © 1990 by Les Éditions de Minuit, copyright © 1992 in the English translation by Arcade Publishing, Inc. By permission of The Harvill Press and Arcade. (11) Michèle Roberts, *Daughters of the House*, Virago, 1993, pp 6–7. Copyright © Michèle Roberts 1992. By permission of Michèle Roberts and Virago Press. (12) Helen Waddell, *Peter Abelard*, Constable, London, 1992, pp 96–97. By permission of Constable Publishers. (13) Ernest Dowson, 'Breton Afternoon', in *The Poems of Ernest Dowson*, Mark Longaker, ed, Oxford University Press, London, 1962, p 125. (14) Marguerite Duras, *Emily L.*, Barbara Bray, trans, Pantheon, New York, 1990, pp 3–4. Translation copyright © 1989 by Random House, Inc. By permission of Random House, Inc. (15) Julian Barnes, *Flaubert's Parrot*, Picador, London, 1985, pp 11–12. Copyright © Julian Barnes 1984. First published in the UK by Jonathan Cape. By permission of Random House UK Ltd. (16) John Evelyn, *The Diary and Correspondence of John Evelyn*, William Bray, ed, Vol 1, George Bell and Sons, London, 1906, p 64. (17) Gustave Flaubert, *Madame Bovary*, Alan Russell, trans, Penguin, London, 1950, pp 274–275. Copyright © The Estate of Alan Russell, 1950. By permission of Penguin Books Ltd. (18) William Shakespeare, *King Henry the Fifth*, in *Complete Works of William Shakespeare*, Peter Alexander, ed, Collins, London, 1951, p 585 (V, ii). (19) Honoré de Balzac, *Eugénie Grandet*, Marion Ayton Crawford, trans, Penguin, London, 1955, pp 36–37. Translation copyright © The Estate of Marion Ayton Crawford, 1955. By permission of Penguin Books Ltd. (20) Annie Ernaux, *Positions*, Tanya Leslie, trans, Quartet, London, 1991, pp 41–43. English translation copyright © by Quartet Books 1991. First published in France as *La Place* in 1983, copyright © by Éditions Gallimard 1983. By permission of Quartet Books Ltd. **Île-de-France:** (1) Raymond Radiguet, *The Devil in the Flesh*, A.M. Sheridan Smith, trans, Marion Boyars, London, 1982, pp 74–75. Translation copyright © Marion Boyars Publishers Ltd, 1968, 1982, 1986, 1988. By permission of Marion Boyars. (2) Paul Valéry, 'Valvins', David Paul, trans, in *The Collected Works of Paul Valéry*, Jackson Matthews, ed, Vol 1, Princeton University Press, Princeton, NJ, 1971, p 39. By permission of Princeton University Press. **Paris:** (1) Marie Cardinal, *The Words To Say It*, Pat Goodheart, trans, The Women's Press, London, 1993, pp 207–208. Copyright © Marie Cardinal 1975. Translation copyright © Van Vector and Goodheart, Inc, 1983. By permission of The Women's Press Ltd, 34 Great Sutton Street, London EC1V 0DX, UK. (2) Marcel Proust, *Remembrance of Things Past*, C.K. Scott Moncrieff and Terence Kilmartin, trans, Penguin, London, 1983, Vol 1, pp 456–457. Translation copyright © by Random House, Inc. By permission of Random House, Inc and Random House UK Ltd. (3) Françoise Sagan, *Aimez-Vous Brahms . . .*, Peter Wiles, trans, Penguin, London, 1962, pp 66–67. First published in France in 1959. Copyright © Françoise Sagan, 1959. English translation copyright © John Murray, 1960. (4) Nancy Mitford, *The Blessing*, Penguin, London, 1957, pp 177–178. By permission of the Peters Fraser & Dunlop Group on behalf of the Estate of Nancy Mitford. (5) Jacques Prévert, *Selections from Paroles*, Lawrence Ferlinghetti, trans, Penguin, London, 1965, p 15. Copyright © Librairie Gallimard, 1949. Translation copyright © Lawrence Ferlinghetti, 1958. (6) Ernest Hemingway, *The Snows of Kilimanjaro and Other Stories*, Scribner, New York, 1987, pp 20–21. Copyright 1936 by Ernest Hemingway. Copyright © renewed 1964 by Mary Hemingway. By permission of Scribner, a division of Simon & Schuster. (7) Raymond Queneau, *Zazie in the Metro*, Barbara Wright, trans, John Calder, London, 1982, pp 92–93. © Librairie Gallimard 1959, 1982. Translation © Barbara Wright 1960, 1982. By permission of The Calder Educational Trust, London, and Riverrun Press, New York. (8) Patrick Süskind, *Perfume: The Story of a Murderer*, John E. Woods, trans, Hamish Hamilton, London, 1986, p 36. First published as *Das Parfüm* by Diogenes Verlag AG, Zurich, 1985. Copyright © Diogenes Verlag AG, 1985. Translation copyright © John E. Woods 1986. By permission of Penguin Books Ltd. (9) Colette, *Claudine in Paris*, Antonia White, trans, Penguin, London, 1963, p 16. Translation copyright © Martin Secker and Warburg Ltd, 1958. By permission of Reed Books. (10) *Love in the Days of Rage*, Minerva, London, 1990, pp 78–79. Copyright © Lawrence Ferlinghetti, 1988. (11) Mavis Gallant, *Paris Notebooks*, Hamish Hamilton, London, 1988, pp 15–16. Copyright © 1968, 1971, 1972, 1973, 1974, 1976, 1977, 1978, 1981, 1982, 1983, 1984, 1985, 1986 by Mavis Gallant. By permission of Georges Borchardt, Inc, and Macmillan Canada. (12) Honoré de Balzac, *Père Goriot*, Henry Reed, trans, New American Library, New York, 1962, pp 8–9. Copyright © 1962 by Henry Reed. (13) John Evelyn, *The Diary and Correspondence of John Evelyn*, William Bray, ed, Vol 1, George Bell and Sons, London, 1906, p 68. (14) Shusha Guppy, *A Girl in Paris*, Minerva, London, 1992, pp 71–72. Copyright Shusha Guppy 1991. By permission of Reed Books. (15) Ezra Pound, 'In a Station of the Metro', *Selected Poems*, Faber and Faber, London, 1948, p 113. All rights reserved: Ezra Pound 1926, 1934, 1937, 1940, 1948, 1949, 1956, 1957, 1975; Ezra Pound Literary Property Trust 1975. (16) Jean Cocteau, *Les Enfants Terribles*, Rosamond Lehmann, trans, Penguin, London, 1961. Copyright © The Estate of Jean Cocteau, 1929. By permission of Penguin Books Ltd. (17) Henry Miller, *Tropic of Cancer*, Panther, London, 1965, pp 162–163. Copyright Obelisk Press, Paris, 1934. By permission of Grove/Atlantic, Inc. (18) Georges Simenon, *Maigret and the Saturday Caller*, Tony White, trans, in *Maigret Victorious: A Sixth Omnibus*, Hamish Hamilton, London, 1975, p 244. First published in France, 1962. Copyright © 1962, 1975 The Estate of Georges Simenon. All rights reserved. By permission of Penguin Books Ltd and The Estate of Georges Simenon. (19) Gertrude Stein, *The Autobiography of Alice B. Toklas*, Penguin, London, 1966, pp 25–26. (20) James Baldwin, *Giovanni's Room*, Penguin, London, 1990, pp 91–92. Copyright © James Baldwin, 1956. (21) Jean Rhys, *Quartet*, Penguin, London, 1973, pp 37–38. Copyright © 1928, 1957 by Jean Rhys. By permission of Penguin Books Ltd and HarperCollins Publishers, Inc. (22) Kay Boyle, *My Next Bride*, Virago, London, 1986, pp 203–204. Copyright © by Kay Boyle 1934. By permission of The Estate of Kay Boyle and the Watkins/Loomis Agency. (23) Henry James, *The Ambassadors*, Penguin, London, 1986, pp 272–273. (24) Charles Baudelaire, 'Morning Twilight', in *Baudelaire's Paris*, Forest Books, London, 1990, p 5. Translation copyright © Laurence Kitchin. By permission of Forest Books. (25) George Orwell, *Down and Out in Paris and London*, Penguin, London, 1975, pp 96–97. Copyright © Mark Hamilton as literary executor of the estate of the late Sonia Brownwell Orwell and Martin Secker and Warburg Ltd. By permission of A.M. Heath & Company Ltd and Harcourt Brace and Company. (26) Jean-Paul Sartre, *Iron in* *the Soul*, Gerard Hopkins, trans, Penguin, London, 1985, pp 90–91. *La Mort dans l'âme* first published in 1949. Copyright © 1949 by Jean-Paul Sartre. By permission of Penguin Books Ltd. (27) Victor Hugo, *Les Misérables*, Norman Denny, trans, Penguin, London, 1982, p 1065. Introduction by Norman Denny. This translation first published by The Folio Society in 1976. Translation copyright © The Folio Society, 1976. By permission of The Folio Society. (28) Katherine Mansfield, 'Feuille d'Album', in *The Collected Stories of Katherine Mansfield*, Penguin, London, 1981, pp 162–163. (29) Louis-Ferdinand Céline, *Journey to the End of the Night*, Ralph Manheim, trans, New Directions, New York, 1983, pp 208–209. Copyright © 1952 by Louis-Ferdinand Céline. By permission of New Directions Publishing Corp. (30) Samuel Beckett, *Dream of Fair to Middling Women*, John Calder, London, 1993, pp 48–49. Copyright © The Samuel Beckett Estate 1992. By permission of The Calder Educational Trust, London, and Riverrun Press, New York. (31) Anatole France, *The Gods Will Have Blood*, Frederick Davies, trans, Penguin, London, 1979, pp 55–56. This translation copyright © Frederick Davies, 1979. By permission of Penguin Books Ltd. (32) Charles Dickens, *A Tale of Two Cities*, Penguin, London, 1970, pp 61–62. (33) 'A Phantom of the Clouds', extract translated by John Edmondson from 'Un Fantôme de Nuées', in *Calligrammes*, 1918. (34) Simone de Beauvoir, *The Prime of Life*, Peter Green, trans, Penguin, London, 1965, p 533. *La Force de l'âge* first published in France, 1960. Copyright © Librairie Gallimard, 1960. Translation copyright © The World Publishing Company, 1962. By permission of Penguin Books Ltd. (35) Milan Kundera, *Immortality*, Peter Kussi, trans, Faber and Faber, London, 1992, pp 270–271. Copyright © Milan Kundera, 1991. English translation copyright © Peter Kussi, 1991. By permission of Faber and Faber Ltd. (36) Georges Perec, *A Man Asleep*, in *Things: A Story of the Sixties, with A Man Asleep*, David Bellos (*Things*) and Andrew Leak (*A Man Asleep*), trans, Harvill, London, 1991, p 160. *A Man Asleep* first published in France by Éditions Denoël, 1967. Copyright © Éditions Denoël, 1967. English translation copyright © 1990 by William Collins Sons & Co Ltd. By permission of The Harvill Press and David R. Godine, Publisher, Inc. (37) Djuna Barnes, *Nightwood*, Faber and Faber, London, 1985, pp 48–49. Copyright © 1937 by Djuna Barnes. By permission of New Directions Publishing Corp and Faber and Faber Ltd. (38) Anaïs Nin, *The Four-Chambered Heart*, Virago, London, 1992, pp 30–31. Copyright © 1950, 1959 by Anaïs Nin. Copyright renewed © 1978, 1987 by The Anaïs Nin Trust. All rights

reserved. By permission of the Author's Representative, Gunther Stuhlmann, and of Peter Owen Ltd. (39) Paul Verlaine, 'Parisian Nocturne', in *Selected Poems*, C.F. MacIntyre, ed and trans, University of California Press, Berkeley, CA, 1948, p 43. Copyright © 1948 by The Regents of the University of California. By permission of the University of California Press. (40) Patrick Modiano, *Honeymoon*, Barbara Wright, trans, Harvill, London, 1992, p 12. First published in France by Gallimard 1990, in Great Britain by Harvill 1992. Copyright © in the English translation Collins Harvill 1992. By permission of The Harvill Press. (41) John Evelyn, *The Diary and Correspondence of John Evelyn*, William Bray, ed, Vol 1, George Bell and Sons, London, 1906, pp 55–56. (42) Hervé Guibert, *My Parents*, Liz Heron, trans, Serpent's Tail, London, 1993, pp 95–96. First published in France in 1986 by Gallimard. Copyright © 1986 by Éditions Gallimard. Translation copyright © 1993 by Liz Heron. By permission of Serpent's Tail.

PICTURE CREDITS

INDEX OF PLACES OUTSIDE PARIS

Index of Paris Streets

INDEX OF PEOPLE

This index includes writers and other prominent people mentioned in the text. (A number of other authors are included in the Booklists.)
(E) = extract; bold type = an entry in 'Lives and Works'